DISCARD

CHICAGO PUBLIC LIBRARY
WRIGHTWOOD - ASHBURN BRANCH
8530 S. KEDZIE 60652

African Americans in the Media Today

African Americans in the Media Today

An Encyclopedia

Volume 2

M–Z

SAM G. RILEY

CHICAGO PUBLIC LIBRARY
WRIGHTWOOD - ASHBURN BRANCH
8530 S. KEDZIE 60652

GREENWOOD PRESS
Westport, Connecticut • London

Library of Congress Cataloging-in-Publication Data

Riley, Sam G.
  African Americans in the media today : an encyclopedia / Sam G. Riley.
    p. cm.
  Includes bibliographical references and index.
  ISBN: 978–0–313–33679–9 (set : alk. paper)—ISBN: 978–0–313–33680–5
  (vol. 1 : alk. paper)—ISBN: 978–0–313–33681–2 (vol. 2: alk. paper)
  1. African Americans in the mass media industry—Encyclopedias.
  2. Mass media—United States—Encyclopedias. I. Title.
  P94.5.A372U568 2007
  302.23089'96073—dc22   2007008192

British Library Cataloguing in Publication Data is available.

Copyright © 2007 by Sam G. Riley

All rights reserved. No portion of this book may be
reproduced, by any process or technique, without the
express written consent of the publisher.

Library of Congress Catalog Card Number: 2007008192
ISBN-13: 978–0–313–33679–9 (Set)   ISBN-10: 0–313–33679–2 (Set)
        978–0–313–33680–5 (Vol. 1)   0–313–33680–6 (Vol. 1)
        978–0–313–33681–2 (Vol. 2)   0–313–33681–4 (Vol. 2)

First published in 2007

Greenwood Press, 88 Post Road West, Westport, CT 06881
An imprint of Greenwood Publishing Group, Inc.
www.greenwood.com

Printed in the United States of America

The paper used in this book complies with the
Permanent Paper Standard issued by the National
Information Standards Organization (Z39.48–1984).

10 9 8 7 6 5 4 3 2 1

This reference work is dedicated to the countless individuals who, due to racial prejudice, were unable to find success of the kind showcased in these two volumes of biographical career sketches.

Contents

List of Entries	ix
Entries of People by Field or Endeavor	xv
Acknowledgments	xxi
Introduction	xxiii
Timeline	xxix
The Encyclopedia	1
Selected Bibliography	547
Index	561

Mabrey, Vicki (c.1956–)

A CBS "60 Minutes II" correspondent since the program's inception in 1999, Vicki Mabrey switched networks to ABC in November 2005 to work as a "Nightline" correspondent. She was born in St. Louis, Missouri, graduated from McCluer High School in 1973 and is a 1977 cum laude graduate of Howard University, where she majored in political science. She entered journalism in 1982 by enrolling in a training program at the CBS Washington, D.C., affiliate WUSA-TV. From 1984 to 1992, she was a general assignment reporter for Baltimore station WBAL-TV, then moved to Dallas to work as a CBS News correspondent. Her biggest story was the siege of the Branch Davidian compound near Waco, Texas, by agents of the FBI and the Bureau of Alcohol, Tobacco and Firearms. On 19 April 1993, a fire in the compound resulted in the deaths of 76 people inside, including leader David Koresh; and four government agents died during the siege. She also reported on political unrest in Haiti. From 1995 to 1998, she worked as a CBS foreign correspondent out of London, reporting on the continuing violence in Northern Ireland, the untimely death of Princess Diana of Great Britain and the prelude to war in Iraq. She also took part in covering two major events in July 1996: the explosion and crash of TWA Flight 800 following takeoff from John F. Kennedy Airport in New York and the terrorist bombing by Eric Rudolph at the Summer Olympics in Atlanta, Georgia. CBS decided to capitalize on the immense popularity of the Sunday evening news magazine show "60 Minutes" by spinning off "60 Minutes II" as a Wednesday night show. The spinoff premiered in January 1999, with Dan Rather in the starring role, assisted by Bob Simon, Charlie Rose and Mabrey. The show's title was later altered to "60 Minutes Wednesday."

Mabrey continued to report for the "CBS Evening News with Dan Rather" as well; in February 2002, she traveled to Yemen to cover a raid against suspected Al Qaeda forces there. In October 2004, she reported on symptoms common to Alzheimer's and Parkinson's patients. Her work for "60 Minutes II" included a January 2003 report on four Ft. Bragg N.C. soldiers accused of murdering their wives, and the suicides of two of those soldiers; the killings were tentatively tied to an antimalarial medicine that was suspected of causing adverse behavioral side effects. An equally sad story in February 2005 was that of Mark Dal Molin, who in 1958 at age three was committed to Sonoma State Hospital in California due to having been born with cerebral palsy, which left him disabled and mentally retarded. There, he became part of a questionable government-sponsored study that involved use of radiation, which caused the experiment's subjects considerable physical pain. In that same month and year, Mabrey did a decidedly more upbeat feature on Jesse James, a descendant of the outlaw of the same name who had made a reputation for himself by building custom motorcycles costing up to $150,000. In April 2005, she reported on a Florida mother who had killed her three-year-old baby, and in June of that year, she did a story about Cohen Syndrome, a genetic disorder that has affected Amish communities in America. Other stories she has done for "60 Minutes II" have been about man-made diamonds, the problem of obesity in America, a family that has taken in at least 25 disabled children, couples who choose the gender of their babies, the last man found alive at Ground Zero after the tragedy of 9/11 and orphaned children in Indonesia following the tsunami there. Another story was about online diploma mills, and an especially enviable assignment sent Mabrey through Europe with travel guru Rick Steves. When CBS decided to cancel the Wednesday night version of "60 Minutes" in the spring of 2005, Mabrey moved to ABC's "Nightline," joining fellow correspondents Lisa Ling, John Donvan and Chris Bury. In January 2006, Mabrey and Sarah Rosenburg teamed to do a story on Florida prisons in general and that state's experiment with the nation's first "faith-based prison" in particular. Mabrey also did a story on composer John Williams.

Mabrey has won four Emmy awards from the Academy of Television Arts and Sciences. Two, in 1996, were for her stories on the Explosion and crash of Flight 800 and the Atlanta Olympics terrorist bombing; the remaining two, in 1997, were for her reporting on the death of Princess Diana. She has also been accorded the Gracie Allen Award from the group American Women in Radio and Television, and she is represented on the McCluer High School Wall of Fame.

Further Readings: "Distinguished Alumni Award Recipients: Ms. Vicki Mabrey." [Online, 3 March 2000]. Howard University Web site www.founders.howard.edu/charterday 2000; Prince, Richard. "Vicki Mabrey Offered 'Nightline' Job." [Online, 29 October 2005]. Richard Prince's Journal-isms. Maynard Institute Web site www.maynardije.org; "Vicki Mabrey." [Online]. ABC News Web site www.abcmedianet.com; "Vicki Mabrey." [Online]. CBS News Web site www.cbsnews.com.

Mabry, Marcus (1968–)

Marcus Mabry is chief of correspondents for *Newsweek* magazine and has worked full time for that magazine since 1989. He was born in Trenton, New Jersey, and was brought up by his mother and grandmother. He credits some of his success to his mother's optimism and his grandmother's pragmatism. His good work in school earned him a scholarship to study at the exclusive Lawrenceville School in Princeton, New Jersey, and there he worked for the student newspaper. His continued success won him a full scholarship to Stanford University, where he got his bachelor's degree in English and French literature and international relations. He planned to go on to law school, but while working on the *Stanford Daily* to earn his livelihood, he began to favor journalism as a career. He was the paper's wire editor and was offered internships by *Newsweek*, *The Los Angeles Times* and *The Washington Times*. He selected *Newsweek* because its editors promised him that he could help cover the 1988 Democratic National Convention, working out of the magazine's Atlanta bureau. While a student, Mabry had also worked in the summers for *The Boston Globe* and *The Trentonian* in his hometown. When the 1988 academic year began, Mabry was off to France to study as an exchange student in Paris. He had a special interest in learning more about the various African Americans who had sought refuge from racism by becoming expatriates in France. Mabry graduated in 1989 and in July of that year, joined *Newsweek* as a writer and associate editor in its business section, working under fellow African American Mark Whitaker, who later became that magazine's editor-in-chief. In 1993, at age 25, Mabry returned to Paris, this time as *Newsweek*'s assistant bureau chief. He was also that magazine's only African-American correspondent at the time. After three years in Paris, Mabry and a colleague won the Overseas Press Club's Morton Frank Award for business reporting. Having traveled to Africa in 1992, Mabry wanted to see more of that continent and in 1996, became *Newsweek* bureau chief in Johannesburg. There, he covered postwar Rwanda, revolution in Zaire and the recruiting of mercenaries in West Africa. Four years later, in 2000, he returned to New York City to begin a nine-month Edward R. Murrow Fellowship with the Council on Foreign Relations. He became senior editor of *Newsweek International* in 2001 and the magazine's chief of correspondents in 2002. Openly gay, Mabry lives in the Hell's Kitchen neighborhood of New York with his partner, a software engineer. His years abroad had made Mabry aware of Americans' lack of interest in, hence ignorance of, international news. He has remarked that the terrorist attacks of 9/11 should open Americans' eyes to the need to pay more attention to events in the rest of the world. He has also commented that U.S. media are falling ever further behind in achieving racial diversity, given the pace at which our population's ethnicity is changing.

Mabry is on the board of governors of the Overseas Press Club and the board of the National Association of Black Journalists. In 2003, the New York Association of Black Journalists awarded him its Trailblazer Award and earlier had presented him its award for personal commentary. He is on the Council on Foreign Relations and is a member of the Chairman's Advisory Council of that organization. He is author of a memoir, *White Bucks and Black-Eyed Peas*, which appeared in 1995. The first part of that odd title was intended to symbolize the "white world" he had joined; the second part symbolized his black roots. In large part, the book examines the phenomenon of "survivor guilt" as felt by minority individuals who grew up poor but went on to succeed in mainstream jobs. In mid-2006, Mabry is at work on a second book, a biography of U.S. Secretary of State Condoleezza Rice. Its tentative title is "Twice as Good: The Souls of Condoleezza Rice," and it is to be published by Rodale Press. Mabry is a fitting choice as Rice's biographer in that both of them were fellows at the Council on Foreign Relations and both pursued Soviet studies at Stanford University, where Rice was later Provost.

In an August 1998 Elizabeth Farnsworth interview of Mabry published on the PBS Newshour Web site, Mabry indicated that while he regarded blacks and whites in South Africa as more divided than ever, he had hope for future race relations in that nation in that children of all races there at last were attending the same schools, singing the same songs and rooting for the same sports teams. He also expressed optimism about the future of the continent as a whole in that most of its nations now have democratic governments and were asking for trade, not aid. His greatest worry, he indicated, was the future of the Congo, rich in resources and located in the center of the continent, but not blessed with a stable government. In 2002, Mabry reviewed a book about another of Africa's more troubled nations: Nigeria. His review of *This House Has Fallen: Midnight in Nigeria* (New York, 2000) by U.S.-born but U.K.-employed journalist and author Karl Maier was mixed. In a 2001 interview Mabry conducted with global trend forecaster Joel Kotkin, the forecaster saw the attacks of 9/11 as intensifying flight from our major cities on the part of computer professionals, creating what Kotkin called suburban "Nerdistans" where these digital workers would feel safer. Mabry was active in covering the presidential race in 2004; some of his work was published on www.msnbc.msn.com. An example was an August 2004 report that centered on President Bush's embarrassing performance when asked about tribal sovereignty for Native Americans in the twenty-first century; Mabry characterized the president as looking like an unprepared schoolboy. In another of these reports, Mabry correctly identified the campaign's eleventh-hour shift in favor of President Bush, and in September, another of these Mabry stories named FEMA head Michael Brown as Hurricane Katrina's first political casualty. Mabry went on to suggest that the ultimate political casualty of the botched handling of relief efforts might well prove to be the president himself. He added to that assessment in November in a story detailing the Bush administration's sinking popularity figures as revealed by recent polls.

Mabry has been an active participant in various panel discussions. In November 2000, he was on a World AIDS Day panel sponsored by the National Lesbian and Gay Journalists Association, Gay Men's Health Crisis and the Lesbian and Gay Community Services Center in New York; the panel examined AIDS in both Africa and the African-American community. In March 2002, he moderated a mediabistro.com panel on the topic of gay editors at mainstream magazines, and in April of that year, he was on a First Amendment panel, "Reporting the World: Whose Rules?" at Columbia University. In October 2003, he was one of three panelists on NPR's "Talk of the Nation" discussing how justice can be done in the glare of media publicity. He was moderator of a Council on Foreign Relations event in September 2004 that featured Dr. Mustafa Osman Ismail, foreign minister of the Republic of Sudan; the topic was genocide, which Osman preferred to downplay as simply tribal conflict. In October 2005, Mabry introduced honoree Thomas Morgan III at his NABJ Hall of Fame induction, and in February 2006, Mabry was the keynote speaker in Raleigh, North Carolina, at a conference of the International Studies Schools Association. He also represented his magazine in March 2006 at the GLAAD Media Awards in San Francisco; on that occasion, *Newsweek* won the award for its coverage of lesbian, gay, bisexual and transgender affairs.

Books by Marcus Mabry: *White Bucks and Black-Eyed Peas: Coming of Age Black in White America* (New York: Scribner, 1995).

Further Readings: "Marcus Mabry." [Online]. Overseas Press Club of America Web site www.opcofamerica.org; "Marcus Mabry, Chief of Correspondents, Newsweek." [Online, 2004]. The Crusade site http://thecrusade.net.

Madison, Joseph Edward (1949–)

Joe Madison does not have the usual smiling facial expression of the television journalist. Although he has worked as a television commentator, he is known mainly for his radio work and his efforts to combat slavery where it still exists as well as genocide in Africa's Sudan. When he is pictured, Madison's usual expression is fully serious, even angry. He currently appears on Radio One and is nationally syndicated on Satellite One, The Power, which is the first 24-7 radio show for African Americans. He was born and raised in Dayton, Ohio, and in high school was a standout running back, baritone soloist and student orator. He holds the B.A. in sociology from Washington University of St. Louis, Missouri, where he was an all-conference running back, and his first job out of college was as a corporate communication specialist. At age 24, he became a civil rights activist, serving as executive director of the Detroit branch of the NAACP. His activist spirit was recognized, and he was named director of the NAACP's Political Action Department nationwide, serving in this office for nine years and concentrating on voter registration. Madison is said to have succeeded in registering around 1 million African-American voters, some who were attracted by the cross-country "Overground Railroad" marches he led for this purpose. He was elected by convention delegates to the board of the NAACP, held that position for the next 14 years and also became chairman of the NAACP Image Awards program, which he made profitable and was able to get syndicated nationally. While working for the NAACP, Madison began doubling as a radio talk show host. His no-holds-barred radio work on WOL-AM in Washington, D.C., earned him the nickname "The Black Eagle"; his morning drivetime show is titled "Madison & Company." He has also written a column that has been carried by many of the nation's historically black newspapers, although his greater public recognition has come from his radio work and from the various hunger strikes, demonstrations and marches he has conducted to bring attention to serious human rights violations that most Americans apparently would prefer to ignore. One of the most dramatic of these events was a march he led in the 1980s from Los Angeles to Baltimore to protest South Africa's practice of apartheid. Prior to that Madison had led other shorter marches, from Richmond to Harlem, San Francisco to Los Angeles and Louisville to Detroit. In the mid-1990s, Madison read a series of stories published in the *San Jose Mercury* that alleged CIA involvement in bringing cocaine into the poor sections of Los Angeles. It was suggested that the CIA played some role in this illicit drug trade as a means of supporting the efforts of the Nicaraguan Contras. To press for an investigation of these charges, Madison joined forces with comedian-turned-activist Dick Gregory, University of Maryland professor and author of *Oswald and the CIA* (New York: Carrol & Graf, 1995) John Newman and Congressional Black Caucus chair Rep. Maxine Waters of California. Madison and Gregory were arrested for picketing outside both the CIA headquarters and the Drug Enforcement Agency, and Madison lost 30 pounds during a fast he conducted to call attention to the matter. In 1998, Madison was tapped to host a new Internet talk show (onlinetalk.com) appearing on Mondays from 7 to 9 PM. The interactive show gave him a worldwide audience and a new way of connecting with his listeners. In 2001, he became associated with another new media venture, NewsMax.com, when he joined that news portal's board. Probably the most adventurous of his civil rights efforts took place in 2000 when he traveled to Sudan to see for himself the slave trade that has flourished there whereby black southern Sudanese were enslaved by the Arabic-speaking residents of that large, extremely poor nation's northern region. Enormous numbers of people had been enslaved during the 16 years of civil war between north and south. Although that war ended in 1972, in 1989 the north, which was better equipped militarily, overthrew the south's government and began a new civil war. With it came a renewed slave trade. The usual policy was to kill the men in what amounted to widespread genocide and to enslave the women and children. In his broadcasts and columns, Madison has described the efforts of some Bedouins to free some of the enslaved captives, operating a sort of underground railroad headed southward.

He adds that the Bedouins count on being reimbursed for this dangerous work by various human rights organizations. Madison has worked with such an organization—Christian Solidarity International, which claims to have helped free more than 38,000 Sudanese slaves. Madison himself reportedly has helped arrange the freedom of more than 4,000 of these people. The stories of rape, mutilation and other mistreatment most of these individuals had suffered affected Madison greatly and made him all the more intent on bringing their story to the American people. He has been especially determined to bring this sad story to the attention of African Americans. In April 2001, Madison, the Rev. Walter Fauntroy and former Reagan administration official Michael Horowitz handcuffed themselves to the entrance door of the Sudanese Embassy in Washington, were arrested and later were represented by the high-powered legal team of Johnnie Cochran and Ken Star. Two months later, the U.S. House of Representatives voted 422-2 to condemn the Sudanese government's record on human rights, and in 2002, the U.S. Congress passed the Sudan Peace Act, which earmarked $100 million to combat that country's ills. Even so, the U.S. government and most of the rest of the world have continued to look away from the horrors of Sudan, and in July 2004, Madison again staged a hunger strike to press for more forceful intervention. In early 2005, Madison again joined Walter Fauntroy, formerly a congressional delegate from the District of Columbia, in urging that states divest their pension funds of stock in corporations that do business with Sudan. Meanwhile, much of the fighting in Sudan has shifted from the south to the central and northern regions. Although the United Nations continues to be ineffective and most of the world continues to look the other way, Madison's many efforts on behalf of the Sudanese are nevertheless a fine example of how one man can make a difference in what is probably the world's most egregious combination of human-rights atrocities: slavery, ethnic cleansing, religious persecution and official corruption.

Other Madison campaigns have centered on such topics as police brutality, racial profiling, efforts to deport Liberians from the United States and the influence of "gangsta rap" music on young Americans. In 1996, he successfully campaigned to get the black singing group The Four Tops a star on the Hollywood Walk of Fame. For all these efforts, he has been listed by *Talker Magazine* as one of the 100 most influential radio talk show personalities in America and by *Ebony* as one of the top 50 leaders of the future. He has won the National Newspaper Publishers Association's News Maker of the Year Award, the Southern Christian Leadership Conference's Journalism Award and the National Political Congress of Black Women's Good Brother Award. In 2005, Madison donated his papers, six linear feet of them, to the Amastad Research Center at Tulane University in New Orleans. A rare exception to Madison's stern public countenance in a world where there is so much to be stern about was a photograph of himself and his wife Sherry that illustrated a *Homes of Color Magazine* story about their newly renovated townhouse in southeast Washington, D.C.—Madison's island of peace in a world full of trouble.

Further Readings: Brown, Peter. "Joe Madison Witnesses the Horror of Slavery in Sudan." *The New Crisis.* November/December 2000; Davidson, Joe. "States Urged to Pull Investments from Sudan." [Online, January/February 2005]. Focus Magazine Web site www.jointcenter.org; Hentoff, Nat. "The Black Eagle Swoops Into Sudan." [Online, May 2001]. The Village Voice Web site www.villagevoice.com; Shaw, Penny. "Nesting with 'The Black Eagle.'" *Homes of Color Magazine,* May/June 2005; "Weekly Internet Program to Feature Joe Madison." [Online, 16 March 1998]. NewsMax Web site www.Newsmax.com.

Madison, Paula Walker (c.1952–)

Paula Madison is president and general manager of Los Angeles station KNBC (NBC 4); when she assumed this position in 2000, she became the first African-American woman to achieve the rank of general manager of a network-owned station in a top-five market. She was born in the Harlem section of New York City and attended Cardinal Spellman High School there. After graduating from Vassar College in 1974, she became a reporter for the *Herald Journal* in Syracuse, New York, remaining there until 1980, when she moved to Texas for an investigative reporter job at the *Fort Worth Star-Telegram.* In 1982 she moved again, this time to become city editor of the *Times Herald* in Dallas. Later that year, she switched media and took her first television job, as community affairs director for Dallas station WFAA-TV. From 1984 through 1985, she was a news manager for that station; from 1986 through 1987, she was news director for Tulsa, Oklahoma, station KOTV-TV. Moving yet again, she worked from 1987 to 1989 as executive news director for KHOU-TV in Houston, Texas. She joined NBC in 1989 as assistant news director of New York City's WNBC, the network's flagship station, and was moved up to news director in March 1996. During the three years she held this job, WNBC became the city's top station as well as the ratings leader for local news programming. Wishing to reward her success, NBC management offered her the job of network vice president for diversity. She later remarked that her goal had been to become a news leader, not a diversity leader, but she accepted the position on the condition that the network allow her to keep her news director job as well. As such, she chaired the NBC Diversity Council, on which she remained a member after stepping down as chair. In November 2000, she was promoted to KNBC's president and general manager and moved to Los Angeles. Her first change was to challenge the station's news staff to do longer stories when the situation warrants it. She sought to give that station's news coverage more respectability by abandoning its knee-jerk response to cover car chases by helicopter and promoted added attention to health issues, environmental concerns and local politics. She also has attempted to cut down coverage of African Americans that shows them mainly in the contexts of violence, arrests or poverty. Reporting that is governed mainly by listening to the police scanner, she has said, is lazy news reporting. She has also expressed concern about those news employees she calls "the indoor people": those who always work inside the station's studio and seldom get out to interact with the community, yet who nevertheless attempt to provide news that satisfies what they imagine to be the public's interests. In April 2002, her job in Los Angeles was expanded when she was named regional general manager of three other stations that NBC had purchased from the Telemundo Communications Group; those NBC/Telemundo stations were KNBC, KVEA and KWHY.

As are most broadcast executives, Madison is active in community affairs and in national organizations. She is a member of the National Association of Black Journalists, the New York Press Club and the New York Vassar Club. She serves on the boards of Vassar College; the National Medical Fellowships Inc., a nonprofit group dedicated to increasing the number of minority medical doctors; the Center for Public Integrity in Washington, D.C.; the California Broadcasters Association and the Maynard Institute for Journalism Education. She is on the advisory boards of the Poynter Institute and the Los Angeles Chapter of the National Association of Women Business Owners and is on the executive committee of the Campaign to Save Cardinal Spellman High School in Harlem. She is president of the Vassar College Alumni Association and is a member of the International Women's Media Foundation. Among her various honors and recognitions are, in 1998, the Ida B. Wells Award from the NABJ, recognition by *Crain's New York Business* as one of New York's Top 100 Minority Executives, the 1999 Ellis Island Medal of Honor from the National Ethnic Coalition of Organizations, and a TRISCORT Award from the Tri-State Catholic Committee on Radio and Television. In 2001, she received the Los Angeles NAACP President's Award and the United Negro College Fund's Frederick C. Patterson Award, and in 2002, she was accorded the National Association of Minority Media Executives' Diversity Award. The Anti-Defamation League presented her with its Deborah Award in 2003; she received the Citizen of the Year Award in 2004 from the City of Los Angeles Marathon; and in 2005, *Black Enterprise Magazine* named her one of the 75 Most Powerful African Americans in Corporate America and the *Hollywood Reporter* included her in its list of the Women in Entertainment Power 100. She has also been honored by *Ebony* magazine as one of its Outstanding Women in Marketing & Communications and by the California Black Women's Health Project as one of its Women Who Dared.

Along the way, Madison has also found herself in the midst of controversy. As NBC's vice president for diversity, she had to take the heat for the network's decision to withhold domestic partner benefits to its gay employees; her response to critics was that the decision hinged more on cost than on homophobia. In December 2002, she fired African-American KNBC weatherman Christopher Nance due to charges that he had exhibited violent, profane, abusive behavior, which he denied. In June of the same year, she was the victim of rumors that she herself had been fired and replaced by Bruno Cohen from NBC's New York operation, and in spring 2005, she fired three KNBC staffers who had been involved in an office affair, including a news producer axed for not reporting the matter.

Further Readings: "Channel Surfing: Paula Madison, President and General Manager of KNBC, Is Used to Challenges." *Los Angeles Business Journal*, 27 May 2002; "Paula Madison." [Online]. San Diego Association of Black Journalists Web site www.sdabj.org; "Paula Madison." [Online, 2005]. NBC4 News Web site www.nbc4.tv/News; "Paula Madison: No More Car Chases." [Online, 12 January 2006]. Vassar College site http://innovators.vassar.edu; Prince, Richard. "Reporter Apologizes for Paula Madison Rumor." [Online, 20 June 2003]. Richard Prince's Journal-isms. Maynard Institute Web site www.maynardije.org; "WNBC-TV News Director Calls Monitoring Police Scanners 'Lazy News.'" [Online, 1998]. National Council of Churches Web site wwsw.ncccusa.org.

Malveaux, Julianne Marie (22 September 1953–)

Outspoken and iconoclastic, Julianne Malveaux is a woman of many parts: PhD economist/professor, syndicated columnist, broadcast commentator, book author and owner of her own multimedia production company. She was born in San Francisco; her first published writing was poetry, which she began writing at age 16. As an undergraduate and graduate student, she studied economics, receiving the B.A. magna cum laude in 1974 and the M.A. in 1975 from Boston College and the Ph.D. in 1980 from Massachusetts Institute of Technology. As with most Ph.D. graduates, she entered academic work upon receiving the terminal degree, teaching economics at the New School for Social Research in New York City from 1980 to 1981 and at San Francisco State University from 1981 to 1985. From 1985 to 1992, she was a visiting professor of economics, public policy and black studies at the University of California, Berkeley. She was also a junior staff economist with the White House Council of Economic Advisors in 1987 and 1988, and in 1990, she began writing a newspaper column syndicated by King Features. The column appeared twice weekly; one concentrated on politics, the other on business and economic issues. Having gained national exposure with her column, she added two columns in black-audience magazines: "Left Coast" in *Emerge* and "Economics and You" in *Essence*. She wrote weekly for the *San Francisco Sun Reporter* and has been a contributor to *Ms.*, *Black Issues in Higher Education*, *Black Scholar*, the *Progressive* and *USA Today*. She has also freelanced for a few dozen other periodicals. As a writer, she has focused on women's roles in the economy, commenting upon the barriers they have faced and have partially overcome in hiring and promotion, and upon the backlash that has accompanied their progress.

In the 1990s, Malveaux began to put more time into broadcast commentary. She has been a panelist on the PBS show "On the Contrary" and CNN's

"CNN and Company"; and she has hosted talk shows, first for KGO radio in San Francisco, then in 1994 with "Malveaux in the Morning" on Washington, D.C., station WPFW-FM. On television, she has appeared on "The News Hour with Jim Lehrer," "Politically Incorrect" and, out of Howard University, "Evening Exchange." She has also made appearances on Fox News and MSNBC. One appearance she appears to regret was on the Sean Hannity show on ABC radio on 11 July 2005. There, she described President Bush as "evil" and "out of control," but later apologized for the intemperate language while continuing to disapprove of the war in Iraq. In 1995, she started her own production company, Last Word Productions, of which she is president and CEO.

Malveaux has run once for public office but lost her bid for a seat on San Francisco's Board of Supervisors. She did, however, meet with success by introducing a California ballot initiative that resulted in the state taking $300 million of state pension funds out of corporations that had continued to do business with South Africa despite that country's policy of apartheid. She has also been active in a variety of organizations and was president of the San Francisco Business and Professional Women's Club from 1987 to 1989 and that city's Black Leadership Forum in 1989 and 1990. In 1995 she became president of the National Association of Negro Business and Professional Women's Club and in 1996, chair of the National Child Labor Commission's board. She has also served on the board of the Center for Policy Alternatives, the Economic Policy Institute, the National Coalition for Black Civic Participation and the National Committee for Responsive Philanthropy and has worked with Stanford University's Institute for the Study of Research on Women and Gender and for the Rockefeller Foundation. She has been accorded at least four honorary degrees—from the University of the District of Columbia, Marymount Manhattan College, Benedict College and Sojourner Douglas College. In recent years, she has held the Sister Julie Cunningham Chair at the College of Notre Dame in San Mateo, California (1998), has been an affiliated scholar at Stanford University and twice has had Woodrow Wilson visiting fellowships: at Ithica College in 1998 and Beaver University in 2000. As of this writing in 2005, she is to be a John A. Hannah Visiting Professor in Integrative Studies at Michigan State University. To date, she has written or cowritten six books, two of which, *Sex, Lies and Stereotypes* and *Wall Street, Main Street and the Side Street*, are collections of her columns. Perhaps her most unusual book, *Unfinished Business*, pits liberal Democrat Malveaux against her conservative Republican coauthor, Deborah Perry, as the two writers examine such issues as how to balance work and family, equal pay and reproductive issues. She has also contributed to the books of others, such as *Race and Resistance* (Cambridge, Mass.: South End Press, 2002), edited by Herb Boyd, and *When Race Becomes Real* (Chicago: Lawrence Hill Books, 2002), edited by Bernestine Singley.

Malveaux, Julianne Marie

"Feeding the Greedy, Starving the Needy"
by Julianne Malveaux

With the federal government operating on little more than fumes, and with our budget deficit ballooning, a group of "tax and spend" Republicans pushed through a bill that increases farm subsidies by about $50 billion over the next decade. The legislation guarantees a more stable income for grain and cotton growers by raising subsidies for them. It also provides new subsidies for growers of peanuts, lentils, and dry peas. When President Bush signed the legislation last week, he called farming our nation's "first industry." The farm bill, though, was the first payoff in an already highly charged midterm election year, providing special benefits to the wealthiest wheat, corn, cotton and rice growers in 10 central and southern states.

Many of us have visions of small family farms when we think of farming, and those who pushed the farm bill through did little to discourage the notion that these subsidies are going to homespun farmers in the heartlands of America. In fact, nearly 80 percent of federal farm subsidies go to corporate farmers who hardly need them. This farm bill is public assistance at its worst, but few call it for what it is—welfare for wealthy farmers.

The only good thing about the farm bill is the fact that it includes the Food Stamp Reauthorization Act of 2002, providing a nutrition safety net for working poor families. But House Republicans are trying to take away some of what the Farm Bill provided by providing "flexibility" to states in the ways they administer the food stamp program. One proposal would allow five states to block grant the Food Stamp program at any time during the 2003–2007 period. Block grant states would be required to provide some food assistance, but they could distribute the food stamps in any way they wanted to, could cut benefits to any group, including legal immigrants, and impose limits on the amount of time people could receive food stamps. The problem with block grants is that they provide states with a fixed sum of money, but the need for food stamps varies with economic conditions. In the name of flexibility, block grant states are gambling on economic stability and putting the nutrition status of its most needy residents up as collateral.

Republicans are also pushing for a "superwaiver" program that would allow states to get around federal rules in a variety of low-income programs like food stamps, childcare, and TANF. States that apply for waivers would be allowed to move money from one program to another, which defeats the purpose of setting aside funds specifically for nutrition. Both block grants and "superwaivers" undermine the food stamp program and potentially make it more difficult for poor people, especially the working poor, to feed their families while they subsist on low-wage jobs.

It is ironic that debate on TANF (temporary aid for needy families) reauthorization follows the swift approval of a different kind of TANF program, temporary aid for needy farmers. The President could not have been more delighted to provide public assistance to his corporate friends; he takes a more parsimonious view toward public assistance when poor families are to be the beneficiaries of federal aid. Instead of boosting the funds to go to poor families, the President proposes increasing work to support training and education. The legislation that President Bush proposes would eliminate an aspect of current law that allows people to count vocational education as work. While farmers are subsidized to protect them from market fluctuations in the price of their crops, there are no employment subsidies available for people at the bottom. Indeed, while the farming wage is rising, thanks to federal subsidies, the federal minimum wage has not increased since 1996!

Why treat farmers with kid gloves, while knocking poor folks around with boxing gloves? The agriculture lobby is better financed and more powerful than the poor folks lobby. Members of Congress get bragging rights when they limit benefits for welfare recipients, a group of people that it is easy to vilify. They also get bragging rights for helping farmers, mainly because many of us retain an outmoded notion of struggling family farmers. The real deal is the farm bill was a giveaway to corporate farming interests that had only the redeeming value of food stamp reauthorization to save it. Now Congress wants to take that small benefit away in its wrangling about welfare reform. At President Bush's urging, they are feeding the greedy, starving the needy, and getting away with it because poor folks don't have the money to fund a lobby to protect them.

Source: This column appeared on Ms. Malveaux's Web site and is reprinted here with her permission.

Books by Julianne Marie Malveaux: With Linda Datcher and Phyllis A. Wallace, *Black Women in the Labor Force* (Cambridge, Mass.: MIT Press, 1980); ed. with Margaret Simms, *Slipping Through the Cracks: The Status of Black Women* (New Brunswick, N.J.: Transaction Books, 1986); *Sex, Lies and Stereotypes: Perspectives of a Mad Economist* (Los Angeles: Pines One Pub., 1994); *Wall Street, Main Street and the Side Street: A Mad Economist Takes a Stroll* (Los Angeles: Pines One Pub., 1999); with Deborah Perry and Soledad O'Brien, *Unfinished Business: A Democrat and a Republican Take On the 10 Most Important Issues Women Face* (New York: Perigee, 2002); with George A. Berzsenyi and Reginna Green, *The Paradox of Loyalty: An African American Response to the War on Terrorism* (Chicago: Third World Press, 2002).

Further Readings: Clark, Robbie. "Malveaux, Julianne." In *Black Women of America, Second Edition*. Edited by Darlene Clark Hine. New York: Oxford University Press, 2005, pp. 3321–322; Hall, Mark. "Malveaux Keynotes African American History Month." [Online, March 1998]. Library of Congress Web site www.loc.gov; "King Is Offering Malveaux Feature." *Editor & Publisher*, 8 September 1990, p. 40; Smith, Jessie Carney. "Julianne Malveaux." In *Notable Black American Women, Book II*. Ed. by Jessie Carney Smith. (Detroit, Mich.: Gale Research, 1996), pp. 425–426.

Malveaux, Suzanne (?–)

Suzanne (The a is pronounced "ah.") Malveaux has compiled an impressive journalistic record and is in 2006 a White House correspondent for CNN. Her academic credentials are also impressive—a cum laude bachelors in Sociology from Harvard and a masters in Broadcasting from Columbia. Her first media-related work was producing documentaries for Blackside Inc. in Boston, Massachusetts. Her work there included contributions to a documentary on the Great Depression and others on Egypt and Kenya. In 1989, she was a television intern in Cairo, Egypt, at the Adham Center for Television Journalism. In 1991, she became a general assignment reporter for Boston's FXT-TV and New England Cable News. In 1994, she worked in the same capacity for NBC affiliate station WRC-TV in Washington, D.C., after which she became a general assignment correspondent for NBC News, working there from 1999 until May 2002, when she joined CNN in its D.C. bureau, taking the place vacated by Major Garrett, who had been abruptly dismissed by the network. While at NBC, she covered the impeachment trial of former president Bill Clinton, the 2000 presidential election, the Elian Gonzalez affair and the Bush administration's early responses to the terrorist attacks of 11 September 2001, including reporting about the war in Afghanistan. She traveled to Africa with President Clinton and to Russia and other parts of the former Soviet Union with First Lady Hillary Clinton. Her White House coverage for CNN has taken her through the entirety of the Iraq war thus far. She has traveled with President Bush to Germany, Belgium and Slovakia and, in May 2005, to Egypt, Jordan and Israel with First Lady Laura Bush. She also contributed to coverage of the 2004 elections for CNN.

Malveaux's reporting is taken to task from time to time by the Internet site Media Matters for America (mediamatters.org). One example appeared in February 2005; Media Matters complained that she had remarked after a Bush speech that the centerpiece of his domestic agenda was the reform of Social Security by introducing private accounts in order to make the system solvent, when even administration officials themselves acknowledge that privatization would not take care of the system's coming shortfall. Another Media Matters complaint came in September 2005 and was aimed at both Malveaux and Wolf Blitzer of CNN. Both broadcasters, the complaint said, had cited improving public opinion poll figures for President Bush, whereas most polls at that time showed the president's numbers falling considerably in the wake of the administration's botched handling of Hurricane Katrina. On the other hand, Malveaux shared in the 1993 Associated Press award for Best Newscast in Boston during her time with New England Cable News, and in 1996, she was awarded an Emmy for her work at NBC.

Further Readings: El Hennawy, Noha. "Alumni Spotlight: Suzanne Malveaux." [Online]. Adham Center for Television Journalism Web site www.adhamonline.com; "Suzanne Malveaux." [Online]. CNN Web site www.cnn.com/CNN/anchors.

Marshall, Pluria W. Sr. (19 October 1937–)

Pluria Marshall Sr. is the only photographer represented in this reference work. He is included here due to his founding in 1973 of the National Black Media Coalition, an organization that has worked for three decades to increase the numbers of African Americans in communication industry jobs, encourage more minority programming and increase minority media ownership. Prior to that time, in 1969, Marshall had founded and run Operation Breadbasket, a Houston-based organization that pressed for minority hiring and minority contracts. He was born in Houston, was an Air Force enlisted man from 1956 to 1960 and studied at Texas Southern University. His work in support of civil rights began around 1962. He was the unpaid executive director of Operation Breadbasket for five years, supporting himself and his family with his work as a photographer. As director of the National Black Media Coalition, he was a panelist at the University of North Carolina in 1989; the panel's topic was "Election '88: Where Do We Go From Here?" In 1993, he criticized the NAACP's request, made through its media lawyer, for the Federal Communications Commission to go easy on an EEO violation at station WTGS-TV in Hardeeville, South Carolina, because the station's owner had been a chair of the National Urban League. In 1998, FCC chairman William E. Kennard was the featured speaker at a Washington, D.C., luncheon celebrating the twenty-fifth anniversary of the NBMC and was highly complimentary of Marshall's work and the way he had always challenged broadcasters as well as state and federal government on behalf of the black community. Kennard pointed out that in the year of the NBMC's founding, only 30 radio stations and no television stations were minority-owned but that by 1998, black-owned broadcasting properties totaled 190. In 2000, after Black Entertainment Television had been sold to corporate giant Viacom, Marshall told the press that he could see possible programming advantages in the move but was doubtful about the company's commitment to African Americans. In 2002, Marshall gave good marks to FCC chairman Michael Powell, remarking that despite Powell being a conservative Republican, he would look out for the interests of African Americans, yet in 2005, Marshall was quoted in the Black World Today Web site, www.tbwt.org, as saying he was pessimistic about the future of minority-owned radio stations.

Marshall has been a member of the United States Commission on Civil Rights. He was given the Community Service Award in 1973 by the National Association of Marketing Developers, and in 1974, Texas Southern University gave him its Ex-student Award. In that same year, the Houston chapter of the NAMD named him Marketer of the Year.

One of Marshall's five children is Pluria Marshall Jr., born in 1962 and owner of a variety of media properties, including Wave Community Newspapers Inc., which publishes seven weekly newspapers serving minority residents of Southern California. When a $4 million loan from a bank that itself went into bankruptcy was called in 2004, Wave, too, had to seek bankruptcy protection. Marshall Jr. was also one of the bidders seeking to purchase the Chicago *Defender* after John Sengstacke's demise and later the *New Pittsburgh Courier*.

Further Readings: "Pluria W. Marshall: Chairman, National Black Media Coalition." [Online, 2002]. BayArea Black Media Coalition Web site www.babmc.org.

Marshall, Sherrie (?–)

In February 2001, Sherrie Marshall became executive editor of Georgia's *Macon Telegraph*. Her hometown is Nashville, Tennessee, and she holds the B.A. in English from Atlanta's Spelman College, the nation's oldest historically black college for women, and the M.A. in journalism from the University of Wisconsin at Madison. Thus prepared, she became a copy editor at the *Minneapolis Star* in 1978 rather than taking a reporting job the way she had assumed she would while in college. Her first job led her to the national desk and the business desk. Then in 1991, she became city editor of the St. Paul Bureau, a job she held for a little more than two years. From 1993 to 1995, she was the paper's acting metro editor and from 1995 to 1999, news content editor. Marshall served as assistant managing editor for news during 1999 and 2000 and was promoted to deputy managing editor of the *Star*, now the *Star-Tribune*, in 2000. In this position, she was in charge of all news coverage, the front page and the news library. After roughly 23 years at the *Star-Tribune*, she accepted the executive editor position at the *Macon Telegraph* in February 2001.

In early to mid-2004, Marshall had to deal with a brace of plagiarism charges. The first incident resulted in the firing of education reporter Khalil Abdullah, who she had hired in September 2002 after a similar unpleasantness at the Fort Worth, Texas, *Star-Telegram*. An investigation showed that at least 20 of his *Telegraph* stories contained material taken from other published works minus attribution, according to a story appearing in the *Washington Times* in March 2004. The firing was doubly embarrassing in that Abdullah had been president of the National Association of Black Journalists' Middle Georgia chapter. The second incident involved reporter Greg Fields, who resigned in June 2004 after complaints that he had lifted material without attribution from a Web site while doing a story on Ringling Brothers Barnum and Bailey Circus. Discussions followed at the paper, and some onlookers recommended that new reporters need to be given more thorough training on the trouble they can encounter if they take material verbatim from Internet sources.

Marshall is a member of the NABJ and its Middle Georgia chapter and previously was active with the Twin Cities Black Journalists. She also belongs to the American Society of Newspaper Editors and the Georgia AP News Council. She sits on the board of the World Press Institute and is a member of the Rotary Club in Macon and a board member of the Girl Scouts of Middle Georgia. In 2002, she was a "Best of Cox" judge for the print media competition, and in 2005, she was a judge in the beat reporting category of the Pulitzer Prize competition.

Further Readings: Marshall, Sherrie. "My First Job." [Online, 5 April 2006]. Chips Quinn Scholars Web site www.chipsquinn.org/jobs/first; Prince, Richard. "Are Journalists Given Enough Ethics Training?" [Online, 30 June 2004]. Richard Prince's Journal-isms. Maynard Institute Web site www.maynardije.org; "Reporter in Georgia Fired for Plagiarizing." [Online, 8 March 2004]. The Washington Times Web site www.washtimes.com; "Sherrie Marshall Appointed Executive Editor of the Macon Telegraph." [Online]. Knight Ridder site http://knightridderinfo.com.

Martin, Michel McQueen (?–)

Michel McQueen Martin was, until mid-January 2006, an ABC News correspondent and is now with National Public Radio; earlier in her career, she was a reporter for both the *Wall Street Journal* and the *Washington Post*. Martin hails from Brooklyn, New York. She is a graduate of the once all-male St. Paul's School in Concord, New Hampshire, is a 1980 cum laude graduate of Radcliffe College at Harvard University and has done some graduate study at Wesley Theological Seminary, as well. She began her career reporting on state and local politics for the *Washington Post*, then moved on to cover the national political scene for the *Wall Street Journal*. For part of her time at the *Journal*, she was the paper's White House correspondent. She first became involved in television work as a panelist on "Washington Week in Review" for the Public Broadcasting System, and she also contributed to "NOW with Bill Moyers." In September 1992, she began her long association with ABC News, for which she has contributed many programs and specials. One of her early stories of note was about black attorney Anthony Griffin, who was fired as general counsel for the NAACP when he agreed to defend Texas Ku Klux Klan Grand Dragon Michael Lowe in what became a much-publicized First Amendment case. She covered other such newsmakers as now-deceased Austin, Texas, golf teacher Harvey Penick, conductor Sir George Solti, actor Dennis Franz and football coach Tyrone Willingham of Notre Dame. She did regular coverage of political conventions, campaigning and election results for ABC and worked on specials such as a "Turning Point" documentary the network did looking back at the 1991 conflict between Anita Hill and Clarence Thomas after the first President George Bush had nominated Thomas to replace retiring justice Thurgood Marshall on the U.S. Supreme Court. She also contributed to a Barbara Walters documentary on AIDS and a network special titled "Cedric's Story," about Cedric Jennings, a bright and resilient student at a low-achievement inner city school in Washington, D.C., who beat the system and was admitted to Brown University. This young man's story also won a 1995 Pulitzer Prize for *Wall Street Journal* reporter Ron Suskind, who later authored the book *A Hope in the Unseen: An American Odyssey from the Inner City to the Ivy League* (New York: Broadway Books, 1998). A 1997 story Martin did for "World News Tonight" examined a range of options that had been suggested for reforming the Social Security system. A 1998 story she contributed to that news show was on the best-defense-is-a-good-offense comments to the press made by Whitewater figure Susan McDougal claiming that she was merely a pawn of independent counsel Ken Starr. In 2001 and 2002, Martin was host of "Life 360," coproduced by ABC's "Nightline" and Oregon Public Broadcasting. She had also worked as a reporter for the network's magazine show "Day One." During autumn 2002 and early 2003, she contributed to the political show "This Week with George Stephanopoulos" and was an interviewer on "Nightline Upclose." Her primary assignment since 1999 was the program "Nightline." Some of her work for this program has been its series titled "America in Black and White," which examined various aspects of the issue of race. Like Brit Hume, Garrick Utley and Cynthia McFadden, Martin has worked as a correspondent for this program, and in 2000, she was a substitute anchor when regular anchor Ted Koppel was away, an assignment shared with Barbara Walters, Cokie Roberts, Forrest Sawyer and George Stephanopoulos. In "Driving While Black," Martin and Koppel examined the humiliation and anger caused by racial profiling that results in traffic stops by police simply on the basis of a driver's skin color. Martin has covered the 1998 bombing of the U.S. Embassy in Nairobi, Kenya, and the 1999 earthquakes in northwestern Turkey that killed around 18,000 people. She contributed to another 1999 "Nightline" story about a contemporary irony: with stock prices higher, fewer Americans were attempting to save for retirement. In 2002, she contributed to a story about the fall from grace of Senate Republican Trent Lott, who had commented at Sen. Strom Thurmond's birthday celebration that the nation would have benefited from having a segregationist president, a remark so blatantly dreadful that even President George W. Bush criticized him for making it. In 2005, she looked back at the firestorm caused by comedian Bill Cosby's remarks critical of the less affluent part of the African-American community. In the year 2000, correspondent McQueen married high-profile attorney William "Billy" Martin of the Blank Rome Law Firm and added Martin to her name. The two met at a New York panel she moderated. She is a frequent speaker and panelist. Examples of those activities are a 1998 panel appearance at Harvard University's Institute of Politics, moderating a 2000 Kaiser Family Foundation discussion of sex education in America, moderating a 2005 panel at the Washington D.C. Multicultural Town Hall and an address in 2006 at Martin University in Indianapolis.

The awards she has won include—1992 Candace Award from the National Coalition of 100 Black Women, the 1995 Joan Barone Award for national broadcast excellence from the Radio and Television Correspondents Association, a citation from the Columbia University Graduate School of Journalism for her work on ABC's "America in Black and White," the 2001 Casey Medal for her reporting on family issues and the American Bar Association's 2002 Silver Gavel Award. Earlier, she had won an Emmy for her "Day One" story on an international attempt to prevent the further use of land mines. She serves on the boards of St. Paul's School in Concord, New Hampshire, and the John Carroll High School in Washington, D.C. In January 2006, ABC announced that both Martin and Ted Koppel would be leaving full-time employment at the network to work with NPR. Martin is to have a role on a new show pitched to African Americans, but she will continue to work with ABC's "Nightline" on a parttime basis.

Further Readings: "ABC News Correspondent Michel McQueen to Deliver Annual Holmes-Hunter Lecture." [Online, 19 October 1998]. University of Georgia Web site www.uga.edu; Graham, Tim. "ABC's Ted Koppel. Michel Martin Join Up With NPR." [Online, 13 January 2006]. NewsBusters site http://newsbusters.org; "Michel McQueen Martin." [Online]. ABC News site http://abcnews.go.com/Nightline/News.

Martin, Roland S. (c.1969–)

A man of diverse accomplishment, Roland Martin is a syndicated columnist, newspaper publisher and television personality who has also worked as a radio reporter, magazine editor and founding editor of an electronic news outlet. Now a Dallas resident, Martin finished in 1987 as a graduate of Jack Yates High

School's Magnet School of Communications and is a 1991 journalism graduate of Texas A & M University. He began his career as a county government reporter and neighborhood reporter for the *Austin American-Statesman*, then worked the city hall beat for the *Fort Worth Star-Telegram*, where he also wrote sports copy. There, he helped cover the 1993 Branch Davidian story in Waco, Texas, and the 1995 bombing of the Oklahoma City federal building. Martin also was managing editor of the historically black Dallas-Fort Worth newspaper the *Weekly* and was editor of another such paper, the *Houston Defender*. Martin was news editor of *Savoy* magazine, a black lifestyle periodical published in New York City, and founding editor of the news site BlackAmericaWeb.com. His writing has also appeared in such outlets as *Honey Magazine*, *USA Today*, Inside.com, and Netnoir.com. In 2004, he took on the job of editor for the venerable but troubled black newspaper the *Chicago Defender*.

Also at home in broadcast media work, Martin was a morning drivetime reporter for Dallas' AM station KRLD, from 1995 to 1998 was news director and morning anchor for KKDA-AM in Dallas-Fort Worth and has been a regular on KPRC-TV's Sunday morning show in Houston, American Urban Radio Network, www.blackradio.com and the sports show "The Fifth Quarter" on WOL-AM for the Washington-Baltimore market. He has appeared on many other news and talk shows on both radio and television. In 2003, he became a nationally syndicated columnist with Creators Syndicate, and he has founded his own multimedia company, ROMAR Media Group, in Dallas.

In his syndicated column, Martin takes an unflinching look at the racial problems that linger in today's America, arguing that whites need to stop looking the other way and realize that despite progress, race is still a concern. African Americans, he writes, even today are treated as second-class citizens. In support of this contention, he cites incidents involving two of America's wealthiest blacks: billionaire Oprah Winfrey, who was not buzzed into a New York jewelry store by a clerk who, unbelievably, failed to recognize anything but her skin color, and magazine mogul John H. Johnson, who, Martin wrote, was once pulled over in his Rolls Royce and asked whose car he was driving. Like many other African-American columnists, Martin was disgusted by media coverage of the Jennifer Wilbanks "runaway bride" story in 2005. What galled him was what he termed the breathless reporting about white women who are reported missing while black women in similar circumstances are accorded far less coverage. Part of the problem, he concluded, is that the gatekeepers are, in the main, male Caucasians.

Occasionally, Martin writes about earlier racial atrocities in the United States, such as the Tulsa Race Riot of 1921, in which, according to Martin's figures, 300 blacks were killed and 1,000 homes destroyed in the Greenwood section of that city. The riot was caused by charges that a black man had assaulted a white woman. Members of the white mob were brought before a grand jury, and all were exonerated. No compensation was paid for the destroyed homes.

Martin wrote an August 2004 column describing what he appeared to view as black-on-black political crime: the Republican Party's desperate last-minute attempt to find a black candidate who would run against heavily favored Democratic senatorial candidate Barack Obama. He has also vented his anger at the double standard in the matter of affirmative action for the disadvantaged versus legacy admissions for the wealthy and well connected. He was appalled in January 2005 when President Bush, meeting with the Congressional Black Caucus, admitted that he was unfamiliar with the Voting Rights Act of 1965. While at the *Star-Telegram*, Martin took part in team coverage of the Oklahoma Federal Building bombing that won an award from the Texas Associated Press-Managing Editors. He has won a regional Edward R. Murrow Award given by the Radio Television News Directors Association, a first place in sports reporting in 1997 from the National Association of Black Journalists and a number of first-place recognitions from the Dallas-Fort Worth Association of Black Communicators.

"Alan Keyes: A Political Hit Man" by Roland S. Martin

Alan Keyes has many titles: former ambassador, two-time presidential candidate, two-time candidate for the U.S. Senate, scholar, interim university president and former TV talk show host.

Now he can add another title to his illustrious resume: political hit man.

How else can you describe the move by the Illinois Republican Party to venture outside of the state to recruit a black man to run against another black man, Democratic Senatorial front-runner Barack Obama? If you think the race issue isn't germane, then you are truly out to lunch.

In the entire history of the Illinois GOP, no one can find a single reference to the party choosing, electing or drafting an African American for a statewide position. But after Jack Ryan's candidacy imploded over allegations that he wanted his then-wife, Jeri Ryan, to have sex with him in clubs in front of others, the party leaders interviewed 13 candidates and "settled" on two: Keyes and Andrea Grubb Bathwell, the former deputy drug czar in the Bush administration. Both are African American.

I would love to say that both are qualified to run, but it's apparent that their race was more important than credentials.

Shortly thereafter, the party chose Keyes, even though he vehemently attacked Hillary Rodham Clinton when she chose to run as a U.S. senator from New York, calling her the ultimate carpetbagger. Back at ya, Mr. Keyes.

But at least Clinton studied the issues of the state. Keyes knows nothing about the issues important to Illinois voters. Heck, he couldn't find the South Side of Chicago if he had a tour guide with him. Yet somehow he expects voters in the state to actually consider his campaign a credible one.

Keyes has said he will focus on the broader issues. In other words, he will spend considerable time attacking Obama at every turn, especially when it comes to the bread-and-butter issues Keyes loves: abortion and homosexuality.

He is very much a darling of the religious right wing of the Republican Party, and he will use his national donor base to quickly raise enough cash to battle Obama, who has spent 17 years in the Illinois Legislature and truly understands the needs and concerns of the electorate.

The bottom line is the Illinois GOP knows that Keyes can't win (maybe they chose him because he has lost four times previously and will be able to keep his chin up on Nov. 2.) But their goal is to tarnish the rising star Obama.

Ever since he gave the keynote address at the Democratic National Convention in July, the man has been on a tear. His Web site is getting tons of hits, folks from across the nation are sending in money by the truckloads, and some have even gone so far as to begin thinking of the White House. While those aspirations are seriously premature—he hasn't even gotten to the Senate—they are understandable considering he would only be the third African American to serve in the U.S. Senate since Reconstruction.

And that's why Keyes has been recruited. The party needs a man—a black man—who isn't accountable to Illinois voters and who can unleash a wave of attacks on Obama, hoping that his credibility and integrity take a hit before he gets to the Senate.

On August 9, one day after he was officially in the race, Keyes showed his hand. During a radio interview, Keyes called Obama's position on abortion the same as a "slaveholder."

Let's be real. Had Obama not been black, that would have never been used. And had Keyes not been black, whites and blacks would have condemned it. Instead, Republicans stood back, smiling at the shenanigans. The greater question is whether President Bush will choose to campaign alongside Keyes. If so, he will readily accept this spectacle of a candidate and his baggage.

If Keyes were serious about his personal integrity, he would stand by his previous comments and not even bother running. He's the kind of carpetbagger who would be vilified by the real Alan Keyes.

Source: The column appears here by permission of Creators Syndicate and Mr. Martin. It originally appeared on 13 August 2004.

Books by Roland S. Martin: *Speak, Brother!: A Black Man's View of America* (Dallas, TX: R. Martin Media Group, 2002).

Further Readings: "About Roland S. Martin." [Online]. Creators Syndicate Web site www.Creators.com; "Biography." [Online]. Roland S. Martin Web site www.rolandmartin.com; Fitzgerald, Mark. "Oprah 'Furious' At 'Chicago Defender' Editor." [Online, 26 August 2005]. Editor & Publisher Web site www.editorandpublisher.com; "TV One to Air Commentaries by Roland S. Martin." [Online, 19 April 2005]. Chicago Defender Web site www.chicagodefender.com.

Mason, Paul S. (c.1956–)

Longtime ABC newsman Paul Mason became senior vice president of ABC News in June 2004. He grew up in the Shaker Heights section of Cleveland, Ohio, where he attended the public schools, starting in kindergarten at that city's Ludlow Elementary School. It was during this time that school integration was taking place in this affluent suburb, and Mason's mother was active in the cause. Mason graduated from Shaker Heights High School in 1973. He was an undergraduate at Wesleyan University, where his B.A. was in Classical Civilizations. Before entering journalism, he taught high school English for a short while. He later earned the masters in journalism from Columbia University in New York. He was in London on a fellowship in 1981 when, following race riots in Liverpool, Manchester and Brixton, he began freelancing for ABC, working as an off-air reporter and later as a producer. He has reported and produced out of New York, Miami, London and Johannesburg, South Africa, where he reported on the postapartheid elections. He has reported on the war against drugs for both "Prime Time Live" and "20/20." He was coproducer of the "Prime Time Live" show "Judgment at Midnight," about an execution at Angola Prison in Louisiana. In 1997, he was a coproducer of another ABC special, "Black in White America," which examined the lives of African Americans, both poor and affluent. He took leave from the network and in 1998, joined the journalism faculty of the University of California at Berkeley as an adjunct professor. He returned to the network after two and a half years of teaching. In May 2000, Mason began producing the weekend editions of "World News Tonight" and, in July 2003, "Prime Time Monday." The innovative concept for this magazine-format show was that it would be produced in a different city each week, starting with such locations as New York, Miami, Hollywood, Las Vegas, New Orleans and Nashville. Mason had been passed over for the position of executive producer for "World News Tonight," losing that job to Jon Banner. In addition to being executive producer of "Primetime," Mason produced Elizabeth Vargas specials. Having proved his abilities over a 23-year career with the network, Mason moved on 9 June 2004 into his present high-ranking position, reporting to ABC News President David Weston and holding sway over "World News Now," "Nightline," "This Week," "World News This Morning," "This Week," ABC News Radio and the news portions of "Good Morning America." He also had responsibility for the network's coverage of the 2004 presidential election and the political conventions that preceded it. A very personal assignment for Mason was producing the 2004 documentary "The Reunion," about the desegregation of the Shaker Heights schools. The documentary appeared on "ABC Primetime" on 18 August. Mason was interviewed by National Public Radio's Michele Norris for the program "All Things Considered" about his having lived this story and then having produced it so many years later. CNN also did a special on the Shaker Heights school integration story as part of its reporting on the fiftieth anniversary of Brown v. Board of Education.

Mason appeared as himself in two documentaries, "The World Is Watching" in 1988 and "Only the News That Fits" in 1989.

Further Readings: Prince, Richard. "Paul Mason Named Sr. VP of News." [Online, 8 June 2004]. Richard Prince's Journal-isms. Maynard Institute Web site www.maynardije.org; Sakya, Sapana. "From Liverpool to Cal: A Profile of Paul Mason." [Online]. University of California at Berkeley journalism program site http://journalism.berkeley.edu.

Mathis, Deborah (24 August 1953–)

Columnist Deborah Mathis was born in Little Rock, Arkansas, studied at the University of Arkansas, finishing in 1972, and in 1973 began her career reporting for the *Arkansas Democrat* in that city. She eventually wrote a column for the *Democrat* and also reported and anchored on television there for KTHV-TV and KATV-TV. From 1976 to 1981 she reported and was assistant news director for KARK-TV, also in Little Rock, and in 1988 began a column for the *Arkansas Gazette*, where in 1990 she was named associate editor. In 1991, Mathis was the sole Arkansas reporter to cover the Persian Gulf conflict. In 1992 and 1993, she was a columnist for the *Clarion-Ledger* of Jackson, Mississippi; thereafter she became the national correspondent for Gannett News Service, covering the White House beat, reporting on other national news, and writing a twice weekly column syndicated nationally by Tribune Media Services and carried by at least 100 newspapers. In 1998, she generated a firestorm of complaints when one of her columns suggested that the religious right was complicit in the hate murder of gay University of Wyoming student Matthew Shepard. During 2000–2001, she was a Shorestein Fellow at Harvard University and later joined the Washington, D.C., faculty of Northwestern University's Medill School of Journalism. Since 2003, her column has appeared on BlackAmericaWeb.com.

Like so many other African-American columnists, Mathis has been no fan of the George W. Bush administration, as is abundantly clear in the TMS column reproduced below. In the 2004 election campaign, she wrote that she simply could not understand how any responsible, self-respecting black person could support Bush for reelection. In many a column she has criticized the president's smug arrogance as well as his preference for preemption and unilateralism. She has criticized his tax cuts for the wealthiest Americans, his stance against gays and his macho posturing. When the United States invaded Iraq, she called his "coalition of the willing" nothing but eyewash. She derided Bush's new attorney general, Alberto Gonzales, as a wolf in sheep's clothing, and she has written about Vice President Dick Cheney as the puppeteer pulling Bush's strings and has blasted Cheney's House voting record against Head Start for children and Meals on Wheels for seniors, establishing a holiday for the Rev. Martin Luther King, and the resolution calling for the release of Nelson Mandela.

Further offending conservatives, she has accused the National Rifle Association of helping make the United States the world's most homicidal nation; and she accused various government figures of trading on the personal troubles of Terri Schiavo and her family during the 2005 feeding-tube controversy. Mathis lambasted 24-hour television news operations for the shameless way they wallowed in the story of runaway bride Jennifer Wilbanks and wondered why missing black women never seem to generate comparable public or media attention. In a column with a similar theme, she contrasted the turning of rescued Pfc. Jessica Lynch, who is white, into a made-for-TV heroine complete with biography and movie deal, with the relegation of captured and released black Army Specialist Shoshana Johnson to a paltry 30 percent disability payment. As to the troubles of entertainer Michael Jackson, Mathis says that he is technically black, but with his whitened skin and nose carved up to look like a teapot's spout, he has become so other-worldly that he is not only unlike blacks, but unlike anybody else at all. Mathis won the Angel Award for commentary in 1994 and 1996.

"Orange Alert and the Politics of Fear" by Deborah Mathis

For the last several weeks, the nation's capital has been flooded by tourists—the usual summer migration of sneakered, T-shirted, visored, camera-slinging visitors who live by the map and the subway passcard.

There are fewer of them around this week. Maybe we just peaked early. But I suspect that Sunday's news from Homeland Security Secretary Tom Ridge had something to do with it. There's nothing like an orange alert to ruin a family vacation.

In a city that is already traffic-choked, already detoured to death, already slowed by barriers and security checkpoints galore, the new alert has added another layer of anxiety and hassle to life in democracy's main factory. Gridlock rules around the World Bank and the International Money Fund headquarters—both near the White House, the State Department and other essential governmental installations—and around the U.S. Capitol, where 14 checkpoints have been set up to protect what authorities surmise to be prime, iconic targets.

The chief of the Metropolitan Police says the stepped up security measures will cost his strapped city $1.5 million for two weeks and that there's no telling how long the alert might burn orange. There have been hints that it will continue up to, and perhaps past, the November elections.

"We need to do everything we can every single day to detect, deter and prepare for" the possibility of another terrorist hit, Ridge said in sounding the alarm.

Although it's costly, nerve-wracking and disruptive, the public tends to be cooperative. What choice do we have?

But there's a glitch in the fear matrix this time. *The Washington Post* reported Tuesday that "more than a half dozen government officials" with access to classified information have said the documents about the buildings in Washington, New York City and Newark—materials they took from a terrorist cell in Pakistan last week—are at least three years old. In other words, the targets may have been options in a plan that ultimately settled on the World Trade Center and the Pentagon.

Surely the unnamed government officials were not the only ones to consider that only awareness of the plan was new, not the plan itself. But conceding that would not be very useful to an administration bent on proving how on-the-case it is now that silly, exaggerative, misleading George Tenet is no longer mussing up the intel.

Howard Dean caught a touch of hell for speculating that the Bush White House was playing politics with terrorism watches and warnings.

Dean, on Sunday's "Late Edition" with Wolf Blitzer on CNN: "I am concerned that every time something happens that's not good for President Bush, he plays this trump card, which is terrorism. His whole campaign is based on the notion that 'I can keep you safe; therefore, at times of difficulty for America, stick with me,' and then out comes Tom Ridge."

Republicans pounced. "The only person politicizing threats to our security is Howard Dean," thundered Rep. Mark Foley, R-Fla. "Dean is trivializing America's security for the sake of politics."

Once upon a time, most Americans would have probably agreed with Foley. But how can you say nowadays that the president of the United States would never mislead, exaggerate, distort or manipulate the facts for the purpose of engendering faith and support for him or his cause?

The critics say Dean was reckless even to have suggested that the timing of the new alert redounds in any way to Bush's benefit or, moreover, that advantage figured into the decision to raise the threat level.

"Daring" may be the more appropriate word, given that Dean said aloud what a lot of us have been thinking for a long time. It is certainly curious that the threat code never goes higher when things are going well for Bush.

Coincidence? We don't know. But we sure should try to find out.

Source: Reprinted with permission of Deborah Mathis.

Books by Deborah Mathis: *Yet a Stranger: Why Black Americans Still Don't Feel at Home* (New York: Warner Books, 2002); *What God Can Do: How Faith Changes Lives for the Better* (New York: Atria Books, 2005).

Further Readings: Astor, David. "Over 10,000 Callers Criticize Column of Gay Man's Murder," *Editor & Publisher*, 24 October 1998, p. 34; "Deborah Mathis." [Online]. Tribune Media Services Web site www.tmsfeatures.com.

Maxwell, Bill (16 October 1945–)

The single most repeated theme in the many columns written by Florida columnist Bill Maxwell is that black youth need to apply themselves to their studies rather than fearing that making good grades is not "cool." In the three cities where he lived and wrote, Maxwell often opened himself to criticism from the African-American community for daring to point out not just the good and progressive, but that community's lingering problems, one of which, Maxwell has said, is the way some members of that community "play to stereotype." Today Maxwell teaches journalism at Alabama's Stillman College.

He was born the eldest of seven children in Fort Lauderdale and spent parts of his youth in Crescent City, Florida, and Chicago. He worked the farm fields until he was 16, attended Wiley College in Marshall, Texas, served in the Marine Corps, then graduated summa cum laude in English from Bethune-Cookman College in Daytona Beach. In 1974 he earned a masters in English at the University of Chicago, did some doctoral level work at the University of Florida and was a tenured English professor at Santa Fe Community College in Gainesville.

Having decided upon a career in journalism, he was a reporter and columnist for *The Tampa Tribune* from 1986 to 1988, when he relocated to Gainesville to write a column for the *Sun*. There, his column was picked up by the New York Times Regional Newspaper Group and began appearing in other newspapers. In 1994 he moved again, this time to the *St. Petersburg Times*. There he remained as full-time columnist until his retirement in June 2004. Since that time, he has been writer in residence, advisor to the student newspaper and journalism instructor at Stillman College in Tuscaloosa, Alabama. His reasons for making this move are explained in his farewell column, reproduced below.

In retirement, he continues to write a monthly column for the *St. Petersburg Times*, plus a weekly column for the *Tuscaloosa News*.

Maxwell is a columnist of fierce honesty who pulls no punches. It would be difficult to find a columnist who in the 2004 election was more anti-George W. Bush. Bush was, wrote Maxwell, a liar and someone unqualified to preside in the Oval Office. He deplored the way the Bush campaign exploited the attacks on the World Trade Center and charged the president with trading on the dead in order to portray himself as the strong, steady leader the nation needed for dangerous times. He had similiar criticism for New York's former mayor, Rudy Giuliani, who managed to convert his public image from adulterer to caring leader during the aftermath of the crisis. Maxwell also took former Secretary of State Colin Powell to task for failing to come clean with the public about the real reasons for invading Iraq. Departing from criticism of individuals, Maxwell described what he called the "Archie Bunker Paradigm" that surfaces during presidential election beginning with the Iowa caucuses and the

New Hampshire primary, where, wrote Maxwell, to locate a black person in either state, one would have to mount a "Negro sighting" expedition. The Archie Bunker Paradigm refers to that bigoted character's assertion that there are Americans and there are *real* [white] Americans.

Maxwell calls the South a region just growing out of its adolescence and frequently has pointed out the region's various contradictions and paradoxes. In a region so proud of its rural roots, for example, Maxwell cites figures showing that in recent times about 75 percent of all Southerners live in metropolitan areas. Another of his columns was headlined "The Ever-Contradictory Southern Redneck"; in it he pointed out that poor white Southerners tend to like individual blacks very well, but not be so fond of blacks as a group.

Not endearing himself to those in the black community who dislike having unpleasant news about their community bandied about, Maxwell pointed out in another of his columns that in the most recent year for which he could find statistics, 1999, 25 percent more black men were in the U.S. prison system than were enrolled in colleges and universities. Among the reasons behind that grim figure, he wrote, are inferior public education, absence of black male role models, low expectations, low self-esteem and homes without books or adults who consider learning important.

Among the awards Maxwell has won are a Mark of Excellence Award for feature writing in 1986, a second place award from the Florida Society of Newspaper Editors in 1987 for both column writing and in-depth reporting (the latter with Cindy Loman and Ron Wiginton), first place in the Florida Press Club competition in 1989 and in 1990, the Community Champion Award from the Civil Justice Foundation of Washington, D.C.

"Farewell; It's Time To Keep a Promise" by Bill Maxwell

Well, folks, today I say farewell.

This is my last column as a *St. Petersburg Times* employee. My last official day on the staff is July 2. I have been here 10 years. Long enough.

I have enjoyed writing for the Times. Mine was a dream job: My salary and benefits were great. I was free to write what I wanted, even when my editor disagreed with me and when he knew that I would bring him dozens of angry telephone calls, e-mails and letters.

I was permitted to travel, and I was pretty much free to make my day. With a company laptop for dummies, I made my office wherever I found myself—Gaza City, Jerusalem, Warsaw, Bucharest, Harlem, Belle Glade, Liberty City, Tallahassee. I cannot count the number of times I wrote columns in airport terminals and while in flight.

So, why am I leaving?

At age 58, and counting, I must fulfill a promise I made while attending historically black Wiley College in Marshall, Texas, and Bethune-Cookman College in Daytona Beach: that I would, at the appropriate time, return to a historically black college or university as a professor, that I would pass on my expertise and knowledge.

That time is now.

Beginning in August, I will become a writer in residence at Stillman College in Tuscaloosa, Ala. Currently, the college has a journalism minor and a student newspaper that is published once each semester.

My short-term goals are to help establish a journalism major and to publish the student newspaper weekly. My long-term goals are to help produce competent African-American journalists who can land jobs with the nation's mainline and minority media outlets and to transform Stillman into a center for journalism excellence, where companies, such as the *St. Petersburg Times*, come to recruit.

While we complain about bias against blacks in the media, an unfortunate truth is that too few of us are in America's newsrooms.

Why did I choose Stillman College, a tiny, Presbyterian-affiliated, private institution? Mainly because the president, Ernest McNealey, is my kind of African-American man and my kind of educator.

His philosophy and policies have become the college's esprit de corps. As I do, he believes that education—true learning—is essential to black survival, upward mobility and positive ethnic identity. To McNealey, learning is hope.

In a society where the odds are against blacks, where opportunities to fail abound, we must be competent in the accepted canons, we must speak standard English and we should write well. We must confound the old stereotypes. By being competent, we are being subversive and revolutionary. Education is a pre-emptive strike against failure. It is preventive medicine.

McNealey rejects easy excuses and discourages students from blaming others, particularly white people, for their predicament. Many of Stillman's students come from low-income homes, receive some kind of federal tuition aid and have low SAT scores. For McNealey and his faculty, these are the best reasons to study diligently and to be "smart."

Stillman's faculty and staff challenge students to beat the odds with determination, hard work and discipline, with respect for the wisdom of ages and with common-sense regard for societal norms and conventions.

After being in St. Petersburg for 10 years with a community of mostly anti-intellectual Midtowners who blame white people for their plight, who are too quick to label as "sellouts" those who insist on honest introspection and self-help to solve our problems, I am ready to return to the scholarly and logical world of the academy.

For me, black St. Petersburg has been a dispiriting force. I have seen too much hopelessness, victimhood, defensiveness and provincialism. I have encountered too many mean-spirited people, both clergy and secular, who pose as leaders.

The time has come for me to return to an environment where my modest talents and willingness to speak out will be treated as benefits rather than as threats and betrayals.

No longer will I tolerate being cast as an enemy of the people for believing that we must change to survive, that we must rekindle the awareness that we, like other groups, have great power over our destiny.

At Stillman College, I will be free to teach this essential lesson each day to young people who have their lives ahead of them, who have the intellectual capacity and the eagerness to look inside themselves and become independent thinkers, successful professionals, law-abiding citizens and nurturing parents.

I also will teach students that they should give back to their communities by writing checks for good causes and programs, by serving.

Again, I will miss my dream job here. But the time has come to keep my promise of 40 years ago: to make a positive difference in the lives of black students who, in turn, will make a positive difference for others.

Source: Reprinted by permission of Mr. Maxwell. This column originally appeared on 27 June 2004.

Books by Bill Maxwell: *Maximum Insight: Selected Columns* (Gainesville, Fla.: University Press of Florida, 2001).

Maynard, Nancy Hicks (1946–)

A former *New York Times* and *New York Post* reporter, former publisher of the *Oakland Tribune* in California, and ex- chair of The Freedom Forum Media Studies Center at Columbia University, Nancy Maynard is now a communications consultant and board chair of the Robert C. Maynard Institute for Journalism Education at Berkeley. She was born in New York City to a jazz musician father and a mother who encouraged her to go into journalism. Her first such experience was working on her junior high school paper. She worked as a part-time copy girl at the *New York Post* while enrolled in the journalism program of Long Island University. She is a 1966 graduate of that university and later, in 1987, earned the J.D. at Stanford Law School. After receiving her bachelor's degree, she became a reporter for the *New York Post* and was at that time, the only black newspaperwoman in the city. Her mentor was Ted Posten, who had been the first black reporter hired by that newspaper; her specialty was the education beat. In spring 1968, her editors turned down her request to be sent to Memphis, Tennessee, to cover the activities of Martin Luther King Jr. King was assassinated that very week, and Maynard decided to seek a new job. She quickly found what she wanted at the *New York Times* and became that paper's youngest reporter. She worked as a domestic policy reporter and Washington correspondent for the *Times* until 1979.

She was married in 1975 to Robert C. Maynard, who died of prostate cancer in 1993. He had been hired in 1967 as the *Washington Post*'s first black correspondent and took a leave in 1977 to cofound, with wife Nancy, the Institute for Journalism Education at the University of California, Berkeley, in order to attract and to further the training of minority journalists. In 1979, the Gannett chain named him editor of the *Oakland Tribune*, making him the first black editor of a mainstream U.S. newspaper. He and Nancy bought the paper in 1983 and became the first black owners of a mainstream paper, as well. Bob Maynard took the title of editor, president and copublisher along with Nancy. In the 1980s, he added to his duties a nationally syndicated newspaper column. The paper enjoyed a national reputation as a writer-friendly place to work, and won many awards, including a Pulitzer for photojournalism after a severe California earthquake in 1989. Due to Bob Maynard's ill health, the couple sold the paper in 1992 to William Dean Singleton. In 1993, the institute at Berkeley was renamed the Robert C. Maynard Institute for Journalism Education; it was first directed by Nancy Maynard and is now directed by the couple's daughter, Dori J. Maynard, who like her father before her, had been a Nieman scholar at Harvard University. Nancy Maynard is president of Maynard Partners Inc., a media consultation and research firm. As have other media consultants, she has remarked on the shaky future of that great American institution, the national evening news. Not only are the networks losing ground due to the competition of on-demand news outlets, but because of encroachment of the day's big stories, which are now being included in the local news shows that precede the networks' 6.30 news shows, and by the additional fact that the networks themselves often save their best material to use on their news magazine programs. In 2000, Maynard published a book titled *Mega Media: How Market Forces Are Transforming News*. She moved to New York City and served as chair of the Freedom Forum Media Studies Center during 1996 and 1997. She sits on the board of the Maynard Institute as well as that of the Tribune Company. She has appeared on "Washington Week in Review," "Face the Nation" and "Meet the

Press." Among her recognitions is the University of Missouri's Honor Medal for Distinguished Service to Journalism.

Books by Nancy Hicks Maynard: *Mega Media: How Market Forces Are Transforming News* (New York: Maynard Partners Inc., 2000).

Further Readings: Cuenco, Yvette. "Maynard to Chair Media Center." [Online]. San Francisco State University Web site www.journlaism.sfsu.edu/www/pubs; "Nancy Maynard." [Online]. Global Business Network Web site www.gbn.com, "Nancy Maynard." [Online]. Maynard Institute Web site www.maynardije.org/programs/history.

McCarthy, Sheryl (31 July 1948–)

An insightful and hard-hitting *Newsday* columnist and professor at Columbia University's Graduate School of Journalism is Sheryl McCarthy, who was born in Birmingham, Alabama. Her B.A., cum laude, is from Mount Holyoke College, and her M.A. and J.D. degrees were earned at Columbia. She is a member of the New York bar. She held a variety of earlier newspaper jobs before reaching her present position with *Newsday* on Long Island, New York. McCarthy was a reporter for the *Boston Globe*, then for the *Baltimore Evening Sun*. She served as reporter and education editor for the *Daily News* in New York, was a national correspondent for ABC News, and was a reporter for New York *Newsday* from 1987 to 1989, then a twice weekly columnist for that paper from 1989 until 1995. When the New York edition closed in 1995, McCarthy became an opinion page columnist for the parent paper on Long Island and in 1989 joined the Columbia journalism faculty as an adjunct professor. She has been a Nieman Fellow at Harvard, is a Mount Holyoke College trustee and has published one collection of her columns.

McCarthy's column topics range from the political to the social, on issues that often, but not always involve race. One that had little to do with race relations appears below and gives her take on the reactions of two old Nixon intimates to the revelation of retired FBI official Mark Felt as the informant "Deep Throat." Both columnist/candidate Pat Buchanan and Christian Conservative Charles Colson regard Felt as a disloyal snitch, but the liberal McCarthy begs to differ. Other examples are her own reaction to the 2005 Edward Kline book about Sen. Hillary Clinton, which McCarthy considers a right-wing hatchet job; her surprise over a study claiming that almost half the Americans eventually will suffer some mental illness or disorder; her defense of allowing cameras in New York courtrooms; and her argument that crass political posturing should be eliminated from public debate about the morning-after pill. Commenting on a case soon to come before the U.S. Supreme Court, she argued that the court should uphold the right of the government to deduct repayment of old, unpaid student loans from Americans' Social Security checks. Her criticism of former columnist Armstrong Williams having accepted government money to promote the No Child Left Behind initiative was as harshly critical as can be found.

As to the war in Iraq, her view is that the present administration is guilty of dreadful duplicity. About the revelations of abuses in Abu Ghraib prison, her view is that few things could be less consistent with democracy than torturing and abusing prisoners, and she has advocated that both President George W. Bush and Secretary of Defense Donald Rumsfeld should be turned out of office. She faults former Secretary of State Colin Powell for having been a team player, albeit a reluctant one, and regards his replacement, Condoleezza Rice, as admirable in intelligence and style, but wrong in her hawkish certainty about the wisdom of invading Iraq. McCarthy is likewise sandpaper-rough on former New York major Rudy Giuliani, who, after the attacks on the World Trade Center Towers, reinvented himself as a resolute beacon of strength and concern. McCarthy has less than fond memories of Giuliani's years of cracking down on crime in the city, saying those years were marked by frequent incidents of police brutality. The more recent misuse of police power, she has written, came during the 2004 Republican National Convention in New York City, where protesters were denied their constitutional right of peaceful protest in the vicinity of the convention.

As to race relations, the columnist describes specific incidents of prejudice and discrimination in New York and opposes laws that disenfranchise felons, arguing that such laws are often misused to dilute voting power among people of color. And she is just as quick to criticize the misdeeds of African Americans, as she did in a column about attacks by black teenagers against Asian-American students in Brooklyn.

McCarthy has been a recipient of Columbia University's Meyer Berger Award for her writing about New York City and has won other awards from the New York Society of Black Journalists and the Education Writers Association.

Books by Sheryl McCarthy: *Why Are the Heroes Always White?* Kansas City, Mo.: Andrews and McMeel, 1995.

McGlowan, Angela (?–)

Young and attractive Angela McGlowan is a staunchly conservative political analyst for the FOX News Channel, host of Fox 5's show "Good Day Street Talk" and also one of the voices of the Independent Women's Forum (iwf.org). She hails from Oxford, Mississippi, and is a public administration graduate of the University of Mississippi, where she specialized in political science and criminal justice, was an Ole Miss Ambassador and was active with Habitat for Humanity and the Mississippi Society. She was also a contestant in beauty pageants and was a Top Ten Ole Miss Beauty and Miss Magnolia. In the latter capacity, she made appearances on behalf of the American Cancer Society and the Just Say No program. In addition, she was a legal researcher for criminal court judge Joe Brown in Memphis, Tennessee, and was a volunteer worker in the Clinton/Gore campaign in 1992. After graduating, her plan was to move to the nation's capital, work for a time for politicians, then return home to attend law school. Instead of pursuing a career in law, however, she chose to work as a broadcast analyst and as a lobbyist. In a story for Washingtonpost.com, McGlowan told interviewer Cathy Areu that when she first arrived in Washington in 1993 and sent her resume to various members of Congress, her job search met with no success. A friend suggested that she gain visibility by entering the Miss District of Columbia pageant. She did, and she won, which suddenly made her an attractive hire for our nation's leaders. In 1994, when her "reign" ended, she took a job as director of outreach and spokesperson for Sen. Bob Dole's Better America Foundation, the purpose of which was to promote community empowerment, and to make Dole a more attractive candidate for the presidency. In 1996, McGlowan took a new job as press liaison for Rep. Roscoe Bartlett of Maryland's sixth district and also worked as correspondent assistant in the offices of Rep. John Ensign of Nevada's first district. By this time, McGlowan's politics had shifted to the right, and she argued for conservative policy in such matters as Social Security, Medicaid, welfare reform, health care and tax relief. Her efforts got her quickly promoted to publicist for Rep. Ensign's reelection race in 1996. From 1999 to 2005, she walked the delicate highwire as a political analyst and at the same time was a registered lobbyist for media mogul Rupert Murdoch's News Corporation. She founded her own lobbying/public relations company, Political Strategies, of which she is the CEO. In her work as a lobbyist, she is a link between Congress and Murdoch's corporate interests. She holds the title Director of Government Affairs and Diversity Development for the News Corporation. Simultaneously, she has done on-air commentary for FOX News and has appeared on such shows as "Tonight" on Black Entertainment Television, "Politically Incorrect" on ABC, "To the Contrary" and "This Is America with Dennis Wholey" on PBS and "America's Black Forum" and "Fox & Friends" on Fox. In all these venues, she has been a consistent supporter of Bush administration policy, both international and domestic. In 2005, she became host of "Good Day Street Talk," a public affairs talk show on Fox 5 WNYW in addition to continuing her work as an analyst for FOX Cable News Channel. In 2006, she also began working as a panelist for the Public Broadcasting System—a job that puts her in the company of fellow panelists such as Michelle Singletary, Thomas Friedman, Georgie Anne Geyer and David Broder. In her work for the Independent Women's Forum, an all-women news forum that first aired in 1992, McGlowan comments on politics, public policy and legal matters that pertain especially to women. Topics have included the gender gap in the work place, the wage gap, combating terrorism, election politics, school choice and the rights of women in other nations. Throughout, she has promoted the conservative agenda, arguing that Americans should let the president do his job as he sees fit rather than dissenting. Many of the "To the Contrary" shows in which she has participated as a panelist, however, have addressed issues that are not directly political: women and depression, the plight of poor children in bad economic times, the sorry condition of women's rights in Afghanistan, why women are so often unkind to one another, prenuptial agreements, breast implants, hormone replacement for menopausal women, virtual child pornography, AIDS and whether hospitals should provide emergency contraception for rape victims. McGlowan also has been a guest speaker for the Institute for Media and Entertainment. Her eventual goal, she says, is to return home to Mississippi and run for public office. She reports that her father, a minister, always wanted to stand for office but due to racial prejudice when he was younger, could not do so, and she hopes to fulfill his unrealized ambition.

Further Readings: "Angela McGlowan, Founder and CEO, Political Strrategies and Insights." [Online]. Institute for Media and Entertainment Web site www.instme.org; "Angela McGlowan." [Online, 26 August 2004]. Fox News Web site www.foxnews.com; "Angela McGlowan." [Online]. Independent Women's Forum Web site www.iwf.org; Areu, Cathy. "Angela McGlowan, Political Analyst and Miss District of Columbia 1994." [Online, 18 December 2005]. Washington Post Web site www.washingtonpost.com.

McGruder, Robert G. (31 March 1942–12 April 2002)

A well-liked boss and a seasoned journalist, Robert McGruder was a man of many firsts, including his having been the first black executive editor of the *Detroit Free Press*. He held that position from 1996 until the effects of cancer required that he retire during his 20-month battle with that disease. His death occurred in April of 2002. He was born in Louisville, Kentucky, and was a 1963 graduate of Kent State University, where he also had been the first African-American editor of the campus paper, the *Daily Kent Stater*. His long career began immediately after college at the *Dayton Journal-Herald*, which is no longer being published. By the end of 1963, he had achieved another first by being the earliest black reporter at the *Plain Dealer* in Cleveland, Ohio. Soon after taking that job, he was drafted into the Army in 1964 and spent the next two years stationed in Washington, D.C. He then returned to his reporting job at the *Plain Dealer*, where he helped organize a strike and served as a Newspaper Guild negotiator. He covered the first black mayor of a large American city, Cleveland's Carl Stokes. He investigated charges that Stokes was "on the take" but found no evidence that the charges were true. Some time later, he assisted Stokes in the writing of that political leader's autobiography, *Promises of Power* (New York: Simon and Schuster, 1973). McGruder also investigated Cleveland's financial difficulties and reported on the city's declaration of bankruptcy. Despite his activism, he rose to city editor in 1978 and to managing editor in 1981. In June 1986, he joined the *Detroit Free Press* as its deputy managing editor; the following year, he was promoted to managing editor, to editor in 1993 and finally to executive editor in 1996. In 1995, he had achieved still another breakthrough by becoming the first African-American president of the Associated Press Managing Editors organization. He encouraged diversity both through the APME and at his newspaper and headed a committee to attract minority hires for the paper's parent company, Knight Ridder. McGruder always made it clear that he was interested in fostering the careers of minority journalists of all kinds, not just African Americans. He appeared to have just as genuine an interest in other under-represented groups: Hispanics, Asian Americans, Native Americans and gays.

McGruder was on Pulitzer Prize nominating committees five times: in 1986, 1987, 1990, 1991 and 1998 and during 1991–1992, was a Knight Ridder/Duke University Fellow. He worked with the Accrediting Council on Education in Journalism and Mass Communication, was a director of the Michigan Press Association and was on the advisory board of Wayne State University's Institute for Minority Journalists. He was a director of the American Society of Newspaper Editors, was active with the National Association of Minority Media Executives, was a board member of the American Press Institute and was a trustee of the Foundation for American Communications. In October 2001, McGruder was awarded the John S. Knight Gold Medal; in his acceptance speech, in his typical modest style, he quoted the words of a Chinese philosopher to the effect that the best leaders do not try to call attention to themselves. Rather, when they have helped accomplish something good, their employees will think that they themselves had done it. McGruder had also received the Helen Thomas Spirit of Diversity Award given by Wayne State University and the William Taylor Distinguished Alumni Award from Kent State University. When McGruder died, Knight Ridder management set up the Robert G. McGruder Scholarship Fund to provide support for students at Wayne State's Institute for Minority Journalists and also established, in partnership with APME and the American Society of Newspaper Editors, an annual Robert G. McGruder Award for Diversity Leadership. Winners of the 2005 McGruder Award were the *Honolulu Advertiser* and the Sioux City, South Dakota *Argus Leader*. Kent State also set up a McGruder Award program for fostering media diversity; winner in 2005 was retired Knight Ridder news executive Albert Fitzpatrick, who also is profiled in this reference work.

Further Readings: "Chairman's Citation." [Online, February 2003]. National Press Foundation Web site www.nationalpress.org; Meriwether, Heath J. "Appreciation: Robert G. McGruder, 1942–2002." [Online, 14 April 2002]. American Press Institute Web site www.americanpressinstitute.org; "Robert G. McGruder." In *The African American Almanac*, 9th ed. Ed. by Jeffrey Lehman. (Detroit, Mich.: Gale Group, 2003), pp. 877–78; "Robert McGruder, a Detroit Newspaper Icon." [Online]. The African American Registry Web site www.aaregistry.com/african_american_history.

Merida, Kevin (c.1957–)

Kevin Merida is an associate editor and writer for *The Washington Post* and is the husband of that paper's columnist Donna Britt. He was born in the Washington, D.C., area to parents who worked for the federal government. He was in fifth grade when busing began to be implemented as a means of achieving racial integration in the nation's public schools. Twenty-five years later, when busing was ended, Merida wrote in his *Washington Post* story "An Era Slowly Rolls to a Stop" (2 September 1998) regarding his ambivalent feelings about busing's effects. He reported that although his grade school and high school were attended primarily by white students, he socialized mainly with his fellow African Americans. He added that the same was true of his college years but that in the work world, his friendships have widened to include many people of other racial and ethnic backgrounds than his own. His children, he has remarked, have a set of friends in their Montgomery County schools so diverse that they resemble a meeting of the United Nations. While a tenth-grade student athlete at Central High School, Merida was notified in mid–basketball season that he would have to be bused, along with roughly 300 other children, to Crossland High in Temple Hills. He recalls the demarcation line between blacks and whites in those school days and how, if a black student made friends with someone white, he was criticized as an "Uncle Tom." He also remembers the small group of confrontational white boys that his friends referred to as the "Grits." Merida has noted that in present-day America, a new form of voluntary busing is being done to allow students to leave their own neighborhoods and attend magnet schools. Merida attended Boston University and was attracted into journalism in the post–Watergate era. He credits one of his high school English teachers and his communication professors at Boston University for having aimed him toward a newspaper writing career; he graduated with the B.A. in 1979. Before being hired by the *Post*, Merida was the *Dallas Morning News*' assistant managing editor of international and national news. He also covered the administration of the first President George Bush and was part of a team that won a Pulitzer Prize for its investigative work on secret wars. He joined the *Washington Post* in 1993 as a national political reporter. He wrote a column for the paper's Sunday magazine section and has been a Style Section feature writer. He has done extensive writing on the work of Congress and has covered two presidential elections. Merida has also been an active political analyst for a variety of radio and television shows on PBS, NPR, CBS and CNN. His honors include the National Association of Black Journalists' 2000 Journalist of the Year award and a 2005 Distinguished Alumni Award from Boston University's College of Communication. He and fellow *Post* writer Michael Fletcher have cowritten a soon-to-appear biography of Supreme Court Justice Clarence Thomas; its title is *Supreme Discomfort*. The two writers have already collaborated on several longform stories about Thomas for the *Post*. Merida was a contributor to the NABJ Task Force report "The L.A. Unrest and Beyond," published in 1992. He was a Best of Cox judge in 2001 and a Hoover Institution Media Fellow in 2004.

In 1999, Merida wrote a story titled "3 Consonants and a Disavowal" for the Institute for the Study of Academic Racism challenging the motives of the Council of Conservative Citizens and Sen. Trent Lott's ties to it. Merida charged racism and agreed with the NAACP's Julian Bond that Congress should be as vigilant about white extremists as they have been about the more extreme views expressed by Nation of Islam officials such as Khallid Abdul Muhammad. In a March 2001 article in the *Post*, Merida wrote approvingly about a Washington area 14-year-old whose ambition was to be a literary figure, a contrast to the many youths who aspire to be sports stars or to achieve "gangsta" or "diva" status. He returned to this theme in 2002 in a story about the need for more youngsters who want to grow up to be the Kobe Bryant of physics or some other science, and he credited astronaut Sally Ride for inspiring more American girls to go into scientific studies. In a March/April 2003 story for the *New Crisis*, Merida wrote about the accomplishments of the chair of the Congressional Black Caucus, Maryland Democrat Elijah Cummings, who had begun life as the child of sharecroppers. In a March 2005 story in the *Post*, Merida aimed his attention at the late defense attorney Johnnie Cochran, picturing him as a larger than life celebrity but one who would defend the underdog, whatever the person's race. In an anecdote in the story, Cochran told of having been stopped by Los Angeles police brandishing drawn guns while he was driving with two of his children in his Rolls-Royce; Merida reported that although Cochran was stung by the incident, he never filed a complaint but instead described the experience in his public appearances to highlight the problem of lingering racism. In October 2005, Merida wrote about Supreme Court nominee Harriet Miers having withdrawn her name and about the loss of conservative support being experienced by President George W. Bush. In June 2006, a story by Merida and *Post* reporter Michael A. Fletcher began a year-long series of articles, "Being a Black Man," to examine the problems and the opportunities for African-American men today. Other *Post* staffers, such as Steven A. Holmes and Richard Morin, have also contributed to the series.

"Johnnie Cochran, the Attorney on the People's Defense Team" by Kevin Merida

What I remember about Johnnie Cochran has nothing to do with O.J.

It has nothing to do with Johnnie's oratorical skills or his panache, though I have never seen another human being so confidently wear an eggplant suit.

The Johnnie Cochran frozen in my mind was riding up an escalator in a Dallas hotel four years ago, and I was trailing him to get an interview for a magazine piece on Supreme Court Justice Clarence Thomas. Johnnie was happy to oblige, but I was not the only one who wanted something from him.

I was joined on that escalator by autograph seekers and picture takers, whose ranks were even thicker at the top of the landing. They had spotted Johnnie from a distance and were waiting for him, pens out, Kodak disposables ready to snap. The knot of Johnnie-followers quickly swelled. Some had business offers. Some wanted a job in his firm. Others recounted a horrible injustice done to a relative that could be rectified by only one man, arguably the most famous criminal defense lawyer in America. One guy simply wanted Johnnie to read his poetry.

I took in this display with wonderment, Cochran's skill at handling his renown like it was a glass of water—and tap water at that. He handed out business cards, told someone to jot down a number, promised a meal next time he was in town. The big shots and the little shots got equal attention, nobody left out or left behind. And then finally Johnnie grabbed my arm, ushering me to a quiet patch of carpet behind a pillar, where he hoped we could escape the attention and I could do the interview. It took half an hour to get to this point, but the moment didn't last long, as the Cochran herd located their man again.

It was a small exercise in observing an outsize American character who retained his authenticity. In the fab-fab world of inflated celebrity, the famous often give very little of themselves to those who adore them. Athletes and entertainers routinely sign their names without even making eye contact, and politicians often appear to be searching for someone more important to talk to. Cochran talked to, took time for, everyone. He was a cheerleader for his craft, the Dick Vitale of the legal profession.

True, we were at the annual convention of the National Bar Association, the nation's preeminent organization of black lawyers and judges. But the gawking an giddiness over his presence went well beyond the gathering. A white woman from the Midwest, on vacation with her family, practically screeched upon coming within fainting range of the smooth attorney. "Oh, my God, that's Johnnie Cochran, isn't it? Oh my God. I just want to meet you."

And so Johnnie introduced himself to the woman and her family, and posed for photos.

Cochran could turn on the charm like crazy. He could make you rethink something you thought you knew. He practiced his principles, one of which was emblazoned on T-shirts for his employees: "Injustice anywhere is injustice everywhere." When he took the case of Reginald Denny, the white truck driver dragged from his cab and beaten by black assailants during the Los Angeles riots, some thought Johnnie had lost it. Was he actually going to represent a white guy against the brothers? Even in his own firm, lawyers tried to talk him out of the case. But Johnnie had it all figured out as he filed a $40 million suit against the city: He argued that Denny's civil rights were violated because the cops had deserted the predominantly black neighborhood during the riots and thus had failed to come to Denny's rescue. The suit was eventually dismissed, but in the name of Denny, he had waged a campaign for better police protection for that neighborhood.

Harvard Law professor Charles Ogletree, who considered Cochran a close friend and mentor, hopes to preserve a legacy for Cochran that transcends his celebrity work of O.J. Simpson and Michael Jackson, Jim Brown and Sean "P. Diddy" Combs.

"He was willing to fight for the underdog to achieve social justice and equality, particularly when it came to police brutality and excessive use of force," says Ogletree. "The reason an O.J. Simpson would even know about Johnnie Cochran," Ogletree adds, "was because he was successful for 25 years before the Simpson case was even on the radar. That is the Johnnie Cochran I hope that people will remember."

They could've formed a line from the Capitol to Washington Monument yesterday, black luminaries with thoughts on Cochran. They hailed from the spheres of civil rights and entertainment, from law and politics. Some were community activists and street preachers; almost anyone Cochran had touched had something to say. The call-in lines on black radio talk shows were jammed. Cochran's death at 67 on Tuesday from an inoperable brain tumor had caught a whole lot of folks by surprise. Of course the newspapers all used the well-worn catchphrase from Cochran's O.J. defense—"If it doesn't fit, you must acquit." New York's Daily News plastered that gem on its cover. But for those who knew him, Johnnie's gifts went beyond glove gambits in open court.

"He became a national frame of reference for the dispossessed," proclaimed Jesse Jackson, who noted that some of Cochran's cases never had to be fought. "The idea that you could call Johnnie, or 'Johnnie is coming to town,' made corporations and violators shake."

Many didn't know that after several lucrative years in private practice, Cochran joined the Los Angeles County prosecutor's office for a few years. He took a cut in pay and figured he could help change the system. But on a Saturday afternoon in 1979, as he was driving his Rolls-Royce down Sunset Boulevard—two of his children in the back seat—he was pulled over by police.

"Get out with your hands up!" Cochran heard an officer scream through a bullhorn.

The cops had their guns drawn. Cochran's children were crying. The officers searched the car, rummaging through the Euro-style leather clutch he always carried. And, *voila*, they found his badge from the district attorney's office.

"It was dehumanizing," Cochran recounted to The Washington Post in 1994. But he never filed a complaint and never demanded an official apology. What he did, in his own shrewd way, was to tell the story over and over and over again. It became a signature Cochran anecdote, forever memorialized in magazines and newspapers across the land. The point: Even a black man with a Rolls-Royce and his own initials on his plates can be stopped by police and treated like a criminal.

Some would argue that Cochran baldly injected race into cases, that he exploited race in his practice of the law. And yet he was often a more subtle negotiator than he was given credit for. He also was someone who never felt the need to apologize for being black.

When we finally did grab some time in that Dallas hotel in 2001, Johnnie said something to me that explained a lot about himself and how he wished to be viewed: "I don't care who you are, you want to be regarded well at home. If you're from our community and you've done nothing to uplift your people, I don't know how happy you could be."

Make no mistake, Johnnie Cochran must have been a happy man. A very happy man.

(Staff writers Hamil R. Harris and Tamara Jones contributed to this report).

Source: © 2005, *The Washington Post*. Reprinted with permission. The above story originally appeared on 31 March 2005.

Further Readings: "Being a Black Man: A Look Behind the Project." [Online, 2 June 2006]. Washington Post Web site www.washingtonpost.com; "Kevin Merida." [Online, 19 January 2006]. Boston University Alumni Web site www.bu.edu/alumni/com/awards; "Live: Style Writer Kevin Merida." [Online, 1998]. Washington Post site http://discuss.washingtonpost.com. McWhorter, John. "Racial Profiling." [Online, 13 September 2002]. Manhattan Institute for Policy Research Web site www.manhattan-institute.org.

Miller, John Xavier (11 September 1955–)

John X. Miller is public editor and twice-weekly columnist for the *Detroit Free Press*. He was born in Henderson, North Carolina, and grew up in Winston-Salem, where his father worked at Winston-Salem State University. He decided to pursue the study of journalism, reasoning that this calling would be one way to help improve upon the stereotypical portrayal of black people in the media. Miller is a 1977 journalism graduate of Virginia's Washington & Lee University and also did some course work toward a law degree there. His career began in 1978 at the *Roanoke Times & World News* (now the *Roanoke Times*). During his three years there, he was, in succession, a copy editor, state layout editor, slot editor, bonus section editor and composing room editor. In 1980, he became a sports copy-and-layout editor at the *Charlotte Observer*, and after 18 months, he relocated again to become one of the original sports staff members of the newly formed national newspaper *USA Today*. He started there in 1982 as a copy editor, directed that paper's coverage of the Olympics from 1986 to 1989 and in 1991, was promoted to deputy managing editor of sports but left that same year to become executive editor for the *Reporter* in Lansdale, Pennsylvania. Five years thereafter, Miller became managing editor of the *Sun News* in Myrtle Beach, South Carolina, where he directed that paper's news coverage. He joined the *Detroit Free Press* in 1999 as its ombudsman, charged with receiving and dealing with readers' comments and criticisms and writing two columns a week to help the paper's readers better understand how newspaper journalism operates. He also organizes and runs reader forums and seeks out ways to increase reader interactivity on the *Detroit Free Press* Web site. Soon after arriving at the *Free Press*, Miller collaborated with executive editor Bob McGruder to change his job designation from ombudsman to public editor. He reports that during a normal week, he fields around 90 telephone calls and perhaps 20 emails and that the most common reader complaints involve factual errors, such as incorrect names, numerical errors, misidentifications and misspellings. Other complaints center around grisly photographs and whether they should have been published, and questionable headlines. One of the latter that resulted in angry complaints from parents was "Warren Santa charged in killing daughter." As public editor, he decides how to deal with such complaints, publishing corrections of factual mistakes and addressing more general complaints in his column, which tries to show readers how the newsroom functions. His job, essentially, is to keep faith with readers and thereby keep the paper's credibility high. He also solicits advice from readers from time to time. Following the Jason Blair debacle in 2003, Miller sent an email to roughly 3,000 of the paper's readers asking their opinions about inaccurate reporting and other credibility issues, then published the results in his column. One reader responded that, in his view, the most significant mistakes in most newspapers are errors of omission. Another suggested that for every 100 stories a reporter produces, 10 of those stories, chosen at random, should be reviewed by an editor so that problems like the one involving Jason Blair could not develop for long. Around that same time, Miller issued invitations for as many as 10 readers a day to come to the paper's conference room and observe the morning news staff meeting. Another Miller initiative has been the creation of accuracy checklists tailored to reporters, various kinds of editors, photographers, staff artists and even page designers. He has also addressed the matter of reporters' use of confidential sources; one of his columns on that topic appears below.

During the time he spent on the Myrtle Beach paper, his reorganization helped that paper win the Knight Ridders Alvah Chapman Jr. Award four years in a row for being the top paper in the chain. He is on the advisory board for the Pew Center for Civic Journalism's James K. Batten Award and is on the boards of the Associated Press Managing Editors and the Maynard Institute for Journalism Education. He belongs to the American Society of Newspaper Editors, the National Association of Minority Media Executives and the National Association of Black Journalists and has been a Pulitzer Prize juror and a facilitator at the American Press Institute in Reston, Virginia. He taught journalism at Howard University while working at USA Today and in Spring 2006 taught as a Donald W. Reynolds Distinguished Visiting Professor for his alma mater, where he offered two courses, Introduction to Reporting, cotaught with Professor Doug Cummings, and a new course titled Race, Gender and the Media.

"You Can't Quote Me" by John X. Miller

The one story line that has been long-running in the media drama—or trauma—of this year has been about the use of anonymous sources in news stories.

Actually, debate over them has been ongoing for years in newspaper circles, but not until this year has it reached a level of the industry deciding "we'd better deal with this now."

With more information available to citizens than ever, the news media need to explain why a source cannot be identified and what steps have been taken to ensure that the information from such a source is accurate.

This trauma became newsworthy after two journalists, the New York Times' Judith Miller and Time magazine's Matt Cooper, were subpoenaed to testify about their confidential sources involving the outing of CIA operative Valerie Plame.

So the issue of anonymous sources—I suggest they should be called confidential sources or people who did not want their names used—is on the minds of newspeople nowadays.

Last month, I was among more than 40 editors, publishers, First Amendment attorneys, journalism educators and citizens who discussed the use of unnamed sources and how such use affects all-important credibility.

The conferees gathered by the American Society of Newspaper Editors and the McCormick Tribune Foundation were an eclectic mix of experts who normally would not have been in a room to discuss such matters.

There was consensus that some abuse of confidential sources happens, and agreement that news organizations cannot perform their watchdog function in today's society without these sources.

That aligns with what the public thinks as well, surprisingly.

The First Amendment Center in Nashville surveyed citizens twice this year about their view of anonymous sources. In the first survey, 69% of Americans said journalists should be allowed to keep a news source confidential. In the second, 72% agreed. A similar survey by the Pew Research Center for the People and the Press found people believe the media are at least sometimes justified in protecting the identity of a source.

After a sigh of relief, conference attendees moved past that, to discuss other relevant factors that affect the use—or overuse—of unnamed sources.

Working journalists have become too blasé about sources, offering confidentiality before it is necessary or even requested. This approach grew out of the Watergate era. Reporters, most notably those within the Washington, D.C., beltway, offered sources the chance to talk on "background" or "off the record" as a way to get them to speak candidly in the hope of uncovering that scoop.

Additionally, more federal agencies are holding off-the-record background briefings, where reporters are invited only on the condition that sources are not identified in stories developed from the information.

Now practiced in newsrooms of all sizes and media persuasions, the "anonymous source" means lots of things. And that's one reason media credibility has taken a hit.

The public's interests are best served when the audience knows a news source's identity and can weigh the information against a source's biases and motivations. The public doesn't quite trust the reporting or the newsroom that overuses unnamed sources.

Knowing this, I was pleased to see a Dec. 2 Free Press story that went beyond just stating the information was from a source that did not want to be identified.

In that front-page article about the troubles facing attorney Geoffrey Fieger, we stated clearly why the unnamed source chose to provide information, but not to be identified. We said our information was "according to people with independent knowledge of the investigation both in and out of government. Those people insisted on anonymity because of ongoing probes."

This statement made clear why the person was not named and put the reasoning in context. That statement reflects the policy of the Detroit Free Press on unnamed sources, which is summarized in the box on Page 1K.

No unnamed sources are allowed in the newspaper unless approved by an executive editor or managing editor, and their job is to get specific answers about who the person is, how much they know, whether the information is verifiable elsewhere, and whether the person is likely to lose or gain in some meaningful way by revealing the information. If necessary, the top editors may ask to talk with the source.

At the conference, other alarming trends were addressed.

There was consensus that uniform standards for using anonymous sources need to be supported by journalism organizations, such as ASNE. These standards need to be communicated broadly, with specific support from news departments at media companies.

Among the newspapers represented at the conference, USA Today had one of the most stringent policies, which is no anonymous sources without the approval of a managing editor. Editor Ken Paulson said the use of anonymous sources is down 80% since the policy was instituted in 2004.

More civil lawsuits and government subpoenas are being issued to compel reporters to testify and name sources, and provide information they have reported. The Reporters Committee for Freedom of the Press reports a national increase of legal attempts to get reporters or their work used in court proceedings.

Journalists are becoming less certain the media companies they work for will defend them in these lawsuits and resist subpoenas.

On the subject of a national shield law, some of the editors who initially opposed it—many have always been in favor—are now reconsidering. Thirty-three states, including Michigan, have some form of such a law for journalists, and the mood of Congress seems to be to leave it as a state issue. However, there is a belief that a national shield law could get passed through a concerted push by journalists, journalism associations, First Amendment lawyers and media companies.

The most troubling result of this year's journalistic meltdowns could be more ominous and far-reaching than just how we deal with unnamed sources. It ultimately may come down to how far courts can go to compel reporters to disclose confidential information to government.

All these factors have put some editors, First Amendment attorneys and journalism academics on high alert. There is a sense that unless something is done now to help restore and reaffirm the public's trust in journalism, it will continue to dissolve until news organizations are imperiled for reasons other than economic.

Source: Reprinted by permission of the *Detroit Free Press*. This column appeared on 11 December 2005.

Further Readings: Finneren, Kate. "Miller Explains Controversial Photo." [Online, 19 April 2004]. Central Michigan University Web site www.c-life.com; "John X. Miller." [Online]. American Press Institute Web site www.americanpressinstitute.org; "John X. Miller to be Reynolds Visiting Professor at Washington & Lee." [Online, 13 October 2005]. Washington and Lee University siet http://news.wlu.edu.

Milloy, Courtland (?–)

A fixture at the *Washington Post*, Courtland Milloy writes a twice-weekly Metro column. He was born in Shreveport, Louisiana, and graduated in 1973 from Southern Illinois University. After graduation, he became a police and court reporter for the *Miami Herald* and took the same beat in 1975 when he was hired by the *Post*. He began a weekly column in 1983 and in 1985, moved to a twice-weekly schedule. More often than not, his writing deals with issues of interest to the capital city's black population. His first column for the *Post* was on one of the city's most interesting public figures, Marion Barry, who first assumed the office of mayor in 1979 with costly pomp that made Milloy uncomfortable. In an interview for Washingtonpost.com, Milloy estimates that he has now written as many as 100 columns about Barry, a man who has had enormous ups and downs but always seems to find a way to turn his life's lemons into lemonade.

On any given day, the Milloy column is apt to concern itself with the ordinary citizens of the city and their travails and triumphs. He does not specialize in political commentary, but does occasionally speak out—sometimes vehemently, as in a column headlined, "If I Hear Bush, Then I Don't Believe Him." In this column, he wonders, with dripping sarcasm, if he needs a hearing aid. He adds that he could have sworn he heard the president say the administration had found weapons of mass destruction and biological laboratories in Iraq prior to invading that nation. Milloy extended his criticism to the then secretary of state Colin Powell for having gone along with the administration's hawkish charade. The column concluded with a remark that it is not a hearing aid that was needed, but a lie detector. In another political column, Milloy asked in connection with the Abu Ghraib prisoner abuse scandal if it is really so easy to become what we Americans used to condemn, bemoaning what "shock and awe" had come down to a year later, and remarking that torturing people to find out their guilt or innocence is itself an act of terrorism. He has also chided the president for the use of lofty rhetoric about ending tyranny and promoting freedom and opportunity in other parts of the world, pointedly suggesting that the president should first try spreading such benefits at home. Milloy was also upset over stalled efforts to erect a memorial in the nation's capital to Benjamin Bannecker, the first black American scientist, who surveyed the city and also built the first American clock. This 2001 column complained that the site was in danger of being conscripted by admirers of Ronald Reagan for yet another memorial to that popular president.

One of Milloy's own favorite columns was the one he wrote in 1983 about a troubled D.C. youth who narrowly escaped death after being bitten by a Gabon viper—because the 16-year-old boy could not read. A 1985 column detailed his "citizen's ride-along" with D.C. police as they dealt with a domestic dispute in which a man was pathetically attempting to assert his authority at home in the face of odds he could not control. In 1994, one of Milloy's column topics was the seemingly miraculous recovery of another 16-year-old who had been shot in the forehead at point blank range on the campus of Howard University. A 2003 column dealt with a "Catch 22" situation involving D.C. drivers on the Capital Beltway who were hauled into traffic court for exceeding the speed limit and required to take a driver safety course, only to be told in that course that on the Beltway, the only safe way to drive is to keep up with the flow of traffic, whatever its speed.

A noteworthy 2005 column dealt with the J.L King book *On the Down Low*, about bisexual black men; Milloy's main concern in the matter is the increased spread of AIDS in the black community caused by this practice. Another day's topic was the problems caused by marketing $160 basketball shoes to teenagers, whose need to belong and to be accepted can be taken advantage of so very easily, and yet another was a tribute to black antiwar activist Damu Smith, who had been struck by colon cancer.

In late 2005, Milloy almost left the *Post* but instead took some time off and returned to continue writing his local column.

"Disturbing Turn for Shock and Awe" by Courtland Milloy

So this is what "shock and awe" has come down to a year later—a hooded Iraqi prisoner standing on a box, his hands connected to electric wires in such a way that he fears he'll be electrocuted if he lowers his arms or falls off.

From the awesome U.S. bombings that were supposed to help quickly end the war to allegations that U.S. forces have resorted to Saddam-style torture now that an end to the war is nowhere in sight, Operation Iraqi Freedom sure has come a long way.

The Bush administration cribbed its popular war chant from a book, "Shock and Awe: Achieving Rapid Dominance," by Harlan K. Ullman and James P. Wade.

"The basis for Rapid Dominance rests in the ability to affect the will, perception and understanding of the adversary through imposing sufficient Shock and Awe to achieve the necessary political, strategic and operational goals of the conflict," they write.

So far, however, that concept appears to have been most effective when applied at home rather than in Iraq. Note, for instance, how skillfully the Bush administration created the perception that Iraq was responsible for the Sept. 11, 2001, terrorist attacks.

"In Rapid Dominance, 'rapid' means the ability to move quickly before an adversary can react," the authors write. "This notion of rapidity applies throughout the spectrum of combat from pre-conflict deployment to all stages of battle and conflict resolution."

That should be clear even to a chicken hawk: When it comes to dominance, landing on the deck of an aircraft carrier and posing beneath a banner declaring an end to the war doesn't cut it.

On March 20, 2003, a day before the high-tech bombing campaign against Iraq was set to begin, Secretary of Defense Donald H. Rumsfeld said,

"What will follow will not be a repeat of any other conflict. It will be force and scope and scale that is beyond what has been seen before."

A mere 58 years after atomic bombs were dropped on Hiroshima and Nagasaki, America listened—and did not even flinch. Awesome.

Today, U.S. forces in charge of the Abu Ghraib prison near Baghdad—Saddam Hussein's old house of terrors—are being accused of behaving like his sadistic sons, Uday and Qusay. Is it that easy to become that which one condemns? Or has something been unleashed that was there all along?

In September 2002, J. Cofer Black, then head of the CIA's Counterterrorist Center, told the House and Senate intelligence committees that "there was a before 9/11, and there was an after 9/11. After 9/11, the gloves came off."

It should not come as a shock that the military might be using third-degree interrogation tactics that involve the use of brass knuckles and broomstick handles, tools not unfamiliar to some police departments here at home.

To be fair, in the case of that widely publicized electric torture stand, U.S. forces might not have been using live wires. The hooded prisoner on the box might simply have been told that they were live. Then again, Saddam's firing squads didn't always use real bullets; just the sound of blanks being fired was sometimes enough to cause his hooded victims to have fatal heart attacks.

The Geneva Convention notwithstanding, the mistreatment of prisoners of war pales in comparison to the mistreatment of Iraqi civilians. Where is the concern for them? At one point during the war, 12-year-old Ali Abbas received international medical attention after being severely burned and losing both arms in a missile attack in Baghdad. The idea was to show sympathy for the plight of such children—even as they continued to be killed after picking up unexploded cluster bombs dropped from U.S. warplanes and to perish when so-called smart bombs went astray.

That is mistreatment. That is torture. That is shock and awe.

And the worst may be yet to come. For torturing people just to find out if they are innocent is an act of terrorism—which the authors of "Shock and Awe" call "a tactic often employed by political actors that have no hope of physically vanquishing their enemies."

What a difference a year makes.

Source: © 2005. *The Washington Post*. Reprinted with permission. This column originally appeared on 3 May 2004.

Mitchell, Everett J. II (1962–)

On 6 December 2004, E.J. Mitchell became the first African American to hold the job of top editor at the *Tennessean* in Nashville. He had spent the prior four years as managing editor of the *Detroit News*. Mitchell was born in Nuremberg, Germany; his father was stationed there in the Army. Most of his upbringing was in Lawton, Oklahoma, and later, Louisville, Kentucky. In high school in Louisville, he was managing editor of the student paper, the *Paw Print*; and in college, he edited the *Communicator*, a campus paper for African-American students. He was a 1985 graduate of the University of Kentucky's School of Journalism and Telecommunications. His career began as a reporter at the *Courier-Journal* in Louisville, Kentucky. From there, he moved east to report for the *Evening Sun* in Baltimore, Maryland, where he worked from August 1985 to August 1986. In 1989, he became a police reporter for the *Detroit News*. There, he was one of the reporters who uncovered and documented corruption in the city's police department. That department's chief eventually was convicted and sent to prison. Mitchell became assistant city editor, and before leaving the paper, he was promoted to deputy city editor. He was assistant managing editor for local news at the *Cincinnati Enquirer* from November 1993 until January 1997, after which he was managing editor of the *News Journal* of Wilmington, Delaware. In 1999, he became executive editor of the Salem, Oregon, *Statesman Journal*, and in March 2000, he returned to the much larger *Detroit News* as its managing editor. There, he directed news coverage, supervising a staff of around 280 people. *The News* was a 2003 Pulitzer finalist for an investigative series of stories on Detroit's criminal justice system. Another influential series was on equipment shortages in the city's fire department. A third series done under Mitchell's direction detailed the effects of lingering racial segregation in Detroit and the ways that racial division was impacting education, crime and property values. A *Detroit News* public service initiative was its 2002 weight-loss challenge, in which Mitchell, a large man, took a personal part. Having held many reporting and editing positions at a variety of Gannett newspapers, and having proved his abilities at directing hard-hitting investigative work, Mitchell was selected in 2004 to be editor and vice president for news at the *Tennesssean*, replacing Frank Sutherland, who retired after holding that job for 15 years, and working under publisher Leslie Giallombardo. His announced goals were to strengthen the paper's investigative efforts and to cover news that directly impacts readers' lives. He specified that he wanted his staff of 170 to function collectively as an effective watchdog of both government and business. A bachelor married to his work, Mitchell said that he planned to be a hands-on editor and to function as a "player-coach" for his reporters and subeditors. A major story for Mitchell and his staff has been TennCare, Tennessee's expanded Medicaid program. The program covered around 1.3 million people, but Gov. Phil Bredesen revealed in 2005 that more than 300,000 of these individuals would have to be taken out of the system to keep TennCare financially viable. the *Tennessean*, the *Chattanooga Times Free Press* and the Tennessee Coalition for Open Government joined in a lawsuit to gain access to TennCare records. Mitchell is on the board of the Tennessee Coalition for Open Government. From 1997 to 2003, he was on the national board of the Associated Press Managing Editors and was chair of its Freedom of Information Committee from 1999 to 2000. He served as a Pulitzer juror in 2002 and 2003 and was honored as a Gannett Supervisor of the Year in 1996 and 1998.

Further Readings: Fisher, Deborah W. "Everett J. Mitchell II from Detroit Named Editor of the Tennessean." [Online, 6 December 2004]. The Tennessean Web site www.tennessean.com; Lawson Richard. "New Editor: Public Service to Be Goal for Tennessean." [Online]. Ten Tennessean Web site www.tennessean.com; Prince, Richard. [Online, 6 December 2004]. Richard Prince's Journal-isms. Maynard Institute Web site www.maynardije.org; Taylor, Dorcas. "The Player-Coach." [Online, February/March 2005]. American Journalism Review Web site www.ajr.org.

Mitchell, Mary A. (c.1949–)

Mary Mitchell worked for roughly two decades as a legal secretary but now writes a weekly column for the *Chicago Sun-Times* and is a member of that paper's editorial board. Her wide-ranging column, launched in 1996, usually covers matters of race, family, politics, and justice. She is a native of Chicago, where she and her twin sister grew up in public housing projects with eight other siblings and their hardworking parents. Light-skinned and having green eyes, the twins were picked on in their all-black schools. Sister Marie was the fighter of the two, while Mary was more of a pacifist who would try to talk her way out of tight spots. Due to the inherent dangers of life in the projects, the two girls used reading as a refuge, especially when they were preteens in a Clarence Darrow Homes high rise. Their upbringing was in an all-black environment, and the twins did not understand racial discrimination until they were 12. They took a bus to the Moody Bible Institute that summer, and one day they left the bus to get a milkshake at a drug store they had noticed. Realizing that they were the only nonwhites there and that they were being stared at in an unfriendly manner, the girls backed out the door and fled, crushed. Mary graduated from Dunbar Vocational High School in 1967; due to racial discrimination, the only job she could get at the time was to work in a mailroom. After many years as a legal secretary, she was denied a promotion at her law firm due to the absence of a college degree and decided to speed up the classes she had been taking at Columbia College. She changed majors from Creative Writing to Journalism, and faculty members Don Hayner and P.J. Bednarski suggested that she apply to the *Sun-Times*, which was just beginning to seek out minority reporters. After getting her degree in 1991, Mitchell was hired by that paper as its education reporter. In 1993, she and her former teacher, Don Hayner, also a *Sun-Times* reporter, cowrote "The Great Divide," a series of stories on race relations in Chicago. In 1994, her editor gave her a column. Since that time she has proved herself a worthy successor to such *Sun-Times* columnists as Mike Royko and Irv Kupcinet and a talented contemporary of fellow columnist Richard Roeper.

Sometimes her column is partly autobiographical, as was the case in January 2003 when she wrote about the death of Mamie Till Mobley, whose son, Emmett Till, was the victim of murder because he had supposedly whistled at a white woman. Mitchell recalled her mother warning her twin and herself that they were so sassy, they would end up like Emmett Till. Another 2003 column of note was about "Ghettopoly," the new variation of the popular board game Monopoly. The controversial new game had proved so sought after that Chicago stores could not keep it in stock. She did not share in the public's enthusiasm, however. Instead, she pointed out that the denigrating, stereotypical images of blacks used in the game had been borrowed from hip-hop videos. Her hope was that the game would at least serve to point out the unfortunate side of the music that young blacks and whites alike were finding so entertaining. In a June 2004 column, Mitchell took the part of entertainer Bill Cosby, who had blasted less affluent members of the black community for not acting in their own best interest. Mitchell pointed out that truth often hurts and that it was time for African Americans to admit the existence of a growing economic and social polarization in their community. Another of her 2004 columns addressed President George W. Bush's refusal to appear before the NAACP, a position he finally reversed in July 2006. She wrote about the Republican Party's use of race to appeal to the underbelly of white culture as a vote-getting device, adding that although she was not a Bush supporter, she could understand why he refused invitations to appear before people so unlikely to vote for him. She also mentioned that to run successfully for the presidency, an American must still be a wealthy white male.

A Mitchell column of early 2005 dealt with the difficulty of "fighting city hall" as manifested in a dispute between a Chicago woman and a female member of the city's police force. The woman had filed complaints against the officer, who then sued her accuser for slander. Around that same time, Mitchell wrote about the misadventures of right-leaning commentator Armstrong Williams, questioning whether commentators should even be called "journalists" and pointing out that many of today's commentators are more nearly entertainers. In spring 2005, she wrote about what she termed "entitleitis," a sense of entitlement felt by middle class youth; what brought her to that topic had been a false hate crime claim filed by a Trinity International University student. Just as unusual was a column about "sugar daddies," older men who use their money to prey on young women and who sometimes give those women more than they bargained for—HIV/AIDS. Lukewarm on the issue of reparations, Mitchell instead favors the idea of blacks attempting to reclaim land, especially in the South, that had belonged to their forebears, but had been forcibly taken away by whites. ROSA, or Reclamation of Southern Assets, she wrote, is an initiative sponsored by the Congressional Black Caucus for that purpose.

The murder in Chicago of a young mother by her husband, who thought she was having an affair, led Mitchell to write on domestic violence in June 2005. At other times, she makes personal admissions in her column. An example was a column about poor blacks having been removed from an area of Chicago that had then been "gentrified"; Mitchell admitted that even though she disapproved of that process, she herself was looking for a new house or condo there. In another column, she wrote that the culture of gangs and drugs had become so firmly engrained in many poor black neighborhoods that people living in such conditions had come to regard the perpetrators as legitimate businessmen. The failure of the justice system to deal with the needs of the mentally ill and the scarcity of blacks holding city jobs in Chicago are two other topics addressed in her columns.

Mitchell has appeared on NPR's "News & Notes" and in February 2006 was a participant in the ABC 7 half-hour special "Black Chicago...Today and Tomorrow." Among her fellow panelists were Don Wycliff and Ronald Martin. Mitchell is a past president of the Chicago Association of Black Journalists, is a member of the Association of Women Journalists and is on the advisory board of the Chicago Children's Advocacy Center. Among her awards have been the Award of Excellence from the National Association of Black Journalists and the Chicago Headliner Club's Peter Lisagor Award.

"Reclaiming Land May Be Bigger Than Reparations" by Mary Mitchell

After reporting on the Rankin family and hearing other stories about Northerners who are fighting to reclaim their inheritances in the South, I'm beginning to believe the reparations movement may be on the wrong track. Some of you may recall the Rankins' story.

The Chicago family are the heirs of former slaves who owned land in Fayette, Miss., and they are trying to prove that several oil companies pumped minerals off the land without compensating all of the heirs.

During my research on the Rankins' claim, I ran into Ray Waters, a teacher at DePaul's College of Law who had an interesting perspective on black people and Southern land.

What do you think would happen if you walked into a bank looking for a loan and produced a portfolio that included 40 acres or more of land in

Mississippi? he asked me. And what if the land had timber or oil? What do you think would happen?

Help Pursuing Claim Offered

Unfortunately, for many of us, our biggest assets are our matchbox houses and our 401(k) plans. But what if we suddenly found out our great-grandparents or grandparents owned land in the South? What if they were run off that land by racists? Reclaiming that land—especially land that ended up as part of property now owned by large estates and corporations—or being adequately compensated for its loss would make a difference in the overall wealth of African-Americans.

That's where the Reclamation of Southern Assets, or ROSA, project comes in.

On June 11 at Kennedy-King College, Chicago area residents who are trying to reclaim property they lost track of in the South can get help.

It's long overdue. Given the progress being made in the reparations movement, I'm not sure why reclaiming stolen land rights isn't a bigger political issue.

"We're trying to move it in that direction," Waters said.

From noon to 3 P.M. on June 11, six law students from DePaul and five from Southern universities will listen to stories from forgotten heirs. They will review documents and compile information needed to research claims. Over the next eight weeks, these future lawyers will arm themselves with deeds and titles.

Instead of marching on picket lines, some of them will march into county seats and take over dusty record books.

Many Were Driven off Land

The ROSA project is funded, in part, by the Congressional Black Caucus Initiative known as WOW. The acronym stands for "With Ownership, Wealth," and is one of three initiatives being pushed by Rep. Bobby L. Rush (D-Chicago). The other projects in Rush's South Side district target homeownership.

"The history of the black community in this country is significantly impacted by the lack of a land-based economy," Rush wrote in a statement supporting the second annual ROSA conference.

"This stems from not only the failure of the American government to keep its promise of 40 acres and a mule, but also the treacherous theft of African-American lands during the Jim Crow era."

In the early 1900s, blacks in the South owned more than 15 million acres, according to a 2001 investigation by the Associated Press. Today blacks own only about 1.1 million acres. The AP documented that thousands of blacks were intimidated, threatened, beaten and even lynched to keep them from owning land in the South.

A lot of lands that remained with black families are still under a cloud.

"There's the good and the bad and the missing," Waters said. "The people down South should have made sure that the 'good' was information as to what was going on at the estate. If you don't write down what is supposed to happen, you may end up sharing property with those you might not see."

An Overlooked Wrong

Besides helping Chicagoans sort through their land claims, the ROSA project allows law students to get a jump on their careers.

Al Bailey, a first-year law student at DePaul, will serve the project as a research assistant. Also a first-year law student, Kimberly Mallett will be one of the people listening to the stories. The students also will tackle disputes involving oil and timber rights.

"Once I spot the issues, I'll pass the information on to a research assistant and prepare a memorandum about whether or not the claim is valid," she said. "I'm not sure what field of law I'm going to go into, but I feel that working on this project, interviewing the claimants, doing the research and assessing the claims will arm me with the skills I'll need."

In the short run, Waters hopes the ROSA project will result in legislation that will make it easier for heirs in Chicago to bring suit in federal court against relatives in the South.

And as Rush pointed out in his statement, it is important that black people look into the abuses and injustices done to black people in the name of the law. The outright theft of land from black citizens in the U.S. is an overlooked wrong that has yet to be addressed.

Source: As published in the *Chicago Sun-Times*. Copyright © 2005 by the *Chicago Sun-Times, Inc.* Reprinted with permission. This column appeared on 5 June 2005.

Further Readings: Astor, David. " 'You've Got Hate Mail' Is What 'Target Zone' Columnists Hear." *Editor & Publisher*, 2 July 1999, pp. 36–37; Silets, Alexandra. "One-on-One with

Mary Mitchell." [Online, 2006]. WTTW 11 Web site www.wttw.com; "Mary Mitchell." [Online]. United Feature Syndicate Web site www.unitedfeatures.com.

Mitchell, Russ (25 March 1960–)

The experienced yet youthful Russ Mitchell in April 2006 became anchor of the "CBS Evening News" on Sunday. He had been coanchor of "The Saturday Early Show" on CBS, one of the anchors of the "CBS Evening News" on Saturdays and a correspondent for "CBS News Sunday Morning." He is from St. Louis, Missouri, and is a 1982 journalism graduate of the University of Missouri. Following graduation, he became a reporter for Kansas City station KMBC-TV, then from 1983 to 1985, was an anchor at Dallas station WFAA-TV. He returned to reporting in 1985 at KTVI-TV in St. Louis, then in 1987, became a reporter and weekend anchor at CBS affiliate station KMOV-TV, also in St. Louis. In 1992, he joined CBS as coanchor for its overnight news show "CBS News up to the Minute," and in 1993, Mitchell began working as a correspondent for the network's newsmagazine-format show "Eye to Eye." He reported on the U.S.-led military intervention in Haiti in September 1994, and he also was dispatched to cover stories in France, Russia, Chile and Indonesia. From 1995 to 1997, he was anchor of the "CBS Sunday Night News." He was named a coanchor of "The Saturday Early Show" in November 1997, presently cohosting that program with Tracy Smith, and became a "CBS News Sunday Morning" correspondent in July 2002. During those years, he reported on the 1996 presidential race, the 1996 Republican National Convention; the massacre at Columbine High near Littleton, Colorado, in 1999; the February 2003 disintegration upon reentry of the space shuttle Columbia; conservative radio figure Rush Limbaugh's substance abuse troubles in 2003; the effects of Hurricane Frances in 2004 and the July 2005 London tube station blasts set off by terrorists. He also conducted an interview in March 2005 with actress Lauren Bacall, who recently had brought out an updated version of her autobiography, *By Myself and Then Some* (New York: HarperEntertainment, 2005). In 1998, Mitchell appeared as a correspondent on the television program "True or False: Teenagers Mean Trouble"; and speaking to a student audience at Brown University, he remarked on the fact that many local news shows are preceded or immediately followed by tabloid-type programming and consequently have been under pressure to compete in entertainment value, at the expense of actual news. His lecture was delivered under the auspices of the A. Alfred Taubman Center for Public Policy at Brown.

Mitchell was honored by United Press International in 1989 with a best reporting award. He won the news award given by the National Association of Black Journalists in 1995, a 2001 Sigma Delta Chi Award for spot news coverage—for his reporting on the Elian Gonzalez case—and the 2002 James Beard

Award for work he did on the "Early Show." Mitchell has won two Emmy awards from the National Academy of Television Arts & Sciences, St. Louis chapter, and a 1997 national Emmy for his reporting on the July 1996 explosion of Trans World Airlines Flight 800, which went down off Long Island, New York, killing 230.

Further Readings: "Famous St. Louisans—Russ Mitchell." [Online]. About, Inc. site http://stlouis.about.com; "Russ Mitchell." [Online]. CBS News Web site www.cbsnews.com.

Monroe, Bryan K. (22 August 1965–)

Former Knight-Ridder assistant vice president for news Bryan Monroe is now vice president and editorial director of the magazines *Ebony* and *Jet*. He also was the 2006 president of the National Association of Black Journalists. He was born in Munich, Germany, and holds a 1987 B.A. in communications with a journalism emphasis from the University of Washington. Monroe began his journalism career at the *Seattle Times* and moved through a variety of jobs at the *Roanoke Times & World News*; United Press International; the *University of Washington Daily*, for which he was editor; and, starting in 1988, the *Sun News* of Myrtle Beach, South Carolina, where he was graphics editor and director of photography. He was assistant project director of Knight Ridder's 25/43 Project, after which, in 1991, he became assistant managing editor of the *San Jose Mercury News*. In January 2001, he was promoted to deputy managing editor. In both positions, he was in charge of the paper's photographic, art, graphics and online work, and in 1992 and 1999, he supervised redesigns of the *Mercury News*. He was also the executive in charge of the paper's reporters and copy editors. A recent promotion, in October 2002, was to Knight Ridder assistant vice president for news, succeeding Larry Olmstead, who became the group's vice president of staff development and diversity; Monroe still works out of the San Jose paper.

Monroe was vice president, print, of the NABJ under President Herbert Lowe of *Newsday* and also vice president of Unity: Journalists of Color. He has served as president of the Bay Area Black Journalists Association and is a member of a mentoring group called 100 Black Men of Silicon Valley. He has been the recipient of awards from the Society of Newspaper Design and the National Press Photographers Association, plus the state press associations of Florida, South Carolina and Washington. Monroe has lectured at the Poynter Institute for Media Studies in Florida and was, in 2003, a Nieman Fellow at Harvard University.

Further Readings: "Knight Ridder Names Bryan Monroe Assistant Vice President/News." [Online]. Knght Ridder site http://66.39.131.116/releases; "MN Promotes Two Editors." *San Jose Mercury News*, 3 January 2001.

Moore, Acel (5 October 1940–)

A columnist, editorial board member, director of recruiting and associate editor of the *Philadelphia Inquirer*, Acel Moore has been with that newspaper since he began there as a copy boy in 1962. His commentary page column, "Urban Perspectives," appeared twice weekly, usually dealing with the effects of public policy on urban people; he is now semiretired. Moore won the Pulitzer Prize for local reporting in 1977 and in 1979, was a Nieman Fellow at Harvard. He was born in Philadelphia and attended the Settlement Music School from 1954 to 1958 and the Charles Morris Price School from 1964 to 1966. From 1959 through 1962 he served in the Army. Even more than for his writing, he will be remembered for his many efforts to organize and educate minority journalists. Beginning in 1968, he was active in the group Black Communicators, which drew its membership from all media and media-related jobs. With Chuck Stone of the *Philadelphia Daily News* and Claude Lewis of the Philadelphia *Evening Bulletin*, Moore cofounded in 1973 the Philadelphia Association of Black Journalists to represent members of the working press. He was on that organization's board and had a term as its president, and in 1975 he was a founding member of the National Association of Black Journalists. The PABJ's constitution and bylaws are said to have been used as the model for the national organization's governance. Moore helped with PABJ community workshops and at the *Inquirer*, started two training programs to attract minority students into newspaper journalism. He began the Art Peters Memorial Fellowship Program in 1979, aimed at providing copy-editing internships for minority candidates, and in 1984, he began attracting the city's minority high school students to the paper's Journalism Career Development Workshop program. He taught in the Summer Program for Minority Journalists at the University of California, Berkeley, from 1980 to 1989 and consulted on the founding of the Maynard Institute in Oakland, California. He has also taught part-time at Temple University and at Florida A&M University and has consulted regarding the founding of minority journalism workshops for Northwestern University, the University of Kansas, Duquesne University and Norfolk State University. Associations of African-American journalists in such other cities as Pittsburgh, Chicago and Kansas City have sought his advice, as well. Moore was the first director of the Knight Ridder Scholarship program and has been a board member of the American Society of Newspaper Editors. He was the 1999 recipient of the John S. Knight Gold Medal based on his efforts to increase newsroom diversity. His efforts at teaching, mentoring and advocating have been considerable, and his column has appeared in the *Inquirer* for more than a quarter century. In the column appearing below, Moore advocates mandating the teaching of black history in the Philadelphia public schools. He has been quoted as advising students that the way to success is not a 100-meter race, but a long-distance race requiring stamina and patience.

"Urban Perspectives: Nay to a Naysayer on Black History" by Acel Moore

As I celebrate the 25th anniversary of writing this column, I am painfully reminded that although there have been some significant and positive changes in the culture and behavior of individuals and institutions in this city and this nation, some things remain the same.

Some habits of mind, for example. Like that of State House Speaker John Perzel in opposing the Philadelphia School District's African American history mandate. And there are many who do.

In an interview and in a letter sent to school officials, Perzel questioned whether black students were sufficiently interested in African American history to justify the mandate. He argued that most such students would never go to Africa. He also said that if the School Reform Commission (SRC) decided to mandate the curriculum, it would divide rather than unite city students.

Nonsense.

The irrational ignorance of some who oppose the teaching of African American history causes me to think that if the jury in the Philadelphia, Miss., trial of Klansman Edgar Ray Killen had stayed hung, they would have been on the wrong side. After a momentary deadlock, the jury on Tuesday convicted Killen of manslaughter in a 41-year-old killing of three civil rights workers who had attempted to register blacks to vote.

Perzel's ignorance and illogic are insults to the memory of all of those black scholars who, for more than a century, struggled to have African American history taught in our institutions of learning.

If Perzel wants to talk about something useful, why doesn't he champion an ethics-reform bill that would make it illegal for elected officials to be involved in pay-to-play?

I salute those responsible for the decision to make Philadelphia city schools the first in the nation to mandate African American history. School district CEO Paul Vallas, and SRC members such as Sandra Dungee Glenn and chairman James Nevels, deserve credit, too. Many others in the community deserve praise, as well—including community organizations such as the Coalition of Education Advocates, which collected 25,000 signatures on petitions, and those who attended the School Reform Commission hearings and meetings that led to the decision. And individuals such as attorney and historian Ed Robinson, an octogenarian who has been involved in this struggle for 50 years. Robinson has been hired as a consultant to help develop the curriculum.

In 1967, a demonstration by Philadelphia high school students calling for classes in African American history was violently broken up by police. That demonstration was a symbolic event with direct ties to what the SRC has done. Two of those arrested and beaten by police later became community leaders and kept the issue alive until their deaths. The late state Rep. David P. Richardson (D., Phila.) and community activist Omjasis Kentu deserve posthumous credit for the SRC decision.

Perzel's ignorance shows why we *need* this mandate.

Including African American history in the public school curriculum will teach all students about the contribution African Americans made to the building, defense and development of all aspects of American culture—despite 246 years of enslavement followed by another 100 years and more of overt racial discrimination.

Teaching African American history would not, as Perzel suggests, exclude the study of other racial and ethnic cultures who have contributed to the evolution of America. In the long run, such knowledge will instead unite people, in the best way possible—by teaching them more about each other and thus fostering mutual respect.

Source: Used with permission of the Philadelphia Inquirer, copyright 2005. All rights reserved. This column appeared on 23 June 2005.

Further Readings: "Acel Moore." [Online]. Philadelphia Association of Black Journalists Web site www.pabj.org; "Acel Moore." [Online]. Philadelphia Inquirer Web site www.philly.com; Prince, Richard. "Philly Columnist Says He Was Misdiagnosed." [Online, 12 November 2004]. In Richard Prince's Journal-isms. Maynard Institute Web site www.maynardije.org.

Moore, Gregory L. (1954–)

Greg Moore has been editor of the *Denver Post* since June 2002; prior to that time, he was the managing editor of the *Boston Globe*. He was born in Cleveland's East Side to a foundry worker/handyman father and a high school graduate mother who was, Moore said in an *Editor & Publisher* interview conducted by Jim Moscou, the best-educated person he knew during his childhood. He credits his parents' lively interest in the news with giving him an early desire for a career in journalism. He attended Glenville High School and due to his admiration for Mohammad Ali, took up boxing. He entered Ohio Wesleyan University in 1972, double-majoring in journalism and political science. Having become dissatisfied with the campus newspaper's coverage of the university's African-American students and organizations, he founded a rival paper, *The Witness*, to improve matters. In summer 1974, he interned at the *Akron Beacon Journal* where veteran black journalist Al Fitzpatrick took an interest in him. Moore did a second summer internship in 1975 at the *Blade* in Toledo, Ohio, where he had the tutelage of another longtime black journalist, columnist William Brower. After graduation, his first job was covering the city hall beat for *The Journal Herald* in Dayton, Ohio. Soon thereafter, he became active in Golden Gloves boxing and was billed as the "Blue Bomber." He suffered an eardrum injury after two matches and had to give up boxing. In February 1980, Moore was hired by his hometown paper, the *Plain Dealer* of Cleveland, where he once again had a mentor, the paper's African-American city editor, Robert G. McGruder. Within two years, Moore was promoted to state political editor. In 1986, Moore moved again, this time to the *Boston Globe* as senior assistant city editor. Passed over for the *Plain Dealer*'s editorship, McGruder also moved, to become editor of the *Detroit Free Press*. Moore was promoted to city editor in 1987, to deputy managing editor in 1991 and to managing editor in 1994. He enjoyed many successes, with his paper winning four Pulitzer Prizes and being nominated for several more, but in 1998, the *Globe* received heavy national publicity of a kind no one wants. Boston's best-known columnist, Mike Barnicle, was accused of plagiarism and fabrication of facts and was forced to resign. Later that year, African-American columnist Patricia Smith was let go by the *Globe* due to fabricated quotes in some of her columns. In 2001, Moore was passed over for the editorship of the *Globe* in favor of Martin Baron, executive editor of the *Miami Herald*. At this point Moore, recently divorced, was dating Black Entertainment Television executive Nina Henderson, who lived in Denver, Colorado, a city having two newspapers locked in a struggle for primacy. The *Denver Post* was operating more profitably than its rival, the *Rocky Mountain News*, and in May 2000, the two rivals worked out a joint operating agreement by which the MediaNews Group-owned *Post* would publish on Sundays and the E.W. Scripps-owned *News* on Saturdays.

MediaNews Group CEO William Dean Singleton took over as the *Post*'s publisher and very soon moved to replace editor Glenn Guzzo. Greg Moore got the nod and took Guzzo's place in June 2002. He began making immediate changes in an attempt to reinvigorate the paper's news coverage, improve photography, deemphasize local commentary and publish a greater number of original feature stories. The *Post*'s Sunday paper by this time had become the nation's fifth largest in circulation, and Singleton's charge to Moore was to make the *Post* one of the top five papers in the country. The paper also changed in that longtime local columnist Chuck Green resigned after 34 years with the *Post*, and another of the paper's columnists, Gene Amole, died soon thereafter. In August, three new editors were brought in from other quality newspapers— the *Chicago Tribune*, *Newsday*, the *Dallas Morning News* and Raleigh's *News & Observer*—and two editors were promoted inhouse. After firing Arnie Rosenberg as assistant city editor in June 2003, Moore made an ill-timed gaffe at a meeting when he remarked that to clean up problems, one cannot simply move manure around the barnyard, or words to that effect. Even so, under Moore's leadership, the *Post* in April 2006 produced a highly detailed ethics policy covering not only questions of taste and fairness, but everything from conflicts of interest to procedure for using anonymous sources.

Another Moore initiative has been to move more quickly into new media applications. Toward this end, the paper's Web site was redesigned and new features added. Despite the publisher's hopes of moving the *Post* up in national reputation, the paper has not been exempt from the cutbacks felt in recent years by most U.S. newspapers. In April 2005, MediaNews Group decreed that the paper's editorial budget would have to be reduced by 5 percent. In his various interviews and speeches, Moore has pointed out that today's newspaper has to deal with a 24-hour news cycle in competition with 24/7 news channels and the Internet. He has also stressed the need to increase the diversity of newsrooms if journalism is to reflect the realities of life in today's United States. In delivering the first annual Robert McGruder Lecture at Kent State University in December 2003, Moore made a strong point that at most U.S. newspapers' editorial board meetings, if a woman or a minority member should be out sick, the result would be a meeting that looked very much the way it would have looked in the 1960s. His emphasis is on retention, and the way he suggests making improvements is to be less slow to give minority journalists some of the really big stories that come along. In an interview with Arlene Notoro Morgan that was published on the ASNE.com Web site, Moore stressed that increasing diversity at the *Post* meant more than simply increasing the number of African-American staffers. He pointed out the great growth in Denver's Hispanic population and talked about the need to employ more staff who can read, write and speak Spanish.

In his McGruder lecture, Moore said that he frequently has to defend himself against readers who accuse him of having a liberal bias or with conspiring to fill the *Post* with antiBush administration copy. His response is that his wish is to run a paper free of favoritism and that he has no idea how his subeditors and reporters vote, and no wish to know. Running a newspaper, he added, is not a matter of right versus left. It is a matter of right versus wrong. He is a proponent of old-fashioned journalism's tradition for sticking up for the underdog, exposing corruption and speaking for people who have little voice. That very approach has made Moore enemies among those who interpret any criticism of the U.S. military as "not supporting the troops." In November 2003, the *Post* printed a three-part story about the failure of the Air Force and other military branches to give serious attention to complaints made by service women about sexual assault or harassment. Mail from women readers, Moore reported, was mostly positive, but the paper also was hammered for being "military bashers." Later, in December 2004, the *Post* so angered Army brass at Fort Carson, Colorado, that the paper's reporters were temporarily banned from the base. The offending story, which appeared on 5 December 2004, concerned charges made by National Guard and Army Reserve troops who claim to have been denied either quality medical care or disability pay. Moore defended the story as carefully researched and objectively written, but the story appeared soon after the paper had obtained an injunction to prevent a closed hearing for three soldiers who had allegedly murdered an Iraqi general. A day later, the ban was lifted after military higherups pointed out the absence of required due process in selectively banning from a military base any specific news medium. Also in 2004, Moore crossed swords with Elizabeth Hoffman, president of the University of Colorado. At issue was a *Post* story reporting that President Hoffman had denied that an alleged 2001 rape incident had ever happened. The *Post* also criticized the Bush administration's secret executive order that allowed the National Security Agency to tap phone calls and Internet traffic without a warrant. On the local level, one of Moore's first challenges to authority as *Post* editor, in December 2002, was in joining the American Civil Liberties Union in filing court action against Denver officials to seek the release of documents detailing the gathering of files on 3,400 persons and groups by the city's police.

Moore has served on the board of the National Association of Black Journalists and that of the American Society of Newspaper Editors. He is on the Pulitzer Prize Board and the Board of Trustees of Ohio Wesleyan University. He is also on the selection committee for Colby College for its Elijah Parish Lovejoy Award. In 1996, he was chosen as Journalist of the Year by the New England chapter of the NABJ, and he was the first recipient of the Robert G. McGruder award given by Kent State University for individuals who foster newsroom diversity. He has been an active campus speaker in the Denver area, describing to students the importance of the news media's roles as watchdog and explainer.

Further Readings: Morgan, Arlene Notoro. "Risky Business." [Online, 3 July 2003]. American Society of Newspaper Editors Web site www.asne.org; Moscou. Jim. "Greg Moore's Plan for The Denver Post." [Online, 21 November 2002]. Editor & Publisher Web site www.editorandpublisher.com; "Pulitzer Prize Board Elects New York Times' Thomas Friedman and Denver Post's Gregory Moore." [Online, 2 February 2004]. Pulitzer Prizes Web site www.pulitzer.org; Roberts, Michael.

"The Message." [Online, 21 April 2005]. Westword.com Web site www.westword.com/issues; Sszatkowski, Jim. "Honoring Yesterday's Pioneers and Today's Leaders." *Kent State Magazine*, 4, p. 16; Wenner, Kathryn S. "Publisher's Pick." [Online, June 2002]. American Journalism Review Web site www.ajr.org.

Morgan, Thomas III (1955–)

Thomas Morgan was a reporter for the *Miami Herald* and the *Washington Post* and assistant metro editor for the *New York Times*, but perhaps he will be best remembered for having been president of the National Association of Black Journalists from 1989 to 1991. He was born in St. Louis, Missouri, to a father who worked with the Postal Service and a schoolteacher mother. One of his English teachers at Ritenour High School encouraged him to write, and he was active with his high school newspaper. After finishing high school in 1969, he secured a ROTC scholarship to the University of Missouri and following graduation in 1973, served as an Air Force officer until 1975. In that same year he became a *Miami Herald* reporter and spent six years reporting for the *Washington Post*. In 1983, he moved to the *New York Times*, where he worked as reporter, editor and business manager until taking early retirement in 1995 due to having contracted HIV. After his retirement, the *Times* honored him by creating an internship in graphics, design and photography in his name. Since that time, he has lived in Brooklyn with his longtime partner, an architect and developer, and has worked in Manhattan as a Gay Men's Health Crisis volunteer.

Morgan, who usually avoided the limelight because of his stuttering, campaigned successfully for the NABJ presidency, winning over television executive Ruth Allen Ollison. In so doing, he became the organization's first openly gay president. One of his accomplishments in office was creating the NABJ Hall of Fame. He also began a new short-course program, advanced the organization's Ethel Payne Fellowship program for travel to Africa and started NABJ TV to help train aspiring minority broadcasters. After his presidency ended in 1991, he convinced the organization to create a Gay and Lesbian Task Force; the vote took place in 1995. Although his illness has prevented Morgan from becoming active in the National Lesbian & Gay Journalists Association, he was inducted into its Hall of Fame in September 2005. When his old high school created its own hall of fame in 1998, Morgan was one of its first inductees. He also has been honored by his alma mater, the University of Missouri. Morgan serves on the boards of Care for the Homeless and the Gay Men's Health Crisis organization in New York.

Further Readings: Gray, Katti. "A Salute to NABJ's Presidents: Thomas Morgan III." [Online]. National Association of Black Journalists Web site www.nabj.rog; Villarosa, Linda. "Thomas Morgan III." [Online]. National Lesbian & Gay Journalists Association Web site www.nlgja.rog.

Morris, Valerie Coleman (25 November 1946–)

Valerie Morris is a CNN Business News correspondent and anchor of the "Smart Assets" personal finance feature of CNN Headline News. She was born in Philadelphia. Her father was a Lt. Colonel in the Air Force, and the family lived in France, England and Japan while she was a child. She holds a bachelor's degree in journalism from San Jose State University and, as a *New York Times* fellow, a master's in Broadcast Journalism from Columbia University. After graduation, she took a job as a researcher at KRON-TV in San Francisco, after which she became a researcher, general assignment reporter and finally anchor in 1982 for that city's station KGO-TV. She was a KCBS radio anchor in 1985 in San Francisco. From 1987 to 1988, she was an anchor for Los Angeles station KCBS-TV and in 1989, was again in San Francisco as a morning drivetime anchor for KCBS Newsradio, also writing and narrating a series of commentaries for KCBS titled "With the Family in Mind." In 1993, she moved to the nation's opposite coast to become a general assignment reporter and weekend anchor for New York City station WPIX-TV and in December of that year, married diversity consultant Robert Morris of Tucson, Arizona. The attractive, smartly turned out Morris joined CNN in 1996 as co-anchor of "The Flip Side" and anchor of the four times daily "Smart Assets," a segment of the Headlines News, both on CNNfn. The thrust of "Smart Assets" is to offer personal finance advice on such topics as online banking and investing, consumer credit issues, estate planning, real estate, mortgages, tax planning and the like. Morris has preached establishing a regular savings program to her viewers, often remarking that America has become a nation of devout spenders. Another theme running through her work is that, given the 49 percent divorce rate, women must take control of their own finances and must become more knowledgeable about handling and investing their money. Still another special interest for Morris has been the problems faced by the so-called "sandwich generation," adults who are raising children and at the same time are called upon to care for aging parents. Morris' work has appeared on CNN Headline News, CNN/US, CNN International, CNN Airport Network, CNN Radio and CNN/Money.com. She has anchored or contributed to such shows as "Take It Personally," "Trading Places" and "In Play."

Morris has taken her message to other venues, as well. In 2003, she was a moderator for a Black Career Women diversity forum and a speaker at the national conference of Women Work! The National Network for Women's Employment. In 2004, she was a guest on the "Road to Wealth" segment of the "Tavis Smiley Show." She has written a personal finance column for *Essence* magazine, as well. She has received three California Emmy awards and two awards from the Radio/Television News Directors Association. She has won the Outstanding Contribution to Broadcasting Award from American Women in Radio and Television and from the National Organization for Women, the Award of Courage and the Outstanding Contribution to Broadcasting Award. In 1989, she was part of the news team that won a Peabody Award for coverage of the California earthquake in that year that damaged San Francisco's Bay Bridge.

Further Readings: Gregory, Deborah. "Show Her the Money." *Essence*, 1 March 1999; "Valerie Morris." [Online]. CNN International site http://edition.cnn.com/CNN/anchors; "Valerie Morris." [Online]. CNN Money site http://money.cnn.com/ontv/anchors.

N

Nelson, Jill (?–)

New York–based freelance journalist Jill Nelson has been writing for the press for at least 20 years and yet is probably best known for the five books she has written. She was born in New York City and holds degrees from the City College of New York and the Columbia University School of Journalism. In 1986, she began working at the *Washington Post*, where she was the first black woman assigned to the Sunday magazine section. After three months, she had had only a single story published and came to feel she was there "to be black and female" rather than to actually do anything significant. In her memoir *Volunteer Slavery*, she reports having felt virtually invisible in that large metropolitan paper's corporate culture and has remarked that she felt she had to walk a careful line between "Uncle Tomming" and "Mau-Mauing." She had been a successful freelancer and had published in the *Nation*, *Essence*, *Ms.*, the *New York Times*, the *Chicago Tribune* and the *Village Voice* and reports that her experience at the *Post* nearly gave her a nervous breakdown. Whereas holding positions on the *Post*'s staff has worked out smoothly for more than a few African-American journalists, clearly it did not suit her, even though she won an award as Washington Journalist of the Year before she parted company with the paper. The book about her unhappy experience at the *Post* sold well and received an American Book Award. She left the *Post* job in 1990 and has since concentrated on her books while also writing for MSNBC.com, Salon.com, *USA Weekend* and *USA Today*. The notables she has interviewed include Oprah Winfrey, Spike Lee, Denzel Washington and Diana Ross. She has also taught journalism for the City College of New York.

Nelson's second book, *Straight, No Chaser*, which came out four years after her first, was largely autobiographical and dealt with empowerment of black women in American society. Next, she edited an anthology titled *Police Brutality* in which writers such as columnists Stanley Crouch and Patricia Williams, black detective Arthur Doyle, legal writer Derrick Bell and historian Robin D.G. Kelley examined the phenomenon of police brutality and its causes. Three years later, in 2003, Nelson produced a work of outrageous comic fiction, *Sexual Healing*, about two young black professional women who, unsatisfied with their romantic lives, decide to open a brothel to serve the needs of African-American women; the book won a PEN Oakland-Josephine Miles National Literary Award in 2004. The award is given by the Bay Area chapter of PEN, an international organization of poets, essayists and novelists. Her latest book, which appeared in 2005, is *Finding Martha's Vineyard*; Nelson herself spends part of her time on this posh vacation island off Cape Cod.

One of Nelson's 2002 stories on MSNBC.com launched a barbed exchange with columnist Andrew Sullivan. She had remarked that in her view, women who parade around wearing a bathing suit in a beauty contest are as oppressed as Muslim women who are forced to wear a full burka in public. Sullivan fired back that Nelson appeared to hate Western society and that her ideas showed an overlap with those of radical Muslims. She in turn responded that she did not care for what she considered the macho "my way is the only way" predilections of Sullivan and President George W. Bush.

Some of her 1999 and 2000 stories on Salon.com echo the content of her anthology about police brutality. One was on the Amadou Deallo case, in which four white New York policemen were found not guilty of the murder of an unarmed African immigrant. About the trial's outcome, Nelson reported winning a $10 bet with her own mother, who, she wrote, had somehow managed to cling to shards of optimism concerning equal justice. Another such story was about New York policeman Justin Volpe's guilty plea in the beating and sodomy of black New Yorker Abner Louima. In a third Salon.com article, Nelson admitted feeling relieved when she learned that the two teenaged shooters at Columbine High School in Littleton, Colorado, were not black. She added that she would have found it hard to bear the smug litany of media pontificating about black predators, pathology, violence and broken homes had the perpetrators been black. She widened her focus in this story to address the pervasiveness of violence in American culture—in films, television, newspapers, magazines and our very language—that transcends race, class and place, then took a jab at the National Rifle Association for its stand on the fundamental blamelessness of guns. A recent story Nelson contributed to *USA Today* faulted Hollywood for its reluctance to cast black women in romantic lead roles, especially in those movies starring a black man. She pointed out that according to Census reports, 96 percent of married black women are wed to black men, and 91 percent of married black men have black wives. She concluded that the reason is Hollywood's stereotypical concept of female beauty: white, long blonde hair, and anorexic thinness. Finally, in a *USA Today* story from 2002, Nelson decried the silent acquiescence to our government's hawkish war policies that was demanded by the conservative right and even some of the left following the World Trade Center tragedy.

Books by Jill Nelson: *Volunteer Slavery: My Authentic Negro Experience* (Chicago: The Noble Press, 1993); *Straight, No Chaser: How I Became a Grown-Up Black Woman* (New York: G.P. Putnam's Sons, 1997); ed., *Police Brutality: An Anthology* (New York, 2000); *Sexual Healing* (Chicago: Agate Pub, 2003); *Finding Martha's Vineyard: African Americans at Home on an Island* (New York: Doubleday, 2005).

Further Readings: "Jill Nelson." [Online, 2005]. Times Warner Bookmark Web site www.twbookmark.com.

Newton, Vickie (c.1966–)

Television journalist Vickie Newton is a reporter and coanchor for "News 4 St. Louis" at KMOV-TV. Newton's mother was an English teacher, which might help account for Newton's interest in promoting literacy. She earned the master's in journalism at the University of Detroit and began her career at station WDIV-TV in that city. She also worked for WDAF-TV in Kansas City and KATV in Little Rock, Arkansas. Prior to coming to Missouri, she was a reporter/anchor for WSB-TV in Atlanta and an anchor for CNN Headline News, also in Atlanta. She joined KMOV-TV in January 2002, where she coanchors with veteran newsman Larry Conners. A year later, she won an Emmy for best anchor, and the station, owned by Belo corporation, won the Emmy for overall excellence in television news. In January 2004, Newton was appointed Region VIII director of the National Association of Black Journalists. In this capacity, she represented the organization's members in Iowa, Kansas, Minnesota, Missouri and Nebraska. She has been an NABJ member since 1994. Soon after arriving at her job in St. Louis, Newton began establishing an active presence in the community. In April 2004, she was honorary chair of a benefit for the city's crisis nursery, which provides help to children endangered by domestic strife and which attempts to combat child neglect and abuse in general. She began making school visits and served as mistress of ceremonies at a career-readiness luncheon. In January 2005, she moderated a discussion on "The State of Black Men" that was part of Black History Month. Also in 2005, she was cohost and honorary chair of a Redevelopment Opportunities for Women fundraiser that featured a combination of blues and jazz performers. She repeated her emcee duties for career-readiness for the Mathews-Dickey Boys' and Girls' Club in 2005; and in 2006, she moderated both a conference held by the local Alzheimer's Association and another such meeting, the Joanne Parrish Knight Caregiving Conference. She is on the boards of the St. Louis Alzheimer's Association and the YWCA and she is active with the area Literacy Roundtable. She is an accomplished pianist and is working toward establishing a program whereby piano teachers would give free lessons to children who otherwise could not afford them.

In 2005, she became involved in controversy within the NABJ as the organization grappled with whether to create a Lesbian and Gay Task Force to speak for its homosexual members. The 46-member task force was approved, but Newton reportedly voted against approval.

Further Readings: "New NABJ Region VIII Director Named." [Online, 12 January 2004]. National Association of Black Journalists site http://members. nabj.org; "Vickie Newton, News4 St. Louis Anchor/Reporter." [Online, 16 February 2005]. KMOV Web site www.kmov.com.

Norman, Art (?–)

Genial, experienced Art Norman is weekday cohost of NBC 5 News in Chicago. His entry into broadcast journalism was unusual in that he took a B.S. degree program in math and physics in college and began his career as a television engineer. Norman is a graduate of Johnson C. Smith University, located near Charlotte, North Carolina. He obtained a first-class FCC license; and his first professional job, in 1969, was as an engineer at Charlotte station WCCB-TV. Later he made a major career shift and became a reporter for another Charlotte station, WPCQ-TV, and still later worked in the same capacity for a third station in that city, WSOC-TV. In 1979, he moved to Baltimore to work as a reporter and weekend anchor at WMAR-TV, remaining there until relocating to Chicago in July 1982 as a general assignment reporter for NBC 5 News. Later, he began anchoring, now sharing that duty with coanchor Zoraida Sambolin. In addition, he does feature stories on Chicago area communities in a feature called "Art Norman's Chicago."

During his extensive career, Norman has won quite a lot of awards, beginning in the 1970s. In 1975, a hot-air balloon crash story won him recognition from the North Carolina Radio and Television News Directors Association, and in 1976, his writing and photography on a story for the NBC program "Weekend Magazine" was honored by a George Foster Peabody Award. A School Bell Award from the National Association of Educators was given to him in 1978 for a documentary he did on the various problems faced by poor children. The RTNDA recognized Norman again in 1984 for his story about the courtroom shooting of a divorce court judge and a lawyer, and he won a 1986 Emmy for his reporting on the hostage crisis in Beirut, Lebanon. Another of his documentaries, this one on gospel music's heritage in Chicago, won the 1987 Wilbur Award given by the Religious Public Relations Council. He won a second Emmy, in 1989, for his reporting on the shooting spree and suicide of troubled 30-year-old woman Laurie Dann in a Chicago suburb. The Associated Press awarded him its Best Investigative Reporting honor in 1992–1993 for his series titled "Cops and Robbers" that revealed the identities of police who had criminal records of their own; the series also won an Investigative Reporters and Editors Award. Later came a third Emmy, this one for his reporting of a fatal 1995 grade-crossing bus crash at Fox River Grove, northwest of Chicago. Norman often hosts community functions in the Chicago area and has been active in fund-raising for the United Negro College Fund.

Further Readings: "Art Norman." [Online]. NBC 5 Web site www.nbc5.com.

Norman, Tony (c.1960–)

Tony Norman's outrageous, trenchantly witty column has appeared in the *Pittsburgh Post-Gazette* since July 1996. Norman was born in Philadelphia in the early 1980s. He went to Calvin College in Grand Rapids, Michigan, majoring in political science. He joined the *Post-Gazette* as a letters-to-the-editor clerk in 1988. After hours, he began to write about popular music for the features desk, and within about a year he was covering that beat full time. In 1990, he became the paper's pop music/pop culture critic and appeared frequently on local radio and television talk shows. In July 1999, after having written his column for three years, he was named a member of the paper's editorial board.

Norman's humorous way with words is evident in the column that appears below in which he pokes not-so-gentle fun at television evangelists and their apparent obsession with the issue of homosexuality. In a 2004 Christmas column, Norman had Jesus appearing as a guest on Fox News, becoming ever more exasperated with the host's inane right-wing prattle. Playing on somewhat the same theme, another of his columns dealt with "conventional wisdom," which relieves news media people from having to actually think, and "talking points," which in a sense become true because they are said a lot. Norman worries about the blurring of the line between journalism and entertainment and took delight in the troubles of commentator Bill O'Reilly of "The O'Reilly Factor" when a female producer brought suit for sexual harassment. In general, Norman has considerable disdain for what he considers the phoniness of politicians who talk a good game about moral values but often do the opposite in their own lives. The religious right, he sees as doing its best to violate the separation of church and state for political gain, and he dares to write what many people merely muse about—that there so many signs of collective dementia in today's news that every day feels like April 1. He prays, he says, that stupidity is not as contagious as it seems to be, sighing that either way, there is no point screaming. He has admitted to having a difficult time writing about a lot of politicians without gagging and was disgusted with fellow columnist Armstrong Williams for allowing himself to become a paid shill for the Bush administration. Norman noted that he had a feeling of reality once removed when writing about the Valerie Plume affair, noting that two journalists who never wrote about the story were facing possible incarceration for refusing to name their sources while Robert Novak, the columnist who actually broke the story, had mysteriously escaped the consequences of having done so.

Norman has described Americans as a credulous people willing to turn a blind eye to the obvious. Such assertions no doubt result in a lot of angry mail, yet he makes his outspoken parries in such a clever way that at least some criticism is diffused. Who could deny that our nation is often a bastion of irony, or that we are usually slow to question the motives or conduct of our leaders? A liberal, Norman is at his vitriolic best when criticizing the George W. Bush White House. In one column he remarked that he is well aware that the movies' John "Bluto" Belushi is dead, but just the same he could swear that Bluto was running the war in Iraq.

Norman won first place in 1999 in the National Society of Newspaper Columnists competition and has won first in the competitions of Golden Quill, Keystone and the Pittsburgh Black Media Federation. He also won second some years ago in column writing from the American Association of Sunday and Feature Editors.

"First They Came for Tinky Winky" by Tony Norman

Now that virtue reigns in the land and morality is enshrined at the heart of American foreign and domestic policy, the jihad against cartoon characters of dubious sexuality can begin with all the ruthlessness such campaigns demand.

Get out your scarlet crayons, boys and girls, the gay branding of your favorite cartoons has already begun.

Picking up where the Rev. Jerry Falwell left off with Tinky Winky and the Teletubbies in 1999, Dr. James Dobson, founder of Focus on the Family, got the ball rolling several nights ago at an inaugural black-tie gala for members of Congress.

"Does anybody here know SpongeBob?" Dobson asked, his question dripping with unintentional irony. Dobson wasn't inquiring as to whether the politicians "knew" SpongeBob SquarePants in the biblical sense, though it would be foolish to rule anything out in the current moral climate.

It's more likely Dobson was inquiring as to whether our lawmakers were hip to the bucktoothed SpongeBob's influence over a generation of couch potatoes ignorant of the sexual politics of animated characters.

Besides occasional hand holding with cartoon sidekick Patrick the starfish, SpongeBob has come under suspicion by Dobson and others for participating in a so-called "pro-homosexual" children's video created by Nile "We Are Family" Rodgers.

Rodgers composed the 1979 disco hit by Sister Sledge that will probably stick in your head for the rest of the day. If that song doesn't scream "hello, I'm gay," I don't know what does.

According to Dobson, SpongeBob SquarePants and like-minded buddies Barney the Dinosaur and Jimmy Neutron appear in a video distributed by the We Are Family Foundation that preaches tolerance and other suspiciously gay values to elementary school children.

Despite Rodgers' insistence that the video—conceived in the aftermath of the Sept. 11, 2001 attacks—addresses multicultural tolerance without mentioning sexual preference at all, Dobson's group stands by its criticism of the project as a "classic bait and switch."

Can't say I really blame them for being suspicious, though. Animated characters have been getting out of line for a long time. Our culture has been a consistent enabler of surreptitious homosexual indoctrination via the funnies ever since Batman and Robin began hanging out unchaperoned in the 1940s.

Now, gay characters are running amok in comic strips and Saturday morning cartoons. We've noticed Peppermint Patty and Marcie playing lesbian footsies when Charlie Brown isn't looking. "Sesame Street's" Bert and Ernie are so gay, they ought to change the name of the show to "Christopher Street."

And we all know that whenever Jughead puts down Betty and Veronica as a couple of "dumb girls," there's more than harmless misogyny at work in Riverdale. Though he masquerades as militantly asexual, Jughead simply wants Archie all to himself. Only evil, hyper-sexed Reggie has his priorities straight when it comes to the fairer sex.

As long as we're "outing" cartoon scoundrels, is there any doubt that half of the characters on "Scooby-Doo" are sexually deviant? Shaggy is gay, Velma is a lesbian and Scooby is into bestiality. And don't get me started on that cross-dressing Bugs Bunny with his weird fixation on kissing Elmer Fudd on the lips.

Of course, this insidious seduction of the innocent began with the Krazy Kat comic strip in 1913. Who can blame poor, straight Ignatz Mouse for using bricks to defend himself against Krazy Kat's sexual harassment?

This brings us back to the animated Sodom and Gomorrah under the sea starring SpongeBob. Though the cartoon's gay agenda has forced Dr. Dobson to denounce it in the strongest terms, at least he hasn't sunk to the level of the Rev. Fred Phelps of the Westboro Baptist Church in Topeka, Kan. No one is talking about marching with signs that read "GOD HATES BOB."

At least, not yet.

Source: Copyright, *Pittsburgh Post-Gazette*, 2005, all rights reserved. Reprinted with permission. This column appeared on 21 January 2005.

Further Readings: "Tony Norman." [Online]. Pittsburgh Post-Gazette Web site www.post-gazette.com.

Norris, Michele (c.1962–)

Michele Norris is known to National Public Radio listeners as one of the three hosts of the popular program "All Things Considered" and prior to joining NPR in 2002, had spent nine years as an ABC News correspondent. She grew up in Minnesota and is a graduate of Washburn High School in Minneapolis, where she wrote for the school paper, *The Grist*. She was an electrical engineering major at the University of Wisconsin but switched majors and schools, graduating with a Journalism degree from the University of Minnesota. Her professional career began not in broadcasting, but in newspaper journalism. From 1985 to 1987 she was a reporter at the *Los Angeles Times*. She moved to the *Chicago Tribune* in 1987 and was a reporter there until leaving for a job as a staff writer at *The Washington Post* in 1988, working there until 1993. While at the Chicago paper, she was one of its staffers who wrote stories collected into the book *Chicago Schools: Worst in America* (Chicago: Chicago Tribune, 1988). The story she did at the *Post* about a six-year-old child living in a crack house was included in the book *Ourselves among Others* (New York: St. Martin's Press, 1988), edited by Carol J. Verburg. During Norris' eight years of newspaper writing, she specialized in covering the problems of urban America, especially concerning education and other issues affecting children. In 1993, she became a correspondent for ABC News and in the new medium, continued reporting on poverty, drugs and other problems of the nation's poor. She covered the murder trial of football great O.J. Simpson, Nelson Mandela's election as president of South Africa, the matter of bilingual education in California schools and the World Trade Center attacks of 11 September 2001. She was a White House reporter for the network and contributed to the "Closer Look" feature on "World News Tonight with Peter Jennings." Working out of Washington, she also contributed to "20/20," "Nightline," "This Week" and "Good Morning America" before moving to NPR. Some of her biggest "Nightline" stories were about AIDS, the effects of violent video games and the grants program of the MacArthur Foundation. In December 2002, she joined Robert Siegel and Melissa Black as cohosts of public radio's longest-running public affairs show "All Things Considered," which runs for two hours every weekday, offering a mix of news, features, commentary and interviews. Education remains one of Norris' main specialty topics, but she also covers many other things. In 2004, for example, she interviewed former heavyweight boxing champion Larry Holmes. In a 2003 interview with Lillian R. Dunlap for Poynter.org, Norris remarked that she likes the collaborative nature of her NPR work and values the give and take of her show's morning editorial meetings. She also said that she very much appreciates the luxury of the reporting time she gets on public radio compared to the dramatic but shallow coverage of commercial television news. The public radio journalist, she said, is given the air time to explain and to make use of storytelling skills. A mild frustration for her in 2004 was NPR management's decision that she should not take part in coverage of the political race between President George W. Bush and challenger John Kerry due to the job as senior adviser to Kerry's campaign held by her husband, Broderick Johnson. Christopher Turpin, executive producer of "All Things Considered," said that because of its public mission and public support, NPR must refrain from any appearance of favoritism or bias in its political coverage. In early 2005, Norris spoke in St. Paul on the implications of "point-and-click journalism" in the Internet Age as part of the Broadcast Journalist Series sponsored by Minnesota Public Radio. In October 2005, she substituted for Gwen Ifill as moderator of "Washington Week." The topic was the Supreme Court nomination of Harriet Miers, which, Norris observed, had the ironic effect of drawing the loudest criticism of all from some of President George W. Bush's most staunch supporters, the Religious Right.

During her career, Norris has been nominated four times for a Pulitzer Prize. She received a Livingston Award in 1989 and a 1990 Federal Bar Association Media Award. Also in 1990, she won a feature writing award in the Chesapeake Associated Press News Executive's Council competition. The work she did for ABC on the 9/11 attacks was recognized by an Emmy and a Peabody Award. She also shared in two awards won by the book *Chicago Schools: Worst in America*: the Peter Lisagor Award for public service and the National Education Association Writer's Award for investigative reporting.

Further Readings: Dunlap, Lillian R. "To Inform and Comfort: Michele Norris and the Culture of All Things Considered." [Online, 16 April 2003]. Poynter Institute Web site www.poynter.org; "Michele Norris." [Online]. ABC News Web site www.abcmedianet.com; "Michele Norris to Co-Host All Things Considered." [Online, 10 October 2002]. National Public Radio Web site www.npr.org/news/specials.

O

O'Brien, Maria de la Soledad (19 September 1966–)

Afro-Cuban-Irish Soledad O'Brien has been coanchor of CNN's morning show "American Morning" since July 2003. Soledad, "Solly" to her friends, was born in Long Island, New York, to an Afro-Cuban school teacher mother and a white Irish-Australian mechanical engineer father. She graduated in 1984 from Smithtown High School in St. James, New York, and studied at Harvard, initially planning a career in medicine but changing her plans after working with radio station KISS-FM in Boston. She dropped out of Harvard's Radcliffe College without a degree to become a news writer and associate producer for Boston station WBZ-TV. Thereafter she relocated to San Francisco's KRON-TV, remaining there for three years as a reporter and East Bay Bureau chief from 1991 to 1993. She also worked for two of those years for the Discovery Channel, hosting "The Know Zone," which won her a local Emmy. She joined NBC as a health and science producer for the "NBC Nightly News" and "Today." In 1996, she hosted an information technology–oriented show called "The Site" on newly created cable news network MSNBC, appearing opposite a computer-generated character called Dev Null, also known as Vile Little Puppet Man, whose voice was provided by Leo Laporte, a network tech manager. This curious show was about the Internet and the ways in which information technology impacts everyday American life. O'Brien was placed in this role despite the fact that she knew very little about computer technology. No doubt the fact that she is remarkably good-looking had a lot to do with it, and the show's creators wanted to do a nonintimidating program aimed not at computer science majors, but the average person trying to find out more about computers and the Internet. Also for MSNBC, she worked as anchor for a two-hour morning weekend talk show, "Morning Blend," was a contributor to MSNBC.com, was a contributing technology editor for "USA Weekend Magazine" and was a technology columnist for Women.com, a Women's Wire Web site. In July 1999, she replaced Paula Zahn as coanchor of "Weekend Today," on Saturday and Sunday mornings on NBC. She has covered many a big story, including the plane crash of John F. Kennedy, Jr.; the Littleton, Colorado, and Springfield, Oregon, school shootings; Pope John Paul II's 1998 visit to Cuba; the World Trade Towers attacks and Taliban prisoners held at Guantanamo Bay, Cuba. She initially cohosted this show with David Bloom, who died in April 2002 while covering the war in Iraq.

In July 2003, O'Brien teamed with Bill Henner to coanchor CNN's three-hour "American Morning," which appears daily and offers reports from CNN correspondents plus interviews with studio guests. O'Brien and Henner's assignment was to boost viewership to catch or overtake "Fox and Friends," a show with viewer numbers more than double the CNN morning program. In this role, she was the only broadcaster to travel to Moscow with first lady Laura Bush. In November 2003, she covered the burial of Palestinian leader Yasser Arafat, she reported the Space Shuttle Columbia disaster and she traveled to Phuket, Thailand, to report on the December 2004 tsunami disaster. O'Brien belongs to both the National Association of Black Journalists and the National Association of Hispanic Journalists and is on the board of The Harlem School for the Arts. She has been named to both *Essence Magazine* and *Crain's Business Reports'* "40 Under 40" lists and has twice been included in *Irish American Magazine*'s list of the Top 100 Irish Americans. *Ebony* magazine has recognized her for her contributions to communications. In addition, *People* magazine placed her on its 50 Most Beautiful People list in 2001, and *People en Espanol* did the same in 2004. Now the mother of four children, O'Brien maintains her beauty by walking and jogging. Having begun her television career as the object of computer geeks' affection, she still wows viewers. Rhyming with her first name, an anonymous Internet poet assured her in 2003 that he loves her "more than she could knowledad."

Further Readings: "CNN Hires Soledad O'Brien for Morning Show." [Online, 12 June 2003]. CNN Web site www.cnn.com; "Soledad O'Brien." [Online, 2000]. American Immigration Law Foundation Web site www.ailf.org; "Soledad O'Brien." [Online]. CNN Web site www.cnn.com; "Soledad O'Brien, the Image of Media Information." [Online, 19 September 2005]. The African American Registry Web page www.aaregistry.com.

P

Page, Clarence Eugene (2 June 1947–)

A highly successful columnist, syndicated by Tribune Media Services to at least 200 newspapers, is Clarence Page, whose home paper is the *Chicago Tribune*. Page was born in Dayton, Ohio, and after high school, worked as a freelance writer and photographer for the Middleton, Ohio, *Journal* and the *Cincinnati Enquirer*. In 1969, Page earned the B.S. in journalism at Ohio University, after which he became a reporter for the *Chicago Tribune*, later moving up to assistant city editor. Page was the second African American to work in that paper's newsroom. He was part of a team investigating voter fraud that won the Pulitzer Prize for investigative reporting in 1973. In 1980, he left the newspaper to become director of community affairs and reporter for Chicago station WBBM-TV, then in 1984 returned to the *Tribune* as an editorial board member and twice-weekly columnist. Page took the place, both as editorial board member and columnist, of his wife Leanita, who committed suicide at age 32. His column is moderate in tone and focuses on a wide range of issues confronting contemporary America. An article in *Columbia Journalism Review* once likened Page's style to that of earlier black leader Whitney M. Young Jr., describing Page's column as a calm voice of reason in a media environment of clamor. Another brief article in that same journal quoted Page as remarking on the increased number of pundits in the nation's capital, saying that now, you cannot swing a dead cat in Washington without hitting one. He referred to Secretary of Defense Donald Rumsfeld as a press briefing entertainer, in that the secretary is diverting but usually reveals nothing. Bemoaning and probably making fun of official Washington's arcane system of leaking news to gauge public reaction, he noted the lessened number of leaks in the secrecy-inclined George W. Bush administration and observed that, in stark contrast, Democratic administrations usually resemble a union hiring hall or a university faculty.

In 1989 Page won the Pulitzer for commentary for his columns on both local and national issues. Since that time, he continues to move all across the news spectrum, from topics such as CIA involvement in the Nicaraguan Contras affair to Bob Dole's lack of appeal for female voters, to the rap artist Tupac Shakur, who ironically died in a driveby shooting in a scenario very much like the word-pictures he painted in his songs. In one 1996 column, Page explored some surprising statistical findings in a *Wall Street Journal* study that revealed the feelings of vulnerability and pessimism among white Americans and surprising optimism among blacks as to their economic prospects.

More recently Page has, in the main, found the Bush administration a disappointment, but he applauds the president's comments critical of a bigotry of low expectations for public school children's learning. More often, though, he has criticized the Bush White House for its secrecy, enormous spending on government public relations, embedding at press conferences of "plants" who ask dependably soft questions, allowing only preapproved crowds at presidential speeches, and the like. And, as are most good columnists, Page is adept at the telling application of good quotes; an example was his use of poet Carl Sandburg's remark to the effect that a politician should have three hats—one to throw into the ring, one to talk through, and one to pull rabbits out of if elected. Reelected George W. Bush, Page wrote, was maintaining a happy face, but was still looking for rabbits. If the first casualty of war is truth, he wrote on another day, then the second casualty must be free speech. Here, Page was concerned with the death threats California Democrat Barbara Lee received after hers was the lone no vote when Congress voted to retaliate for the World Trade Center attacks, and with the firings of two local columnists who dared to criticize President Bush's leadership.

Page also has been active in broadcast news work. In addition to his four years with Chicago CBS affiliate WBBM-TV in the 1980s, he has appeared on the "News Hour," the "McLaughlin Group," "Weekend Sunday" on NPR, "This Week" on ABC and "Lead Story" on Black Entertainment Television. He has been a commentator for Chicago station WGN-TV and has been a host for several documentaries for PBS. He was a founding member of the National Association of Black Journalists and has won many an award. He received the Edward Scott Beck Award in 1976 for his coverage of politics in South Africa and a United Press International award in 1980 for investigative reporting. In 1987, he was the recipient of the James P. McGuire Award from the American Civil Liberties Union, and in 1982, he was selected for inclusion in the Chicago Journalism Hall of Fame. In 1991, he won the L.J. Horton Award that honors the accomplishments of the journalism school at Ohio University. He has served as a foundation board member at that university, and he has written freelance for such periodicals and newspapers as *Washington Monthly*, the *Wall Street Journal*, *Newsday*, *Playboy*, *Chicago Reader* and *Chicago Magazine*.

Page also has been a member of the Chicago Association of Black Journalists, AFTRA and the Chicago Academy of Television Arts & Sciences.

"Check Your Media Lap Dogs, Mr. President" by Clarence Page

If America's mainstream media really were as liberal as conservatives claim we are, we would be ballyhooing the fiasco of James D. Guckert, a.k.a. Jeff Gannon, with Page 1 banner headlines and hourly bulletins.

Sure, Guckert-gate may seem like a tempest in a teapot, at first. But so did the Whitewater land-development deal. Yet conservative commentators and editorialists, aided by heir allies in Congress, rode that Arkansas pony until it ended far afield from a land deal with the impeachment of a president for lying about sex.

Imagine, then, how the conservative choir would sing out at this point if a Democratic White House knocked long-tenured journalists off its press room access lists so that it could give access to a fellow like Guckert, 47, who dependably asks softball questions because he reports for a partisan Web site that supports the Bush administration.

Imagine how they would question the access given by the Secret Service and the White House press office for two years to a guy who used a driver's license that said James Guckert to get into the White House, then switched to his alter ego of Jeff Gannon. The best explanation for this that Bush's press secretary, Scott McClelland, could give to Editor & Publisher magazine was, "People use aliases all the time in life, from journalists to actors."

Guckert wrote under the name Jeff Gannon for Talon News, a conservative online news outlet associated with GOPUSA, a conservative Web site based in Houston and dedicated to "spreading the conservative message throughout America."

He attracted the attention of liberal "bloggers," short for Web loggers, when he asked President Bush a squeezably soft question at a news conference in January: How, he asked the president, could he work "with people who seem to have divorced themselves from reality?" (My answer? "Hey, I'm working with you, am I not?")

Liberal bloggers also uncovered links between Guckert and gay-oriented Web sites with such interesting names as Hotmilitarystud. com, Militaryescorts.com and Militaryescorts4m.com, where he apparently advertised his escort services by describing himself as "military, muscular, masculine and discrete [sic]," according to Howard Kurtz, The Washington Post's media reporter.

But all that's a titillating sideshow compared to the charges that House Democratic Whip Steny Hoyer (D-Md.) has called to the attention of the special prosecutor investigating the leak of Valerie Plame's identity as a CIA operative to columnist Robert Novak. In 2003 Guckert wrote in Talon News that he had asked Plame's husband, Ambassador Joseph Wilson, about "an internal government memo prepared by U.S. Intelligence personnel" that revealed his wife's CIA role.

Revealing a CIA agent's identity is a federal crime. A Time magazine reporter and a New York Times reporter face possible jail sentences for refusing to say who revealed Plame's CIA role to them in an apparent effort to discredit Wilson's criticism of the Bush administration's Iraq war policy. Is the prosecutor putting Guckert's feet to the fire too? If not, why not?

Of course, every administration tries to manipulate the media. Team Bush has elevated it to a high art. Before Guckert, there was the disclosure that three conservative syndicated columnists had been paid handsomely to promote administration programs—payment they had failed to disclose to their readers. And remember those pre-packaged, government-sponsored video news releases featuring fake reporters so local news outlets would be tempted to run them as legitimate news stories, as some did?

We have grown accustomed to those pre-screened rent-a-crowd "Ask President Bush" town-hall-style meetings during last year's campaign and during this year's effort by Bush to promote his proposed Social Security changes.

But I thought the last straw was the unprecedented herding of reporters covering this year's inaugural balls into pens from which they could only venture to interview ball guests if they were escorted by "minders" in the fashion of Saddam Hussein's Iraq.

Tell me again: What was that war about? Oh, yeah: freedom and democracy. Great. I'd like to see a little more of that back here at home.

Palmer, Lutrelle F.

Unfortunately, his administration and its supportive chorus are getting away with less accountability, more secretiveness, partly by demonizing the media. If they succeed in intimidating us from watchdogs into lap dogs, they will have succeeded where previous administrations from both parties failed.

That's why, despite the Guckert fiasco, I do not begrudge Web journalists from the right or the left or the squishy middle their access to government press rooms. I want to see more access, not less, granted to a press corps that is as diverse as the people we serve.

More media access means more government accountability. But, when media watchdogs are intimidated into becoming lap dogs, as some wise wit once said, that's not reporting: That's just taking dictation.

Source: This column appeared on 20 February 2005. Reprinted with permission of TMS Reprints.

Books by Clarence Eugene Page: With Leanita McClain, *A Foot in Each World: Essays and Articles* (Evanston, Ill.: Northwestern University Press, 1986); *Showing My Color: Impolite Essays on Race and Identity* (New York: HarperCollins, 1996).

Further Readings: "Clarence Page." [Online, 21 August 2004]. Tribune Media Services Web site www.latsi.com; "Page, Clarence." 2003 *Current Biography Yearbook*. New York: H.W. Wilson, pp. 403–406; "Clarence Page: Syndicated Columnist; Chicago Tribune Editorial Board Member." *Columbia Journalism Review*, September/October 2002, p. 23; "Clarence Page: The Doors Opened." *Columbia Journalism Review*, November/December 2001, p. 106.

Palmer, Lutrelle F. (28 March 1922–12 September 2004)

Fiery Lu Palmer spent 50 years as reporter, columnist, newspaper publisher and radio commentator—always remaining an unflinching advocate for black America. He was born in Newport News, Virginia, and perhaps began to develop his style of advocacy after his father, a high school principal, was fired for having attempted to secure more equal treatment for black students. Young Lutrelle, who had not yet adopted the shortened "Lu," was reportedly a popular young man who always wore a smile—a contrast to the way he is now remembered as a militant civil rights activist who often had been disappointed with both the white and black press. He studied journalism and sociology at Virginia Union University, graduating in 1942 and going on to get a masters in journalism at Syracuse University. He entered he doctoral program at the University of Iowa, after which he worked briefly in communications at Fisk University. In 1950, he left academe to work as a reporter for the venerable *Chicago Defender*, one of the nation's best-known historically black newspapers. The Maynard Institute's writer Richard Prince once quoted Palmer as saying that he was fired three times from his job at the *Defender* because, Palmer said, he was just too black for them. Concluding that the *Defender*'s management had become too interested in advertising dollars and insufficiently willing to take militant stands on civil rights issues, he parted company with that paper and became a rewrite man at a mainstream newspaper, the *Chicago American*; in so doing, he became one of the early black journalists to work in the predominantly white press. From there, he moved to the *Chicago Daily News*, where he became a columnist. His columns were written in a more militant tone than the paper would tolerate, and after some columns had been spiked and others altered, Palmer resigned on Martin Luther King's birthday in 1973. He was disappointed that the paper, in his opinion, was not interested in going beyond coverage of the black community except for stories of crime, militancy or black celebrities. In a statement upon his retirement from the *Daily News*, he said that honest writing by black journalists and the interests of the mainstream press were incompatible. He added that he intended never again to work for either a white or black newspaper unless he owned it, which he did for 14 months in 1973 and 1974. The community paper he founded, the *Black X-Press Info-Paper*, would not accept advertising from predominantly white-owned businesses, and, unable to attract sufficient advertising from black businesses in Chicago, he closed the paper in 1974.

Palmer saw more hope for honest, hardhitting commentary on another medium—black talk radio, and in 1971, he had begun broadcasting five-minute commentaries on Chicago station WVON on "Lu's Notebook." The show ran until 1983, when his sponsor, Illinois Bell, withdrew its support because of city politics. Palmer, an effective activist/organizer, had, in 1979, founded a group called Chicago Black United Communities and in 1981, the Black Independent Political Organization. Having established this base of voter support, he urged his friend Harold Washington to run for mayor of Chicago as an independent. Palmer coined the campaign slogan, "We shall see in '83" and in that year was successful in turning out the black vote. Washington won the election, defeating supposed frontrunner Jane Byrne to become the first black mayor of Chicago. Once in office, Washington disappointed Palmer by being what the writer considered insufficiently militant. Washington later won reelection but died soon after beginning his second term. It was Palmer's advocacy of Washington for mayor that cost him Illinois Bell's sponsorship. Thereafter, Palmer began another radio show, "On Target," which aired on black-owned WVON-AM in Chicago. He retired from that show on 14 April 2001. In an interview at that time, he pointed out that black journalists working in the mainstream media were in a ticklish position in that they needed to be a racial advocate, which often ran counter to the goal of objectivity they had been taught to strive for in their college journalism programs. Politically, he did not appear to like either the Republicans or the Democrats and became increasingly disenchanted with racial integration and with well-meaning but often uninformed white liberals. Palmer's last major effort on behalf of his city's black population was done in concert with his equally activist-minded wife, Jorja English Palmer. In 1992, the couple founded the Stanford English Home for Boys to aid needy African-American boys in Illinois. Earlier, the Palmers had worked together in establishing the Black Crime Commission to study and combat police brutality in Chicago.

Among the many recognitions Lu Palmer received during his career were induction into the Black Journalists Hall of Fame and the Chicago State

University Black Writers Hall of Fame, Grambling State University's Outstanding Service Award and Bell Labs' Black Achievement against the Odds Award. His considerable influence in Chicago was reflected in the roughly 1,000 people who attended his funeral.

Further Readings: Dawkins, Wayne. " 'Lu' Palmer, 82, a Persuasive Black Voice, Say Observers." [Online, 14 September 2004]. BlackAmericaWeb.com Web site www.blackamericaweb.com; Hooks, Theresa Fambro. "Lu Palmer, Journalist, Dead at 82." [Online, 13 September 2004]. Black America Today.com Web site www.blackamericatoday.com; Kane, Eugene. "Columnist Forced Readers to Confront Race." [Online, 25 September 2004]. Milwaukee Journal Sentinel Web site www.jsonline.com; "Lutrelle F. Palmer." [Online]. The History Makers Web site www.thehistorymakers.com/biography.

Parsons, Richard D. (4 April 1948–)

As chairman and CEO of Time Warner, Richard Parsons is among the most powerful executives in the United States. In 2004, he was also listed as one of only four African Americans who were CEOs of Fortune 500 companies. In 2001, he had been one of three. He was born in the Bedford-Stuyvesant section of Brooklyn, New York, and raised in Queens, the son of a Sperry Rand electronics technician father and homemaker mother. He is a 1968 graduate of the University of Hawaii, where he played basketball, and he holds a 1971 J.D. from the Albany Law School of Union University, where he graduated first in his class. During some of his schooling, he had helped pay his expenses by working as a janitor. Parsons passed the New York bar in 1971, making the highest score of all 3,600 people who took the exam at that time. His climb to the heights of the corporate world began in 1974 when he became an attorney for New York Gov. Nelson Rockefeller. When Rockefeller became U.S. vice president in the Gerald Ford administration in 1974, Parsons and his family moved to Washington, where he was a senior White House aide from then through 1976. He regards Nelson Rockefeller as having been his mentor and worked for Rockefeller's family as a lawyer after the vice president's death. In 1977, the now well-connected Parsons joined the Wall Street law firm of Patterson Belknap Webb & Tyler, where he specialized in banking, product liability and First Amendment law and served as managing partner. He practiced law until 1988, when, at a most challenging time, he became CEO of Dime Savings Bank. The real estate market had just fallen on bad times, and he had to cut around 1,500 jobs and restructure the company to keep the bank solvent. He also led a merger with Anchor Savings Bank. During his banking years, 1988–1995, he gained the reputation of an in-the-trenches executive, or as he himself put it, a "lunch-pail manager"—one who liked to mix with the people he managed. He also became a board member of Time Warner in 1991. In that capacity, his diplomacy, wit and intelligence impressed his fellow board members, and in February 1995, Parsons accepted the position of Time Warner president, working under CEO Gerald Levin. There were significant changes in the company in January 2000, when Time Warner announced a merger with new-media giant AOL (America Online), a merger that executives of both companies assumed would profitably link the old media with the new. At the time of the merger, executives expected that AOL would become the company's main profit center, but the dot.com crash proved otherwise. Part of the merger agreement made Parsons and AOL's Robert Pittman cochief operating officers. In the 2001 advertising slump, and in the wake of the September 11, 2001 attack on the World Trade Center towers, profits and hence stock price were sharply off for the newly merged firm, and shareholders were unhappy. Gerald Levin resigned in December 2001, and Pittman followed in July 2002. Eventually, Parsons was the only one of the merger's architects to survive the downturn, and in May 2002, he was named CEO. Many onlookers had assumed that the company's largest stockholder, Ted Turner, would be tapped for that job. Part of Parsons' responsibility at that time was to defend the company and its 90,000 employees against charges of financial irregularities brought by the Securities and Exchange Commission. In September 2003, the company's board decided to drop AOL from the corporate name and return to Time Warner. To reduce its debt level, Time Warner sold the Warner Music Group in 2003 for roughly $2.6 billion, which pulled the company out of the worst of its financial troubles. By 2005, various lawsuits had been settled for a reported $3 billion and the company announced a $5 billion stock buyback program. Parsons has needed all of his even-keel diplomacy, Washington connections and financial-legal expertise to deal with shareholders still dissatisfied over the per share price of company stock, and particularly with the demands for change made by such billionaire shareholders as Carl Icahn and Ted Turner. Turner has been quite vocal in calling for the breakup of all huge media conglomerates.

In May 2001, Parsons became cochairman, with New York Sen. Daniel Patrick Moynihan, of President George W. Bush's Commission to Strengthen Social Security. Although this added responsibility increased his ties with the Bush administration and Parsons' visibility in general, the Commission's recommendations to partially privatize Social Security were met with stiff resistance from all sides and, at this writing in February 2006, have been more or less tabled by the administration. Another high-profile assignment in 2001 was Parsons' work with the transition team for New York City mayor-elect Michael Bloomberg. Parsons had earlier handled the transition of another New York mayor, his former law firm colleague Rudolph Giuliani, and had turned down the job of assistant mayor. He is on the boards of Citicorp, Estee Lauder, the Museum of Modern Art, the American Museum of Natural History, Howard University, the Colonial Williamsburg Foundation, and the Committee to Encourage Corporate Philanthropy; and he has been chairman of the Apollo Theatre Foundation in New York and chair of the Upper Manhattan Empowerment Zone Development Corporation. He is also a member of the

New York City Partnership. He is owner of a modest-sized vineyard in Italy's Tuscany region, producing around 1,000 cases of wine annually. He is a Republican and considers himself fiscally conservative but socially liberal. In September 2005, Parsons and his wife, the former Laura Bush, a child psychologist, jointly received the Louis B. Marshall Award at a ceremony in New York hosted by The Jewish Theological Seminary; the couple was honored for their efforts to address the needs of children and families.

Further Readings: Halpern, Tim. "Richard D. Parsons." [Online, 2006]. Business Reference: International Directory of Business Biographies Web site www.referenceforbusiness.com/biography; Hu, Jim. "Parsons Aims to Get AOL 'Back on Track.'" [Online, 16 May 2002]. C Net News.Com site http://news.com.com; "Richard D. Parsons." [Online]. The Lauder Institute Alumni Web site www.lauderalumni.com; "Richard D. Parsons." [Online]. Time Warner Web site www.timewarner.com/corp/management/corp_executives/bio; Roberts, Johnnie L. "Prime Time for Parsons." *Newsweek.* 22 December 2003, p. 4; Roberts. Johnnie L. "Crunch Time." *Newsweek.* 22 August 2005, pp. 40–41; "Time Warner Chairman and CEO Richard Parsons and Laura Parsons, Psy.D. To Be Honored by JTS." [Online, 7 September 2005]. The Jewish Theological Seminary Web site www.jtsa.edu; Yang, Cathy. "Richard Parsons Leaps the First Hurdle." [Online, 16 May 2003]. Business Week online Web site www.businessweek.com.

Payne, Leslie (Les) (12 July 1941–)

A man of considerable journalistic accomplishment, Les Payne is associate managing editor for national, science and international news at *Newsday*, a syndicated columnist distributed weekly by Tribune Media Services and a chaired journalism professor in Columbia University's graduate program. Payne was born in Tuscaloosa, Alabama, but was reared in Hartford, Connecticut. He is a 1964 graduate of the University of Connecticut, after which he joined the U.S. Army, reaching the rank of captain and being awarded the Bronze Star. His military service included command of a Nike-Hercules antiaircraft missile battery and work as an information officer. He reached Vietnam at an awkward moment: soon after a federal decision against military discrimination by race. Learning that he was black, administrators in Gen. William Westmorland's Fourth Division decided to reassign him to Plaiku in range of enemy mortar fire, but thanks to an interview with an Air Force colonel, which Payne described in some detail in a May 2005 column, he remained in Saigon and spent his tour there editing the weekly *MACV Observer* and writing pamphlets for Westmorland's GIs.

When his tour of duty was complete in 1969, Payne joined the staff of *Newsday*, serving in a succession of positions: reporter, copy editor, editorial writer, investigative reporter, national correspondent and national editor. In 1974, he and other *Newsday* reporters did a 33-part story titled "The Heroin Trail" that investigated the international traffic in that drug, from Turkey through France to the city streets of America. The series, on which Payne spent half a year in Europe, won the 1974 Pulitzer Prize for investigative reporting. He covered the United Nations and reported out of various locations in Europe, Africa and the Caribbean and in 1978 very nearly won a second Pulitzer, for foreign reporting, for an 11-part series set in South Africa. His series was the choice of the Pulitzer jury, but its decision was overruled without comment by that organization's advisory board. In 1985, Payne again reported on events in South Africa, and in 1990, he was invited back to that country following the release of Nelson Mandela and produced another series of stories. Earlier, in 1978, 1979 and 1981, he covered the changes occurring in Rhodesia-Zimbabwe, and his TMS information sheet indicates that he also has reported out of Nigeria, Uganda, Mozambique, Tanzania, Botswana, Guinea, Zambia, Niger, Upper Volta, Kenya and Namibia. Payne used his extensive experience in Africa during his tenure as the fourth president of the NABJ, the National Association of Black Journalists (1981–1983); he attempted to connect black journalists in the United States with those in Africa, as well as with members of the Caribbean press. He urged the NABJ not to lose its protest component but to keep hammering away at the need for supporting African-American interests, especially following what he considered an outright assault on black America during the conservative Reagan administration. He has remarked that the nation, despite the progress that has been made in civil rights, is in denial about race. His own writing, he once remarked, strives to deflate the powerful and to support their hapless victims.

During his long career at *Newsday*, Payne has covered many a big national story as well, including the assassination of Dr. Martin Luther King, the rise and fall of the Black Panther Party and the Symbionese Liberation Army and the latter's kidnapping of newspaper heiress Patricia Hearst, mistreatment of migrant farm workers on Long Island, and the continuing story of illegal immigration. In 1990, he won cable television's Ace Award for an interview he conducted with New York Mayor David Dinkins on his show "Les Payne's New York Journal," and, like most modern-day columnists, he has made frequent appearances on both radio and television talk shows, including the "Phil Donahue Show," "Meet the Press," "Nightline," "Good Morning America" and "Washington Week in Review." He has also been a panelist on the WCBS show "Sunday Edition." He has coauthored a book on the revolutionary West Coast SLA and the Hearst kidnapping, is at work on a biography of civil rights advocate Malcolm X, holds the David Laventhol Chair at Columbia University's Graduate School of Journalism, and has been awarded two honorary degrees, from Long Island University and Medgar Evers College.

Payne's TMS column has appeared since 1980. Three presidents who probably have pleased the columnist least have been Ronald Reagan, Bill Clinton and George W. Bush. Payne's feelings about President Bush are clear in the March 2003 column reprinted below. He was also displeased when Mr. Bush snubbed the 2004 Philadelphia convention of the NAACP, suggesting that the president probably considered that organization too "uppity" in its assessment of administration policies. He described the president as being unable to see beyond his own nose, and his advisors as so totalitarian as to be Kremlin-like. His overall opinion of President Bush's first four years in office was that he had squandered the nation's money and honor, with Halliburton having emerged the big winner in an unjustified war.

Like many Americans, Payne could find little to approve of in the 2004 presidential race. Describing Al Sharpton's speech at the Democratic convention as "booming," Payne wrote that Sharpton had in him something of Jesse Jackson, but even more of Jesse James as he sought the media spotlight in an attempt to supplant Jackson as national spokesman for his race. A luminary who made a very positive impression on Payne, who is a Baptist, was Pope John Paul II, described by Payne as a warm, engaging, spontaneous man who had provided rockstar excitement for journalists to describe. He found John Paul a stark contrast to his predecessors, who were, he said, frosty as the Himalayas. John Paul, he added, had many of the attributes of the politician, but without the accompanying greed.

In a March 2005 column reflecting on the retirement of Dan Rather as the anchor of the CBS Evening News, Payne's assessment was that while Rather was not a great anchor, he was a great reporter. His description of what constitutes a great television reporter, however, was anything but flattering. He bemoaned the downward trajectory of television news in general and that of CBS in particular and suggested that CBS made a mistake back in 1981 when they chose Rather as anchor over Roger Mudd, Bob Schieffer or his own favorite, Ed Bradley.

Payne has also directed the attention of his readers to less known worthies, such as black judge Bruce Wright, who had to overcome enormous obstacles on his way to becoming a criminal court judge, or Ahmet Ertegun, the son of a Turkish diplomat who embraced American jazz, founded Atlantic Records and gave singer Ray Charles his first big contract. Payne also used his column to report in 2005 that blacks in New Orleans, the cradle of jazz and the blues, were being charged more for drinks in some clubs than were whites, which Payne termed similar to the retro behavior found in that city's housing market. And reflecting on the discomfort of *Newsweek* as regards its discredited story about a copy of the Quran supposedly flushed down a Guantanamo Bay toilet, he reminded readers that much of what journalists report, they did not personally witness and that sometimes, for a variety of reasons, news sources will change their tune after a story breaks. He recounted a major libel suit he was once involved in when a Turkish businessman sued *Newsday* for identifying him as a drug smuggler. Payne's source not only recanted his story, but denied ever having met *Newsday* reporters at all. Payne, however, had had the foresight to get the source to sign his name to the notes he had taken and had photographed the man at his desk, where the interview was conducted. Concluded Payne, "Whew!" the suit had been filed for $20 million.

Payne has been a member of the Committee to Protect Journalists, a judge for the National Academy of Television Arts & Sciences' news and documentary

Emmy awards (1981, 1982 and 1996) and a Pulitzer jury member. His own awards have included Columbia University's Tobenkin Award in 1978, the World Hunger Media Award in 1983, various awards for his commentaries from the Associated Press and United Press International and recognitions from Howard University and Lincoln University. He received an Ace Award for outstanding cable television work in 1990 for an interview he did with New York City Mayor David Dinkins.

"Bible-Thumping War Drums" by Les Payne

The moment this time rode in on a question.

The 43rd president of the United States does not like questions. He avoids them as he avoids the thesaurus. And for good reason. George W. Bush is perhaps the least articulate president since Dwight D. Eisenhower, the most uninformed since Gerald Ford and the most provincial since, say, Warren G. Harding.

The question that brought the moment came toward the end of the president's Thursday night press conference. The tangled question was truly welcomed, as revealed by the president's eyes, as they unbeaded momentarily then nearly teared.

"How is your faith guiding you? What should you tell America or what should America do collectively as you instructed before 9/11? Should it pray?"

The magic word "pray" snapped Bush out of a tailspin of a depressed White House conference that must have sent his most devoted handlers to their rosaries.

"I appreciate that question a lot," Bush said.

Before getting to the studied answer, the president fumbled through snatches of remembered, trite briefing notes about failed Iraq diplomacy, the Saddam Hussein menace and the lessons of 9/11. Then he got down to the part of the question that got him enraptured.

"My faith sustains me," he uttered. "Because I pray daily. I pray for guidance and wisdom and strength. If we were to commit our troops...I would pray for their safety. And I would pray for the safety of innocent Iraqi lives as well. One thing that's really great about our country is there are thousands of people who pray for me who I'll never see—be able to thank. But it's a humbling experience to think that people I will never have met have lifted me and my family up in prayer. And for that I'm grateful.

"I pray for peace, I pray for peace."

Seldom in modern times have we had a U.S. president speak so prayerfully while done up in his war paint. It recalled those memorial services at the Dover Air Base, or Jimmy Carter on Sunday mornings, or Billy Sunday anytime. One might be moved to snicker, or even to laugh, until one recalls what President Bush 41st said of his son.

"He is a man of the spirit," the father once said, trying to allay fears of his son's finger on the nuclear trigger. At one level, the former president meant that the current one is a born-again Christian. At another, more disturbing level, the father knew that his son had substituted the Bible for the bottle. In a timely article, *Newsweek* magazine detailed how President Bush wasted his young years in riotous living and how, at age 40, he went dry with the aid of a Bible-thumping, fundamentalist West Texas religious group. "It was goodbye Jack Daniels, Hello Jesus," according to a friend from those early years.

The problem with middle-aged drunks turned Christians is that they can't sleep without yakking about Jesus, and they won't let anyone else sleep, either. Instead of embracing their religion as a private matter, they flaunt it as a mission to convert. They can become a terrible nuisance, especially to those born into the religion.

The drunk-gone-zealot may be reassuring to the troubled family. But it is not altogether reassuring to a modern world facing such a fanatic on the trigger of weapons of mass destruction that are capable of destroying the Earth several times over.

Is it possible that through religious zealotry Bush might make himself a nuisance when facing a non-Christian menace? Already he shows signs of violating secular doctrine in this republic that constitutionally separates government from religion.

Already the religious talk has stirred the hard Christian right to expect their man to walk the walk and enact favorable legislation. Ministers of the evangelical movement, *Newsweek* points out, "form the core of the Republican Party, which controls all of the capital for the first time in a half century."

With war approaching, *Newsweek* stated, "This president—this presidency—is the most resolutely 'faith-based' in modern times, an enterprise founded, supported and guided by trust in the temporal and spiritual power of God."

Sept. 11 certainly shifted American foreign policy into high gear against global terrorism. Attacking Iraq, as Bush demands, is not, for many, the most effective way to answer that challenge.

The Untied Nations Security Council is split on the impending war against Iraq. The Congress may well oppose it, but it doesn't matter. This legislative body, so-called, has already ceded its war-making influence to the White House. Thus, opposition to the war has been left to the people of the Western world. And, by the millions, they have taken to the boulevards of France, Germany and Rome and the streets of the United States.

"We really don't need anybody's permission" to send American planes, missiles and troops into war against Iraq, Bush said at his press conference.

This is indeed true, and it is indeed scary.

Source: This column originally appeared on 9 March 2003 and appears here by permission of TMS Reprints.

Books by Leslie Payne: With Timothy Findley and Carolyn Craven, *The Life and Times of the SLA* (New York: Ballentine Books, 1976).

Further Readings: Dawkins, Wayne. *Black Journalists: The NABJ Story*. Sicklerville, N.J.: August Press, 1993, pp. 170–172; Estrov, Anya. "Les Payne." [Online]. New York University Web site www.journalism.nyu.edu; Jackson, Derrick Z. "Committed to the Cause: A Salute to NABJ's Presidents: Les Payne, 1981–1983." [Online]. National Association of Black Journalists Web site www.members.nabj.org; "Les Payne." [Online]. Tribune Media Services Web site www.latsi.com.

Payton, Brenda (24 August 1952–)

A fixture in the Bay Area media scene, Brenda Payton has written a column for the *Oakland Tribune* for 25 years and also is a public radio commentator on KQED-FM. She was born in Omaha, Nebraska, and grew up in Chicago, where she graduated from University of Chicago High School. She went on to earn a B.A. in history at Pomona College and an M.A. in journalism at Boston University. Her first job was as a general assignment reporter for the *New Bedford Standard Times* in 1975. Later that year, she became a reporter for the *Boston Phoenix*, and in 1977, she again moved, this time to the *San Francisco Examiner*, where she was a reporter until 1980. She then found a longtime home at the *Oakland Tribune*, where she first worked as a reporter, then since 1981 as a columnist, with the exceptions of several breaks. During 1986 and 1987 and again during 1990–1992, she taught news writing, reporting and feature writing for San Francisco State University. In 1988 and 1989, she was a John S. Knight Fellow at Stanford University. From 1990 to 1992, she worked with the Center for Investigative Reporting, where she was research leader and associate producer of the "Frontline" documentary "Your Loan Is Denied" on discriminatory mortgage lending practices, which aired in June 1992. During this time, she continued writing her *Tribune* column on a freelance basis. For 25 years she has written her twice-weekly column, and she also writes a weekly

Tribune arts feature titled "Eye on the Arts" and does a monthly commentary for PBS radio station KQED. She calculates that she has published around 2 million words in her column, which mainly addresses life, politics and social issues in the Bay Area's African-American community. In 1994, she wrote for the Black Community Crusade for Children of the Children's Defense Fund a report titled "The Challenge," about the problem of youth violence in black America. Her column has addressed many topics during its long history: the disproportional brunt of war borne by poor and minority people, U.S.-led torture as an unfortunate part of the war on terrorism, the link between the constant strains of racial discrimination and heart disease, youth prostitution and the sudden revelation of U.S. poverty pockets revealed by Hurricane Katrina. She also has written about the shameful internment of Japanese-Americans living on the West Coast during the 1940s and, on a happier note, about a social club of long standing in the Oakland area and about a new 4,873-pipe church organ. Especially unusual were columns on an exhibit at Oakland's African American Museum and Library that showcased old Confederate paper money on which were pictured various aspects of slavery and another history-based column, reprinted below, about black paper dolls as historical artifacts.

Payton has published freelance in the *New York Times*, the *Nation* and *Enco* magazine and has contributed to two anthologies: *Thinking Black* (New York: Crown Publishers, 1996), edited by DeWayne Wickham of *USA Today* and *MultiAmerica: Essays on Cultural Wars and Cultural Peace* (New York: Viking, 1997), edited by the prolific Ishmael Reed. She often has been recognized for her contributions to Bay Area journalism. Her column has been honored by the National Association of Black Journalists and the California Newspaper Publishers Association, and in early 2006, CityFlight Media Network named her one of the 10 most influential African Americans in the Bay Area. She has received the John Swett Award for reporting on education, the Meiklejohn Civil Liberties Institute Award, a citation for column writing from the California Newspaper Publishers Association and the Jane A. Harrah Memorial Media Award for her work on the U.S. citizens of Japanese descent interned during World War II. In 2005, she and longtime African-American anchorman Dennis Richmond were honored for their work by the Bay Area Black Journalists Association.

"Black Paper Dolls Offer History Lesson" by Brenda Payton

When I was a little girl, I used to play with paper dolls. It seems like all the little girls did, cutting out the outfits and attaching them with those paper tabs that never really held them in place.

The memory is sweet and simple. I never thought of paper dolls as historic artifacts. But like everything, they can be. Mills College is presenting an unusual black history exhibit of black paper dolls that reflects the status of black people since the first doll was issued 140 years ago.

The dolls are from the collection of Arabella Grayson. The first black paper doll was Topsey, based on the character in "Uncle Tom's Cabin" (spelled Topsy in the book).

In a picture, the doll is about 2 inches tall with three outfits—a red polka-dot dress with a blue-checkered apron, a blue-and-yellow-striped dress with a bib apron, and a dress with a shawl. Surprisingly, her face is not drawn as a racial caricature, a popular style at the time.

A black baby articulated paper doll with movable legs and arms attached with brass bands, made in Germany in 1885 and imported to the United States, also has realistic features. The one in the exhibit is smiling; another version was unsmiling. The dolls were sold in envelopes with tissue and crepe paper.

According to the exhibit, in the early 20th century several magazines printed black paper dolls using the fast-printing method, which combined photography and lithography, creating images from tiny, uniform dots.

One of those was "Mammy and Her Thanksgiving Dinner," printed by the *Delineator* magazine in 1912. Mammy had the stereotypical mammy-face with a wrap- around skirt, a white apron and a red head scarf. Accessories included a turkey and pies.

"Aunt Dinah the Colored Cook comes to join the paper doll family" was published by *McCalls* in 1911. Her image was more distinguished than Mammy's, with a realistic face and a hand on her hip. Paper dolls became popular features in comic strips. the *Philadelphia Record* printed a black make servant doll in 1932 with a Sambo-type face and three servant uniforms.

One of the more interesting black paper doll characters was Torchy Togs, drawn by Jackie Ormes and published in the *Pittsburgh Courier*, an African-American newspaper, in the 1950s. Breaking the mammy or maid model, she was curvaceous with a snazzy short haircut and wore the latest European fashions, including a green silk faille coat, a white sharkskin dress and a red linen suit. "Hi Girls," she says. "This week we pay special attention to those special occasions when dressing up is a must."

A similar character was created by Dale Messick, who also created the Brenda Starr comic strip, and ran in the *Chicago Tribune* in the early '50s. She was leggy with big hoop earrings and costumes that included a cowgirl's outfit and a Hawaiian skirt.

We move to 1968 and a "Julia" paper doll box set based on the breakthrough television series that starred Diahnn Carroll as a widowed nurse raising her son in Los Angeles. It was the first role featuring an intelligent, independent African-American woman on a television series.

And the 1969 "Black Is Beautiful" box of four paper dolls. The dolls have huge brown eyes, but don't yet sport the afros that would become almost mandatory. "Just touch with the wand and the clothes stay on," the set promised, including a thin red plastic wand to do the trick.

Other interesting dolls: a Cecil Williams Paper Doll by Trina Robbins, published in *San Francisco Magazine* in 1991. The reverend is holding a Bible. His outfits include a dashiki with huge angel wings and a halo and a Santa Claus suit carrying a bag full of groceries.

The exhibit offers many other glimpses of how black paper dolls have evolved during the years. What an interesting way to look at the history of black people in America. When we were cutting out our dolls and trying to make those tabs work, who knew?

"Precious Playthings: Black Paper Dolls, 1885–2003" is on exhibit at the Heller Rare Book Room at Mills' Olin Library through February.

Source: This column appeared in the Oakland Tribune on 20 February 2004 and appears here by permission of Ms. Payton and the *Oakland Tribune*.

Further Readings: "Brenda Payton." [Online]. 10 Most Influential site http://10mostinfluential.com. McDonough, Susan. "Oakland Tribune Columnist Holds Sway Over Area." [Online, 29 March 2006]. Inside Bay Area Web site www.insidebayarea.com.

Perkins, Joseph (c.1960–)

San Diego Union-Tribune political columnist and editorial writer Joseph Perkins, syndicated weekly by Newspaper Enterprise Association, was completely predictable in his conservatism, but surprised his newspaper, syndicate and readers in March 2005 by abruptly retiring—in his mid-40s—having succeeded in being published in some 250 newspapers. A graduate of Howard University, he was named the best collegiate editorial writer in the nation by the Society of Professional Journalists, Sigma Delta Chi, which got him hired to write editorials for the *Wall Street Journal*, the newspaper having perhaps the most conservative editorial page in the nation. Thereafter, he joined the White House staff of Vice President Dan Quayle as deputy assistant for domestic policy. Perkins made frequent appearances on such broadcast outlets as MSNBC, Fox News, C-Span, CNN, CNBC, "Good Morning America" and "This Week" on ABC, the "Morning Show" on CBS, plus MTV and "Politically Incorrect" on ABC. Some of his work was posted on RealClearPolitics.com, FreeRepublic.com and Lucianne.com, and he has published one book, a collection of his columns, in 1996.

In his farewell column, which appeared on 4 March 2005, Perkins was veiled as to his reasons for giving up his newspaper job and his highly successful syndicated column, citing only the 15 years of grinding out the column plus 3 or 4 editorials a week. Quoting movie actor Clint Eastwood, Perkins quipped that a man needs to know his limitations. He assured readers that his retirement was strictly voluntary and mentioned that his wife was also taking early retirement. He told readers that he had made it his mission to counterbalance the liberal tenor of American editorial pages, knowing that he would be at odds with the largely liberal residents of Hollywood and of academia. Many of his critics, he reported, considered that he was always giving the Democrats hell, then quoted the late Harry Truman, who said he really did not give his political opponents hell, he merely spoke the truth, and they thought it was hell.

In a 2004 column, Perkins quoted ABC correspondent John Stossel as having remarked that at ABC, the word "conservative" appeared to be on par with "child molester." Perkins complained often about liberal media bias and how it caused the press to ask embarrassing questions of the administration, as when Secretary of Defense Rumsfeld was "put on the spot" with tedious inquiries about lack of vehicle armor for our troops in Iraq. Perkins considered NBC's Kevin Sites wrong for having filmed the shooting of an injured insurgent by a U.S. Marine, and he criticized our media for showing the public shocking footage of prisoner abuse at Abu Ghraib prison while refusing to show beheadings of our own troops or allies by the enemy. He criticized former California Lt. Gov. Cruz Bustamonte for having referred to blacks using the "n" word during a Black History Month appearance but was even more critical of the media for making little of this incident because Bustamonte is a Democrat, the way they also gave Bill Clinton a free pass after he played golf at a whites-only club in Florida. Perkins took a swipe at liberal black spokesman Jesse Jackson following Jackson's love–child revelations, saying that in the Clinton incident, Jackson should have been right there in South Florida complaining loudly, but was too busy changing diapers. In a presidential election marked by more dissembling than ever on both sides, Perkins ignored the Republican lies and complained only that Democrats had used every big lie they could come up with to steer the public away from reelecting George W. Bush. And as to the Bush administration's attempt to load the federal courts with conservative jurists, Perkins came out in favor of using what came to be called the "nuclear option" to end Democratic filibustering, an option that was avoided at the last minute by compromise. Predictably, Perkins favored President Bush's plan to partially privatize Social Security and spoke out against affirmative action for minorities.

Books by Joseph Perkins: Editor, *A Conservative Agenda for Black Americans* (Washington, D.C.: Heritage Foundation, 1987); *Right Like Me* (San Diego, Calif.: Union-Tribune Pub. Co, 1996).

Further Readings: Astor, David. "Conservative Columnist Joseph Perkins Resigns Suddenly." [Online, 3 March 2005]. Editor & Publisher Web site www.editorandpublisher.com; "Perkins Is Doing an Opinion Column for NEA." *Editor & Publisher*, 15 August 1992, p. 36.

Person, David (1963–)

David Person is a young columnist and editorial writer for the *Huntsville Times* in Alabama; a columnist for BlackAmericaWeb.com, the Web site for the Tom Joyner Morning Show; and a freelance reporter/producer for National Public Radio. He was born in St. Louis, Missouri, and graduated in 1985 from Oakwood College, a historically black Seventh-day Adventist college in Huntsville, Alabama. Before joining the *Times*, he worked in Huntsville for NPR affiliate WLRH-FM, CBS affiliate WHNT-TV, and Christian station WOCG-FM. Among his radio productions have been the Black Classical Masters series and two radio documentaries for a national audience: "Uncommon Courage: The Viola Liuzzo Story" in 2003 and "The Afro: Personal Reflections" in 2005. His columns usually address some aspect of race relations. In a November 2004 column headlined "A Confederate President?" he juxtaposed today's red and blue states with the states of the Confederacy, pointing out that those 11 states plus Kentucky and Missouri all voted for the conservative agenda in the 2004 presidential election. Conservative values, he found, seem tightly aligned with Confederate values. Another of his columns from May of the same year reported a sad event–the desecration of the Jasper, Texas, grave of James Byrd Jr., the black man from that town who in 1998 was dragged to his death behind a truck in a racial hate crime. Person found irony in the frequent accusations made by racist whites who complain that blacks keep race a contentious issue by "living in the past." The person or persons who defaced Byrd's grave, he wrote, would seem to be the ones who cannot let racist bigotry rest in peace.

Like many other columnists, Person was offended by the teeming flood of media coverage of the search for Natalee Holloway, an attractive young white woman missing in Aruba, contrasting that coverage to the lack of media attention to another young, attractive woman gone missing: Lori Hacking, who is black. Most media gatekeepers are white, he points out, and we all tend to be most moved by what we know best. Reflecting on the death of an earlier African-American columnist at the Huntsville paper, Ben Johnson, Person remarked on the necessity of writing about race—to help keep the dust of past bigotry from settling again. Yet another column makes a striking point—that black history also contains white history. He writes appreciatively of whites who defied tradition and refused to side with the South's segregationists. An example he mentioned was Inez Marsh of Big Cove, Alabama, who in the 1960s had refused to segregate her two businesses. Another was Juliette Hampton Morgan, who advocated abolishing the state's poll tax and had supported the Montgomery bus boycotts; she was so badly treated by fellow whites that she eventually committed suicide.

In the column reproduced below, Person shames the Alabama Legislature for its stand against gay marriage, gays adopting children, and the like, pointing out that perhaps gays today are in a position similar to that of blacks in the 1950s. He pillories Southern Baptists for characterizing America's public schools as "godless," rascals who prey on the gullible by selling "prayer rugs," and the hypocrisy of Alabamans who vote against a state lottery, then rush to a neighboring state to buy lottery tickets. Person has won awards from the Alabama Associated Press and from the Alabama Press Association.

"Gays: Our New Scapegoats" by David Person

Let's toast the Alabama Legislature. Please, lift your glasses of milk, soda or adult beverage of choice like those British fellows in that beer commercial and join me in commemorating the fine work our elected officials have done so far.

A constitutional ban on gay marriage? Brilliant!

A ban on books that portray homosexuality as positive or normal? Brilliant!

A ban on gays being able to adopt children? Brilliant!

I suspect that if we were in another state—where foot-dragging, obfuscation and avoidance were the preferred work modes for elected officials—we would undoubtedly have missed these critical issues.

I have no doubt that we would instead be wasting time addressing ridiculous matters like, say, I don't know, maybe budget shortfalls or funding issues, crazy stuff like that.

Fortunately, we live in Alabama. And here, thank God, we know what threatens our state's ability to serve its people isn't budget shortfalls and a lack of resources.

It's homosexuality, stupid.

Some of you skeptics out there are probably foaming at the mouth. Wait just a minute, you say.

In order to make the 2004 budget work, Gov. Riley had to propose more than $171 million in cuts.

Riley had to cut more than $1.9 million from the Alabama Network of Child Advocacy Centers; about $11.4 million from the Department of Public Safety; nearly $2.5 million from the Public Health Department.

Veterans Affairs had to take a hit of about $640,000. The Coalition Against Domestic Violence had more than $310,000 cut from its 2004 budget.

And that's not all.

Riley cut nearly half a million dollars from his own budget. He also cut $10.3 million from the state's Mental Health Department and anticipated that Medicaid would lose $30 million.

You silly skeptics just don't get it. Budget cuts aren't important. In hard times, everyone's got to suck it up and tough it out. And that includes abused children and spouses, the indigent and poor who rely on public health services, Alabama veterans who served their nation with honor, and people with mental disabilities.

Not enough state troopers to patrol Alabama's highways? Duh, get a cell phone and call Momma or Uncle Jimmy for help if you have a wreck.

Have a loved one who depends on Medicaid to pay for health care? Hello?—pass the offering plate at church. Get another part-time job or two.

And for goodness sake, stop whining. We taxpayers must pick up the slack and suffer while our legislators deal with the issues that really matter, the ones we don't know how to handle.

If they don't protect us from the gays, lesbians, cross-dressers, transsexuals and the rest of those people, who will?

These homosexuals and people with their so-called "alternative lifestyles" are wrecking it for the rest of us. Don't you get it? Marriage is under attack.

Slightly more than 24,000 Alabamians got divorced in 2002. Who's to blame for that? Philandering husbands? Desperate housewives? Money problems?

Nope. It's the gays.

They're everywhere, you know. They used to hide in their closets of shame, which, of course, is where they belong.

No more. Now they have television shows where they tell us how to dress or kiss on and cavort with each other. And doggone it, it's distracting us heterosexuals.

I don't know about the rest of you straight guys, but I find it very difficult to daydream about the four beautiful women on "Girlfriends" when "Will and Grace" is on. And sometimes, I'm ashamed to say, I've passed up dates with beautiful women in order to see "Queer Eye for the Straight Guy."

I mean, really. A guy has to have his priorities in order.

I fully agree with the stand our brave legislators have taken. It's better that abused women and children, veterans, the elderly and the poor lose state services than that heterosexual relationships continue to be attacked by those gays.

So, my fellow Alabamians, let's fight the gay scourge that threatens to ruin our way of life. And if this seems a little difficult or extreme, just pretend the gays of today are the blacks of the 1950s. That ought to make it real easy.

Source: Copyright 2005 *The Huntsville Times*. All rights reserved. Reprinted with permission of *The Huntsville Times*. The column originally appeared on 18 February 2005.

Peterman, Peggy Mitchell (6 October 1936–19 August 2004)

Peggy Peterman retired from the *St. Petersburg Times* in 1996 after having worked for that paper for 31 years, blazing a trail for other African-American journalists to follow. She was born in Tuskegee Institute, Alabama, the daughter of civil rights activist William P. Mitchell, and she earned both the B.A. in liberal arts in 1958 and the LLB in 1961 at Howard University. Mitchell moved to St. Petersburg, Florida, in or around 1962 and worked as a legal secretary. She wrote a letter to the editor of the *Times* describing how due to her race, she had been refused diaper service for her baby and the services of a photographer to redeem a free-photo coupon. Three years later she was hired by that paper to write for its Negro news page, which was distributed only in the city's black neighborhoods. Segregation was beginning to crumble by that time, however, and by May 1967, she was able to convince her editors to do away with that page, so symbolic of the Old South. She spent around twenty years writing a combination of news and features, often facing the displeasure of diehard segregationists. A 2004 column by the *Times*' Tampa columnist, Ernest Hooper, also African American, described how in 1965, Peterman got hate mail from one anonymous reader who would enclose a penny with each diatribe; the pennies eventually formed a large pile in one of her desk drawers. In the late 1980s, management gave her a column, which she used to write about area blacks' troubles and triumphs, struggles and dreams. She became a member of the paper's editorial board in 1994, just two years before her retirement. In the 1970s, she taught in the Upward Bound program at Eckerd College and later was an adjunct instructor at St. Petersburg Junior College, teaching black studies. She also organized the city's annual Black History Pageant in 1978 and received lifetime achievement awards from the National Association of Black Journalists and from the International Women's Media Foundation. She also was accorded the Meritorious Achievement Award by the FAMU Center at Florida A & M University. One of her last major accomplishments came in 2002, when she became the Rev. Peggy Peterman, a minister in the Baptist Church. After her 2004 death, one of her *Times* colleagues, staff writer Jade Jackson Lloyd, noted that some of her most effective "sermons" had appeared in the newspaper and described her as having a quiet grace but a will of stone. Peterman was one of the contributors of chapters to *Thinking Black: Some of the Nation's Best Black Columnists Speak Their Minds* (New York: Crown Publishers, 1996), edited by DeWayne Wickham.

Further Readings: Andelman, Bob. "Peggy Peterman." [Online, 1989]. Bob Andelman Web site www.andelman.com; Basse, Craig. "Peggy Peterman." [Online, 20 August 2004]. St. Petersburg Times Web site www.sptimes.com; Hooper, Ernest. "Positive Signs Help Muzzle Voice of Hate." [Online, 1 September 2004]. St. Petersburg Times Web site www.sptimes.com; Lloyd, Jade Jackson. "700 Say Goodbye to Crusading Writer." [Online, 29 August 2004]. St. Petersburg Times Web site www.sptimes.com.

Phillips, Julian Martin (5 December 1955–)

Longtime television journalist Julian Phillips has since 2002 worked at the Fox News Channel as an anchor and general assignment reporter. He appears to be a favorite target of right wingers for daring to be a liberal who works for a predominantly conservative media outlet. He was born in New York City and educated at Purdue University, where he earned the B.A. in 1977. He began his career as an ABC Radio Network News desk assistant in 1977, then switched media for a one-year job at *Black Enterprise Magazine* in 1980. In 1981, he returned to broadcasting at WNEW-TV as a production assistant. He moved to WNBC-TV in 1984, working as that station's manager of community relations. In 1993, he went oncamera as a WNBC anchor and reporter. His next job was as an on-air correspondent for WPIX-TV's "News at Ten" in New York City. There, he also hosted "Best Talk," a community affairs show. Phillips was hired by Fox News Channel in October 2002. His most recent job is anchoring the "Fox & Friends Weekend" show on Saturdays and Sundays from 7–10 AM. In spite of Fox's "fair and balanced" slogan, many of its most devoted viewers want and expect heavyhanded conservatism to prevail on that network, and Phillips' liberal views make him a lightning rod for right-wing partisans. A look at various conservative Web sites finds viewers calling him a superficial liberal and a monument to Affirmative Action. Others find his personality grating and criticize him as poorly informed. He was skewered in November 2005 by a viewer who complained that Phillips could not find one good thing to say about the United States' part in the Iraq war. Earlier in 2005, a blogger complained that Phillips often professed his Christian faith yet defends liberals. Still others grumble that he exhibits a sense of unease on the show. In October 2005, however, one of his conservative viewers grudgingly complimented Phillips on a right-wing blog site following a show on which Phillips' cohost, Alisyn Camerota, asked whether neo-Nazis or members of the Ku Klux Klan should be allowed to march in an upcoming Dayton, Ohio, parade. Phillips had responded that this is America, and even those organizations should be allowed to march.

Phillips served from 1985 to 1989 as a regional vice president of the National Broadcast Association for Community Affairs and was on the advisory board of the New York City Department for Aging. He was on the advisory boards of the National Puerto Rican Forum from 1984 to 1990 and the Crohns and Colitis Foundation of America from 1989 to 2002. In 1992, he joined the board of the New York Coalition on Adoptable Children. He is a two-time Emmy winner and in 1988 received the Purdue University Distinguished Alumni Award. In 1994, he won an Edward R. Murrow Award for excellence in journalism from the Radio & TV News Directors Association; and in 1996, he received the Associated Press' First Place News Award.

Further Readings: "Julian Phillips." [Online, 23 June 2004]. Fox News Web site www.foxnews.com.

Pierce, Ponchitta Marie Anne Vincent (5 August 1942–)

Known mainly for her abilities as an interviewer, Ponchitta Pierce has enjoyed a long career in television and magazines and is currently a contributing editor for *Parade Magazine*. She was born in Chicago but spent her early years in New Orleans, the daughter of a contractor and a teacher and a member of a large family of aunts, uncles and cousins. She has remarked on the delights of growing up in the South as part of a big family. Her parents moved to Los Angeles when she was in eighth grade, and there she attended an all-girls Roman Catholic school, Bishop Conaty High School, where the nuns encouraged her writing talent. At the University of Southern California, she majored in journalism, wrote for the campus paper and edited the yearbook before graduating cum laude in 1964. During one of her college summers, 1962, she studied at Cambridge University in England. Upon her graduation in 1964, she was approached by magazine publisher John Johnson about becoming assistant editor of *Ebony* and *Jet* magazines. She was promoted to associate editor in the following year and in 1967, became New York editor of *Ebony* and also New York bureau chief of Johnson Publishing Company. In 1971 she moved on to a contributing editor job with *McCall's* magazine, remaining in that position until becoming a roving editor for *Reader's Digest* in 1977. She freelanced for *Newsday*, *Family Circle*, *Ebony*, *Parade*, *Modern Maturity* and *Ladies Home Journal*, writing about such topics as Martin Luther King, crime, the problems of returning Vietnam veterans, racism, teaching children how to avoid being prejudiced and the difficulties faced by black female intellectuals. From 1971 to 1978 she was also an editorial consultant for the Phelps Stokes Fund. Pierce remained with *Reader's Digest* until 1981.

From 1968 to 1971, the extremely attractive Pierce also worked as a special correspondent for the "CBS Evening News" and as an interviewer for "CBS Morning News." She was hired in 1973 by WNBC-TV in New York City as cohost of the magazine-format program "The Sunday Show." In 1977, she moved on to host a public affairs program aimed at seniors, "The Prime of Your Life," remaining there until 1980. She coproduced and hosted another WNBC show, "Today in New York," from 1982 until 1987 and also did hosting for WNET in New York. Since that time, she has been a freelance writer and television producer, and she is one of *Parade*'s contributing editors. She has been an active volunteer and a member of many boards. She is on the boards of WNET, the Morris-Jumel Mansion Museum in Harlem Heights, the Dance Theatre of Harlem, the Educational Broadcasting Corporation, the Third Street Music School Settlement, the Women's Foreign Policy Group in Washington and the Joseph & Edna Johnson Institute of Ethics. Pierce is on the board of advisors for the Mailman School of Public Health at Columbia University, an organization important in research and education about AIDS, teen pregnancy and providing care for the uninsured. She is a former president of the Women's Forum Inc. of New York, a group of 400 women from business, various professional fields and the arts in the city. She has also been on the board of the Foreign Policy Association and the Council on Foreign Relations and has been active with the Voice Foundation, the Inner-City Scholarship Fund, the International Women's Forum, the National Center for Children in Poverty and the Madison Square Boys and Girls Club. She holds membership in American Women in Radio and Television, the American Federation of Television and Radio Artists, Women in Communication, the Lotos Club and the Economics Club of New York. Pierce has also served on the award selection committee of the Peter F. Drucker Foundation.

Her skills as a moderator have been put to use in a 1985 town hall–session on the search for peace with then Secretary of State Alexander Haig, another such meeting in Atlanta the following year featuring ex-president Jimmy Carter on the subject of foreign policy, a 1991 discussion of free trade held in Mexico City and a 1993 symposium on women's health issues at which Sen. Hillary Clinton spoke.

Among her honors are an honorary doctorate of humane letters from Franklin Pierce College in New Hampshire, the 1967 Penney-Missouri Magazine

Award for her *Ebony* article "The Mission of Marian Wright" (June 1966), the 1968 John Russwurm Award given by the New York Urban League, the 1969 Woman Behind the News Award, the 1970 Headliner Award of Theta Sigma Phi Sorority, and the 1974 American-Italian Women of Achievement Award. In 1987, she won both the Commendation Award from American Women in Radio and Television and the Exceptional Merit Media Award given by the National Women's Political Caucus.

Further Readings: Garrett, Marie. "Ponchitta Pierce." *Notable Black American Women, Book II*. Edited by Jessie Carney Smith. Detroit: Gale Research, 1996, pp. 526–528; Schine, Cathleen. "Thinking Heads Charlie Rose and Ponchitta Pierce: Under Cover of Night, TV Gets Smart." *Vogue* 176 (April 1986): 12.

Pitts, Byron (21 October 1960–)

In February 2006, longtime broadcast newsman Byron Pitts became national correspondent for CBS News; Pitts has been with CBS since 1996. He was born in Baltimore, Maryland, and is a 1982 journalism and speech graduate of Ohio Wesleyan University. His entry into working journalism was in 1983 as a reporter and sports anchor for WNCT-TV in Greenville, a small city in eastern North Carolina. In 1984, he took a new job to report on the military for WAVY-TV in Hampton Roads, Virginia, and from 1986 to 1988, he was a WESH-TV reporter in Orlando, Florida. He was a reporter and relief anchor at WFLA-TV in Tampa, Florida, in 1988 and 1989 and from 1989 to 1994 worked as a special assignments reporter for Boston's WCBV-TV. His final job before moving to the network was at WSB-TV in Atlanta, Georgia, where he worked in general assignment reporting from 1994 through 1996. His first CBS job was with CBS NEWSPATH, the network's affiliated 24-hour news service; he was employed in 1997 and 1998. In May 1988, he became a CBS news correspondent, working first in its bureaus in Miami, then Atlanta; finally, in January 2001, he moved to New York City. He led the network's reporting on the attacks of 11 September and later reported on U.S. actions in Afghanistan and was an embedded reporter with a helicopter squadron in Iraq. He also reported on the controversial use of government force in seizing Cuban boy Elian Gonzalez in 2000 and the boy's eventual return to Cuba. He has covered voting irregularities in Florida, the fires that swept parts of that state in 2000 and the execution by lethal injection of Oklahoma City bomber Timothy McVeigh, who died silent and unrepentant. Pitts remarked that he had wept upon seeing the results of McVeigh's act of domestic terrorism but was unmoved when he witnessed the bomber's execution. Other big stories he has covered include the Central American mudslides of 2000 and, in that same year, the plight of refugees in Kosovo. In October 2003, Pitts and then-anchor for CBS Dan Rather reported on the troubles of conservative commentator

Rush Limbaugh, who had charged that the NFL had shown preferential treatment to Donovan McNabb, quarterback of the Philadelphia Eagles, due to McNabb's African-American ethnicity. Charges of racism leveled at Limbaugh were mild, Pitts reported, compared to the conservative spokesman's problems with drug abuse. Pitts remarked on the poetic justice of a man who has advocated the expulsion of drug users from the nation suddenly finding himself on the other end of the issue. In the 2004 presidential race, Pitts, a liberal, drew fire from the right by criticizing the shameless manipulators who smeared the war record of Democratic candidate John Kerry and, in 2002, had sunk to an even more remarkable low by using the same smear tactics on Georgia's Sen. Max Cleland, a triple amputee from his service in Vietnam. Pitts has been accused of biased reporting by a number of conservative groups, including the Media Research Center and NewsBusters.org. In December 2005, Pitts was a panelist on an episode of "Face the Nation" moderated by CBS News anchor Bob Schieffer. Part of that episode was devoted to discussing the Bush administration's mishandling of the devastation Hurricane Katrina wrought on New Orleans and other parts of the Gulf Coast. Pitts pointed out the lingering issues of race suddenly brought into high relief by the flooding and remarked disapprovingly on the possibility that the Ninth Ward disaster might be seized to profitable advantage by developers wishing to gentrify the area, effectively chasing out its former residents. In February 2006, CBS News made several staff changes. Pitts became national correspondent, Lara Logan was named chief foreign correspondent and Jim Axelrod became chief White House correspondent. In announcing Pitts' new assignment, CBS News president Sean McManus praised him as one of the finest on-scene reporters and best storytellers in broadcast journalism. The changes were announced the day after CBS White House correspondent John Roberts left the network to join CNN.

Pitts won a national Emmy in 1999 for his reporting on a train wreck in Chicago. He has also won six regional Emmy awards and four awards from the Associated Press. In addition, he was named Journalist of the Year in 2002 by the National Association of Black Journalists. Pitts is married to fellow CBS employee Lyne Pitts, producer of "The Early Show."

Further Readings: "Byron Pitts." [Onlline, 28 February 2006]. CBS News Web site www.cbsnews.com. "Emmy Award Winner, OWU Alumnus Byron Pitts Discusses Role of Media." [Online, 4 October 2002]. Ohio Wesleyan University Web site www.owu.edu.

Pitts, Leonard Jr. (11 October 1957–)

Pulitzer Prize–winning *Miami Herald* columnist Leonard Pitts appears in roughly 150 newspapers via Tribune Media Services. His column addresses life as lived in the United States and often has more of an emotional quality than the work of most columnists. Topics range from politics to family issues to racial matters to cultural commentary, and he makes not infrequent use of humor. Pitts was born and reared in Southern California, began his career writing about popular music and edited a now defunct Los Angeles entertainment tabloid titled *Soul*, for which he had freelanced while in college. Pitts wrote and produced "Who We Are," a radio documentary on black history that aired in syndication in 1988, and he also wrote for "Casey's Top 40 with Casey Kasem," a popular radio music show. In 1991, he joined the *Miami Herald* as that paper's pop music critic and from 1991 until 1994, wrote a music column. In 1994, he widened his range of topics and began his present news / features column. In a brief article in *Knight Ridder News*, Pitts's executive editor, Tom Fiedler, remarked that Pitts specializes in issues that touch us emotionally. The columnist himself added that his job is to help readers make sense of issues that trouble Americans. Pitts was distributed by Knight Ridder Tribune News Service beginning in 1995 and was picked up by Tribune Media Services in 1998. In 1999, he published a book about black men and fatherhood, and immediately following the 11 September 2001 attack on the World Trade Center, his verbal response to the terrorists attracted more than 30,000 positive email replies, was reprinted as a poster, and was even set to music. His well-received, personality-rich column writing won the 2004 Pulitzer for commentary. His recognitions have included five National Headliners awards, a first place for commentary writing from the American Association of Sunday and Feature Editors in 1997, the American Society of Newspaper Editors Commentary Award in 2001, GLAAD Media's Outstanding Newspaper Columnist Award in 2002 and the National Society of Newspaper Columnists' Columnist of the Year recognition in 2002. He also has been honored by the Society of Professional Journalists, the National Association of Black Journalists and the Simon Wiesenthal Center. He has published in such periodicals as *Reader's Digest*, *Parenting*, *TV Guide*, *Spin* and *Musician*. During the spring semester of 2004, Pitts taught opinion writing and trends in popular culture as the Scripps Howard Visiting Professional in the Hampton University school of Journalism and Communications.

Leonard Pitts differs from most of his fellow columnists in one respect: he seldom writes about politics or the work of the president. In September of 2004, however, he let his readers know his thoughts on the George W. Bush administration in a column that ran under the headline "A Forgery Rather than a Presidency." This column was written after Pitts returned from travels in Europe and Africa, where he met many locals who asked him how the U.S. president could mislead the American public so blatantly and get away with it. Regarding the war in Iraq, Pitts's answer was that having accepted a forgery as regards weapons of mass destruction, we the public were unwilling to admit what the rest of the world could see. Pitts added that for President Bush, a thing is true if he wants it to be true and that the role of his advisors is to nod in agreement. A later column lambasted Bush's arrogance and described the way the president smirks and trips over his own tongue.

More often, however, Pitts selects nonpolitical items in the news as springboards for his commentary. The Jeff Weise killings on the Red Lake Reservation in Minnesota led him to nazi.org, the hate site favored by 16-year-old loner Weise. Pitts wrote of Weise's complaint that his fellow Native Americans were not "Indian enough," favoring black hip-hop culture over their own traditions. Reflecting on the O.J. Simpson affair, Pitts pointed out that since the alleged killer was black and his victims white, the case became a racial Rorshach test that set loose pent-up anger and racial hostility everywhere. He recalled an unpleasant incident in which a white newspaper colleague accused him of being blinded by blackness, not realizing that Pitts, too, thought Simpson was guilty. Pitts went on to offer an insightful explanation about the vast gulf between white and black reaction to Simpson's having been found not guilty of murdering two people, adding that race has the power to warp perspective and to make itself felt as the only thing of importance in cases like that of O.J. Simpson.

In his column headlined "Black? African-American? Colored?" Pitts reflects on a letter from a white reader asking advice on how best to use these various racial descriptors so as to avoid causing offense. Pitts found himself unable to do so, but instead pointed out that in a saner world, the question would not be necessary. In response to the introduction of a new "Monopoly" board game knockoff called "Ghettopoly," rife with offensive stereotypes about crack houses, pimpin' "hos" and carjacking, Pitts suggests that the more important offense has been the enormously successful reduction to caricature of black America by rap music performers, who, he wrote, had turned black America's greatest cultural contribution, its music, into an open sewer that had done more to perpetuate harmful stereotype than "Ghettopoly" ever could. He has also endorsed the efforts of comedian Bill Cosby to reach black youth and keep them from being passive victims of a street culture that few others dared to criticize publicly. Pitts seemed to be far more affronted by a remarkably tasteless new video game, "J.F.K Reloaded," in which the player gets to simulate assassinating President John F. Kennedy.

Pitts's most emotional columns are about events that he finds galling, such as the backfired effort of Pastor Chan Chandler in Waynesboro, North Carolina, to force his political leanings on his Baptist flock, or, in another North Carolina incident, the refusal of Clarence Stowers to return the finger he found in his frozen custard so that doctors could attempt to reattach it. His gentlest columns are often tributes to deceased Americans who did good things, such as Fred Rogers, the soft-spoken children's show host who gave blanket adult approval to a lot of children who badly needed it, or late-night king Johnny Carson, to Pitts, an icon of a now-splintered American mainstream. Pitts' insertion of humor into his columns has never been better than a January 2006 account of the truly remarkable experiences of Colorado Springs police officer Ron Stallworth, who in 1979 joined the Ku Klux Klan—by phone. The "kicker" was that Stallworth was black. When his membership card failed to arrive, he phoned Klan leader David Duke. He asked Duke how he knew that he, Stallworth, was not an undercover policeman or a black man. Duke answered that he could always tell when he was speaking to someone black by the way the person pronounced the word "are." According the Imperial Wizard, African-Americans always pronounced it "are-uh." Pitts' handling of the comic element of this story was deft and incisive.

"A Forgery Rather than a Presidency" by Leonard Pitts Jr.

In March 2003, Pat Robertson tried to give President Bush some advice about the coming invasion of Iraq. Robertson, founder of the Christian Coalition, supports the president. But he told CNN on Wednesday night that he advised Bush to prepare the nation for the likelihood of casualties.

Bush's reply? "We're not going to have any casualties."

That was 9,100 American casualties ago.

The kicker is that Bush—who has denied the remark—stands for re-election a few days from now and it is not expected that he will lose in a landslide. In fact, pollsters say he could squeak to a second term, which throws into sharp relief the question a British man asked me in August. "How does George Bush get away with it?"

The People Are Perplexed

I spent part of the summer traveling in Europe and Africa and I was accustomed to the fact that people in those places were watching our presidential campaign with perplexity. But it's that question I was asked in a London record store that stopped me.

The "it" he thought Bush had gotten away with concerned irregularities in the 2000 vote. But as Campaign 2004 steams toward the finish line, it occurs to me that the same thing might be asked of Bush's entire presidency—and in particular, the war in Iraq.

Credibility lost, opportunity lost, lives lost and yet, amazingly, re-election is not lost.

That says more about us, I think, than the president.

And here, I am indebted to a reader who sent me a quote a few weeks back. It was an observation that one's willingness to acknowledge a painting is forged is usually inverse to the price one paid to buy it.

That's a neat summation of our present state. After Sept. 11, we wanted nothing so much as to feel safe. So some of us bought what Bush was selling—the idea that security lay not in finding a terrorist who had attacked us, but in deposing a dictator who had not.

We bought a forgery, a fake "War on Terror" for which we paid, and are still paying, a fortune in prestige, money and lives. Now we are loath to admit what anybody else can see.

No one should be surprised. After all, we know this guy.

We know his utter unwillingness to be swayed by facts.

For four years, he and his cronies have blithely changed or suppressed government reports—on health, science, the environment—that counter their world view. Just last month when intelligence agents issued a report whose pessimism was at odds with the party line on Iraq, the president dismissed it by saying they were "just guessing."

How It Is on Planet Bush

On Planet Bush, a thing is true because the president believes it to be. One's job as the president's adviser, apparently, is simply to nod vigorously.

You can infer the president's level of comfort with people who challenge him from reports that those who attend his rallies are asked to first sign a statement of support for him. Or from the fact that he holds press conferences only slightly more often than J.D. Salinger does. Or from that pinched expression on his face during the first debate.

Bush has no use for people who challenge him. He trusts—and asks us to trust—his gut over and above any pesky "facts" or "experts."

If you want to judge the reliability of the president's gut, consider what he reportedly told Robertson. Then consider the latest casualty figures.

And finally, ask yourself why we're keeping that forgery on the wall.

At this point, the only people being fooled are those who want to be.

Source: This column appeared on 22 October 2004. Reprinted by permission of TMS Reprints.

Books by Leonard Pitts: *Becoming Dad: Black Men and the Journey to Fatherhood* (Atlanta, Ga.: Longstreet, 1999).

Further Readings: "Columnist Leonard Pitts Jr." *Editor & Publisher*, 26 November 2001, p. 15; "Leonard Pitts, Jr." [Online, 18 May 2005]. Tribune Media Services Web site www.tmsfeatures.com; "Pulitzer Winner, Commentary: Leonard Pitts Jr., The Miami Herald." *Knight Ridder News*, Summer 2004, p. 18.

Poinsett, Alexander Ceasar (27 January 1926–)

Alex Poinsett was senior staff editor of the Johnson Publishing Company and for 26 years was the editor of *Ebony*. He joined the Johnson organization in 1956. Poinsett was born in Chicago, served as a Navy enlisted man from 1944 to 1947 and holds a 1952 B.S. in journalism and a 1953 M.A. in philosophy from the University of Illinois. At the University of Chicago, he completed the coursework for a M.A. in library science but did not complete his thesis; instead he joined Johnson to work as an assistant editor in 1956. A political independent, he reported from many other nations and at home wrote about such topics as the deplorable condition of black city schools and racial injustices in the criminal court system. He remained as senior staff editor for Johnson Publishing until 1982, then spent part of 1982 and 1983 as manager of editorial services for Grumman Corporation. He also was a speechwriter for Richard Hatcher, mayor of Gary, Indiana. From 1969 through 1975, he wrote speeches for John H. Johnson and made frequent talks at U.S. colleges and universities, speaking on civil rights issues and the black press. In retirement, Poinsett has continued to write occasionally for *Ebony* and, as a Unitarian, also has written on religious news for *UU World*, a periodical of the Unitarian Universalist Association. He has authored two books and has been a contributor to others, including the *Negro Handbook* (Chicago: Johnson Publishing Co., 1966); the *White Problem in America* (Chicago: Johnson Publishing Co., 1966); and *Ebony Pictorial History of Black America* (Chicago: Johnson Publishing Co., 1971). In addition, he wrote *Young Black Males in Jeopardy* (New York: Carnegie Corporation of New York, 1990) and the *Role of Sports in Youth Development* (New York: Carnegie Corporation of New York, 1996), two reports of meetings held by the Carnegie Commission of New York.

Books by Alexander Poinsett: *Black Power, Gary Style: The Making of Mayor Richard Gordon Hatcher* (Chicago: Johnson Publishing Co., 1970); *Walking with Presidents: Louis Martin and the Rise of Black Political Power* (Lanham, Md.: Madison Books, 1997).

Pool-Eckert, Marquita (c.1945–)

In March 2006, senior producer of "CBS News Sunday Morning" Marquita Pool-Eckert retired after 31 years with the network. She had worked for the preceeding six years as a producer of both foreign and domestic stories for the "CBS Evening News with Dan Rather." Pool-Eckert received a B.A. in sociology from Boston University and a 1969 masters from Columbia University's Graduate School of Journalism. Her earliest job, which she held for two years before enrolling at Columbia, was as a Time-Life Books photo researcher, and her first job in broadcasting, after receiving her master's, was producing a public affairs show, "Like It Is," aimed at the black audience in New York. In her master's program, she began in the magazine sequence with dreams of being a *Life Magazine* writer/photographer but changed her plans after taking a broadcast course. Her primary interest at that time was in broadcast documentaries. She joined CBS in 1975 and worked there as a producer until her retirement. During her many years with the network, she has contributed to the coverage of numerous presidential elections and has traveled on story assignments to at least 15 other nations. She took her final CBS job, senior producer of "CBS News Sunday Morning," in 1990. She also produced for the network's magazine-format show "60 Minutes." Although she is an attractive, perky woman whose face bespeaks intelligence, Pool-Eckert has never wished to work in front of the camera.

She has won a number of Emmy awards, beginning in 1983 for two "CBS Evening News" stories—"The Black Family: A Dream Deferred" and "The Bombing of Beirut." An Emmy win in 1986 was for a story on racism, and another in 1988 was on the bicentennial of the Statue of Liberty. A 1998 Emmy was awarded for the story "Diana, Princess of Wales" that ran on "CBS News Sunday Morning." Not long before her 2006 retirement, another "Sunday Morning" segment she produced titled "The Little Engine That Could, Spam" won an Emmy in the business news category. In 2002, she received the Black Career Women Lifetime Achievement Award, and she has also been given Columbia University's Journalism Alumni Award for journalistic excellence. Other recognitions have included the New York Women in Film and Television Muse Award, the National Monitor Award and the International Monitor Award. She has been an active participant in various organizations. In May 1996, she was a Kennedy Center panelist during the Women in Jazz Festival. In November 2000, she appeared with moderator Nancy Maynard and fellow panelists Earl Caldwell and Melba Tolliver in an oral history and archival forum sponsored by the New York Public Library. She again was a panelist in 2003 at a Columbia University journalism reunion, and in 2004, she was a conferee at a Black Career Women conference held in Nassau in the Bahamas. At a Writer's Guild of America, East career expo held during a UNITY convention, Pool-Eckert spoke on various kinds of racial tokenism still all too common in U.S. newsrooms.

Further Readings: "Alumni Awards." *Columbia University Graduate School of Journalism Alumni Journal* (Spring 2002): 1 6; Cain, Joy Duckett. "Not Just a Blue Suit—Prominent African American Women." *Essence*, March 1993.

Poussaint, Renee Francine (12 August 1944–)

Included in this volume for her years in broadcasting and her brief magazine experience, Renee Poussaint is currently her own boss at her multimedia production company Wisdom Works and at Poussaint Communications Inc. She was born in New York City and grew up in the Spanish Harlem section of Queens. On childhood visits to relatives in Tennessee, she listened to family storytellers, absorbing some of the techniques she would later use in her career and that she would record for posterity in her Wisdom Works oral history project. Poussaint graduated from Sarah Lawrence College in 1966 with a B.A. in Comparative Literature and in 1971, earned the M.A. in African Studies at UCLA. While still an undergraduate, she also studied at the Sorbonne in Paris and at Yale Law School. After getting her bachelor's degree, she danced in the Jean Leon Destine Haitian Dance Company in 1967, worked as an editor for *African Arts Magazine* in Los Angeles (1969–1973), and was a University of California translator in 1970. She further did nondegree work at Indiana University in 1972 and Columbia University's Graduate School of Journalism in 1973, then later in 1973, worked at Chicago's WBBM-TV. She was there until 1977 as reporter, news anchor and show host. From 1977 to 1978, she worked for CBS as a Chicago and, later, Washington correspondent, and in 1978, she became a WJLA-TV reporter and anchor and also worked on specials and documentaries and did some freelance writing for *The Washington Post* and *Ms.* magazine. In the late 1990s, she worked as an on-air reporter with ABC's "World News Tonight with Peter Jennings." She has also done broadcast projects for Discovery, Lifetime and A&E. One of her major projects appeared on PBS in 2001: "Tutu and Franklin: A Journey Towards Peace." This documentary, filmed on Goree Island off Senegal, brought together South African Archbishop Desmond Tutu and chair of the White House Advisory Board Dr. John Hope Franklin on Race to address racial healing in the new century. Also involved in this documentary was a group of 13 high school students from three countries. Poussaint's central idea was to meld the wisdom of age and experience with the optimism and enthusiasm of youth in a search to solutions to lingering problems involving race. One of the tangible results of this project was the establishment of an international leadership training initiative, the Tutu-Franklin Fellows Program.

Her current project, accomplished through Wisdom Works, also blends age and youth in a search for better understanding. Done with Camille Cosby, wife of entertainer Bill Cosby, is the National Visionary Leadership Project, made possible by funds supplied by the Cosbys. This oral history project conducts autobiographical interviews with African Americans 70 or older. Poussaint and Mrs. Cosby met while working on a movie and Broadway play about the Delany sisters, Sadie and Bessie, *Having Our Say*. Their idea was to record interviews with elders over a period of years, making them available on the Web at www.visionaryproject.com, and also, with the help of the United Negro College Fund, to bring in 50 African-American college students for a one-week conference, then have the students conduct similar interviews of their own. The project was begun in 2001; the two women felt a sense of urgency, inasmuch as some of the older people they wanted to interview, such as jazz great Lionel Hampton and baseball legend Joe Black, had recently died. Poussaint was confident the interviews would produce excellent results because the subjects of those interviews had reached a stage of life at which they could afford to be more candid than might someone who was in mid-career. The project accepts nominations of people to interview via its Web site and from its advisory board. Wisdom Works is a nonprofit multimedia production firm of which Poussaint is president and CEO. The first 50 interviews in the Leadership Project appeared in a 2004 book coedited by Poussaint and Camille Cosby—*A Wealth of Wisdom: Legendary African American Elders Speak*. The videotaped interviews are available for use by scholars and others at the National Visionary Leadership Project Museum in Washington. Housed there are five collections of Pouissaint and Cosby's Visionary Interviews plus separate interviews with writer Maya Angelou, executive Lee Archer, Sen. Edward Brooke, actor and director Roscoe Lee Browne, artist Elizabeth Catlett, singer Ray Charles, Oblate Sister Mary Alice Chineworth, Congresswoman Shirley Chisholm, actors Ossie and Ruby Dee Davis, dancer and choreographer Carmen De Lavallade, New York City Mayor David Dinkins, artist and art historian David Driscoll, dancer/choreographer Katherine Dunham, historian John Hope Franklin, Admiral Samuel Gravely, comedian/activist Dick Gregory, actor Robert Guillaume, Episcopal Bishop Barbara Harris, jazz musician Jimmy Heath, teacher/activist Dorothy Height, painter/dancer Geoffrey Holder, magazine titan John H. Johnson, civil rights icon Coretta Scott King, architect Leatrice McKissack, federal judge Constance Baker Motley, photographer Gordon Parks, minister Fred Shuttlesworth, lawyer and executive Percy Sutton and politician and U.S. Ambassador to the United Nations Andrew Young.

The Leadership Project also earned Poussaint and Cosby recognition at the 2002 awards dinner of EPIC, Enhancing Perceptions in Culture, which honored the presentation of positive media images of women. Poussaint was also recognized as an honoree in 1997 by Women in Film & Video, and she is a three-time Emmy winner. In addition, her efforts have been recognized by the American Firefighters Association, the U.S. Department of Labor, the Chicago YMCA and the Illinois Mental Health Association; in 1989, she received an honorary doctorate in humane letters from Georgetown University. She is a lifetime member of the NAACP and belongs to the Society for Professional Journalists (Sigma Delta Chi), Women in Communications, and a Omicron Delta Kappa honorary. She is a sponsor of the Black Film Center/Archive at Indiana University and in December 2001, gave the keynote address at a conference of the National MultiCultural Institute, speaking on "The Media's Distorted Multicultural Reality and Its Surprising Consequences." She has also been an advisor to UNICEF and a board member of the Capital Area Food Bank in Washington.

Books by Renee Poussaint: Coeditor with Camille O. Crosby, *A Wealth of Wisdom: Legendary African American Elders Speak* (New York: Atria Books, 2004).

Further Readings: "Renee Poussaint." [Online]. Poussaint Communications Inc. Web site www.wisdomworks.net; "Renee Poussaint." [Online]. The James MacGregor Burns Academy of Leadership Web site www.academy.umd.edu; Stone, Robin. "On the Shoulders of Giants." [Online]. Essence Web site www.essence.com; Ziegler, Dhyana. "Renee Francine Poussaint." *Notable Black American Women.* Ed. By Jessie Carney Smith and Shirelle Phelps (Detroit, Mich.: Gale Research, 1992–2003), p. 866.

Powell, Adam Clayton III (17 July 1946–)

Elder son of the famous politician Adam Clayton Powell Jr. (D-N.Y.), Adam III was the first African American to become a vice president of National Public Radio, worked as a producer for Quincy Jones Entertainment, was vice president of technology and programs for the Freedom Forum, taught at the Annenberg School of Communication at the University of Southern California and is currently director of the Integrated Media Systems Center at that university's Viterbi School of Engineering. He was born into a most remarkable family. His father was, during the 1950s, the most powerful and best-recognized black politician in America; his mother was singer Hazel Scott. Adam Clayton Powell, Sr., was a Baptist minister, for many years pastor of Harlem's Abyssinia Baptist Church. Upon his retirement as pastor in November 1937, his son, Adam Jr., took his place, remaining pastor there until his death on 4 April 1972. At Abyssinia, his pulpit truly proved to be a "bully pulpit," and Adam Jr. entered politics. He became New York City's first black city council member, and his dapper, brashly outspoken presence became known nationwide to most consumers of news during his time as a U.S. congressman for New York. It is said that he was able to gain the office of chair of the House Education and Labor Committee by way of a deal with John F. Kennedy, whereby Powell promised to deliver Kennedy the black vote. Among Powell's accomplishments were helping launch Medicare, Medicaid and Operation Head Start. The white part of segregated America did not know just how to regard the flamboyant Powell, and many were smugly pleased when in March 1967, he was expelled from the House over charges of misappropriation of funds. In 1969, the U.S. Supreme Court ruled his expulsion unconstitutional, but he never returned to Congress. He died in 1972 of causes that were never established with any certainty. In 1961, the twice-divorced minister/politician had married a Puerto Rican woman, Yvette Diago, and in that island country in 1962, had a second son, Adam Clayton Powell Diago, who eventually followed his father into politics. In 1980, Powell Diego had his name changed to Adam Clayton Powell IV, and in 1980, Adam IV was elected to the New York State Assembly. Adam III and his brother, Adam IV, are reportedly close, and Adam IV has taken the family name into another generation by having a son of his own, Adam Clayton Powell V. The two brothers, Adam III and Adam IV, collaborated as coproducers of a 2001 Showtime movie about their illustrious father; it was titled "Keep the Faith, Baby" after the familiar watchwords of the Civil Rights era, and in it, Hollywood star Vanessa Williams played the role of Hazel Scott, Adam Jr.'s second wife. A year earlier appeared a one-hour televised special in which Adam III took part. This was "Scandalize My Name" made for Black Entertainment Television. It portrayed the ways in which black performers were affected by the McCarthy blacklist of the 1950s and how this Red Scare period was manipulated to retard the early civil rights movement; in it Powell appears as himself.

Adam III was not inclined to go into politics. He studied at Massachusetts Institute of Technology but after college decided to go into journalism. From 1973 to 1976, he worked as news director of New York's all-news station WINS, after which he was a producer/manager for radio and television at CBS News from 1976 through 1981. He became vice president of news and information programming at National Public Radio in 1987, holding that position until 1990. From 1985 through 1994, he was a consultant and lecturer for the Freedom Forum Media Studies Center at New York's Columbia University. In 1990 and 1993, he worked there on media projects that examined the media of Africa and organized an exchange between U.S. and African journalists done in cooperation with the National Association of Black Journalists. From 1994 through 1996, he was the Freedom Forum's director, and from then until 2001, its vice president for technology and programs. At the Freedom Forum, he took charge of that organization's computer media technology program and helped put on information technology conferences on five continents. He wrote and edited articles about new media for the Freedom Forum Web site, originated and produced a one-hour magazine-format program, "Newseum Radio," for NPR and was originator and producer of the Freedom Forum radio service via Internet. Also, during 1990 and 1991, he was an executive producer for Quincy Jones Entertainment, producing a weekly show for Jesse Jackson, and was founding general manager of the nation's second PBS television station, KMPT-TV in San Francisco.

Powell then moved to Washington, D.C., to take over as general manager of the nation's oldest black-controlled PBS station, WHUT-TV at Howard University. He remained in that job until 2003, when he joined the faculty of the University of Southern California, initially as a visiting professor of journalism and senior research associate at the Annenberg School of Communication. There, he taught classes having to do with the new media and took part in the USC Annenberg Local Broadcasting Initiative, researching ways that local news media could use the capabilities of the Internet, cable, broadband and digital broadcasting. He was also a visiting professor and senior fellow at USC's Center on Public Diplomacy. Finally, in 2005, he was named director of the Viterbi School of Engineering's Integrated Media Systems Center at that same university. Powell is recognized as a pioneer and expert in new media technology, able to address the field's technological intricacies and its societal implications. His interests mainly revolve around new media, international broadcasting and public diplomacy. He has written about these topics for the *New York Times*, *Wired* magazine, trade periodical *Editor & Publisher* and the *Online Journalism Review* at USC. Powell has authored several reports for the Freedom Forum, which was earlier known as the Gannett Center for Media Studies. Among these are *Getting the Picture: Trends in News Reporting* (New York: Gannett Center for Media Studies, 1987); *New Wave Television: Changing Technology and the New Economics of Broadcast News* (New York: Freedom Forum Media Studies Center, 1993); and *Maintaining Editorial Control in a Digital Newsroom* (New York: Freedom Forum Media Studies Center, 1993). He also contributed to *Death by Cheeseburger: High School Journalism in the 1990s and Beyond* (Arlington, Va.: The Freedom Forum, 1994). In addition, Powell has written for a number of other people's books, such as John V. Pavlik and Everette E. Dennis's *Demystifying Media Technology* (Mountain View, Calif.: Mayfield, 1993; Edward C. Pease and Everette E. Dennis's *Radio: The Forgotten Medium* (New Brunswick, N.J.: Transaction Publishers, 1995), to which he contributed "Ear on America"; Yasmin Hashmi and Stella Plumbridge's *The Internet for Broadcasters* (London: SYPHA, 1996); Graeme Browning and Daniel J. Weitzner's *Electronic Democracy: Using the Internet to Influence American Politics* (Wilton, Conn.: Pemberton Press, 1996) plus the foreword to that book's second edition in 2002; the American Society of Newspaper Editors' *NextMedia Reader: New Technology and the American Newsroom* (Reston, Va.: ASNE, 1999); Kevin Kawamoto's *Digital Journalism: Emerging Media and the Charging Horizons of Journalism* (Lanham, Md.: Rowman & Littlefield, 2003), for which he contributed "Satellites, the Internet, and Journalism"; and the Henry Jenkins, David Thorburn and Brad Sewell book *Democracy and the New Media* (Cambridge, Mass.: MIT Press, 2003), for which Powell wrote "Will the Internet Spoil Fidel Catsro's Cuba?"

His efforts while with NPR won numerous awards, including a Peabody, a Columbia-duPont and an Armstrong. In 1999, he was presented the World Technology Award for Media and Journalism, given by *The Economist* magazine, the Overseas Press Club and Associated Press awards for international and regional reporting and in 2004, *Digital Media* magazine named him one of the nation's "Digital 100."

Further Readings: "Adam Clayton Powell III." [Online]. Freedom Forum Web site www.freedomforum.org; "Adam Clayton Powell, III." [Online]. MediaFriendly Web site www.mediafriendly. com; "Adam Clayton Powell III to Join USC Annenberg Local Broadcast News Initiative." [Online, 14 January 2003]. USC Annenberg School for Communication site http://asweb.usc.edu; "Adam Clayton Powell III, Visiting Professor." [Online, 2005]. USC Annenberg School for Communication site http://asweb.usc.edu.

Powell, Shaun (?–)

Shaun Powell is an accomplished young sports columnist now writing for *Newsday* and is also a frequent guest commentator on a variety of radio and television sports shows. He was raised in Pittsburgh and received a bachelor's degree in journalism from Howard University. He has written sports columns at three other newspapers—the *St. Louis Globe*, the *Dallas Times Herald* and the *Miami Herald*. He came to *Newsday* in 1993. Powell has also written a column about professional basketball for *The Sporting News* and has freelanced for *Basketball Digest* and *Inside Sports*. He has appeared on Madison Square Garden Network, ESPN-TV, CNN, the Metro Channel's "Game Face Show," ABC Sports radio and One-On-One Sports radio. He is a member of the National Association of Black Journalists and is a former president of the Professional Basketball Writers Association. He won first place for best story in the 1986 Associated Press Sports Editors competition and two first place awards for that organization's enterprise reporting category in 1988 and 1996. In 1999, he won the Best Sports Story Award given by the New York Deadline Club.

Powell, like most sports columnists, examines trends and recent trades, such as the change when basketball's Shaquille O'Neal left the New York Knicks for a job with the Miami Heat and the Knicks took Stephon Marbury. Powell playfully asked if this change was a "Steph" in the right direction, or the reverse. He is at his best when writing not about the sports minutiae that diehard sports fans dote upon, but when he examines social issues connected with athletes and athletics. Such a column focused on Patriots' quarterback Tom Brady just before the 2005 Superbowl game, not so much about his game prospects, but about his political aspirations. Brady had indicated an interest in running for Congress after his sports career was done, and Powell's assessment was that with Brady's poise and polish, his scandal-free comportment and personal charm, he might very well be an attractive candidate. The latter part of the column was about earlier football heroes who were or are in politics: former quarterback Jack Kemp, who was a New York congressman and ran for the U.S. vice presidency; Byron "Whizzer" White, running back turned Supreme Court justice; receiver Steve Largent, who became an Oklahoma congressman; and several others. In another 2005 column, Powell discussed the current phenomenon of the most gifted young players skipping college to go directly to the big-money jobs in the pros, which he sees as a loss for the quality of college basketball. He also worries that his city, New York, no longer produces as many "asphalt-grown" basketball players as it once did, and he is very much bothered by two hip-hop rap stars who are part owners of two professional teams, the Charlotte Bobcats and the Nets in New Jersey. His concern is that in a league having 80 percent black players, these recording star owners routinely use the N-word, refer to women as "bitches" and generally promote the thug

"Memo to Mom and Dad: Don't Blame 'Role Models'" by Shaun Powell

Junior weighed only 125 pounds a few months ago, when he tried out for the team, and was so skinny he had to wear shoes in the shower so he wouldn't slip down the drain. Strange thing, though: All of a sudden, he began to swell up fast, and pretty soon he was more ripped than a week-old newspaper.

His muscles were so big they were pregnant. His clothes, once roomy and baggy, were being stretched tighter than a cheapskate's dollar. He gained 50 pounds just like that and was running faster and hitting baseballs farther than anyone in school.

For some reason, his acne spread from his face to his back, but all anyone noticed were the dollar signs in his future, until one day the doctors came with bad news: Junior was taking steroids, and they were destroying him.

So you did what any responsible parent would do: Blame Jose Canseco.

Junior took the Ferrari out for a spin and hours later, he came home in handcuffs. The police wanted to speak with you about Junior's driving habits before they hauled him away for going 125 in a 55-mph zone, and obviously, there's only one organization to blame for Junior getting his license revoked: NASCAR.

The coach put Junior into the game for the big play. Sure enough, Junior's number was called and the football came his way. He caught it, faked his way past a few tacklers and scored easily. Then he went over to the goal post and mooned it, embarrassing you in front of everyone.

What do you do? Of course. Blame Randy Moss.

Some heckler in the stands was giving it to Junior good when he walked to the bench during a timeout, and after taking a little too much verbal abuse, Junior broke away from the huddle, crawled up a few rows and started pounding the guy in the face. The arena security restored order about 30 minutes later, and after sifting through the pile of bloody human rubble, you finally discovered who did this to your son: The Indiana Pacers.

Junior came home one day snapping his fingers and humming a tune through his iPod headphones when he suddenly started dropping F-bombs and screaming the N-word and using a vile vocabulary to describe women.

Out of nowhere, he saw his credibility soar. His street credibility. And you know exactly who to hold accountable for this: Jay-Z, rap master and Nets part-owner.

Junior announced to the family that he finally found a well-paying job. And the gig didn't even demand much of his time. He just had to find game tickets at face value, then sell them at a steep markup, then enjoy the benefits off a huge financial profit without slicing off a cent for Uncle Sam.

This is a scam, you sensed correctly, and you instantly knew who put Junior up to this: Vikings coach Mike Tice.

Junior came to you complaining about pain under his lower lip. You took a look and were horrified by the grotesque signs of decay and sores and all kinds of distressing hints of serious trouble. Junior then came clean about a chronic habit of chewing tobacco, and this was an issue you felt necessary to take up with the people responsible: Half of major league baseball.

Junior came home, staggering and slurring his words, and finally collapsed face-first on the sofa. He'd been out all night and, fortunately for him and every innocent driver on the road, somehow managed to avoid an accident. The smell on his breath said it all.

Junior was binge drinking, and you don't have to look past the TV commercials that air during sports events to find fault with those responsible: The beer companies.

In the sad stretch of a few weeks, Junior cursed out his father, ignored the neighbors, was caught smoking a joint, took the family dog to a secret location for a pit bull fight and disappointed everyone around him with his anti-social and immature behavior. These inconsiderate and crude habits were copied directly from a group of people that you accused of ruining your child: The Portland Trail Blazers.

Junior is sleeping in late, refuses to go to class, can't bring his grades up and is not showing satisfactory progress toward earning a college degree. Unless he straightens himself out quickly, he'll leave school without the proper skills and knowledge that's necessary to go anywhere in life.

Who do you fault? The NCAA.

The sports world is full of distractions, questionable characters, bad influences and people with agendas. But although sports can play on Junior's imagination, sports can't play mother or father.

So if he's getting the wrong messages, there's really only one way to react.

Stop blaming sports.

Start blaming yourself.

Source: This column appeared in *Newsday* on 20 March 2005 and appears here by permission of TMS Reprints.

Further Readings: "Shaun Powell." [Online, 2005]. Newsday.com Web site www.newsday.com/sports.

Pressley, Condace (October 1964–)

Condace Pressley, who in 2001 became the fourteenth president of the National Association of Black Journalists, is assistant program director in charge of operations for news/talk radio station WSB-AM Radio in Atlanta, Georgia. She was born in Marietta, Georgia, and received the bachelor's degree in Broadcast Journalism in 1986 at the University of Georgia. Before being hired in 1986 by WSB, she had gained both reporter and anchor experience with the Georgia News Network/WGST and with WGAU-AM, WNGC-FM and WRFC-AM, all in Georgia. She joined WSB as a local government reporter and anchor, worked in 1987 as a reporter/producer on morning drivetime, and still later as assignment editor and assistant news director. In 1990, she was producer of "Atlanta's Morning News" with Scott Slade. She was promoted to her present job in 1999, and she also is producer and host of "Minority Perspectives," a weekly show. Pressley joined the National Association of Black Journalists in 1987, but her rise to national visibility began in 1992, when she became president of the Atlanta Association of Black Journalists. In 1995, she became Region IV director for the NABJ and in 1998, was inducted into the Region IV Hall of Fame. She was elected vice president–broadcast of NABJ in 1999 and became its fourth female president in 2001. When she assumed office as president, the organization's financial deficit was daunting, partially due to lowered values in its stock portfolio, and one of her greatest challenges was to reverse the losses. A new finance committee was created, and by the end of 2001, the organization was breaking even, although membership had declined. During her two years in office, other initiatives were improving the Web site and going to zoned editions of the monthly electronic newsletter, *NABJ E-News*. Another issue she faced was whether to restrict membership to full-time journalists or to open it to others, such as freelancers. Similar was a debate over how close NABJ ties should be with the umbrella group UNITY; Pressley favored close ties. During her presidency, the national conventions of

NABJ were held in Orlando and Atlanta, and a new procedure was adopted for selecting convention sites five years in advance in order to facilitate getting the best possible rates. Some members were reportedly concerned with the popularity of convention workshops that dealt not with journalism, but with leaving it to become a screenwriter or talk show producer or to go into marketing. Pressley appeared to favor including workshops that focused on non-journalism entrepreneurship and other career opportunities. Being president at times put Pressley in the middle of still other controversies, such as an August 2002 confrontation between largely liberal convention attendees and a conservative activist, the Reverend Jesse Lee Peterson, who had charged the organization with being antiwhite. She also appeared on National Public Radio in June 2003 to take part in a discussion of the Jason Blair plagiarism affair and the subsequent resignation of *New York Times* editor Gerald Boyd; and in July 2003, she was on the CNN show "Talkback Live," debating William McGowan, author of the book *Coloring the News: How Crusading for Diversity Has Corrupted American Journalism* (San Francisco, Calif.: Encounter Books, 2001). As she prepared to leave office, Pressley, ordinarily a quiet, behind-the-scenes type of leader, kicked up a row by taking the unusual step of disparaging two of the three individuals in the running to replace her. She favored candidate Mike Woolfolk, then vice president–broadcast, over the eventual winner, Herbert Lowe of *Newsday*, whom she had defeated in 2001 and a man she characterized as lacking the proper skills for the job. She also let it be known that she questioned the integrity of candidate Cheryl Smith of the *Dallas Weekly*. Some older members of NABJ criticized Pressley's critical remarks as ill advised.

Pressley remained on the board of UNITY after her term as NABJ president and also became UNITY treasurer. She was the regional director for Georgia, Florida, Puerto Rico and the U.S. Virgin Islands for RTNDA, the Radio-Television News Directors Association. She now serves on the board of governors of the Atlanta Press Club and is on the advisory board of the University of Georgia's Henry W. Grady School of Journalism and Mass Communication. She has appeared on MSNBC, CNN, C-SPAN and ABC's "Nightline." Pressley has won recognitions from the Society of Professional Journalists, the Associated Press, and American Women in Radio and Television; and she has received the Edward R. Murrow Award given by the RTNDA. She was a panelist at the RTNDA career seminar in Las Vegas in April 2003.

Further Readings: Barringer, Felicity. "After 27 Years, a Black Journalists' Group Finds Itself at a Crossroads." *New York Times*, 5 August 2002; "Condace Pressley." [Online]. Atlanta Press Club Web site www.atlantapressclub.org; "Condace Pressley." [Online, 17 May 2005]. National Association of Black Journalists Web site www.nabj.org; Prince, Richard. "NABJ Prez Breaks Tradition, Discusses Candidates." [Online, 6 August 2003]. Richard Prince's Journal-isms. Maynard Institute Web site www.maynardije.org; Penn, Charli A. "Pressley Committed to Building on NABJ's Vision." *NABJ Monitor*, 1 August 2002, p. 6; Williams, Brianna. "Diversity: Condace Pressley Takes the Top Job at NABJ." [Online, October 2001]. Radio-Television News Directors Association & Foundation Web site www.rtnda.org.

Prince, Richard E. (26 July 1947–)

A journalist since 1967, Richard Prince is now best known for the long, multitopic "Richard Prince's Journal-isms" column he writes for the Robert C. Maynard Institute for Journalism Education. This column provides a running summary of the problems and accomplishments of America's minority journalists. Born in New York City, Prince earned the B.S. from New York University in 1968, then went to work as a city hall reporter for the *Washington Post*, remaining with that paper until 1977. From 1972 to 1975, he was a *Post* education writer, and from 1975 to 1977, a general assignment metro reporter. During 1977 and 1978, he worked as a freelance writer-photographer in the nation's capital, and in 1979, joined the Gannett Newspapers in Rochester, New York, initially working as a reporter, then serving as assistant metro editor for the *Democrat and Chronicle* from 1979 through 1981 and as that paper's assistant news editor from 1981 to 1985, when he became an editorial writer and columnist. His column began being distributed to other papers via the Gannett News Service in 1988; it was an issues-oriented editorial page column that often addressed issues of interest to African Americans. The column continued to appear until 1993, after which Prince became publications editor for Communities in Schools Inc. In 1998 and 1999, he was interim director of communications for the National Association of Black Journalists and in 1999, was a part-time foreign desk copyeditor for the *Washington Post*. In that same year, he began as editor of the *Public 1*, an online newsletter. Prince's online "Journal-isms" column began in June 2002 and now appears thrice weekly—on Mondays, Wednesdays and Fridays. It chronicles the activities of minority journalists and contains numerous links to further information. Prince also was editor of the *NABJ Journal*, the monthly organ of the National Association of Black Journalists, from 1989 to 1993. He has been a member of both the Trotter Group of African-American columnists and the National Conference of Editorial Writers since 1992. In 1988 he joined the Rochester literary organization Writers & Books, and in 1986 and 1987, he was president of the Rochester Association of Black Communicators.

Proctor, Glenn (1946–)

In October 2005, Glenn Proctor became vice president and executive editor of the *Richmond Times-Dispatch*; his appointment seemed symbolic of social progress inasmuch as Richmond, Virginia, had been the capital of the Confederacy and in the mid-1900s, was a scene of determined resistance to court-ordered racial integration. A Marine, Proctor spent six years on active duty, serving in Vietnam, and six more as a reservist. His career began in 1970 at the *Daily Local News* in the Philadelphia suburb of West Chester, Pennsylvania. He got this job after having witnessed a shootout between a white motorcycle gang and a group of black men in one of Philadelphia's western suburbs and having phoned in his account to a reporter. In 1979, he was press secretary for Florida Congressman Dan Mica and worked in Philadelphia for United Press International. He relocated to Davenport, Iowa, and the *Quad-City Times*, for which he was a reporter and city editor. He was a reporter on the suburban and business beats for the *Akron Beacon-Journal*, where he was part of a team that won a 1987 Pulitzer Prize for coverage of the Goodyear takeover attempt. He was also a weekend and night metro editor for the *Beacon-Journal*, and during his years there, Proctor was an adjunct faculty member in the journalism program at Kent State University. He has continued to present the management and diversity materials he created during that time in seminars around the country. His next move was to the *Louisville Courier-Journal*, where he was night metro editor and business editor. Thereafter, he became assistant managing editor/metro for the *Rochester Democrat & Chronicle* in New York. During the period 1995–2005, Proctor was assistant managing editor for local news, city editor and finally associate editor at *The Star-Ledger* in Newark, New Jersey. Then in November 2005, the former Marine gunnery sergeant, who still looks the part, became the first African American to edit the venerable *Richmond Times-Dispatch*, replacing William H. Millsaps Jr. The *Times-Dispatch*, a property of the Media General Corporation, had remained resolutely white until 1979, when its first African-American writer, Bonnie Wislon, was hired. As executive editor, Proctor hopes to increase diversity in hiring as a means of covering the city more evenly, and he has promised to wage war against dull news coverage. He works in a city having an African-American mayor, L. Douglas Wilder, who earlier had been elected Virginia's first black governor. Proctor's wife had been one of Wilder's legislative aides.

From 2003 to 2005, Proctor was an executive-in-residence for the Maynard Institute of Journalism Education in Oakland, California, and worked with that organization's Media Academy management program. He is on the advisory boards of the American Press Institute and Kent State University School of Journalism. He has also been a board member of the Associated Press Managing Editors, and, in 2000, 2001 and 2006, he has served as a Pulitzer Prize juror.

"The Commandments of B" by Glenn Proctor

Be accountable. Take responsibility for your work and the work of your staff. When you miss opportunities or make mistakes, discuss the situation with the appropriate staff members (if not on that cycle, the next work day).

Be ready to jump in. If major news breaks, especially on a holiday or off-cycle, call the office. If it's a catastrophic event, go to work. Train your staff to do the same. News doesn't take time off—even for family barbecues and ball games.

Be prepared. Just like reporters, copy editors/news editors need to know the major stories of the day and those that will make it to the next cycle.

That means reading your own newspaper and listening to the radio en route to work.

Be flexible. Understand that switching gears is necessary for you and your team. That could mean changing shifts, coming in early or staying late. Or honoring staff requests for time off, especially for family situations and mental health days.

Be visible. Form alliances all over the newsroom, especially with other department heads and other editors. Let your staff see that you are an advocate for them.

Be political. Stay in all loops and understand where the power lies. Embrace change or make a change. If you don't believe it or can't embrace it, leave it.

Be proud of your team. Praise, explain, protect and nurture. Explain the mission and give them the tools (training—in house and off site) to perform. When taking over a new team, embrace everyone until they prove unworthy. Failure is the boss's fault.

Be the boss. The switch from being "one of the troops" to management is difficult for new editors, but trying to play a dual role is worse. Don't play petty games and pout. Favoritism hurts morale and garners little respect—even from the favorites.

Be a thinker. Devise ways to improve efficiency, communication and morale.

Be truthful. Share what you can with staff, but don't lie. And never lie to the face in the mirror.

Be compassionate. But keep an edge in your pocket.

Be a mentor. Find a good one for yourself.

Be curious. Learn to trust your staff. However, the questions don't stop.

Be mentally tough. Cherish the ups; the downs aren't personal.

Be an advocate for your paper. Pride spreads—inside and outside.

Source: The article that appears above was excerpted from a presentation made by Glenn Proctor to attendees at the American Press Institute's News Editors and Copy Desk Chiefs seminar in 2002. The American Press Institute is the newspaper industry's premier leadership development center, located in Reston, Virginia. Glenn Proctor is a frequent speaker to newsroom seminars there on the subjects of leadership and personal responsibility, and a speaker to non-news executives on the subject of First Amendment values. He is also a 2004–2007 member of their newsroom programming advisory board.

Further Readings: Burbach, Mike. "Covering Life Outside the Narrow Lines." [Online, 7 March 2003]. American Society of Newspaper Editors Web site www.asne.org; Folkenflik, David. "Papers Still Grappling with Issues of Diversity." [Online, 25 May 2006]. National Public Radio Web site www.npr.org; "Glenn Proctor." [Online, 2006]. American Press Institute Web site www.americanpressinstitute.org; McRae, F. Finnley. "Paper That Once Championed Resistance to Integration Hires Black Editor." [Online, 4 December 2005]. BlackAmericaweb.com Web site www.blackamericaweb.com; Prince, Richard. "Black Journalist at Helm in Old Dixie Capital." [Online, 6 October 2005]. Richard Prince's Journal-isms. Maynard Institute Web site www.maynardije.org; Rayner, Bob. "Times-Dispatch Names New Executive Editor." [Online, 7 October 2005]. Richmond Times-Dispatch Web site www.timesdispatch.com.

Q

Quarles, Norma R. (11 November 1936–)

Veteran broadcast journalist Norma Quarles was the first female African-American anchor for both NBC and CNN. After 10 years at CNN as anchor and correspondent, she left the network in 1998 and since that time has been a freelance journalist. She was born in New York City and attended Hunter College and the City College of New York. Unlike many of the individuals who appear in this book, she did not immediately go into journalism. She first worked as a buyer for a New York store, then moved to Chicago and from 1957 to 1965, was a real estate agent and broker for Katherine King Associates. In 1965, she got her first taste of media work at Chicago's station WSDM, where for a year she did news and was a disc jockey. In the following year, she was selected as a participant in a one-year NBC training program in New York, and after completing the course of study, she became a reporter and anchor for WKYC-TV in Cleveland, Ohio. In 1970, she returned to New York City and took a new job with WNBC-TV, where she was a news reporter for the "Today" show. A brief stint as a guest hostess on a show aimed at women viewers gained her the approval of management, and she soon became the first black woman to anchor the 6 o'clock news at that station.

A single mother with two children, Quarles made no attempt to become a network correspondent in order to avoid having to travel. She did, however, work for NBC in Chicago for the network's Midwest bureau, and she was producer and reporter for a series titled "Urban Journal" for the network's Chicago station WMAQ-TV. One of her well-known stories in New York was the case of "subway vigilante" Bernard Goetz, who was acquitted of murder in 1987. Another major story, this one in 1988, was the so-called "Baby M" case, the nation's first test of surrogacy, examining the rights of individuals involved in

Quarles, Norma R.

the artificial insemination of a surrogate mother. Earlier, in 1984, she had gained extra national visibility as a panelist in the George H.W. Bush versus Geraldine Ferraro vice-presidential debate sponsored by the League of Women Voters; Quarles appears to have been the first black woman to fill this role. She also was an anchor for the NBC news show "Evening Digest." She switched networks in 1988 after 21 years to work for Cable News Network's New York bureau and coanchored the news shows "Daybreak" and "Daywatch." She was a daytime anchor until 1990, at which time she became a CNN correspondent. Quarles remained in that job until sometime in 1998. In 2001, she did some writing for *Religion & Ethics Newsweekly*, an online affiliate of PBS. She is now retired.

Some of the stories Quarles covered for CNN include the 1995 controversy over questionable Rembrandt paintings owned by the New York Metropolitan Museum of Art, the 1996 death at age 62 of astronomer and PBS television host Carl Sagan, drug-induced abortions offered by Planned Parenthood starting in 1996, the May 1997 "stroller dustup" wherein a Danish mother left her 14-month-old daughter parked outside a Manhattan restaurant while she had lunch, the auction of fabulous objects of art from the estate of Pamela Harriman in 1997 and the fortieth anniversary of the Leo Castelli art gallery in New York in 1998. Quarles has been a member of Sigma Delta Chi, the National Academy of Television Arts & Sciences and the National Association of Broadcast Journalists, on whose board she served. She was inducted into the Hall of Fame of the National Association of Black Journalists in 1990, and in 1993, she won a CINE Golden Eagle award and two recognitions for her CNN shows "The Delany Sisters" and "A House Divided." She also had a cameo role as a reporter in the movie "The Last Days of Disco," which was released in 1998.

Further Readings: "Norma Quarles." *Notable Black American Women*. Ed. by Jessie Carney Smith and Shirelle Phelps. Detroit. Mich.: Gale Research, 1992–2003, pp. 909–910; "Norma Quarles." *The African American Almanac, 9th ed.* Edited by Jefffrey Lehman. (Detroit, Mich.: Gale Group, 2003), pp. 879–880.

R

Ragland, James (?–)

A native of Elysian Fields, Texas, *Dallas Morning News* columnist James Ragland graduated from Texas A&M University in Commerce, Texas, in 1984 having double-majored in journalism and political science. He began his career in 1985 in Dallas as a reporter for the paper where he now works. From 1991 to 1994 he reported for the *Washington Post*, and then returned to the *Dallas Morning News*, serving as editor from 1994 to 1999. During the year 1999–2000, he was a visiting professor at his alma mater, teaching journalism and working as an adviser to the school's president. From 2000 to the present he has worked for the *Morning News* as a columnist, writing for both the Metropolitan and Texas Living sections. His local news columns are written in the standard column essay format, but his work in the Texas Living section uses a modified form of the question and answer format in which he presents the text of questions or comments from his readers, then responds. He writes a total of three columns a week. In 1994, Ragland was honored by being named an Alumni Ambassador for his work with the Texas A&M journalism program, in which he taught later as a visiting professor in 1999 and 2000.

In the local news column reprinted below, Ragland holds the feet of Texas Sen. John Cornyn to the fire, urging him to join the state's other senator, Kay Bailey Hutchison, in signing a congressional apology for having done nothing to stop lynchings, America's most shameful expression of racial bigotry. Another of his concerns is that the U.S. media tend to present a distorted picture of black America, focusing mainly on the troubled residents of our inner cities while writing little about the ever-expanding black middle class and its many success stories. The issue of immigration also interests Ragland; his position is that immigrant workers, who often accept hard-to-fill jobs, are vital to our economy and should be treated accordingly. He also details instances of municipal corruption—bribery, extortion, bankruptcy fraud, misappropriation of public funds, and the like—naming names.

To commemorate Martin Luther King Day, 2005, Ragland noted that rather than coast through the usual speeches by local leaders, parades and other tributes, readers might better read and reflect upon some of Dr. King's addresses apart from the famous "I have a dream" speech, and he applauded King's message calling for brave, but dignified protest. In answer to an inquiry from a reader concerning a black man and his white wife who were considering moving to Dallas but were unsure what their reception would be, Ragland noted that he himself is in an interracial relationship and that the situation in his city is now much more accepting than in earlier times. Another Texas Living column dwells on hair salons as one of the last bastions of segregation, but in this case, segregation by mutual agreement. Ragland is a member of the National Association of Black Journalists and the Trotter Group of African-American columnists. He has served as president of the Dallas-Fort Worth Association of Black Communicators.

"Senator, Quit Stalling and Join the Lynching Apology" by James Ragland

John Cornyn, it's time—past time—to do the right thing.

Do what our other Texas senator, Kay Bailey Hutchison, did—join the overwhelming majority of senators co-sponsoring an apology for Congress' failure to outlaw lynching decades ago.

Sure, it may be just a symbolic gesture at this point, but it's the back-straightening political symbolism we need to help heal a nation that has long suffered from racial animosity.

At its worst, our nation stood coldly by, shamefully really, and watched savage vigilantes and brutal mobs take injustice into their own hands by lynching people, most of whom were black.

An NACP study found 4,742 lynchings in 43 states from 1882 to 1968. Mr. Cornyn, our great state of Texas ranked third with 493.

Shameful.

And senator, here's why you really need to step up to the plate on this issue: In 1922, 1937 and again in 1940, the U.S. House tried to ban lynching.

But Southern Democrats in the Senate deftly and defiantly doomed those measures.

Those senators were on the wrong side of history, standing in the way of an inevitable progress driven by human will and God's mercy.

I am beseeching you, Mr. Cornyn, to get on the bandwagon with Ms. Hutchison because the two of you can help send an important message: This is the New South and, more pointedly, this is a new Texas that doesn't tolerate racial bigotry.

Just think how poetic it would be, and what a powerful statement the Senate would be making, if every senator co-sponsored the measure?

I know you're busy, Mr. Cornyn. By now, you've probably moved on to more pressing matters. Fine and dandy.

But this would take minimal effort, really. You don't have to call a news conference or make a speech on C-Span.

Do it quietly. Do it quickly.

Heck, Ms. Hutchison added her name to the list of co-sponsors on June 20, and the media just took note of it this week.

Ms. Hutchison "abhors lynchings," her spokesman, Chris Paulitz, said yesterday in a telephone interview from Washington. Lynchings "are a horrific part of our past and, from the beginning, she was certainly in support of [the Senate] resolution."

She and others simply weren't personally asked initially to co-sponsor the resolution, so they didn't. Now, all but 10 of 100 senators have co-sponsored the apology.

Mr. Cornyn, there is no reason—read no excuse—for you to remain in this small minority.

When my colleague, Todd Gillman, asked you yesterday why you would not go ahead and co-sponsor it, you responded, "I think it's unnecessary."

Senator, you're wrong.

I'll give you credit for this. You said you favored the resolution and would have cast an aye vote if there had been a roll call.

But, you said, "those who are advocating for co-sponsorship simply don't understand the process."

Senator, you're hung up on process and technicalities.

I want to know where your heart is. I want to know what you feel in your soul.

I want to know that you've reflected on this matter and that you fully understand why co-sponsoring the resolution matters to organizations such as the NAACP.

My colleague asked why you wouldn't want to avoid persistent questions and persnickety columns, and you said, "I have never been one of those people to get along by going along. People can like it or not like [it], but I am not going to be intimidated."

Mr. Cronyn, now is not a time to stick your chest out and wear stubborn pride on your sleeve.

This is a time just to be a man. A human being. An American who extends his hands out mercifully to the descendants of at least 4,742 people who died because our nation failed to protect them. Few had committed any crimes at all.

No one can force you to do the right thing, Mr. Cornyn. That must come from a set of personal and political convictions that lead you down the right path. That requires humility, not haughtiness.

And senator, if I've offended you in any way, I'm sorry.

I'm speaking from the heart.

Source: This column, which appeared on 28 June 2005, appears here by permission of Mr. Ragland and *The Dallas Morning News*.

Further Readings: "James Ragland." [Online]. Dallas Morning News Web site www.dallasnews.com.

Randolph, Toni (c.1962–)

Toni Randolph has been a reporter for Minnesota Public Radio since November 2003 and for the seven years before that, was a WBUR-TV reporter in Boston. Her work has also appeared on BBC, National Public Radio and Voice of America. She grew up in Buffalo, New York, and holds a masters from the Columbia University Graduate School of Journalism. Her career started at WBFO-FM in Buffalo as that station's news director. Later, she moved to Newark, New Jersey, as news director of station WBGO-FM, working there until 1996, when she became a reporter for public radio station WBUR-FM in Boston. Some of the stories she reported for WBUR include a 1997 art theft from the Isabella Stewart Gardner Museum in Boston, the 1999 death of Mr. and Mrs. John F. Kennedy Jr. in the crash of his small plane and the controversy in 2002 over an initiative in Massachusetts to replace bilingual instruction in public schools with an immersion program in English. In 2003, she reported on the replacement of Boston's Cardinal Bernard Law by Archbishop Sean Patrick O'Malley following Law's admission that he had reassigned pedophile priests to new parishes. Also in 2003, she covered the murder of former Catholic priest and convicted child molester John Geoghan by a fellow inmate and a deadly nightclub fire in West Warwick, Rhode Island. Along with continuing coverage of the Roman Catholic Church sex abuse scandals, Randolph covered the slow progress of the so-called Big Dig, a new central traffic artery under downtown Boston that finally was completed in 2003, five years behind schedule. During her years with WBUR, she worked on everything from hard news accounts of election campaigns to a light feature on body piercing.

In the autumn of 2003, Randolph made another move, this time to Minnesota Public Radio in Minneapolis. In 2004, she began covering the ongoing story of Hmong refugees who had been living in a camp near Bangkok, Thailand. She reported that from the year 2000 to November 2004, some 50,000 of these immigrants had settled in Minnesota, and thousands more were expected to arrive. Some of her stories on the Hmong have involved waiting lists for instruction in the English language, and one of her reports in 2006 was about desecration of Hmong graves in Thailand. In a feature story of a happier sort in 2004, she described the origin of the friendship between pianist Andre Watts and conductor and Sommerfest artistic director Andrew Litton. Later that same year she reported on the building of the Winter Carnival ice palace in downtown St. Paul, an effort undertaken by around 200 volunteers who build the palace out of 500-pound blocks of ice. She did stories about the small number of African-American partners in Twin Cities law firms (2 percent of the total), the opening of a time capsule at the University of Minnesota, an album of standards recorded by Lou Rawls as a tribute to Frank Sinatra and the Bronx origins of hip-hop music. Other stories by Randolph have been about Minneapolis' Illusion Theater, which put on a production titled "Undesirable Elements" that dealt with discrimination; preparations in Minnesota for the arrival of Hurricane Katrina evacuees; a change in Minnesota law that helped homeless people be allowed to vote; a self-funding car-repair curriculum at a local technical school; newfound cooperation between St. Paul police and social service workers who deal with the city's homeless population; and distress among less affluent Minnesota residents who found it difficult to pay their heating bills due to the rising cost of energy. She has also written about the Red Lake band of Ojibwas, Native American people living both on a Minnesota reservation and in the Twin Cities.

Randolph twice has been recognized by the National Association of Black Journalists. In July 2003, she won first place for her news feature titled "Grandfamilies House," which was about grandparents who raise their grandchildren. She also stood second in the documentary competition for a report on troubles in the black studies program at Harvard University.

Further Readings: Simon, Clea. "Protests to Body Piercing, a Reporter Has It Covered." [Online, 28 August 2003]. Boston Globe Web site www.boston.com; "Toni Randolph, Reporter." [Online]. WBUR Web site www.wbur.org.

Rashad, Ahmad (19 November 1949–)

Formerly a highly successful football player at both the college and professional levels, Ahmad Rashad has been a sports commentator and television sports show host since 1983. He was born Bobby Moore in Portland, Oregon, the son of a barber and the youngest of six siblings, and grew up mainly in Tacoma, Washington. At the age of six, he developed a strange skin disorder: blood-filled bumps formed on various parts of his body, then burst. The specific malady was never diagnosed, but after the bumps were surgically removed, the problem disappeared. He began playing football at Mount Tahoma High School in Tacoma and in college was the University of Oregon's star running back and wide receiver. He graduated having been a two-time All-American and was drafted by the St. Louis Cardinals. He studied the Muslim faith in St. Louis in the 1970s under a man named Rashad Khalifa, converted to that faith in 1973 and changed his name to Ahmad Rashad. His coaches were unsupportive of his name change and new religion, and he left St. Louis to play for Buffalo, where he suffered a knee injury. As a football player, he is mainly remembered for his exploits with the Minnesota Vikings, which he joined in 1976. As a wide receiver for that team, he caught passes thrown by quarterback Fran Tarkenton, and the team went to four Pro Bowls in a row; Rashad was named most valuable player in 1979. After 11 years of playing professional football, he had tired of the game and also had become increasingly disillusioned about the loose conduct of some of the younger players, who used illegal drugs and appeared to be in the game only for the money. Rashad retired from football in 1983. While still with the Vikings, he had spent time at Minnesota station WCCO-TV with an eye to eventually working in television. Immediately after his retirement, he found a job as a pregame host on "NFL on NBC" and worked in that capacity until 1988, when he became an analyst/commentator. He was host of "Notre Dame Saturday" and anchor for "NBC Sports Update." In 1994, he once again hosted "NFL on NBC" and worked that show through 1998. He has done a considerable amount of Olympics coverage, beginning in Seoul, Korea, in 1988. He also was a host and correspondent during the Barcelona games in 1988 and the Atlanta games in 1996. In March 1998, he "crossed over" to basketball when he became executive producer of "NBA Inside Stuff" and of various NBA special shows. Later he became executive producer and host of "Ahmad Rashad One-on-One," a sports talk show. He continued his football coverage, cohosting the Sunday show "NFL Live" opposite Greg Gumbel.

In 1985, Rashad made headlines by proposing marriage to Phylicia Ayers-Allen during his coverage of a Lions-Jets football game. Ayers-Allen at that time played the role of Claire Huxtable, wife of the character played by the immensely popular actor/comedian Bill Cosby, who also had been a football player. Cosby had introduced the two. Rashad's best man was O.J. Simpson, with whom he had played in 1974 on the Buffalo Bills. The couple's divorce in 2001 was the third for both of them. Rashad stays young looking and fit by playing a lot of tennis and by following an exercise regimen given him by his friend Michael Jordan of basketball fame. Unlike football players today, Rashad never lifted weights while he was a player. His on-screen presence is cheerful and positive, and he is known for his love of expensive cigars. His dapper appearance and easy manner have also found him nonsports work as host of two ABC reality shows: "Celebrity Mole Hawaii" and "Celebrity Mole Yucatan." He has made appearances on other television programs, including "The Cosby Show," "TV Nation," "The Late Late Show with Craig Kilborn" and "A Different World."

Rashad is on the board of trustees of the University of Oregon, which in 1995 gave him its Pioneer Award for outstanding accomplishment as an alumnus. The University of Puget Sound has awarded him an honorary doctorate in journalism. Rashad won an Emmy for his writing during the Seoul Olympics, and he has coauthored one book about his career.

Books by Ahmad Rashad: With Peter Bodo, *Rashad: Vikes, Mikes, and Something on the Backside* (New York: Viking, 1998).

Further Readings: "Ahmad Rashad." [Online]. Capitol City Speakers Bureau Web site www.speakingofsports.com/speakers; "Ahmad Rashad." *The African American Almanac*, 9th ed. Detroit: Gale Group, 2003, pp. 880–81; Shouler, Ken. "Catching It All: Ahmad Rashad Has Gone from All-Pro Receiver to All-Network Announcer." [Online, 2005]. Cigar Aficionado Magazine Web site www.cigaraficionado.com.

Raspberry, William James (12 October 1935–)

The dean of America's black columnists, William Raspberry, wrote a column for the *Washington Post* since 1966 and was syndicated nationally by the Washington Post Writers Group from 1977 until his retirement at the end of December 2005. His column was marked by insight, calm good sense and graceful style. He was born in Okolona, Mississippi, a town he has compared to the one depicted in *To Kill a Mockingbird*, and earned the B.S. in history in 1958 at Indiana Central College. His initial intent was to go into the ministry, but a summer job at the *Indianapolis Recorder* led him to his long career in journalism. He started as a sports writer but almost immediately moved to local news, working as a proofreader, reporter and photographer at the *Recorder* for his last two years of college and two more years after his graduation. In 1960, soon after he had become the *Recorder*'s managing editor, he was drafted into the Army and trained as a public information specialist in Cameron Station, Virginia, outside Washington, D.C.; and when his two-year commitment was up, he took a teletype operator job at the *Washington Post*. Within a few months he was moved to writing obituaries, then to police and court reporting, general assignment reporting, copyediting and a stint as assistant city editor. During 1963 and 1964, when he was a general assignment reporter, Raspberry began specializing in covering the civil rights movement, reporting on local organizing, picketing and the meetings of the NAACP and CORE. The paper sent him to Los Angeles in 1965 to cover the Watts riots, an assignment that he handled adroitly. Soon thereafter *Post* management asked him to contribute to the paper's "Potomac Watch" urban-affairs column. He did so, but used this new platform to continue writing about the sweeping social changes being brought about by desegregation. His column was moved to the op-ed page in 1971, becoming national in scope, and was added to the *Los Angeles Times/Washington Post* news wire. In addition to writing his column, Raspberry taught journalism at Howard University from 1971 to 1973, became a WTTG-TV commentator in 1973 and at WRC-TV in 1974, and also worked as an ABC-TV Evening News contributing editor. In 1985, he became a member of the University of Maryland School of Journalism's board of visitors, and since 1995, he has been Knight Professor of the Practice of Journalism and Public Policy Studies at the DeWitt Wallace Center for Media and Democracy, which is part of the Terry Sanford Institute of Public Policy at Duke University. In 1994, Raspberry won a long-overdue Pulitzer Prize for commentary. He has been awarded at least 15 honorary degrees and has published one book, a collection of fifty of his columns—mainly those on family, education and their importance for African Americans.

In 2005, the shrill pronouncements of the nation's most polarized columnists often get the most attention, yet Raspberry's intelligent, reasoned, conversational approach to public issues kept him one of America's most respected columnists. His column appeared once a week and was reportedly in roughly 100 newspapers. He has referred to himself as a "solutionist," meaning that his hope was to describe existing problems with an eye toward the eventual resolution of those problems. Asked by *Editor & Publisher*'s David Astor which of his columns had brought the greatest reader response, Raspberry replied that it was a 1972 column about discrimination against ugly women. He also mentioned columns about the Rodney King beating and about gays in the military.

The first-person April 2005 column reproduced below addresses the "Foxidation" of the media by, as Raspberry puts it, "verbal ruffians." Another of his columns bemoaned what he called "the death of nuance," or the "all-or-nothing syndrome" in contemporary American politics. He has blamed President George W. Bush for much of this problem, saying that Bush regards nuance as weak and vacillating. The rampant polarization of American voters, he has pointed out, can be seen in surprising ways, as in our reactions to the May 2005 televised report of a five-year-old St. Petersburg, Florida, girl being handcuffed by police after her uncontrollable temper tantrum. Raspberry saw the deep division in public reaction to this story as a "miner's canary"—a warning about the growing problems in our society.

In March 2005, Raspberry said what many Americans had been thinking: that Federal Reserve Chairman Alan Greenspan had become politicized and had for some time been in the pocket of the Bush administration in support of tax cuts for the wealthiest Americans, partial privatization of Social Security and the like. In the past, he wrote, he had believed government figures but often distrusted the administration's interpretation of them; now, he wrote, he doubted the honesty of their figures, as well. In the main, he is a liberal, but in latter-day official Washington, he knew that there was plenty of blame to go around. He blasted the Republicans for pretending that the way to pay for the war in Iraq is to give permanent tax cuts to the rich, but he also blamed congressional Democrats for their "jellyfish" response—so long as they get their share of the pork. One of the columnist's recurring themes was the conservative refrain that privatizing everything possible will be an improvement. In addition to Social Security, a particular concern of Raspberry's has been the privatizing of America's prisons.

Some of Raspberry's most appealing columns were written using a fictitious literary character: the cabbie, an unlettered man who applied good common sense in discussing complex public issues with his "passenger," Raspberry. This is a technique that has been used by many of America's most popular columnists as a way to get around the pompous smokescreen of partisan rhetoric used by politicians and commentators who realize that in confusion there is profit. One of the most enjoyable of his occasional "cabbie" columns appeared in December 1996 and addressed "Ebonics." The educated, worldly Raspberry pretended to be horrified by the notion of legitimizing nonstandard English, then when the cabbie pointed out that it might be possible to pick up extra money by teaching Ebonics, the columnist replied, tongue-in-cheek, that perhaps the cabbie was on to something after all.

Overall, Raspberry's assessment of the present position of African Americans was that for the first time in the history of black America, what African Americans do is more important to their future than what is done to them by others. In addition to his Pulitzer Prize in 1994, he was named Journalist of the Year in 1965 by the Capital Press Club for his coverage of the Watts riots in Los Angeles. He was a member of the Pulitzer Prize Jury from 1975 to 1979 and was on the Pulitzer Board from 1980 to 1986. He has been a member of the National Association of Black Journalists, the Capital Press Club and the Gridiron Club; and he was on the advisory board of the Poynter Institute for Media Studies starting in 1984.

"Fox's Sandstorm" by William Raspberry

The in-your-face right-wing partisanship that marks Fox News Channels news broadcasts is having two dangerous effects.

The first is that the popularity of the approach—Fox is clobbering its direct competition (CNN, CNBC, MSNBC, etc.)—leads other cable broadcasters to mimic it, which in turn debases the quality of the news available to that segment of the TV audience.

The second, far more dangerous, effect is that it threatens to destroy public confidence in all news.

The latter, I admit, is more fear than prediction, but let me tell you what produces that fear. Fox News Channel—though the people who run the operation are at great pains to insist otherwise—is deliberately partisan. It is as though right-wing talk radio has metastasized into cable and assumed a new virulence.

The main difference is that radio's Rush Limbaugh, for instance, doesn't pretend even-handedness. As he has said, he doesn't seek to be balanced but to balance the rest of the media, which he sees as generally dominated by left-of-center attitudes.

Part of the FNC approach, on the other hand, is to promote itself as "fair and balanced." I suppose it does so with a wink and a nod to its far-right audience, who must know it isn't balanced. Certainly those near the center of the political spectrum know it.

So why would I consider Fox such a generalized threat? Because I think the plan is not so much to convince the public that its particular view is correct but rather to sell the notion that what FNC presents is just another set of biases, no worse (and for some, a good deal better) than the biases that routinely drive the presentation of the news on ABC, CBS or NBC—and, by extension, the major newspapers.

For the Foxidation process to work, it isn't necessary to convince Americans that the verbal ruffians who give FNC its crackle have a corner on the truth—only that all of us in the news business are grinding our partisan axes all the time and that none of us deserves to be taken seriously as seekers of truth.

This is huge. As a friend remarked recently, time was when if you found it in the New York Times, that settled the bar bet and the other guy paid off. But if the Times and The Post or any other mainstream news outlet—including the major networks—come to be seen as the left-of-center counterparts of Fox News Channel, why would anyone accept them as authoritative sources of truth?

What is at risk is not a reputation for infallibility; everyone knows that even the best newspapers and most careful broadcasters make mistakes. But it has been generally accepted that the mainstream media at least try to get it right—even when they too grudgingly acknowledge their errors after the fact.

What worries me is that journalism could become a battlefield of warring biases: I'll sock it to your guy, your party or your position on a public issue, and you'll sock it to mine. And we'll both believe we've done a good day's work. Come to think of it, a review of the stories on Social Security suggests that it is already happening to some extent. And one result is that you are less sure than you ought to be as to what the truth about Social Security really is.

Maybe I'm making too much of a small thing—depicting FNC as a huge and menacing ogre when it's only an annoying little pest. A look at a recent week's ratings reveals that Fox News Channel was far from being the most watched among cable shows. It ranked behind the likes of TNT, Disney, USA, Spike TV and TBS for prime-time audiences and even lower for the total day. Its prime-time average of 1.1 million viewers was well behind CBS (12.4 million), NBC (8.3 million), ABC (9 million) and even the Fox broadcast network (9.4 million). Fox News Channel, I am saying, is not the toughest kid in the schoolyard, only the baddest kid in the particular sandbox of cable news.

Still, I'm worried that what is happening in that sandbox may wind up polluting the entire schoolyard. And no one, including the big kids of traditional journalism, seems sure what to do about it.

Source: © 2005. *The Washington Post*. Reprinted with permission. This column first appeared on 19 April 2005.

Books by William James Raspberry: *Looking Backward at Us* (Jackson, Miss.: University Press of Mississippi 1991).

Further Readings: Astor, David. "Columns That Drew the Most Responses." *Editor & Publisher*, 20 February 1993, p. 38; Astor, David. "William Raspberry Talks About His Work." *Editor & Publisher*, 2 February 1991, pp. 36–38; Astor, David. "Writer Wants to See What Is Going Right." *Editor & Publisher*, 24 June, 1995, p. 118; Stein, M.L. *Blacks in Communications: Journalism, Public Relations and Advertising*. New York: Julian Messner, 1972, pp. 46–48; "William Raspberry." [Online]. The Washington Post Writers Group Web site www.postwritersgroup.com.

Reid, Bob (1947–)

A producer and journalist of long experience, Bob Reid is executive vice president and general manager of The Africa Channel; until January 2004, he was executive vice president and general manager of Discovery Health Channel. Reid received a B.A. in political science from the University of Miami. He had attended Miami-Dade Community College, where in 1966 he became the first African-American student body president of a largely white college in the South. In that same year, he also became the first black reporter hired by the *Miami Herald*. His newspaper career was short lived; in 1968, he achieved another first: earliest black reporter to work for Miami station WTVJ-TV. Yet another first for Reid came in 1976 when he became the first African-American network bureau head; he was named chief of the Atlanta bureau of NBC News when he was only 29 years old. Three years later, his visibility earned him a chance to break new ground again when he was elected as the first broadcaster to hold the presidency of the National Association of Black Journalists. He held this office from 1979 to 1981 when the organization was still in its formative stages. A story for NABJ written by *Los Angeles Times* writer Gayle Pollard Terry remarked on Reid's marriage during his years as president to actress Berlinda Tolbert, "Jenny" on the popular television program "The Jeffersons," and his move to Los Angeles, which complicated his contact with the primarily East Coast and Midwest membership of the NABJ. Terry also described the difficulties encountered at the 1980 NABJ convention in Washington, D.C., when some of the scheduled panelists said they had never been notified about their assignments and the person being given the main award, Carl Rowan, failed to attend. During the final year of his presidency, Reid left his job as an NBC field producer to become an investigative reporter for KNXT-TV, now KCBS, in Los Angeles. Three of his initiatives at this time were to build membership by having local organizations of black journalists around the nation affiliate with NABJ, a suggested educational foundation and a scholarship to be awarded by the new and still impecunious organization. Reid also suggested establishing a national office at a university, and a committee selected Florida A&M University as the proposed site. This plan, however, was voted down at the 1981 national convention. Other Reid initiatives were founding a newsletter, the *NABJ News*, and establishing an annual award to recognize excellence in covering events of special importance to the black community. Reid's last national convention, in Louisville, was a well-attended success and helped boost the organization's treasury. After his presidency, Reid worked in a variety of television jobs. He was northeast bureau chief for CBS News, working in New York City, where he also was producer of the "CBS Evening News, Weekend Editions"; and, starting in 1996, he spent more than three years working with Fox News, part of which was as Los Angeles bureau chief. He also worked with Fox's program "Front Page." In addition, he worked with Black Entertainment Television, for which he contributed to "B.E.T. Fashion Preview" and "Africa to America." Other shows he has worked on include MTV's "Entertainment Tonight"; the CBS reenactment show "Rescue 911," which starred William Shatner; and the syndicated show "Inside Video This Week."

From 1991 to 1997, Reid taught advanced television production at the University of Southern California's Graduate School of Journalism. In 1997, he left teaching to join the Discovery Channel as an executive producer. He was executive producer of "Vietnam POWs: A Story of Survival" in 1997, "Live from a Shark Cage" in 1999, the television series "On the Inside: Catching Bank Robbers" in 2000, and the special "The Washington Monument: It Stands for All" in 2000; and he was production director of "The Hindenburg Disaster: Probable Cause" in 2001. By this time, Reid was vice president of production for the Discovery Channel. In August 2001, he became senior vice president and general manager of Discovery Health Channel, replacing Kathy Quattrone. One of the programs he helped produce was a 2003 show about Joseph Merrick, better known as the "Elephant Man." This program, which combined entertainment with information, featured three geneticists from Ohio State University, the University of Oslo and the Kolling Institute of Medical Research in Australia, who debated the probable causes of Merrick's deformities: Proteus syndrome and neurofibromatosis. Reid helped the channel strengthen its ties with the American Diabetes Association, the American Cancer Society, the American Psychological Association, the March of Dimes, the American Dietetic Association and other such organizations. With the APA, the Health Channel launched a 2002 initiative to help people bounce back from stress and adversity: "The Road to Resilience." Another major event in 2002 was "AIDS in the 21st Century."

In 2003, with the March of Dimes, the channel produced a 10-hour special called "Birth Day Live," a live documentary that featured the birth of a number of babies in Orlando, Detroit and Phoenix. He also started an awards program to recognize medical and scientific achievement. Discovery Health's aim was to become the "network of record" for new medical treatments and discoveries, in competition with Fox Cable's The Health Network. Discovery Health had grown during Reid's tenure from 26 million to around 50 million subscribers. By 2005, however, Reid and the channel's president, Billy Campbell, had agreed to disagree on how best to further the channel's aims; and Reid took a new job for The Africa Channel, for which he had been serving as a consultant. The Africa Channel was founded and headed by former NBC News correspondent James Makawa of Zimbabwe. Located in Hollywood, the new channel sought to provide a different kind of programming about the African continent and its peoples—one that went far beyond the usual stories of famine, poverty and strife to bring to the American viewing audience a look at the more positive aspects of life on that continent. Also involved as partners in the new channel were Weller/Grossman Productions of Los Angeles, a major producer of television shows; former UN Ambassador Andrew Young, now head of the Atlanta consulting firm Goodworks International; and two NBA basketball players, Dikembe Mutombo and Theo Ratliff. Reid, as executive vice president and general manager, CEO Makawa and the other channel partners created such programs as "Africa Today," the first daily news show to originate in Africa and have a U.S. audience; a weekly news magazine show titled "Carte Blanche Africa"; a travel show, "Africa Within"; and "All You Need is Love," a romance-oriented show. The channel's launch came in September 2005.

Over his considerable career, Reid has won four Emmy awards. The first was a 1981 Emmy in Los Angeles for investigative reporting. In 1998 and 2000, Emmy awards came for "Discovery News," and in 1998, "Stories of Survival" won a primetime Emmy for best nonfiction special.

Further Readings: "Bob Reid." [Online]. The Africa Channel Web site www.theafricachannel.com; Moss, Linda. "Discovery Installs Reid as Health Chief." [Online, 27 August 2001]. Multichannel News Web site www.multichannel.com; Terry, Gayle Pollard. "A Salute to NABJ's Presidents: Bob Reid." [Online]. National Assoiacation of Black Journalists Web site www.nabj.org; Zeller, Susan. "Discovery Health Names New GM; Bob Reid Moves from the Discovery Channel." [Online, 9 August 2001]. RealScreen Web site www.realscreen.com.

Rhoden, William C. (?–)

William Rhoden is a well-known sportswriter for the *New York Times* and has written the "Sports of the Times" column since around 1996. He is a graduate of Baltimore's Morgan State University and worked while in school as the university's assistant sports information director. From 1974 to 1978, he was an associate editor of *Ebony* magazine, after which he was a columnist at the *Baltimore Sun*. In October 1981, he became a copyeditor for the Sunday Week in Review section of the *New York Times* and began writing sports for that paper in March 1983. His thrice-weekly column, "Sports of the Times," was added in the mid-1990s. More recently, he began recording a weekly audio feature, "Outtakes on Sports," for the *New York Times* Web edition. He has worked for the ESPN "Sports Century" show on a consulting basis and is a commentator on CNN's "The Sports Reporters." In 1996, he won a Peabody Award for having written the HBO documentary "The Journey of the African-American Athlete," about the hard road to fame and fortune endured by the nation's early black athletes; and in 2006 appeared his book *$40 Million Slaves: The Rise, Fall and Redemption of the Black Athlete*. In the book, Rhoden develops the theme of successful sports figures who have achieved wealth, but not control. He paints a picture of black athletes caught in a modern form of physical bondage within a system marked by a plantation mentality on the part of team owners. Rhoden and his family live in the Harlem section of New York City.

At a February 2001 conference at Northwestern University's Medill School of Journalism that was part of its Crain Lecture Series, Rhoden spoke on a theme he would develop in his book: the harsh treatment of black athletes by the predominantly white sports press. He charged that the press was in the forefront of a kangaroo court of public opinion in that it was all too quick to turn on black sports figures who were charged with wrongdoing. In a May 2001 column in the *Times*, Rhoden wrote of Philadelphia as a city starved for a major sports win and built the column around the difficult relationship of basketball star Allen Iverson and his 76ers coach, Larry Brown. A few days later, he wrote a feature-style column on Mets baseball coach Mookie Wilson who, with his family, had recorded a CD of nine gospel songs written by Wilson and his wife, Rosa. Then it was back to the real meat of sports and a June column on the injuries of New York Yankees player Orlando Hernandez, better known as El Duque. Another of his columns around that same time detailed the war of words between towering centers Shaquille O'Neal of the Lakers and Dikembe Mutombo of the 76ers. Next, he focused attention on a talented 76er who was a mere six feet tall: guard Tyronn Lue.

Asked about low university graduation rates for black athletes, Rhoden was quoted in the *Minnesota Spokesman-Recorder* as replying that college basketball is a business, a cash cow, and that worries about graduation rates were mainly pretense. The schools with major basketball programs, he added, had pretty much achieved a disconnect between sports and academics. In December of that year, he addressed what he considered to be racism in the NBA establishment. Professional basketball, he wrote, was too quick to exploit the talent and cash potential of black athletes. In July 2004, Rhoden wrote about the Iraq war protest of Toronto Blue Jays star Carlos Delgado, who refused to stand and remained seated in the dugout during the performance of "God Bless America." Rhoden's 25 May 2006 column concerned one of the unfortunate tendencies of sports fans: to give virtually all their attention to the superstars. The column was not about a human athlete, but about a little-known filly, Lauren's Charm, that died in a race at Belmont, and how the crowd had reacted with a ho-hum attitude, in sharp contrast to the enormous outpouring of sympathy when Kentucky Derby winner Barbaro injured a leg during the 2006 Preakness. Another of his columns, in June 2006, was about the cloud of suspicion that floats over baseball's Barry Bonds and track great Marion Jones, both accused of using performance-enhancing drugs. Another of his columns later that month correctly predicted the loss of the U.S. soccer team to Ghana in World Cup competition.

"Remember the Message, Not the Messenger"
by William C. Rhoden

I couldn't let the weekend pass without noting the latest exploits of Rasheed Wallace, the Portland Trail Blazers' volatile forward.

Wallace hit a nerve last week when he spoke about race and racism in the N.B.A. In an extensive—and raw—interview published Thursday in *the Oregonian*, Wallace said that the N.B.A.'s white establishment had been exploiting young black athletes to enrich itself.

Here are two excerpts:

"I'm not like a whole bunch of these young boys out here who get caught up and captivated into the league. No. I see behind the lines. I see behind the false screens. I know what this business is all about."

He also said: "That's why they're drafting all these high school cats, because they come into the league and they don't know no better. They don't know no better, and they don't know the real business, and they don't see behind the charade."

Wallace added that the N.B.A. looked at black players as if they were not intelligent. "It's as if we're just going to shut up, sign for the money and do what they tell us," he said.

I could do without the racial epithets he used, but in this case the message, and not the messenger's language, is important. Predictably, as Wallace's comments made the rounds, public opinion, processed through the sports news media, came down on him like a ton of bricks. He was called everything from ungrateful to vulgar. More than one commentator made the point that the N.B.A., with eight black coaches and a black owner, was the ultimate meritocracy. On Friday, David Stern, the N.B.A. commissioner, said that "Mr. Wallace's hateful diatribe was ignorant and offensive to all N.B.A. players."

Since when did the commissioner begin speaking for the players? Funny how Stern has the players' best interests at heart—until labor negotiations roll around. Then Uncle David becomes Ivan the Terrible.

In fact, the cold-blooded firing of Michael Jordan last summer by the Washington Wizards' owner, Abe Pollin, was ignorant and offensive to all N.B.A. players. Jordan, the most revered player in N.B.A. history, was treated like a C.B.A. retread. Wallace's comments, on the other hand, were a much-needed slap in the face for a league whose players have become fat, complacent and devoid of a sense of mission.

Since he has the players' best interests at heart, Stern should encourage them to read Oscar Robertson's recently published autobiography. Not only was Robertson one of the greatest players in N.B.A. history, but he also saw behind the lines, behind the N.B.A.'s false screens.

In 1970, the players, led by Robertson, hit the N.B.A. with an antitrust lawsuit when the league tried to merge with the American Basketball Association. That paved the way for free agency.

Wallace apologized Saturday for using strong language to make his point, but he did not apologize for making the point. The N.B.A. establishment—and the sports establishment—is in fact predominantly white. Wallace wasn't making that up. Although a majority of players on the courts and on the playing fields are black, African-Americans are left out of the vast landscape of power and opportunity. Pick up any media guide in any sport—baseball, football, basketball, hockey, professional or college—and pick out the black chief executives, general managers, presidents, trustees. A thimbleful, if that.

I blame Wallace's colleagues for ignoring this imbalance. As for Wallace, he lays out the problem, but does he have a solution or is he just blowing off steam?

I've followed Wallace's career for close to a decade. In the spring of 1995, his North Carolina team was playing Kentucky in the N.C.A.A. tournament in Birmingham, Ala. The game was played in an arena several blocks from the 16h Street Baptist Church, where in 1963 four black girls were killed in a bombing. I asked Delray Brooks, a Kentucky assistant coach at the time, whether he knew about the church and the bombings. He said he did not.

That night, I made copies of the eulogy that the Rev. Dr. Martin Luther King Jr. delivered at the girls' funeral and gave them to Dean Smith, the North Carolina coach. Smith made copies and passed them out to his team. A week later, Wallace came over to me during a shoot-around and said he appreciated the information.

I have watched Wallace's evolution into a tremendous player and, unfortunately, a vaudeville act whose ejections and outbursts have become part of his signature. His comments about race and sports were dismissed as just one more tirade.

Basketball has made Wallace a wealthy man, but there is something beyond the money that makes me glad he's troubled, and wish more of his colleagues would be as well.

Source: Copyright © 2003 by *The New York Times* Co. Reprinted with permission. This column appeared on 15 December 2003.

Books by William C. Rhoden: *The $40 Million Slaves: The Rise, Fall and Redemption of the Black Athlete* (New York: Crown, 2006).

Further Readings: "Rhoden: Sports Guys a 'Kangaroo Court.'" [Online, 20 February 2001]. Northwestern University, Medill School of Journalism Web site www.medill.northwestern. edu; "William Rhoden." [Online]. Medill School of Journalism Web site www.medill.northwestern.edu.

Rice, Linda Johnson (22 March 1958–)

Following the death of her father, John H. Johnson, on 9 August 2005, Linda Johnson Rice came into full control of the Johnson Publishing Company, the nation's largest minority-owned publisher. Her father had introduced national advertisers to the overlooked or underappreciated, yet enormous African-American consumer market, and her plan is to build on his success with *Ebony*, the largest-circulation general-interest magazine directed at the black audience, and *Jet*, the nation's most successful newsweekly magazine for African Americans, by adding to the company's licensing agreements and strengthening its international reach and its appeal to younger customers. She was born in Chicago and from an early age was groomed for running the family business. She earned a bachelor's degree in journalism at the University of Southern California in 1980, working in the summers for her father and traveling with her mother, Eunice, to European fashion shows. Mrs. Johnson was and is director of a company subsidiary, Ebony Fashion Fair. By the time daughter Linda graduated college, she was ready to buy for Fashion Fair on her own and soon was given the title vice president and fashion coordinator, then later, vice president and assistant to the publisher. Her father involved her in more aspects of the business and she enrolled in the MBA program at Northwestern University's Kellogg School of Management, graduating in 1987. At this point she became the company's president and chief operating officer, prompting a July 1987 *Business Week* article headlined "A Nice Graduation Present: Johnson Publishing." In 2002, her title was changed to president and CEO. Still under her father's watchful eye, she was involved in the launch of successful Fashion Fair Cosmetics, a line of makeup and skin-care products for African-American women, and in the E-Style catalog joint venture with mail order marketer Spiegel. She reports taking special pleasure in finding new talent to join the company's many enterprises, strengthening the *Ebony* and *Jet* student intern programs, serving as the company's overall "image," and working to further the company's activities abroad.

The *Chicago Sun-Times* has named her to its lists of the Top 10 Media Women and Chicago's Most Powerful Women, and she has received many other such recognitions, such as the 2003 "Robie" Award for Achievement in Industry, given by the Jackie Robinson Foundation. She sits on the boards of a number of corporations, including Kimberly-Clark and Bausch & Lomb, and is also on the boards of several nonprofit organizations. Some of the latter are the Magazine Publishers Association, the University of Southern California, and the National Museum of African-American History and Culture. She is also on the advisory council for the National Underground Railroad Freedom Center.

Rice belongs to the National Association of Black Journalists, Chicago's Economic Club and The Commercial Club of Chicago. When Nelson Mandela became president of South Africa, she was a member of the U.S. delegation that attended his inauguration. She continues to whittle away at the remaining companies, mainly sellers of luxury items, who remain reluctant to advertise to the black audience, and as head of a company that is worth perhaps $500 million, her influence on publishing and other businesses is likely be felt for a long time to come.

Further Readings: Griffin, Erica L. "Linda Johnson Rice." In *Notable Black American Women, Book II*. Edited by Jessie Carney Smith. (Detroit, Mich.: Gale Research, 1996). pp. 554–55; "Linda Johnson Rice." [Online, 2005]. Kellogg School of Management Web site www.kellogg.northwestern.edu; "Linda Johnson Rice." [Online, 2005]. Johnson Publishing Company Web site www.johnsonpublishing.com; Patterson, Philana. "Ebony's License to Grow." [Online, 23 June 2005]. Black Enterprise Web site www.blackenterprise.com; Ranson, Diana. "At 60, Ebony Magazine Is Branching Out." [Online, 27 June 2005]. New York Daily News Web site www.dnydailynews.com/business.

Richardson, Clem (c.1954–)

Clem Richardson, who joined the *New York Daily News* in 1993, writes the City Beat and Great People columns for that paper. He grew up in Charleston, S.C., and is a 1976 graduate of Duke University, where he majored in English and black studies. In 1979 and 1980, he worked for the *Anderson Independent* and from 1980 to 1983 was a general assignment reporter and neighbors editor at the *Atlanta Journal-Constitution*. From 1983 to 1986 he was a general assignment reporter and national correspondent for the *Chicago Sun-Times*, and in 1986 and 1987 worked for *Miami Herald*. He was assistant city editor and Sunday editor for *New York Newsday* from 1987 to 1993, then moved to the *New York Daily News*, where he was deputy metropolitan editor and deputy city editor, launching his columns in 1999. Whereas most columnists devote their energies to pointing out things that are wrong or need improving, Richardson has the enviable job of writing about the sunny side of life. His most memorable and charming columns tell the stories of New Yorkers who have made a positive difference in their city or elsewhere. The example below is about the exploits of a Holocaust survivor who worked with the American Army's Counter Intelligence Corps after World War II. The column sounds an important warning for present-day Americans lest we turn even more into a two-tiered, polarized society.

Most of Richardson's columns stay clear of politics, however. He has told the stories of such individuals as the operator of a "doggy boot camp," an injured former dancer who has turned to playing the musical saw in the city's subways, a Korean immigrant who has succeeded as a children's book illustrator and the city's director of consumer complaints. Other such columns have described a Bronx professor who teaches "weird science" to motivate his students, a Queens professor whose personal touch made an enormous difference to an immigrant from the Punjab region of India and a generous restaurant owner who supports a program to combat child abuse. He also has written about the "Gates" exhibit in which artist Christo and wife Jeanne-Claude erected 23 miles of fabric-marked pathways in Central Park, the post-9/11 donation of 14 cows to the United States by a tiny village in Kenya and the improved conditions in Queensbridge, the nation's largest public housing project. It would seem that Richardson has a dream job in a city of such limitless variety and true diversity.

"An Army of One: Holocaust Survivor Helped Topple Nazis" by Clem Richardson

Michel Thomas is worried about our country, and that means we all should be.

Thomas has been there as free nations died.

"Democracies are extremely fragile," Thomas said, his voice shaking with passion. "I experienced the collapse of a free society, the collapse of democracy. [Adolph] Hitler did not come to power by force, by terrorism, but by the rules of democratic law. The Germans elected him!"

There are several reasons why Thomas' words carry extra weight.

Born in Lodz, Poland, and reared in Germany, Thomas was a Jew and an only child. He was a teenager when Hitler came to power, and his parents and a cherished aunt and uncle—his second mother and father—all died in the notorious Auschwitz death camp.

Thomas' exploits during World War II are so audacious they seem like fiction. He escaped from two death camps and survived interrogation by Klaus Barbie, the infamous Butcher of Lyon.

Thomas later testified at Barbie's 1987 war crimes trial.

Thomas served with the French Resistance in Vichy, France, and then with the U.S. Army's 45th Infantry Division and later the Army's Counter Intelligence Corps.

As a CIC officer, Thomas was on hand when Allied troops liberated the Dachau concentration camp. He captured Emil Mahl, the Hangman of Dachau.

In May 1945, Thomas raided a paper mill outside Munich and stopped workers from destroying a list of more than 10 million Nazis worldwide. The list was later instrumental in the Nuremberg War Crimes trials.

But his greatest feat came in the years immediately following the war, when a network of former Nazi and SS officers was committing acts of sabotage around the country similar to what fundamentalist militants are now orchestrating in Iraq.

Thomas launched Operation Black Eagle. Posing as "SS Officer Frundsberg," Thomas not only infiltrated the 4,000-man group but eventually rose to lead it, which allowed him to arrest its members.

Thomas' exploits were deemed so incredible that a recommendation that he receive the Silver Star medal for his service was turned down. Then a skeptical review of his 1999 book, "Michael Thomas, The Test of Courage," the review written by Christopher Robbins, prompted a detective to check—and verify—each of Thomas' claims.

With help from Rep. Carolyn Maloney (D-Manhattan/Queens) and Sen. John McCain (R-Ariz.), Thomas, who is now a U.S. citizen, received his Silver Star in May from former Sen. Bob Dole and Sen. John Warner (R-Va.) in front of the World War II Memorial in Washington.

"Mr. Thomas has always deserved our county's greatest respect and appreciation, even if it took 60 years to deliver this honor to him," Maloney said.

"Hollywood does not make war hero movies that match what Mr. Thomas achieved for our country in real life, in a real war. He is truly a shining star from our country's greatest generation."

Thomas fears neglect of our country's educational system is creating two Americas: the educated and the uneducated.

That, he says, will in turn create a two-tiered society. And, as in Germany or Austria, a two-tiered system can lead only to destruction, he said.

"I remember the German teachers saying they did not want an educated proletariat because they thought ignorant people were easier to control," he said. That's why all courses were given in Latin, not in the vulgar languages of the people.

"But then it was the uneducated people who brought Hitler to power.

"I am deeply worried about vulnerability, how highly vulnerable democracy is," he said. "If we don't have an educated citizenry to hold up democracy, then it is very, very easy for it to collapse."

Source: This column appeared on 19 July 2004. New York Daily News, L.P., reprinted with permission.

Riddle, W. Curtis (2 November 1950–)

Curtis Riddle is president and publisher of the News Journal in New Castle, Delaware, and senior group president for Gannett Co. Inc., East Newspaper Group. He was born in St. Louis, Missouri, and grew up in East St. Louis, Illinois. In 1972, he received the B.A. in English literature and journalism at Southern Illinois University. He began his work life as a reporter and editorial writer for the Courier-Journal in Louisville, Kentucky, working there from 1972 until 1976, when he relocated to the Baltimore Sun, where from 1976 to 1982, he progressed through a variety of jobs: local reporter, assistant city editor, night metropolitan editor, counties editor and Washington, D.C., bureau reporter. He was hired away by USA Today, where from 1982 until 1985, he was deputy managing editor for sports. His next move up the management ladder was to become managing editor of the Cincinnati Enquirer, from 1985 to 1987. From 1988 to 1990, Riddle was publisher of the Journal and Courier in Lafayette, Indiana, and from July 1989 to May 1991, he was also vice president of Gannett's Central Regional Newspaper Group. In May 1991, he was promoted to president of the group and held that position until May 1993. Earlier, he had become president and publisher of the Lansing State Journal in Lansing, Michigan, a job he held from June 1990 to June 1994. He served as president of Gannett's East Regional Group from May 1993 until June 1994, after which he took over as president and publisher of the News Journal, which serves the Wilmington, Delaware, area from its base in nearby New Castle. This venerable newspaper was founded in 1785 as the Delaware Gazette. Finally, he was named senior group president of Gannett Co., East Newspaper Group, in June 1994. He is one of seven members of the Gannett Newspaper Operating Committee.

In early 2004, the News Journal launched Spark, a free weekly focused on entertainment, travel, food, the outdoors and fun in general in an attempt to draw younger readers to the newspaper. In autumn of the same year, the paper launched delawareonline.com, a daily interactive Web site having essentially the same purpose as *Spark*. In its more traditional journalistic role, the paper has fought a protracted battle with state officials regarding access to computerized criminal records in Delaware. A sad event for the paper in 2005 was the death at age 66 of its longtime, Pulitzer Prize-winning African-American columnist Norman Lockman. Riddle remarked about Lockman that one of his greatest virtues as a columnist was that he enjoyed making people think. To doomsayers who foretell the demise of print news, Riddle responds that, in his opinion, the newspaper industry will prevail, combined with online material or other new channels of communication. His faith is in the value of the information newspapers provide their readers.

In his position as publisher, Riddle is quite active in civic affairs and in the profession of journalism. He is a founding member of the National Association of Black Journalists and a member of the American Society of Newspaper Editors. He is on the Postal Committee of the Newspaper Association of America and served as a Pulitzer Prize judge in 1986, 1987, 2002 and 2003. He was the Gannett Manager of the Year for 1992 and was a finalist for that award in 2003. Riddle served on the board of trustees of the Delaware Art Museum from 1995 to 2001 and is on the board of First Night Wilmington and the executive board of Forum USA Delaware and is a leadership council member of the Blood Bank of Delaware.

Further Readings: Miller, Beth. "Newspapers' Success a Continuing Struggle: News Journal Looks for Innovative Ways to Win Readers." [Online, 6 November 2005]. The News Journal Delaware Online Web site www.delawareonline.com; Parra, Esteban. "Newspaper Wants Ruling Enforced: Access to Criminal Records Is Sought." [Online, 22 January 2004]. The News Journal Delaward Online Web site www.delawareonline.com.

Rideau, Wilbert (13 February 1942–)

A convicted killer who served hard time in Louisiana's Angola Prison from 1961 to 2000, Wilbert Rideau is mainly known for having taken over the prison's magazine, the *Angolite*, and having made it by far the nation's best magazine of its kind. He was born into abject poverty in Lawtell, Louisiana, and moved with his family to Lake Charles, becoming even poorer when his parents divorced. Rideau dropped out of the eighth grade and worked at menial jobs; at 19, he robbed the Gulf National Bank in Lake Charles, getting away with $14,000 and taking three bank employees hostage. When the three hostages tried to escape, Rideau shot them. One played dead, a second was able to hide, but Rideau caught the third, a woman, and fatally stabbed her. He was quickly captured, and at the local jail, he appeared in a televised interview, answering the questions of law enforcement officials. He was offered no legal counsel and confessed the crimes. The footage was shown repeatedly on local television. Rideau was tried by an all-white, all-male jury and was convicted and sentenced to death, but in 1963, his sentence was overturned by the U.S. Supreme Court in *Rideau v. Louisiana* due to his not having been accorded a fair trial. Damning media publicity had been one problem; another was that his lawyers conducted no cross-examination and essentially presented no defense. Also, no transcript was kept of the trial proceedings. He was re-tried in 1964, once again by an all-white, all-male jury, and again was convicted and sentenced to death; but in 1969, his conviction was overturned by a federal appeals court. He was re-tried for a second time in 1970, once again before an all-white, all-male jury, with the same result, and in 1973, his sentence was reduced to life in prison by the Louisiana Supreme Court. Since that time, four different parole boards recommended his release but were unsuccessful. In 1988, his cause was taken up by the Twomey Center for Peace Through Justice at Loyola University in New Orleans. In 2000, the Fifth Circuit Court of Appeals threw out his conviction on the grounds of racial discrimination, and in 2005, Rideau was re-tried for a third time. This time he was especially well represented by a defense team that included Johnnie Cochran, the nation's best-known black lawyer, and his jury was composed of eight whites and four African Americans. This jury found Rideau guilty not of murder, but of manslaughter, and he was freed due to having served more than the maximum time specified for that crime, 21 years. Rideau had served 44 years. Racial discrimination was not difficult to demonstrate. In the history of Calcasieu Parish, Louisiana, assigning the death penalty when the accused was a black person found guilty of murdering a white was 100 percent, but was only 23 percent in cases of whites who had murdered blacks.

While serving time, Rideau discovered a love for reading, and eventually for writing. He began by writing letters for illiterate inmates who paid him with cigarettes or small amounts of money. His literary pursuits were encouraged by some of his guards, who smuggled books to him. He eventually produced a manuscript for a novel about segregation in the South and began to correspond with New York book editor Clover Swann, who served as his writing coach. In 1973, Rideau asked to work with the prison's mimeographed periodical the *Angolite* but was rebuffed, inasmuch as the periodical had an all-white staff. Instead, he and a few black coworkers started the *Lifer*, whose audience was made up of men serving life sentences. A year later, Rideau began writing a weekly column, "The Jungle," which appeared in a number of black weekly newspapers in Louisiana and Mississippi. His move to the *Angolite* came later that same year when a federal judge ordered reforms at the prison, including racial integration. The warden appointed Rideau as editor of the *Angolite*, and in 1976, a new warden told the editor that he could print anything, including criticism of how the prison was operated, if he could prove his claims. With this agreement; the help of subeditors Tommy Mason, Ron Wikberg and Billy Wayne Sinclair; and a surprising amount of cooperation by prison authorities, Rideau rapidly turned what had been little more than a newsletter into a respected magazine that became known nationwide. Its audience extends far beyond the prison's roughly 5,000 inmates and has 3,700 paid subscribers—2,800 are prisoners—in every state and a few other nations. Some law enforcement and corrections officials also subscribe to find out what the prisoners are thinking. The magazine has won numerous awards, starting in 1977 with the Southern Illinois University School of Journalism's Charles C. Clayton Award. Other recognitions came from the Robert F. Kennedy Foundation, the American Bar Association, the Louisiana Bar Association, Long Island University and the Sidney Hillman Foundation. Seven times, the magazine was a finalist for the National Magazine Award. In 1989, 1990 and 1992, Rideau spoke at the annual convention of the American Society of Newspaper Editors, and in 1991, he and Ron Wikberg teamed with University of Louisiana professor Burk Foster in writing a criminal justice textbook. In 1992, he and by then coeditor Ron Wikberg coauthored a book about life in the prison system. Probably the most widely read of that which Rideau has written appeared in *Time*'s 21 March 1994 issue: "Why Prisons Don't Work," a one-page essay.

In addition to his writing and editing, Rideau appeared in June 1984 on ABC-TV's "Nightline" as part of a panel that also included Chief Justice Warren Burger. He also has spoken to thousands of public-school students who came to visit the prison; his message was about conditions in the penal system and what young people could do to avoid becoming a part of it. Rideau added to his work as magazine editor and prison speaker by doing a limited amount of broadcast work. In 1990 and 1991, he, Ron Wikberg and Dave Isay cowrote and coproduced "Tossing Away the Keys" for National Public Radio; and in 1994, he worked on a short ABC documentary, "In for Life," which won a CINE Golden Eagle Award. In 1998, he codirected "The Farm: Angola, USA," a documentary about the prison that won the best documentary prize at the Sundance Film Festival. Coeditor Wikberg was freed before him, in 1994, but died soon thereafter of cancer. Rideau's own release from prison at age 62 was marred by the resentment still felt by many in the area where his crime had occurred. His success as a prison journalist brought with it envy and resentment, and upon his release, both he and his lawyer received death threats. His hope was to continue to write and hence to further redeem his name. In a January 2005 column, Leonard Pitts of Tribune Media Syndicate remarked that it was natural to have ambivalent feelings about Rideau's release—because he was at the same time both victim and victimizer.

Books by Wilbert Rideau: With Burk Foster and Ron Wickberg, *The Wall Is Strong: Corrections in Louisiana* (Lafayette, La.: Center for Louisiana Studies, 1989); with Ron Wickberg, *Life Sentences: Rage & Survival Behind Bars Survival* (New York: Times Books, 1992).

Further Readings: Fumento, Michael. "A Celebrity Murderer Beats the System." [Online, 20 January 2005]. Richael Fumento Web site www.fumento.com; Haygood, Wil. "The Long Road Out of Lake Charles." [Online, 17 January 2005]. Washington Post Web site www.washingtonpost.com; Masterton, John. "Few Holds Barred for Prison Publication: No Stranger to Top Journalism Awards, The Angolite Is a Four-Time NMA Finalist—National Magazine Awards." *Folio: The Magazine for Magazine Management*. July 1990; Montaldo, Charles. "Wilbert Rideau Released from Prison." [Online, 16 January 2005]. About Crime / Punishment site http://crime.about.com; Nossiter, Adam. "Freed Louisiana Convict Wilbert Rideau Savors Freedom, Faces New Chapter in Life." [Online, 17 January 2005]. San Diego Union-Tribune Web site www.signonsandiego.com/news/nation; "Wilbert Rideau: Biographical Sketch." [Online, 2001]. Wilbert Rideau Web site www.wilbertrideau.com/bio; "Wilbert Rideau's Resume." [Online, 2001]. Wilbert Rideau Web site www.silbertrideau.com/resume.

Riley, Jason L. (8 July 1971–)

Youthful conservative Jason Riley is an editorial writer and member of the editorial board of the *Wall Street Journal*. He comes from Buffalo, New York, and holds a 1994 B.A. in English from the State University of New York at Buffalo. He was a student intern at *USA Today* in summer 1993, where he worked as a copyeditor on the sports desk. His full-time professional career started at the *Buffalo News*, where he was a news desk copyeditor from September 1993 to September 1994. In October 1994, he was hired by the *Journal* as a national news desk copyreader, and in the following year, he was first a copyreader and then a copyeditor for the *Journal*'s remarkably conservative editorial page. Riley became the paper's first editorial interactive editor in April 1996, working with WSJ.com. He became a senior editorial page writer in March 2000 and was elevated to the editorial board in 2005. He was directly involved in escaping the collapse of the World Trade Towers on 11 September 2001 and emailed his first-person account of this harrowing experience to WSJ.com. Realizing that he could not outrun the cloud of dust and debris from the first building's collapse, he first took refuge under a parked van. Unable to breathe, he entered a nearby building but soon had to evacuate. Eventually he joined the stream of people who crossed the Brooklyn Bridge to safety.

In 2002, Riley revealed in a story in the *Weekend Journal* that he had been raised a Jehova's Witness but that he had parted with the church when he was a teenager. The story followed a U.S. Supreme Court decision that struck down a Stratton, Ohio, ordinance that had mandated registering with city authorities for anyone who wished to go door-to-door for any purpose. Riley's story gave a brief history of the church, which had been started in Pennsylvania during the 1870s by Charles Taze Russell. Riley agreed with the court's ruling that found the Ohio ordinance in violation of the First Amendment. In 2003, most African-American columnists and editorial writers used the Jason Blair firing by the *New York Times* to point out the difference in mindset governed by the race of a discredited plagiarist. While acknowledging this tendency, Riley used the firing of Blair as a springboard for arguing that affirmative action strips African Americans of their right to be judged as individuals. Rather than favoring preference or quotas that are race-based, he favors more attention to improving K-12 education for minorities.

In 2004, Riley parted with the nativist wing of the Republican Party and advocated a more welcoming policy toward immigrants. He also disagreed with the 1986 bill that criminalized the hiring of illegal guest workers, former presidential candidate Pat Buchanan's proposal in 1992 to freeze all immigration, and California's now-defeated Proposition 187, which would have cut off education and health-care benefits to people lacking a green card. He pointed out how the far right had aligned itself with advocates of the far left, who wanted to eliminate population growth, and with ultra-leftist environmentalists. Riley credited President George W. Bush with trying to arrive at a sensible compromise, forgetting, as most conservatives will, the way Bush looked the other way on illegal border crossing while courting the Hispanic vote during his two campaigns for the presidency. In that same year, Riley advised Republican politicians to use Black Entertainment Television in campaigning for office. He remarked that black Americans are easy to target in that something like 60 percent watch BET on at least a weekly basis. In a 2006 story headlined "Classy Economist," Riley penned a tribute to long-time conservative columnist and economist Thomas Sowell, clearly one of the younger man's heroes. On occasion, Riley has written for the "de gustibus" column in the *Journal*, where he once described his decision to stop watching the television show "Melrose Place," a show about sex and deception that, he wrote, beautifully illustrates how oddly compelling tasteless television programming can be. He occasionally reviews movies, as well, as in a 2002 critique of "I Am Sam," written for the *National Review*. He found the movie, about a badly retarded man who wanted to be a parent to his young daughter, to be a manipulative, redundant, inept and dreadful tearjerker. Riley has also joined *Journal* editorial page editor Paul Gigot and some of his fellow *WSJ* editorial writers on "The Journal Editorial Report," televised by PBS and, more recently, by Fox News. In a light moment in April 2006, Riley applauded as fitting, a Denver, Colorado, judge's sentence in the case of a man who saved on commuting time by driving in the car pool lane with a mannequin in his passenger seat. The man was required to stand by the road holding a sign that told passersby that the HOV lane should not be used by dummies.

Further Readings: "Jason Riley." [Online]. The *Wall Street Journal* Opinion Journal Web site www.opinionjournal.com/bios.

Riley, Rochelle (c.1967–)

Rochelle Riley has been a thrice-weekly columnist for the *Detroit Free Press* since 1998 and before that wrote a column for the *Louisville Courier-Journal*'s Features section. She is a 1983 journalism graduate of the University of North Carolina at Chapel Hill and worked at the *Washington Post*, *Dallas Morning News* and *Dallas Times Herald* prior to joining the *Courier-Journal*. While in Kentucky, she was an associate editor and deputy managing editor as well as columnist. In Detroit, she also appears weekly on Detroit Public Television on the point-counterpoint public issues program "Am I Right or Am I Right," opposite rival columnist Nolan Finley of the *Detroit News*. Of the two, Riley is the liberal, although her columns show that she is not so vehemently anti-George W. Bush as are many other African-American opinion columnists. Riley doesn't like President Bush's record on the urban agenda, but was generally complimentary of his response to providing aid to the 2005 tsunami victims in Sri Lanka and other Asian nations. She has been far less sanguine, however, about Vice President Dick Cheney, taking him to task for the secrecy with which he surrounded U.S. energy policy planning. As to Condoleezza Rice, when she became national security advisor in 2001, Riley sang her praises, but by the time Rice was promoted to Secretary of State, the columnist was singing a much different tune, as revealed in her column of 21 January 2005, which is reprinted below.

During 2005, Riley has written several columns in reaction to entertainer Bill Cosby's argument for more emphasis on personal responsibility in America's black community. Riley disagreed with Cosby's critics, remarking that her own success could not have been possible without the work of all those who farmed and slaved for people who did not even consider them altogether human. People today who are still enslaved to a self-destructive lifestyle, she wrote, shame their race's hard-fought legacy. In January 2005, when Cosby visited Detroit, Riley noted that he wanted to share the stage with organizations that were already working to improve conditions for the city's poor black citizens; she used most of this column to list and describe eleven such organizations. Like Cosby, she challenges people not to simply accept violence and poverty as a normal way of life, and not to lose pride. One of her column themes is that reducing violence must be a priority in Detroit. On 4 July 2004, she noted 729 shootings in the city during the past six months, adding that most of the shootings were black-on-black. She also has argued for efforts to boost literacy; in November 2003, she wrote that in Detroit, 47 percent of adults are illiterate or read poorly. Riley has published two books of her columns, one in 1998, the other in 2003. She is a member of the National Society of Newspaper Columnists and in 2004, received the Charles E. Scripps Award for service to the cause of literacy, in recognition of her adult literacy campaign that she called "Metro Detroit Reads."

"Respect the Truth, Not the Lies" by Rochelle Riley

Why is it so hard to say the work "lie" in Washington?

Take Condoleezza Rice's confirmation as secretary of state. It gave senators a chance to question the former national security adviser this week about the misleading pronouncements and just plain bull that have been fed to the American people in the past two years.

When Rice asserted that 120,000 Iraqis had received military training in preparation for the withdrawal of American troops, Sen. Joseph Biden, D-Del., called her assessment "malarkey" and cited the true number of 4,000.

And even Sen. Barbara Boxer, D-Calif., who for a few minutes was the only Democrat on the Hill and who came closest to calling her a, well, you know, didn't go far enough. "...Your loyalty to the mission you were given, to sell this war, overwhelmed your respect for the truth," she told Rice.

Stop the rhetoric. Even in Washington, where politicks are legion and candor is rare, somebody just call a lie a lie!

A New Unity?

The American people know there have been lies, even those who think they were justified. President George W. Bush's long-awaited acknowledgement that there were no weapons of mass destruction in Iraq didn't get as much media attention as his $40 million inaugural party (which cost more than the $35 million Bush initially pledged to tsunami victims in southern Asia).

Slowly, and with some deliberateness, the Bush administration is attempting to make the world believe that America is one. He believes if he says it enough, it will become true. Even his adviser, Karen Hughes, just before Bush's inaugural address Thursday, expressed surprise at the tough questions put to Rice this week because they didn't fit with the nation's new unity. What new unity? What country has she been living in?

This campaign to declare unity is supposed to convince the world that all Americans agree on the war in Iraq and that we all support every decision made in the name of fighting terrorism—including the unnecessary death of hundreds of American soldiers.

The scary thing is that the campaign is succeeding. Questions about vote fraud in Ohio were dismissed with an "Oh, be a good patriot and let it go." Complaints from soldiers about their safety and their equipment were dismissed with a reminder that war is hell and you don't always have ice water in hell.

And complaints about this week's inaugural hoopla, which will cost the city of Washington, D.C., anywhere from $12 million to $20 million, were dismissed with a "Take it out of your Homeland Security Budget, why don't ya."

Focus on the Real Issues

Nowhere was the campaign for a new truth more evident than at Rice's hearings, which were a mockery of our governmental process, our expectations on federal accountability and the truth. Even Sen. John Kerry, D-Mass., who truly has nothing else to lose, asked hard questions only after telling Rice that she was going to be confirmed anyway. And still no one used the word "lie."

America's priority shouldn't be the Americanization of the world. It should be to focus on the people's need for truth. The truth won't stop the war. The truth won't reverse the election. It won't end an inaugural party too soon. But in a country founded on truth, justice and the American way, mock hearings, mock press conferences where no real questions get answered and partying while soldiers die—they are not the American way. They are the way of the Bush.

One truth in the history books is worth two truths in the alternative universe that we call America post 9/11. And the truth cannot be recorded until the administration finally admits somebody lied.

Source: Reprinted by permission of the *Detroit Free Press*. This column appeared on 21 January 2005.

Books by Rochelle Riley: *From the Heart, Selected Columns* (Louisville, Ky.: Dream a Little, 1998); *Life Lessons: Essays on Parenthood, America, 9/11 and Detroit* (Detroit, Mich.: Detroit Free Press, 2003).

Further Readings: Astor, Dave. "The 'WE' Generation Combines Writing and Editing Positions." *Editor & Publisher*, 18 December 1999, p. 33; "Muhammad Ali: Coming Home: The Reporter." [Online]. Louisville Courier-Journal Web site www.courier-journal.com.

Roberts, Deborah (c.1960–)

Deborah Roberts is an ABC News correspondent for "20/20," a substitute anchor for "World News Weekend" and "Good Morning America," and host of the show "Lifetime Live" on cable network Lifetime Television, a Hearst Corporation property. Her father had his own business installing carpets, and her mother was a housewife. Roberts holds a 1982 bachelor's degree in broadcast journalism from the University of Georgia; while in college, she worked part-time at a Macon, Georgia, station and for Georgia Public Television. Her early career was in the South. In 1982, she was a reporter for Columbus, Georgia, station WTVM-TV, from which she went to Knoxville, Tennessee, station WBIR-TV to cover the state legislature. She became bureau chief, NASA reporter and weekend co-anchor for WFTV-TV in Orlando, Florida, in 1987, remaining there until she moved on to NBC in 1990. Her initial network duties were in general-assignment reporting. She worked at the network's Atlanta and Miami bureaus and reported out of Kuwait and Saudi Arabia after the Persian Gulf War. She also covered the 1992 Barcelona Olympics and later became a "Dateline NBC" correspondent when that magazine-format show first aired in 1992. In June 1995, having gained the favorable attention of Barbara Walters, Roberts became a substitute anchor at ABC, working with "World News Weekend" and "Good Morning America," and as a "20/20" correspondent. In the latter job, she has done investigative work on alleged incest and other forms of sexual abuse among the Amish in Pennsylvania, reported on the difficulties of growing up as the child of biracial parents and did a profile of civil rights icon Rosa Parks, who died on 24 October 2005. She has also reported on the emotionally difficult visits of African Americans to places in Africa where their ancestors were enslaved, the problem of childhood depression and alcohol abuse as explored in an interview with Darryl Strawberry of baseball fame. More recently she reported on medical issues, gender selection efforts and the difficulties faced by orphaned children and other refugees in Rwanda following the genocide of Tutsis by extremist Hutus there. One of her most unusual stories was an October 2005 report on David Schroer, a former U.S. Special Forces commander who led a covert antiterrorism unit, and how he resigned his commission and became Diane Schroer: transsexual.

Roberts appeared in a 2005 episode of "The Tony Danza Show," playing herself. She is married to genial broadcast weatherman and host Al Roker of rival network NBC. Early in her career, she was accorded a top-anchor award from the *Orlando Sentinel*. She received the 1992 Distinguished Alumnus Award from the University of Georgia, got a sports Emmy for her reporting on the 1992 Olympics and received a Clarion Award for her work on troubles among the Amish.

Further Readings: Edwards, Audrey. "Seeing 20/20 with Deborah Roberts." *Essence*, March 2002; "Deborah Roberts, News Correspondent." [Online]. Jannette Rankin Foundation Web site www.rankinfoundation.org.

Roberts, Osborne "Ozzie" Sinclaire Jr. (8 March 1949–)

A fixture in San Diego, California, is columnist Ozzie Roberts, who has worked for the *San Diego Union-Tribune* since 1974. Roberts is a native

Roberts, Osborne "Ozzie" Sinclaire Jr.

New Yorker, born in Manhattan and educated at Syracuse University, from which he received the B.A. in English composition in 1972. During college, he had a summer job at *Life Magazine* in 1968, and after graduating, he spent 1972 and part of 1973 with *Psychology Today* and the following year with *Ebony Magazine*. In 1974, he joined the staff of the *Union-Tribune*'s predecessor, the *San Diego Tribune*. Roberts characterizes his column as human interest, and he gravitates toward success stories, dealing only rarely with matters that touch on race relations. He is a member of the San Diego Association of Black Journalists, which was founded in 2000; the SDABJ now awards an annual scholarship named for the long-time columnist.

Appearing below is an example of his success-story columns, featuring a bright local teenager who had escaped war-torn Afghanistan. Another such column described the friendship of a black San Diego woman who grew up in segregated Memphis, Tennessee, and a white physician and hospital medical director; their friendship came about through their mutual interest in lung disease. A third told a fishing story—that of a recently deceased Sicily-born commercial fisherman whose best catch ever occurred off the Baja coast one day in the 1970s when he and his crew brought in 35 tons of big eye tuna. Like all human-interest writers, Roberts likes a story about difficulties overcome, such as a June 2005 column about a local man whose last words with his dying father inspired him to overcome a lifetime drug habit, or another column a year earlier about a hulking ex-professional football player who also had to beat his drug addiction to succeed. Stories of people who just will not give up often figure in his columns, such as that of a cerebral palsy victim confined to a motorized chair—a man who had immigrated to California from China not knowing English. Also, many Roberts columns address the need to "give back," as did a column about a 90-year-old man who had volunteered for 30 years as a museum docent. Roberts is a member of the San Diego Association of Black Journalists, which now gives a scholarship in his name.

"Afghan Teen Is Fulfilling a Promise Made to Her Late Father" by Ozzie Roberts

Arian Dyanat is one remarkable 17-year-old.

The junior at Herbert Hoover High School carries a grade point average that is just 0.21 of a point short of perfect.

"I don't like getting B's," she says. "B's are like F's for me. I like trying to do the hard things—I like the challenge."

She also tutors and mentors other youngsters who are refugees, like she was.

Arain came to San Diego by way of Pakistan and Boise, Idaho, with her mother, Suraya, and her younger brother, Ruyin, two years ago. They'd escaped from their native war-and-strife-torn Afghanistan.

Arain, who wants to study at UCLA, UCSD or UC Berkeley and eventually go into medicine, recently won a $7,000 college scholarship and a laptop computer through a San Diego Chargers annual award program.

Chargers Champions recognizes high school juniors for academic excellence, volunteerism and community involvement.

The scholarship and the award are firsts for Arian. So was the formal dinner, at which they were presented May 12.

But looking into her clear, dark eyes that seem to brighten as she speaks with precise English—one of three languages she's already mastered—you're certain that there will be a lot more such honors coming her way.

You're made the more certain, too, when you consider one of Arian's most sacred vows—and all that she's endured to fulfill it.

Her beloved father, Sami, an officer in the Afghan army, always saw great intellect and compassion in his second born of three children. He'd always tell her he wanted her to be a doctor.

And on a cold, clear night in the mountains of Kabul when Arian was just 7, she reaffirmed her oft-repeated promise to her father.

"I will reach for those stars, papa," she said. "I will be the educated person you want me to be."

But the next day, life took a turn into hell for the family Dyanat, and Arian was forced to come to grips with the horrible reality that her father would never be there to see her achieve their dream.

With her mother, Arian found the bodies of her father and her older brother lying in the street near the family home.

The corpses had been thrown there by enemies fighting in the country's civil war who wanted to send a message to anyone and everyone associated with her father.

For a long time, "I wouldn't accept that my dad and brother were dead—I told myself they were just asleep," Arian recalls. "It was just unbelievable to see your father and brother go to the store one night and then to wake up the next day and find them dead."

Yet the young girl had to pull herself together.

She, her mother and her younger brother were in grave danger, and they eventually had to flee to Pakistan, where they would live in hiding for seven years.

Returning home was never an option. Particularly after the repressive Taliban regime came to power in Afghanistan. But living outside their homeland's boundaries was far from a blessing for Arian.

She had to drop out of school in the fifth grade and stay out for four consecutive years while helping her mother support the family through menial office work.

And Arian was tormented.

"We were in abject poverty," she says. "The three of us were living in a one-room apartment, with a bathroom and a kitchen. But more than anything, I'd cry because I wasn't going to school.

"I'd remember the promise I'd made to my father. It would hurt me to know that I wasn't doing what he wanted me to do. It's because of that promise that I'm (in San Diego) today."

When the first opportunity to get into a U.S. refugee resettlement program presented itself in 2002—and upon the relentless strong urging of friends—Arian's mom took it.

After the family landed in Boise for a year and Arian wowed everyone, getting A's and B's and being skipped grades upon her return to school, her mother again followed the advice of friends.

They said go to San Diego, where there are a lot more academic challenges and opportunities for a bright and talented youngster.

Here in San Diego, as in Boise, Arian, who works 30 hours a week in a nonprofit children's bookstore in City Heights to help support her family, constantly counts her blessings.

She also remains resolved to always remember where she came from.

So, in addition to her work for the family and her academic studies, Arian serves as a tutor, a mentor and an all-purpose volunteer in five separate nonprofit programs on the Hoover campus and in the community at large.

"I've learned that when someone goes through bad times," she says, with help from others, "it doesn't have to be the end of the world."

The teenager also immensely enjoys the feeling of living in a free society.

"I love knowing that no one is forcing you to do anything you don't want to do," she says. "And opportunities are unlimited. That's most important to me."

Now Arian's thoughts return to her blessings and the promise.

"It's like I was in a box, not seeing all things around me," she says. "But when I got to San Diego, it's like the box just opened—this is my new land now—this is my home.

"This is the place where I'll become something and where I'll keep giving back to others."

Her father would have loved that.

Source: This column appeared on 22 May 2005 and appears here by permission of *The San Diego Union-Tribune*.

Roberts, Robin (23 November 1960–)

A long-time female sportscaster, Robin Roberts is now one of the three anchors of ABC's news/feature program "Good Morning America." She was born in Tuskegee, Alabama, and reared in Pass Christian, Mississippi, a small town about 13 miles west of Gulfport. Her mother was head of the state's Board of Education, and her father was an Air Force colonel who was a member of the Tuskegee Airmen. Growing up, she always loved sports and was often called a tomboy, although she preferred to be thought of as a female athlete. By age 10 she was a championship bowler, she was a standout athlete in high school and she was an award-winning scholarship basketball player at Southern Louisiana University, where she was inducted into the university's Athletic Hall of Fame for having been both its third all-time leading scorer, with 1,446 career points, and third leading rebounder (1,034) and from which she graduated cum laude with a communications major in 1983. During her junior year, she worked as a sports director at station WHMD/WFPR in Hammond, Louisiana, and was a weekend disk jockey and sports reporter for KSLU-FM. Her first job after graduation, 1983–1984, was as a reporter and sports anchor for WDAM-TV in Hattiesburg, Mississippi. She moved to WLOX-TV, the ABC affiliate in Biloxi, Mississippi, where she worked from 1984 to 1986, then moved on to a sports anchor/reporter job at Nashville, Tennessee, with station WSMV-TV. In Nashville, she won the city's Sportscaster of the Year Award in 1987. Her next move, in 1988, was to WAGA-TV in Atlanta, where she again was a sports reporter/anchor and also worked in radio as a morning personality at WVEE-FM. Then in February 1990, at age 29, she was hired by ESPN to work as an anchor. She was that network's first black on-air personality, hosting "Sports Center." A mere month later, she began working with "NFL Prime Time" and "Sunday Sports Day" and became the first woman to do a National Football League pre-game show. She did play-by-play and hosting for ESPN's coverage of the Women's National Basketball Association from 1997 to 2000, also anchoring "SportsCenter" for the Wimbledon and U.S. Open tennis tournaments and was primary reporter for the winter and summer Olympics in Salt Lake City, Utah, and Sydney, Australia. She also hosted the ESPN interview show "In the Sportslight." In 1995, she joined the staff of ABC's "Wide World of Sports" and was given a nearly $4 million six-year contract with both ABC and ESPN. She was again the first African-American woman to work in this capacity. In that year, she also began contributing to the popular program "Good Morning America," splitting her time between ABC News and ESPN. She has worked with "World News Tonight," "Prime Time Live" and with the "20/20" magazine-format show and has been an occasional host of the series "Vanished." She has done segments on the aftermath of the World Trade Towers attacks, whether to use sky marshals on airline flights, stem-cell research, adoptions arranged by Internet and celebrity interviews with the likes of Sen. Hillary Clinton, movie star Penelope Cruz and sports figures Tiger Wood and Shaquille O'Neal. She covered the inauguration of President George W. Bush and the Scripps Howard National Spelling Bee, and, in 1999, appeared on the "Vintage NBA" weekly hour-long show that spotlights basketball luminaries.

In April 2002, Roberts became the "Good Morning America" news anchor. Her versatility earned her another promotion in May 2005, when, at age 44, she became one of the show's three principal anchors, joining Diane Sawyer and Charles Gibson. The show's ratings have moved upward in competition with NBC's morning "Today" show that starred Katie Couric and Matt Lauer and the CBS "Early Show," which has four anchors. With Sawyer and Gibson on either side of 60, Roberts provides the show a good mix of youth and experience. When Hurricane Katrina struck in summer 2005, Roberts had personal reasons to devote time to the story. Her hometown of Pass Christian was hit hard, and Roberts did on-the-scene reporting on the storm's aftermath. The program set up Web sites through which donations could be raised to help the city's storm victims. Also, Roberts' older sister, whose work in broadcasting had inspired her to major in communications, was working as cohost of a New Orleans morning show on WWL-TV.

Roberts has been the recipient of many recognitions. In 1993, she was accorded the Excellence in Sports Journalism Award, Broadcast, from Northeastern University's Center for the Study of Sport in Society and School of Journalism. The Women's Institute of Sports and Education inducted her into its Hall of Fame in 1994 and in 1996, initiated a Robin Roberts Sports Journalism Scholarship in her honor; and the University of Georgia's broadcasting honorary, Di Gamma Kappa, gave her its Distinguished Achievement Award in that same year. She received the President's Award from the Women's Sports Foundation in 2001 and *Ebony* magazine's Outstanding Journalist recognition in 2002. She is also a three-time Emmy winner. Roberts has published a number of sports-connected books, most of which are short books that appeal to the youth audience.

Books by Robin Roberts: With Nancy Lieberman-Cline and Kevin Warneke, *Basketball for Women: Becoming a Complete Player* (Champaign, Ill.: Human Kinetics, 1996); *Basketball the Right Way* (Brookfield, Conn.: Millbrook Press, 2000); *Basketball Year: What It's Like to Be a Woman Pro* (Brookfield, Conn.: Millbrook Press, 2000); *Careers for Women Who Love Sports* (Brookfield, Conn.: Millbrook Press, 2000); *Sports for Life: How Athletes Have More Fun* (Brookfield, Conn.: Millbrook Press, 2000); *Which Sport Is Right for You?* (Brookfield, Conn.: Millbrook Press, 2000); *Sports Injuries* (Brookfield, Conn.: Millbrook Press, 2001).

Further Readings: "ABC Elevates Robin Roberts to Anchor Status." [Online, 5 October 2005]. Tampa Bay Alive site http://tampabayalive.com; "Robin Roberts." [Online, 21 March 2005]. ABC News site http://abcnews.go.com; "Robin Roberts." [Online, 2003]. National Women's History Project Web site www.nwhp.org; "Robin Roberts." [Online, 4 January 2001]. Women's Sports Foundation Web site www.womenssportsfoundation.org; "Robin Roberts, Good Morning America Correspondent." [Online, 2005]. WCHS8 Web site www.wchstv.com.

Roberts, Troy (9 September 1962–)

Troy Roberts has been a correspondent for "48 Hours" on CBS since 1998. He was born in Philadelphia and is a 1984 political science graduate of the University of California at Berkeley. He began his career in 1985 as producer and host of a weekly news magazine-format show on CBS affiliate station KPIX-TV in San Francisco. In 1987, he moved to Portland, Oregon, to work as a reporter for station KATU-TV and, in 1990, traded that job for a new reporting post with WCBS-TV in New York City. There, he worked with "Channel 2 This Morning" and announced local news items for "CBS News This Morning." In 1993, he became coanchor of "CBS News Up To the Minute," a nighttime show on which he interviewed many a notable; and during 1995 and 1996, he was coanchor of "CBS Morning News." From 1996 to 1998, he was a correspondent for the "CBS Evening News with Dan Rather" as well as for "CBS News Sunday Morning." During that time, he also did investigative reporting for the "Eye on America" feature of the CBS News. He covered the presidential race between Bill Clinton and Bob Dole in 1996, as well as that year's bomb-marred Olympics in Atlanta. Earlier, he had reported and anchored the 1994 Olympics in Lillehammer, Norway, the installation of Nelson Mandela as president of South Africa and the reaching of an ill-fated peace agreement in the Middle East. His current job as a correspondent for "48 Hours" began in 1998. Some of his best reporting for this program has been about hate crimes. He also reported on the seamy story of fugitive serial rapist Andrew Luster, grandson of the late cosmetics magnate Max Factor, and his June 2003 capture in Mexico by the equally colorful bounty hunter Duane "Dog" Chapman. A big story for Roberts was that of another miscreant with a privileged background: handsome "preppy killer" Robert Chambers, who in 1986, killed Jennifer Levin during what Chapman excused as "rough sex." In 2005, Roberts was involved in the reporting of Las Vegas interviews conducted with entertainer Michael Jackson's parents; Jackson had been charged by a teenager with having molested the boy at the singer/dancer's Neverland Ranch home.

Further Readings: "Troy Roberts." [Online, 16 September 2004]. CBS News Web site www.cbnews.com.

Robinson, Eugene (?–)

Seasoned journalist Eugene Robinson is an associate editor of the *Washington Post* and in 2005 began writing a twice-weekly column that is now carried by the Washington Post Writers Group. He was born in Orangeburg, South Carolina, and was one of a handful of African Americans to attend

Orangeburg High School. He is a graduate of the University of Michigan, where he was the first black coeditor-in-chief of the student newspaper, the *Michigan Daily*. After graduation, he found a job reporting for the *San Francisco Chronicle*. There, his first big story was the kidnapping of newspaper heiress Patricia Hearst. In 1980, Robinson joined the *Washington Post* in the capacity of city hall reporter; he covered the first term of Mayor Marion Barry, finding himself in the sometimes ticklish position of middleman between a white-controlled paper and a black-controlled city administration. Robinson was promoted to assistant city editor in 1981, then to city editor in 1984. He was a Nieman Fellow at Harvard University during parts of 1987 and 1988, taking advantage of his time away from the newspaper to learn Spanish, and to a lesser extent, Portugese, which in 1988 got him the job of South America correspondent for the *Post*. He worked out of Buenos Aires, Argentina, and held that job until 1992, when he became the paper's London bureau chief. He came back to Washington in February 1994 to assume the job of foreign editor. Then in 1999, he was named an assistant managing editor and was placed in charge of the *Post*'s Style section, holding that job until 1 January 2005, when he assumed his present job as associate editor and columnist.

Robinson is a liberal and a facile writer. His distribution via the Washington Post Writers Group virtually ensures that his column will be picked up by many newspapers as a replacement for the Writers Group's longtime columnist William Raspberry, who retired at the end of 2005. One of Robinson's early columns, about Secretary of State Condoleezza Rice, is reproduced below by permission of the *Washington Post*; in it, he observes that although he disagrees with her foreign policy, and that of the Bush administration, he thinks her greatest value might be in defying the common archetypes of the American black woman: the angry woman, the sultry temptress, the earth mother and so on. Since Rice fits into none of these stereotypical categories, he writes, she might help give all Americans a new, less encumbered way to look at African-American women. Another really fine column addressed House Majority Leader Tom DeLay and took him to task for his ostentatious religiosity. Robinson called DeLay a theocrat and pictured him as a bombastic combination of Cotton Mather and the "Saturday Night Live" character Church Lady. Also on the subject of religion and politics, Robinson applauded U.S. District Judge John E. Jones III for his 2005 ruling that intelligent design did not have to be taught in science classes. On the continuing troubles of Great Britain's Prince of Wales, Robinson has suggested that the prince might not take the throne until he reaches an age when he would have to be helped into it by a nurse. He further suggested that the current role of the British monarchy is to provide its subjects a continual, dysfunctional soap opera and that Prince Charles fails to understand that his true role is more make-believe than real. The column was headlined "Prince of Wails." In a column on pop star Michael Jackson and his legal troubles, headlined "Adoration's Price," Robinson wrote that the real monster is not Jackson, but Americans' pathetic veneration of celebrity;

he saved his primary denunciation for the parents of the various young boys who were allowed to stay at Jackson's Neverland Ranch. Toward the end of 2005, Robinson leveled even stronger criticism at President George Bush and Vice President Dick Cheney, their claims to unfettered executive power and their tendency to treat laws that might restrain that power as mere nuisances.

Robinson has authored two books. The first, *Coal to Cream* (1999), was researched while he was working in Buenos Aires. It examines the relationships of color, race and class and is in part a memoir of that portion of his life when he realized that Brazil is not really the racial paradise that it seems to be on first glance. He found that, like the Untied States, Brazil has discrimination, although in Brazil, it revolves not around race per se, but around color and class. His second book, *Last Dance in Havana* (2004), examines contemporary Cuba mainly through the lens of music. His view is that our country's Castro-era treatment of Cuba hasn't worked and that we might just as well loosen restrictions on travel to and trade with that island nation. Since 1994, Robinson has been a member of the Council on Foreign Relations, and he is a member of the National Association of Black Journalists.

"Nobody's Archetype" by Eugene Robinson

I thought that by now we had grown accustomed to seeing Condoleezza Rice on the public stage, after her four years as a wartime president's national security adviser. But her first foreign trip as secretary of state has been compelling to watch, and I think that has to do with race, image, archetype and all the things she is not.

She is not the first black U.S. secretary of state, nor the first woman to hold the office. (And *that's* a sentence I thought I'd never get to write.) But she is the first black woman, and that brings into play the whole optician's kit of distorting lenses through which African American women are viewed, both at home and around the world. None of those lenses gives us the view we think we should be getting, and so we try another, and another. Someday we'll give up and take her at face value, for better or worse. I don't think much of her foreign policy or the administration she serves, but I have to give her credit for refusing to be anyone other than who she is.

She doesn't fit any of the silly, often repellent stereotypes that black women get tagged with: There's "Angry Black Woman," personified by Omarosa Manigault-Stallworth, the famous-for-being-famous contestant on Donald Trump's "The Apprentice." Unlike Omarosa, Rice doesn't fly off the handle at the slightest provocation or sideways glance. She isn't constantly telling someone off or storming out of the room, or "assuming the position" of hands on hips, neck moving side to side, as the late Isabel Sanford used to do as "Weezy" in the old sit com "The Jeffersons." When Sen. Barbara Boxer grilled Rice at her confirmation hearings with appropriate, tough questions about Iraq, Rice flashed anger only with her eyes. Her demeanor remained as cold as steel.

There's "Jezebel," perhaps the oldest and most insulting image of all—think of Josephine Baker in Paris, dancing in her skirt of bananas. The image of the black woman as temptress has always been there in American society, either on the surface or just underneath, and it's certainly there in Europe as well. Like most professional women, Rice declines to flaunt her sexuality in the way she dresses and behaves. But neither does she choose frumpiness. She is always put together, conservatively but with a sense of individual style. I leave further judgment to the fashion columnists.

There's "Earth Mother of Us All," which buys into the idea of black women as uniquely nurturing, patient, forgiving, supportive, long-suffering—the notion that the black woman was put on Earth to atone for the sins of all the rest of us. (A subset image is "Nubian Queen.") Rice *destroys* this one. Whatever else you think of her, I can't imagine that, say, Jacques Chirac believes for one minute that she will be any warmer or more nurturing to him than her predecessor Colin Powell was.

There's "Black American Princess," and Rice flirts with this archetype—the piano lessons in her childhood, the figure skating, the doting parents. But she departs from the script by being drawn to football, not cheerleading, and by refusing to play damsel in distress no matter what the circumstances. She may take care with her fingernails, but she's not about to get upset if she breaks one.

Condoleezza Rice is nothing if not different. She's not a Democrat, though most African American women are. She's certainly not a liberal. She obviously is race-conscious, but she puts that consciousness into a box that's more deeply hidden than the one most of us African Americans use to store race when we're on the job. People see her walking next to President Bush and there are ugly snickers of the Jezebel sort; but when Rice is escorted at social events, it is usually by Gene Washington, the former professional football player, a black man.

She is, in short, sui generis—just like every black woman in America.

I don't give her a pass on her performance as national security adviser, and I hold her at least partly responsible for the lies the administration told about weapons of mass destruction in Iraq. Boxer was right to hold her feet to the fire. I can't applaud Rice when she pursues policies that I believe make us more vulnerable, not safer.

But I do recognize her achievement in confounding expectations that were long overdue to be confounded. And now maybe we can begin to see black women through a lens that's not colored or distorted, but crystal clear.

Source: © 2005, The Washington Post Writers Group. Reprinted with permission. This column originally appeared in *The Washington Post* on 8 February 2005.

Books by Eugene Robinson: *Coal to Cream: A Black Man's Journey Beyond Color to an Affirmation of Race* (New York: Free Press, 1999); *Last Dance in Havana* (New York: Free Press, 2004).

Further Readings: "Eugene Robinson." [Online]. The Washington Post Writers Group Web site www.postwritersgroup.com.

Robinson, Maxie (Max) Cleveland Jr. (1 May 1939–20 December 1988)

A pioneer in big-league television news, the late Max Robinson was the first African American to coanchor a network news program and the first to anchor a local news program in the nation's capital. A native of Richmond, Virginia, he was one of four children. His brother Randall became known for his work with the protest group TransAmerica. Max attended three institutions of higher learning: Oberlin College, Virginia Union University and Indiana University, but never completed a degree. His news career began early, at age 20, when, in 1959, he competed successfully with four whites for a job as a news reader for WTOV-TV in Portsmouth, Virginia. In those days of rampant segregation, the station obscured his face behind the station logo. One night he removed the logo so that his friends and relations could see that it really was him reading the news, and the next day he was fired for having done so. He moved to Washington, D.C., and in 1965, got a job as a floor director for WTOP-TV, which is now WUSA. From there, he moved to station WRC-TV, where he was a news reporter for three and a half years. He covered the riots that followed the 1968 assassination of Martin Luther King Jr. and various antiwar protests. He then returned to WTOP-TV in 1969 to become the first black anchor in Washington. Here, he coanchored with Gordon Peterson both the 6 PM and 11 PM broadcasts. In the early 1970s, when hostages were taken by militant Hanafi Muslims and held at the D.C. mosque, they would negotiate only with Max Robinson. Robinson opened himself up to physical risk by performing that task, which was similar to what columnist Chuck Stone was doing in Philadelphia. This role got Robinson interviewed by "60 Minutes," after which he was approached by ABC's president, Roone Arledge, to join the network's news operation as part of a new three-anchor experimental format. In 1978, Robinson became the first black network television anchor when he moved to Chicago and teamed with Frank Reynolds in Washington and Peter Jennings in London. His relationship with network executives became strained, however, when he repeatedly protested the way blacks were portrayed and how their viewpoints were ignored in newscasts. His problem with alcohol became worse, and his personality began to sour. He also got along poorly with Frank Reynolds, whom he considered imperious to underlings. After Reynolds died, the network in 1983 made Peter Jennings the sole weeknight anchor, and Robinson was moved to the weekend news anchor spot. Later that same year, he left the network to work as news anchor for Chicago's WMAQ-TV, but his personal problems continued. He left the station in 1985 and lived for the remainder of his life in a Chicago apartment on the fiftieth floor of Marina City Towers. On top of alcoholism and periodic depression, he contracted pneumonia in 1988 and at that time discovered that he also had AIDS. Robinson did not reveal how he had contracted AIDS, but said it was not because of homosexual or bisexual activity. He never went public about his condition because he did not like the idea of people snickering or speculating about his sex life. The suave, dapper Robinson had always been something of a ladies man and during his retirement, was visited by a woman friend who also had AIDS. Robinson had been married three times and had four children. In 2001, actor/writer/ comedian Aaron Freeman published an online account of Robinson's last days and his own role as the dying newsman's friend. Robinson died in Washington, D.C., after speaking at Howard University's School of Journalism. His final speech was about the indifference of the mainstream media to the bigotry that still remained and about the uncaring policies of the Reagan administration toward minorities. He checked into Howard University Hospital the following day and died there on 20 December 1988. At his funeral, Jesse Jackson delivered the eulogy, and Robinson's former coanchor Gordon Peterson also spoke. In 1992, the Max Robinson Center of the Whitman-Walker Clinic in Washington, D.C., began providing HIV/AIDS services to clients in that city.

Robinson won three Emmys: two in the late 1960s for his documentary "The Other Washington," which was about African-American life in the city, and one in 1980 for his presidential election coverage. He won journalist of the year awards from the Ohio Press Association and from the Capital Press Club, and he taught briefly as an adjunct faculty member at Washington's Federal City College and at the College of William and Mary in Williamsburg, Virginia.

Robinson's pioneering success in mainstream broadcasting provided important inspiration to the many black news figures who were soon to follow in his footsteps.

Further Readings: Freeman, Aaron. "The Last Days of Max Robinson." [Online, 2001]. Aaron Freeman Web site www.afreeman.com; "One of the Best of TV News, Max Robinson." [Online, 1 May 2005]. The African American Registry Web site www.aaregistry.com; Robinson, Mark Cabot. "Biography for Max Robinson." [Online]. IMDB site http://us.imdb.com.

Rodgers, Johnathan A. (18 January 1946–)

A journalist since 1967, Johnathan Rodgers is now the chief executive officer of cable television network TV-One. He was born into an Air Force family in San Antonio, Texas. After living in a number of places where his father was stationed, he finished high school in Rantoul, Illinois, in 1963. There he had been active on the school newspaper and had been a member of the wrestling squad. He again worked for the school paper, where he served as sports editor, at the University of California, Berkeley, and was quarterback of the football team. After graduating in 1967, he became the first African-American writer hired by *Sports Illustrated Magazine*. During 1967 and 1968, he covered college basketball and track and field, then later in 1968 and 1969, he was an urban affairs editor for *Newsweek*. He was drafted into the Army in 1969 and was stationed in South Carolina at Fort Jackson. He rose to the rank of sergeant, and when his period of service was satisfied in 1971, Rodgers enrolled in the communication master's program at Stanford University. Having graduated in 1973, he took a job in New York City as a writer and producer for station WNBC. The following year, he moved to Cleveland, Ohio, and for one year was a general assignment reporter for WKYC-TV. In 1975, he made the move to management when he again relocated to become assistant news director for CBS affiliate WBBM-TV in Chicago. He moved up in the network hierarchy to news director, general manager, CBS News executive producer and finally television station division president. He made another major career change in 1996, when he moved to Discovery Networks as president. Discovery properties include not only the Discovery Channel, but The Learning Channel, Discovery Civilization Channel, Discovery Science Channel, Discovery Health Channel, Discovery Kids Channel, Discovery en Espanol and more. Rodgers had a hand in reviving the Travel Channel and launching Animal Planet. His six years with Discovery saw the network grow substantially in number of viewers and the company's value increase from around $1 billion to $20 billion. Then in March 2003, he accepted the president and CEO position at TV-One, a new venture primarily backed by Comcast Cable and Radio One to target black viewers in the 24 through 54 age range with both lifestyle and entertainment programming. Other backers of TV-One were Constellation Ventures,

Opportunity Capital Partners and Pacesetter Capital Group. TV-One first aired in January 2004 and, like its Atlanta-based competitor Major Broadcasting Channel (now the Black Family Channel), is less youth-oriented than its much larger competitor Black Entertainment Television of Washington, D.C. TV-One is headquartered in Silver Spring, Maryland, north of Washington. Since its debut on Martin Luther King Jr. Day 2004, the new cable network has doubled its number of subscribers and has worked its way into 13 of the 25 largest U.S. urban markets. Rodgers' boss is Alfred C. Liggins III, CEO of parent company Radio One and a major media entrepreneur, having grown his company into the nation's largest radio group that targets African Americans. Rodgers and Liggins were introduced to one another by music great Quincy Jones. Both men recognize the tremendous potential of TV-One, inasmuch as African Americans, on the whole, watch significantly more television and listen to more radio than the general U.S. population and that nearly 70 percent are cable subscribers. They also know that the black community's viewing likes and dislikes differ from those of the general population, creating a large market for programming planned especially for them. The TV-One appeal is mainly geared to urban dwellers, and the music the network features avoids hip-hop and hard rock in favor of musical styles preferred by more mature viewers. As the new network moves toward profitability, only a modest amount of original production has been done; instead, TV-One offers a mix of sitcom and drama reruns, old movies, documentaries and lifestyle programs. The plan is to add more original programming as finances allow. Rodgers is a true believer in the power of television and in 2004, posed the speculation that without the graphic images the medium brought to mainstream America of snarling dogs, howling bigots and baton-wielding police juxtaposed with the passive resistance of civil rights demonstrators, the 1960s Civil Rights Movement itself might not have been able to succeed as well as it did.

Rodgers is on the boards of Proctor & Gamble, The Aspen Institute, the Emma Bowen Foundation, the National Association of Television Program Executives, the International Radio and Television Society, the Cable Television Advertising Bureau and the University of California—Berkeley Foundation. He is a member of the National Association of Black Journalists. While with the Discovery Channel, he was on the board of the Discovery Channel Education Fund, the purpose of which is to help bridge the divide both at home and abroad between people competent in information technology and those who have been left behind in the digital age. He has been identified by *CableFax Magazine* as the seventh most powerful figure in the U.S. cable industry.

Further Readings: Baker, Chris. "BET's Competition." [Online, 19 January 2004]. The Washington Times site http://washingtontimes.com/business; "Jonathan Rodgers." [Online]. The History Makers Web site www.thehistorymakers.com; Penrice, Ronda Racha. "Kings of Cable." [Online, 6 January 2004]. Black America Today Web site www.blackamericatoday.com; Shay, Kevin J. "Top Exec: Future Bright for TV One." [Online, 10 September 2004]. The Business Gazette Web site www.gazette.net.

Roker, Albert Lincoln (20 August 1954–)

Jovial, versatile Al Roker, often called the nation's favorite weatherman, is also a host of the country's most-watched morning talk program, the "Today" show, a celebrity interviewer and a host for various televised specials. He was born in the Queens section of New York City, worked during his last two college years as a weekend weatherman for WTVH-TV in Syracuse, New York, and earned his B.A. in communications at the State University of New York, Oswego, in 1976. After graduating, he took a job as weathercaster for WTTG-TV in the nation's capital and accepted a similar position in 1978 for WKYC-TV in Cleveland, Ohio. His work at those stations earned him a weekend weatherman job in New York City's WNBC in 1983. Portly and genial, Roker joined the staff of NBC's "Weekend Today Show" in 1987; in 1992, he began filling in for weatherman Willard Scott on "Today." In January 1996, Roker took Scott's place as weekday weatherman and feature reporter for "Today." In addition, he does a parenting segment called "Today's Dad," does cooking segments—he describes himself as a "foodie"—and conducts celebrity interviews on the show. More recently, he has produced and hosted a more serious, journalistic series of documentary specials titled "Al Roker Investigates," in which a more serious-faced Roker examines such issues as gang violence, hazing, mishandling or misinterpretation of DNA evidence at the Houston Police Department Crime Lab, and Internet dangers for young people. Finally, he is a host of holiday specials: the Macy's Thanksgiving Day Parade, the Christmas tree lighting at Rockefeller Center, the Rose Bowl Parade. The industrious and versatile Roker had his own talk show, "Al Roker," on CNBC and in the mid-1990s, was host of the MSNBC quiz show "Remember This?" Roker has often made guest appearances on other television shows, including the "Late Show with David Letterman," "Late Night with Conan O'Brien," "The Rosie O'Donnell Show," "Sesame Street," "Seinfeld," "Will and Grace," "Saturday Night Live" and "Mad About You."

In 1994, he launched his own multimedia production company, Al Roker Productions. Some of his productions have been a 1996 special on extreme weather, "Savage Skies"; a 1997 series of travel programs titled "Going Places"; and, in 2003, "Roker on the Road," on which he visited unusual people and places involved with cooking or eating. Others were "Al Roker's World of Weird Restaurants" and "Al Roker's Colonial Christmas." Also in the 1990s, Roker formed another business, RokerWare Inc., selling such items as t-shirts, bibs for babies, keychains, refrigerator magnets, umbrellas and caps, all bearing his name and logo; the items are sold online at AlRoker.com. Also sold on this Web site are the four books Roker has published. Two are about food, the other two, about fatherhood. Both topics are dear to Roker's heart. His love for the former led to gastric bypass surgery in 2002, after which he lost 99 pounds, from 320 to 221. The latter topic resulted from the two daughters and a son of Roker and his wife, "20/20" correspondent Deborah Roberts.

Roker is on the board of the Family AIDS Network and has been honorary chair of the Susan G. Komen Breast Cancer Foundation Race for the Cure. His work has been recognized by such organizations as the Ronald McDonald House, the Children's Defense Fund, the Harlem Boys Choir and the National Urban League Rainforest Alliance. He also has been awarded an honorary doctorate by his alma mater, SUNY, Oswego.

Books by Albert Lincoln Roker: *Don't Make Me Stop This Car: Adventures in Fatherhood* (New York: Scribner, 2000); *Al Roker's Big, Bad Book of Barbecue: 100 Easy Recipes for Backyard Barbecue and Grilling* (New York: Scribner, 2001); *Al Roker's Hassle-Free Holiday Cookbook* (New York: Scribner, 2003); *with Amy Rennert, Big Shoes: In Celebration of Dads and Fatherhood* (New York: Hyperion, 2005).

Further Readings: "Al Roker." *The African American Almanac*, 9th ed. Ed. by Jeffrey Lehman. Detroit, Mich.: Gale Group, 2003, pp. 881–82; "Al Roker." [Online]. Al Roker.Com Web site www.roker.com/bio; "Al Roker." [Online]. Internet Movie Database Inc. site http://us.imdb.com; "Bio: Al Roker." [Online]. Food Network Web site www.foodnetwork.com.

Rowan, Carl Thomas (11 August 1925–23 September 2000)

A major trail-blazer for African Americans in media jobs, Carl Rowan was a newspaperman since 1947, a columnist since 1965 and in between, held three high-ranking positions in federal government. He was born in Ravenscroft, Tennessee, and grew up in another Tennessee town, McMinnville. He was valedictorian of his all-black high school class in McMinnville, then moved to Nashville, where he had grandparents, hoping to go to Fisk University on a football scholarship. Fisk rejected his application, however, and by 1942 he had saved enough money to enroll at Tennessee A&I, now Tennessee State University. During his second year there, he took a Navy officers training examination, passed it, dropped out of school and caned chairs in McMinnville until he got his military orders and became one of the first 15 blacks to become commissioned officers in that branch of the service. Following training, he was deputy commander of communications on the USS *Chemung* during World War II. After his military obligation was complete, he enrolled at Oberlin College, where in 1947 he earned a journalism degree. His first employment was writing for the *Baltimore Afro-American* as a freelancer. He enrolled in the University of Minnesota master's program in journalism, and before completing his M.A. in 1948, wrote for the historically black *Minneapolis Spokesman* and *St. Paul Recorder*, then was the first African American to break the color barrier at the *Minneapolis Tribune*, initially as a copywriter. From 1950 through 1961 he was a *Tribune* general-assignment reporter.

In 1950, Rowan suggested to his editors that he travel the South to report on civil rights there from the minority point of view. During 1951 he logged around 6,000 miles as he visited 13 states, producing an award-winning series of 18 stories, "How Far from Slavery," that established him as a gifted reporter and that was turned into his first book, *South of Freedom*. McMinnville was one of his stops, and he must surely have taken satisfaction in writing a negative portrayal of the rigid segregation still practiced there. Later, he toured the South again for a second series of stories, "Jim Crow's Last Stand," which described several legal cases that led up to the 1954 Supreme Court decision in *Brown v. Board of Education*. A third series, "Dixie Divided," followed, this one about massive resistance. Rowan's scope became international in the early 1950s, when the *Tribune* sent him abroad to cover the Suez Canal crisis and the Soviet-suppressed Hungarian uprising. Then in 1954 he was invited by the U.S. State Department to visit India and other Asian nations as a lecturer on free press practices, while he simultaneously reported for the *Tribune* on Asian affairs and covered the Bandung, Indonesia, conference of smaller Asian nations. By this time his awards were many, his name was known nationally, and he had become the first black member of Washington's Gridiron Club.

Rowan left the *Tribune* in 1961 to become President John F. Kennedy's deputy assistant secretary for public affairs; as such, he was in charge of State Department press relations. In addition to his normal duties, he helped negotiate the release by the Soviet Union of downed U-2 spy plane pilot Francis Gary Powers in 1962, and he was the first black to be a member of the National Security Council. His success in government service not only continued, but increased during the Johnson administration. He had come to know Lyndon Johnson while traveling with him in Asia and Europe while Johnson was vice president. In 1963, President Johnson named Rowan U.S. Ambassador to Finland—the fifth African American to serve as an ambassador—and in 1964, Johnson convinced him to leave that position and take over from Edward R. Murrow as director of the United States Information Agency. In this capacity, he became the highest-ranking African American in federal service, and during the war in Vietnam, Rowan was in charge of psychological warfare initiatives, largely carried out through Voice of America. Rowan was accused of having become too politicized and, like so many other individuals in government, found President Johnson difficult to serve. Rowan once remarked that nothing you could say about Johnson was so bad or so good that it wouldn't be true at one time or another. In one of his disagreements with the president in 1965, Rowan resigned and soon returned to journalism, becoming a thrice-weekly columnist for the *Chicago Daily News*, taking a commentary job with Westinghouse Broadcasting Company and becoming a roving editor for *Reader's Digest*. His *Daily News* column was syndicated to about 180 papers via the Publishers-Hall Syndicate; a personal staff of seven helped him meet all these obligations. Publishers-Hall morphed into the Field Newspaper Syndicate. Later, Rowan was handled by the North America Syndicate, and until his death, was with King Features. He spent approximately three decades as a panelist on the PBS show "Inside Washington," retiring from that job in 1996. Also, he crossed swords with such prominent conservatives as James J. Kilpatrick and George Will on "Agronsky & Co". and made frequent appearances on "Meet the Press."

Rowan's career was crowned by many triumphs. He had, in 1956, been denied entry into South Africa to report on conditions there, but in 1970, the now-famous columnist was able to enter the country to report on the already failing policy of apartheid. He won award after award and was recognized with around forty honorary degrees. Yet his career path was not without its rough spots. In addition to his difficulties with Lyndon Johnson, he had a falling out with Martin Luther King, largely over King's stance against the war in Vietnam. Rowan criticized King in his column and in a widely read *Reader's Digest* article in which he accused King of tripping over his own ego and of going too far by calling the United States the world's greatest purveyor of violence. His attack on King led to counterattacks by other prominent black leaders, such as Andrew Young, who called Rowan an "Uncle Tom." Later, Rowan wondered aloud if the FBI had been involved with King's assassination and in 1969 called for the resignation of that agency's long-time director, J. Edgar Hoover. He was proud of being on Richard Nixon's infamous enemies list, and still later in his career, Rowan remarked that only nitwits could support Reaganomics. He considered himself a moderate and a political independent—he found Jimmy Carter a weak president and clearly disliked most Republicans who occupied the White House—and he warned of a change in media commentary by which purveyors of hate were spreading paranoia throughout the nation.

Rowan's primarily political column addressed a wealth of issues and made him both friends and enemies. He unflinchingly took on gut issues such as capital punishment, which he was against. At his most pessimistic, he wrote his last book in 1996 during the period of racial polarization that followed the murder trial of former football great O.J. Simpson; the book's title was *The Coming Race War in America*. A 1997 column detailing the system of "assembly line justice" that made Texas the nation's leader in public executions made him few friends in that state, and columns like the one from 1998 reproduced below surely lowered his popularity in the tobacco states of the South. One of his most difficult moments came in 1988, when Rowan, an advocate of gun control, shot and wounded in the wrist a young man who had been swimming uninvited in Rowan's pool and who apparently tried to enter his house. The pistol Rowan used belonged to his older son, a former FBI agent. Rowan was charged with firing an unregistered weapon but escaped punishment due to a deadlocked jury. A major professional setback came in 1999, when his longtime employer, the *Sun-Times*, changed ownership and apparently forced him out. Rowan sued for $1 million, alleging that his column had been discontinued because he was too old, too black and too liberal. Management disputed his account of what had occurred, claiming that Rowan had quit voluntarily. The matter was settled out of court after the *Sun-Times* agreed to donate $250,000 to Rowan's "Project Excellence" scholarship program for African-American youths in the nation's capital. By the time of Rowan's death in 2000, this charity had awarded nearly $30 million for college study to around 1,150 young people. Funding had come from Washington businesses, universities, moneyed individuals and, according to a column by Milton Coleman in 2000, the winnings of a race horse named "Just Call Me Carl." Rowan developed diabetes and toward the end of his life, had one leg amputated at the knee due to complications from that disease. He died in the intensive care unit of the Washington Hospital Center at age 75.

Among Rowan's early awards and honors were the 1952 Sidney Hillman Award for newspaper reporting, the 1955 American Teamwork Award given by the National Urban League, and the 1964 Communications Award given by the Anti-Defamation League of the advocacy and service organization B'nai B'rith. Also in 1964, he won the Capital Press Club's Distinguished Service Award and the National Brotherhood Award from the National Conference of Christians and Jews. In 1968, he received the Elijah P. Lovejoy Award from Colby College, and in 1997, the Springarn Medal from the NAACP. Rowan was accorded the National Press Foundation's Distinguished Contribution to Journal honor in 1998 and the National Press Club's Fourth Estate Award in 1999.

"Ban Tobacco Like Marijuana and Cocaine" by Carl Rowan

"Cocaine has been good. We paid for our mansion off cocaine. We educated our kids off cocaine. We paved our old driveway with blacktop off cocaine. We pay our property taxes. We pay the preacher on Sunday morning. We overhaul our vehicles, and we buy tires. We pay our insurance. And we pay our mules and runners, and give them Social Security and Medicare. And we just try to live right and do right off cocaine."

Replace the word "cocaine" with "tobacco" and you pretty much have the emotional speech that tobacco farmer Mattie Mack gave to President Clinton in Brandenburg, Ky., Thursday.

"Aw, come on," you say, "tobacco is legal and cocaine is not, and you can't compare the two."

That's my point. I can compare them in terms of the damage they do to their addicted users, but I can't compare their legal status. Yet I know that there will be no solution to the curse of tobacco in this society until it is banned just like marijuana and cocaine are, and there probably won't be a solution even then.

I never believed last summer that the tobacco companies would pay $368.5 billion and accept the terms of the sate attorneys general, of the president and Congress, and of the health-care industry just to stay in business with curtailed prosperity. Tobacco is such a golden goose that I knew the industry would find some excuse... like Sen. John McCain, R-Ariz., raising the payment to $516 billion over 25 years... to say that it would rather fight than switch.

Clinton said in Kentucky Thursday, "I do not want to put the tobacco companies out of business. I do want to put them out of the business of selling cigarettes to teen-agers."

The tobacco tycoons have always known that if they can't sell cigarettes to teen-agers, they are putting themselves out of business. A 14-year-old who reaches 24 without smoking is very unlikely to take up the filthy, killing habit.

That is why tobacco industry leaders have lied to America for generations about the deliberate boosting of nicotine levels, the ad campaigns targeted at teen-agers, the special lures for minority members. The tobacco industry knows where survival and prosperity lie. And that is why the tobacco bosses have brazenly declared war on legislation that would increase the cost of cigarettes sharply by raising taxes on tobacco products;

would give the Food and Drug Administration power to regulate the levels off additive nicotine in tobacco products; and restrict drastically the advertising and marketing practices of tobacco companies.

Big Tobacco has taken a colossal gamble that farmers like Mack, the millions of people who already are hooked on nicotine and the Republican Party will rise up and help them to maintain something close to the status quo. The tobacco moguls seem to think that handing out a few billion dollars in campaign contributions and sugar-coated bribes will provide more protection than any $516 billion settlement.

But recent exposes of perfidy by the tobacco industry, and revelations of the health tragedies by tobacco, have made it politically impossible for Republicans to provide the shelter that the tobacco industry expects.

So there will be legislation. But it probably won't be the "new Prohibition." It will be tough enough to make a lot of farmers think off growing collard greens, and force a lot of tobacco company employees to look for work elsewhere. But it won't put tobacco in the same pipe with cocaine. So a semi-black market for tobacco will arise, the health problems will endure, and our politicians will wring their hands and give more speeches.

And all the hopes of protecting teen-agers, and of using tobacco settlement money for noble causes, will go up in schoolyard smoke.

Source: Reprinted with permission of King Features Syndicate. The column originally appeared on 10 April 1998 © King Features Syndicate.

Books by Carl Thomas Rowan: *South of Freedom* (New York: Knopf, 1952); *The Pitiful and the Proud* (New York: Random House, 1956); *Go South to Sorrow* (New York: Random House, 1957); with Jackie Robinson, *Wait Till Next Year: The Life Story of Jackie Robinson* (New York: Random House, 1960); *Just Between Us Blacks* (New York: Random House, 1974); *Breaking Barriers: A Memoir* (Boston: Little, Brown, 1991); *Dream Makers, Dream Breakers: The World of Justice Thurgood Marshall* (Boston: Little, Brown, 1993); *The Coming Race War in America: A Wake-up Call* (Boston: Little, Brown, 1996).

Further Readings: Astor, David. "Rowan: 3 Strikes and He Was Out." *Editor & Publisher*, 3 July 1999, p. 6; Bynum, Lynn. *Carl T. Rowan, Journalist Extraordinary*. Bloomington, Ind.: Afro-American Arts Institute, Indiana University, 1975; Coleman, Milton. "Carl's Kids." the *Washington Post*, 26 September 2000, p. A27; Gates, Henry Louis Jr. and Evelyn Brooks Higginbotham. "Rowan, Carl Thomas." *African American Lives*. New York: Oxford University Press, 2004, pp. 731–33; Grauer, Neil A. *Wits & Sages*. Baltimore & London: Johns Hopkins University Press, 1984, pp. 195–212; Lusk, Marvin T. Jr. "Carl Thomas Rowan: a Black Columnist and his Philosophy: Based upon an Investigation of Some of His Writings." M.A. thesis, Tennessee State University, 1978; Matusow, Barbara. "Visible Man." *Washingtonian* 30 (Fall 1995): 44–49; Stein, M.L. "Carl T. Rowan." *Blacks in Communications: Journalism, Public Relations and Advertising*. New York: Julian Messner, pp. 43–46.

Russell, Mark E. (1942–)

After a long career at the *Plain Dealer* in Cleveland, Mark Russell became managing editor of the *Orlando Sentinel* in 2004. He hails from St. Louis, Missouri, and is a 1984 graduate of the University of Missouri School of Journalism, which he attended after having gone through the journalism workshop for black high school youth founded by George E. Curry and run by the Greater St. Louis Association of Black Journalists. While at the university, he was on the reporting staff of the *Columbia Missourian*. His best course, he has said, was basic reporting, and among his most treasured college memories was the late-night work at the campus paper, often followed by even later sessions at a local bar. He credits his late father with having given him discipline and his mother, an optimistic view of his fellow man and the gift of gab. Before deciding on a career in journalism, he had wanted to be a football player or a banker. From 1987 to 1993, Russell was on the staff of the *Plain Dealer*, at first as a business reporter and later on the city desk. He became assistant city editor, then left the paper in 1993 to serve as assistant metropolitan editor of the *Boston Globe*. He returned to the *Plain Dealer* in 1995 as assistant managing editor/metro. He was promoted to managing editor in October 2004 and as such, is responsible for all news operations for Ohio's biggest newspaper, including editing, photography, graphics and media convergence efforts. An example of the latter activity is the paper's use by some reporters of TypePad for live-blogging. In a profile written for the journalism school at Russell's alma mater, he said that the project he was most proud of during his career was a series of three *Plain Dealer* stories that investigated the physical and mental health of less-privileged children in northeastern Ohio.

Today, Russell is on the advisory board of his old journalism school at the University of Missouri. He is an advisory board member for the Institute for Advanced Journalism Studies at North Carolina Agricultural & Technical State University and is a member of the National Association of Black Journalists and the National Association of Minority Media Executives. He also served as a judge in the 2006 Best of Cox journalism competition.

Further Readings: "Mark Russell." [Online, 23 January 2006]. University of Missouri School of Journalism site http://journalism.missouri.edu/alumni; Prince, Richard. [Online, 5 October 2004]. Richard Prince's Journal-isms. Maynard Institute Web site www.maynardije.org.

S

Samuel, Terence (29 May 1962–)

Perhaps best known for his reporting in *U.S. News & World Report* in the early years of the new century, Terence Samuel is now Director of News Programming for news, sports and finance and a writer for AOL Black Voices. He also writes for the *American Prospect* online. He was born in Port of Spain, Trinidad, and after finishing high school, moved to New York City. He attended City College of New York, where he majored in English with a second concentration in communications, graduating in 1984. While a junior and senior, he worked as a writing fellow at the *Village Voice* in New York. Samuel's first job following graduation was as Bedford County reporter for the *Roanoke Times & World News* (now the *Roanoke Times*) in Virginia; he worked there from 1984 until 1988, when he took a new job at the *Philadelphia Inquirer*. There, he began on a suburban beat, then was a general assignment reporter in the city, was for four years a national correspondent working out of New York City, and finally was a banking reporter for that paper. In 1997 he took a third newspaper job, this time as a Washington correspondent for the *St. Louis Post-Dispatch*, writing on urban affairs and racial issues and he remained there until 2000. He entered news magazine work for *U.S. News & World Report* at that time as its chief congressional correspondent. Samuel took a break in the spring of 2003 to be a research fellow at Harvard's Joan Shorenstein Center for the Press and Public Policy. He began writing commentaries for the *American Prospect*'s online edition in fall 2003 and continued to write for *U.S. News* until October 2005 when the magazine began handing out pink slips to some of its writers, including Samuel and chief political correspondent Roger Simon. Since that time, Samuel has been with AOL Black Voices.

Samuel belongs to the International Association of Black Journalists, the City College Communication Alumni Association and that college's Varsity Association. He has been inducted into both the City College Alumni Hall of Fame and that college's Communication Hall of Fame.

As a new *U.S. News* correspondent in 2000, Samuel wrote about liberal California congresswoman Maxine Waters and her dismay over Al Gore's choice of Joe Lieberman as his vice presidential running mate. Four years later, he wrote for the *American Prospect* about what he described as an endangered political species thought to be practically—extinct: the hopeful Democrat. Other topics for that same outlet were 2004 attacks on Sen. Arlen Specter by his fellow Republicans for not having been right-wing enough and the efforts of Barack Obama to become the third African American to be elected to the U.S. Senate since Reconstruction. For *U.S. News*, Samuel produced long accounts of the Bush-Kerry battle for the White House and a profile of Utah's Sen. Harry Reid. In 2005, he wrote more than once about the importance of public relations in the Bush administration's efforts to privatize Social Security. The frequent use of the nation's bankruptcy laws was another of his topics, as was the low, inadequate federal minimum wage. In 2006, the aftermath of Hurricane Katrina was a major subject of his writing for the *American Prospect*, and in another story written for that Web site, Samuel described President Bush as "The Procrastinator-in-Chief." Another 2006 story was about presidential advisor Karl Rove and his continuing ability to find red herrings to drag across the trail of inconvenient news stories of real consequence. Still another favorite topic for Samuel was the gathering public angst caused by high gasoline prices.

"The Outrage Gap" by Terence Samuel

Bob Dole could not have been the first one to ponder the question, but he was on to something when he asked of his fellow Americans: "Where's the outrage?"

Back then, during the 1996 presidential campaign, the country was at peace, the economy was roaring along, President Clinton was talking about building a bridge to the 21st century—whatever the hell that meant—and he was thinking about how to improve race relations in America.

So what if there were skeletons in his closet waiting to come out. There was a feeling that the guy was trying to move the country somewhere, even if he only wanted to take baby steps. So the answer to Dole's question was a shrug, he lost the election, and Clinton's approval ratings stayed high, even when revelations tumbled out of the White House and he got impeached.

President Bush's approval ratings have begun to resemble his waist size, so we know people are tired of him and his way of doing things. But weary voters are not the same as angry voters. These two types of voters don't behave the same way, and Democrats who are counting on the deepening disenchantment with Bush to take them over the top in November need to pay close attention.

Even as the case grows stronger that Bush led us into an expensive, pointless war that was undertaken under a veil of deception, miscalculation and hubris, Americans remain disengaged. Immigration is generating more heat than a bad war and the almost 2,500 body bags that have come home from it.

And while it's increasingly clear that the Republican revolution has devolved into a carnival of self-dealing and self-interest with utter disregard for the public good, Americans are not on edge, polls say. Almost 70 percent of the public believes the country is on the wrong track, according to an AP-Ipsos poll. And even more of those polled, nearly 90 percent, say political corruption is a serious problem. But despair is not driving any action. Americans might be sick and tired, but are they pissed off? Not so much. We're leaving that to the French.

Gas prices continue to rise, and here is where the monster might begin to stir, because when it takes $46 to fill up a Camry, outrage is overdue. The only thing we know for sure is that immigrants and their boosters are a little more miffed than everyone else, and the GOP keeps feeding their anger with one dumb move after another. But everyone else, it seems, has decided to take the bad with the worse. And those who are angry are mad at both sides. Half of independents think the Democratic and Republican parties are equally corrupt, according to the AP-Ipsos poll. This is the textbook definition of cynicism, and Democrats need to be careful that it does not define a fall campaign in which everyone decides to stay home.

After the 2005 elections, when Democrats won governor's races in New Jersey and Virginia, Democratic strategist Cornell Belcher described a very anxious, "on the cusp of being angry" electorate on the fence. These people could go either way, if they show up at all.

Of course, there are those who say there is anger in spades out there and that April 2006 is different from November 2005. "I think we are about to reach the tipping point," says Democratic pollster and strategist Anna Greenberg. "The war in Iraq combined with the scandal, combined with the wiretapping, have left people incredibly frustrated, and they don't see any way out of it, and I think that is the kind of environment that can produce a 1994 kind of result." The Republicans took control of Congress that year, overturning a 40-year Democratic majority.

Greenberg is careful to say that she is not predicting how the election is going to turn out, because so much can change. "This is just a snapshot in time, but if you look at the polls, there may be 40 house seats in play—second-tier seats that you would never think of as being in play are in play."

Democratic National Committee chairman Howard Dean said this week he is looking to generate a wave that can allow Democrats to take back the House. To that end, Dean thinks Democrats need to nationalize the 2006 election and tie Republican candidates to the distemper the White House has engendered in Americans. "We have to have a national message that will play in every district," Dean said.

In general, Greenberg agrees: "Having a nationalized context for this campaign is very important, and it has to have an economic framework and a national security framework." She believes other Democratic advantages are obvious. Using immigration as the example, she said: "No one agrees with [the Republicans] on their approach to any of the issues."

Voters are with Democrats—all that's left is to make them mad enough to vote against the other side in November.

Source: This story appeared on 14 April 2006 in *The American Prospect* Online Edition. It appears here by permission of *The American Prospect*.

Further Readings: Kurtz, Howard. "U.S. News Gives a Top Political Writer the Pink Slip." [Online, 5 October 2005]. Washington Post Web site (www.washingtonpost.com); "Shorenstein Center Names Spring Fellows." [Online]. Harvard University Web site (www.hno.harvard.edu/gazette/2003).

Sanford, Otis L. (1953–)

A pleasant, scholarly looking man, Otis Sanford has been managing editor of the *Commercial Appeal* in Memphis, Tennessee, since October 2002. He was born in Como, Mississippi, attended Northwest Mississippi Community College and became the first African American to be granted a scholarship to study journalism at the University of Mississippi. He graduated from Ole Miss in 1975 and went to work for the *Commercial Appeal*, at first as a copy clerk and later as a reporter. He was the paper's assistant metro editor before he accepted a new job as assistant city editor of the *Pittsburgh Press* in 1987. He moved again to become deputy city editor of the *Detroit Free Press*, then returned to the *Commercial Appeal* in 1994 as deputy managing editor. Eight years later, he was elevated to managing editor, replacing Henry Stokes, who left the job to become assistant to the paper's publisher.

Sanford was honored in 1999 as Northwest Mississippi Community College's Alumnus of the Year and the following year was inducted into the University of Mississippi Alumni Hall of Fame. Also in 2000, he won the William R. Burleigh Award for Distinguished Community Service, an honor named for the retired CEO of The E.W. Scripps Company and given by the Memphis Chamber of Commerce. In 2005, he spoke at Rust College, the school his mother had attended, and was given the school's Journalism Trail Blazer Award. He is a member of the National Association of Black Journalists and helped found a local chapter of that organization in University, Mississippi. In September 1999, Sanford spoke to Ole Miss journalism students as a NABJ representative. He has also been an active member of the American Society of Newspaper Editors and in October 2004, was elected to a three-year term on the APME board. As of 2006, he is also vice chair of the APME First Amendment Committee. Unlike the many "Chicken Little theorists" who predict the demise of the printed media, Sanford believes that newspapers will continue to be an important medium for analysis of public affairs and for in-depth reporting. At the *Appeal*, in cooperation with the Memphis school system, he has been instrumental in publishing a youth newspaper, the *Teen Appeal*, and he has helped organize training for young, aspiring journalists in his city.

Further Readings: "Memphis Commercial Appeal Names Editor." [Online, 9 October 2002]. Editor & Publisher Web site www.editorandpublisher.com; Nesmith, Lydia Katherine. "'Leadership Role Requires Sacrifice'—Otis Sanford, Managing Editor, The Commercial Appeal." [Online, 24 April 2005]. The Rustorian Web site www.rustorian.com; Sullenberger, Amy. "Otis Sanford, ME of Commercial Appeal, to Receive Silver Em Award." [Online, 23 March 2005]. BlackJournalist.com Web site ww.blackjournalist.com/kudos.

Saunders, Barry (c.1958–)

Since 1993, readers of the *News & Observer* in Raleigh, North Carolina, have enjoyed the bold, saucy column of bow tie and bowler hat wearing Barry Saunders. Born in Rockingham, N.C., he is a graduate of Morehouse College. In a 2004 column, he mentioned that he had once considered honoring Martin Luther King Jr. by becoming a preacher, but, having discovered his fondness for women and liquor, he decided it would be more meaningful to honor the

Rev. King by not becoming a preacher. Saunders has published—a collection of his columns as a book.

In the city where Jesse Helms held sway before his long run in the U.S. Senate, Barry Saunders functions somewhat as the "Anti-Helms." Just prior to the summer 2005 arrival in bookstores of Helms' autobiography, Saunders accused the senator of trying to reinvent himself as a moderate, remarking that Mr. Helms had always appeared to view integration the way a snail views an overturned salt shaker. In a column many years earlier, Saunders suggested that Helms had possibly read the book *Roots* backwards so that it could have a happy ending for him, a line that just might be the funniest criticism of the senator ever written.

Prodding sacred cows is a Saunders specialty. The column reproduced below dared to suggest that people should let Martin Luther King Day 2000 pass without any readings of the "I have a dream" speech. The columnist's point was that America needs to recognize that King said a lot more than what he uttered in that one speech. In the same column, Saunders lauded author Michael Eric Dyson, who in his book *I May Not Get There with You: The True Martin Luther King, Jr.* (New York: Free Press, 2000), urged that when writing or speaking about King, we should not deify or Disneyfy him, but present him as the real, fallible human being he was. As to national politics, Saunders is caustic in his criticism of President Bush and the Iraq war, saying that due to the war's apparent pointlessness, he wishes that each time he sees a returning veteran with missing limbs, he could grab the president and Donald Rumsfeld by their collars and admonish them, "Now see what you have done." He was appalled, as well, with the $40 million bacchanalian with which President Bush ushered in his second term, and by the Soviet-style way protesters were kept out of sight of the parade route. Saunders' suggestion for a way to celebrate 4 July 2005, was when grilling out, to invite the family of some member of the armed services now serving in Iraq or Afghanistan.

Of the many African-American columnists upset by the media wallow over the missing white teenager Natalee Holloway whereas missing black girls typically get miniscule coverage, none delivered their criticism as clearly as did Saunders. He noted that the rule of journalistic coverage used to be "If it bleeds, it leads." Now, he added, it was more nearly, "If she ain't white and cute, we don't give a hoot."

Saunders was also upset over the 2004 story of Joseph Scarino, brutally beaten by a 295-pound man in an Akron, Ohio, pizza parlor while not one of several onlookers intervened, called the police or even glanced up from their pizza. People's tendency toward road rage; phony diploma mills at which, he remarked, the only book you have to crack is your checkbook; and the North Carolina State Fair paying instant singing star Clay Aiken $100,000 for a concert also drew Saunders' ire. Something of a contrarian, he has noted with pride that he has never once danced the Electric Slide, watched "American Idol" or bought a Michael Bolton record. He mourned the closing of a notorious strip club called Brothers III in Durham, where Saunders lives, and remarked on the irony of Duke University, a school built by tobacco money, accepting a grant to further cessation of smoking, which, he pointed out in his accustomed style, was like a pimp financing the promotion of sexual abstinence. A 2006 column in which his penchant for humor blossomed into multiple puns involved a proposal that would declare the peach the state fruit of Alabama. His approach to the topic was that the proposal had "pitted" Georgia, the Peach State, against interloper Alabama, and as the proposal was debated, he wrote, the controversy "ripened."

"A Dream of Banning the Speech" by Barry Saunders

I have a dream that I can make it through this whole day without hearing "I Have a Dream."

I don't want to hear some precocious 6-year-old in a school play recite Dr. Martin Luther King Jr.'s speech, nor do I want to hear it on BET when that network takes a pause from airing its daily staple of as-close-as-you-can-get-to-X-rated music videos to "honor" Dr. King.

Chill, Homes. I haven't been kidnapped by some cult and had my brain replaced by Jesse Helms'.

I am just sick and tired of having that speech trotted out yearly, as though it is the only thing King ever said. The speech, the greatest oration ever, now packs about the same emotional wallop as "We Shall Overcome," the anachronistic theme song of the civil rights era: none.

Both, through a combination of overuse, misuse and misappropriation, have been rendered meaningless, almost powerless, because they allow some people to think that merely listening to either and nodding solemnly in the appropriate places makes them a Rosa Parks-like freedom fighter.

That's crap. While criticizing Dr. King's speech will strike some as blasphemous—it would've struck me the same way a few years ago—and invites vituperation upon my head, I mean the big guy no disrespect. The Roman Catholic Church recently named him a candidate for martyrdom, and I'd be the first to say King deserves that and any other honor that can be bestowed upon him.

Criticizing anything about the dude is not something I do lightly, and I wouldn't be doing it now if someone else hadn't done it first.

That someone was the Rev. Michael Eric Dyson. Surely y'all remember Dyson. He is the former University of North Carolina faculty member, now at DePaul University, who had tassels spinning after bravely and justifiably criticizing Michael Jordan at a UNC graduation ceremony.

Dyson is now taking aim, albeit lovingly, I'd say, at the brightest star in black America's firmament. Among other things, he is calling for a 10-year moratorium on "The Speech."

Dyson, who is touring the country promoting his new book on King—"I May Not Get There With You"—feels that the King we purport to honor today bears little resemblance to the one who gave his life for his beliefs.

Dyson and I missed connections all weekend, but in an interview with another reporter, he railed against the "namby-pamby, We-are-the-world-Michael Jackson—and I could add Quincy Jones" revisionist image of King as a "safe Negro" who merely traveled around making eloquent speeches. "Dr. King wasn't killed because he had a dream," Dyson reminds us.

Nowhere in these almost-cartoonish images, Dyson declares, is the King who vehemently opposed the Vietnam War, urged civil disobedience and even favored reparations for descendants of slaves. Dyson bravely writes about the adulterous and plagiarizing King, as well as the one that FBI Director J. Edgar Hoover called "the most dangerous man in America."

Far from diminishing King, Dyson's discomfitingly honest, three-dimensional portrayal is infinitely better than the deification—Disneyfication?—of King to which we are usually subjected on this day. Happy Birthday, Doc.

Source: This column appeared on 17 January 2000 and is reprinted here by permission of The News & Observer of Raleigh, North Carolina.

Books by Barry Saunders: *Do Unto Others and Then Run: A Collection of Columns* (Raleigh, N.C.: News & Observer Publishing Co., 2000).

Saunders, Warner (30 January 1935–)

Now a part-time news anchor for Chicago's NBC owned and operated station WMAQ-TV, Warner Saunders has enjoyed a long broadcast journalism career in his home city. He underwent cancer surgery in 2005. He was born in Chicago, holds a 1957 bachelors from Xavier University and earned a masters at Northeastern University in 1970. When Saunders hit the job market, there were precious few media jobs for black Americans. He was helped into his first media job by a Chicago disc jockey, Holmes "Daddy-o" Daylie of WMAQ radio, in 1968. Saunders was working at the time as executive director of the Better Boys Foundation in Chicago, and when Daylie was asked to plan and host a public affairs show for the city's African-American audience following the assassination of the Rev. Martin Luther King Jr. on April 4 of that year, Daylie invited Saunders to be his cohost on the Channel 7 program. Producer of the show was pioneering black newsman Vernon Jarrett, now deceased but well remembered, especially for his columns in the Chicago Sun-Times. The new show was titled "For Blacks Only," and although management originally intended it to run as a one-time special, response was so positive that WSL-TV kept it on the air until 1979. Saunders left the show in 1972 to become director of community affairs and host of the program "Common Ground" for rival station WBBM-TV. In 1982, he moved to WMAQ-TV Channel 5 as a sports reporter/anchor and covered sports until 1989. In 1990, he became a WMAQ news anchor and cohost of the station's morning show "Chicago Alive." He coanchored the 4:30 PM news on weekdays and in June 1995, moved to cohost the 5 PM news show. He reported from South Africa early in 1990 on Nelson Mandela's release from prison; some of Saunders' work appeared in the documentary "South Africa: What Happens to a Dream Deferred?" He also was host of a public affairs talk show that bore his name, "Warner," from 1983 to 1990 and a magazine show, "You." Later, Saunders took over as coanchor of the 6 PM and 10 PM news. Health problems have caused him to scale back to a part-time schedule. Doctors had discovered a cancerous tumor in his intestines in 2002, for which he received chemo treatments, and his condition finally required surgery in 2005.

Saunders has taught as an adjunct faculty member or lecturer at the National College of Education, Indiana University in Gary and Northeastern University and has lectured as part of the Medill School of Journalism's Crain Lecture Series at Northwestern University. He is on his station's cultural diversity teaching team and has donated time at the Greenbelt Cultural Community Center in North Chicago with an educational program for pupils in grades four through six. He is an honorary board member of the organization Family Focus. A man with a very warm smile, Saunders has been sought out for a few appearances on entertainment television, playing news anchor roles, and has played a role in a one movie. In the movie "Ali," released in 2001, he had a bit role as a customer; he was an anchorman in episodes of "ER" in 1995, 1996 and 2003 and on "The West Wing" in 2000.

Saunders' recognitions have been many. Over the years, he has won 18 local Emmy awards. One of these, in 1980, was for a special titled "Gangs: The New Chicago Mob?" He won Emmy awards for his sports coverage in 1985 and 1986 plus the 1984 Media Award given by the Chicago Association of Black Journalists. An Emmy award in 1988–1989 was for cohosting a series on race issues in Chicago; another, in 1992–1993, was for the half-hour special "Can't Get No Job Without No Degree." His show "Warner" once received the Illinois Broadcasters Association Public Service Award. In 1993, he was inducted into the Chicago Journalism Hall of Fame and in 1994, was a Silver Circle honoree of the Chicago Academy of Television Arts and Sciences. In 1999, he was given the Hull House Jane Addams Award for his extensive community involvement. Two of his stories from early 2005 were about the arrest of Edgar Ray Killen, charged with a Ku Klux Klan murder in 1964, and on the political rising star Sen. Barack Obama of Illinois, whose family home remains in Chicago. In October 2005, Saunders was keynote speaker at the Diversity and Inclusion Days' inaugural event in Chicago, and in April 2006, he and Allison Rosati were emcees of the Jefferson Awards held in the city's NBC Tower. He is a past president of the Chicago Association of Black Journalists.

Further Readings: "NBC5's Warner Saunders: 'Choose Hope Over Despair.'" [Online, 26 April 2002]. NBC5 News Web site www.nbc5.com; Smith, Norine L. "Channel 5's Warner Saunders from Activist to Anchor." [Online, March 1992]. The Chicago Reporter Web site www.chicagoreporter.com; "Warner Saunders." [Online, 27 March 2006]. NBC5 Web site www.nbc5.com; "Warner Sounders." [Online]. The History Makers Web site www.thehistorymakers.com.

Scarbrough, Neal T. (c.1962–)

Former *Denver Post* sportswriter Neal Scarbrough became a senior editor of *ESPN The Magazine* in 2000; was named vice president and executive editor of ESPN.com in 2003; switched to vice president and news editor of ESPN in 2005; and in April 2006, left ESPN to become general manager and editor of sports for AOL. He is a friendly and rather academic looking man. He is a 1984 journalism graduate of the University of Colorado, and he began his career as a copy editor at the *Denver Post*. He held that same position at the *Sacramento Bee* and *Newsday* before becoming national editor of the *National Sports Daily*. From there, Scarbrough became night sports editor of the *Seattle Times* and later moved to be assistant sports editor of the *Chicago Sun-Times*. He was promoted to deputy metro editor of the *Sun-Times* but left to work as assistant managing editor/sports of the *Tennessean*, in Nashville. He returned in 1997 to the newspaper where he had begun his career, the *Denver Post*, as that paper's sports editor, holding that job for about four years until joining *ESPN The Magazine* to work under editor-in-chief John Papanek. Scarbrough was promoted to his present position roughly three years thereafter. By September 2004, he was able to proclaim ESPN.com the nation's number one Web site for sports, thanks largely to the ability of viewers to personalize what they get on the site and to the site's new video offerings. Scarbrough worked out of ESPN headquarters in Bristol, Connecticut. In April 2005, he joined the ESPN Remote Production Unit as vice president and news editor. His most recent move was in April 2006, when he accepted the job of general manager and editor of sports for AOL Sports, working under AOL news and sports editor-in-chief Lewis D'Vorkin.

Scarbrough is Region one director of the National Association of Black Journalists and in 2002, was a member of that organization's Sports Task Force. He was one of the reasons ESPN has won Online Journalism awards for general excellence, commentary and specialty journalism. In 1999, he was named Print Journalist of the Year by the Colorado Association of Black Journalists. In 2005, he lectured as the Hearst New Media professional-in-residence at the Columbia University Graduate School of Journalism.

Further Readings: "Neal T. Scarborough Joins ESPN The Magazine as Senior Editor." [Online, 14 April 2000]. The Write News Web site www.writenews.com; Wynn, Ron. "Neal Scarbrough Makes Sports History." *The Tennessee Tribune*, 8 August 1995.

Scott, Stuart (19 July 1965–)

Sportscaster Stuart Scott is best known for his work as a hip-talking coanchor for ESPN's "SportsCenter." His frequent use of ebonic hip-hop jargon has probably made him the most polarizing sportscaster on television; people seem to either love or hate his catch-phrase banter. He was born in Chicago and is a 1987 graduate of the University of North Carolina at Chapel Hill, where he majored in speech communication and radio, television, film. His earliest work in sports journalism came during his college years as a sports reporter for student station WXYC-FM. He was a news reporter and weekend sports anchor for the Florence, South Carolina, station WPDE-TV from 1987 to 1988 and worked from 1988 to 1990 as a news reporter in Raleigh, North Carolina, for WRAL-TV. From 1990 to 1993, he was a sports reporter/anchor for WESH-TV in Orlando, Florida. Then in August 1993, he joined the staff of ESPN2 shortly before it aired, starting as an anchor of "SportSmash." A year later he became cohost of another ESPN2 program, "Sports Night," and in 1995, he became the first black male anchor of "SportsCenter," an ESPN show that had appeared daily since the network's founding in September 1979. By 2002, 25,000 episodes of "SportsCenter" had appeared, which probably set a record for television shows of all kinds. What Scott—"Double S" to some of his fans—brought to the program was a relaxed, hip, youth-oriented style peppered with such interjections as "Boo-yah!" "Mojo!" and "Big ups!," plus unusual expressions, such as complimenting a player by saying he is "cool as the other side of the pillow" or "Call him Butter, 'cause he is on a roll." When a basketball player is under the basket coiled like a spring and waiting for a free throw to be shot, he is, in Scott's vernacular, doing the "gangsta lean." Sports reporting, already clogged with clichés—"He really came to play"; "She took to the next level"; "You really got to give them credit"—generates fascination when an individual introduces new clichés of his or her own as Scott has done, or speaks in language unlike that of other sports commentators, as did the late Howard Cossell ("Just look at that man register elation!" after a player scored a touchdown, whereas at that same moment Scott might exclaim something about the scorer having "taken it to the house. Boo-yah!").

Scott has had other assignments for his network, including hosting "Monday Night Countdown" and coanchoring "NFL Primetime" with Chris Berman and ex-linebacker Tom Jackson. The show airs every Sunday night during NFL football season, appearing just before "Sunday Night Football." Scott has also hosted an unusual reality show for ESPN: "Dream Job," which first aired in February 2004 and which was the first network reality show to hire its winner. "Dream Job" winners are signed to a one-year contract with sports news program "SportsCenter" and also win a new Mazda sports car. Scott has hosted or appeared as himself in other programs, such as "I Love the '80s" in 2002, "Who's #1?" and "I Love the '90s", parts one and two, in 2004. He has made guest appearances on "The Jersey" in 1999, "Arli$$ Himself" in 1999 and 2000, three episodes of "Soul Food" in 2003 and "One on One" in 2004. He has appeared in such films as "He Got Game" and "Enchanted" in 1998, "The Kid" in 2000, and "Mr. 3000" in 2004.

Scott had eye surgery to correct damage to his cornea sustained in April 2003 at the New York Jets training camp after being hit in his left eye by a ball thrown by a machine that passes footballs to receivers. In 2003, a SportsCenter poll identified Scott as the personality that the most viewers would like to see taken off the show, but he also received the second most votes as a "keeper." The athletes he reports on appear to like his style, whereas some of his more conservative viewers see him as egotistical and dislike his "in-your-face" ethnic attitude, name-dropping, frequent references to his own alma mater and innercity expressions, deriding him as an egotist and as the "king of the catchphrase." Other viewers approve those very same practices and traits and rank him as their favorite sportscaster.

Further Readings: "Boo-yah or Just Boo? Scott Has Fans and Detractors." [Online, 12 March 2003]. USA Today Web site www.usatoday.com/sports; "Stuart Scott." [Online, 1999]. Bock En La Bock site http://bock.bushwick.com.

Shaw, Bernard (22 May 1940–)

Chicago-born Bernard Shaw was, from CNN's inception in 1980 until his 2001 retirement, the principal Washington anchor for that cable network.

Shaw grew up in a news-oriented household; his father usually read four newspapers. Young Shaw also liked television news and wanted to grow up to be like Edward R. Murrow of CBS News. From 1959 to 1963, Shaw was a member of the Marine Corps; he rose to the rank of sergeant and was stationed in Hawaii, where before separating from the service, he managed to arrange a brief meeting with CBS anchor Walter Cronkite, who was there on assignment, to ask about broadcast journalism as a career. Shaw enrolled at the University of Illinois at Chicago in 1963, majoring in history and working without pay at a Chicago radio station, WTNR. He was given a paid position at the station when it converted to all-news format and worked there as a reporter until 1966. A highlight from that part of his career was an interview with Dr. Martin Luther King, Jr. From 1966 until 1968, he was a reporter for Westinghouse Broadcasting Company's Group W and dropped out of college to take a position as Group W's White House correspondent. He covered the latter part of the Johnson administration, reported on Indian affairs in Montana and covered the difficult situation in Memphis, Tennessee, following the killing of Martin Luther King, Jr. He remained in that job until 1971, after which he made the move from radio to television, putting in three years as a Washington reporter for CBS and, from 1974 until 1978, as a CBS correspondent. Breaking into CBS at about the same time were two other future news notables—Connie Chung and Leslie Stahl. Shaw's biggest story during those years was interviewing Attorney General John Mitchell during the Watergate imbroglio. In 1978, he switched networks, going to ABC News as Miami bureau chief and Latin American correspondent. He covered the Jim Jones murder suicides in Jonestown, Guyana, and later the hostage situation at the U.S. Embassy in Teheran. He then came back to Washington and worked as senior Capitol Hill correspondent for ABC until June 1980, when he joined the newly created Cable News Network as its first African-American anchor. CNN was the world's first 24-hour news network, and Shaw became its "senior statesman." By the year 2000, this cable network had grown to employ around 4,000 people and operated 10 U.S. and 27 international bureaus. In his new position with CNN, Shaw covered many important world events. In 1988, he moderated the presidential debate between George H.W. Bush and Michael Dukakis and again served as a presidential debate moderator in 1992. In 1989 he reported live from Beijing when Chinese tanks rolled into Tiananmen Square to put an end to prodemocracy demonstrations by Chinese students. He also covered President Bill Clinton's Economic Summit in Tokyo in 1993. Other big stories were the 1994 Los Angeles earthquake, the funeral of Britain's Princess Diana in 1997 and, also in 1997, the impeachment trial of President Clinton. Very likely his most dramatic and dangerous reporting was done in Baghdad, where Shaw had gone to interview Iraqi dictator Saddam Hussein. The onset of U.S. bombing prevented that interview from occurring, but Shaw, Peter Arnett, John Holliman and cameraman Mark Biello reported from a suite in the Al Rashid Hotel where they were stranded during the bombing of Baghdad that began Operation Desert Storm. A few days later, Shaw left Baghdad and drove by way of dangerous desert roads to Amman, Jordan, where he was able to book a flight back to the United States. On the home front, he covered the bombing of the Oklahoma City Federal Building by domestic terrorist Timothy McVeigh.

Shaw's final assignment for CNN was as coanchor, with Judy Woodruff, of the network's political news program "Inside Politics." He also was the Washington anchor for "NewsStand: CNN & Time," and in his various assignments at CNN, he visited almost 50 nations. At the conclusion of his last "Inside Politics" show, Shaw passed a symbolic *gavel* to Woodruff. He then retired to work on books—an autobiography, essays, fiction, and perhaps a journalism textbook. He was honored with a fancy-dress gala at Washington's Corcoran Gallery of Art soon after he retired in the spring of 2001 at age 60.

Shaw's honors have been many indeed, including at least three honorary degrees—from Marion College, the University of Chicago and Northeastern University, a 1989 Emmy for news and documentary work, several ACE awards, election as a Fellow of the Society of Professional Journalists in 1995 and induction into the Chicago Journalists Hall of Fame in 1997. He was accorded the Distinguished Service Award of the Congressional Black Caucus in 1985, the National Association of Black Journalists' Journalist of the Year Award in 1989, the George Foster Peabody Award in 1990, the David Brinkley Award in 1991, the University of Missouri's Honor Medal for Distinguished Service to Journalism in 1992 and the Congress of Racial Equality's Dr. Martin Luther King, Jr. Award for Outstanding Achievement in 1993. He was the first non-German to receive the Eduard Rhein Foundation's Cultural Journalism Award, which he got in 1991. In 1994, Shaw received the William Allen White Award from the University of Kansas, and in that same year he was awarded a National Headliner Award. In 1997, he was the first recipient of the Tex McCrary Award given by the Congressional Medal of Honor Society.

Further Readings: "Bernard Shaw: A Look Back on the 10th Anniversary of the Gulf War." [Online, 16 January 2001]. CNN Web site www.cnn.com; "Bernard Shaw." *The African American Almanac*, 9th ed. Edited by Jeffrey Lehman. (Detroit: Gale Group, 2003), pp. 884–85; "CNN's Bernard Shaw: A Newsman's Career." [Online, 2 March 2001]. CNN archives http://archives.cnn.com.

Shipp, E.R. (6 June 1955–)

Columnist E.R. Shipp grew up in Conyers, Georgia, and graduated in journalism from Georgia State University in 1976. She went on to Columbia University, where she earned both a 1979 masters in journalism and later a law degree, then was hired by the *New York Times*, working as a national correspondent, legal correspondent, and assistant metropolitan editor between 1980 and 1993. Thereafter she left the *Times* to get a second Columbia University masters, this time in American history, and in 1994 she became an assistant professor at Columbia's School of Journalism as well as a weekly op-ed columnist for the *New York Daily News*. Ms. Shipp, who reportedly dislikes her first name, which she carefully keeps to herself, prefers to be known by her initials or to be called "Shipp" and is occasionally mistaken for a man because of it. In 1996, she won the Pulitzer Prize for commentary for her work on race, welfare and related social issues, which was somewhat ironic inasmuch as she had long resisted doing stories regarding race for fear of being "typecast." Two years later she interrupted her usual duties to serve from autumn 1998 until 2001 as ombudsman for the *Washington Post*; she was the paper's twelfth ombudsman and after Robert C. Maynard, who served during the Watergate era, the second person of color to hold that position. Shipp's immediate predecessor was Geneva Overholser, former editor of the *Des Moines Register*. In this sensitive role, Shipp offended some, but often paused to ask herself where the reporter's imperative ends and exploitation begins. As one might expect from a columnist, she advocated that the *Post* do more stories about ordinary, nonofficial people and that the paper's writers go beyond the standard story topics about well off white people. She also suggested the use of more nonwhites as news sources. Most of the reader complaints she fielded for the *Post*, she said, revolved around fairness—failure to get more than one side of a story, omission of certain facts, loss of a reporter's objectivity and the like.

Fairness of another kind was the topic of one of her January 2005 columns in the *Daily News*; in it, she pointed out that Americans were wonderfully generous in providing private aid to the Asian tsunami victims, but that rather than rest on our laurels, we should not forget the considerable need for charity at home, where children still go hungry and people still live in poverty. In the column reproduced below, Shipp lambastes Columbia University and the U.S. Supreme Court following the court's unpopular 2005 land-use decision. When the Jason Blair scandal broke at *The New York Times*, she was just as quick to blast her old paper for what she saw as its unfortunate tendency toward good-old-boy schmoozing by editors and their more ambitious, ingratiating underlings. As to the Iraq war, she is appalled, both with President George W. Bush and with the news-apathetic U.S. public. Some days, however, her columns accentuate the positive. She has even praised one aspect of hip-hop music, a genre of which she is not usually a fan. She approved the use of this remarkably popular music to lure youngsters into the churches of Harlem, via a group called Hip Hop Church. Along the way, Shipp has coauthored a single book, which was about the Tawana Brawley affair; and she has been a member of the National Association of Black Journalists since 1986 and the New York Association of Black Journalists since 1983.

"Columbia U. Gets to Steal from Li'l Guy" by E.R. Shipp

When the Supreme Court ruled in a land-use case last month, it marked perhaps the first time that two New York activists, Tom Demott and Norman Siegel, agreed with Associate Justice Clarence Thomas.

"I did have to laugh," Demott said.

Of course, the case was no laughing matter. New London, Conn., wanted to displace even longtime homeowners and make the land available to developers who wanted to construct housing and office space. The five jurists in the majority said it was okay for government to seize private property and transfer it to private developers so long as they claim it is for a public purpose.

The ruling had strong relevance for Demott and Siegel, who have been talking to Columbia University as it tries to displace property owners and small businesses to expand northward into the neighborhood of Manhattanville.

Thomas, one of four dissenting jurists, worried that low-income people, especially people of color, would suffer most from the ruling.

He agreed with Associate Justice Sandra Day O'Connor, who in one of the last cases she would hear, wrote the main dissenting opinion. "The government now has license to transfer property from those with fewer resources to those with more," she said.

Frankly, I'm inclined to side with the dissenters. Demott and Siegel see Morningside Heights and other parts of the upper West Side changing as real estate prices—and rent—soar, forcing out longtime residents and business owners.

Columbia, which has a plan that involves the state's use of eminent domain—the power to condemn properties and force current owners out—must be chirping. The majority, in an opinion written by Associate Justice John Paul Stevens, declared of the New London plan: "The city's determination that the area at issue was sufficiently distressed to justify a program of economic rejuvenation is entitled to deference."

The majority opinion is not the greatest news for Demott or Siegel, the lawyer who represents the West Harlem Business Group in trying to hold onto private properties despite Columbia's plans. But neither has given up. The court majority did give them an opening: "We emphasize that nothing in our opinion precludes any State from placing further restrictions on its exercise of the takings power," Stevens wrote.

Siegel sees this as an "invitation for activists to pull together a state coalition and say we should place greater restrictions on the exercise of eminent domain. New Yorkers still believe that their homes and their businesses are their castles and that their elected officials should guarantee that." Siegel envisions a coalition storming Albany and demanding protection of property rights. From the right and the left, he says, "there is great common ground here."

As polite as I have been here, my neighbor has it right. This is rape and pillage of the little person. It's time for legislators to do something about this.

Source: This column first appeared on 10 July 2005. *New York Daily News*, L.P., reprinted with permission.

Books by E.R. Shipp: With Robert D. McFadden, *Outrage: The Story Behind the Tawana Brawley Hoax* (New York: Bantam, 1990).

Further Readings: "Faculty: E.R. Shipp." [Online]. Columbia Graduate School of Journalism Web site www.jrn.columbia.edu; Farah, Joseph. "E.R. Shipp, Where Are You?" [Online, 1999]. World Net Daily Web site www.worldnetdaily.com; "The Pulitzer Prize Winners, 1996: E.R. Shipp." [Online]. The Pulitzer Prizes Web site www.pulitzer.org; Watal, Divya. "Shipp Off the Old Block: Journalist E.R. Shipp Reveals to Brownstone What 'Woman of Color' Means to Her." [Online, 4 November 2004]. Washington Square News Web site www.nyunews.com.

Simmons, Debra Adams (1965–)

Debra Adams Simmons is editor and vice president of the *Beacon Journal* in Akron, Ohio. The newspaper was the first paper in the Knight chain, and in its 164-year history, Simmons is the first African American to serve as its editor. Her career began as a reporter for the *Syracuse Herald-Journal*, after which she was a reporter for the *Hartford Courant*. She was a reporter and assistant metro editor for the *Detroit Free Press*, then moved up to metro editor for the *Virginian-Pilot* in Tidewater Virginia. In January 2003, she became managing editor for the *Akron Beacon Journal*, replacing Thom Fladung, who moved to the *Detroit Free Press*. The paper's editor, Jan Leach, resigned in March of that year due to difficulties in balancing her job with raising three children, and in late July 2003, Simmons became editor of that venerable old paper, which had been founded in 1839 and was bought by the Knight family in 1903. Her promotion created another first for the *Beacon Journal*—the first time a mainstream Ohio paper simultaneously had both an editor and a publisher who were African American. Publisher and president of the paper is James N. Crutchfield, who earlier had been assistant to the publisher of Philadelphia Newspapers Inc. Crutchfield and Simmons selected as their new managing editor Mizell Stewart III, the former African-American editor of the *Tallahassee Democrat*, who had been ousted when that Knight Ridder paper was bought in 2005 by the Gannett group. A bombshell struck in March 2006 with the announcement that Knight Ridder would be sold to the McClatchy Company and that following the sale, 12 of the papers in the old Knight Ridder group would be resold. One of those 12 newspapers was the *Beacon Journal*. McClatchy wanted to retain only the Knight Ridder papers located in growth markets, whereas Akron is in part of the so-called Rust Belt. The future ownership of the *Beacon Journal* is unknown as this entry is being written, but Simmons, a graduate of the Kellogg School of Management at Northwestern University's Medill School of Journalism, will no doubt be well positioned to move should the need arise.

Simmons spoke out as editor in October 2003 urging community respect for gays and lesbians. The occasion was the decision that the *Beacon Journal* would run announcements of same-sex couples who marry or enter into a civil union. In 2004–2005, Simmons was a judge in the Pulitzer Prize competitions for column writing, breaking news reporting and international reporting. In autumn 2005, she dispatched reporters Gary Eastwick and Doug Opplinger and photographer Lew Stamp to provide on-the-scene coverage of the relief effort in New Orleans and Baton Rouge after the devastation caused by Hurricane Katrina. Also in 2005 she came to the defense of African-American cartoonist Aaron McGruder, who draws "The Boondocks" comic strip. A caption about "nappy hair" had stirred criticism from the local chapter of the NAACP and from some *Beacon Journal* readers. Simmons explained that McGruder's purpose was satire.

In March 2004, Simmons and four of her staffers took first place in the National Association of Black Journalists awards competition for the under 150,000 circulation category for their story "Still a Question of Color"; in April of that year Simmons was the keynote speaker at the Press Club of Cleveland's

Media Professionals Conference; and in August 2004, Simmons spoke at a preconvention workshop at the Unity: Journalists of Color convention in Washington, D.C. In May 2005, she won a Harold K. Stubbs Humanitarian Award for social service. Simmons is a member of National Association of Minority Media Executives, and she serves on the board of the Center for Nonprofit Excellence in Akron.

Further Readings: Prince, Richard. "Debra Adams Simmons Named Editor in Akron." [Online, 26 July 2003]. Richard Prince's Journal-isms. Maynard Institute Web site www.maynardije.org; Prince, Richard. "Dropping 12 Papers Puts Some of Color in Jeopardy." [Online, 13 March 2006]. Richard Prince's Journal-isms. Maynard Institute Web site www.maynardije.org; "Two Ohio Newspapers Name New Editors." *Ohio Newspaper Association Bulletin* 16 (1 August 2003): 1, 4.

Simpson, Carole (7 December 1940–)

A broadcaster since 1965, Carole Simpson was from 1988 until 2003 weekend anchor on ABC's "World News Tonight." Having been eased out of this anchor job after 15 years, she remains with the network as a senior correspondent for both the program she anchored and for "World News Tonight." She is also the network's "news ambassador" and in this capacity travels to U.S. high schools to promote journalism and the importance of being an informed citizen—no mean task in our present celebrity-crazed "Age of Entertainment." When she asked one high school group what the media might do to make the news more interesting to them, the well meant but pathetic reply was to have celebrities deliver the news. For most of the year, Simpson's time is mainly taken up with school visits; during summer, she primarily functions in her correspondent role. She has also appeared on C-SPAN, where after the 2004 reelection of President George W. Bush, she produced a map that showed Bush won the former slave states but lost most of the free states, thereby creating an angry reaction from conservatives. An earlier controversy that drew fire occurred in 2001, when remarks she made as an after-luncheon speaker before the International Women's Media Foundation did not agree with network releases about an anthrax scare at the network in which Cokie Roberts had received a suspicious letter. This incident got her suspended from on-air work for two weeks and might have contributed to her removal as anchor, but the more likely reason for her removal was probably the fact that she, like the rest of us, has aged some. Television, even television news, remains fixated on fresh, glamorous youth—a condition that appears to affect women's on-air viability more than men's.

Simpson was born in Chicago, grew up in that city's Hyde Park section, went to high school at Hyde Park Academy and earned a 1962 B.A. in journalism at the University of Michigan, working during summers at a small newspaper. She took graduate work in journalism at the University of Iowa but left without completing the degree. Her original intent was to go into newspaper work, but a graduate school workshop introduced her to broadcasting. She worked as a Voice of America stringer and at Tuskegee Institute, where for two years she taught journalism and was director of the school's Information Bureau. She worked in radio from 1965 to 1968 as a news anchor/reporter for station WCFL in the Chicago area. She also reviewed books and movies for that station. In 1968, she switched stations, working until 1970 as weekend anchor and correspondent for WBBM Radio, also in Chicago. Around that same time, she broke into television, at Chicago's public station WTTW-TV. There she initially worked as a commentator on a minority affairs show called "Our People." Having gained this experience, she moved to WMAQ-TV as a news correspondent and doubled as an instructor in the Medill School of Journalism at Northwestern University. Simpson was at WMAQ from 1970 until 1974, doing a combination of news and features. Then she relocated to the nation's capital to host a women's-interest program, "Her-Rah," on NBC affiliate station WRC-TV. This move proved propitious, inasmuch as she soon got work as a substitute anchor for the "NBC Nightly News," anchored the network's weekend "Newsbreak" and was assigned the high-profile Capitol Hill beat from 1978 to 1981. She joined ABC in 1982, working as a general assignment correspondent and achieving considerable visibility with her coverage of the first President George Bush. In December 1985, she appeared on the popular "Phil Donahue Show" with several other women broadcasters. Then in June 1988, she won the anchor job for "World News Saturday." She contributed stories for the "American Agenda" portion of Peter Jennings' "World News Tonight" and made a few appearances on "20/20" and "Nightline." Simpson was one of the earliest African-American women to deliver the national television news and has said that in that white male-dominated arena, she never found a mentor to help her along. Worse, she reports that some of her coworkers actually made efforts to sabotage her career progress. She especially appears to dislike longtime newsman Ted Koppel. She has, however, spoken kindly of one professor who took a special interest in her career—Wesley Maurer, her department chair while she was studying at the University of Michigan. Maurer encouraged her—his only African-American student at the time—to do graduate work and helped get her the Tuskegee Institute job in the 1960s.

Simpson displayed her versatility on ABC by doing reporting for documentaries and specials. She was a reporter for "Black and White in America" and anchored three specials—"The Changing American Family," "Public Schools in America" and "Sex and Violence in the Media." One of her biggest stories, and probably the most dangerous, came in February 1990 upon the release from prison of South Africa's Nelson Mandela. She was sent to South Africa for two weeks to cover this event for "Nightline." Apparently, the network decreed that the reporting team should include a black reporter, and she was selected. She was there for Mandela's release after 17 years of confinement, yet her primary interest became the plight of black South African women, who were triply oppressed: by race, gender and related tribal customs, and economics. She was surprised when many South African women did not want to be interviewed by her because they considered her not black, but "colored" and hence did not trust her. In a Johannesburg riot, Simpson was knocked to the ground by a policeman wielding a rubber truncheon. Suddenly, she had much too intimate a vantage point from which she could later report about the beatings and use of tear gas by white Afrikaner police who feared that the celebrations of Mandela's release would become riots. Years later, Simpson was the victim of black-on-black violence when her Mercedes was carjacked while she and her housekeeper were grocery shopping near her Chevy Chase, Maryland, home. A handsome, well-dressed young African-American man threatened her and demanded her keys. After taking the car, the man and his confederates, apparently part of a larger gang, used the car in the robbery of a bank in nearby Silver Spring. Other stories Simpson reported for her network were the Clarence Thomas-Anita Hill controversy, the impeachment trial of President Bill Clinton, the Tiananmen Square demonstrations in China, the bombing of the Oklahoma City Federal Building and the Persian Gulf War. In 1992, she also moderated the Richmond, Virginia, presidential debate that broke with tradition by using a town hall format, allowing an audience of uncommitted voters to ask questions directly to candidates George H.W. Bush, Bill Clinton and Ross Perot.

In the early 1980s, Simpson was president of the Radio and Television Correspondents Association, and in 1986, she was chair of the ABC News Women's Advisory Board and vice chair of the International Women's Medical Foundation. She has served on the boards of the Fund for Investigative Journalism, the D.C. chapter of the Society of Professional Journalists and the National Commission of Working Women. She is a member, of the National Association of Black Journalists, the Radio Television News Directors' Association and the Distinguished Journalists Advisory Committee of American University. She has been inducted into the University of Iowa School of Communications Hall of Fame and in 1988, received the Milestone Award in Broadcast Journalism from the National Commission on Working Women. The Ad Council selected her in 1989 for its Silver Bell Award. She also has received Turner Broadcasting's Trumpet Award and, from the Radio and Television News Directors Foundation, the Leonard Zeidenberg First Amendment Award. The National Association of Black Journalists has honored her twice: in 1992 as Journalist of the Year and in 2004 for lifetime achievement. In 1999, she was inducted into the Chicago Journalism Hall of Fame, and universities have awarded her roughly a dozen honorary degrees. Simpson has originated and contributed funds to a number of scholarships for aspiring broadcast journalists. Most of these scholarships are for students at the University of Michigan. She has also set up the Carole Simpson Leadership Institute, which provides training for African women who want to be broadcasters. The institute was launched in 1998, with Simpson providing the initial funding. The institute's short-courses have been offered once yearly in several locations: Johannesburg, South Africa; Nairobi, Kenya; Windhoek, Namibia; and Dakar, Senegal.

Further Readings: "Carole Simpson." *The African American Almanac.* 9th ed. Edited by Jeffrey Lehman. Detroit: Gale Group, 2003, p. 885; Dalrymple, Daniel. "Simpson, Carole." *Black Women in America, Second Edition.* Edited by Darlene Clark Hine. (New York: Oxford University Press, 2005), pp. 121–22; Moorhus, Donita M. Interview with Carole Simpson. [Online, 1994]. Washington Press Club Foundation site http://npc.press.org; "NABJ Applauds Veteran Journalist Carole Simpson." [Online, 28 July 2004]. National Association of Black Journalists Web site www.nabj.org; Prince, Richard. "Carole Simpson Loses ABC Weekend Anchor Job." [Online, 20 October 2003]. Richard Prince's Journal-isms. Maynard Institute Web site www.maynardije.org; Ziellerr, Dhyana. "Carole Simpson." *Notable Black American Women.* Edited by Jessie Carney Smith and Shirelle Phelps. (Detroit: Gale Research, 1992–2003), pp. 1022–24.

Singletary, Michelle (c.1964–)

Washington Post personal financial columnist Michelle Singletary is syndicated nationally by the Washington Post Writers Group. She also does commentaries on her specialty each Thursday for National Public Radio's "Day to Day" and is host of "$ingletary $ays," a weekly show on TV One. Singletary was born in Baltimore, Maryland, and was raised by a grandmother. She holds a 1984 bachelor's degree from the University of Maryland and a 1993 masters in Business and Management from Johns Hopkins University. Her first job in journalism was as a *Baltimore Evening Sun* reporter; her assignments included business, politics, crime, religion and zoning issues. Singletary was hired by the *Washington Post* in 1992 as a business reporter and covered the banking industry and bankruptcy. In 1994, she traveled to West Africa on a National Association of Black Journalists fellowship and reported on small businesses owned by women. She also contributed to coverage of the 1994 presidential election of Nelson Mandela in South Africa. Her twice-weekly *Post* column, "The Color of Money," began appearing in March 1997. Also in 1997, she began a two-year job as a correspondent for Black Entertainment Television's show "Real Business." She added radio appearances as well, on "Insight," an evening news program at Howard University, and on WMMJ-FM in Washington. Other regular appearances were on the public television program "This Week in Business." Singletary has appeared as a guest on other high-profile programs such as "Nightline," "The View," "The Oprah Winfrey Show" and "The Diane Rehm Show"; and in 2000, she began doing financial commentary for MSNBC. She added regular Tuesday appearances on NPR's "Day by Day" and in April 2005, began hosting the weekly half-hour "$ingletary $ays" on TV One, a satellite/cable network targeting the African-American audience. For this show, she sometimes makes "house calls" to people's homes to offer financial advice. In 1999, she began hosting an hour-long interactive "Color of Money Live" session on Washingtonpost.com, sometimes discussing a financial issue or answering readers' questions, but often discussing personal finance with such guests as former IRS commissioner Don Alexander, David Vladeck of the Public Citizen Litigation Group, Kathy Burlison of tax firm H&R Block and Gerri Detweiler of MoneyForMail.com. She also writes an electronic newsletter under the auspices of the *Post*. Singletary became a book author in 2004 with the publication of *7 Money Mantras for a Richer Life*, in which she offers advice, some of which she learned at the knee of the grandmother who raised her and her four siblings, the unlettered yet wise and thrifty woman she refers to as "Big Mama." Much of this advice is good common sense, such as the advantage of dealing in cash rather than credit, setting priorities for one's spending, being careful to separate needs from mere wants and holding down one's consumer urge. Other topics Singletary addresses are more technical, such as the effects of inflation, the use of a reverse mortgage, planning how much tax to withhold from one's paycheck and the impact upon investors of mutual fund fees. Her first book, published in hardback, was quickly followed in the same year by a paperback version, which was retitled *Spend Well, Live Rich*, and in 2006 appeared another book, *Your Money or Your Man*, on one of the columnist/commentator's favorite themes: how women can attempt to square their love life with their financial well being. In early 2006, her syndicated column appears in around 140 newspapers; it was first syndicated by The Washington Post Writers Group in autumn 1999.

Some of Singletary's writing and commentary is done in response to the words and actions of others. In 2005, she replied to the charges comedian Bill Cosby leveled at the less affluent portion of the African-American community. Singletary disagreed with much of what Cosby had said and recommended that her readers buy Michael Eric Dyson's book *Is Bill Cosby Right? Or Has the Black Middle Class Lost Its Mind?* (New York: Basic Civitas Books, 2005), in which Dyson debunks some of Cosby's criticisms. In February 2006, she based a column on the "State of the Black Union 2006: Economic Empowerment—Building and Leveraging Wealth in the African-American Community" symposium hosted in Houston, Texas, by broadcasters Tavis Smiley and Tom Joyner. Singletary was a panelist at the symposium and commented on why so many black Americans failed to benefit by the 1990s run-up of the stock market or the recent sharp rise in the price of residential houses. Some of her comments sounded close to those of Bill Cosby, as when she concluded that African Americans often spend a disproportionate amount of their available funds on nonessential clothes, entertainment and the like. She cited recent studies showing that 48 percent of blacks owned homes, compared to 76 percent of whites, and that 61 percent of blacks owned stocks, compared to 79 percent of whites. Others of her columns have addressed the often unwise use of credit cards by college students. Her recommendation is that a student should not have a card until just prior to graduation and then, not until a job has been secured. She cites figures showing that students who own credit cards are more often delinquent and are more apt to exceed their credit limits than are older cardholders. Inundated with criticism for her stance on students' credit habits, she responded in a later column by pointing out that youth is no excuse for excessive spending, twisting the knife by adding that students who can't afford spring break vacations shouldn't take them. Singletary recommends that young people do a cost-benefit analysis before signing up for a graduate program rather than simply assuming that an advanced degree will result in significantly higher compensation or greater opportunity. Other advice has been directed at the topic of car purchases. While not wishing to vilify the automobile sales business too harshly, she pointed out some of the methods of subterfuge used in the business and noted that even being allowed to see a dealer's invoice will not tell the buyer the whole story. She also quipped that she herself tends to keep a car so long that people begin to feel sorry for her. For older readers, who presumably make up most of her readership, she offers guidance on how to determine one's net worth, and she has often written on various aspects of retirement planning, such as when to apply for Social Security, how to handle distributions from one's pension plan, the advisability of long-term care insurance and the like. She is an advocate of "life cycle investing," whereby mutual fund companies will automatically adjust one's portfolio as one ages. Some of her columns and commentaries get quite personal. In one column, she wrote about her attempts to teach her daughter Olivia the need to be a frugal spender. Singletary has confessed to sometimes saving time by eating in her car, a practice she recommends against for people who want to keep their vehicle in top condition. She also has admitted that she is frequently criticized about being too solemn in offering her financial advice. A February 2006 column offered an antidote by discussing humor writer Dave Barry's book *Dave Barry's Money Secrets—Like: Why Is There a Giant Eyeball on the Dollar?* (New York: Crown Publishers, 2006), in which Barry pokes outlandish fun at the work of personal finance self-help gurus. Her favorite topic, however, is serious enough: the matter of the frequently encountered clash between romance and finance. She cites studies showing that conflicts over money are at the root of more marital problems than is spousal cheating. Unromantic as it may seem, she recommends finding out about an individual's credit history before getting serious romantically and cites the advice of Big Mama, who had told her not to marry a man who had poor saving habits. Another suggestion was to insist on a long engagement to ensure that a couple is not only romantically, but financially compatible. She sometimes recommends other people's books on this subject, such as Jeff D. Opdyke's *Love & Money: A Life Guide for Financial Success* (Hoboken, N.J.: Wiley, 2004).

In 1998, "The Color of Money" took first place in the business writing category from the National Association of Black Journalists, and the next year, the ICI Education Foundation/American University award for personal finance reporting went to Singletary.

"Blacks Still Lag Behind by Key Measures" by Michelle Singletary

What is the economic state of black America?

That is the question radio and television hosts Tavis Smiley and Tom Joyner will be addressing in Houston on Feb. 25. The two men, who have the ears of millions of African-Americans, are hosting a symposium called "State of the Black Union 2006: Economic Empowerment—Building and Leveraging Wealth in the African-American Community."

Smiley invited me to join the panel of black educators, commentators, authors, business owners, and policy makers to find out why blacks did not generally benefit from the stock market boom in the 1990s or the recent housing market explosion.

With the recent deaths of two great civil rights leaders, Rosa Parks and Coretta Scott King, some in the black community have been bemoaning the economic state of black America.

According to Target Market News, which specializes in tracking African-American marketing, media and consumer behavior, blacks spend more per capita than whites on many food, clothing and entertainment products and services.

Many point to the company's survey to criticize black spending. For example, blacks spend about $22 billion of their income on apparel products and services and almost $29 billion on automobiles.

Black households had $679 billion in earned income in 2004, an increase of 3.5 percent over the $656 billion earned in 2003.

If you use the overall earned income figure, it doesn't appear as if blacks are spending wisely. But on a household basis, the annual median income of blacks in 2004 was just $30,134, according to he Census Bureau. Asian households had the highest median income ($57,518). The median income for non-Hispanic white households was $48, 977. For Hispanic households, it was $34,241.

One of the keys, though, to prosperity is through home ownership.

While blacks spend $110 billion on housing, only 48 percent of black households own their own home compared with 75.7 percent for white households, according to the most recent Census Bureau figures. In fact, African-American homeownership has declined one percentage point from the fourth quarter of 2004. That number should be going up, not down.

Another equalizer in this race to prosperity is a college education. And here the news is good for the black community.

The number of black college students in fall 2004 was 2.3 million, roughly double the number 15 years earlier. Education does pay off.

According to Census Bureau statistics, people with a bachelor's degree earn 62 percent more on average than those with only a high school diploma. Over a lifetime, the gap in earning potential between someone with a high school diploma and someone with a bachelor's degree is more than $1 million.

It's also imperative that blacks invest.

After five straight years of steady increases in the percentages of blacks who own stocks, only 61 percent of blacks surveyed had money in the stock market in 2004, down from 74 percent and approaching the 1998 level of 57 percent. White stock ownership, meanwhile, is at 79 percent, virtually unchanged over the last six years.

No question that black households have to do better, as do many households. But I cringe when those in my own community talk as if blacks are genetically predisposed to spending on cars and clothes. I have the opportunity to communicate with hundreds of consumers of all ages, races and economic backgrounds and America is full of conspicuous consumers.

My answer to how blacks can achieve prosperity is to follow the advice of my grandmother, Big Mama. She always told me that it doesn't matter how much you make but how you make do with what you have. This from a woman who retired with more savings and financial strength than folks I know who make more in a few months than she made in an entire year.

Source: © 2006 The Washington Post Writers Group. Reprinted with permission. The column originally appeared in *The Washington Post* on 19 February 2006.

Books by Michelle Singletary: *7 Money Mantras for a Richer Life: How to Live Well with the Money You Have* (New York: Random House, 2004)—paperback edition as *Spend Well, Live Rich: How to Get What You Want With the Money You Have* (New York: Ballentine, 2004); *Your Money and Your Man: How You and Prince Charming Can Spend Well and Live Rich* (New York: Random House, 2006).

Further Readings: "Michelle Singletary." [Online]. Black America Web site www.blackamericaweb.com; "Michelle Singletary." [Online]. The Washington Post Writers Group Web site www.postwritersgroup.com.

Smiley, Tavis (13 September 1964–)

The first person ever to simultaneously host talk shows on Public Broadcasting Service television and National Public Radio, Tavis Smiley is also known for his work as a correspondent for CNN and ABC-TV and for his earlier hosting of "BET Tonight with Tavis Smiley." He was born into a family of 10 children in Gulfport, Mississippi, and spent some of his formative years in Kokomo, Indiana, when his father, an Air Force noncommissioned officer was transferred there. Smiley holds a 1986 B.A. in law and public policy from Indiana University. While in college, he took an active part in student government and interned in Los Angeles with that city's first black mayor, Tom Bradley. In 1984 and 1985, prior to graduating, he had also worked as assistant to Bloomington, Indiana, Mayor Tomilea Allison. After graduating, he moved to the West Coast to work as an administrative aide to Mayor Tom Bradley, holding that position until 1990. He made an unsuccessful run for a city council seat in Los Angeles in 1991 and originated "The Smiley Report," a radio feature that focused on the needs of African Americans. The program first appeared in Los Angeles in 1991 and was nationally syndicated in 1992. He also was cohost of a talk show for a local station in Los Angeles. He then moved to Black Entertainment Television as host of "BET Tonight with Tavis Smiley," a one-hour show offering a combination of news and entertainment especially geared to the African-American audience. The show, although successful, was not renewed in 1999, two months after BET was sold to Viacom by its founder, Robert Johnson. The break with BET was reportedly due to an interview Smiley had conducted with Sara Jane Olson, who had been a member of the Symbionese Liberation Army. BET was angry that he had offered the interview story to CBS rather than to BET; the interview was finally sold to ABC instead, and Tavis took a new job at ABC-TV as a special correspondent for "Good Morning America" and "Primetime Thursday" and as a correspondent and political analyst for CNN, as well. He then joined National Public Radio, where his commentaries on the "Tom Joyner Morning Show" were syndicated nationally. He and Joyner successfully pressured Christie's auction house to cancel plans for an auction of slavery artifacts. Concurrently with his television responsibilities, Smiley in 2001 began hosting his own program, "The Tavis Smiley Show," on NPR. It was the first show in NPR history to specifically target a black audience. Smiley wanted his program to serve as a bridge across the black-white gulf that still exists in America, and, secondarily, he wanted to attract more young viewers than is the norm for public radio programs. The program offered a variety of commentary, interviews and reporting on topics both political and cultural. Joining Smiley were other commentators, including Professor Cornell West of Princeton, author Michael Eric Dyson, lawyer Connie Rice, University of California Regent Ward Connerly and former congressman J.C. Watts. On both his radio and television shows, the liberal Smiley became known for his reasoned, dignified commentary, as opposed to the shrill and hateful brand of commentary that has pocked so much of contemporary conservative talk radio. In late 2004, roughly three years after his radio program began, Smiley announced that he would leave the show due to a disagreement between himself and NPR management regarding efforts to attract more minority listeners to public radio. He was disappointed that management was reluctant to devote to that cause some of the $225 million left to NPR in the will of Joan Kroc, widow of McDonald's founder Ray Kroc. He pointed out that his show had attracted the most multiracial audience of any program in NPR history and the youngest, as well. He also mentioned that when his show began, he had received hate mail for sounding "too black," yet at age 40, he was reaching around one million listeners a week on 90 stations. The last episode of his show aired on 16 December 2004. Around the same time, PBS extended his television talk show contract for a second year. The show, produced at KCET-TV in Los Angeles, had succeeded in attracting a young, well-educated audience and had given that audience visits with a varied mix of political and entertainment figures: Bill Clinton, Jimmy Carter, Pat Buchanan, Newt Gingrich, John McCain, Ted Kennedy, Ann Coulter, Robert Redford, Prince, Maya Angelou, Bill Cosby and many others. Smiley also does the "Tavis Smiley Show" on PRI radio and is a contributor to "The Huffington Post."

The modest, pleasant Smiley has been profiled on CBS' "60 Minutes," is a contributing editor for *USA Weekend* magazine and has appeared on such programs as the "Today" show, "World News Tonight with Peter Jennings" and "Politically Incorrect with Bill Maher." He has authored half a dozen books, beginning in 1996 with *Hard Left: Straight Talk about the Wrongs of the Right*. He has also set up his own Web site, www.tavistalk.com, publishes a newsletter titled *The Smiley Report*, is a frequent speaker before university and corporate groups and has his own charitable foundation, The Tavis Smiley Foundation, founded in November 1999. The foundation's thrust is to help young people realize their potential. An initiative of this foundation is the Youth 2 Leaders program in selected U.S. cities having large African-American populations. Smiley got the idea for this program thanks to single mother Judy Williams, who had heard him speak and wrote to him asking that her son be allowed to follow him around for a day so as to have a positive role model. He granted her request, and after news of the event came out, thousands of similar requests were sent to him. His response was to create a national program, with college scholarships for some of the Y2L participants and a "Follow Tavis For a Day" essay contest for college students. In recognition of his achievements, Texas Southern University in September 2004 named the Tavis Smiley School of

Communications and the Tavis Smiley Center for Professional Media Studies in his honor. He repaid the compliment with a $1 million gift to the school, which was matched by the State of Texas. Smiley also has been accorded a number of honorary degrees, one of which was from his alma mater, Indiana University.

He chaired the operations committee of Young Black Professionals in Los Angeles in the late 1980s and served on the boards of the Inner City Foundation for Excellence in Education, Challengers Boys and Girls Club, the Los Angeles Black College Tour, Kappa Alpha Psi fraternity, the Martin Luther King Center in Atlanta, Scouting USA and the United Way of Greater Los Angeles. He is a member of the NAACP, the National Association of Black Journalists and the American Federation of Television and Radio Artists. He was accorded the Outstanding Business & Professional Award in 1992 by *Dollars & Sense Magazine*, was inducted into the *Vanity Fair* Hall of Fame in 1996, won the 1998 Mickey Leland Humanitarian Award given by the National Association of Minorities in Communications and got the NAACP President's Image Award in 1999.

Books by Tavis Smiley: *Hard Left: Straight Talk about the Wrongs of the Right* (New York: Anchor Books, 1996); *On Air: The Best of Tavis Smiley on the Tom Joyner Morning Show: Thoughts on Culture, Politics and Race* (Los Angeles: Pines One Pub., 1998); *Doing What's Right: How to Fight for What You Believe—and Make a Difference* (New York: Doubleday, 2000); *How to Make Black America Better: Leading African Americans Speak Out* (New York: Doubleday, 2001); *Keeping the Faith: Stories of Love, Courage, Healing, and Hope from Black America* (New York: Doubleday, 2002); *On Air: The Best of Tavis Smiley on the Tom Joyner Morning Show, 2002–2003* (Carlsbad, Calif.: Smiley Books, 2004).

Further Readings: Shipp, E.R. "Tavis Smiley Is Doing It Right." New York *Daily News*, 20 June 2004; "Tavis Smiley." *The African American Almanac*, 9th ed. Edited by Jeffrey Lehman. (Detroit, Mich.: Gale Group, 2003), pp. 885–886; "Tavis Smiley." [Online]. National Public Radio Web site www.npr.org; "10 Questions for Tavis Smiley." *Time*, 13 December 2004, p. 8.

Smith, Clarence O. (31 March 1933–)

Clarence O. Smith will be remembered as cofounder of Essence Communications, the highly successful company he was reportedly forced out of in 2002 after a 32-year association with Edward T. Lewis. Smith's new company is YOU Entertainment, devoted to serving the music needs of people over 25. He is also chairman and CEO of Avocet Travel, a tour operator that specializes in charter service from New York to Brazil. Smith began his career as an insurance salesman for Prudential Life Insurance Company. When he started there in the early 1960s, he was one of only three African-American agents employed by the company. There he developed the sales skills that helped *Essence* magazine attract enough major advertisers to become viable, then very profitable. Smith and Lewis founded Essence Communications in 1968 to fill a void by appealing to African-American women who wanted a magazine of their own that treated them seriously and recognized that they constituted a large and growing market segment. The magazine hit the stands in May 1970 and progressed from initial circulation of 50,000 to around 1.6 million in 2005, establishing itself as the leading magazine of its kind. Smith played a large role in merchandizing this valuable brand by starting spin-off businesses such as the annual Essence Music Festival, Essence Art Reproductions, Essence Books, the Essence-By-Mail catalog, the weekly "Essence" television show, "The Essence Awards" television special and Essence Online, plus a licensing subsidiary that deals in eyewear, hosiery and sewing patterns. Smith's departure from Essence Communications stemmed from the company's takeover by AOL Time Warner, which in 2000, bought a 49 percent interest in the company. Then in March 2005, Time Warner purchased the remainder of Essence Communications for a reported $170 million. It appears that Smith was never keen on becoming part of the gigantic Time Warner conglomerate and that he preferred to follow the keep-control path chosen by magazine mogul John H. Johnson instead. But in June 2002, the announcement appeared that Smith would be stepping aside as president and that Michelle Ebanks would replace him in that position. Smith, the announcement continued, would continue to appear on the *Essence* masthead as Cofounder and President Emeritus. It has been reported that Smith and Lewis no longer speak to each other and that Smith's departure came after a vote of the Essence Communications board. At this writing in early 2006, *Essence* continues in very nearly its same editorial formula. It maintains its preeminence while competing with other similar magazines such as *Upscale* and *Today's Black Woman*, and it has succeeded where other of its competitors failed, notably those operated by Vanguarde Media. Prior to the split, Smith and Lewis had bought the smallbusiness magazine *Income Opportunities* to appeal to African-American entrepreneurs and had become involved in a joint venture publication: *Latina*, published in English and Spanish for America's Hispanic women.

In his new music venture, YOU Entertainment, Smith's first effort was in producing "Love Pages," a mixture of jazz and rhythm and blues, which targets a largely black audience of people older than 25 who do not especially like rap and hip-hop. His new travel company specializes in trips to Bahia, Rio de Janeiro and Salvador. Smith has also chaired the African American Marketing and Media Association in Chicago and was one of the founders of the African American Anti-Defamation Association. In 1997, he was a recipient of the Golden Trumpet Award, given by Chicago's Publicity Club to honor distinguished individual achievement by communications professionals.

Further Readings: Cabell, A.K. "Essence: Right Time?" [Online]. Brand Channel Web site www.brandchannel.com; "Clarence O, Smith." In *The African American Almanac*. 9th ed. Edited by Jeffrey Lehman. (Detroit, Mich.: Gale Group, 2003), pp. 886–87; Daniels, Karu F. "Clarence O. Smith Unleashes His Own Essence." EUR web Web site www.eurweb.com.

Smith, Elmer (2 June 1945–)

With the *Philadelphia Daily News* since 1982, Elmer Smith writes a column for that paper. His column is usually on a serious topic, but on occasion he veers away for a humorous look at something less weighty, such as the poolroom of his youth or his erstwhile efforts to diet or exercise. Some of the topics in his one book collection of his work are Nelson Mandela, Jesse Jackson and his love child, the Clarence Thomas-Anita Hill controversy, the widow of Malcolm X, entertainer Sammy Davis, Jr., and the controversial police bombing of the MOVE headquarters in Philadelphia. Smith advises younger columnists to write about the things they really feel so as to increase their chances of having a strong impact on readers. He also suggests that it's best not to take oneself too seriously and that it is all right to admit it when one's opinions change. The columnist, he has said, should not deal in consensus but should try to reduce reality to understandable terms to help readers think and feel as they read. To his way of thinking, people will like a columnist whose work they can relate to regardless of whether they agree or disagree with a particular day's column.

Smith was born in Madison, Wisconsin, but grew up in West Philadelphia. He studied journalism at Temple University from 1969 to 1973, when he left before graduating to work as a nightside rewrite man for the Philadelphia *Bulletin*. He was a City Hall reporter at the *Bulletin* during the end of the reign of Mayor Frank Rizzo, and when that paper ceased publishing, Smith became a Philadelphia *Daily News* sportswriter. Boxing became his forte, but eventually he was promoted to general sports columnist. In 1988, he claimed the distinction of being the only black general sports columnist for a mainstream daily newspaper anywhere in the continental United States, though he was not the first such black U.S. sports columnist. Smith won the Nat Fleisher award as the nation's top boxing writer before leaving sports to work as an editorial columnist and member of the paper's editorial board.

Until 2002, Smith was an adjunct journalism faculty member at Temple University for 24 years, teaching basic news writing and opinion writing. He was a founding member of the Philadelphia Association of Black Journalists and long has been active with the National Association of Black Journalists, for which he was the first regional director for its Region three. He is also a member of the Trotter Group of black columnists and is on the board of the Institute of Advanced Journalism Studies at North Carolina A&T University.

In his column of 29 October 2004, Smith made an accurate prediction about the outcome of the 2004 presidential election, painting a highly negative picture of President George W. Bush as he did so. On the other hand, a later column gave the president kudos for the increases Mr. Bush had made in humanitarian aid to Africa. Smith also pointed out that aid to the Africans is the sole issue on which the mainstream churches and the far-right fundamentalists agree.

Another of his columns, this one about the revelation of Mark Felt as "Deep Throat," offers a review of how news reporters should treat sources depending upon whether a source's motivations for coming forward are self-serving or otherwise. Weighing all available considerations, he concludes that Felt should be remembered as a hero, not a turncoat. A more frequent object of Smith's columns is his city's municipal government, which he sees as a never-ending breeding ground for corruption. In one column he quips that he has come to expect to see the Jolly Roger fluttering over the defense table at the trials of Philadelphia officials. In the case of the FBI's bugging of Mayor John Street's offices, Smith wrote that the agency caught more underlings than they had expected to, but not the big fish they had hoped to catch.

Considering the potential trouble caused by violence-filled video games such as Mob Enforcer, Hitman, Blood Money, Predator and the like, Smith's position is that official restrictions would be a First Amendment violation, but that parental firmness would be a welcome approach in dealing with the problem. A May 2005 column expressed his appreciation for an organization called Concerned Black Men that had started in Philadelphia and had spread to 20 states and some other nations; CBM's aim is to attempt to reduce the awful death toll from gang-related shootings. When Edgar Ray Killen was finally sentenced in June 2005 for his part in the 1964 murders of three civil rights workers, Smith admitted that his first reaction was to feel sorry for the frail old defendant—until he paused to consider the lives Killen had snuffed out due to racial hatred. And in the case of five-year-old Ja'eisha Akins of St. Petersburg, Florida, the child handcuffed while having an elementary-school tantrum, Smith's position was that the police had not needed the cuffs, but that after the child and her parents had appeared on the television show "A Current Affair," all Ja'eisha had probably learned was how to win an all-expense-paid jaunt to New York.

"Bush Will Win and the United States Will Lose" by Elmer Smith

This presidential election is not as close as the polls say.

In the final analysis, George W. Bush will win by a five-to-10-point margin in the popular vote, by eight to 10 votes in the electoral college, or by a 6–3 vote of the Supreme Court if need be. But, somehow, he will win.

And America will lose.

We will lose because team Bush will claim a mandate to continue the policies of an administration that is reckless, divisive and fundamentally dishonest.

George Bush hasn't just been dishonest in the campaign. We expect that. Shaded truths and even outright lies are a staple of election campaigns. Bush is just better at it than John Kerry.

He's better at the politics of terror too. After a campaign where attack-dog Dick Cheney all but promised a terrorist holocaust if Kerry is elected, and where TV ads feature a pack of slavering wolves poised to attack a nation weakened by the election of Kerry, millions will be frightened into voting for Bush.

He will win despite a domestic policy that even the majority of people who will vote for him see as a failure. The economy continues to be plagued by the longest run of unemployment and under-employment since the Great Depression; the $450-billion deficit he produced out of a $200 billion surplus is mounting almost as fast as his tax giveaways are depleting the budget.

His vaunted No Child Left Behind education policy is all diagnosis and no therapy. For all his lip service, he didn't even believe in it enough to fully fund it.

And the best the President has to offer when confronted with this woeful record is a declaration of victory like the glorious victory he declared in Iraq.

This President is so skilled at diversionary tactics he would have made a great combat commander if he hadn't been too busy to fight.

But he will win even though hundreds of U.S. soldiers and thousands of Iraqi bystanders are being killed and maimed in a post-war occupation that, if anything, has made Iraq and America less secure.

Kerry is wrong. Saying it's so does make it so if it is said often enough and forcefully enough by someone we desperately want to believe. We want to believe the President, whoever he is.

The master stroke in this election was getting the nation to see the war in Iraq and the war on terrorism as the same war. Poll after poll have shown that voters think the administration's Iraq strategy is failing.

But by consistently wide margins, they favor Bush over Kerry to conduct the war on terrorism.

HUH?!

How does that work? When the administration is attacked for diverting resources, especially CIA undercover operatives, from al Qaeda strongholds in Afghanistan and Pakistan to Iraq, they tell you Iraq is a key front in the war on terrorism.

They're selling security and it works. It works even though the 9/11 Commission appointed by this president, albeit under duress, concluded that the administration failed to heed warnings about terrorist cells in the U.S. They failed to heed FBI warnings about pilots who were interested in learning how to fly but not how to land. They made missile defense, not terrorism, their main security initiative.

We have placed our trust in an administration that has trumped up a case for war. The 60,000 aluminum tubes we said could only be used for nuclear reactors, the missing weapons of mass destruction, the alleged Iraqi attempts to buy uranium that turned out to be more yeast than yellowcake are products of an administration that is dishonest.

And one that will be given a vote of confidence by the American people next week.

Source: Used with permission of *The Philadelphia Daily News*, copyright 2004. All rights reserved. This column appeared on 29 October 2004.

Books by Elmer Smith: *Out of My Mind* (Newport News, Va.: August Press, 2002).

Further Readings: Von Stiers, Bruce. "A Mindful of Elmer." [Online, 2002]. BVS Reviews Web site www.bvreviews.com; "Write About What You Feel." *Knight Ridder News*, Winter 2002, pp. 32–33.

Sowell, Thomas (30 June 1930–)

Perhaps the most intellectual of African-American columnists, and certainly the most published, is conservative economist Thomas Sowell. He was born in Gastonia, North Carolina, lived in nearby Charlotte for a number of years, then moved with his family to Harlem, in New York City. The lackluster public schools he had attended in North Carolina caused him to struggle at first after the move to New York, but he overcame that disadvantage and was enrolled in classes for the gifted. Economic necessity caused him to drop out of school during tenth grade to help support his family, and at age 17, he was drafted into the U.S. Marines, serving for two years as a photographer at Camp Lejune, in his native North Carolina. His later writings show that he was not fond of military life, and when his period of service was up, he took advantage of the G.I. Bill and took Howard University night classes while working as a General

Accounting Office clerk in Washington. Three semesters later, he was admitted to Harvard, where again he at first had to struggle to meet academic expectations but succeeded, working part time as a photographer and graduating magna cum laude in 1958 with a B.A. in economics. Next he earned the M.A., also in economics, at Columbia University in 1959 and for the next two years, was an economist with the Department of Labor. He taught economics during 1962 and 1963 at Rutgers University's Douglas College, taught at Howard University in 1964 and spent parts of 1964 and 1965 as an AT&T economist. He returned to academe in 1965 as the only black professor at Cornell University and ran a Rockefeller Foundation–sponsored economics program for students from historically black colleges, but resigned angrily in 1969 over a dispute with his department chairman as to how to handle a disruptive student Sowell had wanted removed from his class. By this time he had completed his formal education with a 1968 Ph.D. in economics at the University of Chicago, where he studied with Nobel Prize winner Milton Friedman.

At this juncture, Sowell moved from job to job, spending 1969 and 1970 on the Brandeis University faculty, 1970 through 1972 with the University of California, Los Angeles and 1972 to 1974 directing a project for the Urban Institute in Washington. During 1975 and 1976, he was an adjunct scholar at the American Enterprise Institute. During this period, he became a prolific book author, writing on various aspects of economics. He also addressed what he considered an educational mistake in his second book, *Black Education: Myths and Tragedies*, by attacking black studies programs, which he considered to be watered-down in quality and a disservice to black students. He returned to UCLA, remaining there until 1980 except for a part of 1977 spent as a visiting professor at Amherst College. By this time, Sowell had adopted a firm conservative line of thought and opposed affirmative action, quotas in racial hiring, subsidies for minorities, forced busing and any form of preferential treatment. His view was that such efforts, well meant as they might be, took away honest pride in accomplishment and hence were self-defeating. He went on leave from UCLA in 1980 to work as a senior fellow at the conservative Hoover Institution on War, Revolution, and Peace at Stanford University, where he remains in 2005 as Rose and Milton Friedman Senior Fellow on Public Policy, and where he continues to be a prolific book author. He was named to a position on the Federal Trade Commission by President Gerald Ford but opted out due to a dispute over his term of office. Still a darling of the Republican Party, he was placed on President Ronald Reagan's economic policy advisory board in 1981, in good company there with the likes of Alan Greenspan and his old professor Milton Friedman.

Throughout his adult life, Sowell has been a frequent contributor to a wide variety of journals, magazines and newspapers. Among the periodicals in which he has published are *American Educator*, the *American Enterprise*, the *American Scholar*, the *American Spectator*, *Black Enterprise*, the *Canadian Journal of Economics and Political Science*, *Change*, the *Chronicle of Higher Education*,

Commentary, Daedalus, Economica, Encounter, Ethics, Ethnic and Racial Studies, Forbes, Fortune, History of Political Economy, Industrial and Labor Relations Review, Journal of Economic Issues, Journal of Ethnic Studies, Journal of Legal Education, Journal of Political Economy, Journal of World History, the *New York Times Magazine, Newsweek, Oxford Economic Papers, Policy Review,* the *Public Interest, Quarterly Review of Economics and Business, Review of Black Political Economy, Southwestern Law Review, Taxing and Spending, Washington University Law Review, Wayne Law Review,* and the *Wilson Quarterly.* In addition, he has written book reviews for some of the above mentioned journals and for quite a few other periodicals.

Sowell is syndicated nationally to around 150 newspapers by Creators Syndicate. He began his syndicated column in 1984 after observing what fellow conservative George Will could accomplish in the short-essay form of the newspaper column. He has also been a *Forbes* columnist and currently does a regular column for *Capitalism Magazine.*

One of Sowell's recurring themes is political correctness. To his way of thinking, this mindset, which is dominant in American colleges and universities, is a forced demand for conformity made by those who preach the gospel of diversity. He faults the rewriting of history for ideological purposes in education and especially detests academic administrators, people he derides as abject cowards in situations that threaten them. Affirmative action admissions policies, quotas and preferential treatment for minorities are anathema to him, and in support of his position, he points out the largely unaided educational and economic success of some dark-skinned ethnic minority immigrants such as Nigerians and West Indians as proof that preferential treatment initiatives are unnecessary. Sowell's view is that the "War on Poverty" launched in 1964 by President Lyndon Johnson started American down that well-known road that is paved with good intentions, and he has an equal dislike for environmentalists, depicting them as preferring to keep the world green rather than fed. Ignorance abounds, he writes, but worst of all is the ignorance of the well educated. He supports drilling for oil in the Alaskan wilderness and defends Wal Mart in that company's battles against localities that have attempted to keep that retail giant out. Like most conservatives, his stance is prolife, he opposed the removal of Terri Schiavo's feeding tube, and he is antigay marriage. An avowed political independent, he has a dim view of politicians in general, has called politics the art of concocting clever reasons for having done stupid things, and in spite of his conservatism, has misgivings about the Bush administration's handling of the war in Iraq and its zeal for spreading democracy worldwide. But as to media mistakes in stories critical of President Bush, Sowell awarded former CBS news anchor Dan Rather his 2004 "Joseph Goebbels award," so named for Hitler's propaganda chief, for Rather's discredited story about the quality of the president's National Guard service, and in 2005 he lambasted *Newsweek* for its reliance on a single source when it ran a later recanted story about a copy of the Koran having been flushed down a Guantanamo prison toilet.

In his columns that stray from politics, Sowell has criticized modern music as lacking in humanity, and in a 2005 column headlined "Black Rednecks and White Liberals," he argued that many characteristics of life in the American South that are usually considered by liberals as distinctive racial characteristics are actually shared by blacks and whites due to cultural rub-off. In 1990, Sowell was awarded the Francis Boyer Award, given by the American Enterprise Institute.

"Looking Back" by Thomas Sowell

Whenever a puff piece praises me for overcoming disadvantages and rising from poverty to a professional career, it makes me feel uneasy—not out of modesty, but because it is not completely true. Being a black orphan born in the Jim Crow South during the Great Depression may not seem like a promising start in life. But that is also not the whole story.

While the family in which I was raised had very little money or education, they had some hings that money can't buy and which expensive government programs cannot create. As the only child in a family with four adults, I was the center of attention.

Many years later, when I had children of my own, I asked my sister how old I was when I first started to walk. Her reply was: "Oh, Tommy, nobody knows when you could walk. Somebody was always carrying you." You can't buy that.

Even when my sister was courting and sitting out on the front porch in a swing with her boyfriend, yours truly was sitting right there with them. It was so romantic—just the three of us.

After she and her boyfriend got married, he took a great interest in me and was my biggest booster and defender. It so happened that he too had been adopted—and he had not always been treated right. So he took it as his job to see that I got all the benefits, including the benefit of the doubt—which I often needed. You can't buy that either.

Some of my happiest times were when we were in the deepest poverty down South. As a child, I had no idea that we were in poverty. There was always food and clothing, though we didn't always have frills like electricity or hot running water.

I was nearly 9 years old before we had both of those things, and by now we had moved to New York, where we lived in Harlem. Although no one in our family was really educated, they understood that now I would have a chance for education and for other opportunities that they never had.

Before I arrived in New York, family members who were there had already picked out a boy that they wanted me to meet, because he came from a more educated background. He took me to a public library for the first time that I had ever set foot in such a place and explained patiently to me what it was and how it worked. His name was Eddie Mapp and, without either off us knowing it, he opened a whole new world for me that day.

In later years, the family's excited reaction when I was promoted to the seventh grade caught me completely by surprise. "Now you have gone further than any of us," I was told.

My teenage years were turbulent, and I left home when I was 17. That was when I learned the hard way that there was no great demand for a black teenage dropout with no skills or experience. Those were tough times, but they taught me things that would benefit me the rest of my life. Here was also no time for me to get hung up on adolescent navel-gazing about "identity" or "finding myself." It was all I could do to find the room rent.

Once, I had to pawn my only suit to get money to eat. My first meal with the money—a knish and an orange soda—was like a banquet. Since then, I have eaten at the Waldorf and in the White House, but no meal anywhere has ever topped that one.

Again, good fortune came my way, though I did not fully recognize its importance at the time. The foreman in the machine shop where I worked was a man named Ed Gally, who took a father's interest in me and gave me some much-needed advice from his store of experience. I learned how good his advice was, not only by following it, but also by not following it and suffering the consequences.

Yet again, this was something you can't buy.

Many years later, I returned to New York from California to give a talk at Columbia University.

After the talk, various people from the audience came up to me for more discussion. One of them was a distinguished-looking black man who was carrying a book of mine that he wanted autographed. Only when he got closer did I suddenly recognize him. It was Eddie Mapp!

Looking back on it all, how "disadvantaged" was I? Like most people, I had windfall losses and windfall gains. Much of what I didn't have turned out not to be really necessary, and much of what I did get was indispensable. Moreover, there was no one to give me a victim mentality.

Source: This column is reprinted here by permission of Thomas Sowell and Creators Syndicate, Inc.; it first appeared on 7 September 2000.

Books by Thomas Sowell: *Economics: Analysis and Issues* (Glenview, IL.: Scott, Foresman, 1971); *Black Education: Myths and Tragedies* (New York: McKay, 1972); *Say's Law: An Historical Analysis* (Princeton, N.J.: Princeton University Press, 1972); *Classical Economics Reconsidered* (Princeton: Princeton University Press, 1972); *Affirmative Action: Was It Necessary in Academia?* (Washington, D.C.: American Enterprise Institute for Public Policy Research, 1975); *Race and Economics* (New York: D. McKay, 1975); *Patterns of Black Excellence* (Washington: Ethics and Public Policy Center, Georgetown University, 1977); ed., *American Ethnic Groups* (Washington: Urban Institute, 1977); ed., *Essays on Data on American Ethnic Groups* (Washington: Urban Institute, 1978); *Markets and Minorities* (New York: Basic Books, 1981); *Pink and Brown People, and Other Controversial Essays* (Stanford, Calif.: Hoover Institution Press, 1981); *Knowledge and Decisions* (New York: Basic Books, 1982); *Ethnic America: A History* (New York: Basic Books, 1983); *The Economics and Politics of Race* (New York: W. Morrow, 1983); *Marxism: Philosophy and Economics* (New York: Morrow, 1985); *Civil Rights: Rhetoric or Reality?* (Stanford, Calif.: W. Morrow, 1986); *Compassion vs. Guilt, and Other Essays* (New York: Morrow, 1987); *A Conflict of Visions: Ideological Origins of Political Struggles* (New York: W. Morrow, 1987); *Choosing a College: a Guide for Parents and Students* (New York: Perennial Library, 1989); *Preferential Policies: An International Perspective* (New York: W. Morrow, 1990); *Race and Culture: A World View* (University Park, Pa.: Pennsylvania State University Press, 1992); *Inside American Education: the Decline, the Deception, the Dogmas* (New York: Free Press, 1993); *Is Reality Optional? and Other Essays* (Stanford, Calif.: Hoover Institute Press, 1993); *The Vision of the Anointed: Self-Congratulation as a Basis for Social Policy* (New York: Basic Books, 1995); *Migrations and Cultures: A World View* (New York: Basic Books, 1996); *Late-Talking Children* (New York: Basic Books, 1997); *Conquests and Cultures* (New York: Basic Books, 1998); *Barbarians Inside the Gates and Other Controversial Essays* (Stanford, Calif.: Hoover Institution Press, 1999); *The Quest for Cosmic Justice* (New York: Free Press, 1999); *A Personal Odyssey* (New York: Free Press, 2000); *The Einstein Syndrome: Bright Children Who Talk Late* (New York: Basic Books, 2001); *Basic Economics: A Citizen's Guide to the Economy* (New Haven, Conn.: Basic Books, 2001); *Some Thoughts About Writing* (Stanford, Calif.: Hoover Institution, 2001); *Controversial Essays* (Stanford, Calif.: 2002); *Applied Economics: Thinking Beyond Stage One* (New York: Basic Books, 2004); *Affirmative Action around the World; An Empirical Study* (New Haven, Conn.: Yale University Press, 2004); *Essays on Classical Economics* (Princeton, N.J.: Princeton University Press, 2005).

Further Readings: "Sowell, Thomas." *Contemporary Authors*, New Revision Series 26, pp. 397–399; "Sowell, Thomas." *Current Biography* 1981, pp. 390–393; "Thomas Sowell." [Online]. Creators Syndicate Web site www.Creators.com.

Spencer, Collins (1966–)

Youthful Collins Spencer is a coanchor for WSB-TV Channel 2 Action News in Atlanta. Prior to this job, he spent two years as a news anchor for

CNN Headline News, also in Atlanta. Spencer was born in Connecticut, spent his youth in the Northeast states and majored in broadcast management at Howard University, finishing in 1987. He began his career working for five years as a lobbyist in Washington. He moved to Richmond, Virginia, where he was for two years a political reporter and anchor at CBS affiliate station WTVR-TV. Returning to Washington, he freelanced for several months as a reporter for WJLA-TV. In 2000, he joined the Fox News Channel, working as a correspondent. There, he reported on the White House, the Capitol and the Pentagon. He covered the much-debated Elian Gonzalez story, which ended with the boy's return to his home in Cuba. Spencer contributed to coverage of the 2000 presidential election and in 2001, reported on the September 11 terrorist attacks in New York and Washington. His move to Atlanta and CNN came in February 2003. As one of CNN's anchors, he reported on security for the Summer Olympics, attempts by the West to restrict Iran's nuclear program, the seemingly endless violence in the Middle East, the burial of President Ronald Reagan, former president George H.W. Bush skydiving at age 80, climbing gas prices and the Far Right's attack-dog treatment of presidential candidate John Kerry's war record. He covered Hurricane Ivan in autumn 2004 and its effects on Florida, North Carolina and West Virginia. As do so many television anchors, Spencer occasionally serves as a master of ceremonies, as he did in April 2004 at the Native American Business Leaders awards luncheon in Atlanta.

Further Readings: "Collins Spencer." [Online, 11 November 2005]. WSBTV Web site www.wsbtv.com; "Collins Spencer Joins Pan Martin and Karen Minton on Channel 2 Action News 'This Morning.'" [Online, 2006]. Atlanta Daybook Web site www.atlantadaybook.com.

Staples, Brent A. (c.1951–)

An insightful man with a University of Chicago Ph.D., Brent Staples is an editorial writer for the *New York Times*. He was born in the tough factory town of Chester, Pennsylvania, the eldest son in a family of nine children. His early life was pleasant and supportive but the later years of his youth were often difficult inasmuch as his father began drinking heavily and had trouble holding down jobs. On occasion, the family had to make rapid moves to avoid the rent collector, his father sometimes became violent, some of his siblings slid into drugs and crime and he was often the picked-on new kid in the various schools he attended. Life hard and money scarce, Staples did not anticipate going to college, but he did so thanks to special instruction at Philadelphia Military College and Penn Morton College, the cadet corps and undergraduate civilian components of what became Widener College, and in 1979, Widener University. He was admitted to Widener and graduated with a B.A., with honors, in 1973. He won a Danforth Fellowship to study psychology at the University of Chicago and received his Ph.D. there in 1977. His psychology training can be seen in his newspaper writing, in which he shows an active interest in the way people think and relate. He attributes his storytelling abilities to his mother, who made it a custom to tell her children a bedtime story on a regular basis. From 1977 to 1981, Staples was an adjunct faculty member, teaching psychology. In 1982, he took a reporting job at the *Chicago Sun-Times*. In 1983, he left Chicago for a position with the *New York Times Book Review*, a job that suited his literary interests. He later became an assistant editor for metropolitan news at the *Times* and in 1990, became a member of the paper's editorial board. His editorials have often addressed matters of education, race and the various effects of the media. Staples has published one book, a well-received memoir of having grown up with one foot in the black world and one in the more sheltered, affluent side where much of white America lives. *Parallel Time: Growing Up in Black and White*, which appeared in 1994, was highly personal in that he contrasted his own career success with the troubled lives of some of his siblings, especially his younger brother Blake, who died at age 22 due to involvement in the illegal drug trade. The book won the Anisfield-Wolf Book Award and was a finalist in the Los Angeles Times Book Prize competition. Staples also has published in other newspapers and periodicals. One of his most striking stories appeared in *Harper's* in December 1986: "Black Men and Public Space." In it, Staples hauntingly described the unintended effect his hefty 6'4" presence has had on some of the strangers he had passed on the street while walking or jogging. He described in graphic terms the way many who encountered him on the streets of Chicago would tense, avoid eye contact and brace themselves for possible assault; the sound of car windows being locked at his approach; and whites crossing to the other side of the street to avoid him. He wrote of enjoying evening walks after he moved to Brooklyn even though he continued to be regarded as a likely mugger there too. In this strange saga of shared public space, he reported feeling outraged, yet feeling obliged to give strangers extra space to avoid frightening them. He added that he had adopted the habit of whistling Beethoven or Vivaldi in order to diffuse the obvious fear of many who shared the dark city streets with him. Staples also has published in the *Los Angeles Times*, *Literary Cavalcade* and *Columbia Journalism Review*.

In his book reviewing for the *Times* and for Slate.com, Staples has written insightfully about books of all sorts. A 1994 example was his review of the prolific V.S. Naipaul's novel *A Way in the World* (New York: Knopf, 1994), which examines, among other things, the legacy of colonialism. Staples credits Naipaul with being one of the best living writers of prose. In 1998, he reviewed Toni Morrison's *Paradise* (New York: A.A. Knopf, 1998), another novel of good and evil. Reviewing Paul Hendrickson's *Sons of Mississippi* (New York: Alfred A. Knopf, 2003), Staples again became personal by introducing readers to his own great-grandfather, John Wesley Staples, born on a plantation in Virginia at the end of the Civil War. His purpose in writing about his forebear was to point out how much more difficult his own rise to a prosperous middle-class lifestyle might have been had his own family been from Mississippi instead. The theme of his review is intolerance and Hendrickson's search for goodness or hope or optimism where these qualities are hard to find. One of his most powerful reviews was on Jennifer Gonnerman's *Life on the Outside: The Prison Odyssey of Elaine Bartlett* (New York: Farrar, Straus and Giroux, 2004). Here, his attention went to the seemingly endless cycle of crime and imprisonment and to the multiple difficulties faced by individuals who are released from prison, often into hope-deprived urban neighborhoods where crime abounds.

Staples' signed commentaries in the *Times* have examined questions such as why African Americans have been so favorably disposed to Bill Clinton. His overall conclusion in this 1998 commentary was that inasmuch as black people have been treated with contempt for so long, any prominent white who is friendly toward them is assumed to be "black inside," an assumption that does not always make literal sense considering their segregated upbringing. In 2001, another of Staples' efforts resulted from his having been summoned for jury duty to the striking new Courthouse and Federal Building in Central Islip, Long Island. The new courthouse was designed by Richard Meier, who was architect for the J. Paul Getty Museum in Los Angeles. Funds to pay for the courthouse came to Long Island courtesy of Republican Sen. Alfonse D'Amato, to whom Staples referred as "Senator Pothole" for his practiced ability to bring home pork-barrel funding. The mammoth grandeur of the new building, for Staples, was rendered less impressive by its skimpy, crowded bathroom facilities.

An advocate for better funded public schools, Staples cited the case of a Florence, South Carolina, woman to argue for supporting quality approaches to helping students who have learning disabilities. A year later, in 2003, he criticized wealthy Californians living in gated communities who supported Proposition 13, which was written to cap property taxes. In 2004, he castigated prison officials and politicians for rules that disallow condoms in 48 of the nation's 50 prison systems, thereby helping along the spread of AIDS and other venereal diseases. A commentary he wrote in 2005 addressed the history of interracial lust in America. Focusing on the relationship between Thomas Jefferson and Sally Hemings, he recognized the one-sided nature of their intimacy but pointed out that the descendants of blacks who worked in close proximity to their owners during slavery became the nucleus of the black intelligentsia of more recent times. As racist as that statement might sound, Staples made a good case for its veracity. Other recent commentaries by Staples have addressed No Child Left Behind and reparations, both of which he supports, and mandatory sentencing and electronic junk mail, of which he does not approve. Like other opinion writers, he is taken to task from time to time by those who disagree with his positions. One of the most rabid attacks on his writing came from *New York Press* columnist Taki Le Maire, who in 2005 called him "Brent Staplebrain" for his support of reparations for those affected by slavery. Le Maire also called the *Times* "The New York Sharpton."

Staples, Brent A.

"Lust across the Color Line and the Rise of the Black Elite" by Brent Staples

The 1998 DNA study that linked Thomas Jefferson to the final child of his lover Sally Hemings has settled one argument and fired up another. Most historians who had argued that Jefferson was too pure of heart to bed a slave have re-evaluated 200 years of evidence and embraced the emerging consensus: that Jefferson had a long relationship with Hemings and probably fathered most, if not all of her children.

Having acknowledged the relationship, these historians are now trying to explain it. This has sent them scrambling back to the 19th-century accounts of life at Monticello by two former slaves: Jefferson's former servant, Israel Jefferson, and the founder's son, Madison Hemings. This represents the rehabilitation of Madison, who was being vilified as a liar even 10 years ago.

Madison's memoir, based partly on family history conveyed to him by his mother, is as close to the voice of Sally Hemings as we will ever come. But neither of these brief accounts, published in an Ohio newspaper in 1873, reveals anything about the intimate texture of the relationship between Thomas Jefferson and Sally Hemings. They tell us a great deal, however, about the circumstances that created the black intelligentsia that sprang to life during Reconstruction and that dominated African-American cultural, intellectual and political life through the first half of the 20th century.

This black intelligentsia did not spring fully formed from the cotton fields. It had its roots in the families of mixed-race slaves like the Hemingses, who served as house servants for generations, often in the homes of white families to whom they were related. Employed in "the big house," these slaves often learned to read, at a time when few slaves were literate. They also absorbed patterns of speech, dress and deportment that served them well after emancipation.

Most of them were set free by their guilt-ridden slave owner fathers long before the official end of slavery. The Hemings children were all free by 1829—or more than a third of a century before slavery was finally abolished. Not surprisingly, mixed-race offspring who were well educated became teachers, writers, newspaper editors. They formed the bedrock of an emerging black elite and were disproportionately represented in the African-American leadership during Reconstruction and well into the 20th century.

Not all of these mixed-race children fared so well, however. Many were sold or passed on as chattel to relatives in their fathers' wills. This was in fact the case with Sally Hemings, one of several children born to a mixed-race slave named Betty Hemings and a white lawyer and businessman named John Wayles—the father of Thomas Jefferson's wife, Martha. When Wayles died, Martha inherited some of her enslaved half siblings, including Sally Hemings.

Sally Hemings was just a child when she accompanied Jefferson and his daughter to France for more than two years. Madison tells us in his memoir that his mother became pregnant by Jefferson in France, where she was considered free. She refused to return to America, he said, until Jefferson agreed to free all of the children born of their relationship.

Madison recalls that he and his siblings were favored at Monticello, and allowed to spend their time in the "great house," where they could be close to their mother. Madison further asserts that they knew of Jefferson's plans to emancipate them. "We were free from the dread of having to be slaves all our lives long, and were measurably happy," he says.

Jefferson's favoritism, however, did not include affection. Jefferson's black children, who seem never to have received so much as an embrace or a peck on the cheek, watched in what must have been painful silence as the great man doted on his white grandchildren. Madison says, "We were the only children of his by a slave woman."

The "great house" at Monticello offered abundant opportunities for encounters with the great minds of the day. Israel Jefferson, for expample, recalls being present when Jefferson and Lafayette debated the question of slavery.

Raised in such a context, the Hemings children—and others like them—were probably better prepared for middle-class life than most people, either black or white. Indeed, historians who have followed the Hemings descendants through time have found that the cultural capital acquired by Hemings children at Monticello translated into upward mobility.

Historians who are now searching for ways to understand the Jefferson-Hemings relationship have several models from which to choose. Some masters developed caring, de facto marriages with enslaved women and tried to leave their children money and property in their wills. Other masters were serial rapists or plantation potentates who made harems in their slave quarters and were profoundly indifferent to their offspring.

For the time being, however, the last word on this issue should go to Madison Hemings, who flatly and dispassionately describes the relationship as a bargain, in which his mother consented to share Jefferson's bed in exchange for the emancipation of her children. That she had the courage to articulate this deal—and stand firm on its terms—makes her more than a mere concubine. It makes her the architect of her family's freedom.

Source: Copyright © 2005 by *The New York Times* Co. Reprinted with permission. The above story appeared on 10 April 2005.

Books by Brent A. Staples: *Parallel Time: Growing Up in Black and White* (New York: Pantheon Books, 1994).

Further Readings: "'Apocalypse Pretty Soon,' Starring Undertaxed California." [Online, 10 November 2003]. Times Watch Web site www.timeswatch.org; "The Distorted Story of Memoir Inc." [Online, 23 July 2001]. Christianity Today Web site www.christianitytoday.com.

Stevens, Shay (?–)

A broadcast newswoman since 1981, Shay Stevens, also known as Sharon McCalister, is overnight anchor for National Public Radio. In this job, she works while most of us sleep, writing, editing and broadcasting news. She was born in Philadelphia to a postal employee father and city worker mother, lived in the neighborhood partially destroyed by the 1980 MOVE bombing and graduated from West Philadelphia High School. She holds a 2000 B.A. in journalism from American University. Much earlier, she had attended both Temple University and California State University at Northridge. Her career began as a disc jockey and newsreader at a radio station in Sioux City, Iowa. After a short stay there, she moved to Philadelphia in May 1981 to work as an afternoon drive-time anchor for WHAT-AM and a part-time news anchor for its sister station, WWDB-FM. In January 1982, she took a new job with that city's WUSL-FM as afternoon drive-time anchor and as evening anchor for its sister station, WFIL-AM. She also covered City Hall for the station and was its entertainment reporter and assignment editor. In January 1985, Stevens became afternoon drive-time anchor and government and education reporter for the Wilmington, Delaware, all-news station WILM-AM, remaining there until July 1987 and from January 1985 until July of that same year, doubled as a part-time news announcer and reporter for Philadelphia station WCAU-AM. In May 1987, she moved to Buffalo, New York, to become live-line reporter for WEBR-AM. She did on-air interviews for this public news station, was a news anchor and also served as a general assignment reporter.

Stevens returned to Philadelphia in February 1988 and was news anchor for WWDB-FM, a news/talk station. In this job, she fed stories to ABC and UPI. She moved again in October 1988, this time to Baltimore as news director of WCBM-AM, another news/talk station. From May 1992 to May 1994, she worked for USA Today Sky Radio, writing for and anchoring hourly newscasts, reporting from the field and producing feature stories that were beamed by satellite to airlines. Stevens began her present NPR job in March 1990 and lives in Glenn Dale, Maryland. She has held memberships in the Philadelphia chapter of the Association of Black Journalists, the National Association of Black Journalists, the Society of Professional Journalists and the Radio and Television News Directors Association. She holds membership in the National Association of Black Journalists, the Society of Professional Journalists and the Radio-Television News Directors Association.

Further Readings: "Shay Stevens." [Online]. National Public Radio Web site www.npr.org.

Stewart, Pearl (?–)

Now a journalism faculty member at the University of Southern Mississippi, Pearl Stewart was, in 1992, the first black woman to become editor of a major metropolitan daily and in 2002, founded Black College Wire to promote the training and job prospects of students attending historically black colleges and universities. Stewart has also taught as an instructor, fellow or journalist-in-residence at a number of other schools, including Harvard University, where she was a Shorenstein Fellow; Louisiana State University; Dillard University; Xavier University and Howard University. She worked as a staff writer for the *San Francisco Chronicle*, but her most outstanding journalistic credentials come from her time at the *Oakland Tribune*, where in the late 1970s, she and fellow reporter Lance Williams reported on the activities and finances of Huey Newton and the Black Panther Party. During this assignment, her car was firebombed in the parking garage of her apartment building. In 1992, Stewart became the *Tribune*'s top editor and as such, was the first African-American woman to reach that level of mainstream newspaper management on a metropolitan daily. In 2000, she joined the faculty of the School of Journalism at Florida A&M University, where she both taught and was director of career development. In January 2005, she took over as managing editor of the financially troubled *Chicago Defender* but resigned after just two months in office. At that time, the venerable *Defender*'s writing was done mainly by freelancers. It had one reporter, one sportswriter, an entertainment writer/editor and two graphics employees, working under editor Roland S. Martin. Before she left the *Defender* in March 2005, Stewart remarked that she had been looking forward to a challenge, but not one that was so completely overwhelming.

Earlier, in 2002, Stewart founded the Black College Wire, a news service that promotes the work and prospects of students from America's black institutions of higher education. The Wire was a project of the Black College Communication Association and was funded by a grant from the John H. and James L. Knight

Foundation, which has continued its support. The project was also supported by the National Association of Black Journalists. Stewart was the Wire's founding coordinator, and its editor is longtime journalist Richard Prince. The idea behind the Wire is to facilitate the linking of academic training with the job market. Stewart has also worked for the Black College Communication Association as a "roving journalist"; her travel to historically black colleges is funded by The Freedom Forum. In 2005, the Black College Communication Association announced the creation of the Pearl Stewart Freedom Fighter Award, to be given to student journalists who demonstrate professional courage and strive to uphold the First Amendment in their work. The first recipient was Hampton University student Daarel Burnette, who had written a story about health code violations at the school's cafeteria that resulted in the ill-advised confiscation by administrators of the paper's homecoming edition. Appearing below is Stewart's own take on that unfortunate, embarrassing situation, which occurred in a school at which the journalism/communications program had just benefited from a $2.3 million grant from the Scripps-Howard Foundation.

Following the Hurricane Katrina disaster in New Orleans and other parts of the Gulf Coast, Black College Wire and the *Black Collegian* magazine combined forces to cover the disaster's wake, especially the hardships being encountered by the area's college students. Also attracting comment from Stewart has been the war in Iraq. Stewart has been quoted as remarking, as have many other journalism faculty, that today's students do not seem to have grasped the realities of the war and are not even interested in doing so. Instead, they are content with staying out of it and continuing to be well entertained at home. This situation has special relevance for African-American students, inasmuch as our nation's military is now disproportionately black. Stewart has further pointed out that war costs have also had the effect of reducing funding for social programs, which also disproportionately affect blacks.

A Stewart article posted on Black College Wire in February 2000 described strains of another kind. The article listed a number of historically black campuses at which not one issue of the student newspaper had appeared during the 1998–1999 academic year, sometimes due to financial problems, sometimes to censorship by nervous administrators who feared the publicizing of negative news. Other college papers, most of which are supposed to be monthlies, had only one to three issues appear during that time frame. The money problems were understandable, she wrote, but she was sharply critical of school administrators who feel threatened by student media and resort to censorship.

Stewart has contributed a chapter to a 1997 book edited by Pippa Norris, *Politics and the Press: The News Media and its Influences* (Boulder, Colo.: Lynne Rienner Publishers); her chapter is "Women of Color as Newspaper Executives."

"No One Won in Hampton Newspaper Crisis" by Pearl Stewart

The agreement reached last week between Hampton University's student newspaper staff and Acting President JoAnn Haysbert was not a victory, but, as editor Talia Buford told the Daily Press in Hampton Roads, Va., simply progress.

The task force that will be appointed will focus immediate attention on a situation that has long needed to change. The Script is currently under the control of the administration, and its content has to be approved before the paper is published. Far too many historically black institutions have these rigid restrictions on student media. Perhaps this incident will lead to changes on those campuses as well.

No one won at Hampton, not Haysbert, who revealed a shocking lack of understanding about the role of student media, and certainly not the student editors, who should not have been forced to place Haysbert's letter on the front page. That action came close to turning the school newspaper into a public relations handout and was an insult not only to the newspaper staff but to the readers, who expect to see news presented in the paper in the appropriate manner. When was the last time anyone saw a letter on the front page of any reputable newspaper? The acting president required the students to do something that diminished the quality and credibility of the paper. The editors' disclaimer that had accompanied the letter was an excellent idea, but it should not have been necessary, because the letter should not have been there.

For several days last week, Hampton's newspaper editors resisted Haysbert's order that her letter of response about the cafeteria violations be published on the front page. Haysbert had the 6,500 copies of the paper removed from The Script office last Wednesday after she learned that her letter was on page three. If the students hadn't agreed to redesign the front page, Hampton would not have had a homecoming issue.

By insisting that the students place her letter on the front page instead of inside, where it belonged, Haysbert made it clear that she is neither knowledgeable nor concerned about proper journalism, and that she is interested only in having her wishes carried out. That is a questionable attitude for the chief executive of a university that houses an accredited journalism school.

The students wrote an accurate story about health code violations in the cafeteria, and in it they focused on the university's hasty response to the citations. The story was not only fair, it was charitable to the administration. The conditions in the cafeteria, which is located in the basement of a 130-year-old building, were deplorable.

In the thirteenth paragraph of the story, The Script reported: "Students complained about seeing dead flies in the dinner plates and roaches crawling across salad bars and from under plates. One student witnessed a roach trapped in the plastic wrap covering a cup of pudding." In many papers, that paragraph would have been the lead.

The acting president's actions had the boomerang effect of publicizing to an international audience the school's disgusting bug infestation. Had she allowed the original issue of the paper to be distributed, the cafeteria's code violations would not be a topic of conversation—along with the censorship issues—all over the Internet. Although the building has been sanitized, many are wondering how it was allowed to reach the point of having 30 violations.

The students were clearly trying to report the story without embarrassing the university on homecoming weekend. However, the gravity of the health issues warranted a hard-hitting news story and an even harder-hitting editorial.

The administrators who condoned the confiscation of the papers should enroll in some of the classes being taught by their outstanding journalism faculty. They should learn how intrepid journalists have exposed human rights violations from lynchings in the South to the killing fields of Cambodia and Bosnia.

Journalism is a noble profession, and Hampton's administrators should encourage the campus newspaper to report the truth and to stand up for what is right.

Source: The above commentary piece appeared on 27 October 2003 on the Black College Wire Web site and appears here with the permission of the administrators of that site.

Further Readings: Coleman, Kate. "The Panthers for Real." [Online, 23 June 2003]. FrontPageMagazine.com Web site www.frontpagemag.com; Hart, Ariel. "How to Find Black Journalists." [Online, May/June 2000]. Columbia Journalism Review site http://archives.cjr.org;

Stone, Charles (Chuck) Sumner Jr.

Lee, Dain. "The Bomb-Bay Doors Open and...Blogs Away." [Online, 27 February 2004]. New York University Department of Journalism ReadMe site http://journalism.nyu.edu; Lennon, Jen. "Journalism Pros Discuss What Went Wrong, Right with Katrina Coverage." *The Athens News*, 10 October 2005; Prince, Richard. [Online, 22 December 2004]. Richard Prince's Journal-isms. Maynard Institute Web site www.maynardije.org; Prince, Richard. "Pearl Stewart Quits Defender." [Online, 25 February 2005]. Richard Prince's Journal-isms. Maynard Institute Web site www.maynardije.org.

Stone, Charles (Chuck) Sumner Jr. (21 July 1924–)

Chuck Stone is best known for having been his city and region's champion of the common man during the 1970s, when he wrote a *Philadelphia Daily News* column, syndicated by Universal Press Syndicate. He is secondarily known for his years as a journalism faculty member at the University of North Carolina at Chapel Hill. He was born in St. Louis, Missouri, and his middle name was given him in honor of Charles Sumner, a prominent abolitionist. He was known as Charlie until he served as a navigator and bombardier in the Air Force from 1943 to 1945, when a friend christened him "Chuck." He earned the B.A. from Wesleyan University in 1948, majoring in political science and minoring in economics, and received the M.A. in sociology 1951 at the University of Chicago. Stone worked from 1952 until 1956 as a field representative for World Politics and American Foreign Policy, then in 1956 and 1957 as a representative in Beirut and India for CARE (Cooperative for American Relief Everywhere). He had a job offer to work for the Asia Foundation, but instead, at age 34 in 1958, he entered newspaper work, at first as an editorial consultant and six months later as editor of the venerable historically black paper the *New York Age*. Many of his readers and colleagues were surprised when he hired two white columnists and a white advertising director. In 1960 he relocated to the Washington *Afro-American* as editor and columnist, and when John F. Kennedy was elected president, Stone made himself the White House correspondent, as well. He moved again in 1963 to edit the *Daily Defender* in Chicago. He was fired from the *Defender* job in 1964 for his criticism of Chicago mayor Richard Daley and in 1965 went to work as a special aide to New York congressman Adam Clayton Powell at a time when Powell was receiving death threats and carried a gun. Stone was instrumental in creating the "Black Power" slogan, and when Powell was ousted from Congress due amidst charges of malfeasance, Stone found a new position as a research assistant for another black congressman, Robert Nix. In 1969, Stone was a visiting faculty member at Trinity College in Hartford, Connecticut, and was an NBC-TV commentator on the "Today" show. From 1970 to 1972 he was minority affairs director for the Educational Testing Service in Princeton, New Jersey, and later in 1972 he joined the Philadelphia *Daily News* and began writing the column that made him the paper's best-known writer. His was a witty and sometimes acerbic column in which he stuck up for disenfranchised African Americans and never hesitated to deflate the pompous or to prod sacred cows—as in the column on evangelist Billy Graham that appears below, one that Stone says elicited an enormous response—both positive and negative. He was inventive and surprising, sometimes writing in different voices, such as those of his fictitious characters "Chief Standing Bull" and "Nicodemus." In his *Daily News* column, Stone lived up to the old saying that journalists should comfort the afflicted and afflict the comfortable. His three favorite luminaries to "afflict" were two-gun Frank Rizzo, Philadelphia's colorful, egotistical police chief and later mayor; black congressman William Gray III; and Wilson Goode, another mayor of the city where brotherly love has been so often tested. Stone's willingness to take on the great and powerful endeared him to much of the city's populace, and he soon had an unusual role thrust upon him: mediator between the city's and region's criminals and the police. His first such mediation was in 1972 when he helped settle a conflict for prisoners at a prison in Wilkes-Barre, Pennsylvania. In 1981, he negotiated the end of a hostage situation at Graterford Prison, and three other such negotiations followed. On 75 occasions, individuals wanted by the police turned themselves in to Stone, fearing mistreatment should they go directly to the authorities. Stone, a natty dresser known especially for his bow ties, looks back upon these experiences as his "life of crime." Stone became a senior editor at the *Daily News*, briefly taught English at the University of Delaware, and achieved syndication with Universal in 1989. Two years later he joined the Chapel Hill faculty, teaching there as the Walter Spearman Professor of Journalism until he retired at age 80 in 2005.

Stone was founding president of the NABJ, the National Association of Black Journalists, in 1975. He has written four books, including a novel and a children's story. In retirement, he is working on a biography of Walter Spearman, another legendary Chapel Hill journalism professor. He has won many an award, starting with the Best Column of the Year award from the National Newspaper Publishers Association in 1960 and the Capital Press Club's Journalist of the Year award in 1961. The Congress of Racial Equality awarded him its Distinguished Citizen Award in 1964. He received honorary degrees from three schools: Wilberforce University in 1977 and both Pembroke State University and Rider College in 1985. In 1983, he was made an honorary federal warden by the U.S. Bureau of Prisons, and in 1989, he received first place in column writing from the Pennsylvania Publishers Association, and from the University of Delaware, the Laubach Excellence in Teaching Award. In 1992, he won the Undergraduate Teaching Award at the Journalism School of the University of North Carolina. In 1995, he received the Lifetime Achievement Award given by the NABJ and was inducted into its Hall of Fame. In 1996, the University of Missouri honored him with its Missouri Honor Medal for service to journalism.

Stone, Charles (Chuck) Sumner Jr.

"Silly Billy Graham: Magnificent Phony" by Chuck Stone

The thundering wrath of his devoted partisans may come cascading down in torrents over my head after I write this, but I'm going to submit it anyhow: Billy Graham is one of the most magnificent phonies in America today.

In this papier mache, assembly-line culture of instant coffee, instant tea, instant mashed potatoes, instant cake mix, and instant house construction, Billy Graham's "instant Christianity" is just about the most nauseating short-cut to heaven anybody's ever manufactured.

Machine-gunning his message in a Walter Winchell-like staccato, the golden-maned evangelist serves up a heaping dish of Southern fried, hominy grits Christianity that is more P.T. Barnum in presentation than it is Christ in inspiration.

Every time he walks to the podium and begins making like a combination of William Jennings Bryan and Willy Loman, thousands of confused, churchless Americans gobble up this wordy garbage and come away with the worst case of spiritual indigestion they have ever had.

They then spend the next few days trying to diagnose why they ever got excited in the first place.

Yes, Billy Graham "saves souls."

The trouble is as lot of these souls get lost the next day.

True product of a society almost totally conceived in the womb of an advertising account executive, Billy Graham merchandises Christianity with an impeccable eloquence that leaves corporation executives gasping in admiration. He is unchallengeably one of the most successful salesmen in America today. Rather than come to specific grips, however, with some of America's critical problems—race hatred, crime, unemployment, unequal education, inadequate housing, poverty, drop-outs—in terms of the precise demands Christ would have placed upon us for their remediation, Billy Graham skirts definitive answers by urging us to "take your burdens to the Lord and leave them there."

His attitude and pronouncements on the racial crisis in America attained their soiled apotheosis a few days ago when he pontificated that the racial problem would be solved at "the foot of the cross of Jesus Christ."

What the sinner is supposed to glean from this kind of vapid, silly declaration is that if he simply kneels down and prays to Jesus Christ, somehow his troubled, racist heart will be changed and he'll love his black brother.

Shucks, Billy Graham himself isn't even able to come out and unqualifiedly denounce racial segregation and those who practice it. Along with his segregated American church and white brothers of the clergy who every Sunday rise up in their lilywhite pulpits and preach to lilywhite congregations, he's too busy praying.

You don't see Billy Graham walking into the Southern temples of racial segregation and telling the racists to get out because they defile God's house with their denial of love and brotherhood: "And Jesus went into the temple and began to cast out them that sold and bought in the temple and overthrew the tables of the money changers and the seats of them that sold doves." (In short, Jesus gave 'em hell.)

You don't see Billy Graham walking any picket lines or even admitting they have a spiritual redemption for the sinner: "Moreover, if hy brother shall trespass against thee, go and tell him his fault between thee and him alone...But if he does not hear thee, then take with thee one or two more that in the mouth of two or three witnesses every word may be established." (The Rev. John F. Cronin, assistant director of the social action department off the National Catholic Welfare Conference, agreed with Jesus about taking along "two or three witnesses" when he said this week that clergymen "should be in the forefront of demonstrations to show our support for the civil rights movement.")

You never see Billy Graham telling white people that Negroes are so unremittingly their brothers that they must live together next door to each other as neighbors and accept Negroes with love as neighbors: "And behold a certain lawyer stood up and tempted him saying, Master, what shall I do to inherit eternal life?...And he answering said, Thou shalt love the Lord thy God with all thy soul and with all thy strength and with all they mind and thy neighbor as thyself...But he, willing to justify himself, said unto Jesus, And who is my neighbor?" Whereupon Jesus told the lawyer the parable of the good Samaritan, then asked: "Which now of these three thinkest thou was neighbor unto him that fell among the thieves? And he said, He that sheweth mercy on him. Then said Jesus unto him, Go and do thou likewise." Negroes fell among thieves when their rights to live anywhere or be served as citizens in public places were stolen from them, but have you heard Billy Graham coming out for mercy-showing laws that would guarantee open occupancy and equal accommodations for Negroes?

And this is the tragedy of a Billy Graham—not his antiseptic evangelism that would keep us enslaved by simply "kneeling at the cross," waiting for a miracle to transform our souls, but his failure and refusal to invigorate the teachings of the Christ of Nazareth with the spiritual requisites of a jet-age society torn asunder by horse-and-buggy racial hatred.

"For God so loved the world that He gave His only begotten Son, that whosoever believeth in Him should not perish but have everlasting life."

When the Reverend Bruce Williams Klunder placed his hand in God's in Cleveland last week and lay down before the terror off that life-crushing bulldozer, he understood in that quick moment of truth more about the soul-saving demands of Christianity than Billy Graham can ever hope to feel in the next twenty-five years with his phony summonses to merely "kneel at the cross" and be saved.

In an era which nurtures middle-class mediocrity and phony religious values, the Reverend Billy Graham is exactly what we Americans deserve in our present inability to find lasting salvation in the true meaning of brotherhood.

Source: This column appears here by permission of Mr. Stone.

Books by Charles (Chuck) Sumner Stone Jr.: *Tell It like It Is* (New York: Trident, 1967); *Black Political Power in America* (Indianapolis, Ind.: Bobbs-Merrrill, 1968); *King Strut* (Indianapolis, Ind.: Bobbs-Merrill, 1970); with Jeannis Jackson, *Squizzy the Black Squirrel: A Fabulous Fable of Friendship* (Greensboro, N.C.: Open Hand, 2003).

Further Readings: Henry, Neil. "A Newsman Who Makes News." *Newsweek*, 16 November 1981, p. 72; Kramer, Staci D. "Election Ombudsman." *Editor & Publisher*, 28 December 1996, pp. 14–15; McBride, Sarah. "Stone's Career: A Study in Charisma and Controversy." *The UNC Journalist*, Fall 1994, p. 10; Villeponteaux, Bess. "Stone to Retire This Spring After a Fruitful Career." *Carolina Communicator*, Winter 2005, pp. 1, 7.

Syler, Rene (17 February 1963–)

The attractive Rene Syler is one of the anchors of the CBS News' morning program "The Early Show." She is said to have been the first African-American woman to work as a morning show anchor. Prior to taking this position in October 2002, she had been in television news work since 1987. She was born at Scott Air Force Base in Illinois and grew up mainly in Sacramento, California. Syler is a 1987 graduate of California State University at Sacramento, where she majored in psychology. She had attended American River College in Sacramento from 1981 to 1983 and Azusa Pacific University in Azusa, California, before transferring to Cal State in autumn 1985. She had registered for graduate school in psychology but decided to attempt a career in television after reading a story about successful African-American newswoman Liz Walker in Boston. Syler took a few basic journalism courses at a community college and got an internship at a Sacramento station, where she learned production skills. Armed with a demo tape made during the internship, she approached Reno, Nevada, station KTVN-TV and was hired later in 1987, working there as a reporter until 1989. During 1989 and 1990, she worked as an anchor at rival Reno station KOLO-TV, after which she was an anchor at Birmingham,

Alabama, station WVTM-TV until 1992. At that time she became morning and noon anchor for WFAA-TV in Dallas, Texas. In 1997, she joined Dallas' CBS-owned station KTVT as noon and 5 PM anchor. She was noon and 6 PM anchor there from 2000 until 2002, when, at age 39, she became one of four anchors for the revamped "Early Show," working alongside news veteran Harry Smith, sports maven Hannah Storm, and Julie Chen. The four were later joined by entertainment reporter Laurie Hibberd, weatherman Dave Price and consumer reporter Susan Koeppen. The previous version of "The Early Show," hosted by Bryant Gumbel and Jane Clayson, had been a flop compared to its rival shows, ABC's "Good Morning America" and NBC's "The Today Show." Announcing the new four-anchor format, CBS News executive Andrew Heywood emphasized that the show would concentrate primarily on news, not entertainment. Time has proved those words hollow, however, and the show has received considerable criticism for its fluffy, entertainment-oriented programming, even though its ratings have improved somewhat. In her early months with the show, Syler interviewed Laura Bush, Colin Powell, Sen. John McCain, Dr. Howard Dean, John Kerry and other bona fide news figures; and she reported from Florida after Hurricane Charley. She also covered the Ronald Reagan funeral from Washington. In October 2003, she started an "Early Show" series on breast cancer, an assignment that had personal meaning to her because the disease had struck members of her own family. In December 2004, she collaborated with *More* magazine editor Peggy Northrup to do an "Early Show" series titled "Reaching for More," on issues important to women over 40. Overall, however, she appears to have specialized in conducting celebrity interviews. In July 2003, she interviewed weight-loss icon Jenny Craig and her husband Sid Craig. Another weight-loss interview, in February 2004, was with celebrity dieter Anna Nicole Smith; and in June of that year, she interviewed "American Idol" winner Fantasia Barrino. A month later, it was the three brothers who sing as "Hanson," and entertainer Prince, who expounded on war, politics and race. In August, she interviewed actor Peter Boyle, who plays the father role in the successful sitcom "Everybody Loves Raymond." In February and March 2005 came a variety of "reality television" personalities who had been voted off the show. The low point must have been her March 2005 interview with buxom blonde Kim Mullen, who talked about such weighty news issues as her "snuggle partner" on the show.

Syler is a member of the National Association of Black Journalists. During her time in Reno, she belonged to the Northern Nevada Black Cultural Awareness Society and while in Dallas, to the Dallas/Fort Worth Association of Black Communicators. She also has been active with the YWCA. She has spoken before the American Women in Radio and Television and served as emcee at the 2004 awards ceremony of the NABJ and as master of ceremonies at the Pink Tie Ball fundraiser of the Susan G. Komen Breast Cancer Foundation's North Jersey Affiliate. She was named Television Personality of the Year in 1997 by the Dallas/Ft. Worth Chapter of AWRT and in 2004, won the Gracie Allen Award for Individual Achievement for her series on breast cancer.

Further Readings: Burton, Valorie. "October Challenge: Listen to Your Life Spotlight." [Online, 5 October 2004]. Black America Web site www.blackamericanweb.com; Pierce, Ellise. "Rene Syler Is (Almost) Ready for Her Close-up." *D Magazine*, 1 January 2003; "Rene Syler." [Online, 21 September 204]. CBS News Web site www.cbsnews.com; "Rene Takes on Her Claustrophobia." [Online, 1 December 2004]. CBS News Web site www.cbsnews.com.

T

Taylor, Susan L. (23 January 1946–)

New York City–born Susan Taylor came to success as editorial director of *Essence*, the nation's premier magazine for African-American women, by a somewhat unusual route. She attended Roman Catholic schools but did not go to college at the usual time of life; and, living in the Bronx as an anxious, just-separated single mother at age 24, she went to cosmetology school, then sold cosmetics in a New York department store. With this background, she launched her own cosmetics company, Nequai Cosmetics, and in 1970, became the beauty editor for *Essence* when the magazine was just two years old. As a licensed cosmetologist, she had a better grasp of the makeup needs of black women than did the predominantly white cosmetics industry, and her monthly column was well received. The magazine added fashion to her responsibilities, and in 1981, she became editor-in-chief, taking over from Marcia Ann Gillespie, and in 1986, was named vice president of Essence Communications Inc., the magazine's parent company. She was named senior vice president in 1993. During her term as editor-in-chief, she continued her monthly column, titled "In the Spirit," to reflect the spiritual leanings that later led her to enroll in Union Theological Seminary. Her upbeat, motivational column has encouraged black entrepreneurship and offered sisterly personal encouragement for her readers; she has often been called a print version of Oprah Winfrey. For balance, she added to the magazine's contents a column written by men titled "Brothers." In 1984, she began taking night classes at Fordham University and in 1991 received the B.A. in sociology. Circulation grew tremendously during her years as editor, from 600,000 to more than a million, and she also hosted and produced the nation's first nationally syndicated magazine-format television show for African Americans, also titled "Essence." Added later were the "Essence Awards Show" and the annual Essence Music Festival, which began in New Orleans in 1995 and featured Stevie Wonder, Luther Vandross and Anita Baker. In the midst of all these efforts, Taylor has graduated from Fordham University, has written or cowritten six books and has been active on the lecture circuit. She has received two honorary degrees, one in 1988 from Lincoln University, the other in 1993 from the University of Delaware.

In July 2001, she stepped down as editor, taking the title of editorial director and continuing to write her column. Taylor has also worked with Amistad Press, a book publisher partly owned by Essence Communications. She also coordinates the company's licensing division, which offers a line of hosiery suited to the particular needs of black women, Essence Eyewear, Essence Art Reproductions and Essence Television Productions. She has been active is support of the fostercare agency Edwin Gould Services for Children and is on the board of the organization Aid to Imprisoned Mothers. She has worked on the Commission on Research in Black Education and, with actor Danny Glover, has cochaired a campaign to raise funds to build housing in rural South Africa. In 1999, she received the magazine industry's highest honor, the Henry Johnson Fisher Award given by the Magazine Publishers of America. In 2002, she was inducted into the American Society of Magazine Editors Hall of Fame.

Books by Susan L. Taylor: *In the Spirit: The Inspirational Writings of Susan L. Taylor* (New York: Amistad, 1993); *Lessons in Living* (New York: Anchor Books, 1995); with Khepra Burns, *Confirmation: The Spiritual Wisdom That Has Shaped Our Lives* (New York: Anchor Books, 1997); with Patricia Mignon Hinds, *Black Men in Their Own Words* (New York: Crown Publishers, 2002); with Patricia Mignon Hinds, *50 of the Most Inspiring African-Americans* (New York: Essence Books, 2002); with Patricia Mignon Hinds, *Wisdom of the Ages: Extraordinary People, 19 to 90* (New York: Essence Books, 2003).

Further Readings: Clark, Robbie. "Taylor, Susan." In *Black Women in America, Second Edition.* Ed. Darlene Clark Hine. New York: Oxford University Press, 2005, pp. 216–17; Edwards, Audrey and P. Mignon Hinds. *Essence: 25 Years Celebrating Black Women.* New York: H.N. Abrams, 1995; Marshall, Dianne. "Susan L. Taylor." In *Notable Black American Women.* Ed. Jessie Carney Smith and Shirelle Phelps. Detroit, Mich.: Gale Research, 1992–2003, pp. 111415; "Susan L. Taylor." In *The African American Almanac.* 9th ed. Ed. Jeffrey Lehman. Detroit, Mich.: Gale Group, 2003, pp. 889–90; "Taylor, Susan L." In 1997 *Current Biography Yearbook.* Ed. Elizabeth A. Schick. New York: H.W. Wilson, pp. 555–57.

Thomas, Pierre (c.1964–)

After 13 years as a newspaper reporter, 10 of which were at the *Washington Post*, Pierre Thomas moved to broadcast news work, first at CNN for three years, then to his present post at ABC News. He hails from Amherst County, Virginia, and is a 1984 graduate of Virginia Polytechnic Institute & State University, better known as Virginia Tech. He came to college with plans to major either in business administration or computer science but discovered how much he liked the information-gathering aspect of journalism.

As a student, he wrote for the campus newspaper, the *Collegiate Times*; was active in campus radio and television; and belonged to a near record-breaking number of other campus organizations. He was the only student in the history of Virginia Tech's Department of Communication Studies (now Department of Communication) to complete four internships. Thomas first set his sights on becoming a television news anchorman, but the internship he did with a Roanoke station showed him that he was probably not "pretty" enough for that job. Next, he did a radio internship and after that, an internship in public relations. Still uncertain that he had found his niche, he accepted a paid newspaper internship after his 1984 graduation at the *Roanoke Times & World News* (now the *Roanoke Times*). To his surprise, he found that he liked the opportunity for reporting in greater depth that newspaper work offered, and his internship turned into a regular job at that paper. Three years later, in 1987, he took a new job, at the *Washington Post*, reporting on state politics and covering the police and court beats for Alexandria and Prince William County. In 1991, having established a sound reputation for careful reporting, he began doing investigative work with the *Post*'s Metro projects team. There, he and his colleagues reported on illegal gun use in the nation's capital, a story that was a Pulitzer Prize finalist. Next he moved to the national desk to cover law enforcement, from local police to the FBI and Justice Department. He reported in 1992 on the FBI assault at Ruby Ridge, Idaho, the 1995 bombing by Timothy McVeigh of the Oklahoma City federal building and the 1996 arrest of the "Unabomber," Chicago-born mathematician Theodore Kaczynski, the sender of letter bombs who killed or wounded 29 victims.

In the following year, 1997, Thomas left newspaper journalism for his original medium of choice, television, to become a CNN correspondent. In the three years he held this job, he covered several major stories, including the April 2000 INS abduction at gunpoint of Cuban boy Elian Gonzalez and his being returned to Cuba three months later, the FBI's Most Wanted list, cyber-crime, school violence in America, the FBI's controversial Internet surveillance system known as Carnivore and ongoing coverage of terrorism, including the as yet unsuccessful hunt for terrorism mastermind Osama bin Laden of Saudi Arabia. Thomas's most recent move was in November 2000, when he joined ABC News, working at that time with the late Peter Jennings. There, too, he has covered big stories, such as the terrorist attacks of September 11; the arrest in 2001 of FBI agent Robert Hanssen, who had sold classified information to the Soviet Union and Russia; and the still-unsolved anthrax attacks, in which letters carrying the powdery substance were mailed to U.S. political figures and media outlets. His biggest story of 2002 was about the Beltway sniper attacks and the arrests for those crimes of John Allen Muhammad and Lee Boyd Malvo. In 2003, Thomas reported on extremist Christian homophobe Eric Rudolph, who had bombed the Atlanta Summer Olympics in 1996 and abortion clinics in 1997; the capture of Ohio truck driver Iyman Farris, an Al Qaeda operative who had plotted to blow up the Brooklyn Bridge; and the disappearance in

Angola of a Boeing 727 jet. An ongoing story has been the treatment of suspected terrorists who are or have been in U.S. custody. In 2005, Thomas gave ABC a scoop: the first photographs showing the results of the London subway bombings, including information on several bombs that had failed to explode; and he covered the debate over and passing of the antiterrorism bill put forward by the Bush administration. An early story he wrote in 2006 involved La Mara Salvatrucha, better known as MS-13, a machete-wielding Latino gang operating in the United States. Thomas has also devoted some of his time in 2006 to the issue of child abuse and to charges of illegal domestic spying by the National Security Agency.

Thomas's careful, detailed reporting has won him a number of major awards. In 1991 and 1992, he won the Mort Mintz Investigative Award for investigative reporting at the *Washington Post*. He was a 1993 finalist for the Livingston Young Journalist Award, and in 1994, his story "Beyond Grief and Fear" won him the National Council on Crime and Delinquency's Pass Award. For his broadcast work, he was part of the ABC team that was recognized for coverage of September 11 and its aftermath by an Emmy, the Peabody Award and the Alfred I. duPont-Columbia University Award. His quiet, serious demeanor, ability to cultivate sources and careful attention to detail have contributed to his success in both broadcast and print work. Of the two, his greater love is broadcast journalism, which, he says, demands not only the skills of the wordsmith, but the added dimension of the visual medium that makes a reporter think about how he or she looks and sounds, as well as how best to mix the words with the visuals. Thomas has also contributed to ABC News specials, "Nightline," "This Week," and "Good Morning America" for his network. He is a member of the National Association of Black Journalists, is on the advisory board of his alma mater's Department of Communication and in February 2006, was the keynote speaker at the *Milwaukee Times'* twenty-first annual Black Excellence Awards Banquet. Thomas has had one brush with legal trouble over the Weh Ho Lee story, about that former nuclear scientist who was accused of leaking classified information to China. Charges against Lee were later dropped, and Lee sued a number of media outlets, including ABC, for invasion of privacy. In June 2006, a $750,000 settlement was reached, which brought Lee's suit to a conclusion.

Further Readings: Crichton, Juliet. "Getting the Source." *Virginia Tech Magazine* (Winter 2004): 18–19; "Pierre Thomas." [Online]. ABC News site http://abcnews.go.com.

Thomas, Wendi C. (c.1972–)

Memphis Commercial Appeal metro columnist Wendi Thomas grew up in Memphis and is a graduate of Butler University in Indiana. A calculus course convinced her to change her major from pharmacy to journalism, and in 1992, she interned at the *Commercial Appeal* in her hometown. Following graduation, she worked as a reporter for the *Indianapolis Star* and as an editor for the *Tennessean* in Nashville and the *Charlotte Observer* for a total of fourteen years before returning to Memphis in August 2003 to begin writing her thrice-weekly metro column for the *Commercial Appeal*. She held this job until March 2006, when she left the *Appeal* to begin a new column at the *Baltimore Sun*. A month later, it was announced that she would be remaining at the Memphis paper. She remarked that she missed her hometown, and the *Commercial Appeal*'s managing editor told Richard Prince's Journal-isms that Thomas' Memphis admirers had been unhappy about her departure, as well.

Thomas' willingness to come right out and say what she is thinking gives her column bite. When the city's mayor criticized the city council as timid and unproductive, she accused him of grandstanding. She also placed the label "resident hot-head" on the council chairman and dubbed an alderman "Old Shoe Leather Sure Is Tasty" due to statements he had retracted in civil discourse that Thomas termed more nearly uncivil. She noted with irony how quickly improvements tend to be made when bad things happen to prominent people; the situation involved the death of a former mayor who had been out of range of proper ambulance service when he suffered a heart attack. She ripped into a local company that was making home-improvement loans to elderly or poor locals, then foreclosing on their homes when they couldn't afford the interest. When a statue of Confederate General Nathan Bedford Hale was erected in a Memphis park, she reminded her readers that despite his admirable military skills, he had also been the Ku Klux Klan's first Grand Wizard. She was bold to add that she harbored suspicions about ugly racist undertones to the fondness of so many white Southerners for Confederate history. On the happy side of the ledger, she has written glowing copy about James Hyter, retired local singing legend whose special song was "Ol' Man River." And in a column headlined "All praise the Lord, doo-wop," she related her encounter with a street evangelist who flapped a Bible in her face and told her she might go to hell for liking jazz and the blues.

Though hers is a metro column, Thomas often strays to a wider focus, as in the column that appears below—her response to the outpouring of tributes to former president Ronald Reagan after his 2004 death. In it, she offers a balanced look at his accomplishments—the bad and the good. Another delightfully headlined column, "A Dark Day in Alabama, by George," describes the sad result of the vote on an amendment to the Alabama constitution that would have stricken its provision mandating separate schools for black and white children. Upon the 2005 conviction of Edgar Ray Killen for the murder of three civil rights workers in 1964, her assessment was that the finding would bolster the public's faith in the U.S. justice system. Her take on people's reaction to the acquittal of O.J. Simpson was clear and probably accurate—for those who see our courts as fair and just, the verdict was a travesty; but for people who think our courts tend to be biased against nonwhites, the not-guilty verdict was just fine. About the firing of *New York Times* reporter Jayson Blair, Thomas pointed out that rather than use that unfortunate incident as a general indictment against Affirmative Action, the public would do well to remember that incompetence, dishonesty and mediocrity come in all colors. On Martin Luther King Day 2005, she wondered in print whether Dr. King would think his work had been in vain if he could see the sleaze and self-degradation displayed on Black Entertainment Television, or if he would look at the accomplishments of Colin Powell and Condoleezza Rice and the fall of apartheid and smile with satisfaction.

"Let's Paint Complete Portrait of Reagan" by Wendi C. Thomas

The deification of the late Great Communicator, President Ronald Reagan, revises history in a way that's unfortunate and unfair to him.

If you listened only to the posthumous reflections on his career, you'd think that all the world was his fan club.

Perhaps while his body is shuttled from California to Washington and then back to California, it's kinder to recall only the good.

But to wade through paragraph after paragraph of platitudes does not befit Reagan or his legacy.

The better tribute is one that's complete, a telling of his shortcomings alongside a telling of his successes.

Reagan, after all, appointed the first woman to the Supreme Court.

Although initially opposed to a national holiday for Martin Luther King Jr., he made the holiday law.

He signed a treaty with the Soviet Union to ban mid-range nuclear missiles, called for the destruction of the Berlin Wall, railed against Communism, and advocated prayer in public schools.

His optimism for America's future was infectious. His devotion to wife Nancy was inspiring.

No disrespect or discredit comes from telling the truth, even if the truth is less than flattering.

As president, he was faced in 1982 with an economy as depressed as it'd been in the 1930s. He promoted widespread tax cuts only to allow a $100 billion tax hike the next year.

During his tenure, he cut federal spending for housing assistance, legal aid, school lunches and tuition reimbursement, gutting programs that helped the nation's poorest while at the same time boosting defense spending.

He coined the phrase "welfare queens," telling the story of a Cadillac-driving cheat scamming he system for $150,000 with multiple identities and Social Security cards. He repeated the tale, even after he was told it wasn't true.

As thousands died of AIDS, Reagan stood silent. It wasn't until the end of his second term that he acknowledged the crisis.

He had only one black person in his Cabinet, and less than 2 percent of his judicial appointments were black.

The Iran-contra scandal. His veto of sanctions against South Africa. His role in the rising deficit. His statement that most air pollution comes from trees, that many of those on the streets are "homeless by choice"—none of these missteps make him unworthy of honor.

Instead, his mistakes make him more of a man. They show him as human, capable of erring, capable of rebounding from errors.

Even the best life lived well meanders on the road to greatness, with foibles that may prefer to be forgotten.

In his farewell speech, given as he left office in 1989, Reagan said this: "We made the city stronger, we made the city freer, and we left her in good hands. All in all, not bad, not bad at all."

The same could be said of his life: All in all, not bad.

Source: Copyright, *The Commercial Appeal*, Memphis, TN. Used with permission. (http://www.commercialappeal.com). This column appeared on 10 June 2004.

Thomas-Graham, Pamela (1963–)

Harvard University-educated writer of Ivy League murder mysteries Pamela Thomas-Graham was until October 2005 president and CEO of CNBC. She was born in Detroit to engineer/real estate agent-social worker parents who made her education a high priority. She attended Lutheran High School in Detroit and was active in choir and drama. She was introduced to Harvard by a family friend and attended Radcliffe College of Harvard University with plans to become a lawyer, worked a variety of internship jobs, graduated magna cum laude with a B.A. in economics, won the prestigious Captain Jonathan Fay prize as the graduating student showing the most promise, then remained at Harvard for law school, where she was an editor of the *Harvard Law Review*. She decided to add a concurrent MBA, finishing at Harvard with both that degree and the J.D. Thus armed with three degrees at age 26, she went into the consulting business in New York City with the firm McKinsey & Company, working there for a decade and specializing in media and entertainment work. At age 32 in 1995, she became that company's youngest person and first African-American woman to make partner. A McKinsey colleague introduced her to General Electric CEO Jack Welch, and in 1999, Thomas-Graham was hired as president and CEO of CNBC.com. CNBC, based in Englewood Cliffs, New Jersey, is owned by NBC, which in turn is owned by General Electric. She had been in that position for only a short time before, at age 41 in July 2001, she was named president and CEO of all CNBC operations. That promotion probably made her the most powerful woman executive in the industry, but at this time, viewership had dropped dramatically in the wake of the dot.com implosion that had sent tech stocks southward. Thomas-Graham moved to inch the network's focus somewhat away from the stock market and toward a broader analysis of business and to coverage of government regulation. Viewer numbers remained down, yet her programming changes appear to have helped keep the company profitable. Even so, the high-profile executive was not without her critics, who complained that she put too much emphasis on polishing her own image and too little time into day-to-day management. She has countered that for someone in her position, speaking engagements are a necessary obligation. Other observers regarded her as an elegant person, a supportive but no-nonsense boss and an intelligent leader. Of the various hires and changes she made, some of the most controversial were her decisions to give CNBC air time to comic Dennis Miller, magazinist Tina Brown and bad-boy tennis star and commentator John McEnroe, all of whose shows were flops. One of her notable successes appears to have been introducing the bombastic market observer Jim Cramer to CNBC. It is possible that when viewers tune in CNBC, they really do want information, not just diverting entertainment—a rarity in the world of television. In October 2003, Thomas-Graham made another big career move, leaving media work to become a group president at Liz Claiborne. Her new challenge will be to keep the clothing lines of Liz Claiborne, Emma James and other company labels profitable during highly competitive times.

Thomas-Graham is on the boards of the American Red Cross of Greater New York, the New York City Opera and Girls Incorporated, known earlier as the Girls Club of America. She has appeared in the *Crain's New York Business* list of the "40 Under 40" business leaders and has been profiled in *Fortune* magazine and named one of the 2004 Women of the Year by *Ms.* and *Glamour* magazines. In April 2005, she and CNBC reporter Maria Bartiromo took part in the Financial Women's Association's Distinguished Speaker Series in New York. By virtue of getting by on around four hours of sleep a night, Thomas-Graham has been able to function as an executive, a mother and in addition, an author of mystery books set in a succession of Ivy League schools. Her first book, published in 1998, was *A Darker Shade of Crimson*, set at Harvard. The center of action for the second was Yale, and for the third, Princeton. Her lead character in these mysteries is Nikki Chase, a young black Harvard professor. The author's busy life is shared by Princeton-educated Lawrence Otis Graham, her husband, who also is a lawyer and author.

Books by Pamela Thomas-Graham: *A Darker Shade of Crimson: An Ivy League Mystery* (New York: Simon & Schuster, 1998); *Blue Blood: An Ivy League Mystery* (New York: Simon & Schuster, 1999); *Orange Crushed: An Ivy League Mystery* (New York: Simon & Schuster, 2004).

Further Readings: "A Better Fit at Liz Claiborne?" [Online, 10 October 2005]. Business Week online Web site (www.businessweek.com); Brady, Diane. "Pamela Thomas-Graham: A Change of Wardrobe." *Business Week*, 3 October 2005; Clarke, Robyn D. "Excellence by the Graham—CNBC President Pamela Thomas-Graham." *Black Enterprise*, September 2001; "First Person Singular: Pamela Thomas-Graham." *Essence* (September 2004); Jenkins, Carol. "Woman of the Year 2003: Pamela Thomas-Graham." *Ms. Magazine* (Winter 2003); "Reflections on Success." [Online]. The Black Collegian Web site (www.black-collegian.com); Shell, Adam. "CNBC Leader Gives New Meaning to Multi-Tasking." [Online, 22 March 2004]. USA Today Web site www.usatoday.com.

Tolliver, Melba (8 December 1939–)

One of the very first African Americans to work as a news anchor in New York City, Melba Tolliver has had a career that took her from nursing to broadcasting and finally to room designing. Oddly, she is often remembered because of a controversy about her hairstyle, which almost ended her job as a broadcaster. Born in Rome, Georgia, to a bellhop father and housewife mother, she spent most of her early years in Akron, Ohio. She moved to New York City after high school and enrolled in New York University's Bellevue School of Nursing, from which she graduated with honors in 1959. She went to work as an operating room nurse but disliked what she was doing and began studying acting at the

American Academy of Dramatic Arts. In 1967, she gave up nursing and took a secretarial job at ABC in New York. As luck would have it, the American Federation of Television and Radio Artists struck in 1968, and she was invited to appear on-camera to deliver a news brief. Her performance was good enough to prompt the network to enter her in a training program at New York University's journalism program, and in autumn 1968, she was hired as a news reporter at WABC, Channel 7. On weekends, she coanchored, and she also cohosted a morning talk program. Another accomplishment was a special she wrote and produced for ABC: "Gordon Parks: A Man for All Seasons," about that famous black photographer.

The late 1960s were still highly segregated times and discrimination against blacks was rampant. Tolliver at first appeared oncamera with her hair straightened, but as she prepared to cover the wedding of President Richard Nixon's daughter Tricia in 1971, she reported to work with her hair worn natural. In a classic case of discriminatory clumsiness, WABC management told her she would have to get her hair straightened or not appear on-camera. She held her ground, and after a flurry of public protest, the station relented. This experience, small and odd though it might seem, was somehow symbolic of the false standard of "whiteness" to which early African-American broadcasters were expected to adhere. Around that same time, Tolliver has recalled, she began using the racial descriptor "black," saying that she preferred it to the old term "Negro," which, she added, had plantation and cotton patch associations.

In 1976, Tolliver took a year off from broadcasting and studied as a National Endowment for the Humanities Fellow at the University of Michigan. She also helped direct a conference, "Kerner Plus 10," on media and minorities ten years after publication of the Kerner Commission Report on domestic unrest. Returning to New York the following year, she switched networks and became a reporter-producer for WNBC-TV. She was given her own show, "Melba and Company," and with Pia Lindstrom, was weekday news coanchor. Later, she was host of "Meet the People"; was, alongside Alan Alda and Bennett Cerf, a panelist on the popular quiz show "What's My Line"; and with actor Robert Kline, hosted the Emmy Awards show. She became directly involved in politics in the mid-1980s, when she served as Jesse Jackson's New York media director for his White House bid. She also branched out into print media work, freelancing for *Good Housekeeping*, *Black Sports*, *Networking* and *USA Today*, for which she did a series of profiles of business people. Her final broadcasting position was with News 12 Long Island, America's first 24-hour news operation. Tolliver was a coanchor during prime time and with chef, food consultant, cookbook author and bon vivant Gene Hovis, also African American, cohosted "Long Island People."

Tolliver returned to school via distance learning and in 1998 received a bachelors degree in cultural studies from Empire State College. In the 1999–2000 school year, she was the Howard R. Marsh visiting professor of journalism at the University of Michigan, offering a seminar course titled "Race in the Media," which examined how racial identification is handled in news stories and how race reflects and structures media reality (and unreality). Also in 1999, she made a brief appearance in the role of anchorwoman in *Summer of Sam*, a movie about serial killer David Berkowitz that had a gargantuan cast. Due to her long experience as a pioneering black broadcaster, Tolliver has been part of many attempts to chronicle the difficulties she and her contemporaries faced in their work lives. She, and her "hair affair," were featured in "A Question of Color," aired in 1993 and written and produced by Kathe Sandler. Tolliver was a participant in a New York Public Library program, "A Black Journalists Oral History and Archival Project Forum", in November 2000 and was guest speaker in the RISE (realistic, inspirational strategies for everyday living) seminar held in spring 2004 at Purchase College of the State University of New York. Over the years, she has received innumerable honors, such as the Torch of Liberty Award given by Long Island's Anti-Defamation League, an honorary doctorate from Molloy College, the Long Island Association's Woman of the Year Award and the Lifetime Achievement Award of the New York Association of Black Journalists. In 1994, she received the Trailblazer Award from 100 Black Women of Long Island Inc., and in 2003, she was inducted into the Gallery of Distinguished Graduates of Empire State College. Tolliver, who lived for many years in Brooklyn, has moved to Bangor, Pennsylvania, to pursue a new interest, room design. She is not the only African-American journalist to be discriminated against because of her hairstyle. In 1981, a full decade after Tolliver's "hair affair," reporter Dorothy Reed at KGO-TV in San Francisco was given a two-week suspension for appearing on camera wearing a "cornrow" hairstyle. It would appear that old discriminatory practices die hard.

Further Readings: Goodson, Martia Graham. "Melba Tolliver." *Notable Black American Women, Book II*. Edited by Jessie Carney Smith. Detroit, Mich.: Gale Research, 1996, pp. 651–53.

Towns, Hollis (23 October 1963–)

Large, imposing Hollis Towns is managing editor of the *Cincinnati Enquirer*. He was born in Fort Valley, Georgia, and was a scholarship linebacker at historically black Fort Valley State University, from which he received the bachelor's degree in mass communications. While in college, he did a National Association of Black Journalists internship at the *Detroit Free Press* and a second internship at the *Atlanta Journal-Constitution*. After graduating in 1988, he took a reporting job at the *Journal-Constitution* and eventually became its assistant city editor. He wrote mainly on matters of race while at the Atlanta paper but held a number of jobs there. He did general assignment reporting for the paper's zoned editions, reported on the Olympics, covered housing issues and headed two bureaus: Rockdale County and Clayton/Henry. He interviewed older African Americans who had taken part in the demonstrations, marches and protests of the early Civil Rights era and reported on hate crimes such as church burnings. He covered the Million Man March, profiled Coretta Scott King and occasionally wrote, not always entirely positively, about the activities of the Southern Christian Leadership Conference and the Center for Democratic Renewal. Towns moved to Michigan in 2000 to become managing editor of the *Kalamazoo Gazette*, replacing Rosemary Goudreau at that Newhouse newspaper. Four years later, in May 2004, he took over as managing editor of the much larger *Cincinnati Enquirer*. An article by Cliff Radel in the *Enquirer* that introduced Towns to the paper's readers reported that the new managing editor keeps in his office an old Royal typewriter that has a symbolic meaning for him. The old machine reminds him of journalism's roots, and it also recalls his mid-Georgia upbringing in that the nearest city to his home was Macon, site of a Royal typewriter factory. Like many newsmen, Towns has a dual fascination with the old and the new technology of the field. In August 2005, he became a mentor in the Maynard Institute's mentoring program and in a similar program run by the organization 100 Black Men of Cincinnati. He is also a member of the diversity committee of the Associated Press Managing Editors organization. He has expressed an interest in encouraging the APME to devote more attention to journalism's digital components.

Further Readings: "Hollis Towns." [Online, 2006]. Associated Press Managing Editors site http://apme.com; Prince, Richard. "Hollis Towns Gets ME Job at Cincinnati Enquirer." [Online, 29 March 2004]. Richard Prince's Journal-isms. Maynard Institute Web site www.maynardije.org; Radel, Cliff. "New Enquirer Manager Is 'Stickler for Excellence.'" Cincinnati Enquirer Web site www.enquirer.com.

Tucker, Cynthia Anne (13 March 1955–)

Atlanta Constitution editorial page editor and syndicated columnist Cynthia Tucker was born in Monroeville, Alabama, and received the B.A. from Auburn University in 1976. After graduation, she became a reporter for the *Atlanta Journal*, working there until 1980, when she was hired as a reporter by the *Philadelphia Inquirer*. Tucker joined the *Constitution* in 1983 as a columnist and editorial writer and in 1986 was promoted to associate editorial page editor. She was a Nieman Fellow at Harvard during 1988 and 1989 and was moved up to *Constitution* editorial page editor in 1992. That same year, one of her twice-weekly "As I See It" columns was picked up by Chronicle Features and soon began appearing in roughly 25 other newspapers. In a 1992 interview with *Editor & Publisher*'s David Astor, Tucker remarked that she wants to avoid being pigeonholed either as a "black columnist" or as a columnist who writes only about politics and public policy. Her column topics range widely: women's issues, the politics of the day, black issues, family matters, social issues and international happenings. In 2003, in her role as editorial page chief, she spiked a Mike Luckovich cartoon that showed Georgia's governor Sonny Perdue next to a flag that bore the words, "I'm With Stupid." Perdue's campaign had included his desire to give the state a new flag more similar to the old Confederate battle flag. Tucker disallowed the cartoon, she said, out of respect to the office of governor. In addition to her newspaper work, the photogenic Tucker has been a frequent presence on the "MacNeil-Lehrer News Hour."

Tucker's political leanings are liberal. In a column headlined "The Fear President," she pointed out how President George W. Bush used the September 11 tragedy to his considerable political advantage by keeping Americans "emotionally stuck" in dread of future attacks, transforming his public image from that of a relatively weak and ineffectual leader who had dodged active military service into the bold, hawkish defender of the nation. This reelection strategy, Tucker wrote, would not work; here, time proved her wrong. Another of her columns pointed out how the sons and daughters of the American working class were bearing the brunt of our military struggles abroad and how the well off had not even had to help pay for the costs of war, but had actually been given big tax breaks. This May 2004 column appears below. Another column from the same year used the term "affluenza" to characterize how "the loosening of civic ties have dampened the sense of duty in an America that wants its wars arranged to be watched on television from the comfort of the couch, and at no extra cost." Tucker's discontent with the Bush administration transcends the war on terror. In an April 2005 column she stated flatly that Tom Delay-style Republicans are on the rise and represent a serious threat to democracy. She considers the far right to be populated by self-righteous individuals who dislike modernity and would like to dictate how we live our lives—just as extremist Muslims want to do in their own countries.

Tucker is not one to see all issues through an "us or them" lens as far as race is concerned. On one hand she points up the unintended but obvious way the nation's media react to a news story depending on the race of the person involved, contrasting the overly intensive coverage of a white Jennifer Wilbanks (the runaway bride of 2005) to the scant coverage accorded a black Stacy-Ann Sappleton, abducted and murdered in Queens, New York, that same year. On the other hand, Tucker spoke out against elevating black California Supreme Court justice Janice Rogers Brown to the federal bench, remarking that Brown's views are similar to those held by Genghis Kahn. In another race-related column, Tucker complimented Coretta Scott King for having taken on the uncomfortable issue of black homophobia and its link to the alarming spread of AIDS among America's black population. African Americans, Tucker agreed, tend to regard AIDS as a "gay disease," and many still fail to realize the risks of unprotected heterosexual sex. Tucker pointed out that AIDS has become the leading cause of death for young black men and the second-leading cause for young black women. Worse, she wrote, is that at a time when AIDS deaths are declining among the nation's population as a whole, they are increasing among blacks, and she criticized black leaders for being afraid to address the issue. On the other hand, Tucker has stuck her chin way out by criticizing the King family for trading on the MLK legacy and making it a profit center. Tucker is, furthermore, uncomfortable with the nation's overall health system, saying that its first, second and third priorities are making money by selling a product: health care. Our national faith in capitalism, she points out, is bumping up against our unspoken conviction that our citizens have a right to decent health care, and she has predicted that as more people lack health insurance, our faith in capitalism will be sorely tested. As to the excesses of capitalism, Tucker points out how even our reformers are quicker to go after the small fish than the big sharks. A 2003 article in *Time* quoted her as likening the CEOs of WorldCom and Enron to Al Capone, whereas Martha Stewart was brought to justice far more swiftly even though her offense was more nearly that of an Oliver Twist.

In 2002, Tucker received the Distinguished Writing Award from the American Society of Newspaper Editors, and in 2005, she was winner of Colby College's Lovejoy Award, named after the abolitionist editor and Colby graduate murdered by a mob in 1837. She delivered that year's Lovejoy Address and also was given an honorary Doctor of Laws degree by the college. She is a member of the National Association of Black Journalists and the National Association of Minority Media Executives. She is on the Council on Foreign Relations and is a board member of the International Women's Media Foundation. She is a member of the American Society of Newspaper Editors and the Atlanta Chapter of the American Red Cross and is on the board of Families First.

"Sons and Daughters of Working Class Bear Burden of Service" by Cynthia Tucker

The other day President Bush stated the painfully obvious: "Our work in Iraq has been hard."

But his suggestion of a national mission—a cause to which all Americans are making a substantial contribution—is misleading. The hard work of fighting and dying in Iraq has been done by a few—the sons and daughters of the working classes. The affluent have hardly been troubled unless they tune in to the nightly newscasts.

The frantic calls to in-laws to scrape together child care before shipping out, the desperate planning to keep the painting business together while the owner is in uniform, the wives' attempts to fend off unpaid bills while the soldiers, fighting a distant war, fend off rocket-propelled grenades—those burdens have been borne by families with modest paychecks and scant savings. So have the grieving and the burying.

The all-volunteer military is drawn from a relatively small slice of America, from families more likely to work at Wal-Mart than on Wall Street, from young men and women more likely to drive a Hyundai than a Hummer. Enlistees tend to come from households with incomes between $32,000 and $33,500, according to a 1999 Defense Department study. Commissioned officers tend to come from slightly more affluent backgrounds, but graduates of trendy private schools and exclusive colleges are rare in the officer corps.

(Before you begin scripting your e-mail protest, let me state for the record that I know that there are exceptions, including former football star Pat

Tillman. Why do you think there was so much coverage of Tillman's death? He was a rare example of sacrifice by the affluent.)

Of all the discordant notes about this war, this is among the most jarring: While President Bush insists, rightly, that the war on terror will last for generations and require great sacrifices, he has asked few Americans to make any. The president won't even ask the wealthy to pay for the war. Instead, he gave them a hefty tax cut.

In that climate of indulgence of the well-off, it's no surprise that neither the Bush administration nor Congress wants to consider a draft. The Pentagon, which always resists change, continues to insist it doesn't want to resume the draft (it also fought ending the draft), even as it becomes increasingly clear that troop strength is stretched to the breaking point.

And that doesn't begin to count the needs here on the home front, where legions off young men and women could be put to work guarding ports, nuclear sites and borders. In a essay in The Washington Monthly shortly after the terrorist atrocities of 9/11, the magazine's editor, Paul Glastris, and military sociologist Charles Moskos wrote:

"Not only are we not drafting our young men. We are not even planning to draft them... That terrorists might poison municipal water supplies, spray anthrax from crop dusters, or suicidally infect themselves with smallpox and stroll trough busy city streets is no longer considered farfetched. That we might need to draft some of our people to counter these threats—now that's considered farfetched," they noted.

Armchair warmongers have denounced draft proponents such as Moskos and Rep. Charles Rangel, D-N.Y., declaring their motives suspect: War critics support conscription knowing its unpopularity would doom any war effort. Wrong. Many strategists have begun to suggest that a draft may be necessary because the U.S. military is too small to confront new threats while also carrying out its current obligations.

But human nature also suggests that Congress (and the press) might have questioned this dubious pre-emptive war more aggressively if the sons and daughters of the affluent classes were subject to conscription. Freedom isn't free, someone has said. But if you're wealthy and well-connected, it's pretty cheap.

Source: This column appeared on 29 May 2004 and is reproduced here by permission of the *Atlanta Journal-Constitution*.

Further Readings: Astor, Dave. "Killed Editorial Cartoon Has Brief Web Life." Editor & Publisher [Online, 16 April 2003]. Editor & Publisher Web site www.mediainfo.com; Astor, Dave. "NFC Speaker Takes a Look at the Future." *Editor & Publisher*, 28 October 1995, p. 34; Astor, Dave. "Out of the South Into Syndication." *Editor & Publisher*, 22 August 1992, pp. 28, 30; "Atlanta Editor and Columnist Cynthia Tucker Receives 2005 Lovejoy Award." [Online]. Colby College Web site www.colby.edu; "Chronicle Has Tucker's Column." *Editor & Publisher*, 23 May 1992, pp. 31–32.

Tutman, Lisa (?–)

Lisa Tutman is a general assignment reporter for NBC5 News in Chicago. She holds both the B.A. and MBA degrees from Alabama Agricultural and Mechanical University in Normal, Alabama. Her first job out of college was as a general assignment reporter for Saginaw, Michigan, station WJRT-TV, where she also did fill-in anchor duties and produced a weekly show, "Monday's Child," that paired children with mentors. Her next job, also as general assignment reporter and substitute anchor, was a two-year stay in Indianapolis, Indiana, at WISH-TV. There, she added sports features and worked on special series assignments. From Indianapolis, she moved to WSB-TV in Atlanta as anchor of the Saturday morning and mid-day news. Next she relocated to Washington, D.C., to NBC5. She was a Cox Broadcasting correspondent reporting on the White House and Congress plus covering other national news for Cox stations around the nation. In May 1997, she came to the NBC5 operation in Chicago as a reporter. At that time, the station, which had gone on the air in 1948 as WNBQ, was using the call letters WMAQ-TV. The change to NBC5 came in 2000. Coincidentally, Tutman's arrival occurred at about the same time that the station, in an attempt to improve ratings, hired talk show host Jerry Springer to do local commentary. Two anchors resigned in protest, ratings went down instead of up and station management had egg on its face. Springer quickly resigned but continued his raucous talk show, taped in the WMAQ-TV studios. Tutman did some anchor duty for WMAQ, but in early 1999, when she took maternity leave, the station got into union trouble for using a daily hire to take her place as weekend anchor.

As a local reporter in Chicago, Tutman has no shortage of news to report—a suspicious fire in the Pilsen neighborhood in November 2003, the shooting of a state trooper who had stopped to help a motorist in December of that year, the dispute between SBC Communications and a striking union in May 2004, a likely case of road rage in which an off-duty policeman was shot in June 2004. Is August 2004, she reported on one of her strangest stories ever: the dumping of 800 pounds of human waste from a bus that was crossing the Kinzie Street Bridge. The bus was under lease to the Dave Matthews Band. The dumping, captured on a surveillance video, hit passengers riding on a passing tour boat. In December 2004, she covered a major fire in the highrise LaSalle Bank building, and in January 2005, she reported on Tamara Mendis, the only Chicago resident to have been a victim of the Asian tsunami. Many of the stories she covers are about human misfortune of one kind or another. Such stories in 2005 were about a Pakistani cab driver who was beaten and then run over with his own cab, a high school English teacher caught having sex with a 17-year-old football player, a Lake Michigan double suicide and a fatal brawl in a Chicago suburb. In March 2006, Tutman covered the biggest Latino demonstration Chicago had ever seen; around 100,000 people demonstrated in protest to a proposed law that would jail illegal immigrants living in the United States. Tutman has a twin sister, Paula, who is a reporter in Detroit, Michigan, for WDIV-TV-4.

Further Readings: "Lisa Tutman." [Onllline]. NBC5 Web site www.nbc5.com.

U

Udoji, Adaora (c.1967–)

Adaora Udoji, of Nigerian heritage, has been a general news correspondent with CNN in New York since December 2003. Immediately prior to that time, she was a foreign correspondent based in London with ABC NewsOne. Her father is head city engineer for Dearborn, Michigan, and her mother is director of the Washtenaw County Library in Ann Arbor. Udoji is a political science B.A. graduate of the University of Michigan and earned a J.D. from the UCLA School of Law. She entered broadcasting in 1995 as an ABC News reporter. Among her stories were the 1995 criminal trial and acquittal of former football great O.J. Simpson as well as his 1997 civil trial, in which he was found liable. She also covered the 1996 explosion over Long Island of TWA flight 800, which killed all 230 aboard; and she reported on the 1996 presidential campaign. In addition to her reporting work, Udoji was an associate producer for ABC. From 1997 to 2000, she worked as a general assignment reporter for ABC-owned station WTVG in Toledo, Ohio. There, she reported on crime and local elections. In June 2001, she joined ABC NewsOne to serve as a foreign correspondent during U.S. military action in Afghanistan, which began in October 2001. She reported out of Pakistan, then covered the later action in Iraq from Qatar and Kuwait and the continuing conflict between Israel and Palestine while based in Israel and in Jordan. She was also assigned stories on Pope John Paul II in Rome and reported on sports events including tennis at Wimbledon in 2000 and 2001, cycling at the 2002 Tour De France, and golf at the 2002 British Open. From her home base in London, she covered a wide range of stories in Africa and Europe as well as in the Middle East. During this period of her career, she reported for the roughly 180 network affiliate stations; international clients such as BBC, ARD in Germany and CTV in Canada; and

"World News Tonight," "World News Weekend," "20/20," "Primetime," "Good Morning America" and ABC Radio. Immediately after moving to CNN in December 2003, she reported on a major snowstorm that struck the U.S. northeast. In 2004, she reported on the trial of Martha Stewart, and in 2005, two of her biggest stories were the life support removal and death of Terri Schiavo and the devastation Hurricane Katrina brought to New Orleans and the Gulf Coast. She reported on the August 2005 death from lung cancer of ABC news anchor Peter Jennings, shark attacks off the U.S. East Coast and developments in the matter of gay marriages and civil unions.

In 1997, Udoji was a member of a team that won the Cine Eagle award for an ABC documentary on death-row prisoners. In 2002 she married broadcast journalist Ron Allen of NBC News and in February 2005, she was selected as a Woodrow Wilson Visiting Fellow to work at Ohio Dominican University.

Further Readings: "Adaora Udoji." [Online, 2006]. ABC News Web site www.abcmedianet.com; Adaora Udoji." [Online]. CNN International site http://edition.cnn.com.

W

Walker, Adrian (1962–)

City and regional columnist at the *Boston Globe*, Adrian Walker was born and raised in Miami and attended Florida International University, majoring in English. He left school without graduating and went to work as a general assignment reporter for the *Miami News*, remaining there until 1988 when he joined the staff of the *Boston Globe*, where he worked as City Hall bureau chief and deputy political editor, and, in 1997, statehouse editor. When *Globe* columnists Mike Barnicle and Patricia Smith left the paper in 1998 amidst allegations of fabricating copy, Walker and Brian McGrory were given columns to replace them. Walker's column now appears on Mondays and Thursdays.

The example of Walker's work that is reproduced below shows that he has a deft touch with human-interest copy; it tells a story about amazing generosity on the part of a Boston bar-owner touched by the plight of an Ecuadorian immigrant who needed a kidney transplant. A column of the same sort also described generosity, this time as shown by the New England Seafood Producers Association, a trade group that has donated hundreds of thousands of pounds of fish to the Greater Boston Food Bank. Still another of his columns dealt with a visit to Boston by New York Sen. Hillary Clinton, there to speak at a benefit for a faith-based social program called the National Ten Point Leadership Foundation. Its head, the Rev. Eugene Rivers III, had attracted the attention of presidents Bill Clinton and George W. Bush. Walker quoted the Rev. Rivers, a political independent, as saying that when whites are bipartisan, they are regarded as sophisticated, but black bipartisans are often assumed to be opportunists who lack loyalty. Many of Walker's columns deal with the local scene, as one would expect. Another such column was about a Boston minister who elected to skip the usual mild protests about gang violence and had put himself in harm's way to deal with that problem on a more personal level. In January 2005, Walker penned a column of tribute to his mentor at the *Globe*, the liberal, Harvard-educated David Nyhan, who had taken an interest in Walker when he first joined the paper and who died while shoveling snow. Walker's columns are not always of the gentle variety; on more than one occasion he has blasted the city's three-term mayor, Thomas Menino, for uttering malapropisms and for acting as though he does not have to do anything he does not want to, such as agreeing to debate a political opponent.

On occasion, Walker departs the confines of his city for column fodder, as when he interviewed Brandeis professor Anita Hill about Martin Luther King or when he gave readers his thoughts about Essie Mae Washington-Williams, who came forward at age 78 to announce that she is the daughter of the late Sen. Strom Thurmond of South Carolina. Her story, Walker wrote, is deeply American—not in the mythologized sense, but because it is a story shared, often in secret, by so many American families.

"Broadening the View" by Adrian Walker

For months, Gerry Quinn had been planning to buy a condominium with a view of the Charles River. Ten days ago, after reading a short newspaper article, his life and that of a man he had never met changed utterly.

Quinn came across the story of Franklin Piedra, an immigrant from Ecuador who shines shoes on Wall Street.

Piedra, 33, had been diagnosed with a kidney disease. In the time since, he had undergone dialysis treatments three days a week, for four hours a day. Between the treatments and the time it took to recover from them, he was able to work only twice a week.

Quinn, 52, is the owner of The Kells, a popular Allston bar. He moved to Boston from his native Galway 30 years ago and has had his own health problems. Piedra's story, reported in the New York Post Jan. 3, struck a chord. Quinn thought about it and slept on it. When he woke up the next morning, he was still thinking about it.

"When I was reading it, I figured this guy was probably desperate," he said. "I found out after I met him that he had written to the president, to everyone, trying to get help."

Piedra, in fact, had been trying to get a new kidney since at least 2001, when his mother offered to become his donor. Because of changes in Medicaid rules, he discovered he was no longer eligible for federal assistance. He couldn't afford the six-figure surgery and had no hope of raising the money it could cost.

After the story detailing his plight appeared, donations began to trickle in, and the company he worked for offered to set up a fund. Still, $100,000 is a lot to raise in $100 increments.

Within a few days, Quinn reached the reporter who had written the story. He told her he wanted to contribute. How much, she asked. All of it, he responded.

He flew to New York that weekend with a check for nearly $100,000, a lot for a man who is comfortable, but not wealthy. He had decided to save the life of a man he had never met.

"I said to myself, 'If I can help this guy live, I'll be so grateful,'" Quinn said yesterday. "Right now, I feel so grateful for him having a second chance at life. He's only 33 years old, and now he has a chance at life."

Quinn's generosity came as no surprise to his many friends. He is well known, especially among the city's Irish transplants.

The Kells runs a free lunch program for neighborhood kids during the school year and hosts meals at Thanksgiving and Christmas for those with nowhere to go. When college student Orla Benson was raped and murdered in 1995, he paid for her burial and arranged for her family to travel to Boston. He is still part of a committee that has continued to raise money for the family, some

$60,000 so far, a modest effort, he says, to keep her memory alive.

Piedra is awaiting his transplant and expects to have the surgery within three to four weeks. He recalled his desperate efforts to find a transplant patron.

"I did a lot of things," he said yesterday, saying that he wrote to "the White House, to Senator Hillary Clinton, to guys who make a lot of money who play for the Yankees, to people on TV." Nothing had clicked.

"When I got the news that Mr. Quinn is going to pay for my transplant, that was very exciting. I'm going to have a chance to be OK. It's my second chance to live."

Piedra looks forward to the day he can return the favor. He says that some time in the future, he wants to help someone, too.

"I'm always in my life going to have [Quinn] in my mind," he said. "If I have a situation where I can do for someone what he did for me, who really really needs it, I'm going to do it."

Quinn is still buying a downtown condo, as he had planned. But his dream has been scaled back a little.

"I decided I don't really need a water view," he said. "I can do without that."

Source: This column appeared on 13 January 2005 and is reprinted here by permission of *The Boston Globe*.

Further Readings: "Globe Replaces Columnists." *Editor & Publisher*, 31 October 1998, p. 6.

Walker, Hal (1933–25 November 2003)

Broadcast journalist Hal Walker died in November 2003 after a career that included 12 years with CBS News followed by 15 years with ABC News. He is said to have been the first African-American correspondent to work at CBS. He had retired in 1995. In the 1960s, Walker was a reporter for Washington, D.C., CBS affiliate station WTOP-TV, later redesignated WUSA. He received a local Emmy as well as the Capitol Press Club's Journalist of the Year award for having anchored a CBS special, "A Dialog with Whitey," concerning the riots that took place in the nation's capital after Martin Luther King's 1968 assassination. His reporting on civil rights efforts at this station also won him notice by network officials, and a month after his special aired, he began working for CBS, covering domestic news, much of which involved the newly asserted rights of African Americans; presidential politics during the Nixon, Carter and Reagan administrations; and some foreign news. His first story was the funeral of Sen. Robert F. Kennedy, and soon thereafter, he was one of the reporters who worked on the CBS seven-part series "Of Black America." He also reported on campus protests at Cornell University. Once Walker's fellow correspondent and later CBS Evening News anchor Dan Rather has been quoted as saying that Walker made little over his status as a pioneering black broadcaster, but preferred to be judged simply by his work. In 1980, Walker moved to rival network ABC. He succumbed to prostate cancer at age 70, dying in his Reston, Virginia, home.

Further Readings: Prince, Richard. "Hal Walker, Pioneer at CBS News, Dies at 80." [Online, 26 November 2003]. Richard Prince's Journal-isms. Maynard Institute Web site www.maynardije.org; "TV Newsman Hal Walker Dies." [Online. 27 November 2003]. CNN Web site www.cnn.com.

Walker, Liz (1952–)

After a 25-year run as an anchor for CBS4 in Boston, Liz Walker now hosts her own news magazine show, "Sunday with Liz Walker," on that station and is also a recent member of the clergy. She was born and raised in Little Rock, Arkansas, before racial integration in that area. Her father was a minister whose church was across the street from a nightspot, the Flamingo Lounge, where black jazz musicians played. She and her brother were forbidden by their highly religious mother from listening to jazz, which the mother regarded as the devil's music. A favorite childhood memory of Walker's recalls the night she and her brother were caught by their father sitting on the steps snapping their fingers to the music coming from across the street. When they asked him what kind of music God likes, he smiled and replied that he thought perhaps the Almighty likes the horns. She holds a bachelor's degree in communications from Michigan's Olivet College and in 2005, added a divinity degree from Harvard. Following her bachelors, she took her first broadcasting job in Little Rock as director of public affairs for station KATV. From there, she moved to Denver, Colorado, and was a reporter and weekend anchor at KMGH-TV. Her specialty areas were court and consumer issues reporting. Later she relocated to San Francisco as reporter and early morning anchor at KRON-TV, also hosting "Midday," a daily magazine-format show. In April 1980, she became weekend news anchor at CBS4 in Boston, which serves the city plus Cape Cod, Worcester and Nashua. She was the station's first African-American anchor. For 20 years starting in 1981, she and Jack Williams coanchored the evening news; from June 2000 until January 2005, she anchored the station's noon news show. Her last day as anchor was 15 January 2005, when she voluntarily departed daily broadcasting at age 53. In early March 2005, she resumed on-air work at the station, this time hosting her Sunday magazine show "Sunday with Liz Walker." Each show is built around a theme, which often has spiritual overtones. In February 2006, she began a blog, on cbs4boston.com/ thinking. Blog topics have included love; listening to one's inner voice, or intuition; childhood memories; her unfulfilled dream of running in the Boston Marathon; her first dance, when she was tall and bookish; people's belongingness needs; and the challenge of restoring public faith in the nation's political and business leaders. One of her career highlights was a summer 2001 trip with Boston area ministers to the Sudan as guests of Christian Solidarity International. She made two more trips to that ravaged nation, taking video footage that earned her the 2002 Edward R. Murrow Award from the Regional Television & Radio News Directors Association. Her exploration of the slave trade in southern Sudan aired as "In the Lion's Mouth," a one-hour documentary she produced independently. Earlier, she had produced other documentaries, such as "Friends Like These," for CBS4.

That work won her a Gabriel Award from the Catholic Academy for Communication Arts Professionals.

Walker has been a frequent speaker at Massachusetts schools and colleges. She was cofounder of "My Sister's Keeper," an organization dedicated to helping the women of Sudan. Another of her initiatives, this one done with state representative Marjorie Claprood, was the Jane Doe Safety Fund, which benefits women and children who are victims of domestic abuse. For many years, she fronted her station's "Stop the Violence" campaign, which targeted not only domestic violence problems, but similar issues in schools and elsewhere. Her community work earned her the 1997 Governor's Award from the National Academy of Television Arts and Sciences, New England branch. Walker also has worked with or served on the boards of the Big Sister Association, The Urban League of Eastern Massachusetts, the Pediatric AIDS Charitable Trust of Boston and the Boston Children's Museum. Her professional memberships include the National Association of Black Journalists, the Society of Professional Journalists, and American Women in Radio and Television. She holds honorary degrees from several Massachusetts colleges and universities, including Northeastern University, Suffolk University, the New England School of Law, Anna Maria College, Bridgewater State College, Curry College, Framingham State College, Merrimack College and Pine Manor College. Pine Manor College also gave her its 2002 Award for Inclusive Leadership and Social Responsibility, and in 2001, The Women's Union gave her its Amelia Earhart Award in recognition of her many good works. Her potential for further good works increased in 2005, when she entered the ministry after finishing at Harvard Divinity School and took a position at the Bethel AME Church in Jamaica Plain.

Further Readings: "Liz Walker." [Online]. CBS4 Boston site http://cbs4boston.com; "Liz Walker in Darfur." [Online, February 2005]. Women Waging Peace Web site www.womenwagingpeace.net; Rodman, Sarah. "Hotline: Liz Walker Returns to the Air." *Boston Herald*, 2 March 2005; Rodman, Sarah. "Tears, Laughs as Liz Walker Says Farewell." *Boston Herald*, 15 January 2005.

Watson, Carlos (1970–)

A man with a big, boyish smile, an outgoing personality and a record of success as an entrepreneur, Carlos Watson has worked at CNN since 2003 and has the potential to accomplish a lot for that network. His father and mother, both teachers, immigrated to Miami from Jamaica. Watson credits his father, who especially liked watching the work of broadcast journalists David Brinkley and Cokie Roberts, with jump-starting his own intense interest in politics. Watson was a bright but bored student during his early years; thanks to the attention of one understanding teacher, he began making grades good enough to get him into Harvard University. He majored in journalism and government, published several articles in the *Miami Herald* and *Detroit Free Press* and took summer employment as an aide to Miami's first Cuban-born mayor, Xavier Suarez. He also worked with Sen. Bob Graham and Ron Brown, the then chair of the Democratic National Committee. After graduating from Harvard with honors, Watson was campaign manager and chief of staff for Representative Daryl Jones of Florida. Next, Watson took a law degree at Stanford University, was an editor of the *Stanford Law Review*, interned at the White House Office of the Legal Counsel and clerked at high-profile law firms. After earning his degree, he remained in the Bay Area in the employ of management consulting firm McKinsey and Company.

In 1997, Watson, his sister and a friend struck out on their own, launching Achieva College Prep Services, a consulting business that targeted urban school districts that needed extra help in preparing their students for standardized tests and with counseling. The new company first operated in Palo Alto and within five years had clients in 75 school districts located in 22 states. In 2002, Achieva was bought by test-prep giant Kaplan for a reported $25 million, and Watson began to get invitations to appear on television talk shows. He reports having made nearly 40 appearances in six months on shows such as "Your World with Neil Cavuto" and "The O'Reilly Factor," where he commented on education, legal issues, politics, and business. He attracted the attention of CNBC and was hired to host one-hour interview specials titled "The Edge with Carlos Watson," talking with the likes of presidential hopeful Howard Dean, "First Brother" Jeb Bush of Florida, designer Vera Wang and baseball star Barry Bonds. In 2003, he was hired away by CNN, which used Watson as a contributor to its coverage of the 2004 presidential election campaign, where he added an enthusiastic air of youth appeal to the work of Wolf Blitzer and other CNN veterans. He is a political analyst for CNN TV and has done additional one-hour specials, this time as "Off Topic with Carlos Watson." The concept that makes these specials different is that on each episode, Watson interviews a celebrity about some subject matter different from his or her own area of expertise. Some of his guests have been California Gov. Arnold Schwarzenegger, Illinois Sen. Barak Obama, evangelist Creflo Dollar, "Desperate Housewives" actress Eva Longoria, and basketball legend Shaquille O'Neal. Watson also writes a weekly political column, "The Inside Edge with Carlos Watson," for CNN.com.

Watson is a member of the California bar and has made frequent appearances on talk radio shows such as NPR's "The Tavis Smiley Show," "The Paul Berry Show," "The Dean's Talkroom with Bernie McCain," "The Jim Bohannon Show," and the "Doug Banks Morning Show." He sits on the board of college preparatory company College Track and is often invited to speak on university campuses and to other audiences. On "The Tavis Smiley Show," Watson expressed the opinion that George W. Bush had proven to be the decade's most talented politician, and later, in 2005, he predicted that Bush would be effective in reforming Social Security, an outcome that thus far has yet to come to pass.

One of Watson's better predictions came in May 2004 on "The Inside Edge" when he discussed the practical difficulty of creating a strong democracy in Iraq and foresaw the Bush administration having to redefine its goals in that country. America's justification for invading that nation indeed has proved to be a textbook exercise in serial redefinition. Two more not-so-fortunate predictions Watson made on "The Inside Edge" were that the issue of gay marriage would not loom large in the 2004 presidential election campaign and that Secretary of Defense Donald Rumsfeld would resign after the election. He was, however, entirely correct in predicting that the 2004 election would turn mainly on the issue of protecting the nation from further terrorist attack by use of military preemption. Here, a nervous nation proved Watson right, but his prediction that erred most was in saying that Sen. John Kerry would win the election by a narrow margin. At this moment, the likable Watson remains a star-in-waiting at CNN.

Further Readings: "Carlos Watson." [Online]. CNN Web site www.cnn.com; Oremus, Will. "See Star." San Jose, California, *Mercury News*, 6 August 2004.

Weathers, Diane Marie (?–)

Former *Essence* magazine editor Diane Weathers hails from Brooklyn, New York. She grew up in Bedford-Stuyvesant, then later the Ft. Greene-Clinton Hill area of that city, attended Brooklyn Friends School starting in tenth grade and went on to get a journalism degree at Syracuse University. Her career began at *Black Enterprise* magazine in 1975; there she wrote mainly for black professionals and owners of small businesses. In 1977, she was hired by *Newsweek* to write on lifestyles, fashion and religion and she later became a correspondent in that magazine's Washington bureau. In 1984 she left *Newsweek* to work in Rome as an information officer for the United Nations World Food Program, and from 1987 to 1992 she traveled with that agency to various countries in the Middle East, sub-Saharan Africa and Southeast Asia. She wrote for UN publications and freelanced for such magazines as the *Financial Times*, the *New York Times* and *Family Circle*. She worked briefly as *Redbook* magazine's senior editor for news features and as a *Consumer Reports* associate editor, then in 1993 joined the staff of *Essence*, the nation's best-established magazine for African-American women. From that time until 2001 she wrote feature stories on a variety of social issues, developed story ideas, worked with freelance writers and led a team of writers and editors who produced the magazine's twenty-fifth anniversary issue.

In July 2001, Weathers succeeded Monique Greenwood as editor-in-chief of *Essence*, a magazine having a circulation of 1.6 million and 40 percent readership among black U.S. women, plus 15 percent of black men, according to its parent company, Essence Communications Inc. The magazine has a broad focus, offering copy on family issues, health, beauty, fitness, careers, food and dining, travel and contemporary lifestyles, plus profiles of African-American celebrities and achievers. In an industry that concentrates so heavily on entertainment, Weathers gave *Essence* a significant nudge toward the serious. Two of her editorial campaigns concentrated on misogyny and the cultural fallout from rap music. Perhaps her main concern has been the ways in which black men hurt black women, which she called the dirty secret that African Americans don't like to discuss in public. The prevalence of black domestic violence, she wrote in an editorial message in July 2003, has deep historical roots; she added that the sexual mistreatment of black women during the slavery years was perhaps even more devastating than slavery's emasculating effect on black men, who have reacted to that effect by adopting toughness as a coping mechanism. The result, she has written, has been the definition of present-day black manhood as hypermasculine—aggressive, unemotional and inclined to treat women as inferior. Linked to that concern was her conclusion that far too much of modern rap and hip-hop lyrics are demeaning to women, tending to show them as mere sex objects and pushing girls toward sexuality at younger and younger ages, even to the point of encouraging childhood prostitution. A third concern during her tenure as editor was the George W. Bush administration's war on terror and the need to focus more on peace and understanding among races and religions. A fourth concern was gun violence in America and its especially high toll among blacks.

Essence's owner, ECI, was founded in 1968 and was black-controlled until 2000, when Time Inc. formed a joint venture with the company. Then in March 2005, Time Inc. bought the rest of the company's stock. Perhaps too serious-minded for what is mainly an entertainment medium, Weathers resigned as editor-in-chief in May 2005, remaining with the magazine as an at-large editor. Also, advertising had declined by the time she stepped down, and circulation had dropped to just more than 1 million. At roughly the same time, cofounder Clarence O. Smith resigned as ECI president and was replaced by Michelle Ebanks. Upon Weathers' resignation, the job of editor-in-chief was done on an interim basis by Susan L. Taylor, and later the position was filled by Angela Burt-Murray. Weathers long had expressed a desire to write a novel and is now likely to do so.

Further Readings: Prince, Richard. "Weathers Stepping Down as Top Essence Editor." [Online, 21 March 2005]. Richard Prince's Journal-isms. Maynard Institute Web site www.maynardije.org; Smith, Stephanie D. "Weathers Steps Down from Essence." [Online, 21 March 2005]. MediaWeek Web site www.mediaweek.com; Stanley, Jeffrey. "Alum Profile: Diane Weathers, '67." [Online]. Brooklyn Friends School Web site www.brooklynfriends.cor/alunmi/profiles.

Weathersbee, Tonyaa (c.1959–)

Jacksonville native Tonyaa Weathersbee is a columnist for the *Florida Times-Union* in Jacksonville and writes for a national audience on the Web site

BlackAmericaWeb.com. After getting her bachelors in journalism from the University of Florida in 1981, she was hired by the *Pensacola News-Journal*, working there until moving to the *Times-Union* in 1985. In addition to her opinion page column, she writes two community news columns a week. Weathersbee has taught journalism for four years at the University of North Florida and has been a journalist-in-residence at Virginia's Washington & Lee University and at Florida A&M University in Tallahassee. Also, she is senior project manager for North Carolina A&T University's Institute of Advanced Journalism Studies in Greensboro, N.C. Her work has allowed her travel considerably. She has made six trips to Cuba to report on the implications of the U.S. embargo; has led groups of journalists to Brazil, Haiti and Panama; and has written from Grenada and Jordan. Weathersbee is a member of the National Press Club, Investigative Reporters and Editors, the Society of Professional Journalists, the William Monroe Trotter Group of black columnists and the National Association of Black Journalists, which in 2005 inducted her into its Region 4 Hall of Fame.

Weathersbee's columns are closely tied to topics of special interest to African Americans. An example of her work that was likely to have trod upon a good many toes, white and black, concerns the difficulties of having "black-sounding" names, such as Da'Quan or LaQuisha. She also worries that conservative presidential administrations' emphasis on "personal responsibility" has morphed into code talk for society turning its back on the disadvantaged, and she considers President George W. Bush to be insensitive and even hostile to racial concerns. She thinks that the U.S. invasion of Iraq has been a victory for Osama Bin Laden in that it has so divided America, and her concern about the Patriot Act is that it is intended more to reduce personal freedoms than to combat terrorists. She likens the act to COINTELPRO, an earlier counterintelligence program run by the FBI in the Cold War era that was utilized to stifle the efforts of Martin Luther King and Malcolm X on the domestic front, whereas its stated purpose was to protect us from outside threats.

Reappearing in her columns year to year is American Beach, a small stretch of seashore on Amelia Island that was purchased in the 1930s by Florida's first black millionaire, insurance company founder Abraham Lincoln Lewis, so that blacks could enjoy beach vacationing during America's many decades of rigid segregation. One such column introduced readers to MaVynee Betsch, Lewis' great-granddaughter who has made preserving this beach her life's work and who so disliked the Reagan administration that she dropped the "r" in her first name, originally spelled MarVynee. Weathersbee has a personal connection to this beach in that her father bought its only restaurant in 1980.

Often, her columns celebrate accomplishments and improvements. One such column reflected favorably about the increasing number of children's books written especially for a multicultural audience, whereas the books she read as a child were mostly reflective of a very white world. Another complimentary column was about a local program called Suited for Success that donates clothing to just-released prisoners in an effort to ease their return to the work force. On the international front, Weathersbee celebrated the first time an African woman was given the Nobel Peace Prize when Kenyan environmentalist Wangari Maathai received the award in 2004 for her efforts to protect Mount Kenya from overly aggressive loggers.

"Bush Helped the Terrorists Gain Mileage from Attacks" by Tonyaa Weathersbee

Wherever Osama bin Laden is now, I'm sure he's smiling.

Not, as Dick Cheney slyly warned, at the prospect of a John Kerry presidency. Terrorists don't distinguish between George W. Bush and Kerry. Not at the fact that, for whatever reason, bin Laden has been able to elude forces out to capture him. Not even at the fact that the war in Iraq has alienated, rather than endeared, the rest of the world to us.

Bin Laden might very well be chuckling at how the Sept. 11, 2001, terrorist attacks that he masterminded have morphed from being a catalyst to unite Americans into a tool to divide them.

Playing the terror card has led us into an unjustified, poorly planned, pre-emptive war in Iraq—a war in which 8,000 Americans have been wounded and more than 1,000 killed. It has led to massive protests and deep resentments. It has led to scant attention to other issues—issues like burgeoning health care costs, a record deficit and record job losses—that also threaten our survival as well.

It has led to a wave of intolerance; a time in which writers can unabashedly argue for interning Arab-Americans for the crime of being Arab, and not bat an eye. A time in which a business owner can lose patrons for having the wrong candidate's sign in front of his or her shop. Fear has us more at each others' throats than on the trail of the terrorists.

I wonder if this is what bin Laden had in mind all along.

This presidential election is tight. Record numbers of new voters have signed up. Last week, the latest polls showed the race between Bush and Kerry as a dead heat. There's no arguing that, after decades of dismal turnouts, the level of interest in a presidential election is refreshing.

Yet, while I want to believe that this news solely reflects a newfound belief in the power of democracy, I also know that it is a testament to the power of fear. People are voting their fears, not their hopes. Against, not for. I'm one of them, in fact.

And I don't like it.

This all started with Bush, though. When he narrowly won the presidency in 2000 by way of a flawed election, he promised to be a uniter, not a divider. He vowed that he'd govern from the center. That was reasonable and admirable. But no sooner than the nation began to heal from its collective grief of Sept. 11, the president forgot that promise.

Instead of building on that unity to not only fight terrorism but to reach out to constituencies that questioned his legitimacy and harbored qualms about him, he began to exploit the fear that emerged from the attacks to pursue an ideological agenda that has sharply divided this country.

After his success in painting Iraq as a great threat to America that needed to be contained immediately, Bush soon began to paint homosexuals as a great threat to marriage. Government responsibility began to morph into privatization. Dissenters weren't just ignored. They were shut out. If you don't believe me, ask the Congressional Black Caucus. Bush didn't meet with these elected representatives for more than three years—and when he finally did regarding the crisis in Haiti, it was because they came to the White House and refused to leave.

This might be the way to run a corporation, or the way Bush runs a corporation, butt it's no way to run a democracy. It certainly isn't the way of a uniter.

Many people, of course, believe Bush's actions in Iraq make him a strong leader. But again, that's fear working—the kind of fear that has too many people confusing recklessness with decisiveness and praising quick reaction over strategic and thoughtful response. But it is also fear that is turning many people against Bush—and driving much of these record registrations of new voters. Based on his record, many believe that he won't just stop after he gets the terrorists in line, but anyone else who dosen't hew to the ideologies that are driving him.

That's not a recipe for national unity. It's a recipe for national discontent.

Whoever wins the election, however, will have to be a uniter. If Bush wins, he'll have to get a lot better at it. And that unity can't be a coerced unity—the kind of unity that demands that suffering people or alienated constituencies ignore their reality and behave themselves. It has to be real. As Martin Luther King Jr. once said: "True peace isn't the absence of conflict, it is the presence of justice."

The next president would do well to heed those words. If he doesn't, we risk having terrorists gloat about how one horrific act they committed not only succeeded in killing more than 3,000 people, but the spirit of America as well.

Source: Copyrighted, the *Florida Times-Union*. Reprinted by permission. This column appeared on 25 October 2004.

Further Readings: "NABJ Founder, Two Columnists To Be Inducted into Region IV Hall of Fame." [Online, 18 May 2005]. National Association of Black Journalists Web site www.nabj.org; "Tonyaa Weathersbee, BlackAmerica.com." [Online]. BlackAmerica.com Web site www.blackamericaweb.com.

Whitaker, Mark (7 September 1957–)

Newsweek editor Mark Whitaker was born in Lower Merton, Pennsylvania, the son of two professors—his father black, his mother white. He lived in his early years in a variety of places: Swarthmore, Los Angeles, Nigeria, London, Princeton, and Norton, Massachusetts. At the age of eight he settled in Norton following his parents' divorce, and he began writing sports for the *Attleboro Sun* while in seventh and eighth grades. He also wrote for the school paper at the George School, the Quaker boarding school he attended. Later he learned French while attending a high school in France, where his mother was on sabbatical. He spent the 1975–1976 school year at Swarthmore College, then accepted a scholarship to Harvard, where he was on the editorial board of the *Crimson*. Starting in 1977, he spent three summers practicing journalism, first as a reporting intern at *Newsweek*'s San Francisco bureau, then as a stringer and intern for *Newsweek* in Boston, Washington, Paris and London. A good scholar, he graduated summa cum laude from Harvard in 1979, then studied in England at Oxford University's Balliol College as a Marshall scholar but left without completing his Ph.D. to take an entry-level job writing sidebars at *Newsweek* in New York. After six months of borrowing desk space from vacationers, he was given a windowless office but soon was reporting from all over the world for the magazine's international section. His original intention to remain a foreign correspondent was altered in 1987 when he was named business editor, a job he held until 1991 when he was elevated to the post of assistant managing editor. In this position he led the magazine's new emphasis on computer technology, spun off a yearly magazine titled *Computers & the Family* and also did some commentary pieces that reflected on race issues. He was promoted to managing editor in 1996 and in September 1997, when editor

Maynard Parker's leukemia became worse, Whitaker took over as interim editor. Upon Parker's death in October 1998, Whitaker was named editor, the first African American to edit one of the three leading U.S. newsweeklies. At age 41, he was also the only African American to edit one of America's top 100 general interest magazines.

In an era of considerable mobility and frequent changes of employment for media people, Mark Whitaker's one-employer career is unusual, yet as he has pointed out, in corporate America staying with one company is not so uncommon. In his years as a writer and those spent as an editor, he has had a hand in a wide range of important stories, including the Black Monday collapse of the stock market, the savings-and-loan debacle, the Michael Milken securities fraud affair, the untimely death of Britain's Princess Diana, and the Monica Lewinsky scandal that rocked the Clinton administration and brought *Newsweek* the National Magazine Award for reporting in 1999. It is ironic that the magazine's other National Magazine Award, this one in 2002 for general excellence, was for its coverage of the 11 September 2001, attacks on the World Trade Center towers, the event that precipitated President George W. Bush's war on terrorism. The irony is that in May 2005, another chapter in this conflict was the low point in Whitaker's editorship. After interviewing a high-level but unnamed government source, *Newsweek* ran a story on May 9 that claimed a Quran had been flushed down a toilet in the U.S. military prison at Guantanamo Bay, Cuba. Angry riots occurred in various parts of the Muslim world including Afghanistan, where 16 people died and more than 100 were injured, plus Gaza, Pakistan and Indonesia. The White House was quick to challenge the story, and on May 23, Whitaker issued a statement that the magazine's source had changed his story and recanted the flushing allegation. The administration, apparently relieved to see some other institution's veracity challenged, demanded a full apology from *Newsweek*. The U.S. commander in Afghanistan gave the magazine some measure of relief by saying that local politics were more to blame for the unrest there than was the magazine's story, and Whitaker revealed that before running the story, it had been vetted by Pentagon officials, who had not disputed the Quran-flushing account.

Blessed with movie-star looks, Whitaker is in demand for television appearances but does only a few, such as occasional guest appearances on "Charlie Rose" and "Hardball." In addition, he has been on the board of the American Society of Magazine Editors since 1999 and in 2004, became its president.

Further Readings: Lindsay, Greg. "So What Do You Do, Mark Whitaker?" [Online, 25 May 2004]. Media Bistro Web site www.mediabisro.com; "Mark Whitaker, Editor." [Online, 2004]. MSBNC Web site www.msnbc.com/modules/newsweek; "Mark Whitaker Elected President of American Society of Magazine Editors." [Online, 4 May 2004]. ASME Web site www.magazine.org/Editorial; "Reflections on Success: Mark Whitaker." [Online, 2005]. The Black Collegian Web site www.black-collegian.com; Schuker, Lauren A.E. "Crimson Colleagues Reunite at Newsweek Magazine." [Online, 9 June 2004]. The Harvard Crimson Web site www.thecrimson.com; Smith, Maureen M. "Whitaker, Mark." In *African American Lives*. Ed. by Henry Louis Gates Jr. and Evelyn Brooks Higginbotham. New York: Oxford University Press, 2004, pp. 876–77; "Whitaker, Mark." In *2003 Current Biography Yearbook*. Ed. by Clifford Thompson. New York: H.W. Wilson, pp. 561–63.

White, Jack E. (1946–)

Talented writer Jack White retired from *Time* magazine in 2001 after a 29-year career there and from 2004 to the end of spring term 2006, taught reporting and news writing at Hampton University's Scripps Howard School of Journalism and Communications. His paternal grandfather was born into slavery near Savannah, Georgia; and his father, the youngest of 17 children, beat the odds to become a physician and a professor at the Howard University Medical School. Jack White was a student at Swarthmore College outside Philadelphia. In 1969 he found a job as a general assignment reporter for the *Washington Post*, then moved to Tennessee to work for the *Race Relations Reporter* in Nashville from 1969 to 1972. White was hired by *Time* in 1972 and was a staff writer for a succession of sections: Modern Living, Economy and Business, and Energy. He was assigned to the magazine's Atlanta bureau in 1974 and to the Boston bureau in 1977 following a leave of absence for a Nieman fellowship at Harvard that began in fall 1976. In 1978, he returned to *Time* headquarters in New York City and wrote for the World section. He served as Nairobi bureau head in 1980 and 1981 and once again came back to New York as bureau chief in May 1982. He reported on the 1984 presidential race and became better known to the nation as one of the panelists who asked questions of vice-presidential candidates George Bush and Geraldine Ferraro in their televised debate. From 1985 to 1987, he worked out of Chicago as the magazine's Midwest bureau chief. In June 1987, he became deputy chief of correspondents and as such, was in charge of 10 domestic bureaus and 51 correspondents. He was Nation editor from July 1990 to July 1992 and at that time left the magazine to work for one year as senior producer of domestic news for "ABC World News Tonight with Peter Jennings." Returning to *Time* in April 1993, White worked as a senior correspondent in the New York bureau and moved to the nation's capital in 1994 as a national correspondent and writer of the magazine's "Dividing Line" column. He broke new ground as the first African American to write a column for one of the major U.S. news weeklies. In May 1995, he was given an additional job: organizing a campaign to recruit more minority journalists for the magazines of Time Inc., which were *Time, People, Sports Illustrated, SI for Kids, Fortune, Life, Money, In Style* and *Martha Stewart's Living*. After 29 years with *Time*, White retired in 2001. In the fall of 2001, he began teaching journalism at Howard University. He began teaching at Hampton University in Tidewater Virginia in 2004 and during the 2005–2006 school year, he held the Scripps Howard Endowed Chair for media professionals at Hampton. In May 2006, White announced that he was leaving the university due to disagreements with Dean Tony Brown and dissatisfaction with the university administration's handling of First Amendment issues. Specifically, he was critical of the administration's confiscation of an issue of the campus newspaper, the Hampton Script, when student editors ran a story inside the paper rather than on the front page, as directed by the university's president, JoAnn Haysbert. White also cited a 2005 incident in which seven students were disciplined for protesting against the policies of the Bush administration. He has published in *Ebony, Black Enterprise, Progressive* and the *Columbia Journalism Review*, is the coauthor of one book on race and corporate America and is married to former NBC News correspondent Cassandra Clayton, who now teaches at the University of Maryland's Philip Merrill College of Journalism. White has also made appearances on such programs as "The Today Show," "Inside Washington with Gordon Peterson," "The McLaughlin Group," "The Point with Greta Van Susteran," "This Week with San Donaldson and Cokie Roberts," "Lead Story" on BET and on WHUT, "Evening Exchange with Kojo Nnamdi."

White, a liberal, has often been quoted as remarking that the far right has fostered a myth: the liberal media, when in reality most of our nation's media display more of a conservative bias. He has especially singled out Brent Bozell and his Media Research Center and Fox News, which is not at all as "fair and balanced" as its company slogan claims. While he has been quick to point out the recidivist views of many white conservatives, he was just as quick to criticize African-American spokesman Jesse Jackson when the Rev. Jackson revealed that he had fathered a child out of wedlock with his biographer, Karin Stanford. The biggest controversy of White's career involved a dispute with neo-conservative white columnist David Horowitz, who had complained about "race hustlers" who made a career of shaking down guilt-ridden whites to further the black agenda. White accused Horowitz of conducting a blanket assault on the black community in a 30 August 1999 *Time* column titled "A Real, Live Bigot." Horowitz countered by bringing a libel action, suing White for $50 million and defending himself in Salon.com, citing his earlier life of public activity in the struggle to achieve equal rights for African Americans. Horowitz recalled his efforts two years earlier that had raised $500,000 to defend black columnist and commentator Larry Elder, whose radio talk show was under threat of cancellation.

In a Web-only special report for Time.com in February 2000, White blistered the four police officers who had shot college student Amadou Diallo, an immigrant from Guinea, as he stood holding his wallet in the vestibule of his apartment building. Diallo had not been armed and was shot 41 times. In December 2000, White wrote about the preelection promise of presidential candidate George W. Bush to fill some high government positions with African Americans; White noted the irony of his doing so after 92 percent of blacks voted against him. In this story, headlined "No Toms Need Apply," White also advised the president-elect to choose independent-minded African Americans.

A February 2001 column concerned the courtroom victory of Marsha Coleman-Adebayo, a MIT-educated black political scientist who had suffered racial affronts while working for the Environmental Protection Agency during the administration of the elder George Bush. Having been told that her supervisors found her "uppity," she filed a discrimination complaint. When the complaint was brushed aside, she went to court, winning a $600,000 judgment, later reduced by a judge to half that amount. In "Lott, Reagan and Republican Racism," published on Time.com in December 2002, White pointed out that black anger at Trent Lott more logically should go back in time to take into account the racial insensitivity of President Ronald Reagan, who had also dealt in thinly veiled resistance to black progress in order to appeal to the more mean-spirited branch of the Republican Party. The above-mentioned stories were brief compared to some of his earlier reporting for *Time*, such as "Segregation Remembered" from 27 September 1976 or the many-page report (17 June 1974) on the growing black middle class written by White and fellow African-American reporter Joseph Boyce. For this story, White interviewed individuals in four U.S. cities. (Part of this lengthy report was written by associate editor Edwin Warner.) White was also chosen by *Time* editors to write the 13 April 1998 portrait of the Rev. Martin Luther King, Jr., that was part of the magazine's selection of the 100 most important people of the twentieth century.

Books by Jack E. White: With Bari-Ellen Roberts, *Roberts v. Texaco: A True Story of Race and Corporate America* (New York: Avon Books, 1998).

Further Readings: "Jack E. White, National Correspondent." [Online, 1996]. CNN Web site www.cnn.com/ALLPOLITICS/1996/analysis/bios; "Jack E. White, Scripps Howard Endowed Chair." [Online]. Scripps Howard School of Journalism and Communications Web site www.hampton.edu; "Journalist Leaves Post at Hampton University." the *Roanoke Times*, 14 May 2006.

Whitfield, Fredricka (?–)

A young broadcaster of considerable accomplishment and potential is Fredricka Whitfield of CNN, one of roughly 30 minority anchors employed by that organization as of early 2006. She holds a bachelor's degree in journalism from Howard University, and her first job was as a morning anchor for Charleston, South Carolina, station WCIV. Like so many young broadcasters, she moved through a fairly rapid succession of other similar jobs: at WTNH in New Haven, Connecticut, and KTVT-TV in Dallas, Texas, as a general assignment reporter, then as an evening anchor at News Channel 8 in Washington, D.C., and WPLG-TV in Miami, Florida. She next was hired by NBC News and was a correspondent for the "NBC Nightly News" and "The Today Show," working out of Atlanta. In 2002 she began her present job with CNN, also in Atlanta. There, the slender, attractive Whitfield is a news anchor for the Saturday and Sunday newscasts, and she also works as a network correspondent. Through her career, some of her biggest stories have been about various aspects of the war on terrorism, including some in-country reporting from the Middle East during Operation Iraqi Freedom in 2003. In addition, she has reported on the case of the Cuban boy Elian Gonzales, who finally was returned by U.S. authorities to his homeland, the West Nile virus threat and the abnormally high number of shark attacks during the summer of 2001. Whitfield has been accorded several recognitions, including the Rookie of the Year Award from the Society of Professional Journalists, the Associated Press Reporter of the Year Award and the Groit Award for excellence in journalism. Some less enthusiastic observers of her work have accused her of being biased or having spent too much time on "fluff stories." In an account written for the Jewish Press Online, writer/editor Jason Maoz characterized her coverage as anti-Israel, pro-Palestinian. Writing for Weeklystandard.com, Victorino Matus criticized the choice of stories on her show, pointing out that really meaningful material gets passed over quickly in favor of celebrity drivel or human-interest material. What set him off was how quickly she had presented a segment about the invention by an Australian of an all-electric gun that has no moving parts, can fire a million rounds a minute and might be useful in missile defense systems. Other of her soft news stories have been about "American Idol" singer Ruben Studdard and children who flushed their pet fish down the toilet after seeing the movie "Finding Nemo." A talk Whitfield gave at an October 2002 meeting of Women in Film and Television was titled "The Television Journalist—Is It What We Look Like or What We Have to Say?" Overemphasis on youth and glamorous looks, she concluded, is a disturbing trend in television today, and one that now affects both anchors and correspondents.

Far more substantive stories Whitfield handled in 2002 included the Bush administration's simplistic plan for two-parent families, abuse of children by U.S. Roman Catholic priests, how the U.S. Homeland Security Department should be structured and the work of the Salvation Army at Ground Zero after the World Trade Center attacks. In 2003, she reported on the Turkish parliament's vote to allow the United States military to use its airspace for air strikes on Iraq, a debate about war in Iraq between students from North Carolina's Davidson College and the University of Baghdad, obesity as a major health problem for Americans, the evacuation of a seriously ill U.S. worker stationed at the South Pole and the possibilities for mad cow disease in the United States. Two 2004 interview stories were with Florida's Gov. Jeb Bush regarding his state's preparations for Hurricane Frances and Yvonne Latty, coauthor, with Ron Tarver, of *We Were There: Voices of African American Veterans from World War II to the War in Iraq* (New York: Amistad, 2004), about 28 selected African Americans who served in both World War II and the current war on terrorism.

Further Readings: "Fredricka Whitfield." [Online]. CNN Web site www.cnn.com.

Whitlock, Jason (?–)

Jason Whitlock is a talented, opinionated, outspoken sports columnist at the *Kansas City Star*, from which he appears in around 400 other newspapers via the Knight Ridder Tribune Service. He grew up in Indianapolis and was captain of the undefeated football team at Warren Central High School his senior year, 1984. A good blocker, he got a football scholarship to Ball State University, where he played for two years before getting a torn anterior cruciate ligament and concluding that he would prefer writing about the game to playing it. He dropped his accounting major in favor of journalism; he wrote for the campus newspaper, the *Daily News*, and graduated in 1990. Whitlock's inspiration was the great Chicago columnist Mike Royko, whose style he emulated, and his goal—never realized—was to write sports for either the *Indianapolis Star* or the *Chicago Tribune*. His initial job was writing sports part-time for the *Herald-Times* of Bloomington, Indiana. Nearly a year later, he moved to the East Coast to cover high school and other children's sports at the Rock Hill, South Carolina, bureau of the *Charlotte Observer*. He also wrote on rap and rhythm and blues music for the *Observer*, which got him noticed and led to his next job, covering University of Michigan football and basketball for the *Ann Arbor News*. In his first column, on 2 October 1994, a month after he joined the *Kansas City Star*, he put his readers on notice that they were likely to find him cynical, negative, argumentative and rude.

Since that time, he has been the kind of columnist who kicks up a fuss often enough to make sure that his words will not be ignored by either his fans or his critics. His tone is often antiestablishment and aimed primarily at the younger reader. Like Royko, he sees himself as a voice for the less privileged; one of his pet peeves is what instant mega-wealth has done to major athletes, especially those who are African American. His concern is that these newly rich objects of public hero worship often seem to forget their roots and feel little obligation to help others. One of his publicity stunts was to pretend that he was seeking membership in the exclusive Kansas City Country Club—just to shake up that organization's comfort level while providing gleeful copy for his column's readers. A large, intimidating figure at 6'4" and at least 300 pounds, he refers to himself as "Big Sexy," and in a 1997 article in *Columbia Journalism Review*, *Sports Illustrated* writer John Garrity dubbed Whitlock the "hip-hop scourge" of Kansas City sports journalism. Whitlock has insulted Kansas State fans by picturing them as hayseeds, crossed swords with Kansas City Royals boss David Glass, criticized African Americans who use the N-word and, in 1995, suggested a boycott of baseball because of the high salary demands of the players. Unlike Royko, who disdained working in any medium besides newspapers, Whitlock has embraced work in broadcasting and from 1999 until March 2005, he hosted his own early morning radio show, "Jason Whitlock's Neighborhood," which began on Sports Radio 810, WHB. In June 2003, Whitlock left WHB for Entercom, a company that wanted to launch an all-sports talk station. His 2005 resignation from 610 Sports was apparently due to a salary dispute. He has also appeared on the ESPN Sunday morning show "The Sports Reporters" and has substituted for the popular Tony Kornheiser on another ESPN program, "Pardon the Interruption." Like Royko, Whitlock is very much an everyday part of his city. He reports taking pleasure and pride in this relationship and has confessed that watching sports and writing about what he sees is too much fun to feel like work.

One of Whitlock's most controversial dust-ups came in March 2005, around the time he left his radio show. The U.S. Congress had opened hearings on the use of steroids by Major League baseball players. The aim of the hearings was to attempt to put an end to this risky practice, ostensibly to set a better example for children. Whitlock saw the hearings as blatant political posturing, staged to get approval of the voters at the expense of a few players, such as homerun-hitting heroes Mark McGwire and Barry Bonds. He called the hearings a witchhunt and likened them to the infamous McCarthy hearings of the 1950s. Whitlock's take on the situation was that despite the photo-op congressional hearings and the pious criticisms voiced by many fans and sportswriters, no one actually cares much about steroid use by athlete-entertainers and, truth be known, prefer to see the greater number of homeruns despite the chemical cheating that produces them. Going beyond the confines of sports, he has criticized the nation's so-called "war on drugs," which began during the Reagan administration, and which, he once pointed out, has spawned a lively market in for-profit incarceration. Many drug offenders, he added, get longer sentences than do convicted rapists or murders. In his view, the George W. Bush administration's push to eliminate steroids will fail due to the constant development of newer and harder-to-detect performance drugs. He charged team owners with being secretly pleased about the effects of steroids and wrote that sports fans just want to be entertained, drugs or no drugs.

Whitlock has also ripped into the relationship of university presidents and their successful revenue-sports coaches. The visibility brought to a school by a winning team, he commented, has made presidents afraid of these coaches, even though the added contributions from hero-worshiping alumni and other boosters tend to benefit only the athletic department, especially the head coaches, whose compensation eclipses that of their universities' presidents. In his view, the primacy of big-time college sports represents a system out of control, a view shared by many university faculty members. As to professional sports, Whitlock sees the players as having too much money and too much adulation, but too few morals. He has sometimes pictured professional athletes as being taken advantage of by dishonest coaches and team owners, greedy agents, uncaring sports writers, overwilling "groupies" and sycophantic fans. Just the same, he adds, the fact that they often act like idiots should not prevent us from enjoying their deeds on the field or court. As to the matter of race in sports, he has criticized consumer advocate Ralph Nader for singling out African-American basketball superstar LeBron James by urging that James should fight to improve the lot of the exploited factory workers in Third World countries who make the athletic shoes that the star endorses. Whitlock complains that black athletes are usually the ones targeted for criticism regarding social issues such as this one, whereas white players are more likely to be left alone to attend only to their game. Criticizing America in general, Whitlock has pointed out that we have become fat, lazy and obsessed with making money to the point that we cannot compete with the athletes of other nations the way we once did. We can now be bested in baseball, long considered an American sport, by teams from Mexico, Japan and Cuba, and many of our top basketball players, he writes, are too unmotivated or too self-centered to represent their country in the Olympics. He cheered the cancellation of the 2004-2005 season of National Hockey League play, contending that the players were in it only for the money, not the wins. Even in golf, he writes, the players are too self-concerned to play the style of team golf needed to win the Ryder Cup. The central problem, he contends, is that our best athletes are too rich, content and arrogant to care—a situation, he adds, that mirrors our society, in which the wealthy are often the least likely to be compassionate or patriotic. There seems to be no end to what he will criticize, but there is always some truth in what he writes. Money, he often points out, is the root of all evil in sports, and the only people not in athletics for the money are the fans.

Once in a while, Whitlock writes something positive about athletes, as in a 2004 column calling the Denver Broncos' quarterback John Elway the game's best player ever—the Michael Jordan of football. He had, wrote Whitlock, the passing arm of Marion, the accuracy of Montana, the running ability of McNabb, the intelligence of Manning, the courage of Favre and the ability to absorb punishment of Simms. Thus far, Whitlock as coauthored one book about his sports writing career.

"Find Heroes Elsewhere" by Jason Whitlock

Whether he doped or not, Floyd Landis, winner of the Tour de France, should make Americans come to grips with an uncomfortable truth.

Charles Barkley was right 13 years ago when he said professional athletes are not role models or heroes.

That's the lesson to take from the performance-enhancing drug controversy engulfing America's latest cycling star. It doesn't mater whether Landis filled his bloodstream with testosterone so that he could pull off the Stage 17 comeback that shocked the cycling world. Those blood-test results will be debated for years.

On Thursday, Landis swore to a Sports Illustrated reporter that he didn't cheat to win the Tour, but he also said he has little faith that a second test will exonerate him. His team, Phonak, has quickly distanced itself from its champion, suspending Landis pending a second test.

I don't particularly care whether Landis cheated. His "guilt" is not germane to the uncomfortable reality we all must confront.

It's foolish for any of us to look for heroes and role models on fields, courts, bike routes, golf courses or anywhere money and sports collide. We'll always be disappointed.

Floyd Landis, with his degenerative hip condition, was an American hero, a symbol of incredible perseverance for what, four days? He won the Tour on Sunday, went into hiding by Tuesday and was disgraced early Thursday morning. We had four days to celebrate Landis, tell our kids how he overcame improbable odds to win a daunting physical test, and then, poof.

One test reduced Landis to rubble and had television reporters hounding his mother for interviews. Charged with the crime of defrauding American sports fans of a hero, Landis has reacted like O.J., sans the White Bronco.

Landis has skipped planned appearances and offered a hole-ridden denial. In his SI interview, he mentioned that medicine he was taking for a "thyroid condition" might have produced the result.

I guess it beats saying his dog ate his testosterone.

Again, I'm uninterested in putting Landis or Lance Armstrong or Barry Bonds or Mark McGwire on trial. I'd just like to see all athletes taken off a pedestal. It's unhealthy. It's improper. It's a position they don't want or deserve.

They're entertainers. They're no different from Jim Morrison or Justin Timberlake or the movie star who goes in and out of rehab.

Athletes and the bad deeds they get involved in are not what's wrong with our kids. We're what's wrong with kids, those of us who keep praying that our children grow up to be professional athletes, those of us who fail to accept responsibility of being role models to the kids within our own families.

It's comforting to blame your child's failure on Barry Bonds' flaws rather than your own unwillingness to make sacrifices.

We can't deny that money has completely perverted the sports world. It's ridiculous that we act outraged every time we learn another athlete has been turned out by the pursuit of athletic fame and wealth. That's what happens.

You want to clean up sports, you want to rid the sports world of performance-enhancing drugs?

Quit worshipping athletes. Quit kissing their rear ends every time you see them at a restaurant.

We know that's not going to happen. And I don't think the sports leagues will ever come up with a testing policy that will keep pace with the medical advances and masking devices that help athletes cheat.

So I say treat 'em like rock stars and movie stars. We don't care that they drink and drug themselves into lives 10 to 20 years shorter than expected. Most people don't put little guitars or movie scripts in their infant's crib.

We enjoy the entertainment actors and musicians provide and ignore their misbehavior.

Source: This column appeared on 28 July 2006. Reproduced with permission of *The Kansas City Star* © Copyright 2006 *The Kansas City Star*. All rights reserved. Format differs from original publication. Not an endorsement.

Books by Jason Whitlock: With Buck O'Neil, *Love Him, Hate Him: 10 Years of Sports, Passion and Kansas City* (Kansas City, Mo.: Kansas City Star Books, 2004).

Further Readings: Blackwood, Kendrick and Andrew Miller. "Big Sexy: Jason Whitlock's Pen Gained Him Local Fame (And a Favorite Nickname)—Then He Took to the Air." [Online, 29 January 2004]. The Pitch Web site www.pitch.com; Garrity, John. "Jason Whitlock Scores in K.C." [Online, May/June 1997]. Columbia Journalism Review site http://archives.cjr.org; "Introducing … Jason Whitlock." [Online, 2000]. Kansas City Star Web site www.kcstar.com/sports; "Jason Whitlock, Columnist's Biography." [Online]. Kansas City Star Web site www.kansascity.com; "Jason Whitlock Quits 61 Sports." Gateway City Radio Web site www.gatewaycityradio.com.

Wickham, DeWayne (22 July 1946–)

A Gannett News Service columnist since 1985 and a *USA Today* columnist since 1988, DeWayne Wickham is an unrelenting advocate for the interests of African Americans. He was born in Baltimore; was in the Air Force from 1964 to 1968, serving in several areas of the war zone in Vietnam and other parts of Southeast Asia and reaching the rank of sergeant; received the B.A. in journalism in 1974 at the University of Maryland; and earned a masters of public administration in 1982 at the University of Baltimore. His journalistic career started during his undergraduate years, when in 1972 he was a reporting intern at the Baltimore *Evening Sun*, and 1973 as a copyediting intern at the *Richmond Times Dispatch*. After graduating in 1974, he was a Capitol Hill correspondent for *U.S. News & World Report*; in 1975, he became a reporter for the Baltimore *Sun*, remaining in that capacity until 1978, when he worked for two years as an assistant to Dr. Mary Frances Berry, President Jimmy Carter's education chief prior to the creation of the Department of Education. Wickham also hosted a talk show on Baltimore's station WBAL-TV from 1976 until 1989. Wickham was one of the founders of the National Association of Black Journalists and was that organization's president from 1987 to 1989. He had run unsuccessfully for that office in 1989, but during his tenure as president, proved himself an accomplished fundraiser. The organization's membership doubled, reaching around 1,900 by the time his term ended. He was also a founder of the Trotter Group, an organization of black columnists. Wickham has chaired the board of visitors of Howard University's journalism program, has served on the advisory board of the multicultural management program at the University of Missouri's School of Journalism, has been on the alumni association board of the University of Baltimore and is a member of the advisory board of the Newseum, the nation's only interactive museum of news and the board of visitors of the University of Maryland's Philip Merrill College of Journalism. He also has been a contributing editor for *Black Enterprise* magazine, appeared as a panelist on "Lead Story," appeared on Black Entertainment Television, and published four books.

Politically, DeWayne Wickham is a liberal and a considerable admirer of former president Bill Clinton. As such, he has taken his share of flak from conservatives, such as columnist Robert Yoho, who has chided Wickham for writing only about race, saying that the Wickham column is a single-note melody in a world of symphony. The very conservative Yoho complains that Wickham's observations on race are cut from the same cloth as those of Jesse Jackson and Al Sharpton, a comment that must have irritated, inasmuch as Wickham has criticized Sharpton as a political second-story man mainly concerned with stealing the media spotlight. Some of Wickham's columns are forceful and direct, but others approach the lingering problems of race relations from the side, as in some of his clever, disarming earlier work featuring his fictitious literary character "Ungawah Jones," whose unlettered common sense is reminiscent of the way Langston Hughes used his own character, Jesse B. Semple, in his longago *Chicago Defender* column. Wickham plucked the name "Ungawah" from the Tarzan movies he watched as a boy, reflecting that this made-for-movies word was, ironically, the best known word to enter the English language "from Africa."

"Battle Ready" by DeWayne Wickham

There he was, dressed in camouflage fatigues, standing in the shadow of "Big Daddy's Topless Bar," in the middle of one of Bourbon Street's bawdy blocks.

Ungawah, Ungawah Jones. What are you doing here, dressed like that? I called out to my longtime friend.

"Hey, brother. Can't be too careful. They're all over the place," he answered.

Who? Ungawah. All over where?

"Them damn conservatives, man. They're thicker than thieves' round here. Got to be on my guard, brother. Got to be ready to throw down with them dudes," he said.

Give me a break, Ungawah. I'm here to cover the Republican National Convention. I don't have time for your war games, man.

"Well, you better make some time," Ungawah snapped. "Cause if them conservatives take over this country black folks are gonna be history."

Ungawah, this is 1988. Ronald Reagan is president and the conservatives are already in control of the government, I said, annoyed that this obvious fact had escaped his notice.

"Not the Reagan conservatives, brother. They're bad enough. But that's not the bunch I'm talkin' 'bout," he said.

"See, that's the problem. It's hard for a lot of folks to distinguish them. I'm tellin' you, man, there is a group of those conservatives who are real extremists—you know, a kind of Christian, Islamic Jihad. And they're determined to finish off black folks."

Yeah, well I don't see it, Ungawah. A conservative is a conservative. They're all the same, I said.

"Damn, man. Did you see the movie Predator? Remember how that creature from outer space was able to make himself look like a tree? Remember how he blended in with the jungle?

"Well, that's what these dudes do. They blend in with all the other conservatives, but they are a much more deadly breed," Ungawah warned.

Now I see, Ungawah. Arnold Schwarzenegger is our enemy, I said with a big grin.

"Listen, geek. I don't have time to play with you. People like Reagan and Bush are decoys. They are just trees in the jungle compared to the guys I'm talkin' 'bout. The predator is that guy Gordon Humphrey," Ungawah said, referring to the ultraconservative Republican senator from New Hampshire. "He's the real Great Satan."

Hey, Ungawah. I can see the light on in your head, but I don't think anybody's home up there. What the heck are you talking about?

"This guy Humphrey is out to trash us, I'm telling you. And he's not alone," said Ungawah, his eyes sweeping the crowded streets for signs of "the enemy."

Is that right? I asked in a condescending voice.

"I ain't jivin', man. He's the one who pressured Bush into puttin' that Quayle guy on his ticket."

You mean Indiana Sen. Dan Quayle? I asked. Bush's vice presidential running mate?

"Right. He's a Humphrey clone. They're both anti-civil rights and anti-affirmative action," Ungawah said. "If these guys had their way, Robert Bork would be the next attorney general."

Even if this is true, Ungawah, I don't see how one man, or two, can be a great threat to 25 million blacks, I challenged him.

"Hey, they're not alone. It's Humphrey and Quayle. And it's also New Hampshire Gov. John Sununu and Jerry Falwell—the Moral Majority head mullah—and a lot more," he explained.

"I saw Cal Thomas, that ultraconservative columnist, out here on Bourbon Street the other day," Ungawah whispered. "I'm tellin' you man, they're all over the place."

OK, Ungawah, I conceded. We're surrounded by hostile conservatives. So what do we do?

"Now you're talkin', brother. We've got to organize. Get the word out. We can't let them predators pick us off one by one," my radical friend cautioned. "If this guy Quayle gets anywhere near the White House, we may all end up on a fast train ride to nowhere, if you know what I mean."

I understand, Ungawah, but...

"No buts, geek. This is war," he said angrily. "And we're only gonna get one shot at these guys this year."

When? I asked.

"Early in November. And we've got to be ready," he answered. "You are registered to vote...right?"

Source: The above column originally appeared on 19 August 1988. It appears here by permission of Mr. Wickham.

Books by DeWayne Wickham: *Fire at Will* (Washington, D.C.: USA Today Books, 1989); Ed. *Thinking Black: Some of the Nation's Best Black Columnists Speak Their Minds*

(New York: Crown, 1996); *Woodholme: A Black Man's Story of Growing Up Alone* (New York: Farrar, Straus, Giroux, 1995); *Bill Clinton and Black America* (New York: Ballentine Books, 2002).

Further Readings: Brooks, Sheila. "Committed to the Cause: A Salute to NABJ's Presidents: DeWayne Wickham." [Online]. National Associationof Black Journalists Web site www.nabj.org; Dawkins, Wayne. *Black Journalists: the NABJ Story*. Sicklerville, N.J.: August Press, 1993, pp. 186–188; Page, Clarence. Introduction to DeWayne Wickham, *Fire at Will*. Washington, D.C.: Gannett, 1989, pp. xv–xvii; "DeWayne Wickham." [Online]. The History Makers Web site www.thehistorymakers.com.

Wilbon, Michael (19 November 1958–)

Michael Wilbon is a longtime sports columnist and reporter for the *Washington Post* and is cohost of the show "Pardon the Interruption" on ESPN. He was born and raised in Chicago and is a 1980 journalism graduate of the Medill School at Northwestern University. While a student, he interned at the *Lafayette Journal and Courier* in Indiana, where he covered the police and courts and wrote basketball sidebar stories. His clips from that experience got him a second internship, this time with the *Post*, in 1979; and he joined the paper's staff directly after his graduation. His first assignment was covering Howard University sports and professional soccer. In 1981 and from 1985 to 1987, he covered Georgetown University basketball. He reported on University of Maryland football from 1981 to 1985 and that university's basketball program from 1982 to 1984. He was assigned to cover the Baltimore Orioles in 1985, Big East basketball and the National Football League from 1987 to 1990 and college football in 1988. In 1990, he was named a full-time columnist for the *Post*. During his many years of sportswriting, Wilbon has covered eight Olympics, 19 NCAA Final Four competitions, 17 Super Bowls and four World Series. In October 2005, Wilbon joined fellow *Post* sportswriter Tony Kornheiser in a sort of good-natured point-counterpoint ESPN sports show, "Pardon the Inerruption." The 30-minute program is done in Washington and airs weekdays at 5:30 PM Both men do guest appearances on ESPN's "The Sports Reporters," and Kornheiser also hosts "The Tony Kornheiser Show" on ESPN Radio. Viewers of "Pardon the Interruption" are able to call in to argue with the hosts or ask questions. Wilbon has also contributed to sports coverage on Channel Four and Washington's WRC, the city's NBC affiliate. He also has been a guest on NPR's "All Things Considered."

Wilbon has joined NBA basketball star Charles Barkley in writing two books: *I May Be Wrong, but I Doubt It* (2002) and *Who's Afraid of a Large Black Man?* (2005). He also was a contributor to *Redskins: A History of Washington's Team* (Washington, D.C.: Washington Post Books, 1997), edited by Thomas Boswell. He played himself in the 2004 movie "Mr. 3000," about a former baseball star who discovers that he had fallen short of 3,000 career hits and who returns in middle age hoping to remedy the situation. Wilbon is an elector for both the Baseball Hall of Fame and the Pro Football Hall of Fame. He is a member of the National Association of Black Journalists and has won awards for various of his columns and stories, including those about the late basketball player Len Bias and the University of Alabama's legendary football coach Paul "Bear" Bryant. Name a major athlete, and Wilbon has probably written about him or her. On one episode of "Pardon the Interruption" in 2005, Wilbon and Kornheiser were asked to name the top five Washington, D.C., athletes of all time. Among the names they debated were Sonny Jurgensen, Patrick Ewing, Michael Jordon, Len Bias, John Riggins, Joe Theismann, Darrell Green, Art Monk and Sugar Ray Leonard. In 2003, the cohosts started their own annual Kornheiser and Wilbon Golf Classic, a celebrity competition to benefit educational causes.

In December 2003, a Wilbon commentary on MSNBC celebrated the retirement of NFL defensive end Bruce Smith, whose record number of quarterback sacks totaled 199. Wilbon pointed out, however, that neither Smith's record nor that of fellow sack artist Reggie White could match that of an earlier player, Deacon Jones, who played before statistics were kept on sacks but is thought to have tallied more than 200. In Athens, Greece, to cover the 2004 Summer Olympics, Wilbon wrote a quirky column that touched on smog, automotive assembling and tardiness, but settled down to reflect on the long history of performance-enhancing drugs. When professional baseball returned to the nation's capital in 2004, Wilbon joined the chorus of fans and sports professionals in suggesting names for the team. Wilbon's suggestions were four: Senators, Nationals, Americans or Grays. The last of the four was in honor of a Negro National League team that won nine consecutive pennants in the 1930s and 1940s. In 2005, when National Hockey League commissioner Gary Bettman cancelled the season, Wilbon used his column to accuse the commissioner of arrogance. A month later, he picked the University of Maryland's team as the year's biggest disappointment in college basketball. The very next day, he offered his reasons why the Atlantic Coast Conference was the nation's best league. A column he wrote about a week later criticized a congressional hearing on the use of steroids in baseball as the biggest waste of time of anything televised since Geraldo Rivera's anticlimactic opening of the vault in Al Capone's house. Around that same time, Wilbon took on a topic that most sports commentators apparently prefer to ignore: the loss of basketball games due to poor foul shooting. His immediate target was the George Washington University team. Part of Wilbon's popularity with readers and viewers is his ability to offer commentary that is at once acerbic and good humored.

"In Athens, the New Can't Hold a Torch to the Ancient" by Michael Wilbon

It's just fine here, thank you. The smog is about the same as it is in Los Angeles. The humidity is only half as bad as most days in Washington. The traffic is what you get on the average weekday driving the I-94 into downtown Chicago. The security is what we have come to expect around the U.S. Capitol or the Holland Tunnel when the threat level is raised. God only knows what the state of the world will bring us between now and the end of these Summer Olympics, so there's no sense in feeling too cocky or naively at ease. But today is as promising as any day ever is one week before the start of the Games.

Yes, with five days to go before the Opening Ceremonies, people are paving and painting and erecting stuff. The most ready of all the stadiums appears to be the Olympic Stadium, but I'm talking about the one built for the 1896 Games, the one whose glistening marble bowl still seats 65,000 people and somehow, despite being 108 years old, is infinitely more attractive and in better shape than, say, RFK Stadium. Maybe the Expos could play here. Otherwise, well, anybody attending an event the first few days might want to wear white, since wet paint will be everywhere.

On the topic of tardiness, Greeks joke openly about how chronically late they are, how dinner at 9:30 really means 10 o'clock for men, 10:15 for women. This seems eerily akin to what we Americans who used to be called colored people refer to as C.P. time, so I'm right at home as it relates to the clock. Anyway, five days is a lot of time to make the final preparations; time enough for the U.S. men's basketball team to get smacked around again by one of the many international teams with more talent and hubris than most Americans understand or appreciate, time enough for Sean Taylor to hire another agent, fire that agent, then hire another.

Still, it seems about time to welcome everybody to our excellent summer adventure in Athens, where I came hoping to experience something radically different than I'd get at home. Instead I've arrived to find young Greek men driving tricked out cars—so what if it's usually a Renault hatchback—with rims spinning like they've all been studying MTV's "Pimp My Ride." Switch on the TV and there's the Greek "Survivor" on Athens's Channel 4 a half-hour past midnight on Saturday. And practically all day the "Mad Video" channel brings everything from Chingy to my new favorite rap group, La Sagrada Familia, where three Greek homeys are not only rockin' the best hip-hop tune in Europe (yes, in Greek, silly) but doing it while wearing Larry Bird and Magic Johnson jerseys. I have no idea what they're saying, but I nave no idea what Juvenile and 'Lil John are saying, either. Walking the streets of Athens you hear so much hip-hop, specifically strains of "In Da Club," it seems as if 50 Cent is to Greece what Jerry Lewis is to France.

This is the space and the time in which Kornheiser used to welcome the *Post* readers to the Summer Olympics, to Los Angeles and Seoul, to Barcelona and Atlanta. He'd take you through the streets, to the sounds and smells of Olympic cities, from Kimchi to tapas. That, of course, was when he was a working sportswriter and long before he became such a diva that Jason Alexander agreed to play him during prime time on television (check local listings after Labor Day). Kornheiser, as soon as he arrived at the Winter or Summer Games, took you through all the intimate details of his excellent adventure, which I won't do. I won't dwell on Santorini being the most soothing place I've ever seen, or walking through the 1,500-year-old ruins of ancient Ephesus or buying a handmade double-knotted rug from a guy named Atilla Aydin, in whose shop I learned that Mike Tyson had been knocked out by another Brit. First Lennox Lewis, then some tea-drinking stiff club fighter nobody ever heard of. If this keeps up the next guy begging Bob Arum for a shot at Tyson will be Hugh Grant.

Nope, I'm not going to mention any of that self-indulgent what-I-did-on-my-summer-vacation stuff, not even the best part of it, which, unquestionably, is getting away long enough to bail on NFL training camps in the United States (specifically Redskins camp) and all the overblown camp stories my brethren in print and TV treat like the moon landing.

So, I'll skip all that junk and tell you about performance enhancement. Specifically, ancient performance enhancement. You think the Bay Area Laboratory Co-Operative is groundbreaking stuff? BALCO is nothing. Somebody has a trainer with a syringe or, better yet, some topical solution to rub in a steroid and the whole thing, as distasteful as it is, barely produces a frown.

You know what the ancient Greek athletes reportedly ate to enhance their performances?

Sheep testicles.

That's right, a taste of that delicacy was said to raise the testosterone level of the boxers, wrestlers, bull-jumpers or anybody else in ancient times who had the nerve to let that pass his lips.

Sheep testicles, baby. That and strychnine reduced with a little bit of wine. The International

Herald Tribune carried a story last week that told of the 1904 marathon winner, Thomas Hicks, needing four physicians to revive him after his victory because he had a little strychnine to go with his brandy and passed out.

Nothing's new. The stadiums certainly aren't new in this part of the world. A soccer stadium that is home to one of the local teams in Istanbul is called "the new stadium" and it's said to have been built in 1917, just after our "ancient" Wrigley Field and Fenway Park were constructed. Older yet, there are ruins in the archeological museum in Athens that include a marble frieze from somewhere between 510 and 500 B.C. depicting a contest that looked remarkably like modern hockey, which served as the headstone of a grave where a great athlete was buried.

The first lesson, then, is one we never seem to learn in America, that old indeed can be good, whether we're talking about stadiums, contests, scheating or brandy—as long as there's enough to wash down a second helping of those sheep testicles.

Source: © 2004, *The Washington Post*. Reprinted with permission. This column appeared on 9 August 2004.

Books by Michael Wilbon: With Charles Barkley, *I May Be Wrong but I Doubt It* (New York: Random House, 2002); with Charles Barkley, *Who's Afraid of a Large Black Man?* (New York: Penguin Books, 2005).

Further Readings: "Michael Wilbon." [Online]. Washington Post Web site www.washingtonpost.com; "Michael Wilbon, Pardon the Interruption Wo-Host." [Online]. ESPN site http://espn.go.com; " Pardon the Interruption with Tony Kornheiser and Michael Wilbon." [Online]. ESPN Page 2 site http://espn.go.com.

Wiley, Ralph (12 April 1952–13 June 2004)

Far more than simply a sports writer, Ralph Wiley will be remembered best for a combination of his work with *Sports Illustrated*, his writing for ESPN.com, and for the nine books he authored or coauthored, only four of which were on sports topics. Wiley died at his Orlando, Florida, home of heart failure at age 52 in 2004 while watching a basketball game. He was born in the "Orange Mound" neighborhood of Memphis, Tennessee; his father died while he was a boy, and he was raised by his mother, a humanities teacher at Owen Junior College. She imparted her love of reading to her son, who was an amateur playwright while at Melrose High School as well as a member of the football and track teams. In 1972, he entered historically black Knoxville College, where he was a business and finance major, a sports writer for the weekly *Knoxville Kayana-Spectrum*, and a wide receiver on the football squad. His hopes of pursuing a career in professional football were dashed by a knee injury, and after graduating in 1975, he took a job as a copyboy with the *Oakland Tribune*. A year later, the sports editor asked him to see how he could do at writing a story about basketball standout Julius Erving, and on the basis of his success with the assignment, Wiley was hired to write about sports. He was later given the city beat for a while, then returned to the sports department to cover boxing. His stylish writing earned him his own column soon thereafter. Wiley, known to his friends as Butch, was hired away by the nation's premier sports magazine, *Sports Illustrated*, in 1982 and during his nine years with the magazine, wrote 29 cover stories and logged roughly 200 bylines. His specialties during these years were football, baseball and boxing. He was known for his personality-profile writing on such sports figures as Sugar Ray Robinson, Thomas Hearns, Cal Ripken Jr., and basketball coach Clarence "Bighouse" Gaines of Winston-Salem State College. He tended to write about the individuals who populate the world of sports; an example of this approach was a story on the death of boxer Duk Koo Kim after a bout with Ray "Boom Boom" Mancini. While still at *Sports Illustrated*, Wiley published his first book, *Serenity: A Boxing Memoir* (1989), the title of which was inspired by a favorite uncle, professional middleweight "Charlie Boy" Wiley, a man he especially admired due to the older man's air of personal serenity. The book was not about a single boxer, however, but about a variety of pugilists, some successful, some not. He brought something special to sports writing, which so often is the stuff of cliché. One thing that informed his writing was a near-encyclopedic knowledge of the sports he reported. Another was his unusually wellread background, and yet another was a sincere interest in people as individuals, not just members of a team. As a writer, he exhibited considerable passion, and he coupled intentional provocation with flashes of wit, a combination that engaged his readers' emotions more than is the case with most sports writing. He appears to have been a natural writer, with a built-in ability to turn a phrase and to capture the rhythm and tempo of subject matter. It is clear that he also thought long and hard about the troubles and opportunities of his fellow African Americans, as is revealed in the titles of some of his books: *Why Black People Tend to Shout* (1991), *What Black People Should Do Now* (1993), *Dark Witness: When Black People Should be Sacrificed (Again)* (1996). With its provocative title, his book of essays titled *Why Black People Tend to Shout* was rejected by about 30 publishers before being accepted by the Carol Publishing Group of Secaucus, New Jersey. Thereafter, he published the two additional books of essays named above. One chapter in the *Why Black People Tend to Shout* was titled "Why Black People Don't Buy Books," in which Wiley argued that African Americans should place more importance on reading. Wiley had meant the title of *What Black People Should Do Now* to be ironic but was disappointed that most people took it literally. A theme to which he often returned in his writing was the supposition that black athletes are superior to whites. Wiley disliked this assertion because, he pointed out, those who made this assertion usually seemed to imply a derogatory flip side: that blacks, so gifted physically, must be inferior to whites intellectually. Appearing in *Dark Witness* was Wiley's take on football great O.J. Simpson and his murder trials. His assessment of Simpson was not flattering, and he remarked that he thought that Simpson was probably guilty as charged. He also disapproved of the celebrity treatment Simpson received from police and the courts as compared to what would have been the case if the accused had been an ordinary citizen.

Starting in 1989, Wiley appeared as a NFL analyst on NBC. He became a sports agent, representing football star Raghib "Rocket" Ismail, and was president of

Heygood Images, a multimedia sports information company based in Washington, D.C. He also wrote a screenplay for a new version of Mark Twain's *Huckleberry Finn* titled "Spike Lee's Huckleberry Finn" and at the time of his death, was collaborating on another screenplay with filmmaker Lee. It was a shared appreciation for the work of Twain that began a friendship between Wiley and literary scholar Shelley Fisher Fishkin; the two men exchanged numerous letters in which they discussed Twain, writing and racism.

When Wiley left *Sports Illustrated* in 1990, he began appearing on "Sports Reporters" for ESPN and also was a sports commentator on ESPN's "Sports Century," where the individuals he covered included Hank Aaron, Willie Mays, Jim Brown, Joe Louis, Arthur Ashe, Pete Maravich, Stan Musial, Charles Barkley, Sugar Ray Leonard, Mike Tyson and Oscar Robinson. Again readers reacted well to his unique combination of humor and anger and to his skilled use of the language peppered with an unusual combination of literary allusions and Ebonic tidbits. He became one of the first columnists for ESPN.com when it was launched in 2000. In his three weekly columns, which totaled around 240, he offered commentary that tried to make his readers think. He held this job for the four years leading up to his untimely and unexpected death in 2004. During his career, Wiley also wrote freelance for *National Geographic*, *Gentleman's Quarterly* and *Premiere* as well as for various newspapers around the nation. Another facet of his writing career involved collaborations with interesting public figures that produced three more books. The first of these, *By Any Means Necessary* (1992), was done with black filmmaker Spike Lee and told the story of militant civil rights leader Malcolm X. Next came *Born to Play: The Eric Davis Story* (1999), written with that baseball great, then *Growing Up King* (2003), with and about Dexter Scott King, who was six years of age when his father, Martin Luther King Jr., was murdered in Wiley's hometown. The book not only described the life of the famous civil rights leader's second son, but the lives of his widow and other children as well. Also by Wiley is the book *Classic Wiley: A Lifetime of Punchers, Players, Punks & Prophets* (2005), published after the writer's death.

In his coverage of boxing, the most brutal of sports, Wiley began as an admirer of "the manly art" but ended more nearly disillusioned with it. Toward the end of his life, he wrote for ESPN.com that he no longer wrote much about the sport because there had come to be so few boxers worth writing about. African-American men who formerly might have become top boxers, he wrote, now gravitated to professional football, whereas in the time of rampant segregation and discrimination, the football option was not available to them. He considered Mohammed Ali to have been the perfect boxer, noting that Ali was protected from the corrupting influence of the Mafia by Malcolm X and the Nation of Islam. An example of Wiley's outspoken and often satiric approach to sports writing was an ESPN Page 2 column headlined "Prima Donnas I've Known," which discussed what Wiley considered the self-infatuation of sprinter Carl Lewis, batter Reggie Jackson, quarterback Joe Montana, rebounder Dennis Rodman, skater Tonya Harding and—his choice for greatest prima donna of them all—running back O.J. Simpson. He added that the most imitated of sports prima donnas was football's Deion Sanders, who reportedly had bragged that he was so fast, the only person who could catch him was himself. Other ESPN columns he wrote were devoted to the unusual topic of sports "trash talk," in which an insult or a putdown demands an immediate snappy "comeback." Wiley liked to provoke iconoclastic thought, as well, as in a column that touted women's basketball coach Vivian Stringer as the right choice to become the next head coach at Georgetown University—for the men's team. One sports figure who both fascinated and saddened Wiley was the relatively short but lightning-fast basketball star Allen Iverson, who had become a sort of urban legend antihero who had sprung from the roughest possible background, from which he never could free himself in his life off the court. You could make the player out of the thug, Wiley noted, but you could not always take the thug out of the player.

Wiley's frequent and effective use of simile and metaphor stood out in a column speculating about which young basketball star would become the next Michael Jordan. After bowing to the talents of LeBron James, Wiley spent the majority of the column discussing Kobe Bryant, who came across as Jordan with no conscience or Luke Skywalker with no Yoda or Obi-wan Kenobe to guide him, and Kevin Garett, the "good Jordan" who had great skill but recognized that for success, basketball must be played as a game of teamwork. Garnett, Wiley wrote, was so selfless that he was like Michael Jordan on Prozac. In his final column for ESPN, Wiley remarked that all a person has is the integrity of his or her work. He himself died with his reputation for integrity intact. What he once wrote about his role model, early black sportswriter Sam Lacy: that Lacy never became full of himself and always had time to encourage younger writers, came back to Wiley after his own death in the form of comments from such younger sports scribes as Jason Whitlock, who considered Wiley his mentor, and Bonami Jones, who wrote that he had called Wiley his "sensei"and that Wiley called him "Grasshopper" as the older man helped the beginner with his reporting and writing. Eric Neel also provided a testimonial to the encouragement and coaching he had received from Wiley and likened Wiley's writing to the rhythmic jazz syncopations of Thelonious Monk. Richard Lapchick recalled when Wiley advised him to improve his own writing by reading as much as possible, and that when he had read all he thought he needed to, then read a little more. Perhaps the finest tribute Wiley received after his death came from Alan Grant, who noted that Wiley had been the first writer he had ever encountered who wrote about African-American athletes not just as hot properties, but as real human beings.

Books by Ralph Wiley: *Serenity: a Boxing Memoir* (New York: Holt, 1989); *Why Black People Tend to Shout: Cold Facts and Wry Views from a Black Man's World* (Secaucus, N.J.: Carol Pub. Group, 1991); with Spike Lee and Malcolm X, *By Any Means Necessary: The Trials and Tribulations of the Making of Malcolm X* (New York: Hyperion, 1992); *What Black People Should Do Now: Dispatches from Near the Vanguard* (New York: Ballentine Books, 1993);

Dark Witness: When Black People Should Be Sacrificed (Again) (New York: Ballentine Books, 1996); with Spike Lee, *Best Seat in the House: A Basketball Memoir* (New York: Crown Publishers, 1997); with Eric Davis, *Born to Play: The Eric Davis Story: Life Lessons in Overcoming Adversity On and Off the Field* (New York: Viking, 1999); with Dexter King, *Growing Up King: An Intimate Memoir* (New York: IPM, 2003); *Classic Wiley: A Lifetime of Punchers, Players, Punks, & Prophets* (New York: ESPN Books, 2005).

Further Readings: Bickerstaff, Brandon M. "Missing Ralph Wiley, For a Reason." [Online, 17 June 2004]. Sun Herald Web site www.sunherald.com; Edwards, Walik. "The Sweet Life of Wiley." [Online, 16 June 2004]. Black Athlete Web site www.blackathlete.com; Fishkin, Shelley Fisher. "In Praise of 'Spike Lee's Huckleberry Finn' by Ralph Wiley." [Online]. Citadel site http://faculty.citadel.edu; Johnson, Roy S. "Young Journalists Should Take a Page from Ralph Wiley's Hymn Book." [Online, 15 June 2004]. Sports Illustrated site http://sportsillustrated.cnn.com; Kimberley, Margaret. " Ralph Wiley." [Online]. Black Commentator Web site www.blackcommentator.com; LeBatard, Dan. "Vintage Wiley." [Online]. ESPN.com site http://sports.espn.go.com; Schudel, Matt. "Sportswriter Ralph Wiley Dies; Essays Probed Black Life." [Online, 16 June 2004]. Washington Post Web site www.awhingtonpost.com.

Wilkins, Roger Wood (25 March 1932–)

Now the publisher of the NAACP's official periodical the *Crisis*, Roger Wilkins is also a lawyer, history professor, book author and National Public Radio commentator and is often remembered for his part in uncovering the Watergate scandal during his years with the *Washington Post*. Wilkins was born in Kansas City, Missouri; when his father died during Wilkins' early years, the family relocated to New York and later moved to Michigan. Wilkins earned both his degrees at the University of Michigan—his B.A. in 1953 and his LLB in 1956. While in law school, he interned at the NAACP's Legal Defense Fund offices under Thurgood Marshall. After graduating, he began his legal career doing casework for the Ohio Welfare Department and later joined the staff of the U.S. Agency for International Development (1962–1966). His next post was as an assistant attorney general during the Lyndon Johnson administration (1966–1969). When Johnson left office, Wilkins worked with the Ford Foundation from 1969 to 1972, then later in 1972, joined the editorial department of the *Washington Post*. His work at that paper with reporters Carl Bernstein and Bob Woodward as well as cartoonist Herbert Block earned these men the 1972 Pulitzer Prize for investigative journalism for their coverage of the downfall and resignation of President Richard Nixon. He was hired away by the *New York Times* in 1974 and was the first African American to serve on that paper's editorial board, remaining there through 1979; he was also a *Times* columnist from 1977 to 1980, after which he became associate editor of the *Washington Star*. In that same year he began doing radio commentary for NPR; he has continued his radio work to the present day but left the *Star* in 1981 and joined the Institute for Policy Studies as a senior fellow, remaining there until

1992. He is now Clarence J. Robinson Professor of History and American Culture at George Mason University in Washington's Virginia suburbs.

Wilkins was chairman of the Pulitzer Prize Board in 1988 and in the 1980s, wrote and narrated the documentaries "Keeping the Faith" (1987) and "Throwaway People" (1989) for PBS. He has been on the board of the University of the District of Columbia and on the District of Columbia Board of Education. He is chairman of The Crisis Publishing Company Inc. and publisher of the *Crisis*, the NAACP's bimonthly journal of opinion and analysis, which was founded in 1910 by W.E.B. Du Bois. Wilkins' association with this organization is somewhat a matter of family tradition inasmuch as his uncle, Roy Ottoway Wilkins, was editor of the *Crisis* from 1934 to 1949 and executive director of the NAACP from 1955 to 1977. Roger Wilkins has written two books and coedited a third, and his commentary pieces and book reviews have appeared in many newspapers and magazines.

Books by Roger Wood Wilkins: *A Man's Life: An Autobiography* (New York: Simon & Schuster, 1982); ed. With Fred R. Harris, *Quiet Riots: Race and Poverty in the United States* (New York: Pantheon Books, 1998); *Jefferson's Pillow: The Founding Fathers and the Dilemma of Black Patriotism* (Boston: Beacon Press, 2001).

Further Readings: "Roger Wilkins." [Online, 2005]. NNDB Web site www.nndb.com/people; "Roger Wilkins." [Online]. The History Makers Web site www.thehistorymakers.com/biography; "Roger Wilkins, Clarence J. Robinson Professor of History and American Culture." [Online]. George Mason University Web site www.gmu.edu/robinson/wilkins.

Williams, Armstrong (5 February 1959–)

One of America's most persistent multimedia proponents of conservative values until he suffered a conflict-of-interest collision in early 2005, Armstrong Williams owns his own Washington, D.C., public relations firm, has been a presence on radio and television and until January 2005 wrote a column syndicated nationally by Tribune Media Services. In an era of media convergence, Williams allowed his journalistic and financial interests to over-converge, and his reputation suffered a heavy blow.

Williams was born in Marion, South Carolina, one of ten children. A good student, he received admissions and scholarship offers from prestigious universities, but he and his family took the position that preferential minority admissions should go to students who were more financially needy than they. His 1981 B.S. was earned at historically black South Carolina State College. While in college, he worked in 1979 and 1980 as a legislative aide to Sen. Strom Thurmond and in 1981 as an aide to both Congressman Carroll Campbell and Congressman Floyd Spence. From 1981 until 1983 he was a legislative analyst for the U.S. Department of Agriculture. He later worked under Clarence Thomas at the Equal Employment Opportunity Commission and in 1991, wrote commentaries for *USA Today* in support of Thomas during the

Thomas-Anita Hill controversy that figured in that jurist's Supreme Court confirmation hearings. Williams also wrote a column for the *Marion Star* and *Mullins Enterprise* in his home state and a few years later was picked up by the Los Angeles Times Syndicate and began appearing weekly in around 50 newspapers. He added a nationally syndicated radio talk show, "The Right Side With Armstrong Williams"; "The Armstrong Williams Show," a television interview show broadcast on America's Voice network, which earlier was called National Empowerment Television; and "On Point," another interview show on black-oriented TV One. He published two values-oriented books in the mid-1990s and founded the Graham Williams Group, a public relations firm in the nation's capital serving clients from politics, business and entertainment. A contract with one of his government clients caused the trouble that lost him his syndicated column and, in January 2005, his syndicated television show "America's Black Forum."

Williams' journalistic undoing dates from 2003, when his PR firm took a $240,000 contract to run a U.S. Department of Education ad on Williams's syndicated television show to promote the George W. Bush administration's No Child Left Behind Act and the use of school vouchers. The tax dollars that paid for this ad came to Williams by way of a larger PR firm, Ketchum Inc. The difficulty, in part, was accepting government funds to promote government policy, a practice of debatable legality on government's part, but worse, taking the money and supporting the school voucher issue in his work as columnist and pundit, a clear conflict of interest in any medium that attempts to be more journalistic than entertainment-oriented. Williams, in a 10 January 2005 column, apologized to his readers and admitted that what he did constituted bad judgment and stepped over the journalistic line. Tribune Media Services promptly cancelled his column, and soon newspaper accounts revealed that what Williams had become caught up in, also happened to other conservative journalists, most notably Universal Press Syndicate columnist Maggie Gallagher, paid $21,500 by the Department of Health and Human Services to research and write on marriage issues, her journalistic specialty. At the same time these abuses were occurring, the Bush administration was also using "plants" in press conferences—non-journalists who would ask the "soft questions" the president wanted to be asked. Williams, already a pariah in some circles of black America due to his conservatism, paid the price while the administration escaped meaningful censure for its covert propaganda practices. He was taken to task even by the Public Relations Society of America, but to that criticism, Williams replied that what he had done was advertising, not public relations.

This unfortunate mixture of journalism and public relations robbed the nation of one of its more lively minded conservative columnists. In February 2005, however, New York radio station WWRL hired Williams to be host of a three-hour show during afternoon drivetime. The program, which features interviews with both conservative and liberal political figures, was a success; and the station's ratings soared. Williams argued adroitly against what he considered the black community's culture of victimhood and in favor of self-reliance and hard work. He considers the public school system to be a government monopoly lacking consequences and accountability for its frequently poor results; opposes stem-cell research, comparing it to the experiments of the Nazis; and opposes the prescribing of drugs such as Ritalin to narcotize the nation's schoolchildren who have trouble behaving or concentrating. He criticized NAACP Chairman Julian Bond for having fired that organization's president, Kweisi Mfume, due to Mfume's ties to the Bush administration. He made a strong argument opposing the University of Michigan's particular brand of affirmative action admissions, whereby being African American was accorded 20 points and a perfect SAT score only 12 points. Instead, Williams advocates an affirmative action system based more on financial need than on race. During the 2004 presidential contest, he roundly criticized Democrat John Kerry for "using" religion to get votes but completely ignored the far more effective job Republican George W. Bush was doing at that very thing. Williams's one break with current government policy was his criticism of our present "class system" of military service. Williams dramatically pointed out that, during the fighting in Iraq, only one of Congress' 535 members had a child or grandchild in the armed services, leaving military duty to those Americans who occupy the lower economic tiers of our society. Williams has served on the boards of the *Washington Afro-American* newspaper and Childhelp USA.

Books by Armstrong Williams: *Beyond Blame: How We Can Succeed by Breaking the Dependency Barrier* (New York: Free Press,1995); *Letters to a Young Victim: Hope and Fear in America's Inner Cities* (New York: Free Press, 1995); *The New Racists: How Liberal Democrats Have Betrayed Minority Americans* (Washington, D.C.: Regnery, 2005).

Further Readings: "Armstrong Williams Promoted Bush Policies in Writing, Too." [Online, 7 January 2005]. Media Matters for America Web site www.mediamatters.org; "Pundit Payola." [Online, 14 January 2005]. On the Media Web site www.onthemedia.org; Astor, Dave. "Armstrong Williams' Column Axed by TMS." [Online, 7 January 2005]. Editor & Publisher Web site www.editorandpublisher.com; Burton, Bob. "The Other Armstrong Williams Scandal." [Online, 14 January 2005]. Center for Media and Democracy Web site www.prwatch.org; Corn, David. "Armstrong Williams: I Am Not Alone." [Online, 10 Jaunary 2005]. The Nation Web site www.thenation.com; Cusack, Bob. "With New Book, Radio Program, Williams Is Making a Comeback." [Online, 28 July 2005]. The Hill Web site www.thehill.com; Kurtz, Howard. "Administration Paid Commentator." [Online, 8 January 2005]. The Washington Post Web site www.washingtonpost.com; Prince, Richard. "2 More Drop Armstrong Williams." [Online, 12 January 2005]. Maynard Institute Web site www.maynardije.org.

Williams, Byron (22 September 1959–)

Both a minister and a columnist, California-born Byron Williams writes a thoughtful twice-weekly column for the *Oakland Tribune*. From 1995 to 2000, his column was selfsyndicated to a variety of historically black newspapers on the West Coast. He was born and raised in Berkeley, California, and received a bachelor's degree in 1982 from Idaho State University. He later returned to academe and in 1997, earned the masters at the Pacific School of Religion of the Graduate Theological Union in Berkeley. Williams speaks French and reads Greek. In 2001, he began serving as pastor of the Resurrection Community Church in Oakland, California.

In his brightly written columns, Williams tries to move readers from passive acceptance of the way things are toward thinking about needed changes. His is a generally liberal orientation; in an April 2005 column, he refers to himself as a fundamentalist Christian who opposes the death penalty, favors marriage equality and thinks that women, not government, should have the choice of abortion. In this same column, he ventured an opinion that, ironically, many conservative evangelical Christians are out of sync with the teachings of Christ. His writing draws a line between religion and religiosity in American life, and his columns often appear in other papers, such as the *Los Angeles Daily News*, *San Francisco Chronicle*, *Atlanta Journal-Constitution*, and *San Mateo County Times*. His work also has appeared in *Tikkun Magazine*, *Christianity Today* and *Public Theology*. He began his *Oakland Tribune* column in May 2004, and in addition, he writes for Arianna Huffington's Web site blog, The Huffington Post (www.huffingtonpost.com). In his varied writing career, the Rev. Williams has interviewed presidential hopeful John Kerry, Massachusetts Sen. Ted Kennedy, Delaware Sen. Joseph Biden, former Oberlin College President Robert Fuller, poet Maya Angelou, social commentator Michael Eric Dyson and Princeton faculty member Cornel West. Williams has appeared on CNN, Fox News, ABC Radio and National Public Radio and was named by *CityFlight* magazine one of the Bay Area's 30 most influential African Americans. He has been a member of the boards of the Oakland East Bay Symphony and African Americans for Telecommunication Equity, and he was cofounder of the Isaiah Project, a coalition of African-American Christians and Jews working for social justice. He is writing a book about public morality in America.

The topics Williams addresses in his columns vary considerably. He has written about his state's recent decline in the attention its officials pay to infrastructure such as highways, bridges, schools and the like and about the U.S. Congress' treatment of Washington, D.C., residents—treatment he considers paternalistic. He has spoken out on the public's lack of interest in voting in California elections, arguing for campaign-spending reform that would, he thinks, reenergize potential voters by making them feel that with special interests no longer in such tight control, individuals' votes would be more meaningful. In a 2003 column about "compassionate conservatism," he indicated that it actually does exist in at least a few places in government, citing the efforts of U.S. Supreme Court Justice Anthony Kennedy to loosen federal mandatory sentencing laws and to promote more frequent use of executive pardons. Another of Williams' columns that year chided gubanatorial candidate Arnold Schwarzenegger for having voted in only 6 of the previous 11 California elections. In another column headlined "What's in a Name?" Williams became personal in his subject matter, telling his readers about his own father having suggested that Williams change his 8-year-old son's name from Malik to something like Sam, Fred or Joe to prevent the boy from being an automatic suspect at airports and elsewhere. Williams remarked that he could not recollect anyone being automatically suspect simply for having the last name McVeigh. Prior to the U.S. invasion of Iraq, the columnist told his readers that going to war in that country was a done deal and that nothing less than North Korea attacking Japan and kidnapping a Bush daughter would stay the president from invading that country.

In "Can Californians Handle the Economic Truth?" which was written in 2006 for the Huffington blog site, Williams introduced the concept of the "Col. Nathan R. Jessup moment," so called for the character portrayed by Jack Nicholson in the film "A Few Good Men," and that character's memorable line about his opposing counsel's not being able to handle the truth. In current California politics, Williams wrote, voters seem to prefer to be told what they want to hear rather than displeasing truths about housing, energy costs, and the like. Williams is no admirer of the Bush White House, which is apparent in the column on "strip mall patriotism" that appears below.

"Strip Mall Patriotism" by Byron Williams

Last week the Dixie Chicks kicked off the U.S. leg of its Top of the World Tour in Greenville, South Carolina, their first since they have become the object of boycotts, ridiculous slurs and satire, plummeting record sales, and non air play on many of the same radio stations responsible for their fame. This unfortunate display of strip mall patriotism when individuals exercise their First Amendment right to free speech that is in opposition to the views of the dominant culture serves only to diminish our collective tolerance for difference.

For those who have forgotten, allow me to refresh your memories. At a March 10 London concert, Dixie Chicks singer Natalie Maines told the audience, with the United States on the brink of war with Iraq, that "We're ashamed that the President of the United States is from Texas." Immediately, the Dixie Chicks were synonymous with unpatriotic, anti-American, and Saddam loving. My particular favorite is a Web site that features Saddam and Natalie Maines in an embrace on a CD cover entitled the "Dixie Duo." And as a promotional event, KRMD 101.1 FM in Bossier, LA, held a "Dixie Chick Destruction Day" as they bulldozed hundreds of the Dixie Chicks' CDs.

Albeit extremely silly, I can at least attribute the unofficial boycott of France, and French products in particular, directly to France's failure to support President Bush's war efforts, but the Dixie Chicks? Since when did the Dixie Chicks influence world opinion? Perhaps French President Jacques Chirac, when addressing his cabinet, said, "Si les Dixie Chicks ne veulent pas la guerre, je ne veux pas la guerrre aussi!" Translation: If the Dixie Chicks don't want the war, I don't want the war either." The prevailing assumption is that the Dixie Chicks were referring to the impending war; what if that were not the case? Suppose the Dixie Chicks were ashamed of President Bush for different reasons? Hypothetically speaking, suppose that no weapons of mass destruction were ever found in Iraq? Would the Dixie Chicks' comments still be considered unpatriotic? Would that not be cause for shame? The president's spokesperson, Ari Fleischer, said on April 10 that the weapons of mass destrucion were "what this war was about." With the reason for going to war changing no less than five times, only to find out that the reason ultimately decided upon for going to war did not exist, I for one would be ashamed.

The criticism of the Dixie Chicks speaks to a faux patriotism that will not tolerate the very things that make this country unique such as freedom of speech. When WTDR-FM in Talladega, Alabama, pulled the Dixie Chicks from the air waves, station owner Jim Jacobs stated: "The emotion of the callers telling us about their fathers and sons and brothers who are overseas now and who fought in previous wars was very specific." Was it specific enough to take the Dixie Chicks off of the air for exercising their freedom of speech?

The fear created by 9/11 has only served to make this country less tolerant of difference. There is a fear of difference, which has been pervasive in this nation since its origin is now exacerbated in a post-9/11 context. Therefore, there is less interest in understanding what makes each of us unique to the American Experiment. We are becoming a carbon copy of the stores that inhabit the majority of strip malls across the country: prefabricated, one size fits all. It is this strip mall patriotism that comes prefabricated with its own set of "bill of rights" that does not lend itself to questioning public policy.

The strip mall patriotism's "bill of rights" conveniently expands the definition of "support the troops" in such a way that it does not allow for any questions concerning the president's war policy. It is a brand of patriotism that resembles a closer allegiance to Mao and Stalin than Madison and Jefferson. It seeks a silence and consent rather than offering authentic engagement by understanding our unique differences. If that prefabricated box created by strip mall patriotism is too small for the Dixie Chicks, how can it fit those of a different color, different religion, different ethnicity, different orientation, or anyone who may simply have a different opinion?

Source: This column appeared on 9 May 2003 and is reprinted here by permission of the Rev. Williams.

Williams, Juan (1954–)

After a 23-year career at the *Washington Post* as a police reporter, White House correspondent, editorial writer and op-ed columnist, Juan Williams became a presence on National Public Radio as both a host and a correspondent and on television as a Fox News anchor and political analyst. Williams was born in Colon, Panama, and grew up in Brooklyn, New York. After ninth grade, he won a scholarship to a private school, Oakwood Friends School in Poughkeepsie, New York. He is a 1976 Haverford College graduate, holding the B.A. in philosophy. Following his years with the *Post*, Williams joined Fox News as a political analyst in 1997. A conservative on many issues—although Michelle Malkin and other media figures sometimes refer to him as a liberal—he has appeared regularly as a panelist on "Fox News Sunday with Tony Snow," a panelist on "Special Report with Brit Hume" and a daytime anchor for Fox News. Another Fox assignment was hosting "America's Black Forum," and he has appeared in several episodes of "ESPN Sports Century." He joined NPR in 2000 as host of the national call-in show "Talk of the Nation," replacing Ray Suarez. In that position, he was part of a year-long NPR project called "The Changing Face of America," which was funded by a grant from the Pew Charitable Trust. The project's thrust was an examination of changes occurring in American life around the time of the new millennium. Williams' part in the project took him to U.S. cities and towns where he hosted town hall-style meetings with live audiences. Material gathered during the period of this project was also aired on NPR programs "All Things Considered" and "Morning Edition." At the conclusion of the project, Williams became a senior correspondent for "Morning Edition," and he also has contributed to NPR documentaries such as "Politics—The New Black Power," "Marian Anderson," and "A. Philip Randolph: For Jobs and Freedom." He has worked as a cohost of CNN's "Crossfire" and has appeared on many other television programs, including "Inside Washington," ABC's "Nightline," "Washington Week in Review on PBS," "Capitol Gang Sunday," "The O'Reilly Factor," "Oprah" and "Arsenio."

Williams has published in such magazines and newspapers as the *Atlantic Monthly*, *Newsweek*, *GQ*, *Ebony*, *Fortune*, the *New Republic*, the *New York Times* and the *Wall Street Journal* and he has authored, coauthored or edited seven books, the first in 1987. That book was *Eyes on the Prize*, an examination of the 1950s and 1960s Civil Rights Movement in the United States. His next, in 1998, was a wellreceived biography of Thurgood Marshall, America's first black Supreme Court justice, the driving force behind Affirmative Action and an important voice in breaking the hold of racial segregation. The book presents Marshall as America's most important radical. Thereafter came three coauthored books: *Thus Far by Faith*, a look at the black religious experience in America; *I'll Find a Way or Make One*, about the struggles of the nation's more than 100 historically black U.S. colleges and universities and the importance of that struggle in the growth of the nation's black middle class; and *Brown v. Board of Education*, on the impact of that crucial decision on education in America. *This Far by Faith* was turned into a six-part television documentary that was aired in 2003. He also edited *My Soul Looks Back in Wonder*, which appeared in 2004 and presented the stories of 50 civil rights activists. In addition, he wrote the essay portion of a book of photographs taken by John Francis Ficara: *Black Farmers in America* (Lexington, Ky.: University Press of Kentucky, 2006). The book points out that today, black farmers make up only 1 percent of all U.S. farmers, whereas in 1920, they accounted for 14 percent of the total. Williams is a member of the boards of the Washington Journalism Center, the Aspen Institute of Communication and Society, the New York Civil Rights Coalition and Haverford College.

Williams' conservatism has garnered criticism, such as when a writer for Blackcommentator.com in 2002 called him a political conjure-artist. When asked if Fox News really is "fair and balanced," as its motto indicates, Williams answered in the affirmative, an assertion fully worthy of conjuration. In 2004, writing for the *New York Times*' op-ed page, Williams predicted that presidential candidate George W. Bush could win at least 20 percent of the black vote by stressing his administration's support for school vouchers and by calling attention to the two African Americans he had appointed to high office, Colin Powell and Condoleezza Rice. Bush, however, did little to reach out to black voters and got a far smaller percentage of the black vote, winning reelection by appealing to white conservatives and the need for protection against terrorism.

An earlier op-ed commentary Williams wrote for the *Wall Street Journal* in April 2002 spoke out against reparations for descendants of former slaves, calling reparations a demeaning, misguided exercise in racial politics. He added that while paying reparations might give African Americans extra funds in the short run, the long-term effect would be to cut off the sense of moral responsibility that well-meaning whites have because of the evils of slavery. A "Talk of the Nation" interview conducted by Williams in May 2000 was with author Jon Entine, speaking about his book *Taboo: Why Black Athletes Dominate Sports—and Why We're Afraid to Talk About It* (New York: PublicAffairs, 2000). Entine's book had drawn frequent charges that it was helping perpetuate harmful racial stereotypes, but Williams provided him a forum to argue the opposite—that the book actually attempted to destroy stereotypical notions about black athletes. The issue is a touchy one, and surely Williams deserves credit for tackling it. Also in May 2000, Williams interviewed fellow pundit and Reform Party presidential candidate Pat Buchanan, who argued against the prevailing free trade and globalization policies that had been supported by both Republicans and Democrats. Later in that same year, Williams did a "Talk of the Nation" show on the equally controversial topic of genetically modified foods; he presented arguments both pro and con: that such foods might help end world hunger but might on the other hand pose health and environmental dangers. NPR interviews he conducted in 2004 with then-White House Security Advisor Condeleezza Rice, Secretary of Defense Donald Rumsfeld and Secretary of State Colin Powell drew barbs from liberal critics who accused him of lobbying softball questions at those high-level proponents of the Iraq war. Despite his support of the Republican administration, however, Williams defended the military service record of presidential candidate John Kerry against the remarkably dishonest attacks launched on Kerry by unprincipled and overzealous Bush supporters.

"Slavery Isn't the Issue" by Juan Williams

Once upon a time, the black reparations movement amounted to 40 acres and a mule for ex-slaves. Now that legendary but long discarded idea has been transformed into lawsuits against several American companies that allegedly profited more than a century ago from the always immoral but once legal trade in slaves. The legitimate offer to help emancipated slaves get a start in life as free men has now been twisted into a strange scheme to squeeze money out of any company with distant ties to the bitter business of slavery.

The real news here is that lawyers and academics behind this effort have apparently given up trying to get the U.S. government to pay reparations for slavery. The statute of limitations has long since expired on any direct claim of reparations for former slaves. And the slaves are long dead. So are the slave owners. Even a federal court dominated by liberal judges has ruled that there is no jurisdiction to hear a reparations case against the federal government. So now the faltering legal spotlight has shifted to pressuring private companies.

The consequences of this misguided adventure in racial politics have not changed. Whether government or industry foots the bill, any payment of reparations will spark waves of racial resentment. Charges of extortion will be made against black people as a whole, not only by whites but also by Hispanics and Asians, especially by the large number of recent immigrants scrambling to make it on their own.

If reparations become a reality, black Americans already battling presumptions of inferiority (they are less hardworking, less intelligent and less patriotic, according to whites questioned by pollsters) will also bear the weight of being demeaned as less able than any Mexican immigrant or Bosnian refugee. The newcomers, after all, are not asking for reparations—they only want a chance to make it in America. The result will be a further segregation of low-income black people from the mainstream.

On a political level, the cost of reparations may be even higher. Reparations will mean an end to the moral responsibility that all Americans, especially white Americans, have for the history of slavery, legal segregation and the continuing racism in our national life. That white guilt opens the door to the idea of national obligation to repair the damage of racism. Once the first reparations check is written, that moral responsibility will disappear, and the door will shut on all claims for affirmative action in private industry, government and academia. It may also bring a collapse of the already tenuous support for social-welfare programs that are a key to repairing the horrors of public schools in big cities, high rates of poverty among children, and jails overflowing with young black men.

Democrats as well as Republicans have rejected efforts to raise the reparations issue in Congress for a dozen years, and polls show that nearly 70% of whites stand in opposition to even an apology for slavery. The minute any company starts writing reparations checks all the collective white guilt that fuels support for social policy to help poor black people will be exhausted. The debt will be paid and forgotten.

Given the devastating consequences contained in this Trojan Horse, why does the reparations movement march on?

On a simple level, it is about the alluring possibility of a bonanza payday for some of the lawyers involved. And there are still people who think they might get a check for thousands of dollars if some company somewhere issues a reparation check. The IRS is dealing with increasing numbers of people who have been duped into believing that they can claim a "Slavery Rebate" on their tax forms. (Last year 80,000 taxpayers made that claim.)

But greed aside, the reparations movement is also evidence of the growing strength of black America. Some of the best-educated, most affluent black people in world history are properly flexing their political muscles. Randall Robinson, author of a best-selling book calling for reparations, has told interviewers that the key issue is that black people have "decided for ourselves that they are our due."

In a diverse nation, the demands of a strong and vocal black community cannot be ignored. No matter how farfetched the legal claim may be, there will be press conferences and college conferences to review the horrors of slavery. The devastation that slavery visited on black people is beyond debate, and so is the history of exploitation of former slaves once they were set free without compensation for their labor.

But that sound argument is now being contorted into claims that black America is still feeling the impact of slavery. That stretch is necessary for the lawyers behind the reparations movement to support the idea that there are victims of slavery alive to serve as plaintiffs in a lawsuit. But while racist attitudes persist, it's hard to make the case that slavery is the issue when black Americans are enjoying record levels of educational attainment and income.

One intriguing way to look at reparations is as an effort by the rising black middle class to take control of the massive budgets dedicated to social-welfare policy. In the current lawsuits the money for reparations is designated for a treasury that would be controlled by a black elite and used as they see fit to improve life in black America. What is now national policy for dealing with black poverty would become a matter of a black nationalist agenda.

That is as sure a road to racial separatism as you can get. Scandals are sure to follow as money goes to black entrepreneurs who may be friends of the people handing out the money. And inevitably some black nationalists will complain that those controlling the money are addressing the wrong needs. Even without infighting and scandals it is obscene to think of this modern generation of black Americans profiting from the blood money drawn nearly 140 years ago from the exploitation of slaves.

There is nothing wrong with a fantasy about every black person getting a check for all that black people have gone through. But too much time spent in fantasy land is wasted time. If this reparations movement goes on much longer, history will view it as self-indulgent hysteria by people intoxicated by their rising power. The passion that currently goes for reparations would better be spent in other areas, such as confronting teachers unions, civil-rights leaders and everyone else involved in our failure to educate minority kids.

Reparations are a dangerous, even evil, idea because they contradict the moral authority of black America's claim to equal rights. Pushing them through would only hurt race relations by encouraging negative stereotypes about blacks at a time when the nation is more diverse and the need for interracial understanding is at its greatest.

Source: This story appeared on *The Wall Street Journal's* online Opinion Journal Web site on 14 April 2002. It appears here by permission of Mr. Williams.

Books by Juan Williams: *Eyes on the Prize: America's Civil Rights Years, 1954–1965* (New York: Viking, 1987; *Thurgood Marshall: American Revolutionary* (New York: Times Books, 1998); with Quinton Hosford Dixie, *This Far by Faith: Stories from the African-American Religious Experience* (New York: William Morrow, 2003); with Dwayne Ashley and Shawn Rhea, *I'll Find a Way or Make One: A Tribute to Historically Black Colleges and Universities* (New York: Amistad, 2004); ed., *My Soul Looks Back in Wonder: Voices of the Civil Rights Experience* (New York: AARP/Sterling, 2004); with Dara N. Byrne, *Brown v. Board of Education: Its Impact on Public Education, 1954–2004* (Brooklyn, N.Y.: Word For Word Pub. Co., 2005); *Enough: The Phony Leaders, Dead-End Movements, and Culture of Failure That Are Undermining Black America—And What We Can Do About It* (New York: Crown Publishers, 2006).

Further Readings: Nelson, Edward. "Digging for Nuggets with Juan Williams." [Online, 2003]. Poynter Institute Web site www.poynter.org; "Juan Williams." [Online, 23 June 2004]. Fox News Web site www.foxnews.com; "Juan Williams." [Online, 2004]. National Public Radio Web. site www.npr.org; "Talk of the Nation Host Juan Williams to Leave Show on Aug. 30." [Online, 2005]. NPR Web site www.npr.org.

Williams, Michael Paul (1958–)

Michael Paul Williams is a columnist and reporter at the *Richmond Times-Dispatch* in Virginia. He was born in Richmond, earned his bachelor's degree at Virginia Union University and received a masters in journalism from Northwestern University. He was hired by the *Times-Dispatch* in 1982 and worked for a decade in its Williamsburg bureau and on the Chesterfield County and Richmond City Hall beats. In 1992 he added a Monday feature-section column and in 2001, a Wednesday column in a newly created part of the paper called Your Section. During 1999 and 2000, he was a Nieman Fellow at Harvard University, and he is a founding member and a former copresident of the Richmond Association of Black Journalists. During his lifetime in Richmond, he has seen the former capital of the Confederacy evolve from oppressive, near-complete segregation to a much improved climate in which at least its middle class African Americans have moved into the city's mainstream and where its white citizens continue fighting the Civil War far less regularly. Williams was his newspaper's first black columnist and has proved to be an enduring writer, in spite of the bad omen that marked his first column on 1 June 1992, when the box atop his column that contains his now-familiar head shot somehow was left empty.

In May 2005, Williams wrote approvingly about a conference on Civil War history being held at Richmond's Virginia Commonwealth University that featured scholars from all over the nation and offered several sessions about the various roles of blacks in that war. Many of his columns try to make sense of a city in which the downtown population continues to decline in favor of the suburbs, yet significant improvements in new construction, renovation and crime reduction also continue. Williams' conclusion is that Richmond's inner-city population will not stabilize until people have more confidence in the city's schools, bringing about a return of families. As to city politics as of summer 2005, he considers it an embarrassing soap opera and pins much of the blame on newly elected mayor Douglas Wilder, who earlier had been Virginia's first black governor, then returned to public life in his early 70s. Williams' columns picture Wilder flexing his political muscles in the manner of a bouncer, displacing lesser city officials right and left, even tossing the school system's offices out of City Hall without providing funding for the expensive move. The columnist is very much put off by the power struggle among the governor, the City Council and the city's upper-echelon business leadership, picturing the resulting situation as grotesque and absurd. When the governor, at his inaugural, spoke of restoring the city to its former "pristine dignity," Williams wondered in print just when that golden period might have been, remarking that calling Richmond's past "pristine" was similar to putting a new coat of paint on an old jalopy.

Williams writes about both the bad and good facets of Richmond life. In June 2005, he wrote sadly about a multicultural triple homicide in which three people were shot dead: a black, a Korean and a Yemini. But shortly thereafter, his column featured good news about a school consolidation that peacefully merged two sets of students coming from rival public housing areas and on another occasion was about a Salvation Army-run program that had helped youngsters paint a large wall mural in the Church Hill section, noting that in Philadelphia, some 2,400 such murals had been painted. He also applauded Gov. Mark Warner's help in restoring the voting rights of at least some former felons, countering a policy that falls especially heavily on the city's black population.

Other Williams columns address the national scene, as when he wrote about convicted civil rights murderer Edgar Ray Killen, recalling the saying that "justice delayed is justice denied," but adding that in view of the nature of Killen's crimes, society today must take what it can get. No fan of the George W. Bush administration, Williams criticized the president's $40 million reelection celebration, comparing it to the wretched excess of an enormous $24 hamburger being advertised and adding that it should be no surprise that the rest of the world so often despises us. He also criticized members of the Bush administration for taking apparent delight in the discredited story about a Koran flushed down a Guantanamo Bay toilet, flogging *Newsweek* for its error while refusing to acknowledge its own far costlier mistakes. Similarly, he fired a volley at far-right former members of the Nixon White House who characterized Mark Felt ("Deep Throat") as a rat and a snitch, predicting that history would place the real blame where it was due.

Williams was a contributor to *Thinking Black: Some of the Nation's Best Black Columnists Speak Their Mind* (New York, 1996), edited by DeWayne Wickham. He won Virginia Press Association recognitions in 1992 and 1994.

"Measuring the City's Vital Signs" by Michael Paul Williams

For a dying city, Richmond sure has plenty of signs of life.

East Broad Street in Church Hill is a construction zone of lofts, town houses and condominiums, including the renovation of the old Nolde Bakery into 77 condos.

Farther south near Shockoe Slip, the renovation of several stately old buildings into lofts is now under way at the long-dormant southwest corner of 14th and Main streets. And high-rise buildings will slake the thirst for condos overlooking the James River.

Who knew all this construction was a façade masking the fact that Richmond is still hemorrhaging residents?

The latest estimates from the U.S. Census Bureau show a 2.7 percent drop in Richmond's population since 2000, from 197,790 to 192,494.

In the meantime, Chesterfield County gained more than 23,000 residents, Henrico County grew by more than 14,000 and Hanover County increased its population by nearly 10,000.

We suburbanites should not feel smug upon reading these figures. Our locales must build schools and roads to accommodate this growth. We must be mindful of the decay of our inner-suburban neighborhoods, which are already experiencing inner-city problems.

Looking beyond our backyards, we need a truly regional mass-transit system, as gas is unlikely to dip below a dollar a gallon again and city folks without cars need access to suburban jobs.

We also must consider that the toll of suburban sprawl on our region's wildlife, water, air quality and, ultimately, our quality of life may prove incalculable.

The idea of Richmond's decline despite signs of rebirth is easy to grasp if you simply do the math. For every single man or woman or young urban couple, the city is losing families with school-age children.

This is not a revelation. When area schools desegregated more than three decades ago, some city residents opted out and relocated in the surrounding counties. The reasons may have once been racial but are now largely economic.

Beneath the facelifts and rehabs, our city's vital signs are not strong. Richmond's 60 square miles contain too many impoverished residents. And this poverty has created too much of a strain on educators.

The school system has made progress in achievement as measured by Standards of Learning text scores (although recent test-score irregularities at Oak Grove Elementary School are not helpful). But Richmond will not experience significant residential growth until residents regain confidence that its schools—and I mean more than a couple—can provide their children with a quality education. Directing resources and attention toward the school system alone won't solve what is largely a problem rooted in poverty.

The school system will remain embattled until the region increases the stock of affordable housing and seriously promotes the dispersal of impoverished residents throughout the region instead of concentrating them in urban pockets.

Richmond's population loss can't be addressed only with bricks and mortar. For decades, the city has functioned with the belief that if we build it, they will come. They might. But they'll also leave when the education of their children becomes a primary concern.

If we want to stop the bleeding, we've got to foster healthy communities and successful schools. Bandaids won't do it.

Source: Copyrighted, *The Richmond Times-Dispatch*. Reprinted with permission. This column appeared on 4 July 2005.

Further Readings: "Michael Paul Williams." [Online]. University of Virginia Center for Politics Web site www.centerforpolitics.org.

Williams, Montel Brian (3 July 1956–)

Host of a daily one-hour nationally syndicated talk show that has more substance than most of its competitors, Montel Williams suffers from multiple sclerosis and is an advocate for medical use of marijuana as a pain reliever—a change to U.S. legal policy that most politicians are reluctant to endorse. He was born in Baltimore, Maryland, and after finishing high school in 1974, enlisted in the Marine Corps. He was trained at Paris Island, South Carolina, and was promoted twice in the enlisted ranks and sent to the Desert Warfare Training Center near Palm Springs, California, before becoming the first African American to be sent to the Naval Academy Prep School at Newport, Rhode Island. Having completed the one-year course of study there, he entered the Naval Academy at Annapolis, from which he graduated with the B.S. in 1980. He majored in general engineering, minored in international security affairs, studied Mandarin Chinese and was the first African American to graduate from both the Prep School and the Naval Academy. Ensign Williams served in Guam for a year and a half as a cryptologist in naval intelligence and in 1982 and 1983, studied Russian at the Defense Language Institute. He worked at the National Security Agency at Ft. Meade, Maryland, and was on a submarine, the *USS Sampson*, during the invasion of Grenada. In 1986 he became the supervising cryptologic officer for the Naval Security Fleet Support Division at Ft. Meade. While in this position, Williams began using his public speaking skills by counseling and giving motivational talks to his men and to other young people. He received the Navy's Commendation Medal, Achievement Medal, three Expeditionary Medals and two Meritorious Service Medals before leaving the service to become a full-time motivational speaker. He traveled widely, speaking mainly before young audiences.

Williams' reputation as a speaker led to the 1991 debut of his single-topic television talk show, "The Montel Williams Show." Williams is said to have been the earliest African-American man to host a daytime television talk show. Unlike those talk shows that cater to pop entertainment or showcase the bizarre and mock-violent antics of deranged exhibitionists, Williams' program explores serious social issues, such as drugs, violence, obesity, foster care problems, domestic abuse and the like. In 1997, AIDS and its prevention became a recurring topic on the show, and the host created an After-Care Program to help his show's guests deal with their various problems—also in marked contrast to those shows that merely exploit the same problems for their entertainment value. He also has campaigned against animal cruelty and has examined the connection between this type of abuse and human-to-human violence. On his long-running show, the host interviews the influential, the experts and the ordinary people who have problems or who help deal with these problems. In 1999, Williams announced on his show that he had been diagnosed with MS, and in that same year, he created the Montel Williams MS Foundation to attract contributions for research into a cure for this debilitating disease. In 2000, while in Idaho, Williams helped save the life of a 16-year-old boy who had been involved in a fiery car accident in the town of Bonners Ferry. In severe pain from MS, Williams began taking marijuana, finding it the most effective drug to ease his discomfort, and in November 2003, he was arrested at the Detroit airport for possessing a small amount of that drug. He was detained only briefly and was fined $100. In 2004, Williams revealed on his own program, and again during an interview with Deborah Norville on her MSNBC show "Deborah Norville Tonight," that his pain had become so acute that he was suffering depression and had even considered suicide. He also revealed that his neurological pain had been misdiagnosed for 15 years before he was told he had MS. Although weakened by this disease, which attacks the central nervous system, Williams, at this writing in October 2005, is still host and coexecutive producer, with Diane Rappoport, of his talk show, a Mountain Movers production done in association with Paramount Domestic Television, a unit of Viacom Inc.

Williams has received many awards and recognitions, including several Emmy awards, a PRISM award given by the National Institute on Drug Abuse/National Institutes of Health and the Entertainment Industry Council for his programs on drugs and teenagers, the Nancy Susan Reynolds Award for a show on teens and AIDS, the Silver Angel Award for a show honoring Mother Teresa and a Genesis Award from the Humane Society of the United States.

The photogenic Williams has also done a modest amount of acting. He starred in the television show "Matt Waters" in 1996 and has made appearances or had roles in such shows as "The Sopranos," "Perry Mason," the "Jenny Jones Show," Dave's World," "American Dreams," "The Peace Keeper" and "Touched by an Angel." He has acted in three episodes of "JAG," playing a Navy Seal, and appeared in eleven episodes of "All My Children." In addition, he directed the movie "Little Pieces" in 2000 and in that same year was executive producer of another film, "The Simian Line," and he acted in the off-Broadway show "The Exonerated." He has written or cowritten five books, which, like his television talk show, revolve around his themes of faith, restraint and responsibility. His two most personal books are his first, his autobiography *Mountain, Get Out of My Way*, and his most recent, *Climbing Higher*, which deals with multiple sclerosis and his experiences with that disease.

Books by Montel Brian Williams: With Daniel Paisner, *Mountain, Get Out of My Way: Life Lessons and Learned Truths* (New York: Warner Books, 1996); *Life Lessons and Reflections* (Carlsbad, Calif.: Mountain Movers Press, 2000); with Jeffrey Roger Gardere, *Practical Parenting* (Carlsbad, Calif.: Mountain Movers Press, 2000); with Daniel Paisner, *A Dozen Ways to Sunday: Stories of Hope and Courage* (Carlsbad, Calif.: Mountain Movers Press, 2001); with Lawrence Grobel, *Climbing Higher* (New York: New American Library, 2004).

Further Readings: "Montel Williams." [Online]. Internet Movie Database Inc. site http://us.imdb.com; "Montel Williams." [Online, 2005]. Military.com Web site www.military.com;

"Montel Williams." *The African American Almanac,* 9th ed. Ed. by Jeffrey Lehman. Detroit: Gale Group, 2003, pp. 890–91; "Montel Williams Diagnosed with Multiple Sclerosis." [Online, 23 August 1999]. CNN.com Web site www.cnn.com; "Montel Williams Pushing Medical Marijuana." [Online, 7 January 2004]. NSU Today Web site www.usatoday.com; "Montel Williams ... Still the Talk of the Town." [Online]. AskMen.com Web site www.askmen.com.

Williams, Walter Edward (31 March 1936–)

Libertarian conservative Walter Williams writes a column that has been syndicated to as many as 140 newspapers; he also holds a chaired position in economics at George Mason University in Virginia. Williams was born in Philadelphia and was raised by his mother in that city's hard-bitten Richard Allen housing project. He served as an Army enlisted man from 1959 to 1961, then worked his way through California State University, graduating in 1965 with a bachelor's degree in economics. Continuing his formal education at UCLA, he earned the M.A. in 1967 and the Ph.D. in 1972, also in economics. He was an economics instructor during 1967 and 1968 at Los Angeles City College, was an assistant professor of economics at Cal State-Los Angeles from 1967 to 1971, worked on the research staff of the Urban Institute from 1971 to 1973, and returned to academe in 1973 with Temple University's economics program. He held a fellowship with the Ford Foundation in 1970 and with the Hoover Institute in 1976, and in 1980 he moved to George Mason as the John M. Olin Distinguished Professor of Economics. He has chaired the department there and in 1984–1985, was named that university's faculty member of the year.

Williams' column writing began in 1978 when he was a columnist for the historically black *Philadelphia Tribune.* His column was picked up in 1981 by Heritage Features and was run under the column title "A Minority View." In 1991, Creators Syndicate took over Heritage, and Williams an influential economist, has remained with Creators since that time. His academic writing has appeared in such journals as the *American Economic Review, Social Science Quarterly,* and *Economic Inquiry;* and he has freelanced for *Newsweek, Reader's Digest* and the *Wall Street Journal.* He has appeared on many a public affairs talk show, including "Rush Limbaugh," where he has worked as a guest host, and "Nightline," "Firing Line," "Crossfire" and "Face the Nation." He has been a prolific book author as well. The whole of his accumulated work argues for individual responsibility and hard work and against welfare, racial preferences, and big government. He holds both liberal Democrat and conservative Republican politicians at fault for their endless thirst for the taxpayers' money, but on balance is highly conservative in most of his views. His view of taxes and government spending is that they constitute legalized theft whereby one person's property is confiscated and given to others to whom it does not belong.

Liberals, he writes, want to confiscate taxpayers' money and give it to the poor, while conservatives want to give it to farmers, insolvent banks and other troubled companies. He faults politicians for telling us what we want to hear rather than the truth, so as to get elected or reelected, and he favors privatizing Social Security. He considers the nation's system of public education so bad that it is beyond repair and finds especially distasteful the self-esteem emphasis propagated by education schools and departments, which he has termed the slums of the American campus. He opposed admitting women to Virginia Military Institute, saying to do so would destroy that program's standards in the same way they had been destroyed at West Point and the Naval Academy. Williams is equally quick to defend or criticize his fellow African Americans. One column in 1996 complained that history has for the most part ignored the contributions of the many thousands of blacks who fought on the side of the Confederacy in the Civil War, yet he sided strongly with comedian Bill Cosby's sharp attacks at black anti-intellectualism and stereotype-enhancing "gangsta rap" music.

Williams is on the advisory boards of the Hoover Institution, the Taxpayer's Foundation, the Reason Foundation, and the National Tax Limitation Committee. He also is on the National Science Foundation's Review Board of Economics Studies. He has been a winner of the George Washington Medal of Honor from the Valley Forge Freedom Foundation and the National Service Award of the Institute for Socioeconomic Studies. He was the 1984–1985 faculty member of the year at George Mason University, a recognition given by the school's alumni. Williams belongs to the American Economic Association and the Mont Pelerin Society and has been a Ford Foundation Dissertation Fellow and a National Fellow of the Hoover Institute of War, Revolution, and Peace.

"Educational Fraud" by Walter E. Williams

While there are some government schools doing a good job, by and large, our educational establishment is corrupt beyond repair. "There you go again, Williams," you say, "beating up on teachers." Let's look at it. Dr. Karl Zinsmeister, fellow at the American Enterprise Institute and editor in chief of its magazine *The American Enterprise*, has written an article in its September/October 1996 edition titled "Doing Bad and Feeling Good."

American students rank No. 1 in the world in how good they feel about their math skills, but a 1992 international study by the Educational Testing Service showed American students ranking last in math achievement (behind Slovenia). Research surveys show self-esteem levels at least as high among black students as white students, but a majority of either are: unable to write a persuasive letter, date the Civil War or calculate simple interest.

Educationists love the humane-sounding idea of self-esteem. It gives them cover for low standards and low effort both on their part and that of students. After all, high standards, at least in the short run, provide grief for everyone. Teachers have to threaten, cajole and punish, and often parents have to be confronted. It's easier just to keep students feeling good about themselves—while they don't know theirs from the one in the ground—and give them social promotions.

Educationists cover up this tragedy with deceit and dishonesty. According to the College Boards, in 1972, 28 percent of college-bound seniors had an A or B high school average. By 1993, 83 percent had an A or B average. During that interval, SAT scores went south. This clearly indicates what some call grade inflation and I call educational fraud. Since SAT scores have gone permanently south, and the public is increasingly aware of that fact, the educational establishment has resorted to "re-norming" the SAT so as to give the appearance of progress.

That's the subtle dishonesty, but there are more blatant forms. Staten Island's Public School 5 ranked first among New York's public schools in standardized reading and math tests. One parent couldn't figure out how her daughter scored in the 99th percentile in reading, yet could not read street signs. An investigation ensued, and it uncovered widespread cheating, but not by students. According to the school's chancellor of New York City, the school's principal, Murray Brenner, altered answer sheets. Wrong answers were erased and punched-out overlay sheets were used to make the correct circles. One student who originally scored in the 99th percentile in math plummeted to the 18th percentile after re-testing.

The half-baked, never-worked-anywhere ideas that have taken over today's education can be readily understood. First, education departments at most colleges are the academic slums of the campus. Students who become education majors have the lowest SAT scores. Students who earn education degrees have lower LSAT, GMAT and GRE scores (tests for graduate school admission) than any other major with the exception of social work majors. People with that kind of academic grounding fall easy prey to half-baked, never-worked-anywhere schemes.

More money, smaller classes and higher teacher pay will not cure our education problems. The long-term solution is privatization—make education subject to competitive pressure. After all, for the most part, production we are happy with is a result of ruthless competition and the profit motive. Think about it. Most of what pleases us (computers, clothing and food) is subject to that kind of pressure, and most of what displeases us is not (post office, police and schools).

Source: This column is reproduced by permission of Walter Williams and Creators Syndicate, Inc. Its date of original appearance was 11 September 1996.

Books by Walter Edward Williams: With Frank L. Cleaver, *Pre-calculus, Algebra and Trigonometry* (New York: Holt, Rinehart and Winston, 1971); with James H. Reed, *Fundamentals of Business Mathematics* (Dubuque, Iowa: W.C. Brown, 1977); *Youth and Minority Unemployment* (Stanford, Calif.: Hoover Institution Press, 1977); with Betty Jane Narver, *Government by Agency* (New York: Academic Press, 1980); *The State Against Blacks: A Minority View* (New York: McGraw-Hill, 1982); *America: A Minority Viewpoint* (Stanford, Calif.: Hoover Institution Press, 1982); *All It Takes Is Guts: A Minority View* (Washington, D.C.: Regnery Books, 1987; *South Africa's War Against Capitalism* (New York: Praeger, 1989); *Do the Right Thing: The People's Economist Speaks* (Stanford, Calif.: Hoover Institution Press, 1995); *More Liberty Means Less Government; Our Founders Knew This Well* (Stanford, Calif.: Hoover Institution Press, 1999).

Further Readings: Edward, Todd. "The' People's Economist' Speaks Out." *Virginia Educator*, July/August 1996, pp. 22–23; Lamb, Chris. "Columnist Doesn't Follow Liberal Agenda." *Editor & Publisher*, 1 September 1990, p. 30; "Williams, Walter E(dward). *Contemporary Authors*, Vol 123, p. 470.

Wilson, Brenda (18 July 1949–)

National Public Radio science correspondent and editor Brenda Wilson has been with NPR since 1979. She hails from Roanoke, Virginia, and she holds a 1971 B.A. in English literature from Randolph-Macon Woman's College in Lynchburg, Virginia. Her early experience was as a Pacifica National News reporter, from 1977 to 1979, and as a news writer/editor in 1984 for the

Washington bureau of ABC Radio. When she was hired in 1979 by NPR, she first worked as an associate producer for the show "Morning Edition." In 1981, she became a reporter for the Washington desk, for which she covered the Reagan White House. She split her time from 1989 to 1992, working both at NPR and as a writer for *Governing Magazine*, and from 1995 to 1998, she was health and medicine editor for the NPR science desk. She now works out of Washington, reporting on national and international public health issues and trends, Washington politics and social issues. She has written about the Nation of Islam, Jesse Jackson, AIDS, drug addiction, tuberculosis and social service reform. Wilson has reported on the AIDS epidemic in Africa and has gone to various locations on that continent to help train journalists. In 1999, she won a Kaiser Media Fellowship that took her to South Africa to report on HIV and AIDS. In addition to her NPR work, she has appeared as an analyst or commentator on public station WHUT's "Evening Exchange," "BET Tonight" and Black Entertainment Television's "Lead Story." She was one of the recipients of a DPont-Columbia Award for the NPR series on AIDS in the African-American community "Breaking the Silence"; that series also won a National Association of Black Journalists award. A series she worked on concerning affirmative action won an American Bar Association award, as well.

In July 1999, Wilson and Linda Wertheimer coanchored a segment of "All Things Considered" on the vicious cycle of global suffering due to disease and poverty. In 2004, she reported on the difficult problems of gay AIDS sufferers in India, where homosexuality is still illegal. Other stories that year concerned issues of reproductive health among Indian women and the uncertain availability of flu vaccine in the United States. A touching "Weekend Edition" story Wilson did in December 2004 was on the orphans of Otukpo, Nigeria, where the Center for Economic Development and Population Activities had run a five-year project to care for thousands of children orphaned by AIDS. The story described those children's plight when the project ended but no local or national Nigerian government organization took its place. Some of her 2005 stories were about the $1 billion for children's vaccines pledged by the Bill and Melinda Gates Foundation, an outbreak of the plague among miners working in the Congo, an enormous increase in the incidence AIDS deaths in South Africa and potential profiteering from AIDS medicines by certain U.S. defense contractors. In November 2005, she did a story on the unfortunate brain drain whereby physicians and trained nurses from Third World countries migrate to wealthier countries to live and work. A March 2006 story she did described efforts to control the spread of tuberculosis in Asia and in other parts of the world. Other 2006 stories have been on an outbreak of mumps among college students in the U.S. Midwest and a United Nations estimate that 38 million people worldwide were infected with HIV and that the infection rate was increasing in Russia and Eastern Europe, whereas it was slowing in at least some parts of Africa and in the Caribbean.

Further Readings: "Brenda Wilson." [Online]. National Public Radio Web site www.npr.org; "NPR Science Correspondent Explains It All For You." [Online, 3 November 2005]. The Center for Nursing Advocacy Web site www.nursingadvocacy.org.

Winfrey, Oprah Gail (29 January 1954–)

Probably the best-recognized and perhaps the most popular woman in America, Oprah Winfrey is many things: host of the nation's most-watched talk show, actress, producer and studio owner, magazine owner, advocate for children and for women's self-empowerment, the nation's highest-paid entertainer and, having become America's first black woman billionaire in 2003 and generous philanthropist. Hers truly is a rags-to-riches story; she was born to unwed parents in the small town of Kosciusko, Mississippi. Oprah was born at home, and, although her name on her birth certificate was spelled correctly as Orpah, after a Moabite woman mentioned in the Book of Ruth, the p and r were transposed in other records of her birth, and her family began calling her Oprah. The name stuck. Her parents separated, and her mother moved north to Milwaukee in search of better employment, leaving the baby on a farm in the care of her stern, Baptist grandmother, who taught Oprah to read by age three and encouraged her to recite Bible verses at church, where she was spoken of as "the little preacher." The precocious Oprah skipped kindergarten, went directly into the first grade and was moved to third grade by the time she was six. At that time, her mother returned for her and took her to Milwaukee, where they lived in a one-room apartment. Oprah was unhappy with her new surroundings and soon left to live in Nashville, Tennessee, with her father, who by then was remarried and owned a barbershop, hence was better able to provide for her. He especially encouraged vocabulary-building and book reading during her fourth-grade school year. She did well academically and continued to perform in church, but eventually her mother came for her again. Back in Milwaukee, now with two siblings, she was the odd child out, especially in relation to her lighter-skinned step-sister, and, worse, she was raped by an older cousin at age nine, then abused by a family friend and by an uncle. She reacted by running away twice and becoming increasingly promiscuous. Her mother tried to have her admitted to a detention facility but was unsuccessful, inasmuch as that institution was full. Instead, Oprah returned to her father in Nashville, where, at age 14, she gave birth to a son, who died shortly thereafter; so far, she has kept the father's identity a secret. This was no doubt the low point in her life, yet she recovered and continued doing well in school, holding leadership positions and winning an Elks Club oratorical competition for a full scholarship to Tennessee State University. She graduated high school in 1971, won the Miss Fire Prevention, Miss Black Nashville and Miss Black Tennessee beauty contests and was a Miss Black America contestant.

Before entering Tennessee State, she began her first media job, as a news announcer for black-owned WVOL in Nashville. Soon she moved to television as a reporter and anchor for WLAC-TV, which later became WTVF. Oprah was the first African American to work as an anchor in Nashville and made a quite good salary while still in college. During her senior year in 1976, she left school without completing all course requirements to take a 6 PM reporter and coanchor job at ABC affiliate station WJZ-TV in Baltimore. The station promoted her arrival with billboards asking the question: "What's An Oprah?" Although photogenic and articulate, she was not well trained in news work and not ideally suited to it in temperament. The station moved her to a new job to take advantage of her naturally warm personality and inherent talent for interviewing, having her cohost a morning show, "People Are Talking." She began sending tapes to stations in larger markets, and in 1984, she moved to Chicago and another ABC affiliate, WLS-TV, to host "A.M. Chicago," which competed with the highly popular "Phil Donahue Show." In just three months, her show's ratings exceeded those of Donahue, who moved his show to New York in 1985. Her growing importance was apparent when, in 1984, she was interviewed for "60 Minutes" by Mike Wallace and showcased to that program's large national audience.

Oprah had always wanted to be an actress, and in 1985, she got her chance thanks to music great Quincy Jones, who with Steven Spielberg, produced the movie "The Color Purple," based on the Alice Walker novel of the same name. Her portrayal of the character Sophia was well-received, and the role earned Oprah an Academy Award nomination. In the following year, she appeared in her second film role, in the less-heralded movie "Native Son," based on the novel by Richard Wright. The year 1986, however, was when Oprah's career really took off. Her morning show went from a half hour to a full hour and was re-named "The Oprah Winfrey Show." The program was an immediate success, netting her a $30 million contract for 1986 and 1987. She became the third U.S. woman to own her own studio (after Mary Pickford and Lucille Ball) when she founded Harpo Productions (Oprah spelled backwards) in 1986, and in September 1988, the show was syndicated to 138 cities. Suddenly Oprah was the best-paid entertainer in the nation and was well on the way to becoming the iconic figure she is today. She had been recognized in 1986 as a Woman of Achievement by the National Organization for Women and in 1988, was named Broadcaster of the Year by the International Radio and Television Society. In 1987, she had made a cameo appearance as herself in the comedic film "Throw Momma From the Train"; and in 1989, Oprah produced and starred in the television movie "The Women of Brewster Place." In the years that followed, she produced other films and made-for-television movies: "There Are No Children Here" in 1993; "Before Women Had Wings" in 1997; "The Wedding," "Beloved" and a remake of "David and Lisa" in 1998; "Tuesdays with Morrie" in 1999; "Amy and Isabelle" in 2001 and "Their Eyes Were Watching God," her favorite love story, in 2005.

In addition to her own show, she has hosted or appeared in many other programs, including a 1988 Christmas special, "Listen Up: The Lives of Quincy Jones" in 1992, "Michael Jackson Talks" in 1993, "About Us: The Dignity of Children" in 1997, "Quincy Jones: The First 50 Years" in 1998, "Tina Turner: Celebrate Live" in 1999, "The Cosby Show" in 2002, "ABC's 50th Anniversary Celebration" in 2003 and "Desperate Housewives" in 2004. She has also been a guest on many other shows, such as "The Tonight Show Starring Johnny Carson," "Saturday Night Live," "The Arsenio Hall Show," "The Fresh Prince of Bel-Air," "The Tonight Show with Jay Leno," "Ellen," "Home Improvement," "Entertainment Tonight," and "Good Morning America."

Throughout most of her remarkable career, Oprah has promoted and contributed to a variety of causes. In 1987, she founded The Oprah Winfrey Foundation to provide grants to organizations that benefit women and children and promote family life. Her Oprah Winfrey Scholars Program gives scholarships to students who want to give back to others after they become established. Her pitch for the "world's largest piggy bank" raised more than $1 million in small-change contributions, which Oprah matched, giving the money to needy college-bound students. The Oprah's Angel Network charitable initiative, started in 1997, raised more than $20 million for scholarships, schools, women's centers and youth centers; and a trip she took to South Africa resulted in her 2002 ChristmasKindness South Africa program that benefited orphanages, libraries and rural schools in that country. Around 50,000 individual South African children also received gifts of clothing, books, toys and food through that program. She has, in addition, joined with the South African Ministry of Education to build the Oprah Winfrey Leadership Academy for Girls in that nation; the school is to open in 2007. Another of her scholarship programs directly benefits Tennessee State University, which gave her a diploma in 1988 in honor of her achievements. Ten students a year receive these funds and must maintain a B average to continue receiving them. Other recipients of her generosity have been the United Negro College Fund, Morehouse College and the Harold Washington Library. Another of Oprah's good works was her advocacy of a national register of convicted child abusers, for which she argued before Congress and which was signed into law in 1993 by President Bill Clinton. She has participated in the Boston-based A Better Chance program that sends promising inner-city students to preparatory programs before they enter college.

Yet another Oprah project has been her efforts to get Americans to read. Her Oprah's Book Club was started in 1996, and lucky authors whose work she liked found their careers touched as though by a magic wand. An example was the author of Oprah's first recommendation, Jacquelyn Mitchard, for her debut novel, *The Deep End of the Ocean* (New York: Viking, 1996). Mitchard was a local columnist for *The Milwaukee Journal Sentinel* and a single mother, doing all right financially but no better. With Oprah's favorable mention, her novel became a bestseller, her column was syndicated and she became known throughout the nation. The books Oprah picks are usually those that might not otherwise be bestsellers and that offer an uplifting message. More recent choices have included *Cry, the Beloved Country* (New York: C. Scribner's Sons, 1948), Alan Patton's novel about race relations in South Africa; *The Four Agreements* (San Rafael. Calif.: Amber-Allen Pub., 1997), by Miguel Ruiz; Sen. Barack Obama's *Dreams from My Father: A Story of Race and Inheritance* (New York: Three Rivers Press, 2004); and Jo Frost's *Supernanny: How to Get the Best from Your Children* (New York: Hyperion, 2005). Her book selections ran into an unexpected buzzsaw in January 2006 when it came to light that author James Frey's memoir *A Million Little Pieces* (New York: N.A. Talese/Doubleday, 2003) contained more than a little fiction. Frey's fictionalizing was uncovered by a story on The Smoking Gun.com. When Winfrey ascertained that the Web site's accusations were accurate, she not only backed away from defending Frey but had him on her show and took him sternly to task.

Earlier, in 1995, Oprah paired with AOL to introduce a new-media presence, "Oprah Online," and she was cofounder of Oxygen Media Inc, a cable network offering programming that had its start on her talk show. The network reached some 53 million homes. The best-known spinoff of them all has been the "Dr. Phil Show," syndicated in 2002. She also became a part owner of Granite Broadcasting, which owns 11 television stations. A more recent broadcasting venture was announced in February 2006: a three-year, $55 million agreement with XM Satellite Radio Holdings to create a new channel, "Oprah & Friends Radio." The channel, launched in September 2006, is geared to self-improvement, health and fitness programming and features a weekly show with Oprah and Gayle King.

In 1999, Oprah and her gentleman friend Stedman Graham taught a course in entrepreneurship at Northwestern University's J.L. Kellogg Graduate School of Management. Due to time constraints, she and Graham were unable to repeat the course. In 2000, television's most famous woman entered the magazine market with *O, The Oprah Magazine*, a joint venture with the Hearst organization. Due to her immense popularity, the women's lifestyle monthly was an immediate success. The magazine offers its readers a combination of inspiration, tips for being all that they can be, and celebrity-watching fodder. Sample stories from recent issues include "Oprah Talks to Charlize Theron," in which the Best Actress Oscar winner discusses the antirape campaign she supports in her native country; "A Lesson Before Dyeing," offering hair color tips; and "Oprah and the Really, Really Good Sandwich," featuring a curried chicken sandwich made by San Luis Obispo, California, café owner Margaux Sky, who had been struggling financially and was about to give up in spite of her delicious food—until Oprah came along, that is. Oprah's admiration for this sandwich was expressed in form of a check that enabled Sky to hire four new employees and continue making what Oprah deemed the world's best sandwich. The magazine now has a circulation of around 2 million. In 2002, an international edition of O was launched in South Africa, and in 2004, the new shelter magazine *O at Home* appeared. Like its competitors, *O at Home* offers stories on such topics as sofa-rug-wall combinations, wining and dining, budgeting for remodeling projects, pairing wines and cheeses and antique or folk-art shopping.

The heart of the Oprah empire, however, is her phenomenally successful talk show, which has made her one of the most loved and trusted persons in the nation. The remarkable degree of her success is hard to explain but certainly stems in part from the highly open, personal way she relates to her guests and to her audience. Oprah herself once remarked that talk shows hosted by men tend to be more informational, whereas her show is more conversational and emotionally charged. Members of her television audience appear to feel that Oprah is not talking to them, but with them, and they see her not only as a friendly celebrity, but as one who has a genuine spirituality as well. Her audience is largely but not exclusively female, and the show combines the light and diverting with the serious and informative. Recent examples of light, celebrity-oriented show segments have been "Ricky Martin Travels to Meet Tsunami Orphans," "How Much Weight Has Kirstie Alley Lost?" and segments that featured cyclist Lance Armstrong, singer Bon Jovi and entertainer Queen Latifa. Quirky segments have included "Pathological Liars Confess," "The Secret Lives of Hoarders," "When the One You Love is a Pedophile" and "When Your Identical Twin Has a Sex Change." Travel-oriented segments have been "Oprah on Location in Mississippi," "Oprah Goes to Paris" and "Oprah's Wildest Dreams Bus Hits L.A. and New York." The show is quick to pick up on items in the news, with segments such as "A Secret Sex World: Living on the 'Down Low'" and "Held Hostage by the Atlanta Spree Killer: How Ashley Smith Survived." Americans love a giveaway, and Oprah has made frequent headlines in this regard. Whereas Elvis was known for having impulsively given Cadillacs to people who admired the one he was driving at the time, Oprah has been far more organized. On one show, she asked all members of the audience to look under their seats to see if they had won a new car. Every one of them had.

Oprah has also created a $100,000 reward for anyone who provides information that leads to the arrest of a fugitive sex offender. The mug shots shown on her program have thus far resulted in two arrests. Other serious show segments have focused on overuse of plastic surgery, prison conditions, mothers who entertain secret dreams of killing their children, the difficulty of being the fat member of one's family, child molestation and racism. The show's mix of light and heavy, happy and sad has made it the nation's favorite talk show for 18 years running, and in September 2002, she added "Oprah After the Show," which gave her fans a half-hour of unscripted material taped after the regular Oprah show ends. By the end of 2004, King World Productions CEO Roger King had concluded a deal with Oprah for several more seasons of her show, plus an assignment that called for her to develop new talk shows for King. She herself plans to star in a new reality series/documentary for which she will have to temporarily live in poverty in a Chicago housing project to show her national audience what people in this condition actually face.

Her popularity has earned her a considerable number of major awards and recognitions. In 1996, she received the George Foster Peabody Individual Achievement Award and the Gold Medal Award from the International Radio & Television Society. In 1997, *TV Guide* named her the Television Performer of the Year and *Newsweek*, the Most Important Person in Books and Media. In the following year, *Time* placed her among the 100 Most Influential People of the twentieth Century, and she received the Lifetime Achievement Award from the National Academy of Television Arts and Sciences, plus the last of her 39 Emmy awards. In 1999, she removed herself from further Emmy competition and did the same for her show in 2000. The National Book Foundation awarded her its Gold Medal in 1999, and in 2002, she was inducted into the Broadcasting & Cable Hall of Fame and also was given the Bob Hope Humanitarian Award. In 2004, she received the National Association of Broadcasters' Distinguished Service Award, and in 2005, she was inducted into the NAACP's Hall of Fame. Although she is arguably America's most beloved and admired woman, even Oprah is not immune from criticism. Former *Ladies' Home Journal* editor Myrna Blyth, in her book *Spin Sisters: How the Women of the Media Sell Unhappiness—and Liberalism—to the Women of America* (New York: St. Martin's Press, 2004) accuses Oprah of being a—gasp—liberal, and, like most celebrities, she has been parodied on "Saturday Night Live" and other comedy shows. A remark she made on a 2004 Oprah show to the effect that North Korean women are obsessed with plastic surgery in order to look more Western ruffled the feathers of Koreans and Korean Americans alike. For the most part, however, Oprah remains on the side of the angels. To this date in 2005, she has collaborated on five books, as well.

Books by Oprah Gail Winfrey: With Robert Waldron, *Oprah* (New York: St. Martin's Press, 1988); with Bob Greene, *Make the Connection: Ten Steps to a Better Body—and a Better Life* (New York: Hyperion, 1996); with Bill Adler, *The Uncommon Wisdom of Oprah Winfrey: A Portrait in Her Own Words* (New York: W. Morrow, 1996); with Janet Lowe, *Oprah Winfrey Speaks: Insight From the World's Most Influential Voice* (New York: Wiley, 1998); with Ken Regan, *Journey to Beloved* (New York: Hyperion, 1998).

Further Readings: Bly, Nellie. *Oprah! Up Close and Down Home.* (New York: Kensington Pub. Corp., 1993); Dunn, Lois L. "Oprah Winfrey." In *Notable Black American Women*. Ed. by Jessie Carney Smith and Shirelle Phelps. (Detroit, Mich.: Gale Research, 1992–2003), pp. 127–376; Farr, Cecilia Konchar. *Reading Oprah: How Oprah's Book Club Changed the Way America Reads.* (Albany, N.Y.: State University of New York Press, 2004); Fuller, Gary J. *The Oprah and Dr. Phil Connection.* (Jefferson, Mo.: Ridgewood Press, 2003); Garson, Helen S. *Oprah Winfrey: a Biography.* (Westport, Conn.: Greenwood Press, 2004); Gates, Henry Louis Jr. and Cornel West. *The African-American Century.* (New York: The Free Press, 2000), pp. 379–82; Hatch, Shari Dorantes and Michael R. Strickland, eds. *African-American Writers: A Dictionary.* (Santa Barbara, Calif.: ABC-CLIO, 2000), pp. 398–400; Illouz, Eva. *Oprah Winfrey and the Glamour of Misery: an Essay on Popular Culture.* (New York: Columbia University Press, 2003); Kramer, Barbara. *Oprah Winfrey: Reaching Out to Others.* (Berkeley Heights, N.J.: Enslow Publishers, 2005); Lowe, Janet. *Oprah Winfrey Speaks: Insight from the World's Most Influential Voice.* (New York: Wiley, 1998); Mair, George. *Oprah Winfrey: The Real Story.* (Secaucus, N.J.: Carol Pub. Group, 1994); Nelson, Marcia Z. *The Gospel According to Oprah.* (Louisville, Ky.: Westminster J, Knox Press, 2005); "Oprah Winfrey: Interview, February 21, 1991." [Online].

Academy of Achievement Web site www.achievement.org; Rivo, Lisa E. "Winfrey, Oprah." In *African American Lives*. Ed. by Gates, Henry Louis Jr. and Evelyn Brooks Higginbotham. (New York: Oxford University Press, 2004), pp. 90–407; Rooney, Kathleen. *Reading with Oprah: the Book Club That Changed America*. (Fayetteville, Ark.: University of Arkansas Press, 2005); Ruuth, Marianne. *Oprah Winfrey*. (Los Angeles, Calif.: Melrose Square Pub. Co., 1996); Wilson, Sherryl. *Oprah, Celebrity, and Formations of Self*. (New York: Palgrave Macmillan, 2003).

Wycliff, N. Don (17 December 1946–)

Since 2000, Don Wycliff has worked as a columnist, editorial page editor and, for the last six years, as public editor (ombudsman) for the *Chicago Tribune*. In February 2006, he left the paper to become associate vice president for news and information at Notre Dame University. He was born in Liberty, Texas, and eight years later moved with his family to Kentucky. He attended Catholic schools and is a 1969 graduate of the University of Notre Dame, where he majored in government. He entered graduate studies at the University of Chicago on a Woodrow Wilson Fellowship but left the program in 1970 to become a general assignment reporter with the *Houston Post*. He later worked for other papers in Ohio, Illinois and Washington as well as at the *Chicago Daily News* and *Chicago Sun-Times*, and from 1985 until 1990 was a section editor, editorial writer and assistant to the editor at the *New York Times: Week in Review* and was a member of the *Times*' editorial board. In 1990 he was hired as deputy editor of the *Chicago Tribune's* editorial page and was moved up to editor of that page in 1991. During his editorship, the page won a Pulitzer Prize, and he himself was a finalist in 1996 in the editorial writing category. He has since served as a Pulitzer juror and from 2000 to 2002 and, was chair of the American Society of Newspaper Editors Writing Awards Committee. In 1997, he won the ASNE Distinguished Writing Award, and in 1996, was inducted into the Chicago Journalism Hall of Fame. He is a member of the National Association of Minority Media Executives and a former member of the National Association of Black Journalists. Wycliff had long wanted to write a column and in 2000 began doing so; at the same time he became the paper's first public editor, charged with fielding reader complaints and monitoring news and editorial practices. Since that time, he was an advocate of greater transparency in the paper's editing and reporting practices. He belongs to the American Society of Newspaper Editors and the National Association of Minority Media Executives. He also has taught media criticism at Notre Dame. He has considered doing more teaching when retired from active newspaper work and has served on advisory committees at both Notre Dame and Northwestern University. Wycliff received an honorary doctorate in 1999 from the University of Portland in Oregon and has been inducted into the Chicago Journalism Hall of Fame. He has also contributed to *Commonweal Magazine*.

Wycliff, N. Don

Many of Wycliff's columns were written to answer readers' questions or complaints or to address his own concerns about *Tribune* stories or practices, but others were written at his own behest about topics that interested him. In September 2002, he defended his paper's decision to fire popular columnist Bob Greene due to indiscretions involving a teenage girl; the credibility of the paper demanded it, Wycliff wrote. Following the 2004 presidential election, he reported having received at least 2,400 messages from readers who questioned how the paper could have endorsed George W. Bush. Wycliff himself has not been an admirer of this president and has been fairly outspoken about Mr. Bush's lack of intellectual curiosity, inarticulate speaking and questionable judgment. Wycliff had a difficult time answering these readers' concerns but pointed out that the endorsement of Bush had been the collective decision of the ten journalists who make up the paper's editorial board. Another more recent column posed the question: Can a journalist be both honest and patriotic as regards the war in Iraq? Again, his was hardly a definitive answer, but Wycliff's main point was that dissent, or reporting about dissent, does not automatically mean disloyalty. Despite his personal misgivings about President Bush, Wycliff wrote in the president's defense after the *Tribune* ran a front-page mug shot of the president making what could only be described as a silly face while meeting with United Nations Secretary General Kofi Annan. In Wycliff's view, this photo was intentionally used to make the president look foolish and thus was disrespectful of the office.

In answer to a reader's letter about a well-written story found on the Internet, Wycliff used his public editor's forum to remark that while he agreed about that particular story, far too many blogs and other Internet postings are garbage. Another column that touched on the same general topic used syndicated columnist Molly Ivins of Texas as an example of a true journalist as compared to the propagandists who occupy much space on the Internet and in other media. Ivins had made a rather large mistake in a column about civilian deaths in Iraq and was responsible enough to correct it in a later column—one sign of a good journalist to be sure. A question that touched off a fine Wycliff column came from his own son, who asked his dad why people were so interested in now-convicted murderer Scott Peterson, whereas so many similar cases fail to catch the public's attention. Wycliff's answer was that such heavy, impassioned public interest is a clue that its object has become a symbol of something larger—in this case, a symbol of domestic violence in general, made all the more media-worthy because of what so many media consumers saw as his all-American whiteness and good looks. Peterson and his late wife were, the columnist wrote, a convenient image of Everyman and Everywoman. And just when Wycliff began to think that he had heard every conceivable reader complaint, out of the blue came a missive sent by a reader upset because the paper had ignored the anniversary of the 1867 coronation of Franz Joseph as king of Hungary.

An example of a Wycliff column not tied to a reader complaint is one that was adroitly headlined "Ask and ye shall receive a bailout" and that expressed

Wycliff's concerns about the post–September 11 $15 billion bailout of the airline industry; he added that in the past, only our nation's farmers had done that well at getting government subsidies. Another such column was his take on the jailing of *New York Times* reporter Judith Miller for her failure to abide by a court order to name a confidential news source. Wycliff is one of many journalists who are not convinced that a national reporters' shield law would best serve the public interest. Yet another such column was inspired by the death of former *San Jose Mercury News* reporter Gary Webb, who wrote about a possible link between the CIA and Nicaraguan Contras who in the 1980s brought large amounts of crack cocaine to sell in the predominantly black sections of Los Angeles. Webb was fired for his assertions, drummed out of journalism and died of an apparently self-inflicted gunshot to the head. Wycliff expressed the opinion that Webb had probably been right about the CIA link. Finally, the column appearing below addresses one of our society's great divides: creationism vs. secularism.

"Moral Values' Divide Has Been Widening for Decades" by Don Wycliff

First, two quick stories. Here's the first:

His name was Cal Beisner and at the time he was editor of a publication called the Pea Ridge Country Times, located in the Ozarks region of northwest Arkansas. I googled his name yesterday and discovered that he since has gone on to bigger things.

We met in 1981, while we both were in Little Rock covering what some people called "the second monkey trial"—the challenge, ultimately successful, to the State of Arkansas' decision to require the inclusion of "creation science" in the public school curriculum, alongside what creationism advocates always made sure to call the theory of evolution. Cal was not a mainstream journalist, a disinterested observer of the proceedings. He was a strongly committed Christian and a defender of the creationist position.

He and I had dinner together one night at the hotel where most of the out-of-town press was staying, and we talked for a long time about the trial and "creation science" and the geological and other evidence that was said to support it.

To tell the truth, I mostly listened and interjected questions. Cal did most of the talking, and that was fine with me, since I learn most when I just listen. As he discoursed on and grew more and more passionate, I had an epiphany. On the surface this court case, this whole creationist movement, was about the validity of certain scientific claims and the constitutional validity of certain actions by Arkansas authorities.

But beneath the surface it was about respect—the respect that comes from being able to claim a scientific basis for what you believe in; the respect that Cal and his co—believers knew that a purely religious, scripture-based claim never could command. Most important of all, it was about the disrespect for people like themselves that creationists and others felt fairly oozed from America's elite newspapers, magazines and television news operations.

Second story:

In the late 1980s, while I was working in New York, I was involved one day in a casual conversation with several colleagues. I don't remember the subject, except that it involved the appearance by some newsmaker on one of those Sunday morning network TV interview shows—"Meet the Press," "Face the Nation" and such.

In the course of this otherwise unmemorable conversation, one colleague uttered a remark that I've never forgotten. "What else is there to do on Sunday morning," he said, "except read the paper and watch the news shows?"

The remark left me dumbfounded. How out-of-touch could a person be?

The temptation is to say, "Typical myopic New Yorker." But the fact is that New York City is full of churches and synagogues and mosques, and New Yorkers by the millions fill their seats and prayer halls weekly, many of them on Sunday mornings, just like their brethren elsewhere in the country. The moral of these stories isn't a look-how-different-New-York-is-from-the-rest-of-the-country thing.

No, the moral is many other things. It's that the great social division over "moral values" revealed in exit polls after last week's election has been in the making for a long time—at least two decades, probably closer to four.

It is a division rooted in issues of epistemology, of what is knowable and what is unknowable. On one side are the secularists, saying that it's time to be done with God-talk and all the theological myths and superstitions that humans have clung to over the centuries, and to live and govern ourselves on the basis of science and rationality.

On the other side are the people of religion, men and women who believe, in Hamlet's words, that "there are more things in heaven and earth than are dreamt of" in the secularist's philosophy, and that God must be served and honored. This conflict, which is epochal in its implications, is being played out in American society as Republicans versus Democrats, coastlands versus the heartland, the highly educated versus the less-educated.

Members of the news media, increasingly well-educated and part of the social elite, find themselves more often than not on the secularist side of this conflict—or presumed to be.

Too often they also find themselves blindsided by developments such as an exit-poll showing the largest percentage of voters cited "moral values" as the reason for their vote—or even the appearance of a soft-spoken Southern governor who uses phrases such as "born again" or "lust in my heart."

We in our news shops may have been blissfully unaware of all the Cal Beisners and his fellow believers out there. But you can bet they've always been aware of us.

Source: This column appeared on 11 November 2004. It appears here by permission of the *Chicago Tribune*.

Further Readings: "About Don Wycliff." [Online]. Chicago Tribune Web site www.chicagotribune.com; "Interview With Don Wycliff, Ombudsman, The Chicago Tribune." [Online, 21 July 2005]. Journalism Jobs Web site www.journalismjobs.com; "N. Don Wycliff: Biography." [Online]. The History Makers Web site www.thehistorymakers.com.

Selected Bibliography

Acham, Christine. *Revolution Televised: Prime Time and the Struggle for Black Power*. Minneapolis, Minn.: University of Minnesota Press, 2004.
Ainley, Beulah. *Black Journalists, White Media*. Stoke on Trent, England: Trentham Books, 1998.
Allen, Donna. "Women, Minorities & Freedom of the Press." *Newspaper Research Journal* 11 (Summer 1990): 10–17.
Andsager, Julie L. and Teresa Mastin. "Racial and Regional Differences in Readers' Evaluations of the Credibility of Political Columnists by Race and Sex." *Journalism & Mass Communication Quarterly* 80 (Spring 2003): 57–72.
Appiah, K. Anthony and Amy Gutmann. *Color Conscious: The Political Morality of Race*. Princeton, N.J.: Princeton University Press, 1996.
Appiah, Osei. "Americans Online: Differences in Surfing and Evaluating Race-Targeted Web Sites by Black and White Users." *Journal of Broadcasting & Electronic Media* 47 (December 2003): 537–55.
Arthur, Abby and Ronald Maeberry Johnson. *Propaganda and Aesthetics: The Literary Politics of Afro-American Magazines in the Twentieth Century*. Amherst, MA: University of Massachusetts Press, 1979.
Atkin, Charles, Bradley S. Greenberg and Steven McDermott. "Television and Race Role Socialization." *Journalism Quarterly* 60 (Autumn 1983): 407–14.
Augoustinos, Martha, Keith Tuffin and Danielle Every. "New Racism, Meritocracy and Individualism: Constraining Affirmative Action in Education." *Discourse & Society* 16 (2005): 315–40.
Beasley, Maureen H. and Shiela J. Gibbons. *Taking Their Place: A Documentary History of Women and Journalism*. Latham, MD: American University Press, 1993.
Beaudoin, Christopher E. and Esther Thorson. "Credibility Perceptions of News Coverage of Ethnic Groups: The Predictive Roles of Race and News Use." *Howard Journal of Communications* 16 (January–March 2005): 33–48.
Bell, Derrick. *Faces at the Bottom of the Well: The Permanence of Racism*. New York: Basic Books, 1992.
Bennett, W. Lance. *News: The Politics of Illusion*, 3rd ed. New York: Longman, 1995.
Bennett, W. Lance and Regina G. Lawrence. "News Icons and the Mainstreaming of Social Change." *Journal of Communication* 45 (3)(Summer 1995): 20–39.
Bennett, W. Lance and Robert M. Entman, eds. *Mediated Politics: Communication in the Future of Democracy*. New York: Cambridge University Press, 2000.

Selected Bibliography

Billings, Andrew C. "Portraying Tiger Woods: Characterizations of a 'Black' Athlete in a 'White' Sport." *Howard Journal of Communications* 14 (2003): 29–37.

Bishop, Ronald. "A Nod from Destiny: How Sportswriters for White and African-American Newspapers Covered Kenny Washington's Entry into the National Football League." *American Journalism* 19 (Winter 2002): 81–106.

Bobo, Lawrence and James R. Kluegel. "Opposition to Race-Targeting: Self-Interest, Stratification, Ideology, or Racial Attitudes?" *American Sociological Review* 58 (1993): 43–46.

Bocage, Aaron and George Waters. *Making Money the Old-Fashioned Way: A Story of Black Entrepreneurship.* Camden, N.J.: EDTEC, Inc., 1997.

Bogle, Donald. *Blacks in American Films and Television: An Encyclopedia.* New York: Simon & Schuster, 1989.

Bogle, Donald. *Prime Time Blues: African Americans on Network Television.* New York: Farrar, Straus and Giroux, 2001.

Booker, Simeon. *Black Man's America.* Englewood Cliffs, N.J.: Prentice-Hall, 1964.

Boyd, Herb. "African-American Images on Television and Film." *Crisis* 103 (2) (February–March 1996): 2–25.

Bramlett-Soloman, Sharon. "Job Satisfaction Factors Important to Black Journalists." *Newspaper Research Journal* 14 (Summer and Fall 1993): 60–69.

Branch, Taylor. *Parting the Waters: America in the King Years, 1954–1963.* New York: Simon & Schuster, 1988.

Brasch, Walter M. *Black English and the Mass Media.* Amherst, Mass.: University of Massachusetts Press, 1981.

Broh, C. Anthony. *A Horse of a Different Color: Television's Treatment of Jesse Jackson's 1984 Presidential Campaign.* Washington, D.C.: Joint Center for Political Studies, 1987.

Brooks, Dwight E. and James A. Rada. "Constructing Race in Black and Whiteness: Media Coverage of Public Support for President Clinton." *Communication Monographs* 4 (Autumn 2002): 113–56.

Broussard, Jinx Coleman. *Giving a Voice to the Voiceless: Four Pioneering Black Women Journalists.* New York: Routledge, 2004.

Broussard, Jinx Coleman. "Saviors or Scalawags: The Mississippi Black Press' Contrasting Coverage of Civil Rights Workers and Freedom Summer, June–August 1964." *American Journalism* 19 (Summer 2002): 63–85.

Brower, William. "The Black War Correspondent." *Media History Digest* 1 (Fall 1980): 47–55.

Brown, Jane D. and Carol J. Pardun. "Little in Common: Racial and Gender Differences in Adolescents' Television Diets." *Journal of Broadcasting & Electronic Media* 48 (June 2004): 266–78.

Brown, Joshua. *Beyond the Lines: Pictorial Reporting, Everyday Life, and the Crisis of Gilded Age America.* Berkeley, Calif.: University of California Press, 2002.

Browne, Donald R. *Ethnic Minorities, Electronic Media and the Public Sphere: A Comparative Approach.* Cresskill, N.J.: Hampton Press, 2005.

Campbell, Christopher P. *Race, Myth and the News.* Thousand Oaks, Calif.: Sage, 1995.

Carmines, Edward G. and James A. Stimson. *Issue Evolution: Race and the Transformation of American Politics.* Princeton, N.J.: Princeton University Press, 1989.

Carter, Bill. "Two Upstart Networks Courting Black Viewers." *New York Times,* 7 October 1996, p. C 11.

Cashmore, Ernest. *The Black Culture Industry.* London; New York: Routledge, 1997.

Chaudhary, Anju G. "Press Portrayal of Black Officials." *Journalism Quarterly* 57 (Winter 1980): 636–41.

Clark, Dorothy A. *Race, Poverty, and the Role of Media: A Review of News Coverage of Boston's Black Community, 1985–1990.* Boston, Mass.: William Monroe Trotter Institute, University of Massachusetts at Boston, 1994.

Selected Bibliography

Clark, Roy Peter and Raymond Arsenault, eds. *The Changing South of Gene Patterson: Journalism and Civil Rights*. Gainesville, Fla.: University Press of Florida, 2002.

Classen, Steven D. *Watching Jim Crow: The Struggles over Mississippi TV, 1955–1969*. Durham, N.C.: Duke University Press, 2004.

Cobb, Cathy J. and David Kenny. "Adolescents and the Newspaper: Images in Black and White." *Newspaper Research Journal* 7 (Summer 1986): 1–8.

Cohen, Sharon. "Sportswriters and the Color Bar." *Media History Digest* 12 (1992): 24–27.

Coleman, Renita. "Race and Ethical Reasoning: The Importance of Race to Journalistic Decision Making." *Journalism & Mass Communication Quarterly* 80 (Summer 2003): 295–310.

Collins, Sharon M. *Black Corporate Executives: The Making and Breaking of a Black Middle Class*. Philadelphia, PA: Temple University Press, 1997.

Cortese, Anthony. *Opposing Hate Speech*. Westport, Conn.: Praeger, 2006.

Cosby, William H. Jr. "50 Years of Blacks on TV." *Ebony* 51 (1) (1996): 215–17.

Cose, Ellis. Does Cosby Help? *Newsweek*, 27 December 2004, pp. 66, 68–69.

Cose, Ellis. "Seething in Silence—The News in Black and White." *Media Studies Journal* 9 (Winter 1995): 22–31.

Cose, Ellis. *The Quiet Crisis: Minority Journalism and Newsroom Opportunity*. Berkeley, Calif.: Institute for Journalism Education, 1985.

Cose, Ellis. *The Rage of a Privileged Class*. New York: HarperCollins, 1993.

Cottle, Simon, ed. *Ethnic Minorities and the Media: Changing Cultural Boundaries*. Buckingham; Philadelphia, PA: Open University Press, 2000.

Cottle, Simon. *The Racist Murder of Stephen Lawrence: Media Performance and Public Transformation*. Westport, Conn.: Praeger, 2004.

Cox, Archibald, Mark De Wolfe Howe and James Russell Wiggins. *Civil Rights, the Constitution, and the Courts*. Cambridge, Mass.: Harvard University Press, 1967.

Cutting, Hunter and Makani N. Themba. *Talking the Walk: A Communications Guide for Racial Justice*. Oakland, Calif.: AK Press, 2006.

Daily, Charles U., ed. *The Media and the Cities*. Chicago: University of Chicago Center for Policy Study, 1968.

Dalton, Jon C. *Racism on Campus: Confronting Racial Bias through Peer Interventions*. San Francisco: Jossey-Bass Inc., 1991.

Daniels, Walter C. *Black Journals of the United States*. Westport, Conn.: Greenwood Press, 1982.

Dates, Jannette L. and Edward C. Pease. "Warping the World—Media's Mangled Images of Race." *Media Studies Journal* 8 (Summer 1994): 89–96.

Dates, Jannette L. and William Barlow, eds. *Split Image: African Americans in the Mass Media*. Washington, D.C.: Howard University Press, 1990.

Davies, David R., ed. *The Press and Race: Mississippi Journalists Confront the Movement*. Jackson, Miss.: University Press of Mississippi, 2001.

Dawkins, Wayne. *Black Journalists: The NABJ Story*. Sicklerville, N.J.: August Press, 1993.

Dawson, Michael C. *Behind the Mule: Race and Class in African-American Politics*. Princeton, N.J.: Princeton University Press, 1994.

Delaney, Paul. "Pop Culture, 'Gansta Rap' and the 'New Vaudeville.'" *Media Studies Journal* 8 (Summer 1994): 97–104.

DeMott, Benjamin. *The Trouble with Friendship: Why Americans Can't Think Straight about Race*. New York: Atlantic Monthly, 1995.

Dennis, Everette E. "Racial Naming." *Media Studies Journal* 8 (Summer 1994): 105–12.

Dennis, Everette E. and Edward C. Pease. *The Media in Black and White*. New Brunswick, N.J.: Transaction Publishers, 1997.

Dijk, Reun van. *Racism and the Press*. London: Routledge, 1991.

Dines, Gail and Jean M. Humez, eds. *Gender, Race and Class in Media: A Text-Reader*. Thousand Oaks, Calif.: Sage, 1995.

Selected Bibliography

Dipboye, Robert L. and Adrienne Colella. *Discrimination at Work: The Psychological and Organizational Bases*. Mahwah, N.J.: Lawrence Erlbaum, 2005.

Dixon, Travis L. and Daniel Linz. "Television News, Prejudicial Pretrial Publicity, and the Depiction of Race." *Journal of Broadcasting and Electronic Media* 46 (March 2002): 112–36.

Dixon, Travis L., Cristina L. Azocar and Michael Casas. The Portrayal of Race and Crime on Television Network News. *Journal of Broadcasting & Electronic Media* 47 (December 2003): 498–523.

Domke, David. "Strategic Elites, the Press, and Race Relations." *Journal of Communication* 50 (Winter 2000): 115–43.

Domke, David, Philip Garland, Andre Billeaudeaux and John Hutcheson. "Insights Into U.S. Racial Hierarchy: Racial Profiling, News Sources, and September 11." *Journal of Communication* 53 (December 2003): 606–23.

Doreski, Carole. *Writing America Black: Race Rhetoric in the Public Sphere*. Cambridge; New York: Cambridge University Press, 1998.

Drotning, Phillip T. and Wesley W. Smith. *Up from the Ghetto*. New York: Cowles, 1970.

Dunnigan, Alice. *A Black Woman's Experience: From Schoolhouse to White House*. Philadelphia, Pa.: Dorrance & Co., 1974.

Dunnigan, Alice. "Early History of Negro Women in Journalism." *Negro History Bulletin* 28 (Summer 1965): 178–79, 193.

Dyson, Michael Eric. *Between God and Gangsta Rap: Bearing Witness to Black Culture*. New York: Oxford University Press, 1996.

Edley, Christopher. *Not All Black and White: Affirmative Action, Race, and American Values*. New York: Hill and Wang, 1996.

Elias, Tom and Dennis Schatzman. *The Simpson Trial in Black and White*. Los Angeles: General Pub. Group, 1996.

Ellison, Christopher G. and Daniel A. Powers. "The Contact Hypothesis and Racial Attitudes Among Black Americans." *Social Sciences Quarterly* 75 (1994): 385–400.

Entine, Jon. *Taboo: Why Black Athletes Dominate Sports—and Why We're Afraid to Talk about It*. New York: PublicAffairs, 2000.

Entman, Robert M. "African Americans According to TV News." *Media Studies Journal* 8 (Summer 1994): 29–38.

Entman, Robert M. "Blacks in the News: Television, Modern Racism, and Cultural Change." *Journalism Quarterly* 69 (1992): 41–61.

Entman, Robert M. *Democracy without Citizens: Media and the Decay of American Politics*. New York: Oxford Univerrsity Press, 1989.

Entman, Robert M. "Manufacturing Discord: Media in the Affirmative Action Debate." *Harvard International Journal of Press/Politics* 2 (1997): 32–51.

Entman, Robert M. "Modern Racism and the Images of Blacks in Local Television News." *Critical Studies in Mass Communication* 7 (1999): 32–45.

Entman, Robert M. "Representation and Reality in the Portrayal of Blacks on Network Television News." *Journalism Quarterly* 71 (1994): 9–20.

Entman, Robert M. and Andrew Rojecki. *The Black Image in the White Mind: Media and Race in America*. Chicago; London: University of Chicago Press, 2000.

Ettema, James S. "Press Rites and Race Relations: A Study of Mass-Mediated Ritual." *Critical Studies in Mass Communication* 7 (1990): 9–31.

Feagin, Joe R. and Melvin P. Sikes. *Living with Racism: The Black Middle-Class Experience*. Boston: Beacon, 1994.

Fearn-Banks, Kathleen. "African-American Press Coverage of Clarence Thomas Nomination." *Newspaper Research Journal* 15 (Fall 1994): 98–116.

Ferguson, Robert. *Representing "Race": Ideology, Identity, and the Media*. London; New York: Arnold, 1998.

Selected Bibliography

Fetter, Henry D. "The Party Line and the Color Line: The American Communist Party, the *Daily Worker*, and Jackie Robinson." *Journal of Sport History* 28 (2001): 375–402.

Fielder, Virginia Dodge. *Minorities and Newspapers: A Survey of Newspaper Research.* Reston, Va.: American Society of Newspaper Editors, 1986.

Fishel, Leslie. *The Black American: A Documentary History.* New York: Scott, Foresman and Co., 1967.

Fisher, Paul L. and Ralph L. Lowenstein, eds. *Race and the News Media.* New York: Praeger, 1967.

Fiske, John. *Media Matters: Everyday Culture and Political Change.* Minneapolis, Minn.: University of Minnesota Press, 1994.

Fisler, Paul L. and Ralph L. Lowenstein, eds. *Race and the News Media.* New York: Praeger, 1968.

Fleming, Karl. *Son of the Rough South: An Uncivil Memoir.* New York: PublicAffairs, 2005.

Fong, Mary and Rueyling Chuang. *Communicating Ethnic and Cultural Identity.* New York: Rowman & Littlefield, 2004.

Franklin, Raymond. *Shadows of Race and Class.* Minneapolis, Minn.: University of Minnesota Press, 1993.

Frazier, E. Franklin. *Black Bourgeoisie.* New York: Collier MacMillan, 1957.

Frymer, Paul. *Uneasy Alliance: Race and Party Competition in America.* Princeton, N.J.: Princeton University Press, 1999.

Fugioka, Yuki. "Black Media Images as a Perceived Threat to African American Ethnic Identity: Coping Responses, Perceived Public Perception, and Attitudes Towards Affirmative Action." *Journal of Broadcasting & Electronic Media* 49 (December 2005): 450–67.

Fugioka, Yuki. "Television Portrayals and African-American Stereotypes: Examination of Television Effects When Direct Contacts Are Lacking." *Political Communication* 16 (April–June 1999): 147–67.

Gabriel, John. *Whitewash: Racialized Politics and the Media.* London and New York: Routledge, 1998.

Gamson, William and Andre Modigliani. "The Changing Culture of Affirmative Action." *Research in Political Sociology* 3 (1987): 37–77.

Gandy, Oscar Jr. *Communication and Race.* London: Arnold, 1998.

Gandy, Oscar Jr. "From Bad to Worse—The Media's Framing of Race and Risk." *Media Studies Journal* 8 (Summer 1994): 39–48.

Gans, Herbert J. *The War Against the Poor: The Underclass and Anti-poverty Policy.* New York: Basic Books, 1995.

Gates, Henry Louis Jr. *Colored People.* New York: Alfred A. Knopf, 1994.

Gates, Henry Louis Jr. *Race, Writing, and Difference.* Chicago: University of Chicago Press, 1986.

Gates, Henry Louis Jr. and Evelyn Brooks Higginbotham. *African American Lives.* New York: Oxford University Press, 2004.

Ghiglione, Loren. "The 1990s—A Time for Frontline Fighters & a New Kind of 'Press Corps.'" *Newspaper Research Journal* 11 (Summer 1990): 2–6.

Gibbons, Arnold. *Race, Politics, and the Mass Media: The Jesse Jackson Campaigns.* Lanham, Md.: University Press of America, 1993.

Gilens, Martin. "Race and Poverty in America." *Public Opinion Quarterly* 60 (1996): 515–41.

Gilens, Martin. *Why Americans Hate Welfare: Race, Media and the Politics of Anti-poverty.* Chicago: University of Chicago Press, 1999.

Gilliam, Frank D. Jr. Shanto Iyengar, Adam Simon and Oliver Wright. "Crime in Black and White: The Scary World of Local News." *Harvard International Journal of Press/Politics* 1 (1996): 6–23.

Ginsburg, Carl. *Race and Media: The Enduring Life of the Moynihan Report.* New York: Institute for Media Analysis, 1989.

Giroux, Henry A. *Fugitive Cultures: Race, Violence, and Youth.* New York: Routledge, 1996.

Gissler, Sig. "Newspapers' Quest for Racial Candor." *Media Studies Journal* 8 (Summer 1994): 123–32.

Selected Bibliography

Gist, Marilyn E. "Minorities in Media Imagery: A Social Cognitive Perspective on Journalistic Bias." *Newspaper Research Journal* 11 (Summer 1990): 52–63.

Glazer, Nathan and Daniel Patrick Moynihan. *Beyond the Melting Pot: The Negroes, Puerto Ricans, Jews, Italians, and Irish of New York City.* Cambridge, Mass.: MIT Press, 1963.

Goodall, Heather and Andrew Jakubowicz. *Racism, Ethnicity, and the Media.* St. Leonards, Australia: Allen & Unwin, 1994.

Gorham, Bradley W. "News Media's Relationship with Stereotyping: The Linguistic Intergroup Bias in Response to Crime News." *Journal of Communication* 56 (June 2006): 289–308.

Gorshorn, Kent and Oscar H. Gandy Jr. "Race, Risk and Responsibility: Editorial Constraint in the Framing of Inequality." *Journal of Communication* 45 (1995): 33–51.

Grabe, Maria Elizabeth. "Television News Magazine Crime Stories: A Functionalist Perspective." *Critical Studies in Mass Communication* 16 (1999): 155–71.

Graber, Doris A. "Seeing Is Remembering: How Visuals Contribute to Learning from Television News." *Journal of Communication* 40 (1990): 34–56.

Graham, Hugh Davis. *Crisis in Print; Desegregation and the Press in Tennessee.* Nashville, Tenn.: Vanderbilt University Press, 1967.

Graham, Lawrence. *Our Kind of People: Inside America's Black Upper Class.* New York: HarperCollins, 1999.

Graves, Earl G. *How to Succeed in Business without Being White.* New York: HarperBusiness, 1997.

Gray, Harman. "Television, Black Americans, and the American Dream." *Critical Studies in Mass Communication* 6 (1989): 76–86.

Gray, Harman. *Watching Race: Television and the Struggle for "Blackness."* Minneapolis, Minn.: University of Minnesota Press, 1995.

Guimary, Donald L. "Ethnic Minorities in Newsrooms of Major Market Media in California." *Journalism Quarterly* 61 (Winter 1984): 827–34.

Gutierrez, Felix and Clint Wilson. "The Demographics Dilemma." *Columbia Journalism Review* 17 (January/February 1979): 53–55.

Hacker, Andrew. "Are the Media Really 'White'?" *Media Studies Journal* 8 (Summer 1994): 81–88.

Harkey, Ira. *The Smell of Burning Crosses: An Autobiography of a Mississippi Newspaperman.* Jacksonville, Fla.: Harris-Wolf, 1967.

Harley, Sharon and Rosalyn Terborg-Penn, eds. *The Afro-American Woman: Struggles and Images.* Port Washington, N.Y.: Kennikat Press, 1978.

Harper, Phillip Brian. *Are We Not Men? Masculine Anxiety and the Problem of African American Identity.* New York: Oxford University Press, 1996.

Hartman, Paul and Charles Husband. *Racism and the Mass Media: A Study of the Role of the Mass Media in the Formation of White Beliefs and Attitudes in Britain.* Totowa, N.J.: Rowman & Littlefield, 1974.

Havens, Timothy. "White Viewers, Black Media, and Disciplinary Boundaries." *Review of Communication* 2 (January 2002): 1–7.

Heath, G. Louis. *Off the Pigs! The History and Literature of the Black Panther Party.* Metuchen, N.J.: Scarecrow Press, 1976.

Henry, Neil. *Pearl's Secret: A Black Man's Search for His White Family.* Berkeley, Calif.: University of California Press, 2001.

Hill, George H. *Black Media in America: A Resource Guide.* Boston: G.K. Hall, 1984.

Hill, George H. and Sylvia Saverson Hill. *Blacks on Television: A Selectively Annotated Bibliography.* Metuchen, N.J.: Scarecrow Press, 1985.

Hines, Judith D. *The Next Step: Toward Diversity in the Newspaper Business.* Reston, Va: American Newspaper Publishers Association, 1991.

Hochschild, Jennifer L. *Facing up to the American Dream.* Princeton, N.J.: Princeton University Press, 1995.

Holtzman, Linda. *Media Messages: What Film, Television, and Popular Music Teach Us About Race, Class, Gender, and Sexual Orientation.* Armonk, N.Y.: M.E. Sharpe, 2000.

Selected Bibliography

Hooker, Robert. "Race and the Mississippi Press." *New South* 26 (Winter 1971): 55–62.

Hooks, Ball. *Ain't I a Woman: Black Women and Feminism.* Boston: South End Press, 1981.

Hopkins, Jeannette. *Black Looks: Race and Representation.* Boston: South End Press, 1992.

Hopkins, Jeannette. *Racial Justice and the Press: Mutual Suspicion or "the Saving Remnant"?* New York: Metropolitan Applied Research Center, 1968.

Hunt, Darnell, ed. *Channeling Blackness: Studies on Television and Race in America.* New York: Oxford University Press, 2005.

Hunt, Darnell. *Screening the Los Angeles "Riots": Race, Seeing and Resistance.* New York: Cambridge University Press, 1997.

Hunt, Darnell. *O.J. Simpson Facts and Fictions: News Rituals in the Construction of Reality.* New York: Cambridge University Press, 1999.

Hurwitz, Jon and Mark Peffley, eds. *Perception and Prejudice: Race and Politics in the United States.* New Haven, Conn.: Yale University Press, 1998.

Hurwitz, Jon and Mark Peffley. "Public Perceptions of Race and Crime: The Role of Racial Stereotypes." *American Journal of Political Science* 41 (1997): 375–401.

Husband, Charles. "Beyond Contesting Racism: Imagining the Polyethnic Media Environment." *Media Development* 47 (2000): 11–14.

Hutchinson, Earl Ofari. *Beyond O.J.: Race, Sex, and Class Lessons for America.* Los Angeles: Middle Passage Press, 1996.

Hutchinson, Janis Faye. *Cultural Portrayals of African Americans: Creating an Ethnic/Racial Identity.* Westport, Conn.: Bergin & Garvey, 1997.

Illouz, Eva. *Oprah Winfrey and the Glamour of Misery: An Essay on Popular Culture.* New York: Columbia University Press, 2003.

Iyengar, Shanto. *Is Anyone Responsible? How Television Frames Political Issues.* Chicago: University of Chicago Press, 1991.

Jackson, Anthony W., ed. *Black Families and the Medium of Television.* Ann Arbor, Mich.: Bush Program in Child Development and Social Policy, 1982.

Jackson, Ronald L. II, ed. *African American Communication & Identities: Essential Readings.* Thousand Oaks, Calif.: Sage Publications, 2004.

Jacobs, Ronald N. *Race, Media and the Crisis of Civil Society: From Watts to Rodney King.* Cambridge, England: Cambridge University Press, 2000.

James, Hunter. *They Didn't Put That on the Huntley-Brinkley!: A Vagabond Reporter Encounters the New South.* Athens, Ga: University of Georgia Press, 1993.

Jeffres, Leo W. *Urban Communication Systems: Neighborhoods and the Search for Community.* Cresskill, N.J.: Hampton Press, 2002.

Johnson, Abby Arthur and Ronald M. Johnson. "Away from Accommodation: Radical Editors and Protest Journalism, 1900–1910." *Journal of Negro History* 62 (October 1977): 325–38.

Johnson, Abby Arthur and Ronald M. Johnson. *Propaganda and Aesthetics: The Literary Politics of Afro-American Magazines in the Twentieth Century.* Amherst, Mass.: University of Massachusetts Press, 1979.

Johnson, Kirk A. "Black and White in Boston." *Columbia Journalism Review* 26 (May–June 1987): 50–52.

Johnson, Phylis. "Black Radio's Role in Sports Promotion: Sports, Scholarships, and Sponsorship." *Journal of Sport & Social Issues* 19 (1995): 397–414.

Johnson, Terry E. "25 Year Report: Black Progress Sure But Slowing." *Jet* 51 (11 November 1976): 34.

Jordan, William G. *Black Newspapers and America's War for Democracy, 1914–1920.* Chapel Hill, N.C.: University of North Carolina Press, 2001.

"Journalism and the Kerner Report." *Columbia Journalism Review* 7 (Fall 1968): 42–65.

Kamalipour, Yahya R. and Theresa Carilli. *Cultural Diversity and the U.S. Media.* Albany, N.Y.: State University of New York Press, 1998.

Selected Bibliography

Kaniss, Phyllis. *Making Local News*. Chicago: University of Chicago Press, 1991.
Katz, Phyllis A. and Dalmas A. Taylor, eds. *Eliminating Racism*. New York: Plenum, 1988.
Kelley, William G. "Jackie Robinson and the Press." *Journalism Quarterly* 53 (Spring 1976): 137–39.
Kellstedt, Paul M. *The Mass Media and the Dynamics of American Racial Attitudes*. Cambridge; New York: Cambridge University Press, 2003.
Kennedy, Liam. *Race and Urban Space in Contemporary American Culture*. Chicago: Fitzroy Dearborn, 2000.
Kern-Foxworth, Marilyn. "Women of Color on the Frontline in the Mass Communication Professions." In *Seeking Equity for Women in Journalism and Mass Communication Education: A 30-Year Update*, ed. by Ramona Rush, Carol E. Oukrop and Pamela J. Creedon. Mahwah, N.J.: Erlbaum, 2004.
Kern-Foxworth, Marilyn and Shirley Biagi. "Minority Newsroom Employment Shows Small Gain." In *Facing Difference: Race, Gender, and Mass Media*, ed. by Shirley Biagi and Marilyn Kern-Foxworth. Thousand Oaks, Calif.: Pine Forge Press, 1997.
Klineberg, Otto. *Race as News*. Paris: Unesco Press, 1974.
Klite, Paul, Robert A. Bardwell and Jason Salzman. "Local TV News: Getting Away with Murder." *Harvard International Journal of Press/Politics* 2 (1997): 102–12.
Kochman, Thomas. *Black and White Styles in Conflict*. Chicago: University of Chicago Press, 1981.
Lamb, Chris. *Blackout: The Untold Story of Jackie Robinson's First Spring Training*. Lincoln, Neb.: University of Nebraska Press, 2004.
Larson, Stephanie Greco. "How New York Times Covered Discrimination Cases." *Journalism Quarterly* 61 (Winter 1985): 894–96.
Law, Ian. *Race in the News*. New York: Palgrave, 2002.
Lawrence, David F. "Broken Ladders/Revolving Doors: The Need for Pluralism in the Newsroom." *Newspaper Research Journal* 11 (Summer 1990): 18–23.
Lentz, Richard. *Symbols, the News Magazines, and Martin Luther King*. Baton Rouge, La.: Louisiana State University Press, 1990.
Leonard, David J. "The Next M.J. or the Next O.J.? Kobe Bryant, Race, and the Absurdity of Colorblind Rhetoric." *Journal of Sport & Social Issues* 28 (2004): 284–313.
Liebler, Carol. "How Race and Gender Affect Journalists' Autonomy." *Newspaper Research Journal* 15 (Summer 1994): 122–30.
Lincoln, C. Eric. *The Black Muslims in America*. Boston: Beacon Press, 1961.
Lind, Rebecca Ann. *Race, Gender, Media: Considering Diversity across Audiences, Content, and Producers*. Boston: Pearson/Allyn and Bacon, 2004.
Lipsyte, Robert. "Covering Ali, Discovering an Era." *Media Studies Journal* 11 (1997): 22–31.
Lomax, Louis E. *The Negro Revolt*. New York: Harper & Row, 1962.
Lusane, Clarence. *Race in the Global Era: African Americans at the Millennium*. Boston: South End Press, 1997.
Lyle, Jack, ed. *The Black American and the Press*. Los Angeles: The Ward Ritchie Press, 1968.
MacDonald, J. Fred. *Blacks and White TV: African Americans in Television Since 1948*, 2nd ed. Chicago: Nelson-Hall, 1992.
Malcolm X. *The Autobiography of Malcolm X*. New York: Grove Press, 1968.
Mallinson, Christine and Zachary W. Brewster. "'Blacks and Bubbas': Stereotypes, Ideology, and Categorization Processes in Restaurant Servers' Discourse." *Discourse & Society* 16 (2005): 787–807.
Marable, Manning. *African-American Studies: Critical Perspectives on the Black Experience*. Boulder, Colo.: Westview Press, 1994.
Marable, Manning. *Beyond Black and White: Race in America's Past, Present and Future*. New York: Lawrence Hill, 1994.
Marable, Manning. *The Crisis of Color and Democracy*. Monroe, Me.: Common Outrage Press, 1992.
Marable, Manning. *Race, Reform and Rebellion: The Second Reconstruction*. Jackson, Miss.: University Press of Mississippi, 1991.

Selected Bibliography

Marable, Manning. "Reconciling Race and Reality." *Media Studies Journal* 8 (Summer 1994): 11–18.
Martindale, Carolyn. "Changes in Newspaper Images of Black Americans." *Newspaper Research Journal* 11 (Winter 1990): 40–51.
Martindale, Carolyn. "Coverage of Black Americans in Four Major Newsrooms." *Newspaper Research Journal* 11 (Summer 1990): 96–112.
Martindale, Carolyn. "Significant Silences: Newspaper Coverage of Problems Facing Black Americans." *Newspaper Research Journal* 15 (Spring 1994): 102–15.
Martindale, Carolyn. *The White Press and Black America*. Westport, Conn.: Greenwood Press, 1986.
Marzolf, Marion. *Up from the Footnote*. New York: Hastings House, 1977.
Massey, Douglas S. and Nancy A. Denton. *American Apartheid: Segregation and the Making of the Underclass*. Cambridge, Mass.: Harvard University Press, 1993.
McCarthy, Cameron, Alicia Rodriguez, Ed Buendia, Shuaib Meacham, Stephen David, Heriberto Godina, K.E. Supriya and Carrie Wilson-Brown. "Danger in the Safety Zone: Notes on Race, Resentment, and the Discourse of Crime, Violence and Suburban Security." *Cultural Studies* 11 (May 1997): 274–95.
McGill, Lawrence. *Newsroom Diversity: Meeting the Challenge*. Arlington, Va.: The Freedom Forum, 2000.
McGowan, William. *Coloring the News, How Crusading for Diversity Has Corrupted American Journalism*. San Francisco: Encounter Books, 2001.
McPhail, Mark Lawrence. "Race in Black and White: Essence and Ideology in the Spike Lee Discourse." *Howard Journal of Communications* 7 (April–June 1996): 127–38.
Mencher, Melvin. "Journalism: The Way It Is, as Seen by Black Reporters and Students." *Journalism Quarterly* 46 (Autumn 1969): 499–504, 544.
Mencher, Melvin. "Recruiting and Training Black Newsmen." *Quill* 57 (September 1969): 22–25.
Merelman, Richard M. *Representing Black Culture: Racial Conflict and Cultural Politics in the U.S.* New York: Routledge, 1995.
Merina, Victor. "Why Race Still Matters." *Media Studies Journal* 14 (Winter 2000): 16–23.
Mickler, Steve. *The Myth of Privilege*. Fremantle, W.A.: Fremantle Arts Centre Press, 1998.
Miles, Johnnie H. *Almanac of African American Heritage: A Book of Lists Featuring People, Places, Times, and Events That Shaped Black Culture*. Paramus, N.J.: Prentice Hall, 2001.
Miller, John J. "Immigration, the Press and the New Racism." *Media Studies Journal* 8 (Summer 1994): 19–28.
Miner, Michael. "Maynard of Oakland." *Quill* 70 (May 1982): 9–15.
Mohamed, Abdul R. Jan and David Lloyd, eds. *The Nature and Context of Minority Discourse*. New York: Oxford University Press, 1990.
Monroe, William and Edmund M. Midura. *Blacks and Whites: Why Aren't We Getting Through? and the Urban Communication Crisis*. Washington, D.C.: Acropolis Books, 1974.
Moorti, Sujata. *Color of Rape: Gender and Race in Television's Public Sphere*. Albany, N.Y.: State University of New York Press, 2002.
Morgan, Arlene Notoro, Alice Irene Pifer and Keith Woods. *The Authentic Voice: The Best Reporting on Race and Ethnicity*. New York: Columbia University Press, 2006.
Morrison, Toni and Claudia Brodsky Lacour, eds. *Birth of a Nation'hood: Gaze, Script, and Spectacle in the O.J. Simpson Case*. New York: Pantheon Books, 1997.
Moses, Wilson Jeremiah. *Black Messiahs and Uncle Toms*. University Park, Pa.: Pennsylvania State University Press, 1982.
Murray, Gene. *Covering Sex, Race, and Gender in the American Military Services*. Lewiston, N.Y.: The Edwin Mellen Press, 2003.
Muse, Benjamin. *The American Negro Revolution: From Nonviolence to Black Power, 1963–1967*. Bloomington, Ind.: Indiana University Press, 1968.
Nadel, Alan. *Television in Black-and-White: America: Race and National Identity*. Lawrence, Kan.: University Press of Kansas, 2005.

Selected Bibliography

Nakayama, Thomas. "The Significance of 'Race' and Masculinities." *Critical Studies in Media Communication* 17 (March 2000): 111–13.

Napoli, Philip M. "Audience Valuation and Minority Media: An Analysis of the Determinants of the Value of Radio Audiences." *Journal of Broadcasting and Electronic Media* 46 (June 2002): 169–84.

Neuendorf, Kimberly A., David Atkin, Leo W. Jeffres, Theresa Loszak and Alicia Williams. "Explorations of the Simpson Trial 'Racial Divide.'" *Howard Journal of Communications* 11 (October–December 2000): 247–66.

Newkirk, Pamela. *Within the Veil: Black Journalists, White Media*. New York; London: New York University Press, 2000.

Newman, Mark. *Entrepreneurs of Profit and Pride: From Black-Appeal to Radio Soul*. New York: Praeger, 1988.

Niven, David. "Race, Quarterbacks, and the Media: Testing the Rush Limbaugh Hypothesis." *Journal of Black Studies* 35 (2005): 684–94.

Noble, Gil. *Black Is the Color of My TV Tube*. Secaucus, N.J.: Stuart, 1981.

O'Kelly, Charlotte Gwen. "The Black Press and the Black Protest Movement: A Study of the Response of Mass Media to Social Change, 1946–1972." Ph.D. dissertation, University of Connecticut, 1975.

Oliver, Mary Beth. "Caucasian Viewers' Memory of Black and White Criminal Suspects in the News." *Journal of Communication* 49 (1999): 46–60.

Oliver, Mary Beth. "Portrayals of Crime, Race, and Aggression in 'Reality-Based' Police Shows: A Content Analysis." *Journal of Broadcasting & Electronic Media* 38 (1994): 179–93.

Oliver, Mary Beth., Ronald L. Jackson II, Ndidi N. Moses and Celnish L. Dangerfield. "The Face of Crime: Viewers' Memory of Race-Related Facial Features of Individuals Pictured in the News." *Journal of Communication* 54 (March 2004): 88–104.

Padgett, George. *New Directions in Diversity: A New Approach to Covering America's Multicultural Communities*. Oak Park, Ill.: Marion Street Press, 2006.

Page, Benjamin I. *Who Deliberates? Mass Media in a Modern Democracy*. Chicago: University of Chicago Press, 1996.

Pan, Zhongdang and Gerald M. Kosicki. "Assessing News Media Influences on the Formation of Whites' Racial Policy Preferences." *Communication Research* 23 (April 1996): 147–78.

Patterson, Orlando. *The Ordeal of Integration: Progress and Resentment in America's "Racial" Crisis*. Washington, D.C.: Civitas, 1997.

Pease, Ted. "Cornerstone for Growth: How Minorities Are Vital to the Future of Newspapers." *Newspaper Research Journal* 10 (Fall 1989): 1–22.

Pease, Ted. "Ducking the Diversity Issue: Newspapers' Real Failure Is Performance." *Newspaper Research Journal* 11 (Summer 1990): 24–37.

Pease, Ted and Guido H. Stempel III. "Surviving to the Top: Views of Minority Newspaper Executives." *Newspaper Research Journal* 11 (Summer 1990): 64–79.

Peffley, Mark and Jon Hurwitz, "Racial Stereotypes and Whites' Political Views of Blacks in the Context of Welfare and Crime." *American Journal of Political Science* 41 (1997): 30–60.

Peffley, Mark, Todd Shields and Bruce Williams. "The Intersection of Race and Crime in Television News Stories: An Experimental Study." *Political Communication* 13 (1996): 9–27.

Penn, Irving Garland. *The Afro-American Press and Its Editors*. New York: Arno Press, 1969.

Phillips, Carolyn L. "Evaluating and Valuing Newsroom Diversity." *Newspaper Research Journal* 12 (Spring 1991): 28–37.

Pinkney, Alphonso. *The Myth of Black Progress*. New York: Cambridge University Press, 1984.

Plous, Scott and Tyrone Williams. "Racial Stereotypes from the Days of American Slavery: A Continuing Legacy." *Journal of Applied Social Psychology* 25 (1995): 795–817.

Poindexter, Paula M., Laura Smith and Don Heider. "Race and Ethnicity in Local Television News: Framing, Story Assignments, and Source Selection." *Journal of Broadcasting & Electronic Media* 47 (December 2003): 524–36.

Selected Bibliography

Potter, W. James and William Ware. "Traits of Perpetrators and Receivers of Antisocial and Prosocial Acts on TV." *Journalism Quarterly* 64 (Summer–Autumn 1987): 382–91.
Powell, Adam Clayton III. "On-Ramps to the Information Superhighway." *Media Studies Journal* 8 (Summer 1994): 113–22.
Pride, Armistead S. and Clint C. Wilson II. *A History of the Black Press*. Washington, D.C.: Howard University Press, 1997.
Pride, Richard A. "Redefining the Problem of Racial Inequality." *Political Communication* 16 (1999): 147–67.
Pulley, Brett. *The Billion Dollar BET: Robert Johnson and the Inside Story of Black Entertainment Television*. Hoboken, N.J.: John Wiley & Sons, 2004.
Rainville, Raymond E. and Edward McCormick. "Extent of Covert Racial Prejudice in Pro Football Announcers' Speech." *Journalism Quarterly* 54 (Spring 1977): 20–26.
Rainville, Raymond E., Al Roberts and Andrew Sweet. "Recognition of Covert Racial Prejudice." *Journalism Quarterly* 55 (Summer 1978): 256–59.
Reed, Adolph L. Jr. *The Jesse Jackson Phenomenon: The Crisis of Purpose in Afro-American Politics*. New Haven, Conn: Yale University Press, 1986.
Reed, Ishmael. *Airing Dirty Laundry*. Reading, Mass.: Addison-Wesley, 1993.
Reeves, Jimmie L. and Richard Campbell. "Coloring the Crack Crisis." *Media Studies Journal* 8 (Summer 1994): 71–80.
Reeves, Jimmie L. and Richard Campbell. *Cracked Coverage: Television News, the Anti-Cocaine Crusade, and the Reagan Legacy*. Durham, N.C.: Duke University Press, 1994.
Reeves, Keith. *Voting Hopes or Fears? White Voters, Black Candidates and Racial Politics in America*. New York: Oxford University Press, 1997.
Rhodes, Chip. *Structures of the Jazz Age: Mass Culture, Progressive Education, and Racial Discourse in American Modernism*. London; New York: Verso, 1998.
Riggins, Stephen H., ed. *Ethnic Minority Media*. Newbury Park, Calif.: Sage, 1992.
Riley, Sam G. *The American Newspaper Columnist*. Westport, Conn.: Praeger, 1998.
Riley, Sam G. ed., *The Best of the Rest: Non-Syndicated Newspaper Columnists Select Their Best Work*. Westport, Conn.: Greenwood Press, 1993.
Riley, Sam G. *Biographical Dictionary of American Newspaper Columnists*. Westport, Conn.: Greenwood Press, 1995.
Romer, Daniel, Kathleen H. Jamieson and N.J. deCoteau. "The Treatment of Persons of Color in Local Television News—Ethnic Blame Discourse or Realistic Group Conflict?" *Communication Research* 25 (1998): 286–305.
Romer, D.K., K.H. Jamieson and S. Aday. "Television News and the Cultivation of Fear of Crime." *Journal of Communication* 53 (December 2003): 88–104.
Rooks, Noliwe M. *Ladies' Pages: African American Women's Magazines and the Culture That Made Them*. New Brunswick, N.J.: Rutgers University Press, 2004.
Ross, Karen and Peter Playdon, eds. *Black Marks: Minority Ethnic Audiences and Media*. Burlington, Vt.: Ashgate Publishing, 2001.
Rothbart, Myron and Oliver P. John. "Intergroup Relations and Stereotype Change." In *Prejudice, Politics, and the American Dilemma*, ed. by Paul M. Sniderman, Philip E. Tettlock and Edward G. Carmines. Stanford, Calif.: Stanford University Press, 1993.
Rubin, Bernard, ed. *Small Voices & Great Trumpets: Minorities & the Media*. New York: Praeger, 1980.
Rudwick, Elliott M. "Race Labeling and the Press." *Journal of Negro Education* 31 (Spring 1962): 177–81.
Ruscher, Janet B. *Prejudiced Communication: A Social Psychological Perspective*. New York: Guilford Press, 2001.
Russell, Cheryl. *Racial and Ethnic Diversity: Asians, Blacks, Hispanics, Native Americans, and Whites*, 4th ed. Ithaca, N.Y.: New Strategist Publications, 2002.
Russell, Katheryn K. *The Color of Crime: Racial Hoaxes, White Fear, Black Protectionism, Police Harassment, and Other Macroaggressions*. New York: New York University Press, 1998.

Selected Bibliography

Russell, Kathy, Midge Wilson and Ronald Hall. *The Color Complex: The Politics of Skin Color among African Americans*. New York: Harcourt Brace Jovanovich, 1992.

Said, Edward W. *Covering Islam*. New York: Pantheon Books, 1981.

Santos, John Phillip. "(Re)Imaging America." *Media Studies Journal* 8 (Summer 1994): 143–52.

Schultz, Janie. "Reading the Catsuit: Serena Williams and the Production of Blackness at the 2002 U.S. Open." *Journal of Sport & Social Issues* 29 (2005): 338–57.

Schuman, Howard. *Racial Attitudes in America: Trends and Interpretations*. Cambridge, Mass.: Harvard University Press, 1985.

Schuyler, George S. *Black and Conservative*. New Rochelle, N.Y.: Arlington House, 1966.

Sears, David O. and Tom Jessor. "Whites' Racial Policy Attitudes: The Role of White Racism." *Social Science Quarterly* 77 (1996): 751–59.

Shah, Hemant and Seugahn Nah. "Long Ago and Far Away: How US Newspapers Construct Racial Oppression." *Journalism* 5 (2004): 259–78.

Signorielli, Nancy. "Aging on Television: Messages Relating to Gender, Race, and Occupation in Prime Time." *Journal of Broadcasting & Electronic Media* 48 (June 2004): 279–301.

Silberstein, Sandra. "Teaching Culture: Imagined Communities and National Fantasies in the O.J. Simpson Case." *Journal of Language, Identity & Education* 4 (2003): 319–30.

Simmons, Tim. "Reporting on the Minority Education Beat." *Nieman Reports* 57 (Fall 2003): 22–25.

Skrentny, John David. *Color Lines: Affirmative Action, Immigration, and Civil Rights Options for America*. Chicago: University of Chicago Press, 2001.

Smallwood, David, Stan West and Allison Keyes. *Profiles of Great African Americans*. Lincolnwood, Ill.: Publications International, 1996.

Smiles, Robin V. "U.S. Newsrooms: Still a Long Way from Racial Parity." *Black Issues in Higher Education* 15 (15 July 2004): 24–25.

Smith, Erna. *Transmitting Race: The Los Angeles Riots in Television News*. Cambridge, Mass.: The Joan Shorenstein Barone Center for Press, Politics and Public Policy, 1994.

Smith, Erna. *What Color Is News? An Ethnic Content Analysis of Bay Area News Media*. San Francisco, Calif.: New California Alliance, 1991.

Smith, Reed. "Sports Illustrated's African American Athlete Series as Socially Responsible Journalism." *American Journalism* 23 (Spring 2006): 45–68.

Smith McCoy, Sheila. *When Whites Riot: Writing Race and Violence in American and South African Cultures*. Madison, Wis.: University of Wisconsin Press, 2001.

Smith-Shomade, Beretta E. *Shaded Lives: African-American Women and Television*. New Brunswick, N.J.: Rutgers University Press, 2002.

Sniderman, Paul M. and Michael Gray Hagen. *Race and Inequality: A Study in American Values*. Chatham, N.J.: Chatham House, 1985.

Snorgrass, J. William, comp. *Blacks and Media: A Selected Annotated Bibliography*. Tallahassee, Fla.: University Presses of Florida, 1985.

Snorgrass, J. William. "Freedom of the Press and Black Publications." *Western Journal of Black Studies* 4 (Fall 1990): 172–78.

Snorgrass, J. William. "Pioneer Women Journalists from the 1850s to the 1950s." *Western Journal of Black Studies* 6 (Fall 1982): 150–58.

Sonenshein, Raphael J. *Politics in Black and White: Race and Power in Los Angeles*. Princeton, N.J.: Princeton University Press, 1993.

Staples, Brent. *Parallel Time: Growing Up in Black and White*. New York: Pantheon Books, 1994.

Steeh, Charlotte and Maria Krysan. "Affirmative Action and the Public, 1970–1995." *Public Opinion Quarterly* 60 (1996): 128–58.

Stein, M.L. *Blacks in Communications: Journalism, Public Relations, Advertising*. New York: Julian Messner, 1972.

Stevens, John D. "From the Back of the Foxhole: Black Correspondents in World War II." *Journalism Monographs* No. 27 (February 1973).

Selected Bibliography

Stone, Vernon. "Race Yields to Education As Predictor of Newspaper Use." *Newspaper Research Journal* 15 (Winter 1994): 115–26.

Stone, Vernon. "Women Gain, Minorities Lose in TV News." In *Facing Difference: Race, Gender and Mass Media*, ed. by Shirley Biagi and Marilyn Kern-Foxworth. Thousand Oaks, Calif.: Pine Forge, 1997.

Streitmatter, Roger. *Raising Her Voice: African-American Women Journalists Who Changed History*. Lexington, Ky.: University Press of Kentucky, 1994.

Stroman, Carolyn A. *Black Families and the Mass Media*. Washington, D.C.: Institute for Urban Affairs and Research, Howard University, 1986.

Tan, Alexis S. "Evaluation of Newspapers and Television by Blacks and Mexican-Americans." *Journalism Quarterly* 55 (Winter 1979): 673–81.

Thorn, Dale. "In the South—Press, Courts and Desegregation Revisited." *Media Studies Journal* 8 (Summer 1994): 61–70.

Tinney, James S. and Justine J. Rector, eds. *Issues and Trends in Afro-American Journalism*. Latham, Md.: University Press of America, 1980.

Torres, Sasha. *Black, White, and in Color: Television and Black Civil Rights*. Princeton, N.J.: Princeton University Press, 2003.

Tucker, Lauren R. "Black, White, and Read All Over: Radical Reasoning and the Construction of Public Reaction to the O.J. Simpson Criminal Trial Verdict by the Chicago Tribune and the Chicago Defender." *Howard Journal of Communications* 8 (October–December 1997): 315–27.

Ullman, Victor. *Martin R. Delaney: The Beginning of Black Nationalism*. Boston: Beacon Press, 1971.

Valentino, Nicholas A. "Crime News and the Priming of Racial Attitudes During Evaluations of the President." *Public Opinion Quarterly* 63 (1999): 293–320.

Vincent, Theodore G., ed. *Voices of a Black Nation: Political Journalism in the Harlem Renaissance*. San Francisco: Ramparts Press, 1973.

Virtanen, S.V. and L. Huddy. "Old Fashioned Racism and New Forms of Racial Prejudice." *Journal of Politics* 60 (1998): 311–32.

Wachtel, Paul L. *Race in the Mind of America*. New York: Routledge, 1999.

Waerden, Stanley T., Barbara J. Hipsman and John Greenman. "Racial Diversity in the College Newsroom." *Newspaper Research Journal* 11 (Summer 1990): 80–95.

Ward, Brian. *Media, Culture, and the Modern American Freedom Struggle*. Gainesville, Fla.: University Press of Florida, 2002.

Ward, Brian. *Radio and the Struggle for Civil Rights in the South*. Gainesville, Fla.: University Press of Florida, 2004.

"Washington Post Reporter Disowns Pulitzer: Resigns." *Jet* 60 (30 April 1981): 12.

Weill, Susan. *In a Madhouse's Din: Civil Rights Coverage by Mississippi's Daily Press, 1948–1968*. Westport, Conn.: Praeger, 2002.

Wenner, Lawrence A. "The Good, the Bad, and the Ugly: Race, Sport, and the Public Eye." *Journal of Sport & Social Issues* 19 (1995): 227–31.

West, Cornel. *Race Matters*. Boston: Beacon Press, 1993.

Whittemore, Katherine and Gerald Marzorati, eds. *Voices in Black and White: Writings on Race in America from Harper's Magazine*. New York: Franklin Square Press, 1993.

Wilkie, Curtis. "Too Hot to Handle: The Mississippi Story Editors Wouldn't Touch." *Washington Journalism Review* 2 (March 1984): 38–58.

Williams, Julian. "The Truth Shall Make You Free: The *Mississippi Free Press*, 1961–63." *Journalism History* 332 (Summer 2006): 106–13.

Williams, Linda. *Playing the Race Card: Melodramas of Black and White from Uncle Tom to O.J. Simpson*. Princeton, N.J.: Princeton University Press, 2001.

Williams, Linda D. "Sportswomen in Black and White: Sports History from an Afro-American Perspective." In *Women, Media, and Sport: Challenging Gender Values*, ed. by Pamela Creedon. Thousand Oaks, Calif.: Sage, 1994.

Selected Bibliography

Williamson, Don. "From the Minority View." *The Masthead* 33 (Fall 1981): 22–23.

Wilson, Clint. *Black Journalists in Paradox: Historical Perspectives and Current Dilemmas.* Westport, Conn.: Greenwood Press, 1991.

Wilson, Clint and Felix Gutierrez. *Minorities and Media: Diversity and the End of Mass Communication.* Beverly Hills, Calif.: Sage, 1985.

Wilson, David. *Inventing Black-on-Black Violence: Discourse, Space, and Representation.* Syracuse, N.Y.: Syracuse University Press, 2005.

Wilson, William J. *When Work Disappears: The World of the New Urban Poor.* New York: Knopf, 1996.

Wolseley, Roland E. *The Black Press, U.S.A.* Ames, Iowa: Iowa State University Press, 1990.

Wong, William. "Covering the Invisible 'Model Minority.'" *Media Studies Journal* 8 (Summer 1994): 49–60.

Zilber, Jeremy. *Racialized Coverage of Congress: The News in Black and White.* Westport, Conn.: Praeger, 2000.

Zook, Krystal Brent. *Color by Fox: The Fox Network and the Revolution in Black Television.* New York: Oxford University Press, 1999.

Index

Page numbers in **bold** indicate main entries.

ABC, 9, 10, 11, 59, 116, 117, 154, 155, 232, 233, 251, 269, 270, 286, 290, 299, 334, 351, 384, 404, 407, 413, 439, 445, 460, 474, 538; ABC News, 10, 56, 60, 61, 117, 284, 285, 289, 297, 333, 403, 407, 433, 472, 473, 487, 491; ABC NewsOne, 487; ABC 7, 49, 179, 314; Radio Network, 61, 204, 235, 279, 355, 488, 536; WABC, 55, 204, 479; WJLA, 43, 49
"About Us: The Dignity of Children" program, 539
Abu-Jamal, Mumia, **1–4**; *All Things Censored*, 3; in Black Panther Party, 1; *Death Blossom: Reflections from a Prisoner of Conscience*, 3; on death row, 1–3; *Faith of Our Fathers: An Examination of the Spiritual Life of African and African-American People*, 3; *Live from Death Row*, 3; Peabody Award, 2; in WDAS-FM, 2; *We Want Freedom: A Life in the Black Panther Party*, 3
Adams, John Quincy, 61
Adams-Wade, Norma, **4–6**; Juanita Craft Award, 5; Lifetime Achievement Award, 5
Affirmative action, 34, 45, 65, 76, 172, 174, 288, 356, 400, 452, 453, 476, 521, 525, 536
Afghanistan War, 198, 281
African Arts Magazine, 365
Agnew, Ronnie, **6–8**; at *Cincinnati Enquirer*, 7; at *Hattiesburg American*, 7; at *Sun Herald*, 7
Akron Press Club, 135
"Alan Keyes: A Political Hit Man," 288–89
Alexander-Sellers, Tina, **9**; chamber of commerce Pinnacle Award, 9; Inside East Texas, monthly public affairs program, 9; at KTRE-TV, 9; Outstanding Community Service award, 9; Outstanding Woman in Broadcasting award, 9; Woman of the Year, 9
"All My Children" episodes, 532

"All Things Considered," 45, 66, 84, 85, 96, 134, 161, 243, 290, 333, 334, 511, 525, 536
"All Together Now," 88
Allen, Ron, **9–11**; Associated Press awards, 10; for CBS News, 10; Emmy, 10; George Foster Peabody Award, 10; on Hurricane Hugo, 10; National Headliner award, 10; Overseas Press Club award, 10; Robert F. Kennedy award, 10; on Rwandan genocide, 10; UPI award, 10
"A.M. Chicago," 538
"Amazon Women on the Moon," 169
American Copy Editors Society, 17
"American Morning," 335, 336
American Prospect, 185, 423, 424
American Society of Newspaper Editors (ASNE), 13, 17, 47, 48, 73, 74, 111, 135, 171, 177, 181, 194, 301, 306, 318, 322, 369, 397, 399, 426, 483, 543
"American Stories," 179
American's Black Forum, 44, 116, 299, 520, 524
Amsterdam News, 139, 140
Anderson, Monroe, **11–12**; *Chicago Tribune*, reporter for, 11; *National Observer*, writer for, 11; *Savoy* magazine, editor, 11; UPI's best community service award (1980), 12
Anderson Independent, 394
Andrews, Caesar, **12–13**; *Detroit Free Press*, executive editor of, 12; *Florida Today*, staff writer for, 12; *Reporter*, executive editor of, 12; *Rockland Journal-News*, executive editor of, 12; *Tribune*, managing editor of, 12
Angolite, 397–98
"Another Viewpoint" column, 255
AOL, 130, 343, 430, 448, 540
AOL Black Voices, 230, 423
"Archie Bunker Paradigm," 293, 294

Index

"Architecture Is a Gumbo of Cultures" column, 121
Arkansas Democrat, 290
"The Armstrong Williams Show" radio talk show, 520
"The Arsenio Hall Show" program, 169, 539
"Arson for Profit," (film), 172
Asim, Jabari, **13–16**; *Drumvoices Revue* journal, assistant editor of, 13; *Eyeball*, founding editor of, 13; *Phoenix Gazette*, commentaries in, 13; *Post-Dispatch*, copy editing for the editorial section, 13; *Washington Post Book World*, senior editor of, 13
ASNE. *See* American Society of Newspaper Editors
"At Bob Jones U., A Disturbing Lesson about the Real George W" column, 216–17
Atlanta Constitution, 206
Atlanta Daily World, 28, 99
Atlanta Journal, 206, 481
Atlanta Journal & Constitution, 7, 104, 121, 143, 190, 230, 394, 480, 522
Atlanta Olympics terrorist bombing, 269, 270
Atlanta Voice, 174
Atlantic Monthly, 31
Attleboro Sun, 499
Aubespin, Mervin Raymond, **16–19**; Black College Communication Association award, 17; in the *Courier-Journal*, 17; Ida B. Wells Award for leadership, 18; Kentucky Journalism Hall of Fame in 1995, 17; at the *Louisville Courier-Journal*, 16; NABJ Hall of Fame in 1994, inducted into, 17; 1991 Distinguished Service to Journalism Award, 17
Austin American-Statesman, 287

Baghdad bombing, 433
Bailey, Isaac J., 21–23; *Charlotte Observer*, freelancing for, 21; *Sun News*, business editor of, 21
Baltimore Afro-American, 254, 255, 417
Baltimore Evening Sun, 104, 209, 297, 311, 441, 509
Baltimore Sun, 78, 136, 143, 390, 396, 475
Baquet, Dean P., **23–25**; *Chicago Tribune*, 23; Hurricane Katrina, coverage by, 23; John Jay Award, 25; *Los Angeles Times*, editor of, 23; Pulitzer Prize, 23; as *Times*' executive vice president, 23; *Times-Picayune*, editor of, 23
Basketball Digest, 370
"Battle Ready" column, 510–11
Bay Street Independent newspaper, 87
Bayé, Betty Winston, 25–27; for *Courier-Journal*, 25
BBC, National Public Radio, 381
Beacon Journal, 72, 73, 134, 135, 320, 375, 436, 437
"Before Women Had Wings," 538
"Beloved," 538
"The Belva Davis Show" on station KDIA, 87
Bennett, Lerone, **27–30**; American Book Awards' Lifetime Achievement Award, 29; at *Atlanta Daily World*, 28; *Before the Mayflower*, book, 28; Carter G. Woodson Lifetime Achievement Award, 29; *Forced Into Glory: Abraham Lincoln's White Dream*, book, 28; *Jackson Advocate*, 27; Lamplighter Award for Corporate Leadership, 29; Literature Award of the American Academy of Arts and Letters in 1978, 29; *Mississippi Enterprise*, 27; Salute to Greatness Award, 29; *What Manner of Man*, production, 28
"Benson" show, 228
"BET News with Ed Gordon," 155
"BET Nightly News," 229
"BET Tonight," 155
BET Weekend newspaper, 63
"Beyond the Norm" column, 262
Big Red News, 115
Black College Wire, 461, 462
Black Enterprise Magazine, 107, 115, 123, 156, 200, 243, 277, 355, 495, 509
Black Entertainment Television, 60, 63, 74, 96, 131, 154, 227, 251, 283, 368, 389, 401, 415, 441, 445, 476, 509, 536
"Black in White America," 289
Black Muslims, 99
Black Panther Party, 1, 53, 88, 345, 461
"Black Perspective on the News" program, 262
Black Sports magazine, 162
Black Stars, 225
Black World magazine, 65, 225
Black X-Press Info-Paper, 341
BlackAmericaWeb.com, 91, 92, 236
Blackistone, Kevin B., **30–33**; as a *Boston Globe* reporter, 30; with the *Chicago Reporter*, 30; for the *Dallas Morning News*, 30
Blackside Inc., 281
Blade, 41
Blade of Toledo, 40
Bloomberg Markets magazine, 108
Bombing of Kosovo, 104
Boston Globe, 30, 139, 184, 186, 215, 262, 271, 297, 320, 422, 489
Boston Herald-American, 209
Boston Phoenix, 348
Boyd, Gerald M., **33–35**; for *Atlantic Monthly*, 31; *The New York Times*, 33
Bradley, Edward "Ed" R., **35–37**; Alfred I. DuPont-Columbia University award, 36; for "CBS Reports," 36; George Foster Peabody Award, 36; George Foster Peabody Broadcasting Award, 36; Lifetime Achievement Emmy, 36; National Association of Media Women's Distinguished Commentator Award, 36; NCAA Anniversary Award, 36; Overseas Press Club Award, 36; Paul White Award, 36; Peabody Award, 36; Pioneers in Broadcasting Award, 36; Robert F. Kennedy Journalism Award, 36; "60 Minutes" correspondent, 35; Sol Taischoff Award, 36; WCBS radio, 35
"Breaking the Silence" NPR series, 536
Britt, Donna, **37–40**; for the *Detroit Free Press*, 37; joining *USA Today*, 37; in the *New York Times*, 38
"Broadening the View" column, 490–91

Index

Brower, William A., **40–43**; *Blade of Toledo*, 40; for the *Norwalk Journal & Guide*, 40; *Philadelphia Afro-American*, editor of, 41; *Richmond Afro-American*, 41
Brown, James, **43–44**
Brown, William Anthony "Tony," **44–46**; American Psychiatrists Association's Solomon Fuller Award, 46; *Black Lies, White Lies*, book, 45; Black Psychologists' Community Service Award, 46; *Detroit Courier*, 44; Frederick Douglass Liberation Award, 46; International Key Women of America Award, 46; National Urban League Public Service Award, 46; Operation PUSH Communicator for Freedom Award, 46; on WNET-TV, 45
Buchanan, Patrick, 116, 173, 196, 401, 446, 526
"Buffalo Soldiers Wrapped in Steel," 249
Bulletin, 449
Bunting, Kenneth F., **47–49**; at the *Corpus Christi Caller-Times*, 47; with the *Post-Intelligencer*, 47
Bunyon, Maureen, **49–50**; Emmy awards, 50; founder of International Women's Media Foundation, 50; founder of the National Association of Black Journalists, 50; Immigrant Achievement Award, 50; for the *Milwaukee Journal*, 50; Ted Yates Award, 50; Women in Communications Matrix Award, 50
Burial of Palestinian leader Yasser Arafat, 336
Bush, George W., 4, 47, 76, 151, 193, 196, 197, 245, 279, 286, 288, 291, 293, 334, 345, 360, 385, 401, 411, 424, 438, 449, 485, 494, 502, 521, 529, 544; administration, 38, 74, 75, 101, 104, 130, 136, 222, 244, 263, 272, 322, 332, 337–38, 352, 359, 504, 506; No Child Left Behind policies, 60, 100–101, 520; and Iraq War, 84, 90, 117, 173, 181, 192, 215, 222, 262, 427, 435, 453, 497; polarizing influence, 84; Social Security plan, 119, 282; tax policies, 57, 151, 386; war on terrorism, 251, 474, 496
"Bush Helped the Terrorists Gain Mileage from Attacks" column, 498–99
Business Tokyo, 107
BusinessWeek Online, 200

Caldwell, Earl, **51–54**; The Caldwell Chronicle radio feature, 51, 54; as a CBS Radio Network commentator on Spectrum, 54; *Herald Tribune*'s city editor, 52
Caldwell Chronicle radio feature, 51, 54
Call & Post, 184
Callaloo journal, 121
Cape Cod Times, 150–51
Capehart, Jonathan, **54–56**; Angel Award of GMAD, 55; *Daily News*, work at, 54; George Polk Award, 55; Pulitzer Prize, 55; Today Show researcher at NBC, 54; WABC-TV's political pundit, 55; at WNYC Foundation, 54
"Capital Sunday" at ABC7/WJLA-TV, 179
Carol Publishing Group of Secaucus, 515
Carter, Jimmy, 36, 88, 99, 151, 211, 245, 357, 419, 446, 491, 509

"The Cathy Hughes Show" Own daily talk program, 201
CBS, 9, 35, 43, 76, 85, 96, 106, 161, 162, 165, 167, 170, 269–70, 346, 352, 358, 364, 365, 389, 409, 433, 491; CBS News, 10, 75, 168, 248, 269, 358, 359, 368, 388, 433, 467, 468, 491; CBS Sports, 43; CBS4, 492; KCBS radio, 324; KCBS-TV, 198, 324, 388; KTVT, 468; Radio Network, 10, 54; WBBM-TV, 11, 158, 248, 338, 414; WBCS-TV, 192, 198; WUSA-TV, 50
"CBS Evening News," 36, 106, 316, 346, 357, 364, 388,491
"CBS News Sunday Morning," 106, 316, 363, 364
"CBS Reports," 36
"CBS Sunday Night News," 36, 316
"Cedric's Story," network special, 285
"The Changing Face of America" NPR project, 524
Charleston Gazette, 184
Charlotte Observer, 21, 78, 104, 305, 475
Chicago Daily Defender, 124
Chicago Daily News, 340
Chicago Defender, 254, 287, 340, 461
Chicago Reporter, 30
Chicago Sun-Times, 220, 312, 393, 394, 429, 430, 457, 543
Chicago Tribune, 11, 23, 74, 220, 333, 337, 505, 543
Chideya, Farai, **56–59**; AlterNet New Media Hero, 58; Gay and Lesbian Alliance Against Defamation award, 58; GLAAD Award, 58; Marketing Opportunities in Business and Entertainment Internet and Technology award, 58; *Newsweek Magazine*, 56; as a political analyst for CNN, BET, MSNBC and Fox, 57; PopandPolitics.com, 56; Pulitzer Prize winner, 58; *Vibe* and *Spin*, music for, 57; *Vibe* magazine, correspondent for, 57; Young Lion award, 58; Young Women of Achievement award, 58; Your Call, a talk/interview, host of, 57
Chirac, Jacques, 3
Christmas Kindness South Africa program, 539
Ciara, Barbara, **59–60**; Edward R. Murrow Award, 60; Emmy nomination, 60; Excel awards, 60; Pilot 13 News, 59; *Virginian-Pilot* newspaper and cable television, 59; for WAVY-TV, 59; WTKRNewsChannel 3 managing editor and primary anchor for, 59; WVEC-TV, 59
Cincinnati Enquirer, 7, 311, 337, 396, 481
City Sun, 264
Civil rights, 7, 16, 25, 28, 35, 52, 99, 101, 183, 218, 221, 222, 258, 282, 345, 368, 385, 417, 491
Civil War, 17, 18, 79, 274, 457, 528, 529
Claiborne, Ron, **60–62**; Emmy for reporting on the Elian Gonzalez controversy, 62; Good Morning America weekend edition anchor for, 60; *Los Angeles Sentinel* article, 61; for the *New York Daily News*, 61; *Richmond Independent*, 61; at WNYW-TV in New York, 61

Index

Clarion-Ledger, 6, 7, 212, 291
Clinkscales, Keith T., **62–64**; American Advertising Federation Hall of Fame, 64; *BET Weekend* newspaper, 63; for *Fortune*, 63; Savoy Life, 63; for *Sports Illustrated*, 63; *Vibe*, 62
Clinton, Hillary, 104, 119, 281, 297, 357, 408, 489
Clinton, William, 29, 55, 57, 74, 104, 131, 163, 170, 172, 173, 197, 226, 227, 351, 409, 458, 509; impeachment story, 248, 251, 281, 433, 440, 500; reaction to 9/11 attacks, 150
CLM Global News Group, 1
CNN, 11, 37, 55, 117, 127, 150, 167, 168, 179, 195, 208, 281, 290, 302, 324, 335, 336, 359, 373, 377, 378, 390, 432, 433–34, 445, 472, 473, 487, 493, 494, 503, 525; D.C. bureau, 127, 281; News Group, 168; Headline News, 324, 329, 456
"CNN and Company" show, 279
"CNN Live Today," 179
"CNN/Sports Illustrated," 195
"Cobb: A Detroit Legend" (documentary), 249
Cockfield, Errol A. Jr., **64–66**; *Black World*, 65; *Los Angeles Times*, 65; *Newsday*, 64
"The Color Purple" (movie), 538
Columbia University, 95
Comcast Networks, 131, 203, 414
Commercial Appeal, 425, 474–75
"Common Ground" program, 182
Communicator, 311
"Conversation with Ed Gordon" interview program, 155
Cooper, Desiree, **66–68**; *Detroit Free Press* columnist, 66
Corley, Cheryl, **68–69**; for NPR station WCBU, 68; at WEEK-TV, an NBC affiliate station, 68
Corpus Christi Caller-Times, 47
"The Cosby Show" program, 539
Courier-Journal, 17, 25, 94, 190, 212, 311, 396
Courier-Post, 92
"Court TV" program, 233
Cox Community Newspapers, 180
Creators Syndicate, 118, 287, 453, 533
The Cricket, 70
"Crime Scene," 190
Crisis magazine, 84, 125, 220, 518, 519
Crouch, Stanley, **69–72**; *Ain't No Ambulances for No Nigguhs Tonight*, a collection of poetry, 70; *The All American Skin Game, Or, the Decoy of Race*, 70; *Daily News*, 71–72; for *JazzTimes* magazine, 70; *Los Angeles Free Press*, *The Cricket* and the *SoHo Weekly News*, 70; *New York Daily News* columnist, 69; *Notes of a Hanging Judge* book, 70; for the *Village Voice*, 70
Crutchfield, James N., **72–73**; in *Beacon Journal* in Akron, 72; for the *Detroit Free Press*, 72; *Philadelphia Inquirer*, 72; for the *Pittsburgh Press*, 72; Pulitzer Prize competition, 73
"A Current Affair" show, 129, 130, 450

Curry, George E., **73–78**; correspondent for the *Chicago Tribune*, 74; as a *Sports Illustrated* reporter, 74
Curtis, Mary Cecelia, **78–80**; *Arizona Daily Star*, 78; *Charlotte Observer*, 78; Green Eyeshade Award, 79; *New York Times*, 78; *Observer* weekly columnist, 78; *Sun* staff, 78; Thomas Wolfe Award, 79

Daily Argus, 91
Daily Cardinal, 139
Daily Challenge, 115
Daily Kent Stater, 300
Daily Local News, 375
Daily News, 54, 71–72, 176, 192, 204, 212
Daily Press in Newport News, associate editor for, 92
Dallas Morning News, 4, 30, 302, 321, 379, 401; *Quick*, 97
Dallas Times Herald, 370
Dallas Weekly, 267
Dash, Leon DeCosta Jr., **81–83**; Award from the National Council on Crime and Delinquency, 83; George Polk Award, 83; 1996 Emmy Award, 83; Honors received, 83; PEN/Martha Albrand citation, 83; President's Award for excellence in reporting urban affairs from the Washington Independent Writers, 83; Robert F. Kennedy book award, 83; *Rosa Lee: A Mother and Her Family in Urban America* book, 82; *The Shame of the Prisons*, book project, 81; Social Services Administration's Distinguished Service Award, 83; UNITA guerilla movement, reporting, 81; *Washington Post*, as a copy boy, 81; *When Children Want Children*, 81
"David and Lisa," 538
Davidson, Joe, **83–85**; "All Things Considered" National Public Radio, commentary for, 84; BET.com, political columnist for, 84; *District Extra*, as editor of, 84; *Focus Magazine*, editor of, 84; "Morning Edition," National Public Radio, commentary for, 84; Pulitzer Prize juror, 84; Trailblazer Award, 85; *Wall Street Journal*, correspondent for, 84; *Washington Post's District Extra*, editor of, 84
Davis, Allison J., **85–86**; Boston's WBZ, reporter for, 85; Emmy nominations, 86; *Global News: Perspectives on the Information Age*, book, 86; at KDKA-TV in Pittsburgh, 85; KingWorld, vice president–creative of, 86; MSNBC online, executive producer of, 85; NBC News' "Today" show, writer/producer for, 85; "NBC Nightly News," 85; 1997 Boston University's Distinguished Alumni Award for Service, 86; "The Reading Club," an educational venture of PBS, 85; "The Scholastic NBC News Video," originated and produced, 85; "The Science of Sport" (documentary), 85; Women in Communication awards, 86
Davis, Belva, **86–89**; "All Together Now," televised public affairs shows, hosting, 88; at *Bay Street Independent* newspaper, 87; Belva Davis Diversity Scholarship awarded, 89; "The Belva Davis Show,"

Index

on station KDIA, 87; Emmy awards, 89; KRON-TV, narrator and consultant for documentaries for, 86; at KQED-TV, 86; Lifetime Achievement Award from the International Women's Media Foundation, 89; Lifetime Achievement Award, 89; Lifetime Achievement ward of the National Association of Black Journalists, 89; PBS station KQED, anchoring the news shows, 88; *Sun Reporter*, columnist and women's editor, 88

Davis, Merlene, **89–91**; *Herald-Leader*, as a reporter, 90; Lyman T. Johnson Alumni Association award from the University of Kentucky, 90; 2003 National Headliners Award competition for column writing, 90; Women of Achievement Award, 90; YMCA's 2002 Black Achievers Community Achievers Award, 90

Dawkins, Wayne J., **91–93**; BlackAmericaWeb.com, contributing editor for, 91; BlackAmericaWeb.com, managing editor of, 92; *Courier-Post* in Camden/Cherry Hill, reporter for, 92; *Daily Argus* in Mount Vernon, reporter for, 91; *Daily Press* in Newport News, associate editor for, 92; *The NABJ Story*, 92; *Post-Tribune* in Gary, Indiana, editor for, 92; received awards from Columbia University, 92; *Rugged Waters: Black Journalists Swim the Mainstream*, 92; Thomas Fortune Lifetime Achievement Award, 92; "Tom Joyner Morning Show" hosting, 92; Trans-Urban News Service in Brooklyn, reporter for, 91

Days, Michael, **93–95**; at *Courier-Journal* in Louisville, Kentucky, 94; *Democrat and Chronicle*, as a journalist, 94; on NJN Public Television, 95; *Philadelphia Daily News*, editor and executive vice president of, 93; 2005 Pulitzer Prize, 94; at *Wall Street Journal*, 94

Dayton Daily News, 99

Dayton Express, 180

The Deep End of the Ocean, novel, 539

Defender, 147

Deggans, Eric, **95–99**; Best Newspaper Columnist, 96; Chuck Stone Award, 96; Columbia University, speaker at, 95; Emmy awards, 96; finalist for criticism in the Atlanta Society of Professional Journalists' Green Eyeshade Award competition, 96; Let's Do It Better! Award, 96; *Pittsburgh Press*, as a reporter for, 95; racial sensitivity training program creation for the State Troopers Academy in Pennsylvania, 95; *St. Petersburg Times*, as full-time media critic for, 95; "The Tavis Smiley Show" Black Entertainment Television, appearance on, 96; "The Tony Cox Show," 96; *Times* columnist and editorial writer, 95

Delaney, Paul, **99–100**; "as the *Times*" Madrid bureau chief, 99; *Atlanta Daily World*, reporter for, 99; "Was Columbus a Whiner?" story by, 99; *Dayton Daily News*, reporter for, 99; New York club, founded by 1924, 100; *New York Times*, correspondent and editor of, 99; on Palestine Liberation Organization, 99; *Our World News*, editor for, 100

Democrat and Chronicle, 94, 374

Denver Post, 172, 173, 320, 430

"Desperate Housewives" in 2004 program, 539

"Detroit Black Journal" public affairs show, 155

Detroit Courier, 44

Detroit Free Press, 12, 37, 66, 72, 172, 301, 306, 494

Detroit News, 190, 311

"A Dialog with Whitey," 491

Discovery Channel, 335, 389, 414, 415

District Extra, as editor of, 84

"Disturbing Turn for Shock and Awe" column, 310–11

Diuguid, Lewis Walter, **100–102**; joined the *Star*, 100; *Kansas City Star*, columnist for, 100; 2000 Missouri Honor Medal for Distinguished Service in Journalism, 101

"Dividing Line" column, 501

"Dr. Phil Show," 540

Donovan, Kyle, **102–3**; business schools of Columbia University, speaker at, 103; Envy Publishing Group and launched *NV* magazine, 102; Howard University, speaker at, 103; a member of the U.S. delegation, 103; University of Pennsylvania, speaker at, 103

Douglas, William, **104–6**; *Charlotte Observer*, general assignment reporter for, 104; *Newsday*, reported for, 104; *Newsday*, staff of, 104; *Observer*, education beat for, 104

Dow, Harold, **106–7**; as CBS reporter, 106; "48 Hours" show, CBS correspondent for, 106–7; KCOP-TV in Los Angeles, freelance reporting for, 106; at KETV in Omaha, 106; as Los Angeles bureau correspondent, 106; Theta Cable TV in Santa Monica, a reporter and anchor for, 106; WPAT Radio in Paterson, a news anchor for, 106

Dreyfuss, Joel P., **107–9**; *Black Enterprise* magazine, editor of, 107; *Bloomberg Markets* magazine, as senior editor and writer for, 108; *Business Tokyo*, managing editor of, 107; *Fortune* magazine, as associate editor of, 107; at *Fortune* as a senior editor, 107; *InformationWeek*, editor-in-chief and later editorial director and associate publisher of 107; in KPIX-TV station, 107; as *New York Post* reporter, 107; *Our World News*, an online weekly, editor of, 107; *PC Magazine*, editor-in-chief of, 107; as Pulitzer Prize juror, 108; *Red Herring* magazine, editor-in-chief of, 107; *Red Herring*, editor-in-chief of, 108; *Urban Box Office*, editor-in-chief of, 107; *Washington Post*, reported for the, 107

Drumvoices Revue journal, 13

Dunlap, Karen Brown, **110–13**; Best Newspaper Writing series, editing and contribution to, 110; *The Editorial Eye*, coauthor of, 110; *The Effective Editor: How to Lead Your Staff to Better Writing and Teamwork*, cowritten, 110; at *Florida Trend*, regional business

565

Index

magazine, 110; *Nashville Banner*, minority youth program, as associate editor of, 110; as a Pulitzer Prize juror, 111; *St. Petersburg Times*, a staff writer for, 110; *St. Petersburg Times, Congressional Quarterly*, owner of, 110; University of Tennessee's Hileman Award, 111; *Warner Robins Enterprise*, editor of, 110

"Early Edition," 179
Ebony Jr., 225
Ebony magazine, 11, 27, 46, 125, 132, 148, 221, 224–25, 267, 317, 336, 356, 363, 390, 393, 405
Ebony South Africa, 225
"The Edge with Carlos Watson" interview specials, 494
Edmond, Alfred Adam, Jr., 115–16; at *Black Enterprise*, 115; *Big Red News*, as managing editor, 115; *Black Enterprise* magazine, editor-in-chief and senior vice president of, 115; *Daily Challenge*, associate editor of, 115; Griot Award from the New York Association of Black Journalists, 116; Lincoln University's Unity Award for Excellence in Media, 116; *MBM/Modern Black Men Magazine*, senior editor of, 115; at *Rutgers Alumni Magazine*, 116; at *Teenpreneur*, 115
"Educational Fraud" column, 534–35
Edwards, Tamala, **116–18**; ABC News, correspondent for, 117; CNN's "Take Five," panelist on, 117; *Time Magazine's* bureau, as a reporter at, 116; "World News Now" anchor of, 116; "World News This Morning" anchor of, 116; WPVI-TV, news anchor at, 116
Eisenhower, Dwight, 101, 154, 186, 226
Elder, Laurence (Larry) A., 118–20; *Is Bill Cosby Right? Or Has the Black Middle Class Lost Its Mind?* book, 119; on KABC Talk Radio in Los Angeles, 118; on "Larry King Live," talk show, 118; "Oprah," talk show, 118; PBS and Fox, hosting a talk show for, 118; "60 Minutes" profiled on, 118
"Eleanor: The Life and Times of Eleanor Roosevelt" (documentary), 220
Elie, Lolis Eric, **120–22**; "Architecture Is a Gumbo of Cultures," column, 121; *Atlanta Journal & Constitution*, reporter at, 121; *Cornbread Nation 2: the United States of Barbecue*, authored barbecue book, 121; in *Callaloo* journal, 121; *Smokestack Lightning: Adventures in the Heart of Barbecue Country*, book, 121; *Times-Picayune* columnist, 120
"Ellen," program, 539
Ellington, E. David, **122–24**; *Black Enterprise* magazine's Entrepreneurs Award for having been Innovator of the Year, 123
EM:Ebony Man, 225
Emerge, 278
"Emery King Show," 249
Empire State Pride Agenda group, 55
"Entertainment Tonight," program, 539
Envy Publishing Group, 102

ESPN, 165, 195, 390, 407, 430–31, 432, 506, 511, 516, 517
"ESPN Sports Century," 524
ESPN The Magazine, 430
ESPN.com, 430, 431, 514, 516
ESPN2, 431
Essence Communications, 260, 261, 447, 448, 471, 472, 495
Essence magazine, 260, 495–96
Estes-Sumpter, Sidmel Karen, **124–25**; *Chicago Daily Defender*, reporter for, 124; "Good Day, Atlanta" executive producer of, 124; at Guam Cable TV, 124; Lifetime Achievement award, 125; Media Woman of the Year, 125; Pioneer Black Journalist Award, 125; WAGA-TV/Fox Five News, 124
Evening Sun, 311
Eyeball, 13

Fancher, Faith, **127–29**; in CNN's D.C. bureau, 127; KTVU-TV station, on the 10 o'clock news, coanchoring, 127; 1998 Excalibur Award, 128; 1993 Beverly Johnson Award, 128; Scripps-Howard Foundation's National Award for Journalistic Excellence in Radio News, 128; Sojourner Truth Award, 128; at WSM-TV station, 127
"Farewell; It's Time to Keep a Promise" column, 294–95
Faulkner, Harris, **129–30**; "A Current Affair" show, correspondent for, 129; *Breaking News: God Has a Plan. An Anchorwoman's Journey Through Faith*, 130; Emmy awards, 130; Fox News, news anchor of, 129; "Harris Faulkner Show," hosting, 130; KCLP-TV, reporter for, 129; *L.A. Weekly*, freelance business writer for, 129; at WDAF-TV, 129; WNCT-TV, as a general assignment reporter at, 129
"Feeding the Greedy, Starving the Needy" column, 280–81
Fennell, Arthur, **131–32**
Ferguson, Renee, **132–33**; American Women in Radio and Television's Gracie Award, 133; as CBS reporter, 132; Best Investigative Reporting Award, 133; *Indianapolis News*, as a reporter for, 132; National Alfred I. DuPont-Columbia Award, 133; NBC5 News at WMAQ-TV, general-assignment reporter for, 132; WBBM-TV, reported at, 132; WLWI-TV, reporter at, 132
Field Newspaper Syndicate, 418
Fields, Michael, **133–34**; "Jihad in America," PBS documentary, producer of, 134
"The Fifth Quarter" sports show, 287
"Find Heroes Elsewhere" column, 507–8
Fitzpatrick, Albert E., **134–36**; in Akron Press Club from, 135; American Journalism Historians Association Local Journalists Award, 135; *Beacon Journal*, reporter for, 135; Community Service Award from Kent State University, 135; Frederick Douglass Lifetime Achievement Award, 135; Ida B. Wells Award, 135; as NABJ's executive director, 135;

Index

NABJ Hall of Fame, inducted into, 136; Outstanding Alumnus Award, 135; Robert G. McGruder Award, 135
"Flashpoint: On the Road to Mackinac," 249
"Flashpoints with Bryant Gumbel and Gwen Ifill," 209
Fletcher, Michael A., **136–39**; *Washington Post*, reporter for the, 136; World Trade Center disaster examined by, 136
Florida Times-Union, 496
Florida Today, 12, 212
Florida Trend, regional business magazine, 110
"Focus," 250
Focus Magazine, 84
Ford, Gerald, 211, 342, 452
Fort Worth Star-Telegram, 276
Fortune magazine, 63, 107, 230, 478, 501, 525
"48 Hours," 106–7, 198, 199, 409
Fox, 43, 44, 57, 118, 129, 130, 150, 159, 168, 169, 199, 389
"Fox & Friends," 158, 159, 299, 336
Fox News, 55, 129, 130, 149, 158, 159, 168, 256, 279, 298, 299, 331, 355, 388, 401, 456, 502, 524, 525
"Fox News Sunday with Tony Snow," panelist on, 524
Fox Sports, 44
Fraser, Charles Gerald Jr., **139–42**; at *Amsterdam News*, 139; as a *Boston Globe* copy boy, 139; *Daily Cardinal*, wrote for the student paper of, 139; lifetime achievement award by the New York Association of Black Journalists, 140; at the *New York Daily News* and *The New York Times*, 139; *San Diego Earth Times*, writer for, 139
"The Freedom Train" (documentary), 249
"The Fresh Prince of Bel-Air" program, 539
Fulwood, Sam III, **143–45**; for *Atlanta Journal & Constitution*, 143; at *Baltimore Sun*, 143; Livingston Award for international reporting and, 144; *Los Angeles Times* as a Washington reporter for, 143; *Plain Dealer*, columnist for, 143; Salute to Excellence Award, 144; *Waking from the Dream: My Life in the Black Middle Class*, book, 143
FXT-TV, 281

Gannett News Service, 7, 12, 25, 176, 190, 213, 261, 291, 296, 311, 374, 396, 437, 508
Gentleman's Quarterly, 516
Georgia News Network/WGST, 372
Gibson, Althea, 14
Gilliam, Dorothy Pearl Butler, **147–49**; at *Defender*, 147; at *Ebony* magazine, 148; *Jet*, associate editor, 147; *Post*, freelance for, 148; *Tri-State Defender*, a reporter for, 147; *Washington Post*, 147; WTTG-TV talk show, 148
Goler, Wendell, **149–50**; FOX News, correspondent for, 149; WKHM radio station, director for, 149; at WRC radio in Washington, 149

Gonsalves, Sean, **150–52**; *Cape Cod Times*, reporter/columnist with, 150–51
"Good Day, Atlanta," 124
"Good Day Street Talk" show, 298
"Good Morning America," 60, 243, 539
Goode, Malvin "Mal" Russell, **153–54**; *Pittsburgh Courier*'s circulation department, 153
Gordon, Ed, **154–56**; Award of Excellence, 156; "BET News with Ed Gordon," anchoring, 155; "BET Tonight," 155; Communication Excellence to Black Audiences award, 156; "Conversation with Ed Gordon" interview program, 155; "Detroit Black Journal" public affairs show, hosting, 155; "Lead Story," 155; "On Point with Ed Gordon," talk radio with ABC show, 155; Outstanding Man of the Year award, 156; "60 Minutes" on CBS, 155; at WTVS, Channel 56 in Detroit, 155
Governing Magazine, 536
Graham Williams Group, 520
Graves, Earl Gilbert, **156–58**; *Black Enterprise* magazine, founder of, 156; *FOLIO*'s 1996 award, 157
Green, Lauren, **158–59**
The Grist, 333
Grosvenor, Vertamae, **159–61**; Communications Excellence to Black America award, 161; duPont-Columbia Award, 161; in the *National Geographic Explorer* series documentary "Gullah," 160; National Association of Black Journalists award, 161; Ohio State Award, 161
Guam Cable TV, 124
Gumbel, Bryant, **161–64**; Emmy, 162; NAACP Presidents Award, 162; Overseas Press Club's Edward R. Murrow Award, 162; "Today Show," 162; with *Black Sports* magazine, 162
Gumbel, Greg, **165–66**; "SportsCenter," coanchoring, 165

Hair, Princell, **167–68**; at CNN, 167; at KCBS-TV, 167; at Orlando's Channel 6, WCPXTV, 167; at WBBM-TV, 167; at WMAQ-TV, 167; at WPLG-TV, 167; for WBAL-TV in Baltimore, 167
"The Half Hour Comedy Hour" 169
Hall, Arsenio, **169–71**; in "Amazon Women on the Moon," 169; "The Arsenio Hall Show," talk show, hosting 169; on "The Half Hour Comedy Hour," 169; "Intimate Portrait: Josephine Baker" narration, 170; MTV Video Music Awards, hosting, 170; on "Motown Revue," 169; on "The New Love American Style," 169; on "Solid Gold" series, 169; on "Thicke of the Night" series, 169; "World's Greatest Commercials," cohosting, 170
Hall, Charlotte H., **171–72**; *Newsday*, copy chief for, 171; at *Orlando Sentinel*, 171; as Pulitzer Prize jury, 172; Robert G. McGruder Award for Diversity Leadership, 172; Tribune Values Award, 172

Index

Hamblin, Ken, **172–74**; "Arson for Profit," produced and filmed, 172; *Denver Post* columnist, 172; *Denver Post*, weekly column for, 173; *Detroit Free Press*, as a photographer for, 172; *Pick a Better Country*, book by, 174; *Plain Talk and Common Sense from the Black Avenger*, 174; on WTVS-TV, Channel 56, 172

Hampton Roads Black Media Professionals, 131, 266–67

Hanif, C.B., **174–75**; at *Atlanta Voice*, 174; *Palm Beach Post*, editorial columnist for, 174; "War Appealed to Americans' Fear" column by, 175

Harpo Productions, 538

Harris, Jay T., **176–79**; *Daily News*, executive editor of, 176; Gannett News Service, a columnist and national correspondent for, 176; *News-Journal* papers by, 176; on the Pulitzer Prize Board of Directors, 177; *San Jose Mercury News*, as chairman and publisher of, 176; *San Jose Mercury News*, as chairman and publisher of, 176

Harris, Leon M. Jr., **179–80**; "Capital Sunday" at Abc7/WJLA-TV, cohost of, 179; "Early Edition," "CNN Live Today" and "American Stories," 179; 5 PM, 6 PM and 11 PM news, anchor of, 179; Los Angeles riots, covering, 179; 1995 Oklahoma City bombing, 179; "Prime News," reporter and coanchor for, 179; tornado damage in 2003, coverage, 179; "The World Today" reporter and coanchor for, 179; World Trade Center attacks of 2001 coverage by, 179

"Harris Faulkner Show," 130

"Harry Truman" (documentary), 220

Harshaw, Karla Garrett, **180–82**; "Best of Cox" award for column writing, 181; Cox Community Newspapers, senior editor of, 180; *Dayton Express*, editor of, 180; editor of the *Springfield News-Sun*, 180; NABJ Region IV Hall of Fame, inducted into, 181

Hartford Courant, 437

Hartman, Hermene Demaris, **182–84**; "Common Ground" program, 182; N'Digo Foundation, 182 posts held, 183

Hartman Group, 11, 182, 183

Harvard Law Review, 477

Hattiesburg American, 7

Haygood, Wil, **184–89**; *In Black and White*, 186; *Call & Post*, job reporting at 184; *Charleston Gazette*, copy editor at, 184; Great Lakes Book Award, 186; James Thurber Literary Fellowship, 186; *King of the Cats*, 186; National Association of Black Journalists Award, 186; New England Associated Press Award once, 186; Ohioana Book Award for nonfiction, 186; Pulitzer Prize finalist, 186; Sunday Magazine Editors Award, 186; *Two on the River*, 186; *Washington Post*, staff writer for 184

HBO, 44, 162, 228, 390

Henderson, Angelo B., **189–92**; *Courier-Journal*, business writer for, 190; "Crime Scene" story by, 190; *Detroit News*, business reporter and columnist for, 190; *Detroit News*, special projects reporter for, 190; Detroit Press Club Award, 191; "Inside Detroit," talk show, 190; *Journal*, special page one writer for, 190; on the *Kentucky Kernel* campus newspaper, 189; NABJ award for coverage of the black condition, 191; 1999 Pulitzer Award, 190; training workshops conducted by, 190; Unity Award for excellence in minority reporting for public affairs and social issues, 191; at *Wall Street Journal*, 190

Herald Statesman, 196

Herald Tribune, 52

Herald-Leader, 90, 242

Herald-Times, 505

Herbert, Bob, **192–95**; in *Daily News*, 192; "Hotline" television show, hosting, 192; Meyer Berger Award, 194; for "NBC Nightly News," 192; as Pulitzer Prize jury, 194; *Star-Ledger*, reporter for, 192; "Sunday Edition," weekly news show, panelist on, 192; teaching journalism at Columbia University and at Brooklyn College, 194; for "The Today Show," 192

Hickman, Fred, **195–96**; CableACE awards for excellence in sports hosting, 195; CNN show, as host of, 195; "CNN/Sports Illustrated," senior anchor for, 195; KLWW-AM, as news anchor at, 195; NBA studio program, anchor duty for an, 195; "Sports Tonight," cohost of, 195; WDIV-TV, sports anchor for, 195; WICS-TV, sports director and anchor for, 195; "Yankees Magazine" weekly show, host of, 195; YES Network, sports anchor for, 195

Holmes, Steven A., **196–98**; as a *Herald Statesman* police beat reporter, 196; *Time Magazine*, a national correspondent for, 196; at the *Washington Post*, 196

Holt, Lester, **198–200**; on "48 Hours," CBS magazine-format show, 198; KCBS-TV, as a reporter and weekend anchor, 198; "Lester Holt Live" anchoring, 198; MSNBC, anchor for daytime news and breaking news on, 198; "Newsfront" coanchoring, 198; "Today" show, hosting, 198; WBBM-TV, as evening anchor and reporter, 198; WCBS-TV, reporter for, 198; "Weekend Today," as cohost, 198; "Weekend Today," cohost of, 198

"Home Improvement," program, 539

"Hotline" television show, 192

Houston Post, 543

Howard University, 103

Hudson Dispatch, 200

Hughes, Alan J., **200**; *Black Enterprise* magazine, editor of, 200; *BusinessWeek Online*, as editor at 200; in *Black Enterprise*, 200; *Hudson Dispatch*, news editor for, 200

Hughes, Catherine "Cathy" Liggins, **201–3**; Advertising Club of Metropolitan Washington's Silver Medal Award, 203; Baltimore NAACP chapter's Parren J. Mitchell Award, 203; "The Cathy Hughes Show," Own daily talk program, 201; Department of Commerce's Ron Brown Business of

Index

the Year Award, 203; Golden Mike Award of the Broadcasters' Foundation, 203; honorary degrees, 203; at KOWH radio station, 201; Lifetime Achievement Award from the Washington Area Broadcasters Association, 203; National Association of Broadcasters Distinguished Service Award, 203; National Media Coalition's 1988 People's Champion Award, 203; 1996 Thomas A. Dorsey Leadership Award, 203; Radio One network, founder and chairperson of, 201; "Tom Joyner Morning Show," 203; Turner Broadcasting System's Trumpet Award, 203; "TV One on One" talk show, 203; WERQ-AM/FM in Baltimore, 202; at WMMJ-FM, 202; Women of Power Award, 203

Hunter, Karen, 203–5; *Daily News*, sports staff of, 204; Hunter College film and media program, an assistant professor in, 204; Rabbi Shea Hecht show, cohosting, 204; WABC radio talk show, hosting, 204; WWRL Morning Show, a radio talk show, hosting, 204

Hunter College film and media program, 204

Hunter-Gault, Charlayne, 205–8; American Women in Radio and Television Award, 207; Amnesty International's Media Spotlight Award, 207; Broadcast Personality of the Year Award, 207; Emmy awards, 207; Journalist of the Year Award in 1986, 207; Lincoln University's Unity ward for reporting about unemployed teens, 207; "MacNeil/Lehrer NewsHour," 207; "MacNeil/Lehrer Report," 207; "MacNeil/Lehrer Report" television, correspondent for, 205; 1986 George Foster Peabody Award, 207; Pulitzer Prize for jazz, 208; Sidney Hillman Award, 207; Tom Paine Award, 207; two awards given by the Corporation for Public Broadcasting for excellence in local programming, 207; Woman of Achievement Award, 207; WRC-TV, reporting and anchoring the news for, 206

Huntsville Times, 352
Hurricane Charley, 468
Hurricane Frances, 316, 504
Hurricane Frederick, 12
Hurricane Hugo, 10
Hurricane Ivan, 456
Hurricane Katrina, 24, 58, 76, 84, 137, 185, 193, 236, 244, 256, 257, 272, 282, 349, 359, 382, 408, 424, 437, 462, 488

"Idlewild: A Place in the Sun," 249

Ifill, Gwen, 209–12; *Baltimore Evening Sun*, as reporter, 209; *Boston Herald-American*, as a food writer at, 209; "Flashpoints with Bryant Gumbel and Gwen Ifill," cohost of, 209; NBC News, as the network's chief congressional correspondent and political reporter, 210; "The News Hour with Jim Lehrer" as a correspondent, 210; "The News Hour with Jim Lehrer," senior correspondent for, 209; *Washington Post*, as political reporter, 209; "Washington Week in Review," as moderator for, 210; "Washington Week in Review," program, moderator and managing editor of, 209

"In Athens, the New Can't Hold a Torch to the Ancient" column, 512–14

"In the Lion's Mouth" (documentary), 492

Income Opportunities, 260

Indianapolis News, 132

Indianapolis Star, 475, 505

InformationWeek, 107

"Inside Detroit," talk show, 190

Inside East Texas, monthly public affairs program, 9

"The Inside Edge" show, 495

"The Inside Edge with Carlos Watson" weekly political column, 494

Inside Sports, 370

Internet talk show, 274

"Intimate Portrait: Josephine Baker" narration, 170

Iraq war, 24, 58, 68, 74, 96, 104, 105, 181, 192, 198, 210, 215, 218, 222, 248, 279, 298, 336, 356, 360, 386, 391, 435, 453, 462, 504, 523, 526

"It's Time to Keep a Promise" column, 294–95

Ivory, Bennie, 212–14; *Courier-Journal*, executive editor and vice president for news of, 212; *Courier-Journal*, executive editor and vice president of, 212; *Daily News*, managing editor of, 212; Florida Today in Melbourne, executive editor of, 212; *News-Star-World*, assistant city editor of, 212; Pulitzer Prize juror four times, 212; Robert G. McGruder Award, 213; *Sentinel-Record*, general assignment reporter for, 212; *St. Cloud Times* in Minnesota, executive editor of the, 213

Jackson, Derrick Z., 215–17; "At Bob Jones U., A Disturbing Lesson about the Real George W" column by, 216–17; *Boston Globe*, columnist for, 215; *Kansas City Star*, sports stories for, 215; *Milwaukee Courier*, sportswriter for, 215

Jackson Advocate, 27

"JAG" episode, 532

James Thurber Literary Fellowship, 186

Jamieson, Robert L. Jr., 217–20; "Persecution of Muslim Chaplain Was Petty and Malicious" column by, 218–20; *Seattle Post-Intelligencer*, columnist for, 217; *Sunnyvale Valley Journal*, worked for, 217

Jarrett, Vernon D., 220–21; *Chicago Tribune*, columnist at, 220; "Eleanor: The Life and Times of Eleanor Roosevelt," documentary, in, 220; "Harry Truman" documentary in, 220; James P. McGuire Award to, 221; James Weldon Johnson Award to, 221; "Meet the Press" program, in, 220; National Literary Hall of Fame at the University of Chicago Gwendolyn Brooks Center, inductee into, 221; "The News Hour with Jim Lehrer" program, in, 220; "Nightline" program, in, 220; "60 Minutes" program, in, 220; President's Award to, 221

Index

"Jason Whitlock's Neighborhood," radio show, 506
JazzTimes magazine, 70
Jazzy Communications, 11, 183
Jean Leon Destine Haitian Dance Company, 365
Jefferson, Stebbins, **221–24**; *Palm Beach Post*, columnist for, 221; "Purging Ethics from Voter Rolls?" column by, 223–24; on Rush Limbaugh, conservative radio provocateur, 222
Jefferson, Thomas, 458
"The Jeffersons" show, 228
Jet, 147, 226, 317, 356
"Jihad in America," PBS documentary, 134
Johnson, John Harold, **224–27**; Arkansas Business Hall of Fame, inducted into, 226; *Black Stars*, 225; *Black World* magazine by, 225; *Ebony Jr.*, 225; *Ebony South Africa*, 225; *Ebony*, philanthropist and publisher for, 224–25; *EM:Ebony Man*, 225; honorary degrees to, 227; *Jet: The Weekly Negro News Magazine*, 226; NAACP's Springarn Medal to, 226; NABJ's Lifetime Achievement Award to, 226; National Newspaper Publishers' John Russwurm Award to, 226; *Negro Digest* magazine by, 224; Presidential Medal of Freedom to, 226; *Succeeding against the Odds*, autobiography of, 227; *Tan Confessions*, 225; *True Story, True Romance*, 225; Wall Street Journal/Dow Jones Entrepreneurial Excellence Award to, 226
Johnson, Lyndon, 226, 418, 419, 453, 518
Johnson, Robert L., **227–30**; "Benson" show in, 228; "BET Nightly News," 229; *Honey, Heart & Soul* and *Impact*, publisher of, 229; "The Jeffersons" show in, 228; "Let's Talk Church," "Treligious programs" in, 229; 1997 Hall of Fame Award to, 229; "The Parkers" show in, 228; wealth of, 228
Johnson, Roy S., **230–32**; *Atlanta Journal & Constitution* magazine, 230; *Fortune* magazine, 230; *Money* magazine, 230; *New York Times*, 230; *Savoy* magazine, 230; *Sports Illustrated*, 230–32
Johnson Publishing Company, 225, 357, 363, 393
"Jones and Jury" show, 233
Jones, Starlet Marie, **232–34**; "Court TV" program, 233; "Jones and Jury" show, 233; "NBC Nightly News" appearance on, 233; "The Today Show" appearance on, 233; "The View," an ABC talk show, 232, 233–34
Journal Herald, 320
Journal Sentinel, 239
Joyner, Thomas, **235–37**; Best Urban Contemporary Air Personality award to, 236; BlackAmericaWeb.com, 236; Essence Award to, 237; Hubert Humphrey Award to, 236; *I'm Just a DJ but— It Makes Sense to Me* book, 237; Leadership Conference on Civil Rights, 236–37; "Little-Known Black History Facts," 235; Mickey Leland Humanitarian Award to, 237; NAACP's President's Award, 237; National Association of Broadcasters Education Foundation's Good Samaritan Award to, 237; Radio Hall of Fame, inducted into, 236; "Real Fathers, Real Men," 235; Texas and Illinois Broadcasters organizations, inducted into, 236; "Thursday Morning Mom," 235; "The Tom Joyner Morning Show," 235; "The Tom Joyner Show," 235–36; "Tom Joyner Platters" album, 236; WBMX-FM, 235; WGCI-FM, 235; WJPC-FM, 235; WVON-AM, 235
"Judgment at Midnight," 289
Jungle Media, Inc., 11

KABC Talk Radio, 118
Kalamazoo Gazette, 481
Kane, Eugene A., **239–42**; *Journal Sentinel*, 239; *Philadelphia Bulletin*, reporter for, 239
Kansas City Star, 100, 215, 505
KATU-TV, 409
KCBS-TV, 167, 198, 324
KCLP-TV, 129
KCOP-TV, 106
KDKA-TV, 85
"Keep Up the Fight" column, 265–66
"Keeping the Faith" (documentary), 519
Kennedy, John F., 154, 226, 361, 367, 418, 464
Kennedy, John F. Jr., 55, 179, 336, 381
Kennedy, Tonnya, **242–43**; *Herald-Leader*, assistant managing editor of, 242; *State*, managing editor of, 242; *Virginian-Pilot*, managing editor of, 242
Kennett News & Advertiser, 261
Kentucky Kernel campus newspaper, 189
KETV, 106
Keyes, Allison, **243–44**; *Black Enterprise Magazine*, reporter for, 243; "Good Morning America" ABC program, 243; Newswoman's Club of New York Front Page Award for Breaking News, 244; Radio News Award to, 244; "The Tavis Smiley Show," reporter for, 243; "Weekend Edition," reported for, 244; "World News Tonight" ABC program, 243; WBEZ, at, 243; World Trade Center attacks, reporting by, 244
King, Colbert, **245–48**; *Washington Post* columnist, 245
King, Emery, **248–50**; "Buffalo Soldiers Wrapped in Steel," 249; "Cobb: A Detroit Legend," 249; "Emery King Show," 249; "Flashpoint: On the Road to Mackinac," 249; "The Freedom Train," 249; "Idlewild: A Place in the Sun," 249; "Paradise Lost, Paradise Found," 249; "Rosa Parks: Path to Freedom," 249; "The Rouge: the Factory and the Workers," 249, 250; "You can't keep a good man down," 249
KingWorld, 86
Kirk, Beverly, **250–51**; "Focus," 250; "NBC Nightly News," 251; "PBS/NPR Newsbrief," 251; "PBS/NPR Newsbrief" newscaster for, 250; WKYU-FM, 250; WLEX-TV, 250
KISS-FM, 335
KLWW-AM, 195

Index

KMOV-TV, 329
Knight Ridder Group, 73, 437
Knight Ridder News, 360
"The Know Zone" 335
Knoxville Kayana-Spectrum, 514
KOLO-TV, 467
KOWH radio station, 201
KPIX-TV, 107, 409
KQED-FM, 348
KQED-TV, 86, 349
KRON-TV, 86, 335, 492
KSLU-FM, 407
KTRE-TV, 9
KTVN-TV, 467
KTVU-TV station, on the 10 o'clock news, 127

L.A. Weekly, 129
Lacy, Sam Harold, **253–56**; "A to Z" column, 255; "Another Viewpoint" column, 255; *Chicago Defender*, assistant national editor for, 254; *Fighting for Fairness* memoir, 255; *Washington Tribune*, 253
"Larry King Live," talk show, 118
"Lead Story," 155
Leadership Conference on Civil Rights, 236–37
Lemon, Don, **256–57**; "NBC News," correspondent for, 256; "The Today Show," correspondent for, 256; WBRC-TV, reporter at, 256; "Weekend Today," correspondent for, 256; WTVI-TV, reporter at, 256
"Lester Holt Live," 198
"Let's Talk Church," 229
Lewis, Dwight, **257–59**; Living Legends Award to, 258; Making Kids Count Award to, 258; 1994 award for commentary, 258; Omega Psi Phi Fraternity Citizen of the Year Award to, 258; Philanthropist Award for Mass Media Outreach, 258; *Tennessean*, affairs columnist for, 257
Lewis, Edward T., **259–61**; *Essence*, 260; *Income Opportunities*, 260
Lexington Herald-Leader, 89, 190
Life Magazine, 364, 406
Limbaugh, Rush, 204, 222, 359
Lincoln, Abraham, 28
"Listen Up: The Lives of Quincy Jones" program, 539
"Little Pieces" (movie), 532
"Little-Known Black History Facts," 235
Lockman, Norman Alton, **261–64**; "Beyond the Norm" column, 262; "Black Perspective on the News" program, panelist at, 262; *Kennett News & Advertiser*, sports coverage for, 261; *News Journal* column in, 261; *News Journal*, reporter at, 262; "White House Talks Gibberish about Iraq" column by, 263
London subway bombing, 316, 474
Los Angeles bureau, 106
Los Angeles Free Press, 70
Los Angeles riots coverage, 143, 163, 179

Los Angeles Sentinel article, 61
Los Angeles Times Syndicate, 57, 520
Los Angeles Times, 23, 47, 48, 57, 65, 143, 271, 333, 388
Lost Word Productions, 279
Louis, Errol T., **264–66**; *City Sun*, 264; "Keep Up the Fight" column by, 265–66; *New York Daily News*, 264; *New York Sun*, 264; *Our Time Press*, 264; *Wall Street Journal*, 264
Louisville Courier-Journal, 16, 25, 53, 206, 375, 401
Lowe, Herbert, **266–68**; "Committed to the Cause" organization's booklet, 267; *Dallas Weekly*, editor of, 267; *Newsday*, staff writer for, 266

Mabrey, Vicki, **269–70**; CBS News correspondent, 269; Emmy awards to, 270; Gracie Allen Award to, 270; "60 Minutes" show, 269; "60 Minutes II" show, 269; WBAL-TV, general assignment reporter for, 269
Mabry, Marcus, **271–73**; *The Boston Globe*, 271; *Newsweek International*, senior editor of, 271; *Newsweek* magazine, 271; *Stanford Daily*, 271–73; *This House Has Fallen: Midnight in Nigeria*, review by, 272; *The Trentonian*, 271; *White Bucks and Black-Eyed Peas*, 272
McCall's magazine, 357
McCarthy, Sheryl, **297–98**; *Baltimore Evening Sun*, 297; *Boston Globe*, 297; *Newsday* columnist, 297; on war in Iraq, 298
McClatchy Company, 73
McGlowan, Angela, **298–300**; "Good Day Street Talk" show, hosting, 298
McGruder, Robert G., **300–301**; *Daily Kent Stater*, editor at, 300; *Detroit Free Press*, 301; Helen Thomas Spirit of Diversity Award to, 301; John S. Knight Gold Medal to, 301; *Plain Dealer*, reporter at, 300; Robert G. McGruder Award for Diversity Leadership to, 301; 2005 McGruder Award to, 301; William Taylor Distinguished Alumni Award to, 301
"MacNeil/Lehrer NewsHour," 207
"MacNeil/Lehrer Report," 205, 207
Macon Telegraph, 283, 284
MACV Observer, 344
Madison, Joseph Edward, **273–76**; Internet talk show, 274; NAACP, at, 273–76; National Newspaper Publishers Association's News Maker of the Year Award to, 275; National Political Congress of Black Women's Good Brother Award, 275; Southern Christian Leadership Conference's Journalism Award to, 275; travels, 274
Madison, Paula Walker, **276–78**; Citizen of the Year Award to, 277; community affairs and in national organizations, activity in, 277; *Fort Worth Star-Telegram*, reporter job at, 276; Ida B. Wells Award to, 277; Los Angeles NAACP President's Award to, 277; National Association of Minority Media Executives' Diversity Award to, 277; *Times Herald*, city editor of, 276; TRISCORT Award

Index

to, 277; United Negro College Fund's Frederick C. Patterson Award to, 277; WNBC, assistant news director of, 276

Malveaux, Julianne Marie, **278–81**; broadcast commentary, 278; "CNN and Company" show, panelist, 279; "On the Contrary" show, panelist, 278; *Emerge*, columns in, 278; "Feeding the Greedy, Starving the Needy" column by, 280–81; honorary degrees to, 279; organizational activities, 279; on President Bush, 279; *Sex, Lies and Stereotypes*, 279; *Wall Street, Main Street and the Side Street*, 279

Malveaux, Suzanne, **281–82**; Blackside Inc, producing documentaries for, 281; Boston's WFXT-TV, general assignment reporter for, 281; Bush administration, coverage by, 281; impeachment trial of former President Bill Clinton, covering, 281

Mandela, Nelson, 3, 30, 156, 207, 291, 333, 345, 394, 409, 429, 439, 440, 441, 449

"Marian Anderson" (documentary), 525

Marion Star, column, 520

Marshall, Pluria W. Sr., **282–83**; Community service Award to, 283; Ex-student Award to, 283

Marshall, Sherrie, **283–84**; *Macon Telegraph*, executive editor of, 283; *Minneapolis Star*, copy editor at, 283; *Star*, deputy managing editor of, 283; *Star-Tribune*, deputy managing editor, 283

Martin, Michel McQueen, **284–86**; "Cedric's Story," network special, 285; *A Hope in the Unseen: An American Odyssey from the Inner City to the Ivy League*, 285; Emmy award to, 286; "Nightline," 285; 1995 Joan Barone Award to, 286; 1995 Pulitzer Prize to, 285; 1992 Candace Award to, 286; "Turning Point" (documentary), 285; 2001 Casey Medal to, 286; 2002 Silver Gavel Award to, 286; *Wall Street Journal*, reporter for, 284; *Washington Post*, reporter for, 284

Martin, Roland S., **286–89**; "Alan Keyes: A Political Hit Man" column by, 288–89; *Austin American-Statesman*, neighborhood reporter for, 287; *Chicago Defender*, editor of, 287; "The Fifth Quarter" sports show, 287; on Tulsa Race Riot of 1921, 287

Mason, Paul S., **289–90**; "Black in White America," coproducer of, 289; "Judgment at Midnight," coproducer of, 289; "Prime Time Live," coproducer of, 289; "Prime Time Monday," 290; "World News Tonight," 290

Mathis, Deborah, **290–92**; Angel Award for commentary in 1994 and 1996, 291; *Arkansas Democrat*, reporting for, 290; offending conservatives, 291; "Orange Alert and the Politics of Fear" column by, 292

"Matt Waters," television show, 532

Maxwell, Bill, **293–95**; "Archie Bunker Paradigm," 293; "Farewell; It's Time to Keep a Promise" column by, 294–95; *St. Petersburg Times*, 293; *The Tampa Tribune*, reporter and columnist for, 293; *Tuscaloosa News*, column for, 293

Maynard, Nancy Hicks, **295–97**; *Mega Media: How Market Forces Are Transforming News* book by, 296; *New York Post* at, 295; *Oakland Tribune*, editor of, 295

MBM/Modern Black Men Magazine, 115

Media Woman of the Year, 125

MediaNews Group, 320–21

"Meet the Press" program, 220

Merida, Kevin, **302–5**; Pulitzer Prize, to, 302; *Supreme Discomfort*, cowritter of, 302; *Washington Post*, associate editor and writer for, 302

Miami Herald, 308, 323, 360, 370, 394, 494

Miami News, 489

"Michael Jackson Talks" program, 539

Michigan Daily, 410

"Midday," a daily magazine-format show, 492

Miller, John Xavier, **305–8**; *Charlotte Observer*, 305; *Detroit Free Press*, in, 306; *Roanoke Times & World News*, at, 305; "You Cant Quote Me" column by, 307–8

Milloy, Courtland, **308–11**; Colin Powel criticized by, 309; "Disturbing Turn for Shock and Awe" column by, 310–11; *Miami Herald*, court reporter for, 308

Milwaukee Courier, 215

Milwaukee Journal Sentinel, 50, 215, 239, 539

Minneapolis Star, 283

Minnesota Public Radio, 334, 381, 382

Minnesota station WCCO-TV, 383

Miss Black America contestant, 537

Mississippi Enterprise, 27

Mitchell, Everett J. II, **311–12**; *Cincinnati Enquirer*, editing at, 311; *Communicator*, editor at, 311; *Courier-Journal*, reporter at, 311; at *Detroit News*, 311; *Evening Sun*, reporter at, 311; at *The News*, 311; *Statesman Journal*, executive editor at, 311; at *Tennesssean*, 311

Mitchell, Mary A., **312–16**; *Chicago Sun-Times* columnist, 312

Mitchell, Russ, **316–17**; "CBS Evening News" anchor of, 316; on "CBS News up to the Minute" news show, 316; "The Saturday Early Show," coanchor of, 316; 2001 Sigma Delta Chi Award to, 316 ; 2002 James Beard Award to, 317

Money magazine, 230

Monroe, Bryan K., **317**; at *Ebony*, 317; at *Jet*, 317; *San Jose Mercury News*, assistant managing editor of, 317 ; at *Seattle Times*, 317

Montel Williams MS Foundation, 532

"The Montel Williams Show" 531

Moore, Acel, **318–19**; at *Philadelphia Inquirer*, 318

Moore, Gregory L., **320–23**; at *Boston Globe*, 320; at *The Journal Herald*, 320; 1996 Journalist of the Year, 322

Morgan, Thomas III, **323**; *Miami Herald*, reporter for, 323; at *New York Times*, 323

"Morning Edition," NPR program, 84, 525

Morning News as a columnist, 379

Morris, Valerie Coleman, **324–25**; California Emmy awards, 324; at KCBS-TV, 324; at *New York Times*, 324; Outstanding Contribution to Broadcasting Award, 324
"Motown Revue," 169
MOVE house, police bombing of, 95, 449, 460
Ms. Magazine, 365
MSNBC, 10, 57, 155, 198, 199, 256, 279, 335, 441, 512, 532
MultiAmerica: Essays on Cultural Wars and Cultural Peace, 349

NAACP, 273–76
NABJ. *See* National Association of Black Journalists
NABJ Journal, 267, 374
The NABJ Story, 92
Nashville Banner, minority youth program, 110
National Association of Black Journalists (NABJ), 5, 9, 11, 13, 17, 24, 41, 50, 59, 60, 65, 69, 79, 83, 84, 86, 92, 96, 100, 108, 124, 131, 135, 148, 220, 230, 266, 267, 272, 277, 284, 317, 318, 322, 323, 329, 338, 345, 368, 370, 372, 374, 386, 388, 397, 411, 415, 424, 426, 431, 435, 440, 461, 465, 468, 474, 509, 512, 543
National Black Media Coalition, 282
National Geographic Explorer series documentary "Gullah," 160
National Geographic, 516
National Observer, 11
National Public Radio (NPR), 1, 45, 50, 56, 57, 58, 66, 68, 69, 84, 96, 100, 127, 133, 134, 155, 166, 243–44, 334, 369, 446, 518, 524–25, 526, 535–36; WCBU, 68; WEZ, 243; WLRH-FM, 352
The Nationalist Movement, 173
"Native Son" (movie), 538
NBA studio program, 195
NBC, 9, 10, 43, 59, 68, 85, 162, 165, 170, 210, 233, 256, 267, 277, 336, 377, 383, 404, 429, 511; KNBC, 276, 278; MSNBC, 10, 57, 155, 198, 199, 256, 279, 335, 441, 512, 532; NBC News, 209, 248, 256, 281, 388, 502, 503; NBC 10, 131; NBC5 News, 132, 330, 256, 330, 484, 485; WNBC, 276, 355, 357, 416, 479
"NBC Nightly News," 10, 11, 85, 86, 192, 233, 251, 335, 439, 503
N'Digo, 11, 182–83, 230
Negro Digest magazine, 224
Nelson, Jill, **327–29**; American Book Award, 327; in the *Nation*, *Essence*, *Ms.*, the *New York Times*, the *Chicago Tribune* and the *Village Voice*, 327; *Sexual Healing*, 328; *Volunteer Slavery*, 327; *Washington Post*, 327
NetNoir Inc., 122, 123
New Bedford Standard Times, 348
"The New Love American Style," 169
New York Age, 464
New York club, 100

New York Daily News, 53, 54, 58, 61, 69, 139, 140, 149, 264, 394, 435
New York Post, 107, 295
New York Sun, 264
New York Times, 33, 38, 53, 65, 76, 78, 99, 139, 140, 173, 192, 196, 197, 207, 209, 230, 265, 296, 323, 324, 349, 369, 390, 400, 435, 456, 476, 518, 525
New York Times Regional Newspaper Group, 293
New York Times Syndicate, 172, 173
The News, 311
News & Observer, 243, 321, 426
"The News Hour with Jim Lehrer," 209, 210, 220
News Journal, 26, 176, 261, 262, 311, 396, 497
Newsday, 58, 64, 65, 104, 171, 237, 266, 267, 297, 317, 344, 345, 346, 370, 394
"Newsfront," 198
News-Star-World, 212
Newsweek International, 271
Newsweek magazine, 11, 56, 58, 271, 273, 346, 414, 453, 495, 499, 500, 529
Newton, Vickie, **329–30**; for CNN Headline News, 329; Emmy for best anchor, 329; at KMOV-TV, 329; WDAF-TV, 329; WDIV-TV, 329; WSB-TV in Atlanta, 329
"NFL on NBC," 383
"Nightline," 61, 160, 220, 269, 270, 285, 286, 290, 334, 345, 373, 399, 439, 441, 474, 525, 533
Nixon, Richard, 226, 297, 419, 491, 518
NJN Public Television, 95
Norman, Art, **330–31**; A School Bell Award, 330; Best Investigative Reporting honor in 1992–1993, 330; WCCB-TV, 330; Emmy award, 330–31; George Foster Peabody Award, 330; Investigative Reporters and Editors Award, 331; NBC 5 News, 330; "Weekend Magazine," 330; at WMAR-TV, 330; Wilbur Award, 330; WPCQ-TV, 330; WSOC-TV, 330
Norman, Tony, **331–32**; *Pittsburgh Post-Gazette*, 331
Norris, Michele, **333–34**; ABC News correspondent, 333; "All Things Considered," 333; *Chicago Schools: Worst in America*, 333; *Chicago Tribune*, 333; *The Grist*, 333; Livingston Award in 1989, 334; at the *Los Angeles Times*, 333; 1990 Federal Bar Association Media Award, 334; *Ourselves among Others*, 333; Peabody Award, 334; Peter Lisagor Award for public service, 334; Pulitzer Prize, 334; at *The Washington Post*, 333
North America Syndicate, 418
Norwalk Journal & Guide, 40
NPR. *See* National Public Radio
NV magazine, 102

Oakland Tribune, 151, 217, 295, 348, 461, 514, 521, 522
O'Brien, Maria de la Soledad, **335–36**; "American Morning," 335; on the burial of Palestinian leader Yasser Arafat, 336; coanchor CNN's three-hour

Index

"American Morning," 336; "Fox and Friends," 336; KISS-FM in Boston, 335; "The Know Zone," 335; KRON-TV, 335; "NBC Nightly News," 335; "Solly," 335; on Space Shuttle Columbia disaster, 336; on Taliban prisoners held at Guantanamo Bay, Cuba, 336; on tsunami disaster, 336; on World Trade Towers attacks, 336; WBZ-TV, 335

Observer, 78, 104

"Of Black America" series, 491

"Off Topic with Carlos Watson," one-hour specials, 494

Offending conservatives, 291

Oklahoma City bombing of 1995, 130, 134, 179, 287, 288, 434, 440, 473

"On Point with Ed Gordon," talk radio with ABC show, 155

"On the Contrary" show, 278

"Oprah," talk show, 118

"Oprah & Friends Radio," 540

"Oprah After the Show," 541

"Oprah Online," 540

"Oprah Talks to Charlize Theron," 540

Oprah Winfrey Foundation, 539

Oprah Winfrey Leadership Academy, 539

Oprah Winfrey Scholars Program, 539

Oprah's Angel Network, 539

Oprah's Book Club, 539

"Orange Alert and the Politics of Fear" column, 292

"The O'Reilly Factor," 494

Orlando Sentinel, 75, 171, 172, 421

Orlando's Channel 6, WCPXTV, 167

"The Other Washington" (documentary), 413

Our Time Press, 264

Our World News, 100, 107

Ourselves among Others, 333

Page, Clarence Eugene, **337–40**; On Bush administration, 337; *Chicago Tribune*, 337; *Cincinnati Enquirer*, 337; Edward Scott Beck Award, 338; James P. McGuire Award, 338; L.J. Horton Award, 338; Ohio, *Journal*, 337; Pulitzer Prize, 337; on World Trade Center attacks, 337

Palestine Liberation Organization, 99

Palm Beach Post, 174, 221

Palmer, Lutrelle F., **340–42**; Bell Labs' Black Achievement against the Odds Award, 341; Black Journalists Hall of Fame, 341; *Black X-Press Info-Paper*, 341; *Chicago Daily News*, 340; *Chicago Defender*, 340; Chicago State University Black Writers Hall of Fame, 341; Grambling State University's Outstanding Service Award, 341; at WVON on "Lu's Notebook," 341

Parade Magazine, 356

"Paradise Lost, Paradise Found," 249

"Pardon the Interruption," 506, 511

"The Parkers," 228

Parsons, Richard D., **342–44**

Payne, Leslie, **344–48**; Ace Award, 345–47; MACV *Observer*, 344; at *Newsday*, 344; *Newsday*, 344; Pulitzer award, 345–47; Tobenkin Award, 347; World Hunger Media Award in 1983, 347

Payton, Brenda, **348–50**; *Boston Phoenix*, 348; Jane A. Harrah Memorial Media Award, 349; John Swett Award for reporting on education, 349; KQED, 349; Meiklejohn Civil Liberties Institute Award, 349; *MultiAmerica: Essays on Cultural Wars and Cultural Peace*, 349; *New Bedford Standard Times*, 348; *New York Times*, freelance in, 349; *Oakland Tribune*, 348; on KQED-FM, 348; *San Francisco Examiner*, 348; *Thinking Black*, 349; *Tribune* column on a freelance basis, 348

"PBS/NPR Newsbrief," 250, 251

PC Magazine, 107

"People Are Talking," show, 538

Perkins, Joseph, **350–52**; CBS affiliate WHNT-TV, 352; *Huntsville Times* in Alabama, 352; as MSNBC, Fox News, C-Span, CNN, CNBC, 351; for NPR affiliate, 352; *San Diego Union-Tribune* political columnist, 350; *Wall Street Journal*, 351; WLRH-FM, 352

"Persecution of Muslim Chaplain Was Petty and Malicious" column, 218–20

Persian Gulf War, 61, 164, 218, 440

Peterman, Peggy Mitchell, **354–55**; Meritorious Achievement Award, 355; *Thinking Black: Some of the Nation's Best Black Columnists Speak Their Minds*, 355

"Phil Donahue Show," 538

Philadelphia Afro-American, 41

Philadelphia Bulletin, 84, 239

Philadelphia Daily News, 72, 93, 95, 318, 449, 464

Philadelphia Inquirer, 72, 84, 94, 245, 266, 318, 423, 481

Philadelphia Society of Black Journalist, 1

Philadelphia Tribune column, 533

Phillips, Julian Martin, **355–56**; an ABC Radio Network News desk assistant, 355; Associated Press' First Place News Award, 356; at *Black Enterprise Magazine*, 355; Edward R. Murrow Award, 356; Emmy winner, 356; Fox News Channel as an anchor, 355; Purdue University Distinguished Alumni Award, 356; WNBC anchor and reporter, 355; for WPIX-TV, 355; at WNEW-TV as a production assistant, 355; WNBC-TV station's manager of community relations, 355

Phoenix Gazette, 13

Pierce, Ponchitta Marie Anne Vincent, **356–58**; American-Italian Women of Achievement Award, 358; Penney-Missouri Award, 357–58; "CBS Evening News," special correspondent for, 357; Commendation Award, 358; *Ebony* and *Jet* magazines, assistant editor of, 356; Exceptional Merit Media Award, 358; in WNBC-TV, 357; John Russwurm Award, 358; *McCall's* magazine, editor job

Index

with, 357; *Parade Magazine*, editor for, 356; *Reader's Digest*, editor for, 357; Woman Behind the News Award, 358
Pilot 13 News, 59
Pitts, Byron, **358–59**; for Boston's WCBV-TV, 358; CBS news correspondent, 358; for CBS News, 358; Emmy awards, 358; Journalist of the Year in 2002, 358; network's reporting on the attacks of September 11th, 358; for WAVY-TV, 358; for WNCT-TV in Greenville, 358; a WESH-TV reporter in Orlando, 358; at WFLA-TV in Tampa, 358; at WSB-TV in Atlanta, 358; worked in general assignment reporting, 358
Pitts, Leonard, **359–63**; American Society of Newspaper Editors Commentary Award, 360; GLAAD Media's Outstanding Newspaper Columnist Award, 360; in *Knight Ridder News*, 360; In *Miami Herald* as that paper's pop music critic, 360
Pittsburgh Courier, 153, 190, 254, 283
Pittsburgh Post-Gazette, 72, 95, 184, 331
Pittsburgh Press, 72, 95, 426
Plain Dealer, 143, 190, 300, 320, 421–22
Poinsett, Alexander Ceasar, **363**; *Ebony Pictorial History of Black America*, 363; *Ebony*, editor of, 363; Johnson Publishing Company, 363; *Negro Handbook*, 363; *Role of Sports in Youth Development*, 363; speechwriter for Richard Hatcher, mayor of Gary, 363; *White Problem in America*, 363; *Young Black Males in Jeopardy*, 363
"Politics—The New Black Power" (documentary), 525
Pool-Eckert, Marquita, **363–64**; Black Career Women Lifetime Achievement Award, 364; of "CBS News Sunday Morning," 363; Columbia University's Journalism Alumni Award for journalistic excellence, 364; Emmy awards, 364; International Monitor Award, 364; National Monitor Award, 364; New York Women in Film and Television Muse Award, 364
PopandPolitics.com, 56
Post-Dispatch, 13, 33, 35, 423
Post-Intelligencer, 47
Post-Tribune, 92
Poussaint, Renee Francine, **365–67**; for *African Arts Magazine*, 365; at Chicago's WBBN-TV, 365; Emmy winner, 366; in the Jean Leon Destine Haitian Dance Company, 365; at Poussaint Communications Inc., 365; *The Washington Post* and *Ms. Magazine*, freelance writing for, 365
Poussaint Communications Inc., 365
Powell, Adam Clayton III, **367–69**; at CBS News, 368; at National Public Radio, 367; Quincy Jones Entertainment, as a producer for, 367
Powell, Shaun, **370–72**; Best Sports Story Award, 370; *Dallas Times Herald*, 370; for *Basketball Digest* and *Inside Sports*, 370; for *The Sporting News*, 370; *Miami Herald*, 370; *St. Louis Globe*, 370
The Poynter Institute, 95, 110, 168, 177, 213, 217

Premiere, 516
Pressley, Condace, **372–73**; *Coloring the News: How Crusading for Diversity Has Corrupted American Journalism*, book, 373; Edward R. Murrow Award, 373; with the Georgia News Network/WGST, 372; with WGAU-AM, WNGC-FM and WRFC-AM, 372; WSB as a local government reporter and anchor, 372
PrideFest, 55
"Prime News," 179
"Prime Time Live," 289, 407
"Prime Time Monday," 290
Prince, Richard E., **374**; *Democrat and Chronicle*, editor for, 374; *Washington Post*, reporter for, 374
Proctor, Glenn, **374–76**; *Daily Local News*, 375; for the *Akron Beacon Journal*, 375; for the *Beacon Journal*, 375; for the *Rochester Democrat & Chronicle* in New York, 375; *Richmond Times-Dispatch*, editor of, 374; at *The Star-Ledger*, 375
Provendor Capital Group, 63
Publishers-Hall Syndicate, 418
"Purging Ethics from Voter Rolls?" column, 223–24

Quarles, Norma R., **377–78**; at Chicago's station WSDM, 377; CINE Golden Eagle award, 378; NBC and CNN, 377; Quarles covered for CNN include, 378; for *Religion & Ethics Newsweekly*, 378; for the "Today" show, 377; for WKYC-TV in Cleveland, Ohio, 377
Quarles covered for CNN include, 378
Quincy Jones Entertainment, 367
"Quincy Jones: The First 50 Years" program, 539

Race in sports, 506–7
Race Relations Reporter, 501
Radio One network, 201
Ragland, James, **379–81**; *Dallas Morning News*, serving as editor, 379; *Morning News* as a columnist, 379; for the *Washington Post*, 379
Randolph, Toni, **381–82**; on BBC, National Public Radio, 381; for Minnesota Public Radio, 381; WBFO-FM in Buffalo as that station's news director, 381; a WBUR-TV reporter, 381; with Minnesota Public Radio in Minneapolis, 382
Rashad, Ahmad, **383–84**; during the Barcelona games, 383; Minnesota station WCCO-TV, 383; on "NFL on NBC," 383
Reader's Digest, 357
"The Reading Club," 85
Reagan, Ronald, 119, 144, 163, 211, 216, 239, 309, 345, 413, 456, 468, 475, 491, 497, 503, 506, 536
"Real Fathers, Real Men," 235
"Real Sports with Bryant Gumbel," 44, 161, 162
Red Herring magazine, 107, 108
Religion & Ethics Newsweekly, 378
Reporter, 12

Index

Rhoden, William C., **390–93**; at the *Baltimore Sun*, 390; *$40 Million Slaves: The Rise, Fall and Redemption of the Black Athlete* book, 390; *Ebony* magazine, 390

Rice, Linda Johnson, **393–94**; with *Ebony*, 393; 2003 "Robie" Award for Achievement in Industry, 393

Richardson, Clem, **394–96**; for the *Anderson Independent*, 394; at the *Atlanta Journal-Constitution*, 394; for *Miami Herald*, 394; *New York Newsday*, editor for, 394

Richmond Afro-American, 41

Richmond Independent, 61

Richmond Times Dispatch, 374, 375, 509, 528

Richmond's life, 529

Riddle, W. Curtis, **396–97**; of the *Cincinnati Enquirer*, 396; for the *Courier-Journal*, 396

Rideau, Wilbert, **397–400**; for *Angolite*, 397–98; Charles C. Clayton Award, 399; National Magazine Award, 399

"The Right Side with Armstrong Williams" radio talk show, 520

Riley, Jason L., **400–401**; at *Wall Street Journal*, 400

Riley, Rochelle, **401–3**; Charles E. Scripps Award, 402

Roanoke Times & World News, 305, 317, 423, 473

Roberts, Deborah, **403–4**; Clarion Award, 404; 1992 Distinguished Alumnus Award, 404; for WBIR-TV, 404; for WTVM-TV, 404

Roberts, Osborne "Ozzie" Sinclaire Jr., **404–6**; at *Life Magazine*, 406; for *San Diego Union-Tribune*, 405

Roberts, Robin, **407–8**; Distinguished Achievement Award, 408; Excellence in Sports Journalism Award, Broadcast, 408; for KSLU-FM, 407; President's Award, 408; at station WHMD/WFPR, 407; at WAGA-TV, 407; WLOX-TV, 407; at WVEE-FM, 407

Roberts, Troy, **409**; KATU-TV, 409; KPIX-TV, 409; WCBS-TV, 409

Robeson, Paul, 148, 240

Robinson, Eugene (Max), **410–12**; with *Michigan Daily*, 410

Robinson, Maxie (Max) Cleveland Jr., **412–14**; "The Other Washington" (documentary), 413; for WTOP-TV, 412

Rochester Democrat & Chronicle, 375

Rockland Journal-News, 12

Rodgers, Johnathan A., **414–15**; with WBBM-TV, 414; for WKYC-TV, 414

Roker, Albert Lincoln, **416–17**; WKYC-TV, 416; for WTTG-TV, 416; for WTVH-TV, 416

Role of Sports in Youth Development, 363

ROMAR Media Group, 287

"Rosa Parks: Path to Freedom," 249

"The Rouge: The Factory and the Workers" (documentary), 249, 250

Rowan, Carl Thomas, **417–21**; *Baltimore Afro-American*, as a freelancer, 417; Capital Press Club's Distinguished Service Award, 420; Elijah P. Lovejoy Award, 420; National Press Club's Fourth Estate Award, 420; 1955 American Teamwork Award, 420; 1952 Sidney Hillman Award, 420; 1964 Communications Award, 420

Russell, Mark E., **421–22**; of the *Orlando Sentinel*, 421; at the *Plain Dealer*, 421–22

Rutgers Alumni Magazine, 116

Rwandan genocide, 10

St. Cloud Times, 213

St. Louis Globe, 370

St. Petersburg Times, 95, 110, 190, 191, 293, 354

Samuel, Terence, **423–25**; for the *American Prospect* online, 423; at the *Philadelphia Inquirer*, 423

San Diego Earth Times, 139

San Diego Union-Tribune, 350, 400, 404

San Francisco Chronicle, 410, 461, 522

San Francisco Examiner, 348

San Jose Mercury News, 176, 317, 545

Sanford, Otis L., **425–26**; of the *Commercial Appeal*, 425; University of Mississippi Alumni Hall of Fame, inducted into, 426; William R. Burleigh Award for Distinguished Community Service, 426

"The Saturday Early Show," 316

"Saturday Night Live," program, 539

Saunders, Barry, **426–28**

Saunders, Warner, **429–30**; Chicago Journalism Hall of Fame, 430; Emmy awards, 430; Illinois Broadcasters Association Public Service Award, 430; WMAQ-TV, 429

Savoy magazine, 11, 62, 63, 182, 183, 230, 231, 244, 287

Scarbrough, Neal T., **430–31**; of the *Chicago Sun-Times*, 430; with *ESPN The Magazine*, 430; Print Journalist of the Year, 431

"The Scholastic NBC News Video," 85

"The Science of Sport" (documentary), 85

Scott, Stuart, **431–32**; "SportsCenter," ESPN's, coanchor for, 432

Seattle Post-Intelligencer, 47, 151, 217

Seattle Times, 317

Sentinel-Record, 212

Shaw, Bernard, **432–34**; with CNN, 433–34 ; Distinguished Service Award, 434; Dr. Martin Luther King, Jr. Award for Outstanding Achievement, 434; Eduard Rhein Foundation's Cultural Journalism Award, 434; National Headliner Award, 434; 1989 Emmy award, 434; Tex McCrary Award, 434; William Allen White Award, 434

Shipp, E.R., **434–36**; with *New York Daily News*, 435; Pulitzer Prize, 435

SI.com, 230, 231

"Simian Line" The, (film), 532

Simmons, Debra Adams, **436–38**; for the *Akron Beacon Journal*, 437; Harold K. Stubbs Humanitarian Award, 438; for the *Hartford Courant*, 437; National Association of Black Journalists awards, 437; with *Tallahassee Democrat*, 437

Index

Simpson, Carole, **438–41**; Leonard Zeidenberg First Amendment Award, 440; Milestone Award, 440; Silver Bell Award, 440; Turner Broadcasting's Trumpet Award, 440; at WMAQ-TV, 439; at WTTW-TV, 439

Singletary, Michelle, **441–45**; as a *Baltimore Evening Sun* reporter, 441; *7 Money Mantras for a Richer Life*, book, 442; at *Washington Post*, 441; *Your Money or Your Man*, book, 442

"60 Minutes," 35, 36, 37, 47, 118, 155, 156, 220, 269, 270, 364, 413, 446, 538

"60 Minutes II," 269, 270

Slave trade exploration, 61, 235, 274, 492

"Slavery Isn't the Issue" column, 526–28

Smiley, Tavis, **445–47**; for CNN and ABC-TV, 445; *Hard Left: Straight Talk about the Wrongs of the Right* book by, 446; NAACP President's Image Award, 447; 1998 Mickey Leland Humanitarian Award, 447; Outstanding Business & Professional Award, 447; *USA Weekend* magazine, editor for, 446

Smith, Clarence O., **447–48**; Golden Trumpet Award, 448

Smith, Elmer, **449–51**; for *Bulletin*, 449

SoHo Weekly News, 70

"Solid Gold" series, 169

"Solly," 335

Sowell, Thomas, **451–55**; *Black Education: Myths and Tragedies*, book by, 452; 2004 "Joseph Goebbels award," 453

Space Shuttle Columbia disaster, 336

"Special Report with Brit Hume," 524

Spencer, Collins, **455–56**

The Sporting News, 370

Sports Illustrated, 63, 74, 230–32, 414, 505, 514, 515, 516

"The Sports Reporters" 506, 511, 516

"Sports Tonight," 195

"SportsCenter," 165, 432

Springfield News-Sun, 180

Stanford Daily, 271–73

Stanford Law Review, 494

Staples, Brent A., **456–60**; *New York Times*, editorial writer for the, 456

Star, 100, 283

Star-Ledger, 192, 375

Star-Tribune, 283

State, 242

Statesman Journal, 311

Stevens, Shay, **460–61**; WHAT-AM, anchor for, 460; WWDB-FM, anchor for, 460; at WCAU-AM, 460

Stewart, Pearl, **461–64**; with *Chicago Defender*, 461; *San Francisco Chronicle*, staff writer for, 461

Stone, Charles (Chuck) Sumner Jr., **464–67**; Best Column of the Year award, 465; Capital Press Club's Journalist of the Year award, 465; Congress of Racial Equality awarded him its Distinguished Citizen Award, 465; Laubach Excellence in Teaching Award, 465; Lifetime Achievement Award, 465; Missouri Honor Medal, 465; with *New York Age*, 464; Undergraduate Teaching Award, 465

"Stop the Violence" campaign, 493

"Strip Mall Patriotism" column, 523–24

Summer of Sam, role of anchorwoman in, 480

Sun Herald, 7

Sun News, 21, 22, 306

Sun Reporter, 88, 278, 441

"Sunday Edition," weekly news show, 192

"Sunday with Liz Walker," 492

Sunnyvale Valley Journal, 217

Syler, Rene, **467–69**; Gracie Allen Award for Individual Achievement, 469; at KOLO-TV, 467; with KTVN-TV, 467

"Take Five," 117

Taliban prisoners held at Guantanamo Bay, Cuba, 336

"Talk of the Nation," 524

Tallahassee Democrat, 437

The Tampa Tribune, 293

Tan Confessions, 225

"The Tavis Smiley Show," 96, 243, 494

Taylor, Susan L., **471–72**; Henry Johnson Fisher Award, 472

Teenpreneur, 115

Television Performer of the Year, 542

Tennessean, 27, 257, 311, 312, 430, 475

Terrorists attacks: on Atlanta Olympics, 269, 270; on London subway, 316, 474; on Oklahoma City, 130, 134, 179, 287, 288, 434, 440, 473; on World Trade Center, 34, 150, 156, 271, 281, 360, 456, 173

"Their Eyes Were Watching God," 538

"There Are No Children Here," 538

Theta Cable TV, 106

"Thicke of the Night" series, 169

This House Has Fallen: Midnight in Nigeria, 272

Thomas, Pierre, **472–74**; at ABC News, 473; Alfred I. DuPont-Columbia University Award, 474; CNN correspondent, 473; Mort Mintz Investigative Award, 474; National Council on Crime and Delinquency's Pass Award, 474; Peabody Award, 474; Young Journalist Award, 474

Thomas, Wendi C., **474–76**; *Charlotte Observer*, editor for, 475; *Indianapolis Star*, reporter for, 475; *Tennessean*, editor for, 475

Thomas-Graham, Pamela, **477–78**; *Harvard Law Review*, editor of, 477

"Throw Momma from the Train" (film), 538

"Throwaway People" (documentary), 519

"Thursday Morning Mom," 235

Time Magazine, 116, 196, 234, 501

Time Warner, 44, 62, 130, 228, 342–43, 448

Times, 23, 95, 99

Times Herald, 276

Index

Times Picayune, 23, 25, 120, 121
Times-Union, 496, 497
"Tina Turner: Celebrate Live" program, 539
TMS. *See* Tribune Media Services
"Today" show, 10, 54, 85, 161, 162, 192, 198, 233, 256, 377, 408, 468, 503
Tolliver, Melba, **478–80**; freelancing jobs, 479; Lifetime Achievement Award, 480; Long Island Association's Woman of the Year Award, 480; *Summer of Sam*, role of anchorwoman in, 480; Torch of Liberty Award, 480
"The Tom Joyner Morning Show," 92, 203, 235
"Tom Joyner Platters" album, 236
"The Tom Joyner Show," 235–36
"The Tonight Show Starring Johnny Carson" program, 539
"The Tonight Show with Jay Leno" program, 539
"Tony Brown's Journal," 44, 45
"The Tony Cox Show," 96
"The Tony Kornheiser Show," 511
Tornado damage in 2003, coverage, 179
Towns, Hollis, **480–81**; at *Cincinnati Enquirer*, 481; at *Kalamazoo Gazette*, 481
Trans-Urban News Service in Brooklyn, 91
Trentonian, 271
Tribune, 12, 348
Tribune Media Services (TMS), 57, 291, 337, 344, 345, 359, 360, 519, 520
Tri-State Defender, 147, 190
Trotter Group, 84, 92, 100
True Story, True Romance, 225
Truman, Harry, 182, 351
Tsunami disaster, 150, 270, 336, 402, 435, 485
Tucker, Cynthia Anne, **481–84**; *Atlanta Journal*, reporter for, 481; Colby College's Lovejoy Award, 483; Distinguished Writing Award, 483; *Philadelphia Inquirer*, 481
"Tuesdays with Morrie," 538
Tulsa Race Riot of 1921, 287
"Turning Point" (documentary), 285
Tuscaloosa News, 293
Tutman, Lisa, **484–85**
Tutsi Forces in the First Congo War, 10, 11
"TV One on One" talk show, 203
TWA Flight 800 explosion and crash, 269, 270
"20/20," 2, 289, 334, 403, 404, 407, 417, 439, 488

Udoji, Adaora, **487–88**; with ABC, 487; Cine Eagle award, 488
UNITA guerilla movement, 81
Universal Press Syndicate, 150, 151, 464, 520
University of Pennsylvania, 103
Urban Box Office, 107
U.S. abuse of Iraqi prisoners, 68
U.S. Embassy bombing in Nairobi, 285
U.S. News & World Report, 423, 509

USA Today, 12, 37, 76, 107, 151, 212, 278, 287, 305, 307, 327, 328, 394, 396, 400, 461, 479, 508, 519
USA Weekend magazine, 327, 336, 446

Vibe magazine, 57, 62–63, 64, 66, 96
Vietnam War, 106, 117, 192, 218, 418, 419
"The View," 232, 233–34
Village Voice, 13, 70, 96, 160, 327
Virginian-Pilot, 59, 242, 266, 437

WABC radio talk show, 204
WABC-TV's political pundit, 55
WAGA-TV, 407
WAGA-TV/Fox Five News, 124
Walker, Adrian, **489–91**; *Boston Globe*, regional columnist at, 489; "Broadening the View" column, 490–91; *Miami News*, 489
Walker, Hal, **491**; ABC News, 491; anchoring "A Dialog with Whitey," 491; CBS News, 491; "Of Black America" series, reporting, 491
Walker, Liz, **492–93**; Amelia Earhart Award to, 493; Gabriel Award to, 493; KRON-TV, reporter and early morning anchor at, 492; "Midday," a daily magazine-format show, hosting, 492; slave trade exploration (as "In the Lion's Mouth" documentary), 492; "Stop the Violence" campaign, fronting, 493; "Sunday with Liz Walker" magazine show, hosting, 492; "Sunday with Liz Walker," own news magazine show, 492; 2002 Award for Inclusive Leadership and Social Responsibility, 493
Wall Street Journal, 84, 85, 94, 97, 189, 190, 191, 192, 217, 226, 264, 284, 285, 338, 351, 400, 525, 526, 533
"War Appealed to Americans' Fear" column, 175
War on drugs, 506
War on terror, 193, 251, 349, 482, 496, 500, 504
Warner Robins Enterprise, 110
"Was Columbus a Whiner?" story, 99
Washington Post, 81, 107, 136, 147, 184, 196, 209, 245, 284, 302, 327, 333, 365, 374, 379, 441, 501, 511, 518
Washington Post Book World, 13
Washington Post Writers Group, 13, 37, 38, 384, 409, 410, 441
Washington Post's District Extra, 84
Washington Star, 518
Washington Tribune, 253
"Washington Week in Review," 209, 210
Watson, Carlos, **493–95**; *Detroit Free Press*, articles in, 494; "The Edge with Carlos Watson" interview specials, 494; "The Inside Edge" show, 495; "The Inside Edge with Carlos Watson," weekly political column, 494; *Miami Herald*, articles in, 494; "Off Topic with Carlos Watson," one-hour specials, 494; "The O'Reilly Factor," show appearance, 494; *Stanford Law Review*, editor of, 494; "The Tavis

Index

Smiley Show," radio show, 494; "Your World with Neil Cavuto" show, appearance, 494
WAVY-TV, 59, 358
WBAL-TV, 167, 269
WBBM-TV, 132, 167, 198, 365, 414
WBEZ, 243
WBFO-FM in Buffalo as that station's news director, 381
WBIR-TV, 404
WBMX-FM, 235
WBRC-TV, 256
WBUR-FM, 134, 381, 382
WBZ-TV, 85, 335
WCAU-AM, 460
WCBS radio, 35
WCBS-TV, 198, 409
WCBV-TV, 358
WCPX, 167
WDAF-TV, 129, 329
WDAS-FM, 2
WDIV-TV, 195, 329
Weathers, Diane Marie, **495–96**; *Essence* magazine editor, 495–96
Weathersbee, Tonyaa, **496–99**; "Bush Helped the Terrorists Gain Mileage from Attacks" column by, 498–99; *Florida Times-Union*, columnist for, 496; *Times-Union* in 1985, 497
"The Wedding" 538
"Weekend Edition," 244
"Weekend Magazine," 330
"Weekend Today," 198, 256
WEEK-TV, an NBC affiliate station, 68
WERQ-AM/FM, 202
WESH-TV, 358, 431
WFLA-TV, 358
WGAU-AM, 372
WGCI-FM, 235
WHAT-AM, 460
Whitaker, Mark, **499–501**; *Attleboro Sun*, writing sports for, 499; *Newsweek* editor, 499
White, Jack E., **501–3**; "ABC World News Tonight with Peter Jennings," senior producer of domestic news for, 501; Brent Bozell and, 502; David Horowitz and, 502; "Dividing Line" column, writer of, 501; *Race Relations Reporter*, 501; *Washington Post*, general assignment reporter for, 501
"White House Talks Gibberish about Iraq" column, 263
Whitfield, Fredricka, **503–4**; "NBC Nightly News," correspondent for, 503; "The Today Show," correspondent for, 503
Whitlock, Jason, **505–8**; *Chicago Tribune*, writing sports for, 505; "Find Heroes Elsewhere" column by, 507–8; *Herald-Times*, writing sports for, 505; *Indianapolis Star*, writing sports for, 505; "Jason Whitlock's Neighborhood," radio show, 506; *Kansas City Star*, columnist at, 505; "Pardon the Interruption," 506; on race in sports, 506–7; "The Sports Reporters," 506
WHMD/WFPR, 407
Wickham, DeWayne, **508–11**; "Battle Ready" column by, 510–11; politically, 509; *Richmond Times Dispatch*, intern at, 509; *USA Today* columnist, 508
WICS-TV, 195
Wilbon, Michael, **511–14**; "In Athens, the New Can't Hold a Torch to the Ancient" column by, 512–14; *I May Be Wrong, but I Doubt It*, 511; "Pardon the Interruption," ESPN sports show, 511; "The Sports Reporters," ESPN sports show, 511; "The Tony Kornheiser Show," ESPN sports show, 511; *Washington Post*, sports columnist and reporter for, 511; *Who's Afraid of a Large Black Man?*, 511
Wiley, Ralph, **514–18**; *Born to Play: The Eric Davis Story*, 516; *By Any Means Necessary*, 516; *Classic Wiley: A Lifetime of Punchers, Players, Punks & Prophets*, 516; *Dark Witness: When Black People Should be Sacrificed (Again)*, 515; *Gentleman's Quarterly*, freelance for, 516; *Growing Up King*, 516; *Knoxville Kayana-Spectrum*, sports writer for, 514; *National Geographic*, freelance for, 516; *Oakland Tribune*, copyboy with, 514; *Premiere*, freelance for, 516; *Serenity: A Boxing Memoir*, book by, 515; *Spike Lee's Huckleberry Finn'* screenplay by, 516; *Sports Illustrated*, 514; on "Sports Reporters," 516; *Sports Illustrated*, with, 514; *What Black People Should Do Now*, 515; *Why Black People Tend to Shout*, 515
Wilkins, Roger Wood, **518–19**; "Keeping the Faith," documentary, narration, 519; "Throwaway People," documentary, narration, 519; *Washington Post*, 518; *Washington Star*, associate editor of, 518
Williams, Armstrong, **519–21**; "The Armstrong Williams Show," radio talk show, 520; "America's Black Forum" television show, 520; *Marion Star*, column for, 520; *Mullins Enterprise*, column for, 520; "The Right Side with Armstrong Williams," radio talk show, 520; *USA Today*, commentaries for, 519
Williams, Byron, **521–24**; *Oakland Tribune*, column, 521; "Strip Mall Patriotism" column by, 523–24
Williams, Juan, **524–28**; "A. Philip Randolph: For Jobs and Freedom," documentary, 525; "All Things Considered," NPR program, 525; "America's Black Forum," hosting, 524; *Black Farmers in America*, 525; *Brown v. Board of Education*, coauthored book, 525; "The Changing Face of America," NPR project, 524; "ESPN Sports Century," 524; *Eyes on the Prize*, book by, 525; "Fox News Sunday with Tony Snow," panelist on, 524; *I'll Find a Way or Make One*, coauthored book, 525; "Marian Anderson," documentary, 525; "Morning Edition," NPR program, 525; "Politics—The New Black Power," documentary, 525; "Slavery Isn't the Issue" column by, 526–28; "Special Report with Brit Hume,"

Index

panelist on, 524; "Talk of the Nation," 524; *Thus Far by Faith*, coauthored book, 525

Williams, Michael Paul, **528–30**; at *Richmond Times-Dispatch*, 528; on Richmond's life, 529; *Richmond Times-Dispatch* in Virginia, 528

Williams, Montel Brian, **531–33**; After-Care Program, host creating, 531; "All My Children" episodes, 532; *Climbing Higher*, 532; Emmy awards to, 532; Genesis Award, 532; "JAG" episode, 532; "Little Pieces" movie direction, 532; "Matt Waters," television show, 532; Montel Williams MS Foundation, creating, 532; *Mountain, Get Out of My Way*, autobiography of, 532; "The Montel Williams Show," talk show, 531; Nancy Susan Reynolds Award to, 532; PRISM award to, 532; Silver Angel Award to, 532; "The Simian Line" (film), 532

Williams, Walter Edward, **533–35**; "Educational Fraud" column by, 534–35; *Philadelphia Tribune*, column by, 533

Wilson, Brenda, **535–37**; "Breaking the Silence" NPR series, 536; *Governing Magazine*, writer for, 536

Winfrey, Oprah Gail, **537–43**; "ABC's 50th Anniversary Celebration" program, 539; "About Us: The Dignity of Children" program, 539; "A.M. Chicago," WLS-TV, 538; "Amy and Isabelle," 538; "The Arsenio Hall Show," program, 539; "Before Women Had Wings," 538; "Beloved," 538; Christmas Kindness South Africa program, 539; *Cry, the Beloved Country*, 540; "The Color Purple" movie production, 538; "The Cosby Show" program, 539; "David and Lisa," 538; *The Deep End of the Ocean*, novel, 539; "Desperate Housewives" in 2004 program, 539; "Dr. Phil Show," 540; "Ellen," program, 539; "Entertainment Tonight," program, 539; "Their Eyes Were Watching God," 538; "The Fresh Prince of Bel-Air," program, 539; George Foster Peabody Individual Achievement Award to, 542; Gold Medal Award to, 542; "Good Morning America" program, 539; Harpo Productions, 538; "Home Improvement," program, 539; Lifetime Achievement Award to, 542; "Listen Up: The Lives of Quincy Jones" program, 539; "Michael Jackson Talks" program, 539; Miss Black America contestant, 537; Miss Black Nashville beauty contest winner, 537; Miss Black Tennessee beauty contest winner, 537; Miss Fire Prevention beauty contest winner, 537; Most Important Person in Books and Media, 542; "Native Son" movie, 538; "Oprah & Friends Radio," 540; "Oprah After the Show," 541; "Oprah Online," 540; "Oprah Talks to Charlize Theron," 540; Oprah Winfrey Foundation, 539; Oprah Winfrey Leadership Academy, 539; Oprah Winfrey Scholars Program, 539; Oprah's Angel Network, 539; Oprah's Book Club, 539; "People Are Talking," show, 538; "Phil Donahue Show," 538; "Quincy Jones: The First 50 Years" program, 539; "Saturday Night Live," program, 539; talk shows, specialty, 541; Television Performer of the Year, 542; 39 Emmy awards to, 542; "The Tonight Show Starring Johnny Carson," program, 539; "The Tonight Show with Jay Leno," program, 539; "The Wedding," 538; "The Women of Brewster Place," television movie, 538; "There Are No Children Here," 538; "Throw Momma from the Train" (film), 538; "Tina Turner: Celebrate Live" program, 539; "Tuesdays with Morrie," 538; wealth of, 537; WLAC-TV, reporter and anchor for, 538

WJLA, 43, 49
WJPC-FM, 235
WKHM radio station, 149
WKYC-TV, 377, 414, 416
WKYU-FM, 250
WLAC-TV, 538
WLEX-TV, 250
WLOX-TV, 407
WLRH-FM, 352
WLWI-TV, reporter at, 132
WMAQ-TV, 167, 429, 439
WMAR-TV, 330
WMMJ-FM, 202
WNBC, 276, 355, 357
WNCT-TV, 129, 358
WNET-TV, 45
WNEW-TV, 355
WNGC-FM, 372
WNYC Foundation, 54
WNYW-TV in New York, 61
"The Women of Brewster Place" television movie, 538
"World News Now," 116
"World News This Morning," 116
"World News Tonight," 61, 117, 243, 285, 290, 334, 365, 401, 438, 439, 446, 448, 501
"The World Today," 179
World Trade Center attacks, 336, 337
World War II, 41, 119, 130, 161, 185, 218, 224
"World's Greatest Commercials," 170
WPAT Radio, 106
WPCQ-TV, 330
WPIX-TV, 355
WPLG-TV, 167
WPVI-TV, 116
WRC radio, 149
WRC-TV, 206
WRFC-AM, 372
WSB-TV, 329, 358, 372
WSDM, 377
WSM-TV, 127
WSOC-TV, 330
WTKR News, 59
WTOP-TV, 412

Index

WTTG-TV, 148, 416
WTTW-TV, 439
WTVH-TV, 416
WTVI-TV, 256
WTVM-TV, 404
WTVS, Channel 56, 155, 172
WVEC-TV, 59
WVEE-FM, 407
WVON-AM, 235; on "Lu's Notebook," 341
WWDB-FM, 460
WWRL Morning Show, a radio talk show, 204

Wycliff, N. Don, **543–46**; ASNE Distinguished Writing Award, 543; *Chicago Tribune*, public editor for, 543; *Houston Post*, reporter with, 543; Pulitzer juror, as, 543

"Yankees Magazine" weekly show, 195
YES Network, 195
"You can't keep a good man down," 249
"You Can't Quote Me" column, 307–8
"Your Call," a talk/interview, 57
"Your World with Neil Cavuto" show, 494

About the Author

SAM G. RILEY is Professor of Communication Studies at Virginia Polytechnic Institute and State University.